THE
MANAGEMENT
OF
MAINTENANCE
AND
ENGINEERING
SYSTEMS IN
THE

HOSPITALITY
INDUSTRY

WILEY SERVICE MANAGEMENT SERIES

TOM POWERS
Series Editor

THE
MANAGEMENT
OF
MAINTENANCE
AND
ENGINEERING
SYSTEMS IN
THE

HOSPITALITY
INDUSTRY

FOURTH EDITION

Frank D. Borsenik
Professor Emeritus
William F. Harrah College of Hotel Administration
University of Nevada, Las Vegas

Alan T. Stutts
Dean
Conrad N. Hilton College of Hotel and Restaurant Management
University of Houston

JOHN WILEY & SONS, INC.
NEW YORK • CHICHESTER • WEINHEIM • BRISBANE • SINGAPORE • TORONTO

Copyright © 1997 by John Wiley & Sons, Inc.

Library of Congress Cataloging in Publication Data:

Borsenik, Frank D.
    The management of maintenance and engineering systems in the
hospitality industry / Frank D. Borsenik, Alan T. Stutts. -- 4th ed.
        p.   cm.
    Includes bibliographical references and index.
    ISBN 0-471-14105-4 (alk. paper)
    1. Hotels--Maintenance and repair. 2. Restaurants--Maintenance
and repair.   I. Stutts, Alan T.   II. Title.
TX928.B575 1997
647.94'068'2—dc21   96–39997

Printed in the United States of America

10 9 8 7 6 5 4 3 2

CONTENTS

Technical installations in hotels

APPENDIXES

PREFACE

Hospitality energy, maintenance, building environment, and engineering costs have stabilized during the 1990s. However, they should continue to be of major concern to hospitality management in the future because of past periods of escalating costs. To be properly prepared for a management career in the hospitality industry, students and prospective managers must acquire a basic understanding of electromechanical systems and their energy consumption and constraints. In addition, environment concerns of the 1990s have redirected engineering management efforts and focused attention on a "smoke-free" environment and the potential discharge of groups of chemicals from some electromechanical systems found in hospitality industry buildings. The following are now common to management and especially to the property manager and chief engineer: EPA, OSHA, and ADA requirements, all of which have maintenance/engineering implications. The fundamental purpose of this book is to provide a basic understanding of these systems and energy and environment concerns. Since the first edition, the challenge has been to cover energy, maintenance, and engineering management in sufficient depth for managerial decision making, without necessarily assuming an engineering background on the part of the student/reader.

This text can be used after the first year of any two-year or four-year college program in hospitality management. The student should have taken at least an introductory course in hospitality management. Since there are several food-related examples and a chapter on foodservice equipment, a student should have had some academic exposure to, or experience in, foodservice management.

The fourth edition has been revised and supplemented with critical new subjects and industry concerns. A glossary of key words with definitions and example applications appears at the end of the book (the glossary was only available in the student and instructor manuals with previous editions). The overall flexible organization remains the same: Chapters 1 and 2 have been expanded to cover a larger range of hospitality businesses and to provide the management background to facilitate the organization of a maintenance-and-engineering department for a lodging, foodservice, health-care, club, institutional building complex, office/professional buildings, shopping centers/malls, sporting complexes, and casino/gambling activities. In addition, these chapters introduce the student and prospective manager to recent environment concerns affecting the hospitality building and industry, for example, EPA, OSHA, and ADA requirements. The remaining chapters may be covered in whatever order the instructor wishes. There are only four interdependent chapters—Heating Concepts and Heat Management (Chapter 7), Management of Refrigeration Systems (Chapter 8); Management of Ventilation Systems (Chapter 9); and Management of Air-Conditioning Systems (Chapter 10). These chapters are designed to be covered in the sequence presented, since each builds on the previous ones.

The fourth edition features a major and significant chapter revision, Life Safety Systems (Chapter 6). The chapter was written by Raymond Ellis, Professor, University of Houston, who is considered the foremost expert in hospitality safety management in the United States. Professor Ellis also addresses the compliance requirements for the ADA (USA) and the effects on the engineering design and maintenance requirements to satisfy the act.
Each appendix is a complete managerial model. The appendixes are optional for study. A comprehensive course, with minimal mathematical requirements for students, can be given without them. They are included for instructors or students who wish to evaluate in greater depth some of the general conclusions presented in the text.

A comprehensive Instructor's Manual including a test bank and a CD-ROM is available to instructors who adopt this text. The CD-ROM includes files of all text diagrams (PCX and WPG formats) for making transparencies, and test bank files for each of the chapters.

The authors are indebted to instructors who adopted the first three editions, and to their students, for valuable advice. We are very grateful to the manuscript reviewers for their recommendations and constructive criticism. We assume final responsibility for the book's content and for any errors.

A special word of thanks to our own former students for their suggestions, to the editorial staff at John Wiley & Sons, Inc., and to the Series Editor. Their assistance, encouragement, prodding, and guidance have made the development of this fourth edition possible.

Frank D. Borsenik
Alan T. Stutts

August, 1997

THE
MANAGEMENT
OF
MAINTENANCE
AND
ENGINEERING
SYSTEMS IN
THE

HOSPITALITY
INDUSTRY

CHAPTER 1

Courtesy of Holiday Inns, Inc.

HOSPITALITY MAINTENANCE AND ENGINEERING

ABSTRACT

Modern hospitality buildings are expensive. These buildings have technological systems that increase building cost and require a "new" type of maintenance. Furthermore, a "new" type of worker-manager is required to operate these modern systems. Today's hospitality manager has building investment, building technology, and maintenance responsibilities beyond what was thought possible from the recent past. In addition, there are increased government regulations concerning the operation, maintenance, and safety of the building. These regulations may be difficult to implement and costly for older hospitality buildings. Hospitality buildings are being built bigger and more service intensive each year. For example, the 5000-guest-room complex, the MGM Grand in Las Vegas, Nevada, could not have been built 10 to 15 years ago, because the technology to interlink 5000 guest rooms with complete hotel services was not available or feasible. This chapter goes beyond lodging units, it reviews foodservice buildings, healthcare facilities, club buildings, and institutional-type buildings. It reviews the organization of maintenance for the wide spectrum of hospitality services and addresses the management of the maintenance function for these buildings and technological systems.

Key words: Alternative I; Alternative II; Alternative III; American Hospital Association (AHA); American Hotel & Motel Association (AHMA); Americans with Disabilities Act (ADA); budget; Club Managers Association of America (CMAA); energy expenses; engineering; executive chief engineer; goal; HVAC; improvement; kitchen steward; maintenance; modification; National Restaurant Association (NRA); Occupational Safety and Health

Act (OSHA); organization; plant maintenance; preventive maintenance; property manager; property operation and maintenance expenses; renovation; repair; replacement; service contract; Uniform System of Accounts for Hotels and Motels; working chief engineer.

INTRODUCTION

Managing the maintenance and engineering systems of a hotel, restaurant, club, hospital, or other hospitality building is not a new or difficult concept to understand. Early in life most persons have had and understood the experience of caring for some possession, becoming upset when it did not operate properly, and paying to have the possession repaired or replaced.

The importance of maintenance and engineering systems is easy to define and evaluate. For example, try turning off the air conditioning for one hour on a hot, humid day; or turn off the heat for one hour on a cold, subzero winter day. It also does not take any specific technical credential or education to identify when something is working or when it has failed.

The terms *maintenance* and *engineering* have different meanings to different people. In some hospitality companies in recent years, the terms have been combined under the heading of facilities management or facilities engineering. Some managers have precise definitions, others loose, others vague, and a few people have lumped all the undesirable aspects of the hospitality industry into their definition of maintenance and engineering. The maintenance-and-engineering department has been treated as a catch-all department, which literally means that if a problem is not related to food, marketing or sales, housekeeping, or accounting, it must be a maintenance-and-engineering responsibility.

Many operations define maintenance and engineering by its areas of responsibility. Other operations rely on normal dictionary definitions. Regardless of the definition or responsibilities of an organization, the basic purpose of the department can be stated as: keeping the structure, its machines, its systems, and its products in an existing or specified state of readiness. This definition assumes that everything is kept in repair, that it is operating at a high efficiency level (low energy consumption), and that there are minimal breakdowns. For a hotel, it means keeping guest rooms and public space salable, at a low cost.

HOSPITALITY MANAGERS

Future hospitality managers will have to learn basic maintenance-and-engineering management concepts, how to analyze engineering data, and most important, the language necessary to communicate with maintenance-and-engineering personnel. One purpose of this text is to provide the awareness and basic knowledge needed in order to make appropriate decisions in engineering, maintenance, and energy management.

Hospitality building engineering and maintenance systems include: life safety; heating, ventilation, and air conditioning; electrical; water; transportation; exterior; environment; and special facilities equipment. In this book the future hospitality manager will become familiar with each system and strategies for effectively managing each system.

There is no glamour in managing the maintenance and engineering systems in a hotel, restaurant, club, hospital, or other hospitality building, but properly managed systems from design to operation can result in considerable long-term savings; or, on the contrary, the failure to manage such systems can result in significant long-term costs.

Lodging and foodservice managers know that their management role has changed because of the increasing importance of engineering, maintenance, and energy requirements in their industry. The health-care administrator has the same building-management problems as a hotel manager, but he must also cope with complex medical equipment. Changing technology in health care has been extremely rapid. The cost of providing space for a bed in a hospital is equivalent to the cost of a deluxe hotel room. Lodging and foodservice managers have complained about the high energy requirements per customer and how energy costs have reduced profit-making potential. They are frequently amazed to learn that their counterparts in health care consume 50 to 100 percent more energy per person to provide modern health-care facility services. Many of these nonprofit institutions now offer services—expensive in the eyes of patients and clients—that have resulted in shorter patient stays, quicker recoveries, higher turnover, and a rash of statistics that make health-care units look like high-occupancy transient hotels. Health-care units are frequently compared with resort hotels in terms of their services and costs.

Lodging units, foodservice operations, and health-care facilities have felt the maintenance/engineering/energy crunch. Costs in these three areas have increased three to five times faster than revenue, giving rise to price increases that offset at least part of these increased costs. This solution, however, is not available for institutional buildings, which are often heavily dependent on government funding, or for clubs, which may be unable to make the necessary adjustments in membership dues. In these last two cases, it is all too easy to cut back on maintenance and repairs, to delay repairs until they are absolutely necessary or until a piece of equipment has broken down. The money saved by postponing maintenance can be partially used to pay energy bills. To compound the problem, a large and significant number of these institutional buildings and clubs are located in areas of very high labor and energy costs.

Maintenance policy and energy consumption are usually dependent on each other; for example, if a piece of equipment is not maintained, its energy consumption increases and its life expectancy declines. Delaying normal maintenance results in very short-term savings. Many clubs and institutional operations that have delayed maintenance now face abnormally heavy maintenance, repair, and equipment replacement costs. Unfortunately, some lodging and foodservice operations have also followed this temporary cost-cutting technique.

MANAGEMENT FACTORS

Whatever the job title, facility manager, chief engineer, or maintenance supervisor, management is a critical element of the job. Whereas in past years the person holding the job of facility manager, chief engineer, or maintenance supervisor could be a good technician and be successful, the investment in facilities and the costs associated with the operations of such facilities require the person holding the position today to also be a strong manager. When evaluating the effectiveness of the management of the engineering-and-maintenance unit, particular attention should be directed toward the established goals and objectives of the unit, organizational structure of the unit, budget decisions, safety and security, workload identification and scheduling, controls and reports in use, and how computers are being utilized to manage the unit.

The remainder of this chapter will consider goals and objectives, organizing, budgeting, and safety and security. Chapter 2 will detail workload identification, workload scheduling, controls, and reports. In Chapter 5, the reader will find a detailed discussion on the utilization of computers to manage the engineering-and-maintenance unit.

GOALS AND OBJECTIVES

Managing the maintenance and engineering systems for hospitality building(s) might be defined as: design, construction, occupancy and use, repair, renovation, and disposal. The manager of the engineering-and-maintenance unit will have a difficult time keeping the unit on track if there is no end goal or set of guiding objectives. It is difficult to apply a common standard to all facilities. Goals for an engineering-and-maintenance unit may vary considerably depending on the intended use of the facility and the business of the user.

However, the goals for an engineering-and-maintenance unit must conform to the overall strategy for the hospitality business and must meet two industry-wide goals. The first goal, which is both strategic and operational, is to ensure that customers, guests, employees, and other constituencies are able to visit or work in a certain type of location and, along with that, a specific type of environment. At a minimum, it is likely to include that the environment be safe and clean and that any facility-related problems are attended to promptly. If this goal is ignored, the business may have difficulty attracting and retaining employees, customers, and guests, thereby decreasing revenues and increasing costs.

The second important goal should target financial performance in terms of costs per square foot, costs per employee, costs as a percentage of revenues, costs as a percentage of total expenses, and costs in relation to prior period and budgeted costs.

Objectives for an engineering-and-maintenance unit typically are directed toward preventive maintenance, repair, replacement, improvement, and modification.

Preventive Maintenance

Preventive maintenance is any work performed on an operational device or facility to continue operating at its proper efficiency without interruption. The interval between preventive maintenance actions on a particular device is typically established by manufacturer's recommendations or measurements that show the declining performance of a piece of equipment or facility components. When analyzing the engineering-and-maintenance unit, there should be an objective that provides for a program of routine inspection and service of equipment to prevent premature failures.

Repair

Typically, repairs must be made immediately, at the expense of other scheduled engineering- and maintenance-related activities. Thus, often objectives that relate to repairs are directed toward the urgency of completing the repair. Thus, in establishing objectives for completing repairs, it is often necessary to set priorities. For example, a typical objective for repair work might be to complete 90 percent of all repair work within prescribed limits.

Replacement

Replacement is performed when a piece of equipment or a facility component has reached the end of its useful life, that is, when the equipment or facility component can no longer perform effectively and repair is no longer cost effective. Typically, the replacement objective for the engineering-and-maintenance unit might focus on executing a program of planned replacement of major facility components, which replaces failing equipment before failure with new or rebuilt components that have a lower life-cycle cost. In Chapter 2 there is a detailed discussion on life-cycle costing and renovation/replacement.

Improvement

Improvement projects enhance the proper operation or reduce the operating cost of a facility. Such projects might include the installation of energy- and utility-conserving devices or the replacement of properly operating but maintenance-intensive equipment with similar but more reliable products. Thus, the engineering-and-maintenance unit should have an objective to identify and execute any improvement project that will provide a payback of the initial investment in 3 years or less.

Modification

Modification projects alter the basic facility or facility component to accommodate a new function. Modification projects differ from improvement projects by their point of origin. Modification projects are initiated from outside of the engineering-and-maintenance unit, whereas improvement projects are initiated from within the unit. However, because modification projects are in large part driven by estimated costs, the engineering-and-maintenance unit should have an objective to estimate accurately the costs of modification projects at or under budget.

ORGANIZING

Organizing work means setting priorities. What are the critical tasks that should receive priority attention and what are the components that need to be scheduled in order to complete a priority task? Each chapter in this text identifies the key components of a particular system and the requirements of each component associated with that system to sustain its effective and efficient operation. Organizing people includes charts, job descriptions, and daily, weekly, monthly, and annual schedules.

Three alternative organizational structures might be considered for the engineering-and-maintenance unit. Each alternative is a function in large part of the size and complexity of the building(s). Alternative I is most appropriate for multiple, large buildings with considerable surrounding acreage; Alternative II for systems involving one to four medium-sized buildings and limited surrounding acreage; and Alternative III is for single buildings with limited square footage and surrounding acreage.

Alternative I

The first alternative is structured around an emerging concept defined as *facilities engineering*. Facilities engineering may typically include up to four subunits: engineering design, maintenance control, maintenance execution, and utilities management. Major facilities with multiple, large buildings and extensive property will generally require a facilities engineering organization. Examples include a major medical center, large school district, university campus, metropolitan airport, commercial office/shopping center, and large resort hotel complex, all of which include hundreds of acres and millions of square feet of buildings. While facilities engineering structures are most typically found in large, complex buildings, they include the basic components of any effective and efficient organization. These components include: design, managing utilities, controlling maintenance, and performing maintenance.

A facilities engineering office is usually headed by a professional engineer, called a facilities engineer. Since, as previously mentioned, design can often determine maintenance costs, a key role for the facilities engineer is to ensure that designers and maintenance employees work closely together.

The engineering design staff is typically headed by a professional architect or engineer. The unit may vary in size depending on the magnitude of the facility and the frequency of the need for engineering systems modifications. Often such services are contracted from outside architectural and engineering firms because they are infrequently required.

A utilities unit is typically only included when the facility is engaged in the self-generation of major utility services. This unit is responsible for the management of potable water treatment plants, electrical power plants, central steam or cooling plants, and water treatment systems. This unit is typically directed by an electrical, mechanical, or environmental engineer.

Maintenance control monitors and coordinates the overall effort. The unit estimates the costs of maintenance activities, which are used to evaluate the merit of modification and improvement projects and also reviewed to determine the scope of the work and the type of work to be performed.

In addition, the unit determines the correct quantities and types of material, personnel, and equipment needed to complete the maintenance task. This is a critical function in any maintenance organization and must be done before a task is assigned to the maintenance work force for completion.

The maintenance control unit may also schedule projects that may involve more than one working unit in the maintenance work force. Also found in the maintenance control unit is a work tracking and monitoring function (i.e., identifying new work through a trouble desk, receiving input from the facility users, and tracking project assignments to completion).

Another key component of the maintenance control unit is a materials and supplies office, which is responsible for ensuring that the required construction materials, spare parts, and consumable products are available in the correct quantity and at the right time for use by the maintenance work force.

The maintenance work force unit may be further divided into several shops such as: electrical; plumbing; carpentry; paint; landscape and grounds; and heating, ventilation, and air conditioning. However, it is important that a maintenance supervisor, maintenance foreman, or general foreman coordinate the maintenance work force unit and the activities of the various shops.

Alternative II

Alternative II organizations usually consist of one to four, medium to large physical structures with limited surrounding acreage. Facilities are usually fixed in size at initial construction, and thus have a limited need for modification. Because such changes are infrequent and do not justify hiring an in-house engineering staff, these transient needs are handled by outside consultants. The manager of the facility such as the hotel manager, restaurant manager, or hospital administrator becomes the point of contact and coordinator for outside engineering projects. The contents of the chapters in this text are written for the manager of a facility with an Alternative II maintenance-and-engineering organization.

The basic elements of control that apply to an Alternative I organization also exist within Alternative II organizations. However, operations are less structured than those of an Alternative I organization. More time is expended in emergency response, remedying minor discrepancies; less time is expended in modification and improvement projects; and due to the contracting of services for major systems, less time is expended on classical preventive maintenance.

The maintenance work force consists of a limited number (e.g., 12 or less) of craftsmen typically described as maintenance mechanics or maintenance men. These individuals are typically multitalented and are able to work in a variety of areas. Service contractors often perform work other than minor troubleshooting and repairs on the various building systems.

Alternative III

In an Alternative III organization, only one or two persons are involved in maintenance and the manager of the overall facility becomes involved to a greater extent in the decisions that involve the maintenance and engineering systems. In such facilities, the maintenance man, a "jack of all trades," works directly for the facility manager. An Alternative III organization utilizes contracted services to a greater extent than Alternative II organizations. In Alternative III organizations, major system components are repaired almost exclusively by service contractors.

Organizational Structures in the Hospitality Industry

Lodging.   On an organization chart, the chief engineer has always held a high-level position in a lodging establishment. Figure 1.1 shows an organization structure for a lodging establishment of 200 to 300 guest rooms with food and beverage service. The chief engineer appears to be part of the total management team. In the past, however, the general manager typically spent very little time discussing operational problems with the chief engineer, seldom visiting or inspecting the engineering department. Many general managers knew little about engineering, maintenance, and energy. Chief engineers tended to know even less about management and management systems. This situation persisted for years.

Since 1950, the average number of guest rooms per lodging establishment has increased. The average new lodging establishment generally has more than 100 to 150 guest rooms, with some food and beverage facilities.

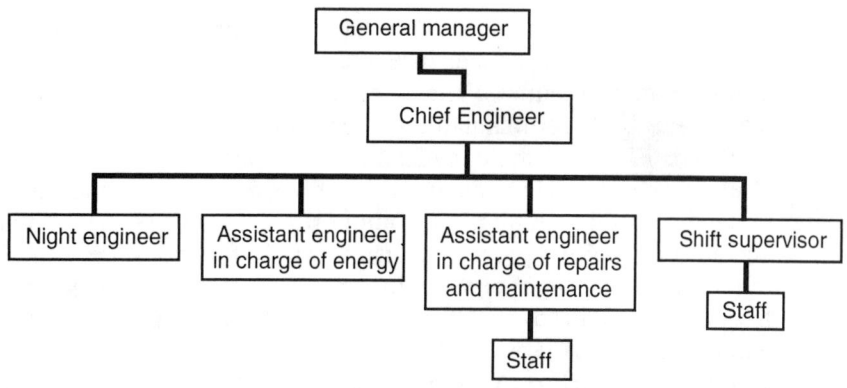

FIGURE 1.1 Organization chart for engineering-and-maintenance department for a hotel with complete and expanded service and having 200–300 guest rooms.

⟨ Tor Departments ⟩

These new properties, as well as older units with equivalent services, require a working chief engineer. A chief engineer is normally required for a property of 200 or more guest rooms with food and beverage and meeting room facilities. All units, regardless of size and facilities, have property maintenance requirements.

Foodservice. Freestanding, or nonlodging, foodservice units seldom have a separate maintenance-and-engineering department. The foodservice manager is generally charged with this responsibility and frequently establishes a series of maintenance service contracts for the unit. The maintenance responsibility for kitchen-production equipment may be delegated to a kitchen steward.

Some of the better foodservice maintenance and energy-management organizations follow the Alternative III organization, discussed above. The kitchen steward, or a "utility" person, has minor maintenance responsibilities. The utility designation may also mean that this person does the general cleaning of the dining areas, outside areas, and rest rooms. Most of these activities, however, are housekeeping tasks.

The unit foodservice manager, like the manager of a smaller lodging establishment, must possess a variety of skills and maintenance/energy knowledge to be effective in reducing costs.

Health Care. Many health-care operations have two or even three departments involved with maintenance, engineering, and energy management. The major department is plant maintenance, which is similar to the engineering department of a hotel. The other related departments, again similar to lodging, are housekeeping and laundry. Foodservice may also be included, and its problems are similar to those of a commercial foodservice operation. Health-care and lodging units have an advantage over foodservice units in that some type of maintenance-and-engineering department is frequently available on the premises. The plant maintenance department may also have the responsibility for maintaining kitchen equipment.

Figure 1.2 shows the organizational structure of a large health-care unit. The engineering and maintenance functions are usually under the organizational control of an assistant administrator. The assistant administrator becomes in reality a property manager whose functions are similar to those of the general manager of a lodging unit. The intensive-care health facility is frequently organized as Alternative I or, for an operation with a smaller number of beds, Alternative II. An extended-care facility frequently follows either Alternative II or Alternative III.

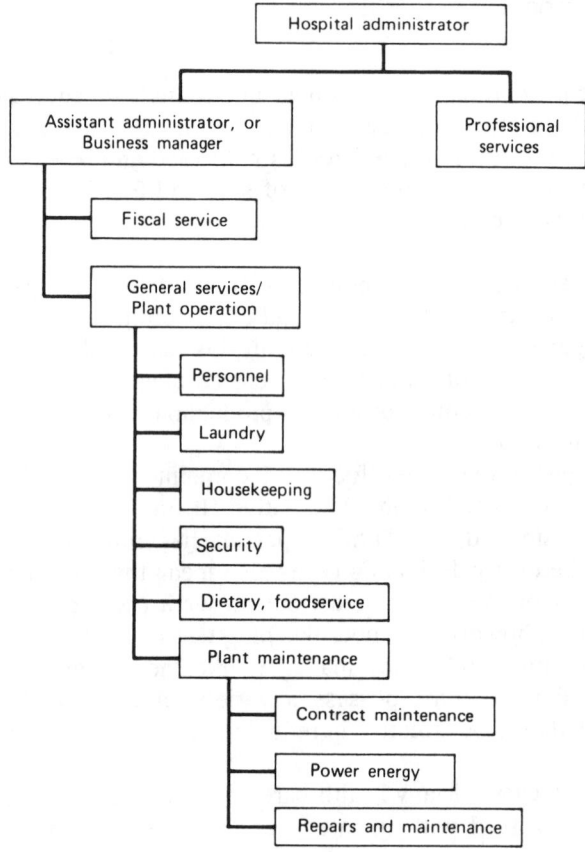

FIGURE 1.2 Typical organizational structure for a hospital with more than 300 beds.

Clubs. Clubs vary according to the services offered to the membership. They also vary with respect to engineering, maintenance, and energy expenses. Some clubs are similar to foodservice units; others offer services similar to those of larger hotels, especially resort hotels. Each service component—food, beverage, banquet facilities, meeting space, and recreational services—has inherent maintenance-and-engineering policies, procedures, and problems. Like the foodservice manager, the total maintenance and energy responsibilities usually fall on the club manager. He must keep abreast of activities and advancements in engineering, maintenance, and energy. Frequently, in larger clubs these activities are delegated to a maintenance head. If the foodservice operation is large enough, there may be a kitchen steward who has the maintenance responsibilities for foodservice equipment (see the foodservice section in this chapter).

The club manager is unique among managers in being responsible to a house committee. This committee sets policies, goals, and general operating procedures for the manager to follow. The committee can set maintenance and energy standards, which may be recommended by the club manager. One or more of the committee members may provide special skills and knowledge in these important areas and may be of great assistance to the manager.

In addition to the house committee, the club manager can join the Club Managers Association of America and enlist in its manager certification program. One of the requirements of the program is a standardized competence level in maintenance and energy management. Program completion is based on seminar participation, written exams, and a service record. The results of the program have been very encouraging. (Other special management areas in the hospitality industry have developed somewhat similar programs, but, in the author's opinion, the CMAA program is one of the most successful in developing a positive maintenance/energy management attitude for a large and significant number of its managers and potential managers.)

Institutional Buildings. Schools, office buildings, penal institutions, colleges, and noncommercial lodging units are defined as institutional buildings. The institutional area of the hospitality industry has generally given the most consideration to engineering, maintenance, and energy. One reason for this is that a large percentage of the operating cost of these units is for the physical plant. Tremendous thought is devoted to the initial design of institutional buildings, hence their often Spartan look. These buildings are very functional; the profit goal may be totally nonexistent.

Many large institutional complexes still generate their own electric power (total energy systems, or co-generation). These units are concerned primarily with the generation of steam or hot water for building heat. Electric energy is a secondary benefit and, with slightly higher energy consumption, both electric energy and steam (or hot water) can be produced. In recent years, co-generation has been encouraged by many industry consultants for smaller hospitality buildings, such as lodging and foodservice facilities.

BUDGETING

To accomplish the objectives of the engineering-and-maintenance unit, personnel, materials, tools, and equipment are required. Since a business does not have unlimited resources, the costs of personnel, materials, tools, and equipment must be accurately understood and predicted as far in advance as possible in order to maintain reasonable control and to apply limited resources for the greatest benefit. The total amount of all estimated costs for a particular period comprises the budget.

Expense trends developed for lodging are generally applicable to many other hospitality areas. Related industries frequently review lodging expense trends, because they are reported annually and other industries can make fairly accurate future projections based on these data.

Volumes of material have been written over the past several years on trends, future developments, and operating statistics in the lodging industry, more than in any other hospitality industry. In this text, however, only trends relating to engineering, maintenance, and energy will be examined.

Lodging

Industry Brief. In the United States, the average size of a lodging unit, in terms of guest rooms per unit, has increased. The average new lodging unit has about 150 guest rooms. This is very large in comparison to most international hotels. This large average size suggests that such properties usually have some type of maintenance department.

Figure 1.3 indicates the range in development costs for hotel properties. While the development costs have declined since 1990, still over 60 percent are basic building system costs, including electromechanical, furnishings, and fixtures, which may be the responsibility of the chief engineer.

Maintenance Department Expenses. In 1976, the American Hotel & Motel Association updated the Uniform System of Accounts for lodging units. Engineering, maintenance, and energy expenses are tabulated in two major classifications: property operation and maintenance, and energy. Figure 1.4 shows the subaccount expense percentage breakdown of each of the classifications. Bear in mind that there can be large variations within each

Luxury	$93,900	$182,300
Standard	57,500	99,100
Economy	31,400	59,000

FIGURE 1.3 Dollar costs per available room for hotel properties.[1]

Expense Item	Percent of Total
Property operation and maintenance expenses	
Payroll	43
Building, general	6
Electrical and mechanical	19
Furniture	3
Grounds	5
Supplies	4
Painting and decorating	4
Waste removal	3
Other	13
Total	100
Energy Expense	
Fuel (natural gas, oil, coal)	23
Electricity	63
Water and sewage	9
Steam	5
Total	100

FIGURE 1.4   Lodging property operation and maintenance expenses; energy expenses.[2,3]

category because of one or more of the previously discussed business activity or operating variables.

Energy Expenses.   In 1990, energy costs represented approximately 4.4 percent of the operating costs for hotels and motels in the United States. Energy as a percentage of operating costs remained the same in 1994. Energy costs per available room are illustrated in Figure 1.5.

	Number of rooms		
Type of hotel	Under 125	125–200	Over 200
Full service	$1250	$1281	$1602
Limited service	NA	688	782
Resort	NA	2218	2714
Suite	1138	1243	1382
Convention	NA	NA	1728

FIGURE 1.5   Annual energy costs per available guest room.[3]

Property Operation and Maintenance (POM) Expenses. Property operation and maintenance (POM) expenses represented approximately 5.4 percent of operating expenses for U.S. hotels and motels in 1990. POM was 5.3 percent of operating expenses in 1994. POM expenses are illustrated in Figure 1.6.

Engineering and Maintenance Employees. The number of employees in the maintenance department is influenced by the property size and the maintenance alternatives selected by the manager. Larger properties, with Alternatives I and II, will average 4.2 employees per 100 occupied guest rooms, or 3.1 employees per 100 available guest rooms.

The chief engineer spends large sums of money each year. The actual amount depends on the age of the property, its facilities, and business activity level. Regardless of the measurement base—the percentage of revenue or actual dollars per room—these variables represent significant figures and have increased for several successive years. Projections indicate that these costs will continue to increase.

Foodservice

Maintenance and energy expenses for a foodservice operation depend on one or more of the following factors:

1. Type of foodservice operation.
2. Basic construction and age of the building, especially whether the building is freestanding or contained within another building.
3. Sources of energy for the property.
4. Geographic location.
5. Age and type of kitchen equipment.

Type of hotel	Number of rooms		
	Under 125	125–200	Over 200
Full service	$1157	$1229	$1879
Limited service	597	711	861
Resort	NA	NA	2714
Suite	1183	1365	1644
Convention	NA	NA	2963

FIGURE 1.6 Annual property and maintenance expenses per available guest room.[3]

The foodservice manager's attitude, knowledge, and maintenance/energy skills are probably as important as any single factor listed above. Unlike the lodging manager, who is dependent on a separate department to carry out maintenance tasks and an energy-management policy, the foodservice manager is responsible for these items. If the manager is fortunate, and if the operation is large enough, the manager may be justified in hiring a maintenance person to perform minimal tasks.

Foodservice managers must generally develop and administer a series of maintenance service contracts for the major electromechanical parts of the building. Without such contracts, a manager must be prepared to contact local tradespeople directly whenever a repair is required. As most foodservice operations are open during the early evening hours, dependable, qualified tradespeople must be available when they are needed. It is very important for managers to develop good working relationships with maintenance contractors and tradespeople who understand the special needs of foodservice operations and can respond quickly in an emergency.

Industry Brief. The National Restaurant Association (NRA) has researched the energy requirements of various types of foodservice operations. The NRA foodservice categories are: cafeteria, full-menu dinner house, limited-menu dinner house, expanded-menu fast food, limited-menu fast food, coffee shop, and pizza unit. Energy consumption data for these operation types will be reported in the next section.

Maintenance and Energy Expenses. Until the 1970s, maintenance and energy expenses in foodservice were very low when expressed as a percentage of sales. They were so low that management was not concerned if energy costs increased by one-third or one-half (33 to 50 percent). Energy expenses were around 1 percent or less of sales. (Hence, if energy expenses were one-half of 1 percent [0.5 percent] of sales, and if they increased by 50 percent in one year, the net effect was that they had increased to three-fourths of 1 percent [0.75 percent] of sales.) Maintenance expenses were usually less than 2 percent of sales or, more typically, 1 percent.

During the early 1970s, the costs of energy doubled in one 3-year period, then doubled again in less than 5 years. As a result, energy costs are now anywhere from 2 to 8 percent of sales, depending on the type of table service and menu theme. Maintenance expenses have risen but not as fast as energy costs. One reason for the large increase in maintenance is that many smaller operations have hired a maintenance person. The result is that maintenance expenses, on average, may now be 2 to 6 percent of sales. In most cases, that part of the kitchen steward's time that is spent on maintenance of kitchen equipment is still not charged to maintenance.

The foodservice industry continues to spend about 3 percent of its sales for the purchase of new equipment in an effort to reduce maintenance and energy consumption. Thus, as reported by Borsenik in 1983, foodservice management is spending an average of 9 percent of sales for maintenance, energy, and new foodservice equipment (3 percent for maintenance, 3 percent for energy, and 3 percent of new equipment—all average percentages).[4] Isolated foodservice corporation data indicate that these percentages have not changed significantly since 1983.

When these percentage-of-sales figures are related to percentage of initial investment, the meaning of energy and maintenance costs can be fully realized. For example, if energy and maintenance expenses are each 3 percent of sales, this is equivalent to 30 percent of the total foodservice investment. This is a considerably higher percentage than in other hospitality businesses.

Figure 1.7 shows the average breakdown of energy expenses for various types of foodservice units by energy use areas: food preparation, sanitation, food refrigeration, lighting, and HVAC (heating, ventilation, and air conditioning). There has been minimal change in recent years from the statistics reported in 1984. Similarly, minimal change has occurred from the statistics reported in 1984 concerning average energy consumption by foodservice establishments, as illustrated in Figure 1.8, which shows the relative energy

Foodservice type	Percentage energy consumption					
	Food preparation	Sanitation	Refrigeration	Lighting	HVAC[a]	Total
Cafeteria	40.5	28.5	3.5	7.2	20.3	100.0
Coffee shop	35.0	18.6	3.8	15.7	26.9	100.0
Dinner house (full menu)	33.6	21.7	7.1	11.2	26.4	100.0
Dinner house (limited menu)	24.9	19.5	10.7	18.6	26.3	100.0
Fast food (expanded menu)	35.8	6.8	6.6	12.9	37.9	100.0
Fast food (limited menu)	45.0	8.1	4.4	19.2	23.3	100.0
Pizza	32.3	17.2	8.4	12.1	30.0	100.0
Average	35.8	20.4	5.9	12.5	25.4	100.0

[a]HVAC: Heating, ventilation, and air conditioning.

FIGURE 1.7 Foodservice percentage energy consumption by function area.[5, 6]

Foodservice type	6-month energy consumption		% of average
	Btu (millions)	Watts (thousands)	
Cafeteria	3,128	916,504	194
Coffee shop	1,100	322,700	68
Dinner house (full menu)	2,500	732,500	155
Dinner house (limited menu)	1,600	468,800	100
Fast food (expanded menu)	1,200	351,600	75
Fast food (limited menu)	1,150	336,950	70
Pizza	583	170,819	36
Average	1,600	468,800	100

FIGURE 1.8   Average energy consumption for different types of foodservice establishments for a 6-month period.[5,6]

consumption of various types of foodservice operations. It indicates that, of all the units listed, a limited-menu dinner house has the average total energy consumption, whereas a cafeteria consumes twice the average energy, and a pizza unit uses only about one-third of the average.

Health-Care Units

Construction costs in health-care centers follow lodging cost trends. The American Hospital Association reports that the physical-plant investment per patient bed was equivalent to about 50 percent of the cost of a new lodging room. This is a first cost, not a replacement cost. Assuming a typical health-care patient room to have two beds, the patient-room value is equivalent to the investment in a new lodging guest room. Approximately 80 percent of the investment is for the structure and its related equipment, including medical equipment and special furnishings. A new health-care unit, or a unit's replacement cost, may range from $75,000 to $250,000 or more per two-bed room for intensive-care units.

The costs of health-care services have risen more than 10 percent per year during the past 10 to 20 years. This means that costs double every 6 to 8 years. Maintenance, engineering, and energy expenses have increased at even higher rates.

Normal plant maintenance cost is close to 10 percent of total expenses. If housekeeping and laundry expenses are included, the cost could reach 16 percent of total income. It should be noted, however, that several housekeeping functions are performed by the nursing staff and that many units of equipment are leased or may have contract maintenance.

The percentage figures just cited vary with the type of health-care property. They are frequently slightly lower for new health-care facilities, high-occupancy units, high census counts, and extended-care facilities. The activities and related costs of maintenance, engineering, and energy are generally considered as fixed, or set-dollar, amounts. The percentage figure may increase to 20 or 25 percent of the total expenses for older health-care buildings.

Figure 1.9 compares the maintenance expenditures of an average hospital and a nursing home. The percentage figures are lower for a nursing home because of limited medical equipment and services.

Clubs

Industry Brief. Clubs may be classified as country or city clubs. The primary differences are facility services and the setting, or site, of the facility. The presence of a golf course may distinguish a country club from a city club. Clubs can be further divided into tennis, athletic, or social clubs, to mention only some classifications. It is not the intent of this text to discuss all the possible variations or associated problems of such clubs. Emphasis is placed on the operation of the physical plant. Because the services and purposes of clubs vary with their membership, there can be large differences in operating data among clubs.

It is almost impossible to develop construction cost data for clubs, as each is built for a slightly different purpose. Most have food and beverage service; hence, they have typical foodservice expenses. Some have guest rooms; hence, they are similar to hotels. Some provide special services—such as a swimming pool, a golf course, tennis courts, and other facilities—

Expense item	Hospital	Nursing home
Depreciation of physical plant	3.0%	NA[a]
Plant operation	4.0	5.0%
Maintenance payroll	2.5	3.0
Laundry	2.5	2.0
Subtotal	12.0%	10.0%
Housekeeping	4.0	3.5
Total	16.0%	13.5%

[a]Not available.

FIGURE 1.9 Comparsion of typical hospital and nursing home plant-maintenance expenses; expenses are shown as a percentage of total operating expenses.[7]

and thus are similar to resort hotels. Therefore, average construction costs are generally meaningless. Decor and furnishings can vary significantly between two similar properties. The services demanded by two different memberships can vary. They all use energy, however, and all properties must be repaired and maintained. The amount and degree of renovation vary from one year to the next. Unlike hotels and foodservice units, the income structure can be adjusted each year through membership dues. These variables make it difficult to compare cost figures and percentages between clubs and other hospitality industry operations.

Country Club Expenses. The two primary expense categories in engineering, maintenance, and energy are: (1) energy—heat, light, and power; and (2) repairs and maintenance. In addition, there are two other maintenance-related categories for country clubs: (3) grounds and maintenance, excluding golf course greens; and (4) golf course maintenance. Such expenses are reported as a payroll ratio on total sales and income excluding dues. Figure 1.10 illustrates the differences in the costs of energy and maintenance at country clubs. Energy costs rose 10.8 percent between 1991 and 1992 at country clubs, while maintenance expenses declined approximately 2.6 percent.

Golf course maintenance is normally expressed as a cost per hole. The latest data indicate that this could average over $34,000 per hole per year. For example, golf course maintenance for an 18-hole golf course would be 18 x $34,000 = $612,000 per year. The average cost per hole increased 4.1 percent from 1991 to 1992.

City Club Expenses. In Figure 1.10, the average energy and maintenance expenses as a percentage of total sales and income are illustrated for a city club. Energy expenses increased 19.6 percent at city clubs and maintenance expenses increased approximately 0.6 percent.[8] One reason for the percentage increase is the frequent location of clubs in cities and suburbs, areas where energy and labor costs are typically high.

Expense category	Type of club	
	Country club percent	City club percent
Energy	0.3	0.5
Maintenance	3.9	2.6

FIGURE 1.10 Energy and maintenance expenses as a percentage of total sales and income.[8]

Institutions

Maintenance, engineering, and energy costs are more difficult to analyze in the institutional area of the hospitality industry. Costs are frequently expressed as a percentage of the building budget or as dollars per square foot (or square meter) of space. In the case of rental or leased space, the basic charge per square foot (or square meter) may include normal repair and maintenance, while extraordinary repair and maintenance may be charged back to the renter as an assessment. In addition, many rental or lease contracts may specify an energy surcharge that increases if energy costs increase. Often the utility company (electric, gas, or steam) bills renters or leased-space users directly.

Energy and repairs and maintenance generally represent 10 to 20 percent of the budget for an institutional building.[9] This excludes replacements, rehabilitation, or major changes in the building. Another method of allocation is to charge $6 to $20 per square foot ($65 to $215 per square meter) of space per year for normal energy and maintenance charges. Since some areas of the building have more volume than others, as measured in cubic feet per square foot (or cubic meters per square meter) of floor area, some property managers use a cubic foot (or cubic meter) space charge for energy, repairs, and maintenance. This technique appears to be superior to other methods for fair energy and cost allocations.

In institutional buildings that have limited hours of operation, it is easy to reduce energy consumption significantly during unoccupied hours by shutting off energy-consuming systems. Public utilities have developed excellent guidelines for buildings with limited hours of operation, and these rules should be followed. Guidelines vary with geographic area.

SAFETY AND SECURITY

Safety and security are primary concerns of management. Crime and accidents cannot always be prevented, but risks can be reduced by taking certain precautions. Correcting and preventing safety hazards should be primary maintenance concerns. The safety of customers and employees is a high priority.

Safety programs for employees should comply with the Occupational Safety and Health Act (OSHA), which imposes comprehensive, detailed safety and health standards and record-keeping requirements for employers. The act states that each employer shall furnish to each of his or her employees a place of employment that is free from recognized hazards that can cause death or serious physical harm. Employees are also required to comply with OSHA standards and all rules, regulations, and orders issued pursuant to this act that are applicable to their own actions and conduct. A copy of the act can be obtained from the U.S. Department of Labor.

In 1990, President George Bush signed the Americans with Disabilities Act (ADA) into law. This act entitled disabled people to the same rights and access as other U.S. citizens. The ADA required that facilities be modified to make them accessible to disabled people. Particular attention was focused on parking spaces, entrances, level changes, elevators, lifts, rest rooms, meeting rooms, foodservice, controls and equipment, signage, and hotel guest rooms.

In addition, the ADA required employers to identify the requirements that are bonafide occupational qualifications of a job, such as the physical or mental requirements. Before an applicant for a particular position can be denied the position because of a physical or mental disability, there must be evidence to show what are the necessary physical and mental requisites of the job.

SUMMARY

The hospitality industry is large and varied. The following chapters will be limited to the lodging, foodservice, club, health-care, and institution segments of the hospitality industry. While the book itself is limited to these industry areas, its application is not restricted to them. Principles and concepts are presented that are applicable to the larger domain of property management as well.

Various types of hospitality organizations were reviewed and the need for competent property management was stressed. It was determined that most segments of the service industry require a working knowledge of maintenance, engineering, and energy management.

The costs of engineering, maintenance, and energy have been increasing and many projections indicate that these costs will continue to increase in the future. Rising costs have made management aware of this important area. Clearly, costs must be controlled with more efficient systems than those used in the past.

The role of the maintenance-and-engineering department head was discussed. This is a difficult department to manage. It was determined that a manager should not be totally dependent on the chief engineer and that the two must be able to discuss problems in the engineer's language.

The chief engineer, as head of an essential department, must be a manager, as well as a technician. The chief engineer of the future will have to master fundamental management skills. At the same time, the building manager must have basic knowledge and skills in engineering, maintenance, and energy management in order to manage the chief engineer.

REFERENCES

1. Rushmore, S., "Investment Today," *Lodging Hospitality*, March 1993.
2. Laventhol & Horwath, CPA, *U.S. Lodging Industry*, Philadelphia (annual ed.), 1985.
3. PKF Consulting, San Francisco, CA, *Trends in the Hotel Industry*—USA Edition, 1995.
4. Borsenik, F. D., "Energy and Foodservice Equipment," *The Consultant*, Vol. 16, No. 1, Winter 1983, pp. 12–24.
5. "Energy Update," *Foodservice Equipment Specialists*, Vol. 37, No. 5, September 25, 1984, pp. 52–53.
6. National Restaurant Association, *PREP Study*, Washington, DC, 1984.
7. American Hospital Association, *Hospital Statistics*, Chicago (annual ed.), 1995.
8. Pannell, Kerr, Forster, *Clubs in Town and Country*, New York (annual ed.), 1993.
9. "Annual Energy Management and Operating Guide," *Buildings*, November 1995 (November issues are comparative volumes for each year).

QUESTIONS/PROBLEMS

1. Diagram the organizational structure of a local lodging establishment, health-care facility, or club. Compare your organizational structure with those that have been suggested in this chapter.

2. Discuss and compare energy, maintenance, and engineering costs and the problems of lodging, foodservice, club, health-care, and institutional buildings.

3. Upon arriving at the office, your secretary hands you a telephone message from the general manager indicating that he needs projected annual costs in the next half hour for maintenance and energy expenses for the 900-room hotel. Your secretary is in a panic. The original records are nowhere to be found and the chief engineer is on vacation for the next three days. What do you tell the general manager?

4. Interview a chief engineer, plant manager, or head maintenance manager for a building, and attempt to determine the functions of management in which he or she is actively involved. Also attempt to

determine if the role of the engineer or manager within the organization could become more effective if that person could practice a larger number of the principles of management presented in this chapter or implement them more fully.

5. In what account would you expect to find information about your lodging maintenance department payroll?

CHAPTER 2

Courtesy of Holiday Inns, Inc.

MANAGING THE MAINTENANCE-AND-ENGINEERING DEPARTMENT

ABSTRACT

Managing a nonrevenue-generating department may not be a very exciting prospect for a young potential manager of a large establishment. However, this young manager should view the department as a challenge and look at cost savings, which is more than revenue generating, it is profit generating. Several larger lodging corporations have viewed maintenance-and-engineering departments as cost centers. However, when management is asked questions about these cost centers (housekeeping is another example), it is really looking at these departments as profit-generating centers. The primary purpose of this chapter is to create a maintenance-and-engineering department that is a profit generator for the business.

Cost reduction or profit generation is dependent on a highly acceptable product or service. The maintenance department keeps the physical assets attractive and acceptable to the customer at a reasonable cost. There are three objectives of this chapter: (1) to create a first-class, or world-class if possible, maintenance-and-engineering department; (2) to set standards or benchmarks and the procedures (forms, computer software programs, etc.) to measure the department's performance against these goals; and (3) to review and select analysis procedures to evaluate the department's output of product and services maintenance.

Key words: backlog work order; benchmark; budget (comparison) report; chief engineer evaluation; cross-training; emergency work order; energy/maintenance correlation; energy management; equipment inventory card; internal customer; inventory control; journeyman status; life-cycle costing; management inspection; management report; manpower forecast; master status; novice sta-

25

tus; preventive maintenance; property renovation; repair and maintenance log; replacement cycle for items that fail; replacement cycle for items that wear out; return on assets (ROA); routine maintenance and repairs; routine work order; service contract; standard deviation; Total Quality Management; value added per employee (VAE); variance; work activity report; work order; work plan; work priority; work productivity; world class.

INTRODUCTION

If you are looking for an interesting and different type of position in the hospitality industry, you should seriously consider becoming a chief engineer, a property manager, the director of a physical plant, or a head maintenance person. The position is interesting because of the variety of problems that must be solved. The position is different because of the interacting triad of the physical plant, employees, and the guest or client. Typically, the guest is not satisfied with some aspect of the physical environment or plant (the temperature is not correct or a unit of equipment does not work). The employee attempts to correct the guest problem in the quickest time period. However, the equipment may not respond to the adjustments. The guest may think the employee does not understand the equipment, or may place the blame for the problem on management and the owners for not providing the appropriate equipment. Seldom will the guest ask, "Am I asking for something that cannot be done?"

Chief engineer turnover is minimal. While there is turnover in other department-head positions, created by promotions and moves to different properties, the chief engineer or equivalent frequently stays at a property for extended time periods. Random-sampling studies of larger hotels (800 guest rooms or more) indicate the position (title) job life expectancy is longer for the chief engineer than any other hotel department head. There are several reasons for this long job life expectancy, some of which are: (1) Who knows more about the physical facilities? (2) What would happen if the "chief" were not there when an emergency engineering problem arises? (3) Who can communicate with, guide, and direct the specialized tradespeople who work in the department? (4) Who knows what is going on in the department, and who really understands what the chief engineer does and why? Finding a qualified chief engineer may be a difficult task.

Generally, the chief engineer does not want the manager's job, but the manager is very dependent on the chief engineer. Wise managers quickly learn the basics of maintenance, engineering, and energy management and acquire the necessary language to become effective in this important area. The relationship between managers and chief engineers should be one of mutual respect and usually results in a well-run maintenance-and-engineering department.

Good managers spend time with engineers, share problems with them, assist them in planning work, ask them for management input, and make the engineers responsible for their departments. Some managers spend a set amount of time each day or, at a minimum, each week with the chief engineer. The success or failure of the maintenance-and-engineering department frequently depends on the working relationship between the manager and the chief engineer.

Stag turnover is minimal.

DEPARTMENT ACTIVITIES

Maintenance department activities include: routine (daily and weekly) mainte-nance and minor repairs; preventive maintenance, which is normally scheduled at weekly, monthly, quarterly, and annual intervals; ordering, inventorying, and issuing department supplies and replacement parts; maintaining energy records and administering energy-management programs; minor rehabilitation, such as painting and repairing guest rooms and public spaces; and administration and management of the department. While these are the major activities for an on-premises staff, some of these functions are handled through service contracts for properties with smaller staffs. This list is not meant to be all-inclusive, as groundskeeping and swimming pool maintenance, for instance, may be an activity of the department. Some departments are also required to handle con-vention, exhibit, meeting room, and special activity space setups.

The remainder of this text covers the details of a majority of these activities. For example, many of the following sections of this chapter deal with adminis-tration and management. Various chapters summarize technical maintenance activities and energy-management concepts.

To manage the maintenance-and-engineering department effectively and direct its future performance, the manager should analyze current and past department activities. Activities must be designed to fulfill departmental respon-sibilities. The primary responsibility of the department is to keep the property in mechanical readiness, so that the building can provide the services for which it is intended. Actually, the department regulates, controls, and operates the physi-cal aspects of the property according to the policies established by management. The department should have some input regarding these guidelines, because its personnel know the limitations of the systems under their control.

A reporting system is essential for communication and eventual control by the building manager. Recommended reporting procedures will be detailed in the next section.

There is normally a very high inverse correlation between energy consump-tion and maintenance: For electromechanical systems, as maintenance increas-es, energy consumption generally decreases. Therefore, the consumption of water, electricity, fuel, and other energy resources should be recorded. These records not only assist in measuring the impact of an energy-management pro-gram but, because they reveal characteristics of the property, they also provide valuable insights for future building design and renovation. If possible, utility requirements should be measured for each major energy consumption area of a building.

TOTAL QUALITY MANAGEMENT FOR MAINTENANCE-AND-ENGINEERING DEPARTMENTS

Total Quality Management (TQM) concepts were introduced and accepted in several hospitality maintenance-and-engineering departments in the early 1990s. While the definition of TQM is very basic and comprehensive (TQM has been defined as the systematic method of developing products and services that meet the needs and expectations of customers), its application to hospitality maintenance and engineering is very specific. TQM is action oriented.

The essentials of a TQM program include, but may not be limited to: The *customer is first*; teamwork and cooperation are essential; the internal customer (other employees) is important; the emphasis is on long-term improvement; *facts and data count*; the objective is a *final solution*, and not in finding fault; everyone is involved; TQM is not a separate program; TQM is people intensive.

An objective of TQM is to empower workers to make spot decisions with the goal of fixing something once. This objective is best reached with good employee training and cross-training programs. When the employee is not required for maintenance activities, he or she is being trained or is being exposed to refresher training, or is being educated about related department activities. TQM programs are guided by *benchmarks*. A benchmark is a changing goal. The department compares itself to recognized "world-class" departments and attempts to become "world class." The department must first establish where it is, or how close it is to a "world-class maintenance-and-engineering department." These world-class departments have similar characteristics and these become benchmarks for departments to follow or achieve.

TQM BENCHMARKS

Management must consider where its maintenance-and-engineering department fits, or how it ranks. The following TQM test was developed for hospitality maintenance-and-engineering departments. The test asks the following:

1. Are emergency tasks (work orders) less than 5 percent of the department's workload?
2. Is planned and scheduled maintenance greater than 70 percent of the department's workload?
3. Do continuous improvement programs require more than 25 percent of the department's workload time?
4. Is there cooperation among all the departments that interact with maintenance?
5. Is there cross-training of employees?
6. Is there a routine maintenance program?
7. Is there a continuously changing 3- to 5-year plan for the department?
8. Is maintenance considered with renovation, design, and new equipment purchases?

If the answer to *all* of the above questions is *yes*, the department is world class. Only 2 percent of hospitality maintenance-and-engineering departments are world class. World-class departments have comparable benchmarks or performance standards. There are two sets of benchmarks: cost and productivity measures; and quality standards. (Remember, benchmarks are continuously changing goals and that only 2 percent of the world's departments are world-class. To become world class, your department must replace one of the present world-class departments.)

Cost and Productivity Measures

The common cost and productivity measures follow. Maintenance cost is expressed as a percentage of asset replacement value. Laborer-to-supervisor ratios are determined. Maintenance labor and supplies costs are determined. Maintenance labor hours per unit of product output are determined.

Quality Measures

The common quality-related measures follow. Planned and scheduled worker hours are determined as a percentage of all maintenance hours. The percentage of jobs (work orders) requiring rework is determined. The average time for a repair is measured. The time between equipment failures is another measurement factor.

The preceding ratios and ratio ranges are used to develop various "status" levels. The levels are *novice, journeyman,* and *master.* The master level is world class.

Novice Status.   The novice characteristics follow. Business return on assets (ROA) is less than 2 percent. Value added per employee (VAE) is less than $47,000. There is some employee involvement, there is some employee training, there is limited teamwork, and the employee is empowered to resolve some customer complaints. The normal benchmarks are to copy the competition. Customers are used for new product requirements. Supply purchases are based on price and then reliability. New products are purchased that will reduce costs. Managers reward employees for teamwork and quality work output. There is an apparent reduction in work turnover; that is, the time between product repairs increases. There are benchmark improvements with time. If a department is not at the novice status, management's objective should be to work with the department to achieve novice status. This represents the largest group of hospitality maintenance-and-engineering departments worldwide.

Journeyman Status.   Journeyman status characteristics follow. ROA increases from less than 2 percent to 2 to 6.9 percent. VAE increases to between $47,000 and $73,999. Employees are continuously finding ways to do their jobs better. Some departments even establish quality-assurance committees. New benchmarks are established; the department attempts to upgrade to market leader ratios and selected world-class ratios. A market research program is used for new product adoption. Supplies are purchased with quality certification being foremost; price is secondary. Department head and employee evaluations are based on teamwork and quality contributions and improvement. Gains are documented and work practices are redefined to improve the value added per employee. The percentage of hospitality maintenance-and-engineering departments in the journeyman status can only be estimated at this time. Most estimates place the percentage at 15 percent or less.

Master Status.   The master status only includes the world-class departments, or 2 percent of the total number of maintenance-and-engineering departments. The common characteristics follow. ROA is greater than 7 percent. VAE is greater than $74,000. Employees are generally self-managed, multiskilled, and are used to train new hires. New products are researched to determine if the latest acceptable technology is used and product quality is a major purchasing specification. Department evaluation is based on quality standards. All gains are documented and practices are redefined to improve VAE.

The records, logs (forms), and department procedures that follow are all designed so TQM can be implemented in a hospitality maintenance-and-engineering department. TQM programs and standards have been implemented by some larger hospitality establishments and corporations. TQM can be applied to foodservice corporations but generally not to individual smaller foodservice outlets. If TQM is to be implemented by a department, there is an apparent minimum maintenance department size level such as three or more employees. However, this is not meant to limit or restrict TQM to medium or larger properties. Basic TQM concepts apply to all businesses and departments, regardless of size.

RECORDS, LOGS, AND DEPARTMENT PROCEDURES

WORK-ORDER SYSTEMS

A work order reports that something is wrong and has to be corrected. It is used as a request for work to be done, usually maintenance or repair. A basic work-order form is shown in Figure 2.1a. It can be used for hotels, foodservice units, clubs, health-care facilities, and institutional buildings. The top section of the form indicates what is wrong, where the problem exists within the building, the unit of equipment that is not working, the date and time the request is made, and who is making the request. Figure 2.1b shows a completed sample form. Some buildings have detailed, printed work-order forms or computer-coded cards. If a form lists items that may require repair, the person filling out the request, such as a hotel housekeeper, merely checks off what is wrong.

Figure 2.2 shows how the work order can be transmitted to the maintenance-and-engineering department. Once the work-order request is received, some

2.1*a*   Work-order form.

Number:
Date: Time:
Building: Section: Room:
Request made by:
Reason for request:

Do not mark below this line

Time received: By whom:
Action:
Work report:
  Time start:
  Work completed:
  Parts required:
  Time work completed:
  Remarks or special problems:

2.1*b*   Typical request for work.

Number: 1234
Date: March 14   Time: 2:00 p.m.
Building: Tower   Section: 16th floor   Room: 1605
Request made by: JDD
Reason for request: No heat—
about 45°F (7.2°C) in room

Time received: 2:15 p.m.   By whom: KLM
Action: Emergency order: John J
Work report:
  Time start: 2:45 p.m.
  Work completed: Yes
  Parts required: Thermostat and convector, water-control valve, cleaned convector
  Time work completed: 5:15 p.m.
  Remarks or special problems: Convector—dirty, lint, paper, ashes.

Filling out the work-order form when the work is assigned and completed by the maintenance-and-engineering department.

FIGURE 2.1   (*a*) Work-order form. (*b*) Completed work-order form.

response (action) is required. However, before any work is done, each work order must be reviewed, and two basic questions must be answered. First: How important is the requested work? This is called a work priority, or rating. Second: Who is best qualified to service the work request? And what person or persons can perform the requested work at the lowest cost?

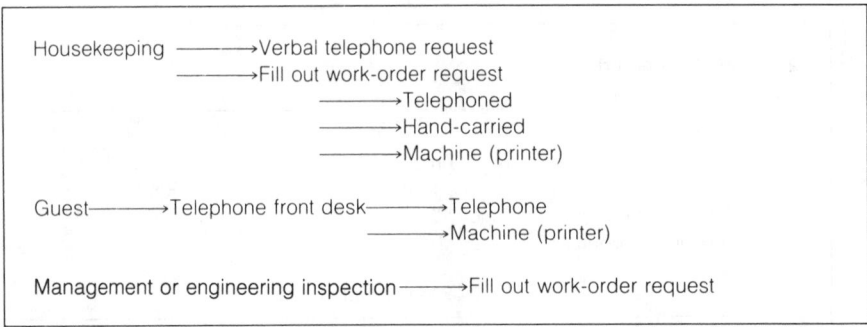

Housekeeping ⟶ Verbal telephone request
⟶ Fill out work-order request
⟶ Telephoned
⟶ Hand-carried
⟶ Machine (printer)

Guest ⟶ Telephone front desk ⟶ Telephone
⟶ Machine (printer)

Management or engineering inspection ⟶ Fill out work-order request

FIGURE 2.2 Transmitting a work-order request to the engineering department.

The least effective work-order system is an oral request between a supervisor from another department and the chief engineer (e.g., the lodging manager and the head maintenance person). Normally, records are not maintained with this system.

Work Priority

There are usually three work priority levels: emergency, routine, and backlog. It is extremely important that these work priorities be accepted and approved by management. The approval of a priority system by the general manager can resolve many potential conflicts between the chief engineer and other department heads.

Emergency Work Orders. These work requests must be handled immediately and, if necessary, by all available staff, including the chief engineer. Human safety or the prevention of a major maintenance expense indicate the need for emergency work.

Routine Work Orders. Most work done by the maintenance-and-engineering department falls into this category, and there may even be subpriorities developed for routine work orders. A routine work order is handled as quickly and efficiently as is feasible.

Backlogging Work. In some cases, requested work cannot be completed because replacement items have not yet been received. Hence, the work request is backlogged, to be completed when replacement parts are received. The work request can then be completed as regular building maintenance.

Dispatching Maintenance Workers

After the work priority is established, a dispatcher or supervisor must send a worker to do the job. In some cases, the decision is automatic. In the case of a water leak, the plumber may be sent. If the leak is within a wall partition, a carpenter is sent to the open wall before the plumber can deal with the leak.

In some cases, a maintenance supervisor is sent to inspect what is wrong. Requiring that a supervisor decide what is wrong and what personnel are necessary to repair the system can be a slow and cumbersome procedure, but it is often required to minimize labor costs.

Some large buildings may have as many as 8 to 12 separate trade unions in the maintenance-and-engineering department. (It should be noted that the large number of trade unions in one maintenance-and-engineering department is being phased out and a common procedure is to use one trade union such as "Operating Engineers.") This is another reason why a supervisor frequently inspects the work that must be done, estimating what parts are needed and the approximate labor requirements to make the repair.

Often, several work requests are given to one worker, who goes to one section of the building and completes a series of tasks. A worker may also be sent to a specific location and asked to report back when the job is finished or to give a time estimate of when the required work will be completed. When the task is completed, the worker calls the departmental dispatcher for another assignment.

The worker then completes the bottom half of the work-order form, indicating what was done, the time required to complete the project, and the materials used. The work-order request can also be used as a storeroom requisition to get replacement items when they are needed.

Analyzing Work Orders

Work-order forms should be tabulated and analyzed. The analysis can provide data that can be used for projections of future labor and material. They also form the basis for the management report (to be discussed in a later section). Figure 2.3 shows the distribution of work orders for three different hotels by hotel function areas (guest rooms, food and beverage, and public/other hotel areas). The work orders are normalized to a common base, work orders per day per 100 rooms, so relative comparisons between properties can be made. Hotel

Work requests/day/100 rooms			
Hotel area	Hotel		
	A	B	C
Guest rooms	6.8	4.8	2.1
Food and beverage	4.5	2.3	1.0
Public and other	4.0	2.1	1.1
Total	15.3	9.2	4.2

FIGURE 2.3 Work requests per day per 100 guest rooms for three selected hotels.

C was the oldest (built in 1965) property of the three. Hotel C also had an excellent preventive-maintenance program. Hotel B was built in 1989, and Hotel A was built in the mid-1970s and is in need of a major renovation.

Figure 2.4 shows the types of work orders and the workload percentages for type of work order for the three hotels shown in Figure 2.3 for the guest room function category. There are three types of work orders with large or unusual workload percentages that should be explained. First, Hotel C's "doors/locks" percentage is much higher than Hotel A or B's. Hotel C had non-fire-rated doors that were easily damaged and it also had the key–lock system. Hotel guests frequently walked off with the guest room key after checking out of the hotel and the lock had to be rekeyed. Second, Hotels A and B had a significantly higher number of lighting work requests than Hotel C. Hotel C assigned one maintenance person the task of checking all hotel electric light bulbs each day (five days per week) and replacing all burnt-out bulbs. The percentage of lighting work orders for Hotels A and B is very "normal" for most lodging establishments. Third, the number of plumbing work requests appears to be very high for all hotels. Once again, the percentage is very "normal" for hotels, regardless of their age. Clogged drains are very common and appear to be a never-ending problem in hotel guest room bathrooms.

Figure 2.5 shows lodging food and beverage work-order types by percentage, repair time (hours), and variance (standard deviation). While Figure 2.5 is for a specific hotel, the data are normal for hotels of 300 to 1500 guest rooms in the United States.

Figure 2.6 shows public space and casino work-order types by percentage, repair time (hours), and variance (standard deviation) for a casino hotel. While Figure 2.6 is for a specific hotel, the data are normal for casino hotels of 300 to 1500 guest rooms with conference and meeting rooms in the United States.

Types and percentage of work orders for three hotels			
Type of repair	Hotel A	Hotel B	Hotel C
Heat/cooling	14.1%	7.7%	11.6%
Doors/locks	5.7	5.5	14.6
Windows/drapes	2.3	7.1	3.0
Lighting	34.1	32.6	8.3
Other electric	1.4	2.4	2.8
Plumbing	21.1	30.0	31.9
Smoke alarm	1.4	1.9	0.6
Television	10.8	4.3	7.0
Other	9.1	8.5	20.2
Total	100.0%	100.0%	100.0%

FIGURE 2.4   Types of work requests and percentage of total work requests for three hotels for guest rooms.

Work orders for a lodging food and beverage department			
Repair type	Percent	TIme	Variance
Cooling/heating	4.58%	1.17	±0.56
Appliance	36.21	1.04	±0.53
Caulking (seals)	1.25	2.25	±0.53
Drain, sewage	11.37	1.01	±0.64
Electric	4.02	0.75	±0.29
Floor	2.08	2.50	±1.41
Furniture	10.40	1.04	±0.64
Ice machine	1.94	1.50	±0.58
Light bulbs	11.65	1.11	±0.55
Fans	6.38	0.53	±0.20
Beverage machine	5.96	0.63	±0.27
Water pipes	4.16	1.25	±0.71
Total	100.00%		
Time and variance (standard deviation) in hours			

FIGURE 2.5 Lodging food and beverage department work-order data showing repair type, average time for a repair, and the variance (standard deviation) for a repair in hours.

Work orders for casino and public areas			
Repair	Percent	Time	Variance
Cooling/heating	7.37%	2.11	±2.14
Equipment checks	22.90	1.04	±1.61
Electric	3.38	0.67	±0.29
Elevator	8.29	1.25	±0.61
Fire alarm	1.84	0.50	±0.32
Furniture	15.82	1.19	±0.82
Keno machine	0.92	2.00	±0.10
Light bulbs	17.05	0.77	±0.59
Parking area	10.45	1.91	±1.78
Pool/spa	3.38	1.88	±1.41
Restroom	5.99	1.88	±0.64
Water/plumbing	1.53	1.50	±0.10
Other	1.08	0.67	±0.26
Total	100.00%		

FIGURE 2.6 Work orders for casino and public areas for casino hotels with conference and meeting rooms indicating types, time per work order, and variance (standard deviation) in hours.

The final-work order data figure shows the number of work orders for the three casino hotel function areas—guest rooms, food and beverage, and casino/public—by day of the week, including an overall average and variance (standard deviation) by function area. See Figure 2.7.

The preceding information can be used to simulate work orders for various hotel types. While not shown, the average time for a guest room work order for the three hotels was 1 hour and the variance was ± 0.50 hours. Good preventive-maintenance programs should reduce the number of work orders per 100 guest rooms.

EQUIPMENT INVENTORY AND MAINTENANCE LOGS

The accounting department usually issues an equipment inventory form (e.g., a separate card, a component of a property management computer software program, or created by the accounting department and kept on a spreadsheet, such as Lotus or Excel). Each piece of equipment of a prescribed value (say, $100 or more) should be inventoried on a form. Frequently, all guest room furnishings and equipment will be placed on one inventory form. One side of the form indicates various specifications of the piece of equipment; an example is shown in Figure 2.8.

The form must contain the location of the unit and all information concerning a warranty. If an installation manual is available, its location may be included on the form. When the unit is discarded, the form is removed from the current equipment file in the maintenance-and-engineering department and returned to the accounting department with the reason the equipment was discarded.

All repairs and maintenance are indicated on the equipment inventory form. A typical format is indicated in Figure 2.9. The form indicates the complete maintenance history of the equipment, including what repairs were made to it and when, man-hour requirements for the repairs, replacement components, and

Day	Work orders/100 guest rooms/day for a casino hotel		
	Rooms	Food/beverage	Casino/public
Monday	5.96	2.23	4.66
Tuesday	5.96	4.65	4.46
Wednesday	6.15	6.70	4.10
Thursday	9.31	3.17	5.02
Friday	5.77	3.17	2.98
Saturday	5.24	3.91	4.66
Sunday	7.26	5.02	5.02
Average	6.52	4.12	4.42
Variance	±1.37	±1.49	±0.71

FIGURE 2.7   Work orders per 100 guest rooms per day by function areas for a casino hotel by day of week with weekly average and variance (standard deviation).

Inventory number:	Location:
Type of unit:	
Application:	
Equipment data:	Serial number:
Model:	
Manufacturer:	
Energy data:	
Warranty information:	
Service contract:	
Date purchased:	
Date installed:	
Manual reference:	
Maintenance schedule:	

FIGURE 2.8 Equipment inventory card.

	Unit	Inventory number	
Date	Type of repair	Equipment or parts cost	Labor requirement
___	_____	_____	_____
___	_____	_____	_____
___	_____	_____	_____

FIGURE 2.9 Repair and maintenance log form (reverse/opposite side of equipment inventory form, Figure 2.8).

labor and repair parts costs. The inventory indexing system is generally computerized for future management use.

Equipment inventory form data are generally used to develop preventive-maintenance schedules for equipment. If the inventory system is computerized, a simple computer program (or a property management software program) can be developed that groups together all equipment requiring monthly maintenance. The equipment list is printed each month and, if the system is properly programmed, a computer printout can also indicate exactly what maintenance is required. All the chief engineer has to do is to assign preventive maintenance work to one or more workers.

In addition, computer printouts and maintenance procedures can be made for bimonthly, quarterly, semiannual, and annual requirements. Once the chief engineer receives such a printout, it serves as a work-order request and authorization to complete these tasks.

Many properties (50 guest rooms or less) use a color-coded, noncomputerized system. For example, equipment that requires monthly preventive maintenance would be inventoried on white index cards; bimonthly preventive maintenance on yellow cards; quarterly maintenance on orange cards; and semiannual and annual maintenance requirements on different colors. The color coding can correspond to a yearly calendar that is similarly color coded. Hence, a white-orange month would require preventive maintenance for all units of equipment having white and orange cards. The system simplifies scheduling preventive maintenance.

ENERGY RECORDS

All energy consumption figures from utility companies must be verified. This may be done by the chief engineer, who then authorizes payment of the various utility bills. Since payments are usually monthly, this procedure implies that energy consumption meters are read at least once a month. In most operations, utility meters are read more frequently in an initial effort to control energy consumption. More frequent meter reading also serves as a check on any energy conservation program being used for the property. A form similar to Figure 2.10 can be used for recording utility meter readings.

Date: Electric meters	Reading	Last reading	Difference (consumption)
Kilowatt-hours			
Meter (1)	_____	_____	_____
Meter (2)	_____	_____	_____
Meter (3)	_____	_____	_____
Meter (4)	_____	_____	_____
Demand meters			
Meter (1)	_____		
Meter (2)	_____		
Meter (3)	_____		
Meter (4)	_____		
Power-factor meters			
Meter (1)	_____		
Meter (2)	_____		
Meter (3)	_____		
Meter (4)	_____		
Gas meters			
Meter (1)	_____	_____	_____
Meter (2)	_____	_____	_____
Water meters			
Meter (1)	_____	_____	_____
Meter (2)	_____	_____	_____

FIGURE 2.10   Energy consumption report. It can be expanded or reduced to fit the building. In some cases, this report is replaced by a similar form generated by a property management software program.

Several electric utilities may retrieve energy consumption readings daily. This can be done with minicomputer electric meters and electromagnetic tape, with radio-transmitting minicomputer electric meters, or with a combination device. The lodging establishment may request a daily readout of its energy consumption if the electric utility makes daily readings. These readouts provide a 24-hour energy consumption record by 15-minute periods for each electric meter. (Note: While these data are available for larger buildings, the authors have found very few property managers and chief engineers who request this information.) In some cases, the lodging establishment, office building, or hospital is given direct access to the minicomputer electric meter readout. If this information is available, there is very little need for the form shown in Figure 2.10.

Energy consumption by selected units of equipment should be measured and monitored for various time periods in order to determine operating efficiency. The results should be indicated on the equipment log. The equipment log can be analyzed to determine if equipment should be overhauled or replaced. Energy use in various sections of a building can also be measured; hence, large energy consumers can initially be isolated within a section of the building. Figure 2.11 shows the results of energy consumption monitoring for various sections of a building. Figure 2.12 indicates selected equipment results, and Figure 2.13 shows the energy consumption record for a unit of equipment over a period of time.

Date: April 16 Last reading: April 1 Electric meters	Reading	Last reading	Difference (consumption)
Kilowatt hours			
Meter (1)	234,567	012,345	222,222
Meter (2)	345,678	234,567	111,111
Demand meters			
Meter (1)	890		
Meter (2)	542		
Power-factor meters			
Meter (1)	0.72		
Meter (2)	0.81		
Gas meters			
Meter (1)	890,123	789,012	101,111
Meter (2)	456,789	389,453	67,336
Water meters			
Meter (1)	666,666	555,555	111,111
Meter (2)	444,444	394,444	50,000

FIGURE 2.11   Energy consumption records and data for a section of a building (part of Figure 2.10 form), for example, guest room energy consumption.

Electric meters	Reading	Last reading	Difference (consumption)
Kilowatt hours			
Meter (1)	113,333	111,111	2,222
Meter (2)	255,666	233,444	22,222
Gas meters			
Meter (1)	055,444	032,111	23,333
Meter (2)	—	—	—
Water meters			
Meter (1)	123,000	102,111	20,889
Meter (2)	108,000	100,000	8,000

Date: April 16
Last reading: April 1

FIGURE 2.12   Energy consumption data for two units of equipment: (1) dishwasher and booster hot-water heater; (2) dining area air-conditioning unit.

Unit: Booster hot-water heater

Date	Energy use (kilowatt-hours)	Meals	Kilowatt-hours per meal
April 1	1098	1098	1.00
April 2	874	950	0.92
April 3	849	758	1.12
April 4	1114	1103	1.01
April 5	1079	1212	0.89
Total	5014	5121	0.98

FIGURE 2.13   Energy consumption for a booster hot-water heater connected to a dish-washing machine.

WORK PLAN AND ESTIMATED EXPENSES

The preparation of a department work plan enables the chief engineer to develop an employee work schedule, set department goals and benchmarks for a specific time period, estimate expenditures for a given time period, and communicate with management. The manager should require such a work plan for two reasons: (1) to be informed of the department's activities and (2) for management control, when necessary.

It was suggested earlier in this chapter and in Chapter 1 that management may not be properly trained in the specific areas of engineering, maintenance, and energy management and that chief engineers may not be trained in necessary management concepts. The use of a work plan helps to minimize these potential problem areas.

If a work plan is properly used, management will approve a proposed work activity plan or provide input. Management will be kept informed regarding the status of special project work, such as guest room renovation, as well as the cost of the work. The form has also resulted in breaking down communication barriers between managers and chief engineers. Figure 2.14 is a suggested format for a work plan and budget. (Note: Several property management software computer programs also generate similar forms.) The time period can be initially set for weekly reporting; then, as the manager gains confidence in the chief engineer, the report interval can be decreased to twice a month.

Management Inspections

Management must schedule frequent inspections of the physical property. It is highly recommended that these inspections be done with the chief engineer. Management is also encouraged to spot-check the department randomly. Inspections are required for management control.

Rental spaces and public areas must be frequently checked by an inspection team. For larger properties, the team should include the manager (or manager's representative) and the chief engineer. At least 10 percent of lodging guest

Time period _____
Repair work orders
   Estimated number   _____
   Estimated man-hours   _____
   Estimated supplies/parts budget   _____
Special projects
   Rooms or areas to be renovated   _____
     (specify rooms or areas)   _____
   Estimated man-hours   _____
   Materials/supplies budget   _____
Preventive maintenance
   Estimated man-hours   _____
   Estimated supplies/materials   _____
Other activities   _____
   Specify activities   _____
                            _____
                            _____
   Estimated man-hours   _____
   Budget   _____
Summary
   Estimated man-hours   _____
   Budget   _____
Management approval   _____

FIGURE 2.14 Typical engineering department work plan and budget format.

rooms should be inspected each year for very large properties, which amounts to about 1 percent of the guest rooms per month. At least 30 percent of the guest rooms should be inspected per year for medium-sized properties, which is about 2.5 percent of the guest rooms per month. All of the guest rooms should be inspected at least once per year for smaller properties, or almost 10 percent of the guest rooms per month.

An inspection program has several purposes. First, it serves as an evaluation device for various departments; the manager can determine how well each department is doing its work. Second, it allows the manager to assess the physical plant. Third, and probably most important, it is a communication device between the manager and a department head. Fourth, and related to purpose 3, it sets standards. Something may look entirely satisfactory to the chief engineer and entirely unsatisfactory to the manager. Two standards of evaluation are being used. The manager's standard and the chief engineer's standard should coincide. This agreement can occur only when both serve on the same inspection team. The manager can tell the chief engineer what he or she considers acceptable and, if need be, the chief engineer can tell the manager what that standard compliance would cost in man-hours and materials. This alone can reduce management's standard. Management communication is greatly improved.

The inspection process must result in corrections; otherwise, inspections are not really necessary. Why inspect if everything is perfect? Actually, when inspection reveals no problems, the frequency of inspections is reduced. The opposite is also true; if numerous corrections have to be made after a detailed inspection, then the inspection frequency should be increased. A suggested guest room maintenance inspection form—not to be confused with a housekeeping inspection form—is shown in Figure 2.15.

The previous paragraph may generate a question regarding acceptable inspection reports. Each item requiring attention, not meeting an acceptable maintenance or management standard, generates a work order. Consider the following two situations: (1) a wall covering is loose and falling down from one upper corner of a guest room; (2) there is a slight wall covering tear less than 1 inch (25 millimeters) in length in a corner above the baseboard. It should be apparent that item 1 should result in a work order to reglue the wall covering before it falls or is torn from the wall. Item 2 would not probably require a work order and would be noted and when the wall-covering person is in the room on another work order, this tear would be fixed at that time.

The major question regarding the frequency of inspections must be answered. The best answer refers back to the TQM section of this chapter. What do world-class establishments accept? In general, if the inspection results in less than 5 percent corrections, the management inspection cycle can be increased. If 10 percent corrections are required, this is generally considered acceptable to very good. Most world-class operations would accept 5 to less than 10 percent corrections, with no major items (the falling wall covering in the preceding

```
 Room number:        _____
 Inspection date:    _____
 Inspection item:    _____              Satisfactory    Repair

Painting
   Seal/sand cracks, holes
      Guest room                             _____      _____
      Foyer                                  _____      _____
      Closet                                 _____      _____
      Bathroom                               _____      _____
   Wood furniture                            _____      _____
   Paint colors (specify)                    _____      _____
      Guest room         _____
      Foyer              _____
      Closet             _____
      Bathroom           _____
Carpentry
   Baseboards                                _____      _____
   Doors                                     _____      _____
   Closets                                   _____      _____
   Broken furniture (specify)  _____
   Tile
      Counters                               _____      _____
      Floors                                 _____      _____
      Walls (bathroom)                       _____      _____
Electrical
   Sockets/outlets (specify)   _____
   Switches                                  _____      _____
   Light bulbs (specify)       _____
      Correct-size lamps (specify)  _____
   Air-conditioning unit                     _____      _____
   Heating unit                              _____      _____
   Television                                _____      _____
   Telephone                                 _____      _____
   Other appliances (specify)  _____
Plumbing
   Chrome fixtures (specify)    _____
   Traps                        _____
   Water leaks (specify)        _____
   Valves (specify)             _____
   Hot water:
      Adequate flow                          _____      _____
      Temperature                            _____      _____
   Caulking around fixtures (specify)  _____
Special items:  _____
                _____
                _____

Notes to maintenance supervisor:  _____
                                  _____

Inspection completed by:  _____
   Date:                  _____
```

FIGURE 2.15 Guest room maintenance inspection form.

paragraph would not be acceptable and is not considered world class). Likewise, if corrections account for 20 percent of the items checked, there are definite problems and the inspection schedule should be increased until corrections are reduced to at least one-half of the present level.

The following recommendations are made:

1. Very good to "world class:" 5 percent or less corrections.
2. Good: 5 to 10 percent corrections.
3. Fair: 10 to 15 percent corrections.
4. Poor: 15 to 20 percent corrections.
5. Major problems: 20 percent or more corrections.

MANAGEMENT REPORTS

There are two basic types of management reports: (1) the budget comparison report and (2) the work activity report.

Budget Comparison Report

The budget is an estimate and, as such, is not perfect. A good budget has an acceptable variance. A *variance* is an acceptable deviation from the expected expense. (Note: If adequate data are available, the variance is the statistical standard deviation; most property management programs can generate a standard deviation after a period of time.) For example, if the maintenance-and-engineering department has a budget of 20,000 annual man-hours, the acceptable variance could be 1000 man-hours (5 percent). If the work actually required 20,499 man-hours, this would cause no major problem because the actual figure is within the acceptable variance. Any variances larger than acceptable would require an explanation in the budget comparison report.

If, however, the chief engineer used only 15,000 of the 20,000 man-hours estimated, he would have to supply a reason for this unacceptable variance. (In other words: Why was the original budget figure so far off, particularly since 5000 man-hours is equivalent to 2.5 workers?) Figure 2.16 shows a working budget and includes energy data.

Work Activity Report

The work activity report is a summary of the activities of the maintenance-and-engineering department for a defined period, usually a month. The report, as illustrated in Figure 2.17, should include the following: work orders, shown by numbers and man-hours in priority order; special projects by room numbers and man-hours; preventive maintenance by man-hours; and other activities by man-hours. In addition, employees may be listed, with total man-hours worked by each one. There should also be space provided for any comments or recommendations. In this space the chief engineer can justify excessive or overestimated man-hours and explain any significant deviations from the budget.

Manpower report: Week Feb. 14	Man-hours	Parts cost	Energy use, Btu (watt) equivalent						
			Water	Gas	Electric	Steam	Oil	Other	Total
Monday	112	$750	5M	20M	21M	17M	10M	5M	78M
Tuesday	112	928	6	20	18	15	14	2	75M
Wednesday	112	1142	7	7	17	14	13	0	58M
Thursday	112	1717	6	8	25	16	15	0	70M
Friday	64	178	4	18	15	14	12	4	67M
Saturday	64	521	3	11	14	10	6	1	45M
Sunday	64	394	2	5	16	12	5	0	40M

	Man-hours	Man-hours		
Total for week:	640	Goal: 625	Difference:	15 +2.4%
Month to date:	1250	Goal: 1200	Difference:	50 +4.2%
Year to date:	7725	Goal: 7800	Difference:	−75 −1.0%

FIGURE 2.16 Typical maintenance department budget form, showing actual man-hour and energy consumption data for one week.

Time period _____		
Repair work orders	Number	Man-hours
Emergency	_____	_____
Routine	_____	_____
Backlog	_____	_____
Special projects	Room numbers	Man-hours
Rooms (specify)	_____	_____
Other (specify)	_____	_____
Preventive maintenance		_____
Other activities		
Administration		_____
Purchasing/supplies		_____
Inspections		_____
Other (specify) _____		_____
_____		_____
Total man-hours worked		_____
Comments or recommendations _____		

Employee	Hours worked
1. _____	_____
2. _____	_____
3. _____	_____
4. _____	_____

Include: Department budget with energy data (Fig. 2.16)

FIGURE 2.17 Format for maintenance-and-engineering department work activity report.

The form becomes a primary source of information for department and chief engineer evaluations. Some managers may require from the chief engineer a bimonthly report or a report that coincides with a payroll period.

It should be noted that the previous reports do not include lodging or business activity. Unless the budget included a business activity index, there could be large deviations between actual and budgeted activities and expenses. A property management computer software program normally includes business activity with its generated reports. The preceding forms are adequate if the budget is correct. It is recommended that the budget comparisons should be adjusted by a business activity index (lodging occupancy, meals served, meetings, and banquets), and the energy consumption data should also be adjusted by both business activity and environment changes (colder or warmer than normal weather). Appendix 6A shows such a technique for energy consumption adjustments; Appendix 6B shows a similar technique for both business and environment energy consumption adjustments.

EVALUATING THE MAINTENANCE-AND-ENGINEERING DEPARTMENT

WORKER PRODUCTIVITY

Several techniques for measuring worker productivity are available. The correct measurement technique depends on the department's objectives, the property's characteristics, to some extent customer requirements, and whether a TQM program has been implemented by the property.

Work-Order Production

One measure of worker and department productivity is based on the number of work orders. The total number of completed work orders is compared to the number of available workers. However, some work requests require much more time than others, and the manager must recognize this. A new building, or one that has been recently renovated, will probably have a high work-order requirement. After a period of time, work requests should decrease, increasing again as the age and use of the building increase.

Preventive-maintenance productivity is difficult to measure. It is normally measured by man-hours of work, which should be rather constant each month. Preventive maintenance can be estimated from manufacturer's equipment manuals, by checking with the manufacturer's local representative, and by reviewing the department's past records. It should also be apparent that there is a very high correlation between work orders and preventive maintenance. A high level of preventive maintenance reduces work orders (recall the TQM test earlier in this chapter).

Budget Comparison

Another productivity measurement standard is the department budget. Unfortunately, it may not show the real picture because budgets generally depend on sales. This technique results in a major preventive-maintenance scheduling problem for the chief engineer. For example, when sales are high, the engineer's budget is high, so that preventive-maintenance procedures can be completed. However, some preventive-maintenance jobs require shutting down electro-mechanical systems that are needed when the property is fully occupied. Ideally, preventive-maintenance procedures should be undertaken when the building is at partial occupancy; at such times, however, the budget is frequently too low to permit preventive maintenance.

Again, TQM measures such as ROA and VAE are generally better monetary productivity measures. For example, preventive maintenance keeps guest rooms in service, which increases both ROA and VAE, whereas, a high work-order level reduces both ROA and VAE because breakdowns are more costly than preventive maintenance. Scheduled maintenance is preferred over work orders.

Manpower Forecast

Productivity should be based on manpower forecasts that depend on preventive maintenance, backlog work, special projects, and limited emergency repairs (work orders). Past records can be used to estimate emergency, routine, and backlog work requests at various levels of building occupancy. Preventive-maintenance routines are determined by the equipment in use and its maintenance schedule. Supervisors can estimate manpower requirements from this information. These estimates are then compared to actual manpower requirements. The variance between estimated and actual work should be less than 5 percent in a world-class maintenance department. Figure 2.18 shows how to make these comparisons.

Total estimated man-hours   1320
Total actual man-hours   1500
Difference   180

Variance = difference/actual man-hours
         = 180/1500
         = 12 percent

Departmental productivity = 100% − variance
                           = 100% − 12%
                           = 88%
Departmental productivities of 80 percent or more usually indicate a well-run engineering department.

FIGURE 2.18 Determining the variance between actual and estimated work for a well-managed maintenance-and-engineering department.

Man-Hours and Building Use, or Occupancy, Correlation

Another productivity measure is the correlation between man-hour data and building use, or occupancy. Such a correlation may be developed with an acceptable management variance. The chief engineer can make estimates based on forecasts of building use and manpower availability, and schedule work in an effort to utilize the work force fully at a very high level of performance.

CHIEF ENGINEER EVALUATION

It may be very difficult to state that any one item in a personnel evaluation list is most important when evaluating a chief engineer. Evaluation factors may be grouped as work environment factors, such as the physical plant and business function areas, and management environment factors, such as management organization, management style, and employee trade unions.

It is possible that a "good" chief engineer (as viewed from outside of the organization) will be considered a poor one (as viewed from within the organization) because a poor management policy has been set for the department. It is critical to know the goals or purposes of the organization because they reflect the management style and the policies under which the department is operating. For example, it may be management's intent to operate at an absolute minimum cost to generate a very short-term maximum profit. The chief engineer does not have an adequate working budget in this case and cannot keep the building in proper operation; 80 percent or more of the workload is emergency work orders. In this case, a "good" chief engineer stays within the budget and satisfies management's goals. We will assume that this is not the typical operation.

The chief engineer (or equivalent) must be evaluated with respect to several factors, generally as follows: adherence to budget, work activity reports, TQM evaluators, guest reactions regarding the property, condition of the physical property as determined through management inspections, cooperation with other departments, and innovation and cost savings. Each will be briefly reviewed as a potential evaluation standard.

Budget

The chief engineer's ability to stay within a reasonable budget is of primary importance. For a fair evaluation, all items in a budget must be weighed. Budgeted man-hours, for example, reflect department productivity. Estimated materials and parts cost reflect the ability to anticipate expenses, since it is assumed that the chief engineer has budget input and can keep the physical plant in operation with adequate budgeted funds. Energy consumption data reflect on the efficiency and maintenance of the electromechanical equipment under the engineer's control. (*Note*: Energy consumption *data* are stressed, not energy *costs*, as energy costs could increase with a significant reduction in energy consumption.) A good chief engineer controls costs and energy consumption.

Work Activity Reports

The work activity report indicates the activities of the department. This report and the engineer's budget must be evaluated together, as they both indicate how funds are being spent. Not only work orders but also special projects indicate general building improvements being done by the department. It is assumed that necessary preventive maintenance is being performed. If preventive-maintenance activities are light or inadequate, this will result in higher than normal work orders, and even special project work, usually within one to four months. The chief engineer's recommendations in these reports are valuable indicators of his or her management capability.

TQM Evaluators

TQM evaluators could be used to replace many of the chief engineer's evaluators. TQM stresses the following: increasing ROA and VAE ratios, which should be improving from one evaluation period to the next; a reduction in emergency work orders, which should eventually decrease to 5 percent of the department's workload; preventive maintenance, which should approach 70 percent of the department's workload; continuous improvement of property quality and employee quality, which should approach 25 percent of the department's workload; and increasing the time between equipment breakdowns.

Guest Reactions

Guest complaints often show up as work orders called in by guests. A review of these work orders reveals items of concern to guests. Some properties have forms available for guests to fill out. A quick analysis of these forms may reveal specific aspects of the building that are of general concern to guests and that could be the result of a substandard preventive-maintenance program.

General Condition of the Property

It is easy to see that a property is deteriorating. Generally, the initial clue is the guest reaction forms. The management inspection form is critical to the general condition of the property. The chief engineer has the ability to look at a piece of equipment, a roof surface, or a door frame and to point out to the manager during the inspection what is likely to go wrong if certain corrective actions are not taken in the near future. Recall, equipment generally wears out with age and preventive maintenance only ensures that the equipment will provide services during the estimated equipment life. There is a time when the best maintained equipment should be replaced or, at a minimum, may require a major restoration. It is the duty of the chief engineer to make management aware of these factors.

Department Cooperation

Do other property functional departments have engineering and maintenance problems? Are their work requests promptly handled? If such questions do not arise, then departmental cooperation is probably adequate or acceptable. Finally, is there a sense of mutual professional respect between the chief engineer and other department heads? If there is, there is generally very good to excellent department cooperation.

Innovation and Cost Savings

Has the chief engineer made cost-saving recommendations? Has the quality of the physical assets been maintained, or better yet, has the quality been continually improved? Does the chief engineer develop alternatives that appear to be original or creative and practical? Does the chief engineer show improvement as a manager and the potential to move up in the organization? If a chief engineer is doing an outstanding job, the answers to these questions will all be positive. Likewise, if management is not aware of any major facilities problems, it should also be apparent that the chief engineer is doing a good job.

Computer Applications

Work-order systems, equipment inventory, maintenance logs, energy records, work plans, estimated expenses, budget comparisons, work activity reports, and productivity evaluations are items now included in property management computer software programs. There are numerous software packages for preventive-maintenance functions alone, ranging in cost from several hundred to several thousand dollars. Some hotel chief engineers have worked with the hotel's director of information systems in developing cross-department property management software systems. One such system interfaces with 28 departments and provides the chief engineer with updated information so that he or she can schedule equipment preventive maintenance and work orders around employee work schedules and department functions.

Generally, a good property management system upgrades the quality of maintenance, improves employee and department productivity, standardizes maintenance procedures, provides planning information, tracks equipment downtime, and reduces inventory carrying costs.

However, system user-friendliness, capability, flexibility, portability, and end-user support and service will be critical to successful implementation. Chapter 5 explores a variety of computer applications for the engineering operation.

ADVANCED MANAGEMENT CONCEPTS

DEVELOPMENT OF REPLACEMENT CYCLES

Data (maintenance history and energy consumption) recorded in equipment logs are generally valuable in determining an equipment replacement cycle. Generally, there are two types of equipment operating patterns. Equipment may fail, apparently without warning. A common example is an electric lamp. If adequate numbers of units are available and in use within the property, data can be generated and accumulated on failure rates for that property. In some cases, manufacturers have accumulated extensive failure data for such units of equipment as sealed refrigeration units, television sets, small appliances, and electric lamps (incandescent and fluorescent).

Another type of failure is the gradual wearing out of a unit. As a unit wears, it generally becomes less efficient and its maintenance requirements increase. This is one reason for periodic energy measurements of selected pieces of equipment. The equipment log can be analyzed to uncover valuable data on wear that help to anticipate replacement needs.

Both types of failure can be computer programmed to determine a cycle of replacement. If a computer is currently being used for inventory purposes and work-order-request record keeping, it can also be used to determine cycles of replacement for any unit or group of units. If manual data record-keeping systems are maintained, the following analyses can be made. The complete analysis will be reviewed in the following sections and examples and formats are shown in Appendixes 2 and 3.

Items That Fail

The only certain fact regarding equipment is that someday it will fail. The exact time can only be estimated from probability theory. A classic example is the incandescent lamp, which has an average life of 1000 hours for normal-life lamps of certain wattage ranges. All this means is that the probability that a particular lamp will operate for 1000 hours is 50 percent. If 1000 lamps were installed at one time and if all were operated for an equal length of time, only 500 would still be in operation after 1000 hours of use. Figure 2.19 represents a failure, or mortality, curve for these items. Most failure curves look like Figure

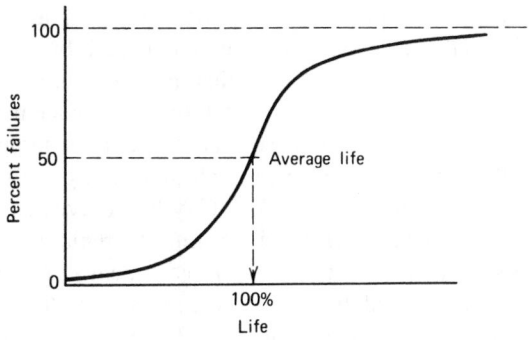

Average life is when one half of the items have failed.

FIGURE 2.19   Normal item failure curve (electric incandescent lamps.)

2.19. A manufacturer's warranty is normally based on such a curve. Warranty periods increase as the estimated life of the product increases.

If manufacturer's data are not available and if a large number of units are installed in a building, similar mortality curves can be developed. Figure 2.20 shows failure data for a particular group of items, such as television sets in a lodging establishment. In this case, a mortality is any failure of the set. Many of these failures can be repaired, but the normal procedure is to have an inventory of replacement television sets for the building. If a simple adjustment by a maintenance person does not provide a satisfactory picture, the television set is removed and replaced with another. The unit is repaired—on or off the premises—and placed back in inventory, to be used in another room at some future date. This type of exchange represents an item that fails; it is replaced with another item, and service is quickly reinstated, much as with a replaced electric lamp.

The replacement procedure becomes economically feasible when labor costs are high in relation to the cost of the item being replaced. The cost of labor includes the preparation, removal, installation, and cleanup man-hours for replacing items. It also assumes that if items fail prematurely, they will be replaced on a routine basis. This is called spot replacement. Or, it may be better to replace all the lamps in the room while a maintenance person is in the room (group replacement). This lowers the average replacement cost per lamp. See Figure 2.21 for a comparison of spot versus two types of group replacement.

The complete replacement model should provide an ideal replacement cycle. The replacement cycle can be expressed in hours, days, months, or years. Figure 2.22 shows some typical replacement cycles for incandescent and fluorescent lamps and for carpeting.

Cost data are required to complete the analysis. Unit or equipment cost of, for example, incandescent lamps, fluorescent lamps, carpets, and television sets is considered. Two equipment cost figures are required. One cost is for the purchase price of a single item, which is called the base unit cost. If a large number of items are replaced at one time, quantity purchasing discounts may be available, so that each unit has a lower unit cost. Furthermore, replacing a large number of items at one time implies that some units being replaced still work. The best of these are retained for future spot replacement.

The second set of cost data is the labor requirement for the replacement. Replacing a single incandescent lamp in a guest room usually has a high labor cost. (A study of a New York City hotel revealed that it required an average of 45 minutes of an electrician's time to replace a lamp in a guest room.)[2] The labor cost per unit for group replacement is generally lower. (The same study revealed that if all the lamps were replaced in the same guest room, the total time requirement was 52 minutes for 12 lamps, or an average time of 4.33 minutes per lamp.)

The complete analysis will reveal the least costly policy. The alternatives are:

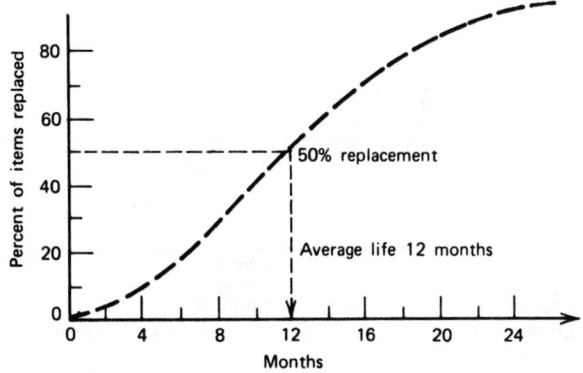

Month	Number of items replaced	Total items replaced	Percent
1	2	2	2
2	2	4	4
3	3	7	7
4	2	9	9
5	2	11	11
6	4	15	15
7	6	21	21
8	10	31	31
9	5	36	36
10	8	44	44
11	2	46	46
12	4	50	50
13	6	56	56
14	4	60	60
15	5	65	65
16	8	73	73
17	2	75	75
18	4	79	79
19	3	82	82
20	2	84	84
21	2	86	86
22	2	88	88
23	0	88	88
24	2	90	90

FIGURE 2.20   Developing a mortality curve from item failure data.

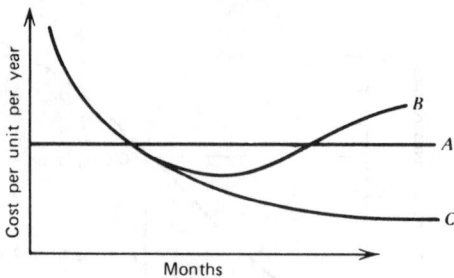

A: spot replacement, replacing items as they fail
B: group replacement at a definite cycle, replacing individual items as they fail
C: group replacement of items at definite cycles, with no replacement of items that have failed.

FIGURE 2.21   Costs of replacing items as they fail and group replacement at definite cycles of replacement.

1. Spot replacement, replacing items as they fail.
2. Group replacement at various time periods, with spot replacement of items that fail. Group replacement alternatives are numerous, as indicated in Figure 2.22, such as replacing incandescent lamps at four months, five months, and at monthly intervals through eight months.
3. Group replacement at various time periods (same replacement cycles as in alternative 2), but spot replacements are not made. Group replacement occurs when 5 to 10 percent of the devices have failed.

The complete application of this technique is shown in Appendix 2. In general, alternative 3 has the lowest cost, if one can live with a possible 5 to 10 percent burnout rate for electric lamps; see Figure 2.21, curve C. If not, alternative 2 results in significant savings over alternative 1; see Figure 2.21, curve B. Unfortunately, alternative 1 is generally practiced in most segments of the hospitality industry; see Figure 2.21, curve A. Many institutional buildings utilize group replacement concepts, and a high percentage of lodging units practice group replacement of stairwell lamps.

Items That Wear Out

Many items become less efficient with use, for example, air conditioners. This occurs even if the units are overhauled on a regular schedule. Repairs may also become excessive with equipment use and age. So, what should one do? Purchase a new unit? Continue to invest money in the present unit? The answers to these questions depend on accurate records that can be found in the maintenance log. The log should contain all repair costs and energy consumption data.

Figure 2.23 shows a record of maintenance repair and energy costs for a unit of equipment. There is no apparent pattern to these costs other than a tendency to increase with time. The rate of cost increase is a critical analysis factor. The

A. Lamps in meeting rooms:

1. Incandescent lamps:
    Rooms are in use 10 hours per day and an average of 4 days per week.
    Consider that there are 4.33 weeks per month.
    Average use per month: $10 \times 4 \times 4.33 = 173$ hours.
    If lamps have an average life of 1000 hours, the average life in a meeting room will be $1000/173 = 5.8$ months, or 6 months.
    Replacement cycles can be estimated as follows:
    4 months: 67 percent of rated lamp life
    5 months: 83 percent of rated lamp life
    6 months: 100 percent of rated lamp life
    7 months: 117 percent of rated lamp life
    8 months: 133 percent of rated lamp life

2. Fluorescent lamps:
    Same data as indicated for incandescent lamps except that the lamp life is estimated at 6000 hours.
    Replacement cycles can be estimated as follows:
    21 months: 62 percent of rated lamp life
    24 months: 70 percent of rated lamp life
    27 months: 79 percent of rated lamp life
    30 months: 88 percent of rated lamp life
    34 months: 100 percent of rated lamp life
    37 months: 109 percent of rated lamp life
    40 months: 118 percent of rated lamp life

B. Carpet in guest rooms:

Assume that data have been accumulated and it was determined that the average life is 7 years, based on 70-percent room occupancy.
The room-use life of the carpet is $7 \times 0.7 \times 365 =$ about 1800 room uses.
Typical replacement cycles may be:
1200 room-nights: 67 percent of rated use
1500 room-nights: 83 percent of rated use
1800 room-nights: 100 percent of rated use
2100 room-nights: 116 percent of rated use
2400 room-nights: 133 percent of rated use
2700 room-nights: 150 percent of rated use

FIGURE 2.22   Establishing the cycle of replacement.

total cost of operation, excluding depreciation and opportunity costs, is plotted in Figure 2.24. The rate of increase refers to the gradual increase in operating cost with time and use (the slope of the straight line).

Appendix 3 shows the complete procedure for items that wear out and an example problem. The procedure can be programmed for quick spreadsheet computer analysis.

Quarter	Maintenance cost	Energy cost	Total cost
1	$ 0	$100	$ 100
2	75	125	200
3	150	150	300
4	200	175	375
5	250	200	450
6	400	250	650
7	500	300	800
8[a]	1000	175	1175
9	200	225	425
10	350	250	600
11	500	300	800
12	1000	350	1350

[a] Major overhaul of equipment.

FIGURE 2.23 Quarterly maintenance and energy cost log for a unit of equipment.

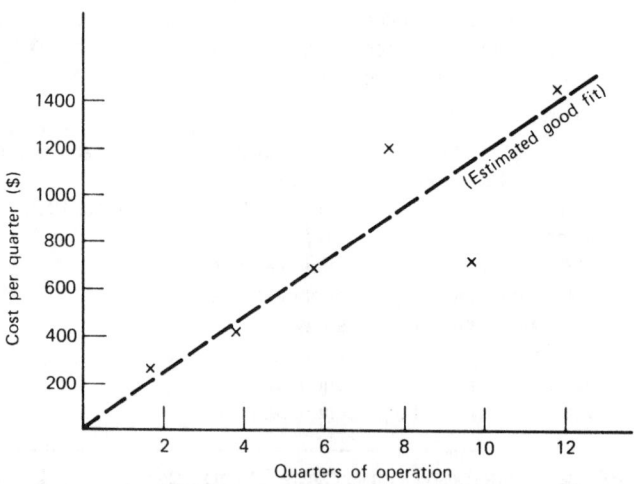

FIGURE 2.24 Graph of Figure 2.23 data, indicating a positive rate of increasing operating costs.

LIFE-CYCLE COSTING

Life-cycle costing considers all costs (present and future) for a unit of equipment, building section, or an entire building. The concept of life-cycle costing is not new. It was recognized as a useful concept in the hospitality industry in the early 1970s when energy costs were increasing. Its application became more widespread in the late 1970s when interest rates in the United States, as well as other countries, reached double digits (10 percent or higher on borrowed money). Life-cycle costing is very useful in analyzing or determining which alternative from a list of two or more is most economical, when each alternative has a different initial cost and different operating costs.

The technique, which is shown in Appendix 4, considers all costs, including future cost estimates, as present costs. It assumes, for example, that if you were to place $20,000 in an interest-earning account at the present time, you could purchase the equipment and pay for all its repairs, maintenance, and energy costs in the future from this account without adding any more money to the account.

The initial purchase price is a present cost. If repair and maintenance costs are estimated at $500 per year over the life of the unit, the present cost of repairs and maintenance can be determined by applying an appropriate factor that represents the time value of money (current interest rates when borrowing money). Future energy consumption can be estimated. Suppose that the cost of energy has been increasing. Another factor can be applied to future energy costs that represents both rates of increasing costs and the time value of money. Future taxes, insurance, and other costs can also be treated as a present cost. All these future costs are added together and represent a single present cost. This cost is calculated for each alternative, and the alternative with the lowest present cost is frequently selected as the most feasible. The complete procedure is shown in Appendix 4. Most construction alternatives for institutional building now require this analysis. Building renovation and equipment replacement analysis should also make use of this management technique.

SUMMARY

The management of the maintenance-and-engineering department can be relatively simple if it is properly organized and supervised, if it is accountable for its activities, and if it is given appropriate goals and benchmarks. Otherwise, its management can be very difficult.

The building manager must specify the department's responsibilities. One way to do this is by means of an acceptable property management record-keeping system, which minimizes customer complaints and results in a desirable physical property. The system should aid in developing the chief engineer's management ability and improve communication between management and the department.

A records system also allows the manager to evaluate the department and its head, the chief engineer. The chief engineer must be evaluated both as a manager and as a technician.

A good chief engineer should be an innovator. Innovation results in high department productivity, which quickly translates into lower costs. The chief engineer should also be receptive to new ideas and must be willing to apply them. Application of the concepts presented in this chapter will lead to these desirable results.

Finally, overall department benchmarks should be based on world-class maintenance-and-engineering departments of comparable establishments. The implementation of a Total Quality Management program accomplishes all of the concepts covered in this chapter and provides the framework for continuous property and department improvement. Such a program is highly recommended for all hospitality establishments, regardless of their size.

REFERENCES AND BIBLIOGRAPHY

1. Barrier, M., "TQM: Total Quality Management," *Nation's Business,* May 1992.
2. Borsenik, F. D., "A Study of the Maintenance Department and Its Management at the XXX Hotel," Howard Hughes Development Corporation (unpublished), 1984.
3. Borsenik, F. D., "A Study of Worker Productivity in the Maintenance Department of the Sahara Hotel, Las Vegas, Nevada," Sahara Hotel Corporation (unpublished), 1982.
4. Borsenik, F. D., Engineering Department Analysis, High Sierra Hotel, Stateline, Nevada, and Hospitality Research Center, University of Nevada, Las Vegas, 1986.
5. Borsenik, F. D., Gold River Gambling Hall and Hotel Food and Beverage Employee Productivity, Gold River Gambling Hall and Hotel, Laughlin, Nevada, and Hospitality Research Center, University of Nevada, Las Vegas, 1992.
6. Borsenik, F. D., Employee Productivity, Horseshoe Hotel and Casino, Las Vegas, Nevada, and Hospitality Research Center, University of Nevada, Las Vegas, 1994.
7. Henkoff, R., "Companies That Train Best," *Fortune,* March 22, 1993.
8. McCanney, J., "Structured Training Becomes Necessary for Effective Maintenance Management," *IMPO Magazine,* Detroit, April 1992.
9. McCanney, J., "How Does Your Maintenance Operation Compare to World-Class Organizations?" *Fortune,* March 22, 1993.
10. Muroff, C., "Maintenance Benchmarking Leads to Lower Repair Costs and Improved Quality," *IMPO Magazine,* Detroit, April 1992.
11. Shepard, S. B., "The Quality Imperative," *Business Week,* Bonus Issue, 1991.

QUESTIONS/PROBLEMS

1. Which of the forms shown in this chapter may be applied to each of the following units?

    a. Lodging
    b. Foodservice
    c. Health-care facility
    d. Club
    e. Institutional building

2. Assume that a lodging maintenance department falls into the novice status when compared to "world-class" maintenance departments. You are to make a series of recommendations to move the department into the journeyman status within the next 3 years. What type of Total Quality Management program would you recommend to upper management and the owners to meet the 3-year objective?

3. If the rate of increasing operating cost is $200 per year for a unit of equipment, the original cost of the unit was $5000, and its current salvage is $2000, determine when it should be replaced. What is its annual cost at the determined replacement cycle?

4. To what extent does the maintenance-and-engineering department of a local hotel, club, foodservice establishment, or health-care facility use a work-order system, maintain an equipment inventory/log, plan/estimate work expenses, conduct maintenance inspections, and evaluate department and employee productivity?

5. You are instructed by your supervisor to prepare a rationale/plan for the implementation of a work-order system (e.g., advantages/disadvantages, how it would be implemented). How would you respond?

6. To what extent can repair and maintenance records facilitate manpower schedules?

7. Using the information shown in the energy forms of this chapter, prepare a management report for your supervisor, summarizing trends in energy consumption.

8. Determine the extent to which a local lodging, health-care, or club facility has computerized its work reporting, scheduling, inventory, and reporting systems for the maintenance-and-engineering department. Speculate on the future role of computers in these areas.

9. As a manager, would you agree that the correct operating policy concerning maintenance/engineering is to hire a very good chief engineer and let him or her operate the department without troubling you with the details of departmental operations?

CHAPTER **3**

USDA Photo by George A. Robinson.

ENERGY AND ENERGY-MANAGEMENT SYSTEMS

ABSTRACT

The hospitality industry was unprepared and not properly motivated to cope with the energy problems of the 1970s. While segments of the industry started to react to energy issues in the late 1970s and early 1980s, some industry units are still following the guidelines of the past: doing very little. Industry surveys have revealed that while energy is a problem area for the industry, measures to deal with it are not fully developed.

Energy resources for the hospitality industry will not change greatly in the near future. Oil, gas, and electricity will continue to be basic resources to about the year 2010. However, oil and gas may be synthetic in the future, and electricity could be generated by less conventional sources. The effects of energy-related technological advances may not be very noticeable in our buildings. More water will be heated by solar devices, and building design may increasingly reflect solar potential.

Management's goal will be to keep energy costs in line or at some stabilized level. In order to do this, energy-management programs and systems are, and will continue to be, a fact of life. Energy costs will rank in importance with those of labor and food. Management will also be more concerned with property maintenance and repair as data suggest a high correlation between energy consumption and maintenance.

Key words: active solar heating; biomass energy; co-generation; computer energy control; electric demand controller; energy goals; fission; fossil energy resources; fusion; geothermal; LNG; load cycling system; LPG; OTG (ocean thermal gradient); passive solar heating; Phase 1; Phase 2; Phase 3; quad; shale oil; SNG; synthetic oil; tidal energy; time clock system.

INTRODUCTION

ENERGY COSTS: A SHORT HISTORY

In the 1960s, the price of gasoline averaged about 25 cents per gallon ($0.066 per liter). A gallon of heating oil cost less than 20 cents and some grades could be purchased for 8 to 12 cents per gallon ($0.021 to $0.032 per liter). Natural gas was about $1 per therm—100,000 Btu (29,300 watts, or $0.034 per 100 watts). The cost of electricity was generally less than 3 cents per kilowatt-hour, and even less than 1 cent in some regions of the United States. Energy costs were normally less than 1 percent of revenue for most hospitality industry buildings. Energy costs just barely kept pace with inflation and frequently lagged behind annual inflation rates throughout the world. Energy was not a major expense item. Hardly anyone cared if it increased 10 percent in any one year. Little time or effort was devoted to the control of such an available and low-cost resource.

During the 1960s, there were numerous technological and energy advances in building systems. It was not feasible, however, to replace equipment that was still performing satisfactorily with new and more efficient equipment. The vacuum-tube television sets of the 1960s usually consumed anywhere from 300 to 600 watts per hour. Television printed-circuit technology using transistors was developed during the mid-1960s. These sets had one-tenth the energy consumption of vacuum-tube sets. However, the older sets were still satisfactory, and operating energy cost was not a significant expense. So why change?

Efficient refrigeration systems were also available and were installed only to replace a less efficient unit that had failed and could not be quickly repaired. Cars in the United States were getting only 7 to 12 miles per gallon (3 to 5 kilometers per liter) of gasoline, but at a cost of only 2 to 3 cents per mile ($0.012 to $0.019 per kilometer). Energy conservation was not important. Few hospitality managers were properly prepared for what was to happen during the 1970s.

Within the next 10 years (1970s), the cost of energy increased 500 to 800 percent. Energy cost now became a significant cost in the hospitality industry. In the United States, energy rationing, especially of natural gas and gasoline, was practiced through regional allocation. An unprepared hospitality industry was caught without adequate energy alternatives. The words "energy conservation" were replaced by "energy management."

It took almost a decade (1980s) to educate the people and industry in general, and the hospitality industry in particular, in energy management. The process was slow, difficult, and costly.

Energy prices stabilized during the late 1980s and many hospitality industry executives reduced their energy-management programs. A Mideast (oil nation) crisis, however, could result in very unstable energy pricing. In less than 30 days, the cost of energy could increase 30 percent. It is very difficult to manage hospitality energy in this environment.

U.S. ENERGY POLICY

Prior to July 29, 1973, there was no U.S. energy policy. On that date the U.S. Energy Policy Office was created. In October 1973, a Mideast crisis developed that resulted in the Organization of Arab Petroleum Exporting Countries (OAPEC) declaring an oil embargo against the United States. The embargo and crisis led to rising energy costs and pricing history as presented in the previous section.

The Federal Energy Office replaced the Energy Policy Office in December 1973. In May 1974, the Federal Energy Administration replaced the Federal Energy Office. Later that year, the Energy Reorganization Act of 1974 created the Energy Research and Development Administration, the Nuclear Regulatory Commission, and the Energy Resources Council. It appears that 1974 was a very important U.S. energy policy year as two departments, a commission, and a council were established to look into U.S. energy problems. However, it was not until April 1977 that a National Energy Plan was presented by the president. The Department of Energy replaced the Federal Energy Administration and the Energy Research and Development Administration in October 1977.

The late 1970s and early 1980s saw the passage of several federal acts, which established specific energy and energy-related policies (e.g., National Energy Conservation Policy Act, Powerplants and Industrial Fuel Use Act, Public Utilities Regulatory Act, Energy Tax Act, Natural Gas Policy Act, U.S. Synthetic Fuels Corporation Act, Biomass Energy and Alcohol Fuels Act, Renewable Energy Resources Act, Solar Energy and Energy Conservation Act and Solar Energy and Energy Conservation Bank Act, Geothermal Energy Act, and Ocean Thermal Energy Conservation Act). The basis for developing a U.S. energy policy was in place in 1981. Various policies were stated and partially initiated from 1982 through 1991. In the opinion of the authors none of these was significantly successful because of political unrest in the Mideast. Each new crisis resulted in increased energy prices and changes in U.S. government efforts and policy.

The Energy Policy Act of 1992 allowed the Department of Energy to establish policy and the setting of strategic goals to meet the policy statements. The DOE (Department of Energy) publication *Sustainable Energy Strategy* clearly states the current U.S. energy policy. The following is taken from this publication.

> Our Nation's progress depends on our ability to use energy resources in ways that help the economy grow, protect the environment, and keep our Nation secure. A sustainable energy policy improves our standard of living today and expands future opportunities by maximizing energy productivity, preventing pollution, and reducing our vulnerability to global energy disruptions.
>
> Although Americans tend to focus on energy issues only in periods of energy crises, as a Nation we should be concerned about energy at

all times. Energy's continuing importance is grounded in three central facts:

1. *Energy Fuels a Competitive Economy.* Our standard of living and industrial productivity require reliable and competitively priced energy supplies. U.S. businesses and consumers directly spend more than $500 billion per year on energy.
2. *Energy Affects the Quality of the Environment.* The United States has made significant strides in reducing energy production and use. These impacts include air and water pollution; nuclear, toxic, and other waste disposal; disruption of wilderness and natural ecosystems; and greenhouse gas emissions. But to make additional progress in reducing environmental risks, we need new, more cost-effective approaches to address the problems we have already tackled, along with innovative methods to counter emerging risks.
3. *Energy Affects Our National Security.* Disruptions in global oil markets and energy price shocks have been followed by three recessions in the past 20 years. Energy policy can help reduce the economic and national security risks of relying on oil produced in unstable regions of the world.

The concept of "sustainable development"—development that meets the needs of today without compromising the ability of future generations to meet their own needs—guides the formulation of the Administration's energy policy and motivates three strategic goals:

1. *Maximize energy productivity* to strengthen our economy and improve living standards.
2. *Prevent pollution* to reduce the adverse environmental impacts associated with energy production, delivery, and use.
3. *Keep America secure* by reducing our vulnerability to global energy market shocks.

The Administration pursues a wide range of programs to attain the goals of national energy policy. The following are the strategic components of sustainable energy policy:

1. Increase the Efficiency of Energy Use.
2. Develop a Balanced Domestic Energy Resource Portfolio.
3. Invest in Science and Technology Advances.
4. Reinvent Environmental Protection.
5. Engage the International Market.

ENERGY CONSUMPTION

The basic energy consumption and reserve term is the *quad*. A quad is one quadrillion Btu (0.293 quadrillion watts), or 10^{15} Btu (0.293×10^{15} watts). This number of Btu is equivalent to 0.293×10^{12} kilowatts, or 0.293×10^{9}

megawatts, or 0.293 x 10^6 gigawatts. To get some idea of how large these numbers are, suppose that all the people in the world were to do hard work for eight hours a day with no breaks or rest periods and were to continue this for three consecutive months. They would generate approximately 1 quad of energy (see Figure 3.1).

In 1994 (latest available data), U.S. energy consumption was 88.5 quads, as compared to 70.5 in 1975; see Figure 3.2. The annual energy cost of $505 billion was equivalent to 8 percent of the gross domestic product. Also, 10 percent of the value of all U.S. imports was for oil. Fifty percent of the oil consumed in the United States was imported, and this figure is expected to rise to 60 percent by the year 2010.

Figure 3.3 compares energy consumption by end-use sector. Hospitality industry buildings are included in the residential and commercial buildings sector. Figure 3.4 shows lodging energy consumption by building function

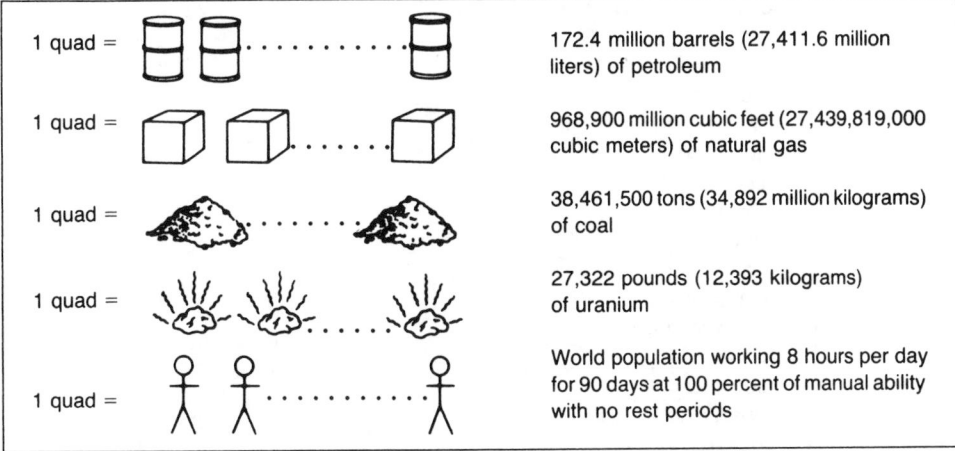

1 quad =	172.4 million barrels (27,411.6 million liters) of petroleum
1 quad =	968,900 million cubic feet (27,439,819,000 cubic meters) of natural gas
1 quad =	38,461,500 tons (34,892 million kilograms) of coal
1 quad =	27,322 pounds (12,393 kilograms) of uranium
1 quad =	World population working 8 hours per day for 90 days at 100 percent of manual ability with no rest periods

FIGURE 3.1   A quad of energy.

Resource	1975		1994	
	Quads	Watts (x10^15)	Quads	Watts (x10^15)
Coal	12.7	3.72	19.6	5.74
Natural gas	19.9	5.83	21.2	6.21
Domestic oil	20.2	5.92	17.5	5.13
Imported oil	12.5	3.66	17.1	5.01
Nuclear	1.9	0.56	6.8	1.99
Hydro and other	3.3	0.97	6.2	1.82
Total	70.5	20.66	88.5	25.93

FIGURE 3.2   U.S. energy consumption for 1975 and 1994[1].

End-use sector	1975		1994	
	Quads	Watts (x10^{15})	Quads	Watts (x10^{15})
Transportation	18.3	5.36	23.5	6.89
Residential/commercial				
Fuels	10.0	2.93	11.3	3.31
Electric	13.9	4.07	20.0	5.86
Industrial				
Fuels	22.4	6.56	22.9	6.71
Electric	6.4	1.88	10.8	3.16
Total	70.5	20.66	88.5	25.93

FIGURE 3.3   U.S. energy consumption by end-use sector for 1975 and 1994.[1]

Function area	Normal estimate energy consumption
Guest rooms and corridors	
Cooling	1.9%
Heating	11.9
Hot water	3.1
Lighting and appliances	8.1
Subtotal	25.0
Public space	
Cooling	3.3
Heating	8.4
Ventilation	7.9
Elevator	1.8
Storage areas	2.8
Other	0.8
Subtotal	25.0
Kitchen and laundry	
Process heat	27.4
Environment heating	5.7
Environment cooling	1.3
Equipment and lighting	15.6
Subtotal	50.0
Total	100.0%

FIGURE 3.4   Normal estimate of lodging energy consumption by function areas.[2]

areas. (Refer to Chapter 2 for similar foodservice energy consumption data.) There will probably be very little changes in the patterns of energy consumption for the United States during the next decade. It should be noted that natural gas and oil reserves are being depleted and this results in increasing prices. It is also known that there is a significant correlation between the price of oil and other energy prices. Hence, if the cost of a gallon of oil increases, this triggers a price increase for natural gas, coal, and electric power. A national energy policy should minimize these effects in the near future.

This chapter has two major purposes: (1) to develop a managerial energy awareness and learn energy terminology and (2) to develop the basis for a hospitality property energy plan.

ENERGY RESOURCES

One important task of this chapter is to review basic energy resources, current and future, and to indicate what effect these may have on the hospitality industry.

FOSSIL ENERGY RESOURCES

The primary fossil resources are oil, natural gas, and coal. Oil and natural gas are primary heat resources, whereas coal is used chiefly for the generation of electric energy, which is the primary source of energy in the hospitality industry.

Oil

Oil represents almost 40 percent of the total energy consumption in the United States. A single barrel of oil may be used in many products; heating oil is only one of them. Other products include natural gas, solvents, gasoline, kerosene (including diesel, jet, and stove fuels), lubricating oil, and residue.

The primary heat from oil is derived from its carbon and hydrogen content. Heating oil (#2 fuel oil) contains about 21,000 Btu per pound (13,673 watts per kilogram), or about 140,000 Btu per gallon (10,851 watts per liter).

The primary pollutant from oil is sulfur. Ideally, if low-sulfur oil is burned, the pollution problem is minimal. Limited amounts of sulfur can be removed in the refining process; however, this is difficult and frequently expensive. The United States has required higher grades of oil for heating, which contain less sulfur and produce less air pollutants.

The U.S. dependence on oil is alarming. Figure 3.2 indicates that the country is consuming about 35 quads of oil per year. Figure 3.5 shows the current known world oil reserves as of 1994. The United States only has 2 percent of the known world oil reserves. However, known oil reserves are a very conservative estimate of the total resources. Total U.S. anticipated oil reserves including marginal recovery oil (economic and technological resources are critical for recovery) and reserves not yet found, but likely to be found, could triple U.S. oil reserves (perhaps up to 6 percent of the known world resources).

Region	Percent	Billion barrels	Quads	Watts (x10^{15})
Middle East	66.4	663	3812	1117
North America	7.9	79	454	133
(United States)	(2.3)	(23)	(133)	(39)
Central\South America	7.4	74	426	125
Africa	6.2	62	357	105
Eastern Europe and former Soviet Union	5.9	59	339	99
Far East\Oceania	4.5	45	259	76
Western Europe	1.7	17	98	29
Total	100.0	998	5739	1168

FIGURE 3.5   World crude oil reserves, January 1, 1994. [1]

Shale Oil.   The United States has significant oil reserves contained in shale, or rocks. These reserves are estimated to be more than five times the known oil reserves in the United States. While world data on shale oil are not generally available, it can be safely estimated that world oil reserves contained in rocks are far in excess of known world oil reserves. There is one major problem with this vast source of energy: How can it effectively be removed from the rock?

At present, two techniques appear to have the most potential. One process involves mining, or bringing oil-rich rocks to the surface. Heat, chemical reactions, and mechanical energy are all used in the attempt to extract oil from the rock. The process is slow and costly.

A second process leaves most of the shale in the ground. Diesel oil, obtained by the mining process just described, is fed back down into the ground and is used to start a slow underground fire, fed with air at a controlled rate. The process produces heat and pressure, which forces the heavy oil contained in the shale to flow into pits; from there it is pumped to the surface for additional refining. The output is called synthetic crude, and the final product, synthetic oil, has properties very similar to oil in current use and possibly causes less pollution.

Synthetic Oil from Coal.   The production of oil from coal is possible, but the process is not very energy efficient. If all the U.S. coal reserves could be converted to oil, with current low-efficiency technology the U.S. oil reserves could be extended by 20 or 30 years.

Petroleum from Biomass Resources.   A more feasible alternative is to obtain oil from biomass wastes. It has been estimated that almost 16 percent of the average biomass wastes in the United States could be converted to synthetic oil.[3] The raw material biomass resources are manure, urban refuse, logging and wood manufacturing wastes, agricultural and food crop wastes, and municipal sewage solids. A synthetic natural gas can also be produced from these wastes.

Gas

Gas energy resources include natural gas (NG), liquid natural gas (LNG), liquified petroleum gas (LPG), and synthetic natural gas (SNG). During the 1970s, the demand for natural gas exceeded the supply in the United States. As a result, there was a temporary shift to LPG to cover the shortage of NG. U.S. imports of LNG rose sharply, and the development of SNG was greatly accelerated. As all these changes were taking place, the price of LNG increased 500 to 600 percent over a 10-year period.

Natural Gas and LNG. The primary source of heat in natural gas is methane (CH_4). When methane is combined with oxygen (contained in air), the by-products are carbon dioxide, water vapor, and heat—no pollutants. It is therefore an ideal source of energy. Natural gas provides about 1000 Btu per cubic foot (1035 watts per cubic meter). (The cubic foot is standardized at 14.7 pounds per square inch and 60°F; the cubic meter at 100 kilopascals and 15.6°C.)

Large amounts of NG contained in the earth are not counted as potential reserves because conventional well-drilling techniques cannot tap them. It is known that NG is contained in coal reserves, in tight sands, and in Devonian shale and is trapped in geopressurized zones deep within the earth. If these sources can be tapped in the future, U.S. natural gas reserves could be increased by a factor of 4 to 5.[4]

Liquid natural gas is obtained when natural gas is placed under very high pressure. Some LNG is produced when oil is refined. The United States currently imports LNG. When the high pressure is released, LNG converts to NG.

LPG. Liquified petroleum gases are primarily propane, butane, and isobutane and are usually extracted from NG. LPG is an ideal substitute for NG since gas-burning equipment can consume either NG or LPG with very simple adjustments in equipment.

SNG. Synthetic natural gas can be produced from either petroleum products or coal. Coal or petroleum products could be used to produce naphtha, the primary source of heat for SNG.

The primary advantage of SNG is that it can be piped throughout the country through existing NG pipelines. Although it can be currently produced, it is expensive. The conversion process is not very efficient, with less than 50 percent of the heat value of coal converted to usable SNG heat. It is thought that coal could be left in the ground to produce SNG. Through a somewhat similar process, it may also be possible to obtain SNG from "unrecoverable oil" that is left in the ground.

Coal

Eighty-six percent of the coal in the United States is used to generate electricity. The second most common use is as a source of energy for industry. Some large institutional complexes utilize coal to produce electric energy, with heat as a secondary output (co-generation).

Coal is one of the most abundant fossil fuel reserves in the United States, and coal reserves are available to many sections of the country. U.S. coal reserves are almost equal in energy to the known oil reserves of the Middle East.

The price of coal is always quoted at the mine and does not include transportation costs. Depending on the location of the mine and the destination of the coal, transportation costs can almost equal the price.

The heat value of coal is derived from its carbon content. One pound (kilogram) of carbon (C), when combined with sufficient oxygen (O_2), produces carbon dioxide (CO_2) and will liberate 14,000 Btu per pound (9050 watts per kilogram).

The major classifications of coal are: anthracite, 2 percent of U.S. reserves, with low sulfur content and a high heat value; bituminous, 52 percent of U.S. reserves, generally high in sulfur and with a high heat value; subbituminous, or brown coal, 38 percent of U.S. reserves, very low in sulfur (0.7 percent or less) and with a medium heat content; lignite, about 8 percent of U.S. reserves, with low sulfur and a low heat value. Peat can also be classified as a form of coal, but it has a low heat value and, with a moisture content of 70 to 90 percent, requires drying before combustion.

Coal and Sulfur. Sulfur contained in coal becomes a pollutant when coal is burned. Sulfur is one of the sources of acid rain. Several techniques can reduce the effects of pollution caused by the burning of coal: low-sulfur coal can be used; one-half to two-thirds of the sulfur can be removed from coal before combustion through various expensive processing techniques; and sulfur can also be partially removed from combustion exhaust gases. These are all costly alternatives.

NUCLEAR ENERGY

Nuclear energy can be obtained by fission or fusion. Fission requires the splitting of the uranium atomic nucleus, which results in the release of large amounts of energy. Fusion is the union of atomic nuclei to form heavier nuclei, resulting in the release of enormous quantities of energy.

Fission

Nuclear energy is currently used to produce electric energy. Present nuclear reactors use uranium, which is plentiful in the United States, as an energy source. The energy potential of 1 gram of uranium is 7.66×10^7 Btu (2.24×10^7 watts). Older uranium fission reactors, however, are only 2 to 3 percent efficient. The converter reactor is three times more efficient. A 70 percent efficient breeder reactor may become available in the near future.

Naturally, reactors have inherent disadvantages because of the radioactive properties of uranium. There is a potential environmental pollution problem while the reactor is in operation. Current reactors are water cooled, which creates a thermal pollution problem. And radioactive materials must be disposed of, which results in a very long-term waste storage problem.

Fusion

The reactions of the sun are fusion; the source of the sun's energy is hydrogen, which has a potential heat output about eight times that of uranium, with minimal radioactive output. When the fusion process is fully developed, it could meet future energy requirements with no pollutants—an ideal situation.

SOLAR ENERGY

It has been estimated that an average of 117 quads of solar energy strike the United States each day throughout the year.[5] This is greater than the nation's yearly consumption of energy. If less than 1 percent of this potential could be utilized, it would provide the United States with over 300 quads per year.

Some major problems will have to be solved before this large heat potential can be utilized. One problem is heat quality, or temperature. Present solar collectors provide temperatures of 110 to 200°F (43.3 to 93.3°C). Most building heating systems in use today require much higher-temperature energy resources. So far, the greatest use of solar energy has been for domestic and swimming pool water heating.

The second problem is that heat conversion efficiency is relatively low. If 400 Btu (117 watts) of solar energy are available, we are fortunate to convert 25 percent of this to useful heat. Related to low efficiency is a heat storage problem. This is more than a day–night storage problem. It is a season-to-season problem. Ample solar energy is available during the summer months; the problem is storing it for use during the cold winter months.

The biggest problem today is the cost of utilizing solar energy with existing mechanical systems. The cost of solar-powered systems is much greater than that of conventional energy systems. In addition, at their present state of development, solar energy systems require conventional energy systems as backups. Contributing to this initial cost are several variables and unknown factors, such as: (1) system life expectancy; (2) system efficiency;

(3) maintenance and repair costs over the life of the system; (4) expected solar energy at the site; (5) future government incentives; and (6) rate of improved technology, which may soon make existing solar energy systems obsolete. So many unknown factors, all bearing on costs, make it difficult to analyze the prospects of solar energy systems.

Basic Solar Energy Systems

Solar energy systems are classified as passive or active. Passive systems do not have mechanical components. A structure is built to utilize solar energy, to capture it for immediate warmth, and to store it for moderate nighttime temperatures.

Passive solar design principles include: building positioning; adequate ventilation, thereby reducing hot and cold spots; building structures that have thermal inertia; providing air locks at the building entrance, such as double-entry doors and revolving doors.

All buildings should be designed utilizing one or more of the listed passive solar principles, thereby reducing heating and cooling requirements for both conventional and active solar systems.

Active systems require some type of electromechanical device to capture, convert, utilize, and store energy. These are the costly systems. The system must have some type of solar cell, or receiver. The more common cells are flat-plate thermal collectors that heat fluids, water, or air.

Solar cells can also be used to convert solar energy directly to electricity, which has instant utilization. Electric energy can be conveniently stored in batteries for future use. These direct, electric energy conversion systems are called photovoltaic systems. The average American household would require about 6000 current solar photovoltaic cells to provide electric energy, even excluding its heating and cooling needs.

Other Solar Energy Systems

Under the definition of solar energy used by the Department of Energy, the following systems are now classified as solar energy systems: hydroelectric energy, tidal energy, wind energy, and ocean thermal gradients.[5]

Hydroelectric Systems. Hydroelectric systems are totally dependent on solar energy. The sun vaporizes water that is transported as clouds. Cooled clouds dissipate water as rain; excess rainfall produces streams of water, which flow to, and are retained by, dams; water from the dams flows through hydroelectric generators, which generate electric energy; hence, hydroelectric systems are classified as solar energy systems. In the mid-1990s, hydroelectric systems provided about 5 percent of the nation's energy requirements. (Switzerland obtains about one-third of its electricity from dammed water.)

One way to improve hydroelectric output is to increase either the number of dams or their output. The total hydroelectric systems in the United States produce about 52,000 megawatts of electric energy.[6] The estimated potential of U.S. hydroelectric systems is about 180,000 megawatts. That is the practical development limit. Hydroelectric systems cannot solve the country's increased energy requirements.

Tidal Energy.   The movement of water in large masses depends on the relative position of the sun and moon with respect to the earth. Because the sun is involved, tidal energy has been classified as a potential solar energy system. The tide takes roughly six hours to move one way and six hours to reverse. It may be possible to convert this movement of large water masses to useful energy as a form of hydroelectric energy.

There is a geographic constraint with tidal systems: Ideal natural harbors and maximum tide heights are generally located in rather remote areas, far from densely populated areas with high energy consumption.

Wind Energy.   Because of the role of sun-heated air currents, wind energy is also classified as solar. Two processes are potentially available for utilizing wind energy. On land, windmills are used to generate electricity or pump water. On water, hydrogen and oxygen can be produced from wind-driven electric generators.[6] Hydrogen is an excellent energy resource because it reverts to water after complete combustion.

Ocean Thermal Gradients.   Ocean thermal energy conversion (OTEC) is also classified as solar because water masses absorb up to 75 percent of the solar energy received by the earth. Hence, upper water layers are warmer than lower layers (producing the thermal gradient). This temperature difference represents an energy resource that could be used to drive electric turbines.

SECONDARY ENERGY RESOURCES

Geothermal Energy

Geothermal energy in the form of hot water or steam is trapped within the earth. Geothermal heat is also contained in subsurface rock formations. The following temperature gradients exist below the surface of the earth: One thermal layer, the level of hot rocks, is 194 to 608°F (90 to 320°C); at the 572°F (300°C) level, there is hot water, along with layers of natural gas; a deep, or magma, layer has a temperature of about 2200°F (1200°C).

There are two pollutants contained in geothermal reserves: hydrogen sulfide and salts. At a level of 0.025 ppm (parts per million), hydrogen sulfide smells like rotten eggs. Many geothermal sources have hydrogen sulfide contents of 330 to 490 ppm.[3] Some geothermal water and steam sources have a 20 percent salt content, which quickly corrodes metals.

With these problems solved, though, geothermal sources could be used for direct space heating, cooling, and electric-energy generation.

Hydrogen as a Secondary Fuel

If adequate hydrogen can be produced, it can be formed as a fuel. Its uses would be similar to gas. Hydrogen combustion is nonpolluting to the environment. As a matter of fact, upon combustion, the by-product of hydrogen is water vapor, which is returned to the environment as water for recycling.

Biomass Resources

Almost any plant or animal waste can be converted to either synthetic oil or SNG. These fuels were discussed earlier in this chapter. The biomass energy potential is rather small in the United States.

One working biomass project, located at Disney World, in Orlando, Florida, is unusual and particularly interesting. Waste water purification is a problem in Florida because of the very high water table. In this project, water hyacinth is grown in channels or ponds of waste water. The plants digest the impurities from the waste water, making it pure in a short six-day cycle. The plants are then harvested in digesting tanks to produce methane (CH_4). The concept appears to work well here, although large water areas are required to produce such energy.[7]

Electricity

Fundamentally, electricity is the by-product of another energy resource. It is produced from energy reserves. The major problem is waste. The conventional generation of electric energy utilizes coal, oil, gas, or nuclear reactors to heat water, producing high-temperature pressure steam. The steam flows through an electric turbine generator. Lower-temperature pressure steam leaves the turbine generator; this steam contains adequate energy to heat or cool buildings. When this steam is available for building heating and cooling, it is called city steam, or street steam.

City Steam

City steam, where available, is a very reasonable source of energy for heating and cooling buildings and for heating water for commercial and apartment use. Co-generation systems, which produce electric energy and at the same time provide heat, are feasible when city steam is not available. Nuclear reactor efficiency could be greatly increased if its thermal waste could be utilized rather than dissipated to the environment. With more and more energy reserves being used to generate electricity, the future development of city steam systems could be very important to the hospitality industry.

ENERGY RESOURCES SUMMARY

Oil, gas, and electricity will continue to be the primary energy resources for the hospitality industry in the near future. City steam could become an important energy resource in larger cities. Active solar energy will probably be used chiefly for heating water in existing buildings. However, solar potential can be designed in new buildings as has been done in the 1980s and 1990s. The other potential energy resources will eventually result in forms of oil and gas for direct consumption or for generating electricity. From the user's standpoint in our industry, switching from one energy resource to another will be barely perceptible.

DEVELOPING AN ENERGY-MANAGEMENT PROGRAM

THE PROPERTY ENERGY COMMITTEE

Energy management is not a one-person or one-department effort. It involves everyone in the organization, from the manager down to each employee at every level. An energy committee is usually selected, made up of one person from each major department in the property. The committee is charged with planning, implementing, and monitoring an energy program for the property. The property's manager normally indicates to the energy committee his or her energy-management philosophy, as well as the owner's. The details of the energy program, including how they are to be accomplished, are left to the committee.

The committee must be made aware that energy management is a three-phase program. The first phase includes those things that can be done now, with a minimum of organization and customer inconvenience, to conserve energy. The payoff of this phase is usually fairly large for the effort. The second phase involves readjustment of operational practices, such as adjusting environment temperatures in some areas. The money savings generated from the first two phases should be fed back into the operation so that the third phase can be implemented. The third phase, which may require additional owner investment, plus the savings from the first and second phases, involves changes in the physical property.

Committee members prepare a format and preliminary plans for each department or building service area. Department employees must be given a chance to respond and to offer program suggestions before each phase of the energy-management program is implemented.

THE ENERGY-MANAGEMENT PROGRAM

ENERGY DATABASE

A property energy base must be established or developed prior to the creation and implementation of an energy-management program. Property energy consumption records and business activity records must be obtained and correlated. Energy-management programs require a starting point, or an energy database. The data types are used to develop program goals and finally, after a predetermined time period, energy consumption is monitored and compared to the original database and goals to determine the program effectiveness.

The following sections are taken from operating hotels located in the Southwest (geographic area from Houston, Texas–San Diego, California–Salt Lake City, Utah–Albuquerque, New Mexico, and cities in between). The hotels are all in the same hotel corporation; hence, all were subject to the same basic corporate business operating policies. Only selected data are shown for comparison purposes and only partial conclusions are indicated.

Comparison of Various Energy Ratios between Hotels

Various figures will be shown that provide specific annual energy information for each of the seven hotels in the study. The presented data are for one year. The following hotel designation code is used:

SST = Seattle, Washington
ANM = Albuquerque, New Mexico
SDH = San Diego, California
WHC = Woodland Hills, California
SLC = Salt Lake City, Utah
SFF = San Francisco, California
HOUS = Houston, Texas

Energy Consumption per Occupied Guest Room Night. Figure 3.6 shows the energy consumption per occupied guest room night. The following terms are used:

Occupied Rooms = Occupied guest room nights per year
KWHR = Total kilowatt-hour consumption per year per occupied room
Gas Therm = Natural-gas therm units per occupied room
Total Therm = Total therm units per occupied room
Water = Gallons of water per occupied room
Average = Average per occupied room

Note: A "therm" is 100,000 Btu (29,300 watts). Total therm units include natural gas and the electric conversion of kilowatt-hours to therm units.

Hotel	Occupied rooms	KWHR	Gas therm	Total therm	Water
SST	6805	27.73	1.9934	2.9345	200.75
ANM	86762	37.70	1.2044	2.4910	293.25
SDH	51020	29.23	3.4817	4.4793	229.93
WHC	34791	32.18	0.9274	2.0258	255.40
SLC	39798	46.31	3.0712	4.6518	293.65
SFF	162173	26.01	0.9036	1.7915	183.19
HOUS	70565	67.00	2.2103	4.8970	578.74
Average		38.02	2.0274	3.3244	290.70

FIGURE 3.6 Energy consumption per occupied room night for seven hotels for a one-year period.

There were no statistical significant differences between any of the hotel location variables compared to the group average (KWHR, gas therm units, total therm units, and gallons of water per occupied guest room night).

Energy Consumption per Guest Room per Year.   Figure 3.7 shows the energy consumption per guest room per year. The following terms are used:

Guest Rooms = Total number of guest rooms in the hotel

KWHR = Total kilowatt-hour consumption per year per room

Gas Therm = Natural-gas therm units per room

Total Therm = Total therm units per room

Water = Gallons of water per room

Average = Average per room

Hotel	Guest rooms	KWHR	Gas therm	Total therm	Water
SST	255	7400	532	783	53585
ANM	367	8912	285	589	69328
SDH	203	7346	875	1126	57787
WHC	129	8680	250	546	68881
SLC	160	11520	764	1157	73043
SFF	563	7453	259	513	52488
HOUS	356	13280	517	971	114715
Average		9227	497	812	69975

FIGURE 3.7   Energy consumption per guest room per year for seven hotels.

There were no statistical significant differences between any of the hotel location variables compared to the group average (KWHR, gas therm units, total therm units, and gallons of water per guest room per year).

Energy Consumption per Square Foot per Year. Figure 3.8 indicates the energy consumption per square foot of building area per year. The following terms are used:

Square Feet = Building square feet within the hotel

KWHR = Total kilowatt-hour consumption per square foot

Gas Therm = Natural-gas therm units per square foot

Total Therm = Total therm units per square foot

Water = Gallons of water per square foot

Average = Average per square foot

Hotel	Square feet	KWHR	Gas therm	Total therm	Water
SST	124075	15.21	1.0935	1.6098	110.13
ANM	146244	22.36	0.7145	1.4778	173.98
SDH	83959	17.76	2.1157	2.7220	139.72
WHC	63898	17.52	0.5050	1.1030	139.06
SLC	80649	22.85	1.5155	2.2955	144.91
SFF	338343	12.47	0.4331	0.8587	87.81
HOUS	174042	27.17	1.0584	1.9855	234.65
Average		19.34	1.0623	1.7218	147.18

FIGURE 3.8 Energy consumption per square foot per year for seven hotels.

There were no statistical significant differences between any of the hotel location variables compared to the group average (KWHR, gas therm units, total therm units, and gallons of water per square foot per year).

Energy Consumption per Cover (Meal). Figure 3.9 shows energy consumption per cover (meal). The following terms are used:

Cover = Total number of covers per year, including breakfast, lunch, dinner, and banquet covers

KWHR = Total kilowatt-hour consumption per cover

Gas Therm = Natural-gas therm units per cover

Total Therm = Total therm units per cover

Water = Gallons of water per cover

Average = Average per cover

There were no significant differences between any of the hotel location variables and energy consumption per cover (total covers). In addition, similar statistical tests were made for each of the variables for each of the hotels for breakfast, lunch, dinner, and banquet covers and no significant differ-

Hotel	Cover (meals)	KWHR	Gas therm	Total therm	Water
SST	136984	13.78	0.9905	1.4581	99.75
ANM	225359	14.51	0.4637	0.9590	112.90
SDH	107109	13.92	1.6585	2.1337	109.52
WHC	46147	24.26	0.6992	1.5273	192.55
SLC	100208	130.94	8.6833	13.1524	830.27
SFF	235897	82.43	2.8635	5.6770	580.51
HOUS	155848	30.34	1.1819	2.2173	262.04
Average		44.31	2.3629	3.8750	312.51

FIGURE 3.9 Energy consumption per cover (meal) per year for seven hotels.

ences could be found for any of these meal periods and energy consumption per cover.

Energy Cost ($) as a Percentage of Total Hotel Revenue ($). Figure 3.10 shows annual energy cost ($) expressed as a percentage of total hotel revenue. The following terms are used:

$ Total Revenue = Total hotel revenue for the year

%KWHR = Total kilowatt-hour cost per year as a percentage of total hotel revenue

%Gas = Natural-gas cost per year as a percentage of total hotel revenue

%Water = Gallons of water per year as a percentage of total hotel revenue

%Total = Energy cost per year as a percentage of total hotel revenue

Average = Average per year as a percentage of total hotel revenue

Hotel	$Total revenue	%KWHR	%Gas	%Water	%Total
SST	4984115	1.8790	1.1208	0.8859	3.8856
ANM	5238543	4.9022	0.7828	0.8291	6.5141
SDH	3984022	2.4281	1.6392	0.7559	4.8232
WHC	2619469	3.7467	0.8083	0.6752	5.2303
SLC	2408758	3.7064	1.7209	0.7710	6.1982
SFF	14713308	2.0065	0.5141	0.6468	3.1674
HOUS	4729237	4.7451	1.9497	2.5233	9.2181
Average		3.3448	1.2194	1.0125	5.5767

FIGURE 3.10 Energy cost expressed as a percentage of total revenue for seven hotels.

The variables are not significantly different; for example, there is no significant difference between any of the KWHR percentages when expressed as a percentage of total hotel revenue.

Energy Cost ($) as a Percentage of Hotel Room Revenue ($).

Figure 3.11 shows annual energy cost ($) expressed as a percentage of hotel room revenue. The following terms are used:

$ Room Revenue = Hotel room revenue for the year

%KWHR = Total kilowatt-hour cost per year as a percentage of room revenue

%Gas = Natural-gas cost per year as a percentage of room revenue

%Water = Gallons of water cost per year as a percentage of room revenue

%Total = Total energy cost per year as a percentage of room revenue

Average = Average per year as a percentage of room revenue

Hotel	$Room revenue	%KWHR	%Gas	%Water	%Total
SST	3897402	2.4029	1.4333	1.1329	4.9690
ANM	4085623	6.2856	1.0037	1.0631	8.3524
SDH	3219362	3.0048	2.0286	0.9355	5.9689
WHC	2372398	4.1369	0.8925	0.7456	5.7750
SLC	1952092	4.5734	2.1235	0.9513	7.6482
SFF	12874914	2.2930	0.5875	0.7392	3.6196
HOUS	3622101	6.1954	2.5457	3.2946	12.0357
Average		4.1274	1.5164	1.2660	6.9098

FIGURE 3.11 Energy cost expressed as a percentage of room revenue for seven hotels.

There were no significant differences for KWHR, gas, or water costs when expressed as a percentage of total room revenue. The only significant difference was for total energy costs; in this case, Houston had higher total energy costs, and San Francisco had lower total energy costs. San Francisco's room revenue was over three times as high as the next largest room revenue hotel; this large room revenue resulted in a lower energy cost percentage figure. Houston had a low room rate, high unit energy costs, and a different hotel energy system.

Energy Cost ($) per Guest Room per Year.

Figure 3.12 shows energy cost ($) per hotel guest room per year. The following terms are used:

Rooms = Total hotel guest rooms

$KWHR = Total kilowatt-hour cost per year per guest room

$Gas = Natural-gas cost per year per guest room

$Water = Gallons of water cost per year per guest room

$Total = Total energy cost per year per guest room

Average = Average per year per guest room

Hotel	Guest rooms	$KWHR	$Gas	$Water	$Total
SST	255	367	219	173	759
ANM	367	700	112	118	930
SDH	203	477	322	148	947
WHC	129	761	164	137	1062
SLC	160	558	259	116	933
SFF	563	522	134	168	823
HOUS	356	630	259	335	1225
Average		573	210	171	954

FIGURE 3.12 Energy cost ($) per guest room per year for seven hotels.

There were no significant differences for energy cost per guest room per year for the seven hotels.

Energy Cost ($) per Cover (Meal).

Figure 3.13 indicates energy cost ($) per cover (meal). The following terms are used:

Covers = Total covers per year

$KWHR = Total kilowatt-hour cost per cover

$Gas = Natural-gas cost per cover

$Water = Water cost per cover

$Total = Total energy cost per cover

Average = Average energy cost per cover

There were no significant differences in the data. It should be noted that some of the energy cost figures per cover look very large, others relatively low. This leads to a very large variance and the resulting lack of significance among the data units.

Hotel	Cover (meals)	$KWHR	$Gas	$Water	$Total
SST	136984	0.6837	0.4078	0.3223	1.4138
ANM	225359	1.1395	0.1820	0.1927	1.5142
SDH	107109	0.9031	0.6097	0.2812	1.7941
WHC	46147	2.1268	0.4588	0.3833	2.9689
SLC	100208	6.3425	2.9449	1.3193	10.6067
SFF	235897	5.7686	1.4781	0.7657	8.0124
HOUS	155848	1.4399	0.5917	0.7657	2.7972
Average		2.6292	0.9533	0.7320	4.3145

FIGURE 3.13   Energy cost ($) per cover (meal) for seven hotels.

Energy Cost ($) per Maintenance Worker per Year.   Finally, Figure 3.14 shows energy cost ($) per maintenance worker (excluding the chief or head maintenance person) at each hotel. The following terms are used:

$$
\begin{aligned}
\text{Number} &= \text{Total number of maintenance personnel} \\
\text{\$Elec} &= \text{Total electric cost per maintenance person} \\
\text{\$Gas} &= \text{Natural-gas cost per maintenance person} \\
\text{\$Water} &= \text{Water cost per maintenance person} \\
\text{\$Total} &= \text{Total energy cost per maintenance person} \\
\text{Average} &= \text{Average energy cost per maintenance person}
\end{aligned}
$$

Hotel	Number	$Elec	$Gas	$Water	$Total
SST	5	18730	11172	8831	38732
ANM	8	32101	5126	5429	42656
SDH	6	16122	10885	5020	32027
WHC	4	32715	7058	5869	45669
SLC	3	29759	13817	6190	49767
SFF	6	49203	12607	15861	77671
HOUS	7	32058	13173	17047	52278
Average		30098	10548	9182	49828

FIGURE 3.14   Energy cost ($) per maintenance worker for seven hotels.

Once again, there were no significant differences in the data.

Phase 1 Energy Program

The committee must meet to discuss employee responses to overall program objectives and review employee suggestions. Phase 1, with employee suggestions incorporated, is adopted. It includes all the items that are easy to implement and that result in minimal inconveniences. A total Phase 1 program is shown in Appendix 5. An appropriate time period is established to give Phase 1 innovations a chance to work. Results are then measured, and monitoring continues during the first phase of the program.

Employees must be reminded of the committee's efforts; otherwise, individual efforts may fall off and energy consumption may rise. As with all new programs, some setbacks are to be expected.

While the Phase 1 recommendations shown in Appendix 5 are generic and applicable to all hospitality industry units, specific recommendations for temperature reduction and other measurable recommendations must be provided for a successful Phase 1 energy-management program. As an example, the following information and recommendations were taken from a Phase 1 energy-management program developed for Holiday Inns, Inc. Hotel Group.[8] Property energy consumption was correlated to seven variables: occupied guest rooms; breakfast, lunch, dinner, and banquet covers; heating degree days; and cooling hours. See Appendix 6 for the analysis and results. An analysis of variable coefficients suggested Phase 1 recommendations. For example, energy consumption was highly dependent on heating degree-days and cooling hours; therefore, reducing building temperatures during the heating season and increasing building temperatures during the cooling season could significantly reduce energy consumption.

The Phase 1 energy reduction goal was to reduce property energy consumption by 10 percent for Holiday Inns. Partial specific Phase 1 recommendations for Holiday Inn lodging units were as follows: guest room temperature control during the heating season was 55°F (12.8°C) for unsold guest rooms and 65°F (18.3°C) for unoccupied sold guest rooms, and during the cooling season was 85°F (29.4°C) for unsold guest rooms and 80°F (26.7°C) for unoccupied sold guest rooms; public corridors were set at 65°F (18.3°C) during the heating season and increased by 5°F (2.8°C) during the cooling season; food chiller and freezer temperatures were increased by 5°F (2.8°C) and it was noted that food chiller temperatures could not be set above 40°F (4.4°C); air filters were replaced or cleaned whenever air flow was reduced by 10 percent; guest room and public rest-room hot water was provided at 115°F (46.1°C) maximum; the maximum swimming pool temperature was established at 80°F (26.7°C) and the maximum spa temperature was established at 103°F (39.4°C); spa and swimming pool filter operation was limited to 12 hours per day or less to a minimum of 8 hours, when acceptable. The results of these specific recommendations and the remaining items listed in Appendix 5 for Phase 1 programs are also shown in Appendix 6.

Energy Monitors. In many cases, energy monitors are appointed by the committee. In a TQM program, each employee becomes an energy monitor. The energy monitor checks on the progress of the plan and reminds others of the program, its results, and what it means to them. An employee reward-and-penalty program may be established. The reward program can be very important. Energy management must become an operational system that is reflected in future policies and work guidelines. Energy programs are actually employee-retraining programs.

Phase 2 Energy Program

When the first phase of the program is operational and has been producing desirable results, the energy committee can recommend the adoption of the second phase of the program. A complete Phase 2 program is also shown in Appendix 5. Once again, the purpose of the program is stressed to the employees. They must be told that temporary inconveniences may occur.

Phase 3 Energy Program

The critical third phase of the program starts when the second phase is completed. Phase 3 can present major inconveniences, as the building's physical systems may change. New investments in equipment, structural changes, and changes in service techniques may result. Once again, program results must be regularly communicated to employees. A complete Phase 3 is included in Appendix 5.

Phase 3 can result in some guest or clientele adjustments. For example, individual guest room ice machines may be removed and replaced with a corridor ice machine. Guest room hot-water temperature may have to be reduced to 105°F (40.6°C). The guest room air-conditioning system may shut off automatically when the balcony sliding door is opened or is left open. The property is still offering the same services as in the past, but it is now controlling their use.

Program Follow-Through

Many programs fail because of inadequate follow-through. Energy management is not a fly-by-night program. Stating that such a program is in effect is an initial step. Results are most important. Energy consumption must, at the very least, level off and, if at all possible, decrease. A zero-growth energy consumption rate will save money in future years and usually indicates that energy reductions can also be obtained.

Program follow-through is dependent on management. A positive management attitude is the key to the success of the entire program. Any one service or device that consumes more energy should be carefully considered before its use or purchase, and the device could be rejected on the grounds that it will increase property energy consumption. The general outline of a successful program is shown in Figure 3.15. Examples of energy committee membership are shown in Figure 3.16. Finally, Appendix 5 represents a summary of a comprehensive three-phase program that is applicable to most hospitality industry properties.

A. Implement Phase One of the program
  1. Establishment of an energy committee
  2. Committee establishes basic overall objectives
  3. Establishment of what can be done now to conserve energy
  4. Employee feedback and suggestions
  5. Adoption of Phase One
  6. Implementation of Phase One, one step of the energy conservation program at a time
  7. Measurement of the results
  8. Feedback of the results to the employees
  9. Energy monitors may be appointed to reinforce program
  10. Adoption of employee reward-and-penalty system, if necessary.
B. Adoption of Phase Two of the program
  1. Informing employees of the objectives and plan of action
  2. Employee feedback and suggestions
  3. Adoption of Phase Two
  4. Implementation of Phase Two, one part at a time
  5. Measurement of the results
  6. Feedback of the results to the employees
  7. Energy monitors may be appointed to reinforce the program
  8. Adoption of employee reward-and-penalty system, if necessary.
C. Adoption of Phase Three of the program
  1. Informing employees of the objectives and plan of action
  2. Employee feedback and suggestions
  3. Adoption of Phase Three
  4. Implementation of Phase Three, one part at a time
  5. Measurement of results
  6. Feedback of the results to the employees
  7. Energy monitors may be appointed to reinforce the program
  8. Adoption of employee reward-and-penalty system, if necessary

FIGURE 3.15 Essentials of a successful energy-management program.

ENERGY REDUCTION GOALS

One of the most important tasks of the property energy-management committee is to develop energy reduction goals. An energy goal must be based on what is practical and realistic for each area of the property. If one department has low energy requirements, it may not be possible to obtain large savings. A very realistic goal is an energy consumption percentage reduction; goals should not be based on energy costs.

Energy-management goals must also be realistic from the customer's, guest's, patient's, and client's points of view. While it is outstanding to reduce energy consumption by large amounts, the services offered by the property must not be drastically affected. If it can be safely assumed that the

A. Lodging
 1. Resident manager
 2. Food and beverage manager
 3. Director of sales
 4. Controller
 5. Chief engineer
 6. Additional person appointed by manager
B. Foodservice
 1. Manager or owner
 2. Accountant
 3. Steward in charge of kitchen equipment
 4. Chef, or person in charge of food preparation
 5. Beverage manager
 6. Host or hostess
C. Club
 1. General manager
 2. Head maintenance person
 3. Food and beverage manager
 4. Controller
 5. Groundskeeper
 6. Lodging manager, if club has rooms
 7. House-committee chairman
D. Health-care facility
 1. Assistant administrator, or business manager
 2. Controller
 3. Head of plant maintenance
 4. Laundry manager
 5. Housekeeping manager
 6. Head of foodservice
 7. Representative from professional services, usually head of nursing services
E. Institutional building
 1. Assistant manager
 2. Property manager
 3. Controller
 4. Director of foodservice
 5. Housekeeping manager
 6. Sales manager or public relations manager

FIGURE 3.16 Typical membership of energy conservation committee.

clientele may experience some minor inconveniences, special notices should be posted regarding the possible inconvenience.

The previous figures were developed to show how energy data can be fitted to a property and how data from each figure could be used as an energy reduction goal (energy per occupied guest room, energy per guest room per year, energy per square foot, only to mention some examples). You should select a measurement base that allows you to compare your property to another similar unit in your geographic area. Selected energy reduction goals follow.

Energy Percentage Reduction Goals

Energy percentage reduction goals should be used initially. Eventually, energy percentage reduction goals are limited to the maximum operating efficiency and requirements of the system, so additional percentage reductions may no longer be possible. This goal is shown in Figure 3.17. Energy percentage reduction goals are also used when energy data are analyzed

---

Case 1:

Original lighting:
    100 lamps
    100-watt rating each lamp
    Energy consumption: 100 x 100 = 10,000 watts

New lighting:
    100 lamps
    75-watt rating each lamp
    Energy consumption: 100 x 75 = 7500 watts

Savings: 10,000 – 7500 = 2500 watts

Case 2:

Cannot reduce lamp size below 75 watts, because lighting level would drop to an unsafe level. However, the lighting hours can be reduced.

Present lighting hours: 10 hours per day
    Energy consumption: 7.5 x 10 = 7.5 kilowatt-hours
                7500 watts = 7.5 kilowatt-hours per hour of operation.

New lighting hours: 8 hours per day (turn on lamps only when needed).
    Energy consumption: 7.5 x 8 = 6.0 kilowatt-hours

Savings: 7.5 – 6.0 = 1.50 kilowatt-hours per day
Total savings: 2.5 (Case 1) + 1.5 (Case 2) = 4.0
                (4000 watt-hours) kilowatt-hours per day

Percentage reduction (savings): 4/10 = 0.4 or 40 percent

FIGURE 3.17   Energy consumption percentage reduction goal.

with linear and multiple regression techniques. An application of the linear regression technique follows in the section on fixed and variable energy goals and the multiple regression technique is shown in Appendix 6.

Energy Sales Percentage Goals

Energy sales percentage goals may become meaningless in a short period. Sales percentage goals may be easily met by increasing the sales price, as shown in Figure 3.18. Large percentage reductions are possible even when energy consumption increases; Figure 3.18 shows this effect.

Energy-per-Customer Goals

Many properties have used an energy-consumption-per-customer goal. This goal is better than the energy sales percentage goal but, as shown in Figure 3.19, it could also be a goal that is easy to achieve and that has short-term usefulness. Advertising and adjustments in marketing programs may increase counts and lower energy consumption figures per customer.

Fixed and Variable Energy Goals

If reliable data are available, it may be possible to separate fixed and variable energy consumption based on customer counts. For example, a hotel consumes energy even at zero occupancy; this energy is fixed energy consumption. Energy consumption goes up as building occupancy increases; this energy is variable energy consumption. This procedure can be very enlightening to management.

Basic data and information for a foodservice establishment:
  Sales: $100,000 per month
  Energy cost: $3000 per month
  Current energy cost percentage: $3000/$100,000 = 0.03 or 3 percent
Goal: Reduce energy consumption to 2.75 percent of sales

Case 1:

Sales do not change
Energy cost is reduced to $2750 per month
Energy cost percentage:$2750/$100,000 = 0.0275 or 2.75 percent
Energy goal is reached!

Case 2:

Sales increase to $112,750 per month
Energy cost: $3100 per month
Energy cost percentage: $3100/$112,750 = 0.02749 or 2.75 percent
Energy goal is reached! However, cost of energy increased from $3000 to $3100 per month for an increase of $100 or 3.33 percent.

FIGURE 3.18　Energy consumption as a percentage of sales goal.

Basic energy-per-customer data and information for a foodservice establishment:

  Gallons (liters) of water (fuel) per customer
  Kilowatt-hours per customer
  Btu (watts) per customer
  Pounds (kilograms) per customer
  Cubic feet (cubic liters) of natural gas per customer
  25,000 customers per month

Typical examples:

  Water consumption: 400,000 gallons (1,514,000 liters)
                       400,000/25,000 = 16 gallons (62 liters) per customer
  Goal: Reduce water consumption to 15 gallons (58 liters) per customer per month
  Electric consumption: 100,000 kilowatt-hours
                       100,000/25,000 = 4 kilowatt-hours per customer
  Goal: Reduce electric consumption to 3.75 kilowatt-hours per customer per month

FIGURE 3.19   Energy consumption as energy-per-customer goal.

Analysis of past data can also be used to distinguish fixed and variable energy consumption. This is shown graphically in Appendix 6. While this procedure is complex, it does provide a database for fixed and variable energy consumption. Both sets of data may now serve as separate energy reduction goals for the business.

Reduction of fixed energy consumption should provide the largest energy savings, and efforts to reduce variable energy consumption frequently have less effect, unless customer volume levels are very high. The procedure relates absolute energy consumption figures and customer, guest, client, or patient counts for one property. Careful analysis of past data is the key to the usefulness of this system in establishing cost reduction goals. It is important to compare similar time periods, for example, December versus December—two heating months—rather than December versus July—a heating versus an air-conditioning month.

The procedures described in the preceding sections indicate that in order to develop, implement, and control an energy-management program, a good database must be developed and analyzed.

Multiple Regression Applied to Energy Reduction Goals

Redlin applied a multiple regression technique to property energy consumption in two studies.[9,10] He determined that occupied guest rooms, heating degree days, cooling hours, and covers were all correlated to property energy consumption. Appendix 6 shows an application of multiple regression for a hotel. Actual energy and estimated energy consumption are plotted monthly for one year. The hotel variables are: occupied guest rooms; covers by meal period, breakfast, lunch, dinner, and banquet service; heating degree days; and cooling hours. The correlation between actual and estimated data is generally very high for multiple regression. Hence, if an energy reduction goal was set at 10 percent for a property and if there had been an unusually cold month, the procedure automatically adjusts for different input variables, and would yield a meaningful result that could be compared to the actual energy consumption for the month. The procedures shown above all assume normal conditions.

Multiple regression is currently the most accurate procedure that can be used to analyze energy data for a property. Most PC (personal computer) software spreadsheet programs have built-in multiple regression analysis capabilities.

ENERGY-MANAGEMENT CONTROL SYSTEMS

There are four common energy-management control systems: time clock, load cycling, electric demand, and computer control.

TIME CLOCK SYSTEMS

Time clock systems are the simplest and least costly energy-management control systems. They have been available for years. They turn devices on and off at predetermined or programmed time intervals. A common application is outside lighting. The timer is set for sunrise and sunset. Timers can be manually reset every 45 to 60 days. In the case of outside lighting, time clocks have now been replaced by light sensors. Most hospitality buildings have some type of time clock energy control system.

Photoelectric cells are also used as sunset and sunrise timers. They do not have to be reset for changing sunrise/sunset times. They are also activated if it becomes very dark during normal daylight hours because of a storm.

LOAD CYCLING SYSTEMS

Some control systems are load cycling. These control several large energy-consuming devices so that they do not all operate at the same time. They can also be programmed to allow only certain devices to operate within specified time periods. In this manner, they limit the length of time an electro-mechanical device is in operation, thereby controlling energy consumption. For example, dining room air conditioning could be cycled to operate only when the room is in use (much like a time clock system). At the same time, load cycling may shut down another major energy consumption system, such as electric hot-water heaters, while the dining room air conditioner is in operation.

These systems ensure that the energy delivery system will nc
tended during any time period. Thus, they are similar to a comb
control (discussed in the next section) and time clock system.

These systems are ideal for controlling energy in multiunit buildings o.
zoned buildings. In the case of a zoned building, each building section is
called a zone, with a separate heating or air-conditioning system. Assume
that a building has three zones. The controller allows only two zones to be
heated or cooled at the same time. If the third zone requires heat or cooling,
it will not be activated until the heater or cooler is shut off in one of the first
two zones. Many hospitality properties utilize load cycling control systems.
Most computer control systems have load cycling that can be programmed
by the operator.

ELECTRIC DEMAND CONTROLLERS

Electric demand controllers are very similar to load cycling in that a maximum electric demand, or energy requirement, is set. Initially, every electromechanical device that is turned on operates until a preset demand is
reached. Now, no additional device can operate until another is shut off.
During peak demand periods, many devices will not operate at the same
time, so both demand charges and energy consumption are reduced (this is
especially important for electric energy). However, in some cases, if the
central air-cooling system is not operated for a period of time the building
could warm up. Then, when the air-cooling system is finally activated, it
may have to remain on for a long time to remove excess building heat. In
this way, net energy consumption figures may not necessarily be reduced by
large amounts, but energy demand surcharges are greatly reduced.

Almost all computer control systems have electric demand programs that
can be installed by the operator. These programs can be complex because the
electric utility (supplying electric energy) may have different electric demand
charges for various times of the year and/or hours throughout the day. Hence,
the installation of the PC electric demand program will require considerable
management input. Electric demand is discussed in Chapter 11.

COMPUTER ENERGY CONTROL

The complete computer energy control system will cycle loads, control
demand, and reduce total energy consumption. The cost of the system is
usually large, but fire, security control, and occupancy sensor subsystems
can be added to the basic system with little additional cost. Some of these
complex systems can control air temperatures within definite set points in
separate rooms of a building, so that the system can reduce the excess temperature rise that occurred with the older system. When the system is properly programmed and maintained, substantial energy savings can result.

Computer systems can also be expanded to include maintenance scheduling that is dependent on operating hours, since these systems can accumu-

late operating times of such electromechanical devices as air conditioners. The high system cost results from connecting, or interfacing, each controlled device with a computer. Telephone lines or electric lines are most frequently used for this interfacing.

Several computer software programs are available for energy-management systems (see Chapter 5). Some can be operated with a PC for smaller properties, while others require a mainframe computer. Generally, larger properties, in excess of 500 guest rooms with complete services, incorporating security, life safety, and maintenance programs, require a larger PC or minicomputer. Selected computer system applications are discussed below.

The simplest computer control that does not require a PC or mainframe computer is a thermostat computer chip. It is directly attached to an energy consumption device, such as a hot-water heater.[11] The control is extremely accurate, controlling temperature to within $\pm 1°F$. It can be set to operate during selected hours (to control electric demand for electric hot-water heaters) and to provide for different temperatures of hot water throughout the day or for different days of the week. One hotel corporation installed these units in its properties and reduced hot-water energy requirements by 37 percent.

A similar unit can be used in guest rooms and can be connected to an occupancy sensor (infrared or motion detector) to control room temperatures during the heating and cooling seasons for occupied and nonoccupied rooms.

One potential installation problem with a computer system is the interface network between the devices in the rooms being controlled, central-heating and/or air-conditioning units, and the computer. At least two feasible techniques have been utilized in lodging units: telephone lines and the electric wires supplying energy to electromechanical units (wireless systems). Radio waves are sent through wires from the computer to various interface devices (thermostats, occupancy sensors, electromechanical equipment controls) to detect temperature, occupancy, or start/stop equipment. Hence, if the temperature of a guest room is above a preset limit, a signal is sent to the computer that verifies the room status; and if the room is occupied, then a signal is sent from the computer to the electromechanical control device.

One wireless computer energy control system allows the operator to establish one of three alternatives for guest room status: (1) Occupied room status measured by the room sensor, which sets the room heating temperature to $72°F \pm 3°F$. (2) Unoccupied sold room status, which sets the room heating temperature to $65°F \pm 3°F$. This system component must be interfaced with the front desk, where an operator notifies the computer that a specific guest room has been sold. When the guest checks out, an operator or cashier notifies the computer of the unsold room status. (3) Unoccupied and unsold status, which sets the room heating temperature to $55°F \pm 3°F$. In addition, the computer controls the status of the heating system by operating it at maximum efficiency for various occupancy loads during the heating season. It also operates the air-cooling system at maximum efficiency during the day. This system can also be used to survey the property for smoke detection and to control electric demand, security, grounds irrigation, the flow of ventilation air, the lighting levels for outside areas, and water chemistry for swimming pools, spas, water cooling towers, and kitchen steaming equipment. The system continuously monitors all interfaced components during a 24-hour period.[12] (*Note*: The previous system represents an example of the capabilities of one system and does not imply an endorsement of the referenced system.)

SUMMARY

The hospitality industry was unprepared and not properly motivated to cope with the energy problems of the 1970s. While segments of the industry started to react to energy issues in the late 1970s and early 1980s, some industry units are still following the guidelines of the past: doing very little. Industry surveys have revealed that while energy is a problem area for the industry, measures to deal with it are not fully developed.

Energy resources for the hospitality industry will not change greatly in the near future. Oil, gas, and electricity will continue to be basic resources until the year 2010. However, oil and gas may be synthetic in the future, and electricity could be generated by less conventional sources. The effects of energy-related technological advances may not be very noticeable in our buildings. More water will be heated by solar devices, and building design may increasingly reflect solar potential.

Management's goal will be to keep energy costs in line or at some stabilized level. In order to do this, energy-management programs and systems are, and will continue to be, a fact of life. Energy costs will rank in importance with those of labor and food. Management will also be more concerned with property maintenance and repair, as data suggest a high correlation between energy consumption and maintenance.

REFERENCES

1. *Sustainable Energy Strategy: Clean and Secure Energy for a Competitive Economy,* National Energy Policy Plan, U.S. Government Printing Office, Washington, DC, July 1995.
2. Turner, W. C., ed., *Energy Management Handbook,* Wiley, New York, 1982. (Only best-estimate energy consumption was extracted from this reference.)
3. Stoker, H. S., S. L. Seager, and R. L. Capener, *Energy from Source to Use,* Scott, Foresman, Glenview, IL, 1975.

4. *Foodservice and the Energy Outlook* for 1985 and Beyond, National Restaurant Association, Washington, DC, 1984.

5. *Energy Policy: Choices for the Future*, Energy Research and Development Administration, Office of Public Affairs, Washington, DC, 1976.

6. Energy, Special Report, *National Geographic Magazine*, February 1981.

7. "Energy Update," *Foodservice Equipment Specialist*, Vol. 37, No. 7, November 25, 1984, pp. 68–69.

8   Borsenik. F. D., Series of research reports: *Holiday Inn, Inc.—Hotel Group, Energy Management Project: Hotel Energy Data Base; Energy Management Program Phase I; Energy Management Program Phase II*, Hospitality Research and Development Center, William F. Harrah College of Hotel Administration, University of Nevada, Las Vegas, 1989.

9. Redlin, M. H., "Energy Consumption in Lodging Properties: Applying Multiple Regression Analysis for Effective Management," *Cornell Hotel and Restaurant Administration Quarterly*, Vol. 19, No. 4, February 1979.

10   Redlin, M. H., and J. A. deRoos, "Gauging Energy Savings: Further Applications of Multiple-Regression Analysis," *Cornell Hotel and Restaurant Administration Quarterly*, Vol. 20, No. 4, February 1980.

11. "Case Study/Energy Management," *Building Operating Management*, Vol. 34, No. 11, November 1987.

12. "Building Management Strategy in Hotels," ISI Wireless Incorporated, Las Vegas, 1990.

13. Aulbach, R. E., *Energy Management*, Educational Institute of the American Hotel & Motel Association, East Lansing, MI, 1984.

14. Fehner, T. R. and J. M. Hall, *Department of Energy 1977–1994: A Summary History*, Office of Scientific and Technical Information, U. S. Department of Energy, Oak Ridge, TN, November 1994.

QUESTIONS/PROBLEMS

1. Indicate several energy reduction goals for:
    a. Lodging units
    b. Foodservice establishments
    c. Country clubs
    d. City clubs
    e. Health-care facilities

2. What potential future effects may fluctuations in the availability of fossil energy resources, nuclear energy, solar energy, and secondary energy resources have on operations in the hospitality industry?

3. Apply Phases 1, 2, and 3 to a foodservice unit that is heated with oil and has electric and natural-gas cooking appliances.

4. Apply Phases 1, 2, and 3 to a club that is heated with natural gas and has electric and natural-gas cooking appliances.

5. Apply Phases 1, 2, and 3 to an institutional building that is heated with city steam and does not have foodservice facilities.

6. Determine the extent to which energy-management control systems are being used by a local lodging, health-care, foodservice, or club facility.

7. Check with a local foodservice establishment and make a list of all of its major energy-consuming devices. Indicate the energy resource required for each device and the energy consumption of each unit. (Note: Limit your list to the 25 major items in the building, counting the dining room lighting as one item, kitchen lighting as another item, and each oven as one unit):

  a. What type/types of energy reduction goals would you recommend for the unit?

  b. How can these goals be obtained?

  c. What types of energy control equipment could be used to meet these goals? Prepare an oral (or written) report of your findings and recommendations.

CHAPTER 4

Copyright © Ken Karp.

READING BLUEPRINTS FOR ENERGY MANAGEMENT

ABSTRACT

The lodging manager of the future must possess several skills and abilities. Many current managers feel that a blueprint-reading skill level will be necessary in the future. The ability to look at, to review, and to understand basic blueprints can be learned and is the primary purpose of this chapter. If the manager is involved with new construction or with building renovation, a blueprint-reading skill is a necessity. Blueprints show what is in a building, how these items are placed and arranged within the building, and provide information that is required to determine if these items can be moved or changed. This chapter discusses the purpose of blueprints, shows how they can be used, and reviews the basic types of blueprints.

Key words: *architect; benchmark; blueprint; clearance; contour line; detail view; dimension; elevation view; fire wall; full scale; hidden lines; mechanical view; model; perspective view; plan view; plot view; scale; section view; SIU; structural wall; survey view; utility wall; written specifications.*

INTRODUCTION

A blueprint of a building is a series of drawings showing the layout of building components: rooms, their sizes and shapes, doors and windows, and details that would require thousands of words to communicate to a reader. Lines, symbols, some words, and numbers are the language of the blueprint. Looking at a blueprint for the first time is a new learning experience.

Managers are frequently misled by blueprints. If they misread their messages, the result may be an incorrect picture in their minds. If they authorize work based on the incorrect image for changes to be made in a building, the outcome may be quite different from what they expected. They can now do one of two things: live with the changes and probably grow to hate them, or spend additional money to correct the structure. Most hospitality industry managers can communicate adequately in words and with numbers, but blueprints frequently present a major communication problem.

Nevertheless, blueprints are critical. If managers must rely on someone else to interpret drawings for them, errors, distortions, and filtering may appear in each step of the proposed change. Figure 4.1 shows what can happen. Which image do you think represents a better blueprint? Figure 4.1*a* shows a reader and a second person receiving messages. Figure 4.1*b* shows

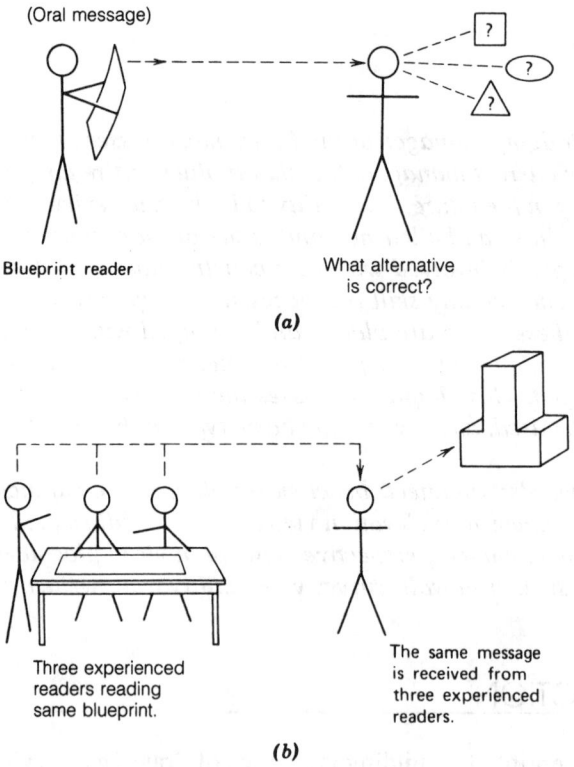

FIGURE 4.1   Reading a blueprint and conveying its message. *(a)* Confusion could result when one person reads a blueprint and relays the message to another person. *(b)* The drawing shows three expereinced blueprint readers looking at the same blueprint—all three are relaying the same message to a second person.

the same process, but with three experienced blueprint readers relaying the same message to the owner or manager. You may think that Figure 4.1*b* represents a better blueprint with clearer instructions. Actually, the same blueprint was used in each case. Only the readers differed. How would you like to be the manager in this case? A good blueprint should convey the same technical information to all readers.

The architect is a key person in developing blueprints. The architect develops your ideas and conveys them to a draftsperson, who actually makes the drawings that are reproduced as blueprints. Various engineers may be required to develop designs for building electromechanical systems. Or, properly programmed computers (with CADD software; see Chapter 5) can be used to draft building plans and many electromechanical systems. Plans for many lodging buildings have been partially generated by computers, which also print out blueprints.

BLUEPRINT USES

CONSTRUCTION AND RENOVATION

The primary purpose of a blueprint is to convey detailed instructions to people in the building trades. They read, understand, and construct according to specifications contained in these documents. The plumber looks at the plumbing mechanical views and installs the correct types and sizes of pipes in exact locations, so that when walls are enclosed, every plumbing fixture can be connected in its correct location with minimal problems. In addition, material lists are developed from the same blueprints. These material lists reduce waste and help to avoid shortages.

Managers are frequently required to supervise remodeling. A key factor in remodeling is the limitations of the existing building. Blueprints make those limitations clear. Blueprints also serve as the basic "talking point" between the manager and the architect. Managers have been known to ask architects to do the impossible because they do not understand basic building constraints. There is only so much that can be done with a given space, especially if utilities—ducts, wires, and pipes—are fixed within that space. Managers who can study blueprints can work more independently and can have preliminary estimates made without initially perhaps hiring an architect or professional engineer who, after days or weeks, might determine that nothing could be done anyway. Or, what about the manager who wants to combine two rooms into one by eliminating a wall between the rooms? The blueprint quickly indicates the likelihood that it can or cannot be done. The wall the manager wants to eliminate may be a fire wall, a structural wall, or a utility wall. A fire wall is a fireproof wall that extends upward through the entire height of the building so that, in theory, if fire destroys a room on one side of the wall, the room on the other side suffers minimum damage (see Figure 4.2*a*).

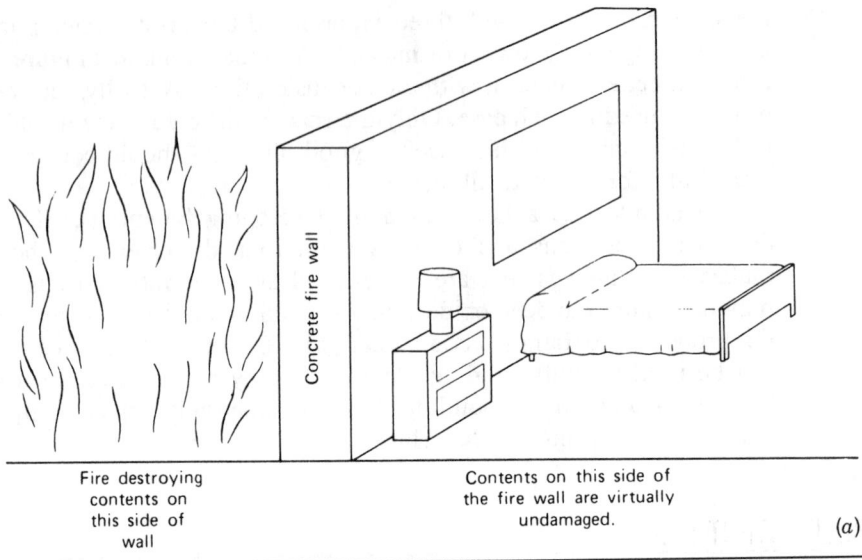

Concrete fire wall

Fire destroying contents on this side of wall

Contents on this side of the fire wall are virtually undamaged.

(a)

FIGURE 4.2(a) Fire wall stops fire from spreading throughout the building. It cannot be removed or changed unless another fire wall is built to replace it.

A structural wall provides support for the roof and the upper levels, and it cannot be removed without first constructing another means of support (see Figure 4.2b).

A utility wall encloses water, sewage, electrical, heating, ventilation, or air-conditioning conveyance systems. Removing a utility wall is costly because alternate routes have to be developed for these utilities (see Figure 4.2c).

If an idea that seemed excellent at first involves rerouting heating ducts and plumbing, it may have to be abandoned because it costs too much. For the manager with an exciting new idea for remodeling the facilities, the blueprint files should be the first stop.

For older buildings, blueprints are frequently inaccurate because renovations, or minor changes, were made several years ago and the blueprints were never updated. This can be critical if you start to knock down a wall and find that a natural-gas pipeline or high-voltage electric line was enclosed within it. Think of the potential damage, danger, expense, and inconvenience that can result from failure to update blueprints when any changes have been made.

CONVEYING IDEAS

A second use of a blueprint is to convey or sell ideas. An owner expresses ideas to an architect. The job of the architect is to present these ideas on

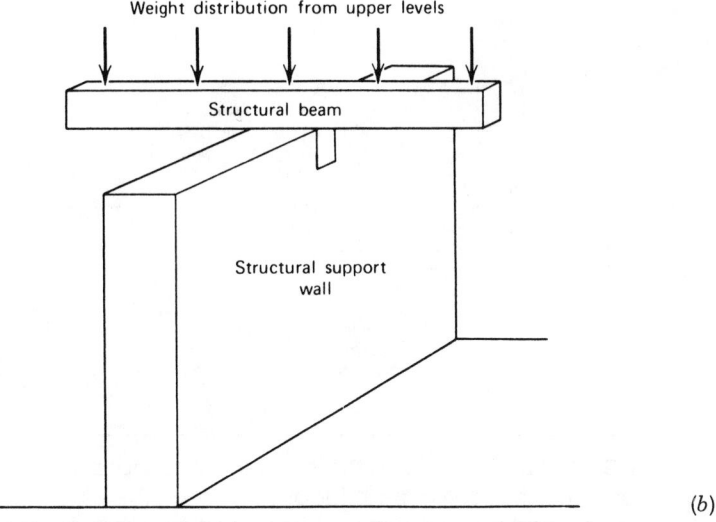

(b)

FIGURE 4.2(b) Structural wall that supports weight from upper levels cannot be removed unless a new structural support is constructed.

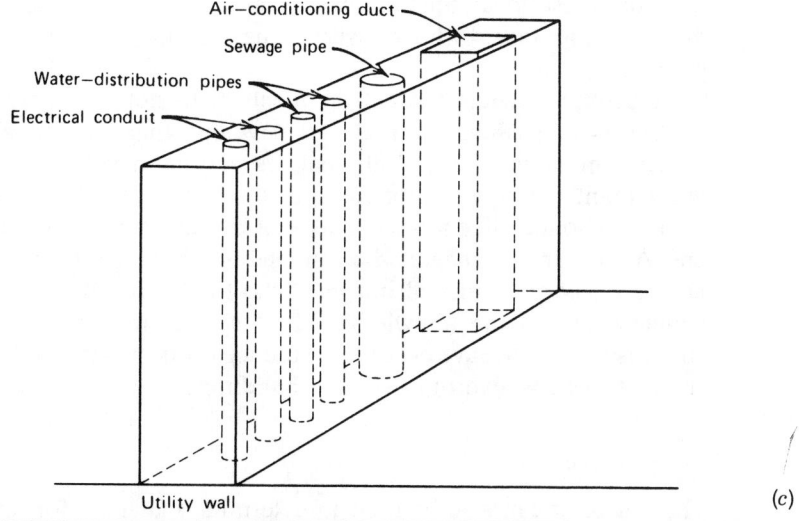

(c)

FIGURE 4.2(c) Utility wall with electric wires, water pipes, sewage pipes, and air-conditioning duct within the wall. If the wall is to be removed, alternate energy paths must be developed.

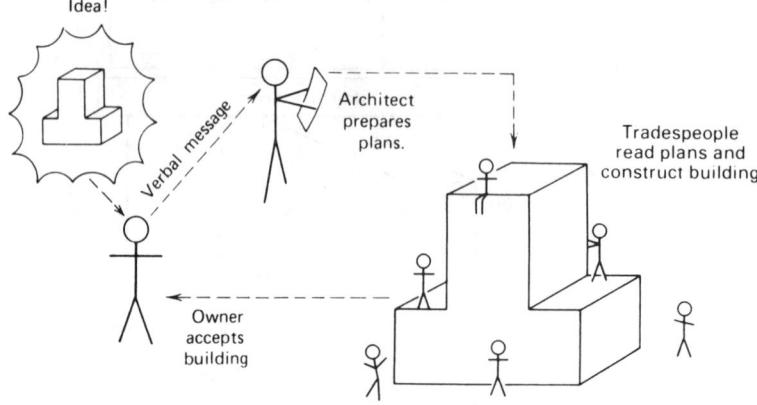

FIGURE 4.3 The role of the architect is to obtain ideas from the owner. The architect translates these ideas to paper—the blueprint. The blueprint is read by the tradespeople who construct the building. The owner observes the final product.

paper so that they have the same meaning for all readers. Blueprints that spell out these ideas for the owner may eventually be read by workers in the building trades who construct the building. Figure 4.3 shows this process.

Sometimes owners present architects with nothing more than an idea. Architects must then interpret and develop what they consider to be the owners' intentions. Several alternatives may be developed, each representing a slightly different impression of the basic idea. This may confuse the owners, who may like more than one of the alternatives but must select only one. An owner or manager who can read blueprints will make a decision and have a fairly good mental image of the final product. The same owner or manager with some knowledge of blueprints may be able to point out changes that could save energy and reduce costs. Many good blueprint readers have low cost overruns for their buildings.

MATERIALS

The blueprint can also be used to determine materials for refurbishing and redecorating. Figure 4.4a shows some examples of this technique.

The exact size of furnishings and equipment can be scaled to the size of the room, and layouts can be worked out using templates, that is, scaled patterns or outlines of furnishings, rather than arranging for a crew of workers to try several different arrangements within the room before a final decision is made. Templates can also be used to determine the size of furnishings or equipment to be placed within the rooms. The amount or sizes of floor cov-

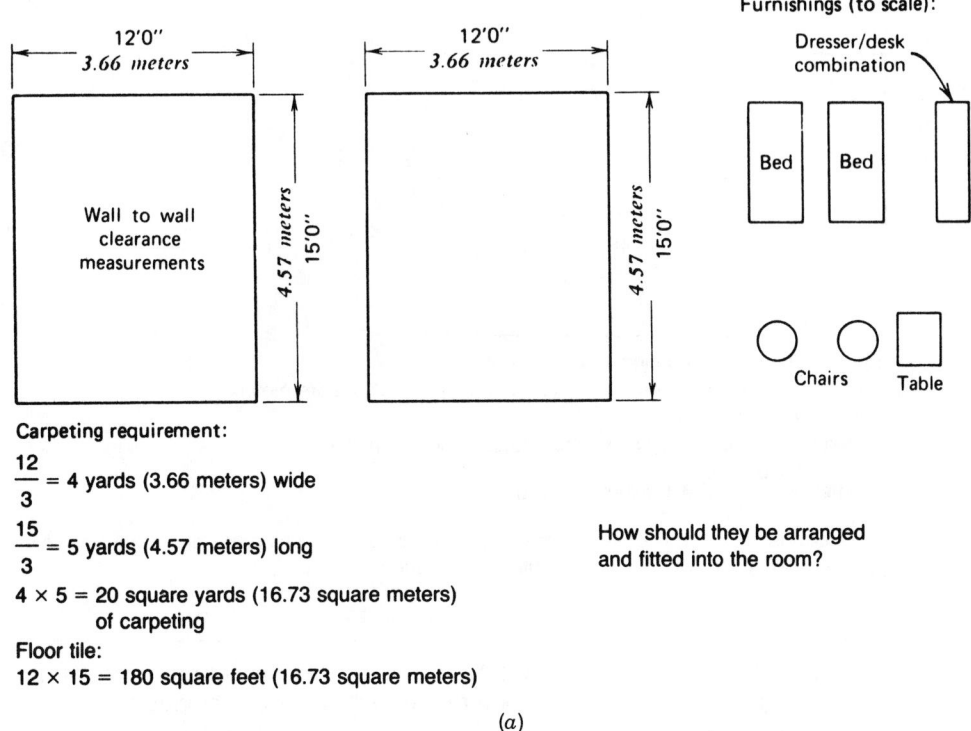

Carpeting requirement:

$$\frac{12}{3} = 4 \text{ yards (3.66 meters) wide}$$

$$\frac{15}{3} = 5 \text{ yards (4.57 meters) long}$$

$4 \times 5 = 20$ square yards (16.73 square meters)
   of carpeting

Floor tile:

$12 \times 15 = 180$ square feet (16.73 square meters)

(a)

FIGURE 4.4(a) Use of a plan view to determine floor-covering requirements for a room and the appropriate layout of furnishings within the room.

erings, wall coverings, paint, plaster, wallboard, and drapery can be developed from blueprints. Knowing the exact size will result in accurate pricing, installation, and timely quotations from suppliers.

MANPOWER REQUIREMENTS

Maintenance and housekeeping manpower requirements can be determined from blueprints if standard times (time required to do a task) are available. Figure 4.4b shows such an application. From this information, labor budgets can be established, personnel schedules developed, and optimal crew sizes and manpower needs estimated.

ENERGY SAVINGS

One of the many uses of blueprints is as a basic tool in energy management. Many of the example blueprints in this chapter indicate energy-saving ideas. Some of these ideas will be expanded in the following chapters.

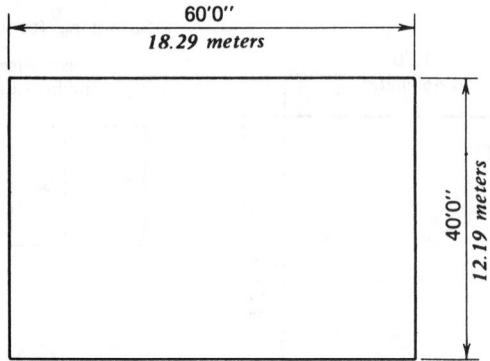

Standard time for vacuuming an empty room:
   15 minutes per 1000 square feet (0.25 hours per 92.9 square meters)
Manpower requirement:
   Area = 40 × 60 = 2400 square feet (222.96 square meters)

Time: $\dfrac{2400 \times 15}{(1000)}$ = 36 minutes (0.6 hours)

*Plus allowance for worker travel time and break time; if assumed at 25 percent, the total time allowance for the task is 45 minutes (0.75 hours).

(b)

FIGURE 4.4(b)   Determining from a blueprint the manpower requirements for vacuuming a carpet floor for a conference room or empty banquet room.

All proposed energy-consuming devices should be challenged by management before they are installed. If the devices are already in the building, the blueprint and its specifications provide information that directly indicates energy data or that is referenced so that energy data can be obtained and alternate systems evaluated. An energy-saving building renovation plan can be developed almost entirely by reviewing blueprints.

Some basic energy conservation techniques are shown in the following figures: Figure 4.5, roof insulation and alternate methods of increasing insulation thickness; Figure 4.6, insulated piping, both hot-water pipes and air-conditioning ducts; Figure 4.7, replacing incandescent with fluorescent lamps.

SCALES AND DIMENSIONS

Only very small devices or spaces are drawn to full scale on a blueprint. *Full scale* means that the item shown in the blueprint is exactly the same size as in real life. (Imagine a full-scale blueprint layout of a golf course.)

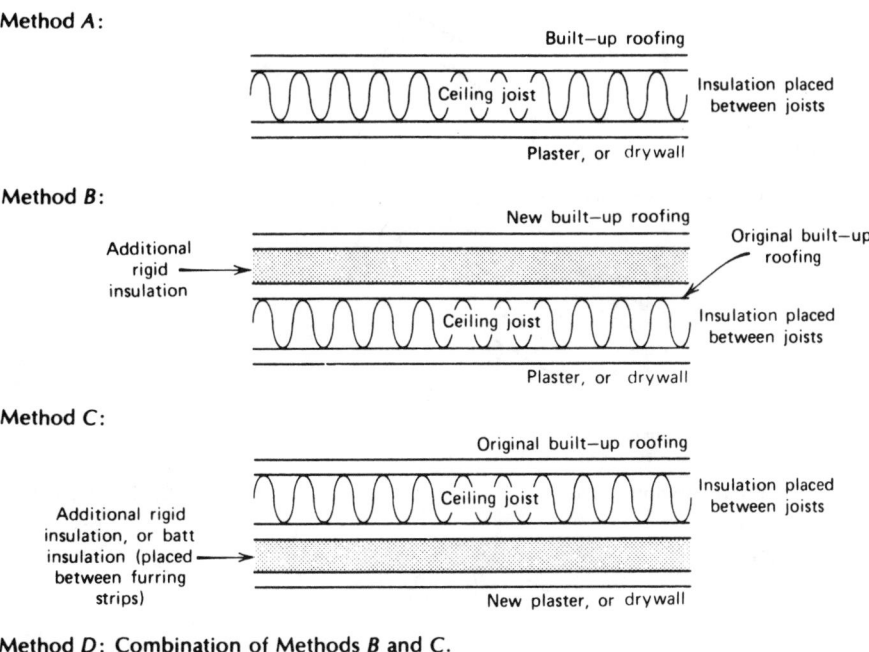

Method *D*: Combination of Methods *B* and *C*.

FIGURE 4.5 Roof insulation designation and alternate techniques of increasing insulation thickness in a roof to save energy (heating and cooling).

Even a blueprint drawn to full scale would not be very lifelike. In the golf course example, one blueprint is required for the overall layout; this would show the relative positions of the holes and the distances from the tees in the scaled drawing in Figure 4.8.

Another blueprint may be required to show the original contour and shape of the land before excavation (see Figure 4.9).

Another would be developed to show the final contour of the land (see Figure 4.10).

What about sand traps, trees, and other natural and artificial features of the course? It is very hard to get a feel for the course from a couple of sheets of paper. Yet, an experienced blueprint reader can study a detailed blueprint and actually start to develop a game plan for playing the course. (If the game plan works, the blueprint was excellent.)

At this point, it becomes necessary to reduce the actual size of the plan to a size that can be understood and is convenient to use. This reduction of size is called *scaling*. Scaling preserves the proportions and relationships of the larger image; only the size is changed.

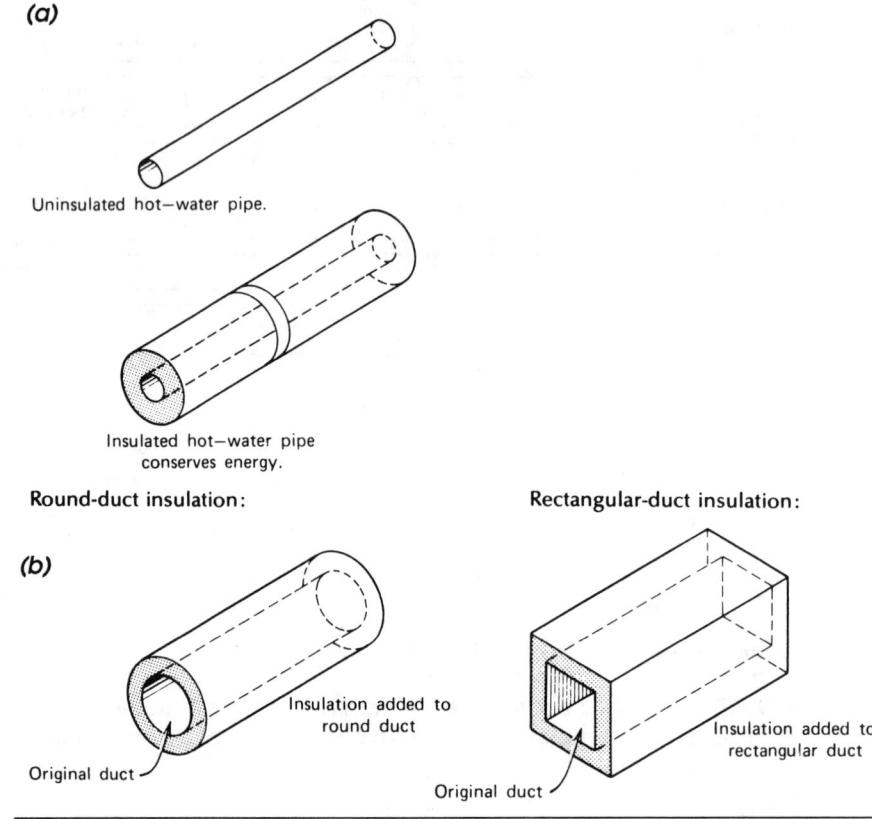

(a)

Uninsulated hot—water pipe.

Insulated hot—water pipe
conserves energy.

Round-duct insulation: **Rectangular-duct insulation:**

(b)

Insulation added to
round duct

Original duct

Insulation added to
rectangular duct

Original duct

FIGURE 4.6 Adding insulation to conserve energy. *(a)* Adding insulation to hot-water pipe to conserve energy (heat and water). *(b)* Adding insulation to air-conditioning ducts to conserve energy (heat and cooling),

Scaling is one reason people have a hard time reading and understanding blueprints. Basically, if you can read a road map, you can read a blueprint. A road map is a blueprint. A globe or model may be thought of as a three-dimensional blueprint. These representations are all reduced in scale so that the real thing is shown in sufficient and useful detail, but generally much smaller than in real life.

Scales used in the United States and other English-speaking countries can be very confusing. If the metric, or Standard International Unit (SIU), notation is adopted, blueprint scales will be greatly simplified. Standard inch–feet, or the so-called English system, will be used in this chapter and throughout the text, followed by the equivalent metric notation. These are not exact because of the difficulty of converting fractional inch scales to

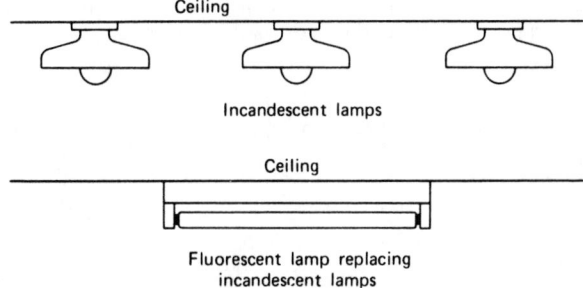

FIGURE 4.7 Replacing incandescent lamps with fluorescent lamps to conserve energy (lighting and cooling energy).

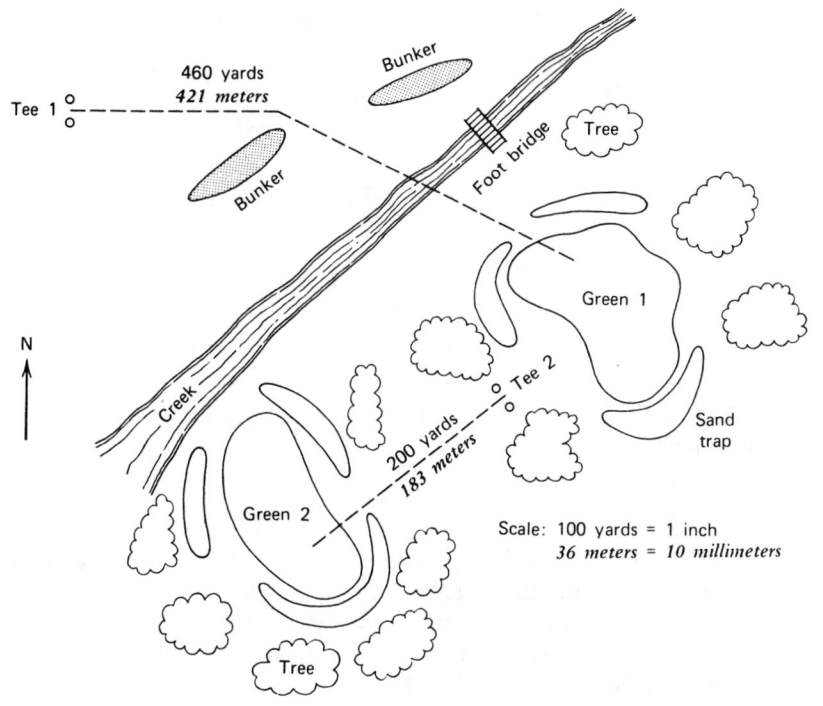

FIGURE 4.8 Partial golf course layout using a plot view.

Contour lines are lines of equal elevation from a point of reference, the benchmark. The benchmark may be indicated in feet, yards, or *meters*.

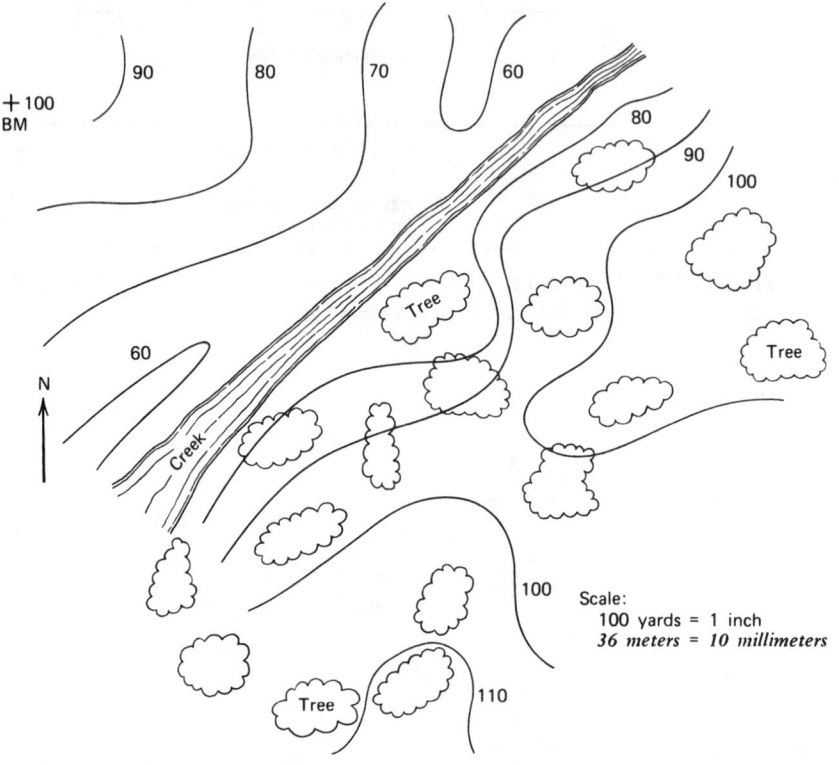

FIGURE 4.9 Contour of land before construction of golf course shown in Figure 4.8.

common SIU scales. Figure 4.11 shows how this problem develops between the standard notation in inches and its SIU equivalents.

Several common scales are shown in Figure 4.12.

Each line represents the same length of real wall, but each is drawn to a different scale. To determine the length or width of a room, all one has to do is measure the length of a line with a regular ruler, look for the scale indication, and do the simple arithmetic shown in Figure 4.13.

Figure 4.14 shows two common procedures for determining the size of a room.

Careful observation reveals that one procedure shows the clearance between the interior surface of the walls, while the alternate procedure includes the full dimensions, or thickness, of the outside wall, and one-half

Refer to Figs. 4.8 and 4.9

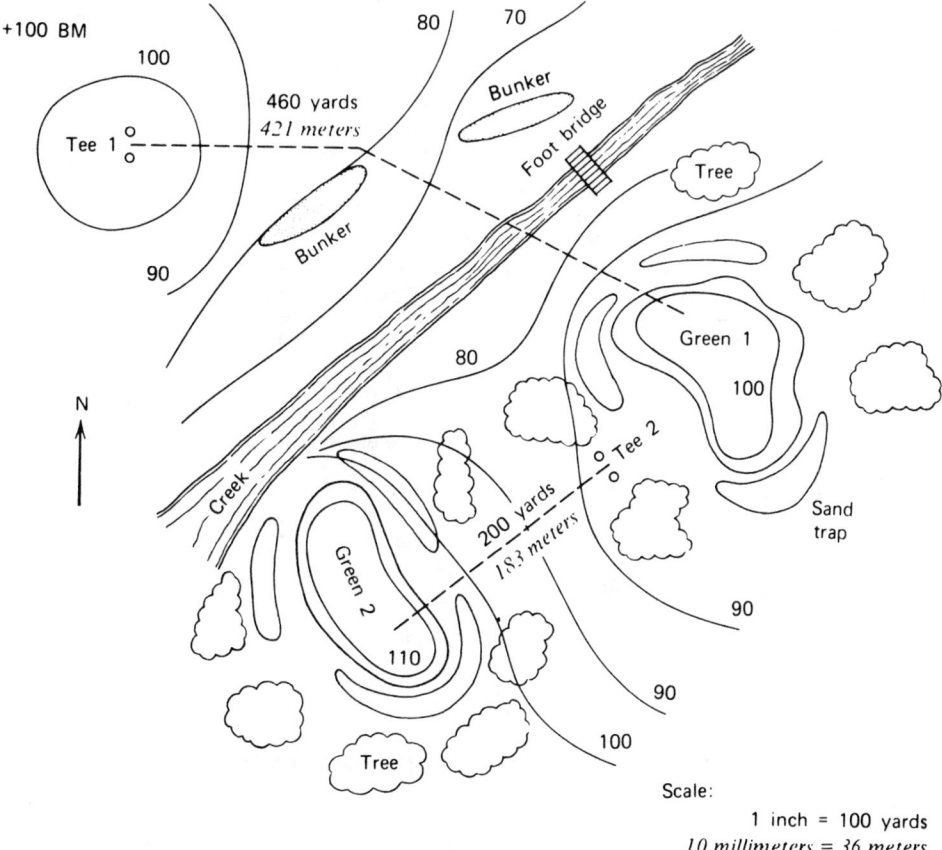

FIGURE 4.10   Partial golf course layout showing final contour lines.

Common English Designation	Standard International Designation
$\frac{1}{4}$ inch = 1 foot	8 millimeters = 1.0 meter
25 inches = 100 feet	203.2 millimeters = 30.5 meters
$\frac{1}{8}$ inch = 1 foot	4 millimeters = 1.0 meter
12.5 inches = 100 feet	151.6 millimeters = 30.5 meters
$\frac{1}{16}$ inch = 1 foot	2 millimeters = 1.0 meter
6.25 inches = 100 feet	75.8 millimeters = 30.5 meters

FIGURE 4.11   Comparison of English and Standard International length designations on blueprints.

English	Standard International
½" = 1'0"	25 millimeters = 1 meter
¼" = 1'0"	10 millimeters = 1 meter
⅛" = 1'0"	5 millimeters = 1 meter
¹⁄₁₆" = 1'0"	2 millimeters = 1 meter

Actual length 4"

About 100 millimeters

Scale (English)	Scale (Standard International)
$\frac{1}{2}$" = 1'0"	25 millimeters = 1 meter
$\frac{4}{\frac{1}{2}}$ = 8'0" (Actual)	$\frac{100}{25}$ = 4 meters
$\frac{1}{4}$" = 1'0"	10 millimeters = 1 meter
$\frac{4}{\frac{1}{4}}$ = 16'0" (Actual)	$\frac{100}{10}$ = 10 meters
$\frac{1}{8}$" = 1'0"	5 millimeters = 1 meter
$\frac{4}{\frac{1}{8}}$ = 32'0" (Actual)	$\frac{100}{5}$ = 20 meters
$\frac{1}{16}$" = 1'0"	2 millimeters = 1 meter
$\frac{4}{\frac{1}{16}}$ = 64'0" (Actual)	$\frac{100}{2}$ = 50 meters

FIGURE 4.12 Common English and Standard International scales for blueprints.

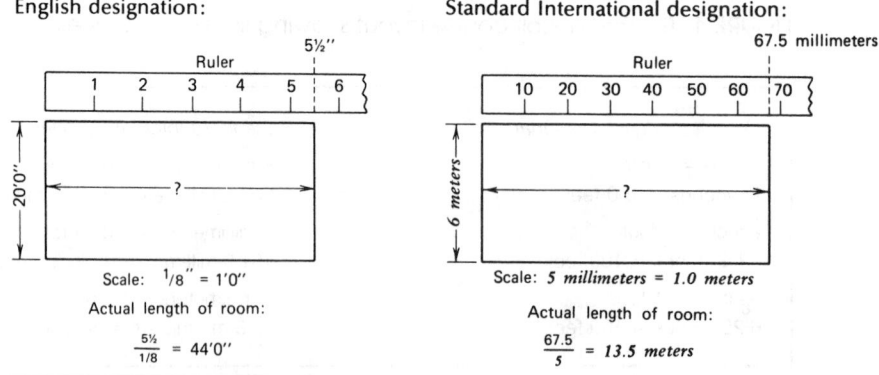

English designation:

Ruler   5½"

1 2 3 4 5 6

20'0"

?

Scale: ⅛" = 1'0"

Actual length of room:

$$\frac{5\frac{1}{2}}{1/8} = 44'0"$$

Standard International designation:

67.5 millimeters

Ruler

10 20 30 40 50 60 70

6 meters

?

Scale: 5 millimeters = 1.0 meters

Actual length of room:

$$\frac{67.5}{5} = 13.5 \text{ meters}$$

FIGURE 4.13 Use of an ordinary ruler to measure the length of a room when dimensions are not indicated.

Note: not drawn to scale.

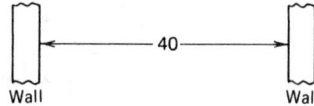

Dimension is actual clearance between walls.

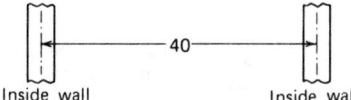

Dimension includes one-half thickness of inside walls.

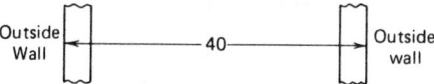

Dimension includes full thickness of outside walls.

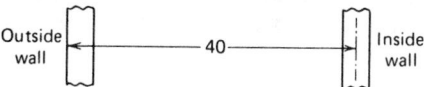

Dimension includes full thickness of outside wall and one-half thickness of inside wall.

FIGURE 4.14   Common procedures used to indicate the length of a room.

the thickness of all interior walls. While these two procedures provide the same basic information, complications can arise if you are trying to determine accurately the equipment layout in a room and fail to consider the thickness of the walls; this is shown in Figure 4.15. If you had used the wall clearance procedure, the equipment would fit as indicated in the figure.

Another example involves the determination of floor-covering materials. The example shown in Figure 4.16 is for one room. If you use dimensions for quantity determinations, make sure that wall clearance dimensions are used. They are fairly accurate.

Not all dimensions are shown on blueprints, but only those the architect considers necessary to indicate the size of each room, area, or surface. One of two procedures can be used to determine missing dimensions; both are shown in Figure 4.17. The ruler method should not be used for small scales, as any error could represent one or more feet (meters), depending on the scale.

Dashed lines on blueprints indicate locations and dimensions of important hidden surfaces: a wall, supporting structural post, or column. You cannot see it in the finished room, but if you were to cut into the indicated wall,

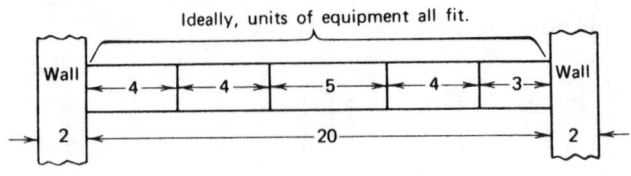

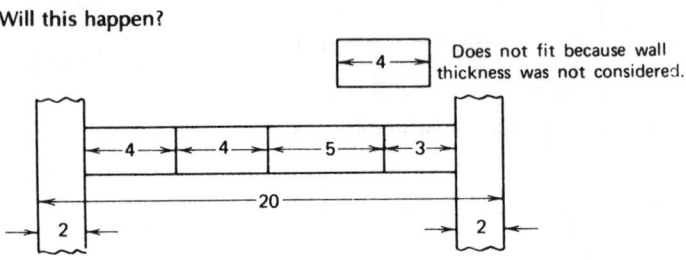

FIGURE 4.15 Problems could develop when attempting to place units of equipment between two walls if wall clearances and thicknesses are confused.

Total area to be covered: 20 × 30 = 600 square units

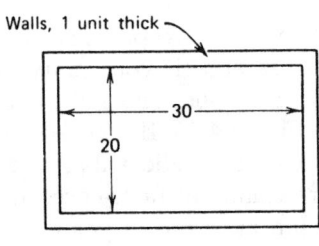

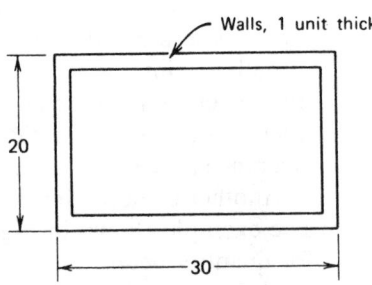

Actual clearance between walls:
30 − 1 − 1 = 28
20 − 1 − 1 = 18
Actual area: 18 × 28 = 504 square units
Difference: $\dfrac{600 - 504}{504} = \dfrac{96}{504} = 19.05\%$

FIGURE 4.16 Floor-covering material requirements vary with the dimension-designation technique.

Method *A*:

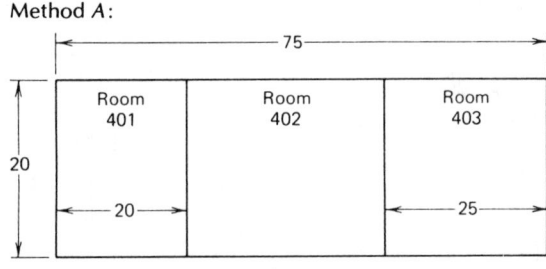

Width of Room 402: 75 − 20 − 25 = 30 units

Acceptable Method *B*, not recommended:

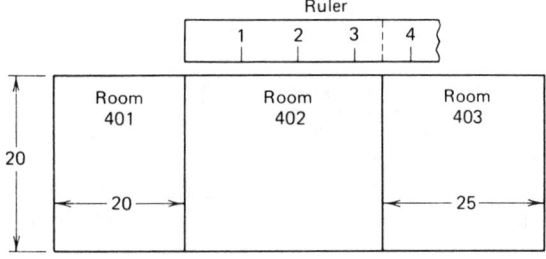

Scale: ⅛ = 1

Length: $\dfrac{3.75 \text{ units}}{⅛} = 30 \text{ units}$

FIGURE 4.17 Missing dimensions can be determined by one of two methods.

the structural member would be there, and generally it can be removed only at great expense. Figure 4.18 shows two such dashed-line dimensions. The second series of lines represents an underground room, with no apparent surface openings to the outside.

Architects should be requested to use the wall clearance dimension procedure. Then the reader will not have to remember to subtract wall thicknesses from the overall dimensions when using the blueprints for future determinations. This could become very important, especially for room layout work, as was shown in Figure 4.15.

TYPES OF BLUEPRINTS

One drawing cannot show all the construction procedures and details for a building, or even a room. It would become a mass of lines, notes, and symbols, and serious reading errors would probably result. Therefore, a series of

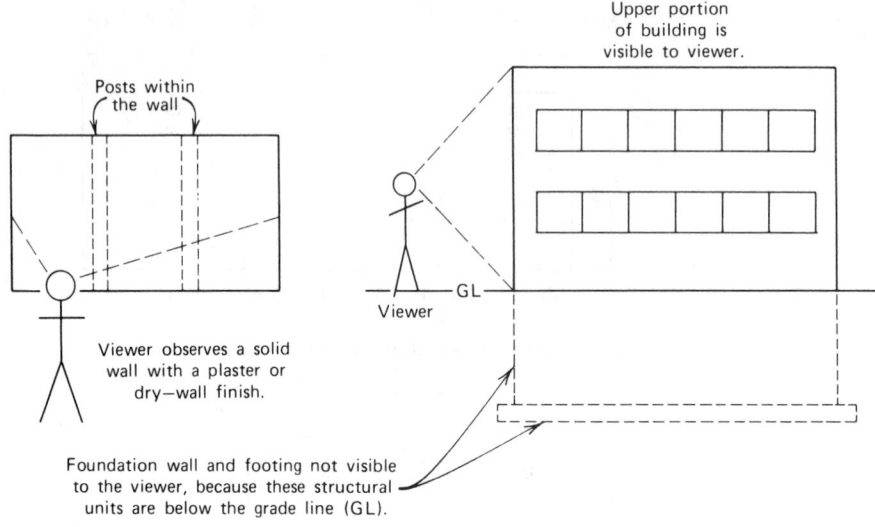

FIGURE 4.18 The use of dashed lines on a blueprint indicating hidden obstructions, or solid walls that are not visible to the viewer.

blueprints is used for each building. Each drawing is labeled and shows specific information of interest to workers in a particular building trade. Information that cannot be shown graphically, perhaps because it would be confusing, can be included in the written specifications that accompany the drawings. Generally, the combination of blueprints and written specifications are called *construction documents*.

The term *blueprint* is still used today, and its meaning is the same, but the look of the blueprint has changed. At one time, a blueprint was drawn with white lines on a blue background. The common blueprint today has blue or black lines on an off-white background. It is easier to make changes, additions, and corrections on the white background.

The more common types of drawings are plan, elevation, detail, perspective, section, mechanical, plot, and survey views. Some of these are very specialized, such as heating mechanical views, heating detail views, heating plan views, or perspective detail views. The architect must decide carefully which views should be drawn to instruct the skilled tradespeople concerning the installation procedures to be followed. As everything cannot be shown on drawings, the written specifications are an important aspect of blueprints. In some cases, the architect will make a note on a blueprint to refer to the written specifications or to local building and fire codes. Each view may also have a special set of symbols that apply only to a given type of blueprint. Some examples will be shown in the following sections. Of course, not all procedures, symbols, or terminology can be shown—entire texts would be needed to do that. Only those aspects that may be appropriate to hospitality industry management will be included.

PLAN VIEWS

The *plan view* is a top, or bird's eye, view. You see the plan as if you were looking down from above a room or area with no ceiling or roof. Figure 4.19 is such a view. The figure has circled items and additional notes that would not be necessary on an actual blueprint but that assist you in "reading" the kinds of information that can be shown on such a view.

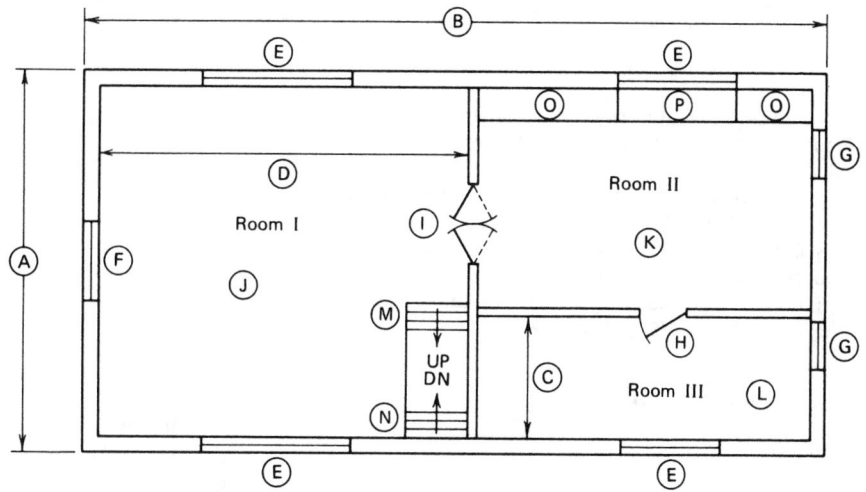

Width of total floor : Ⓐ
Length of total floor: Ⓑ
Width of room: Ⓒ
Length of room: Ⓓ
Windows, three different types or sizes: Ⓔ, Ⓕ, and Ⓖ
Door opening into Room III: Ⓗ
Double doors that open into Rooms I and II: Ⓘ
Types of floor coverings for each of the three rooms: Ⓙ, Ⓚ, and Ⓛ
Stairwell going up to the next level: Ⓜ
Stairwell going down to the lower level: Ⓝ
Cabinets on wall, built-in, wall-to-ceiling: Ⓞ
Cabinet on wall, built-in, floor-to-table height: Ⓟ

FIGURE 4.19 Plan view with additional notations to assist the reader.

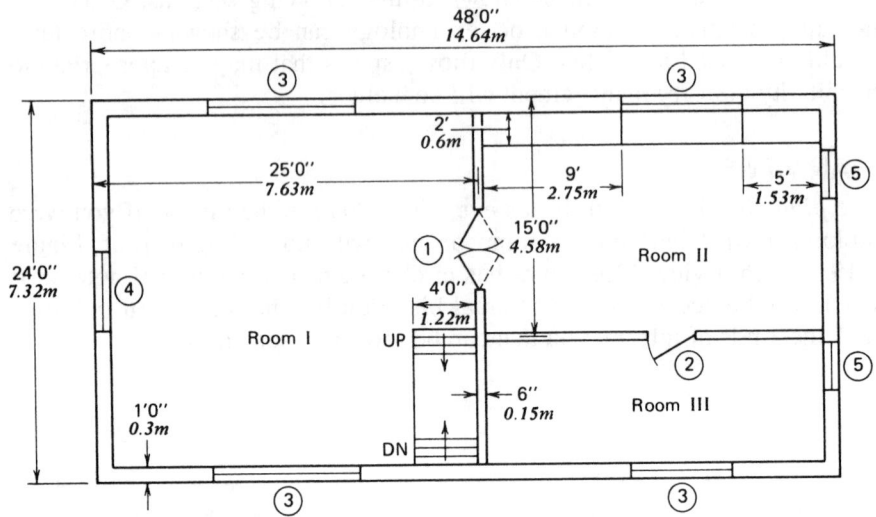

Scale: 3/32″ = 1′0″ (2.4 millimeters = 1 meter.)
  Floor coverings: I—carpet; II—tile; III—wood.
  Window schedule:
    ③ Double-hung: 42″ × 24″/24″ (1.07m × 0.6 m/0.6m)
    ④ Double-hung: 36″ × 24″/24″ (0.92m × 0.6 m/0.6m)
    ⑤ Double-hung: 24″ × 24″/24″ (0.6m × 0.6 m/0.6m)
  Door schedule:
    ① Double doors, each 2′6″ × 6′8″ (0.76m × 2.03m)
    ② Doors 3′0″ × 6′8″ (0.92m × 2.03m)

Can you answer the following?

	Answers
1. Scale	(3/32″ = 1′0″)
2. Width of total floor-plan	(24′0″)
3. Length of total floor-plan	(48′0″)
4. Size of Room I	(24′ × 25′)
5. Size of Room II	(23′ × 15′)
6. Size of Room III	(23′ × 9′)
7. Type of door between Rooms I and II	(Double)
8. Types of windows in Room I	(Double-hung)
9. Types of windows in Room III	(Double-hung)
10. Width of door opening between Rooms I and II	(5′0″)
11. Width of stairwell	(4′0″)
12. Width and depth of floor-to-ceiling cabinets in Room II.	(2′ × 9′ and 2′ × 5′)
13. Floor covering in Room I	(Carpet)
14. Wall thickness, outside walls	(1′0″)
15. Wall thickness, inside walls	(0′6″)
16. Wall-to-wall clearance of Room III.	(7′6″ × 21′6″)

FIGURE 4.20 Plan view of one floor of a building.

Figure 4.20 shows a plan view with architectural notations. Below the figure are items that the reader should be able to find on the view. You should determine the required information and compare your results with those shown in the figure. A primary use of the view is to show room layouts. Even more important, the plan view serves as a basis for various calculations, such as floor-covering sizes, electrical outlets, security-alarm-system requirements, sizes and number of furnishings, and heating, cooling, and air-conditioning determinations. It is the most common view and is frequently shown in books and magazines.

ELEVATION VIEWS

If you placed yourself outside a building and looked at an outside wall and drew a picture of that wall, you would have an *elevation view*. Figure 4.21 shows a plan view with each of the outside walls indicated by a circled letter.

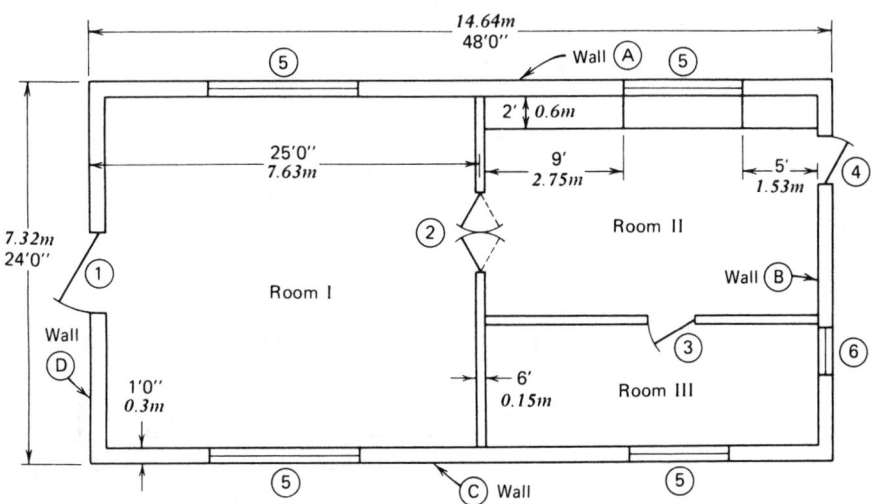

Scale: 3/32" = 1'0" (2.4 millimeters = 1 meter)
Floor coverings: Window schedule:
  Room I: Carpet   ⑤ Double-hung: 42" × 24"/24" (1.07m × 0.6 m/0.6m)
  Room II: Tile   ⑥ Double-hung: 24" × 24"/24" (0.6m × 0.6 m/0.6m)
  Room III: Wood
Door schedule:
  ① 4'0" × 6'8" (1.22m × 2.03m)
  ② Double doors, each: 2'6" × 6'8" (0.76m × 2.03m)
  ③ 3'0" × 6'8" (0.92m × 2.03m)
  ④ 3'6" × 6'8" (1.07m × 2.03m)

FIGURE 4.21 Plan view of a single-floor building.

Each letter refers to a specific wall elevation view; see Figure 4.22.

Frequently, only one elevation view is shown on a single drawing, as in Figure 4.23.

Once again, only vital information is indicated. Figure 4.24 shows another elevation view with more information. Below the figure are items that you should be able to find on the view. You should determine the required information and compare your results with those shown in the figure.

This view can be very important for the architect, who usually prepares a number of alternate elevation views from which the owner will eventually make a final decision.

There are several important energy conservation techniques that can be built into the outside walls. The wall is a critical item because heat loss and

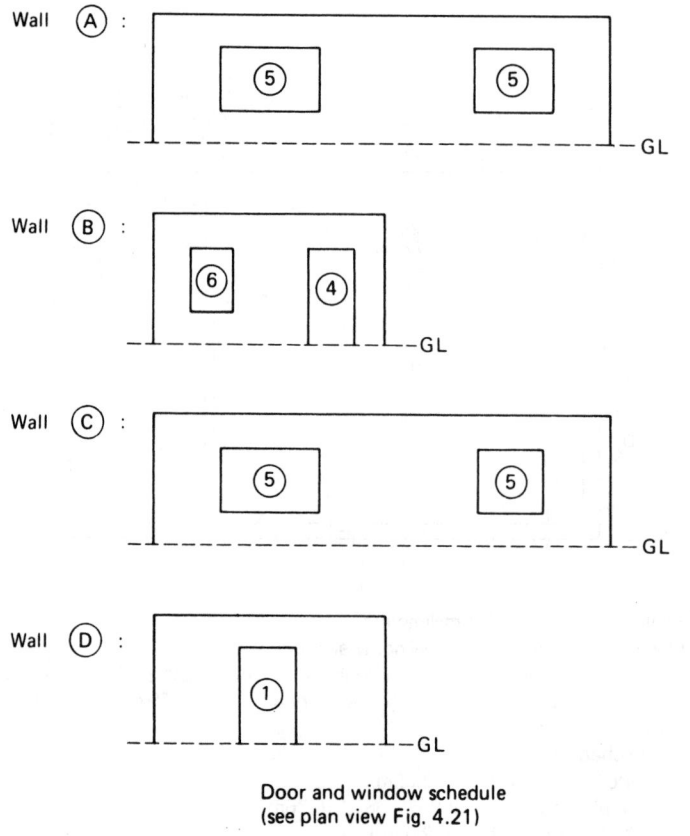

Door and window schedule
(see plan view Fig. 4.21)

FIGURE 4.22 Elevation views of the walls indicated in Figure 4.21.

Wall Ⓑ from Figs. 4.21 and 4.22

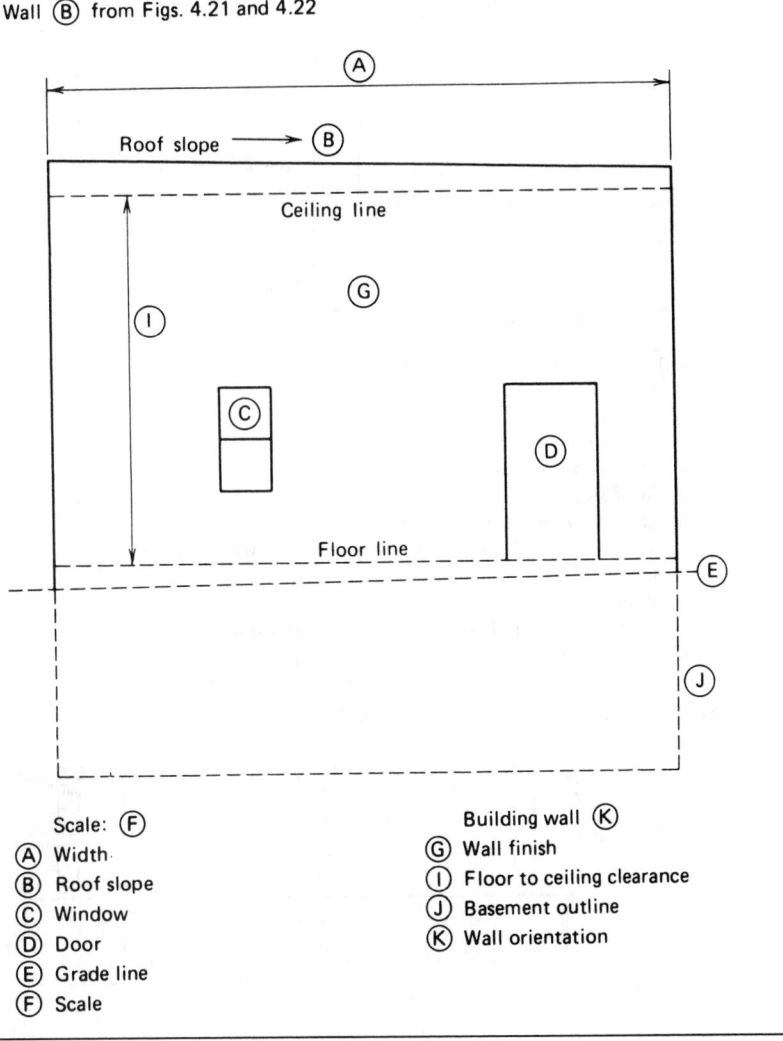

Scale: Ⓕ
Ⓐ Width
Ⓑ Roof slope
Ⓒ Window
Ⓓ Door
Ⓔ Grade line
Ⓕ Scale

Building wall Ⓚ
Ⓖ Wall finish
Ⓘ Floor to ceiling clearance
Ⓙ Basement outline
Ⓚ Wall orientation

FIGURE 4.23   Elevation view with additional notations to assist the reader.

gain depend largely on wall construction. Referring to Figure 4.25, notations should be made on the following items for energy conservation: percentage of wall area that is glass, types of windows, exterior finished material on the wall, height of interior rooms, orientation of the wall, percentage
of usable space below the grade line versus that above the grade line, balcony areas, and, most important, whether the balcony will provide an
awning effect for the lower level.

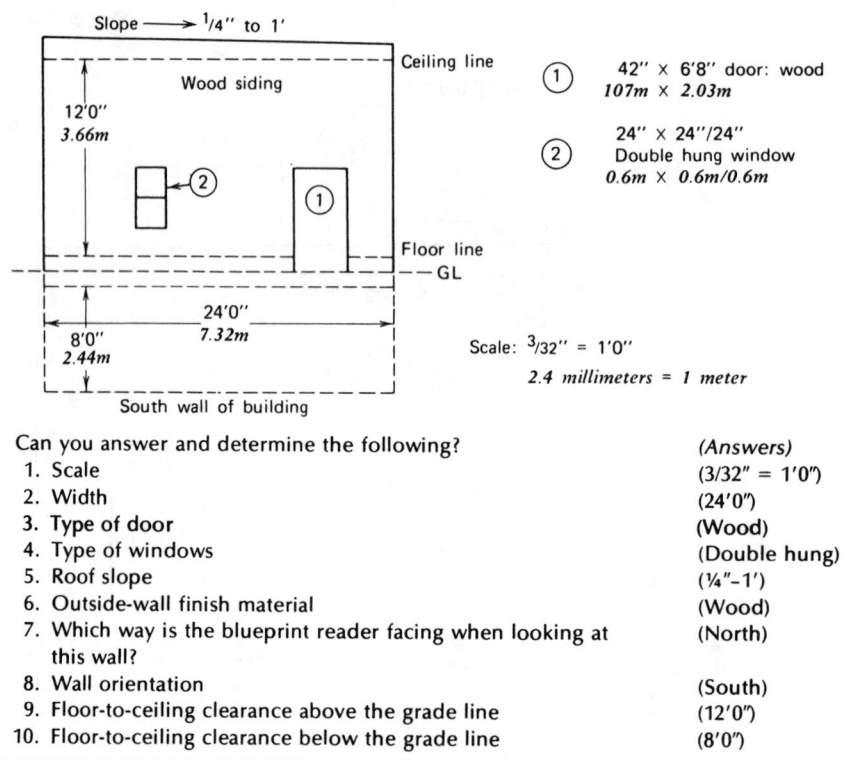

Can you answer and determine the following?   (Answers)

1. Scale   (3/32″ = 1′0″)
2. Width   (24′0″)
3. Type of door   (Wood)
4. Type of windows   (Double hung)
5. Roof slope   (¼″–1′)
6. Outside-wall finish material   (Wood)
7. Which way is the blueprint reader facing when looking at this wall?   (North)
8. Wall orientation   (South)
9. Floor-to-ceiling clearance above the grade line   (12′0″)
10. Floor-to-ceiling clearance below the grade line   (8′0″)

FIGURE 4.24   Elevation view of a building.

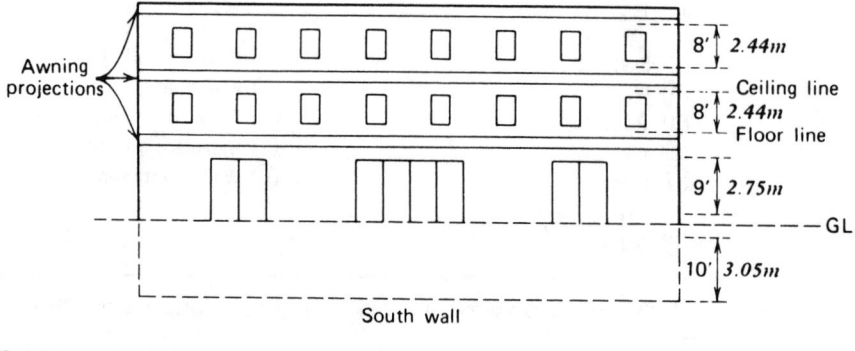

Special notations:

1. Percentage of glass area in wall   (Less than 20 percent)
2. Types of windows   (Thermal double glaze)
3. Wall-finishing material   (Wood, or insulated metal)
4. Wall color   (White, or highly reflective)
5. Interior room height (clearance)   (8′0″ 2.44 m)
6. Orientation of wall   (South)
7. Percentage of usable area below grade line versus that above the grade line   (About 30 percent)
8. Balcony areas   (Covered with awnings)

FIGURE 4.25   Elevation view with special energy conservation notations.

120

DETAIL VIEWS

The *detail view* can be a plan view or an interior-elevation drawing of an item that cannot be shown in sufficient detail in other views. As its name indicates, it shows details of construction and layout. The details of a unit of equipment are shown in Figure 4.26.

The detail of a wall is shown in Figure 4.27, while Figure 4.28 details a cabinet area on an interior wall.

A realistic view of stairs appears in Figure 4.29, and below it are various items the reader is to determine from the figure.

Frequently, there is a notation on other views (plan or elevation) that refers the blueprint reader to a specific detail view that should clarify an idea and reduce potential misunderstandings. One typical situation (Figure 4.30) actually shows a line of information flow and how a misunderstanding could develop. Detail views of interior walls, equipment location, or the relative position of permanent items and their utility connections may be of special importance for future building renovation. Detail views serve as a vital communication link between the architect and the builder.

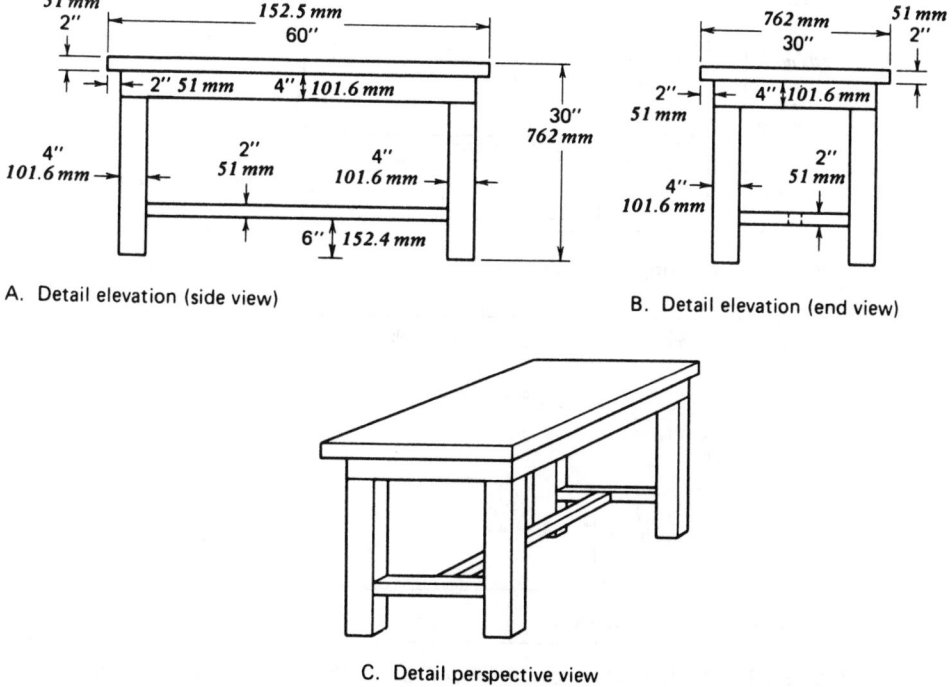

A. Detail elevation (side view)

B. Detail elevation (end view)

C. Detail perspective view

FIGURE 4.26 Detail views of a table.

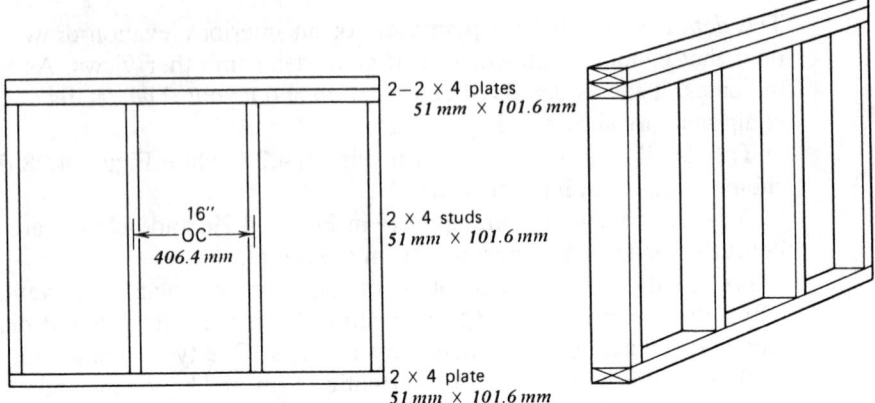

A. Detail elevation view of interior wall construction

B. Detail perspective view of interior wall construction

FIGURE 4.27 Detail views of an interior wall.

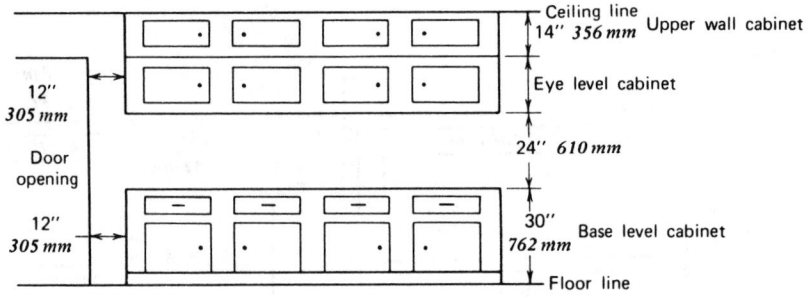

A. Detail elevation, side view

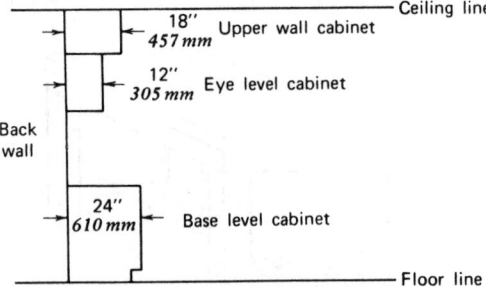

B. Detail elevation, end view

FIGURE 4.28 Detail elevation view of the location of a cabinet on a wall.

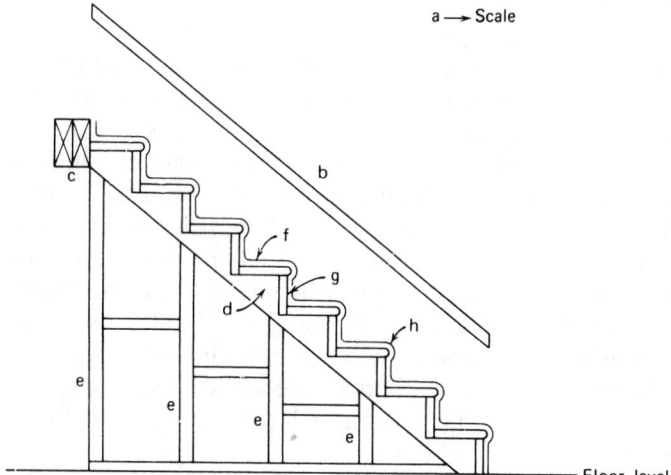

Information shown on the above view:
a. Scale
b. Handrail
c. Upper support for carriage
d. Size of carriage
e. Carriage supports
f. Tread
g. Rise
h. Carpet on tread and rise

FIGURE 4.29 Detail view of stairwell construction.

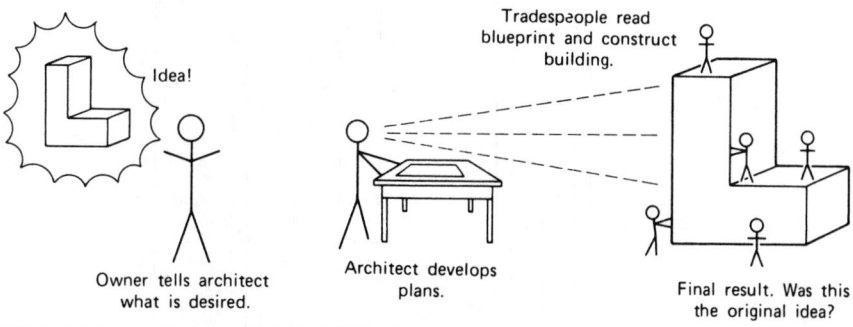

FIGURE 4.30 Blueprints communicate ideas.

PERSPECTIVE VIEWS AND MODELS

Originally, the *perspective view* was a technique to show the owner a three-dimensional rendering, or view, of a proposed building. It was normally one of the first views in a set of blueprints. The perspective view shows two elevation views and a roof plan in one drawing, as shown in Figure 4.31.

It shows nothing more than the previous elevation views. It may be dressed up with tree locations, sidewalks, parking areas, and perhaps lines of people waiting to enter the building. It is amazing how an architect can push his or her personal preference on an owner and influence a manager's decision by showing one perspective view with a parking lot full of cars and people walking toward the building (the "full house" rendering), a second view with some people and a limited number of automobiles, and a third with no people or automobiles. The architect should place the same number of people and automobiles on each perspective view. In any event, a manager should be aware of this tactic.

Many architects show perspective views and also have three-dimensional models prepared of one of the alternate exterior finishes. Figure 4.32 is a photograph of such a model. It is an impressive technique for selling ideas. The model's purpose is to replace some of the drawings so that "readers" can easily visualize and place themselves in the setting. Models also serve as blueprints. Many models are elaborate, showing sidewalks, parking areas, green grass, scaled trees, and even the contour of the land. Some are built so that the roof level can be removed and one can observe a three-dimensional plan view of an entire floor of the building.

Figure 4.33 shows a perspective detail view. This represents a combination of views that show three separate drawings on one view. These three separate views are also shown in the same figure here. However, perspective

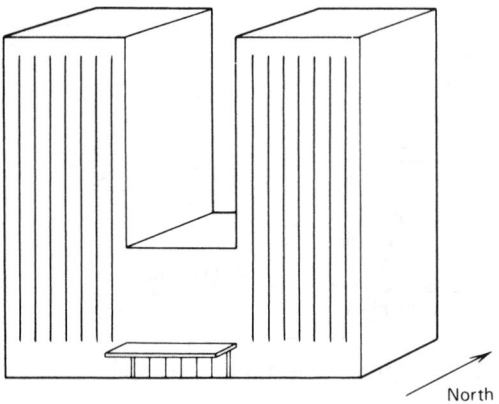

North

FIGURE 4.31 Perspective view of a building.

FIGURE 4.32   Photograph of a model.

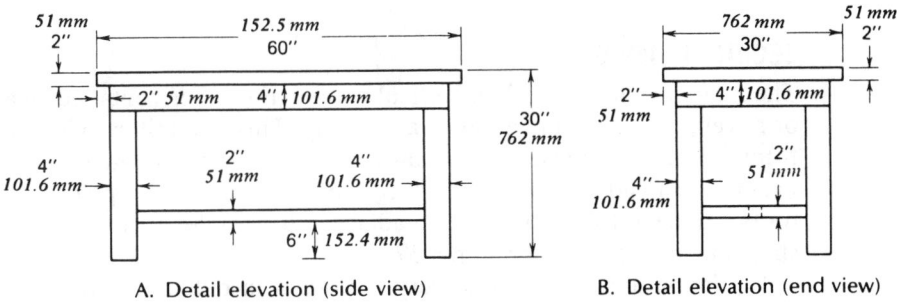

A. Detail elevation (side view)   B. Detail elevation (end view)

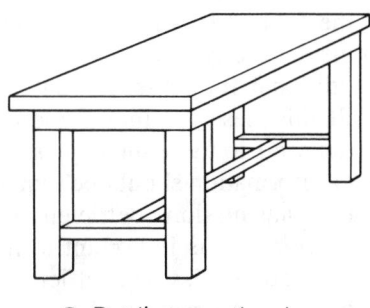

C. Detail perspective view

FIGURE 4.33   Detail elevation and perspective views.

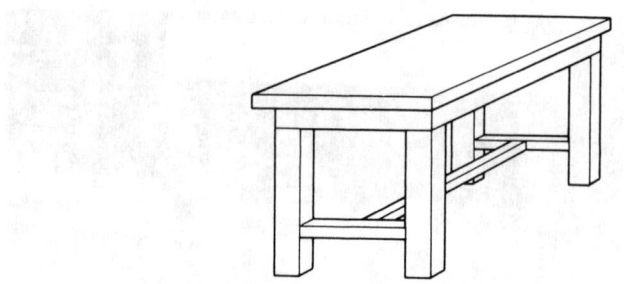

FIGURE 4.34   Detail perspective view.

detail views do not normally show all the views indicated in Figure 4.33 but are more like Figure 4.34.

SECTION VIEWS

The *section view* is usually a vertical or sometimes horizontal cutaway view of a wall, roof, or foundation of a building. This is a critical view because, from an energy conservation standpoint, it indicates what construction materials should be used, including the insulation to be placed in walls, roofs, or near foundation walls adjacent to usable areas. Examples are shown in Figures 4.35 through 4.37.

Insulation thickness can be very important in reducing energy costs. An economical insulation thickness for the present may be inadequate for the future. Two questions should be asked: What is the additional cost of adding more insulation now? Is the design flexible so that insulation can be conveniently added in the future? If walls and ceilings are plaster or drywall, it may be better to insulate fully now. Also, is the space within the wall adequate to allow additional future insulation? If not, you should consider increasing the wall thickness for future energy conservation. The section views provide the answers to these three questions.

Another piece of information should be requested when section views are shown; it is the heat transmission coefficient, the importance of which will be discussed in Chapter 7. It is important to have exterior structural walls and roofs with low heat transmission coefficients.

Figure 4.38 shows a detail section view of a window area. The primary function of the view is to show the window components and how they are to be assembled, including everything down to the size and length of the fasteners. This may be useful in the future, especially if these units are to be replaced with more energy-efficient windows. A review of the blueprint will indicate what is in the wall and how components are fastened.

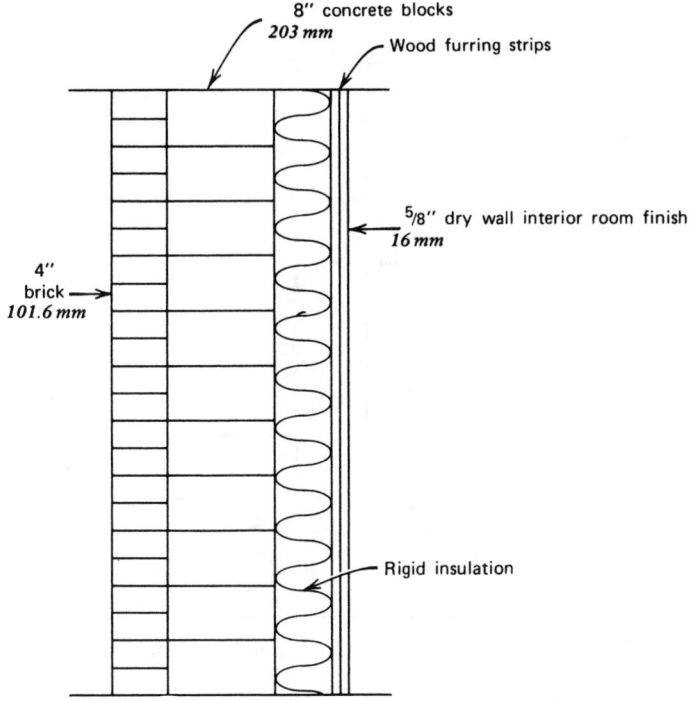

8" concrete blocks
203 mm

Wood furring strips

5/8" dry wall interior room finish
16 mm

4"
brick
101.6 mm

Rigid insulation

FIGURE 4.35 Section view of a partial wall, showing full insulation within the wall cavity.

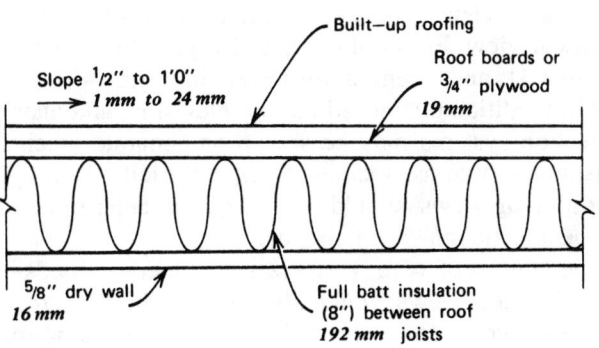

Built—up roofing

Slope 1/2" to 1'0"
1 mm to 24 mm

Roof boards or
3/4" plywood
19 mm

5/8" dry wall
16 mm

Full batt insulation
(8") between roof
192 mm joists

FIGURE 4.36 Section view of a roof.

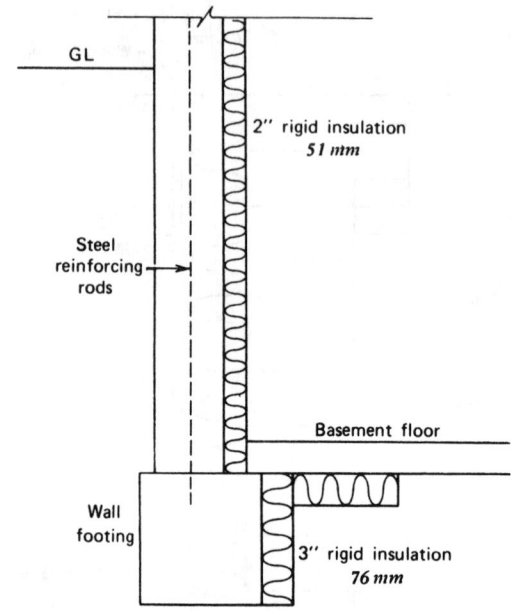

FIGURE 4.37 Section view of a foundation basement wall, showing insulation.

MECHANICAL VIEWS

Each mechanical/electrical system in the building will be shown on a separate mechanical view. Any of the previously mentioned blueprint types can be used for these views. The most frequently used is the plan view. Each mechanical view may use a special set of symbols. Figure 4.39 shows an electrical view. Figure 4.40 shows a plumbing view. Heating is shown in Figure 4.41, and a ventilation system in Figure 4.42.

Air-conditioning, closed-circuit television, antennas, and security and fire protection systems may be shown on separate mechanical views. Energy-consuming systems, such as water, electricity, heating, ventilation, and air-conditioning views, should be analyzed to determine if modern energy-management techniques are being used.

The lengths of wire, wire sizes, and electric loads can all be determined from electrical views, which also provide the basis for future computer-controlled networks for electric demand and consumption. They will indicate the best location and relative capacity of these systems. It is much quicker to conduct the preliminary survey with an existing blueprint than going to the affected areas and gathering data for a new blueprint.

Many of the energy conservation techniques presented in the following chapters are dependent on the accessibility of system components. Blue-

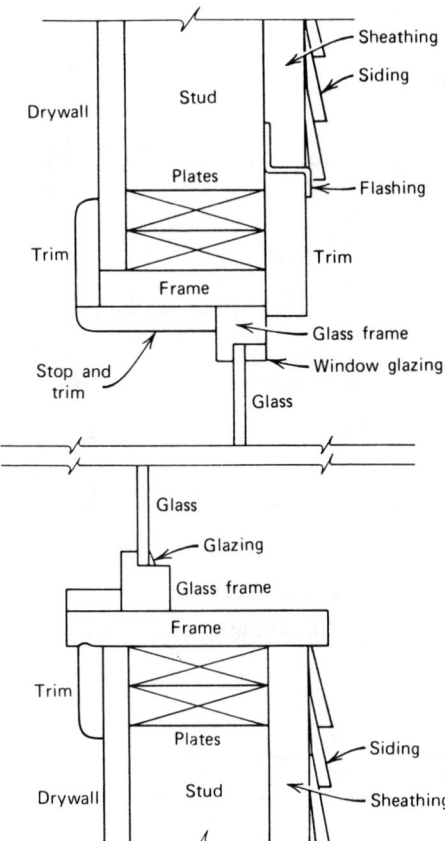

FIGURE 4.38 Detail section of a window.

prints will indicate if components can be serviced or repaired and how much time and effort will be required.

PLOT AND SURVEY VIEWS

The last major classifications of blueprints are the *plot and survey views*. The survey is a drawing made by a registered or licensed surveyor. It shows the legal boundaries of the property. Usually, other information must be requested before the survey is conducted. The customary minimum information shown on the survey is indicated in Figure 4.43.

Figure 4.44 shows the same basic data plus additional required information. The contour lines could be of special significance because they indicate the lay, or slope, of the land. Each point on a given contour line represents a point of equivalent elevation above some given point called a

See electrical specifications for:
    lighting fixtures
    wire sizes
    wire types
    outlet types and sizes
    lamp types and sizes
    switch types
    number of circuits

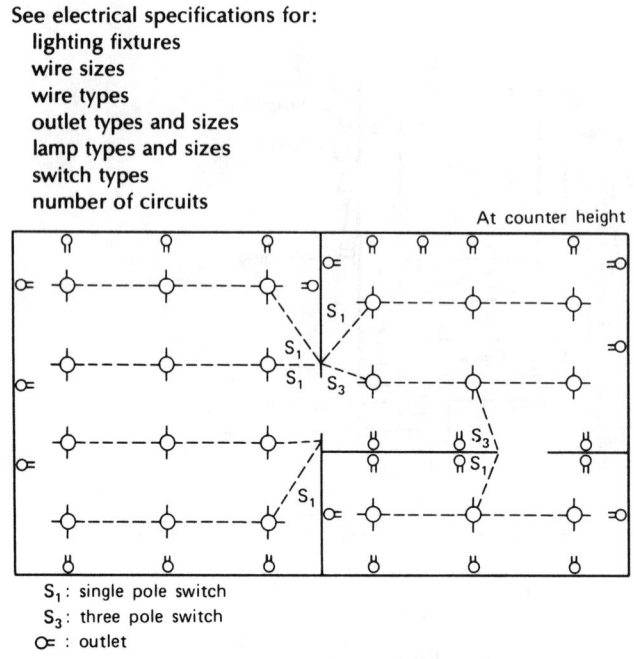

S_1 : single pole switch
S_3 : three pole switch
O= : outlet

FIGURE 4.39 Electric mechanical view for one floor of a building.

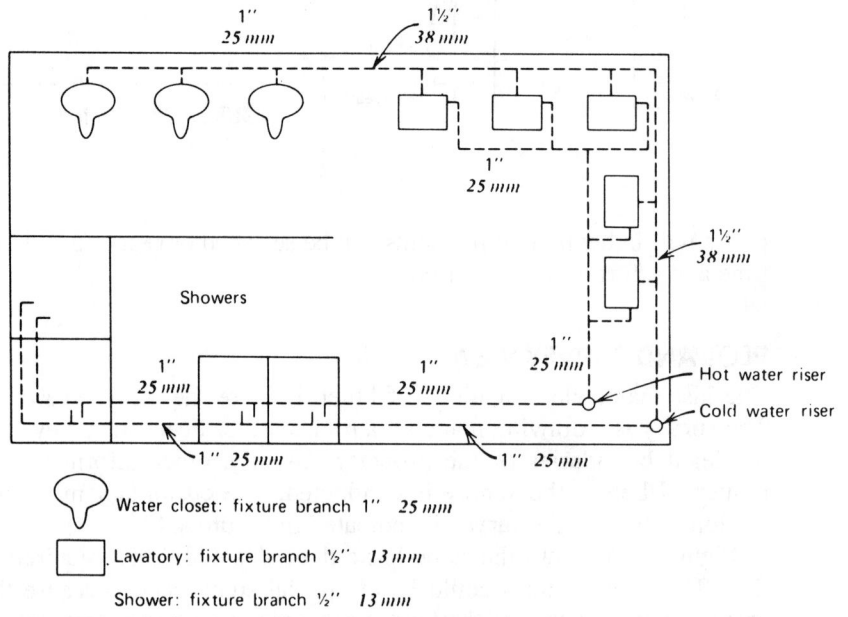

Water closet: fixture branch 1″ *25 mm*

Lavatory: fixture branch ½″ *13 mm*

Shower: fixture branch ½″ *13 mm*

FIGURE 4.40 Plumbing mechanical view for a small rest room, showing hot- and cold-water supply pipes.

130

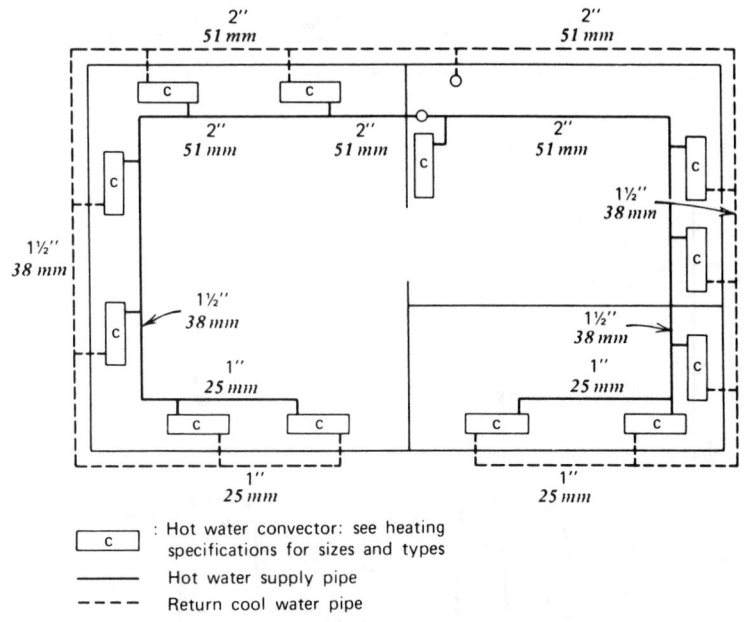

FIGURE 4.41 Heating mechanical view for one floor of a building.

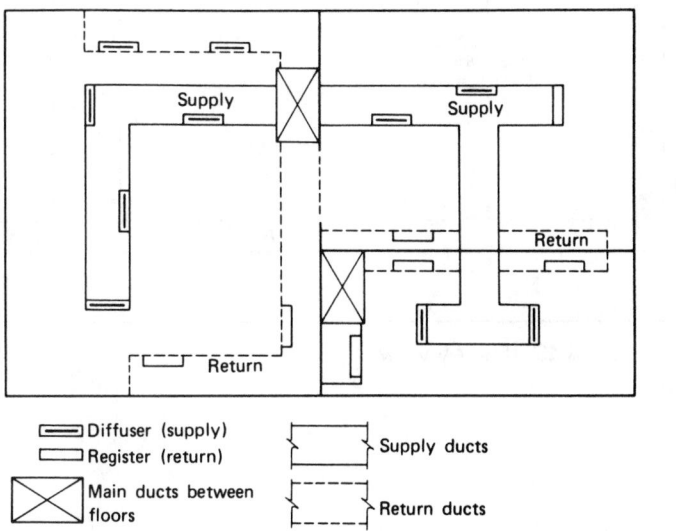

FIGURE 4.42 Ventilation mechanical view for one floor of a building.

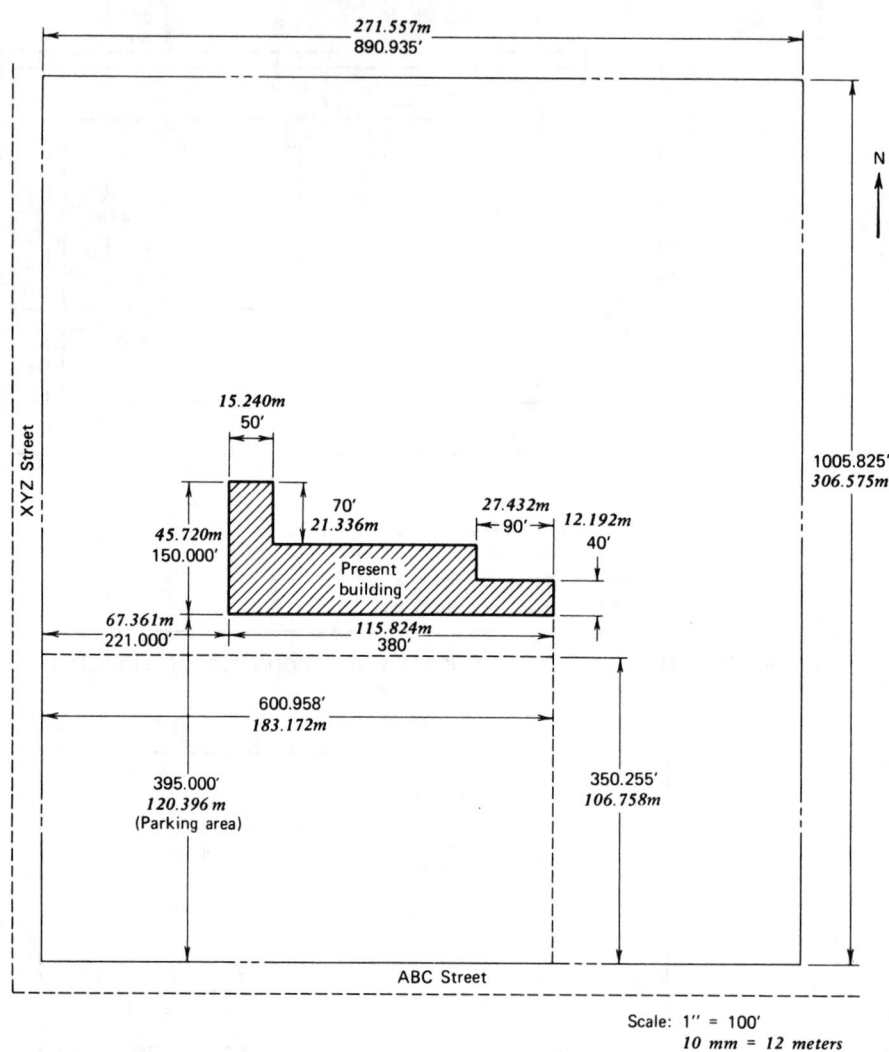

FIGURE 4.43 Survey view.

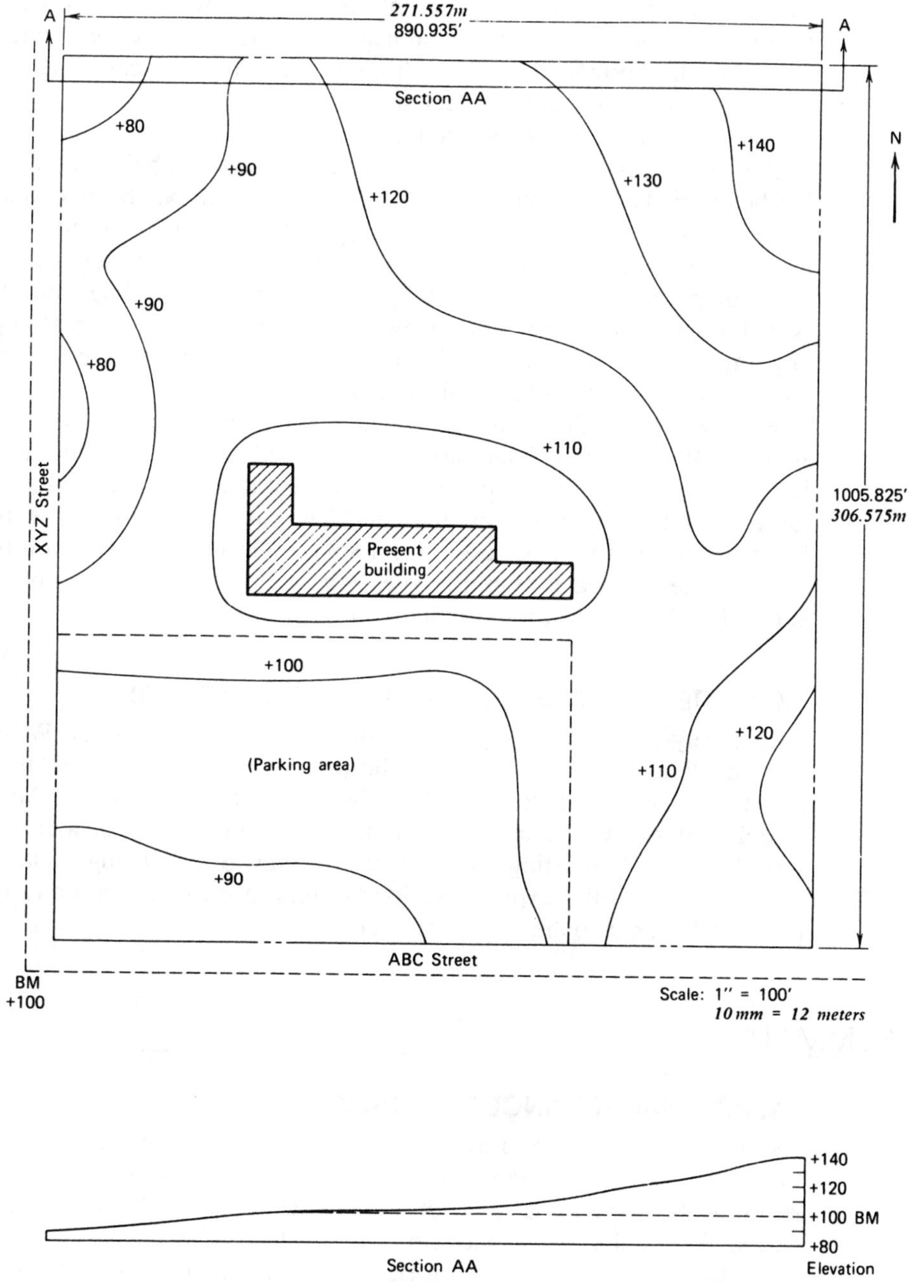

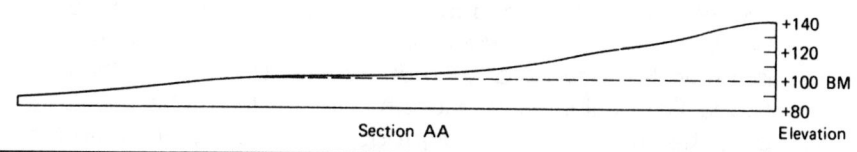

A ←――――――――― 271.557m ――――――――→ A
890.935'

Section AA

+80

N

+90

+120

+130

+140

+90

+80

+110

1005.825'
306.575m

XYZ Street

Present
building

+100

(Parking area)

+120

+110

+90

ABC Street

BM
+100

Scale: 1'' = 100'
10 mm = 12 meters

+140
+120
+100 BM
+80

Section AA

Elevation

FIGURE 4.44 Survey view with contour lines.

benchmark, which is a location point. Directly below the survey view is a contour, or elevation, view of the indicated area across a section of the land. Note that the horizontal scale is different from the vertical scale on this drawing; this constitutes a technique frequently used when elevation changes are not as large as horizontal distances.

If a building is to be constructed, an addition is to be built onto an existing building, the shape and contour of the land are to be changed, a swimming pool is to be added, or other changes on the property are to be made, the architect will start with a survey view and show these changes on a plot view. In most areas, a plot view is required before building permits are issued. Figure 4.45 shows a plot view of a new building on a parcel of property. Figure 4.46 shows an addition to a present building. Figure 4.47 shows the addition of a swimming pool for a private club.

Energy conservation can also be advanced with the use of plot views. Figure 4.48 shows how landscaping can be used around a building to assist in energy conservation, by planting the correct kinds of trees and knowing the angle of the sun on the parcel of land. The basic view can also be used to indicate the probable best location for solar collectors. The location of private sewage and water-pumping sites is also determined from plot views, some of which are shown in Figure 4.49.

COMPUTER-AIDED DESIGN AND DRAFTING (CADD)

A relatively new technology for the engineering unit is CADD. While not cost effective in its entirety for most hospitality enterprises, CADD provides tremendous potential for cost-effective drafting and design. Currently, CADD software with a drafting-only potential can prove to be a cost-effective alternative to existing labor-intensive means of producing a plan print. Chapter 5 more fully explores various factors in the consideration of computer applications to the engineering unit.

SUMMARY

ENERGY MAINTENANCE SUMMARY

The key to energy management is knowing the current conditions in a building. Blueprints are valuable aids, as they show if insulation is present in the walls, the types and amount of insulation, and if there is adequate space for additional insulation. In addition, the written specifications indicate the types and thermal properties of all insulators used in the building. The specifications should also indicate acceptable insulation substitute products.

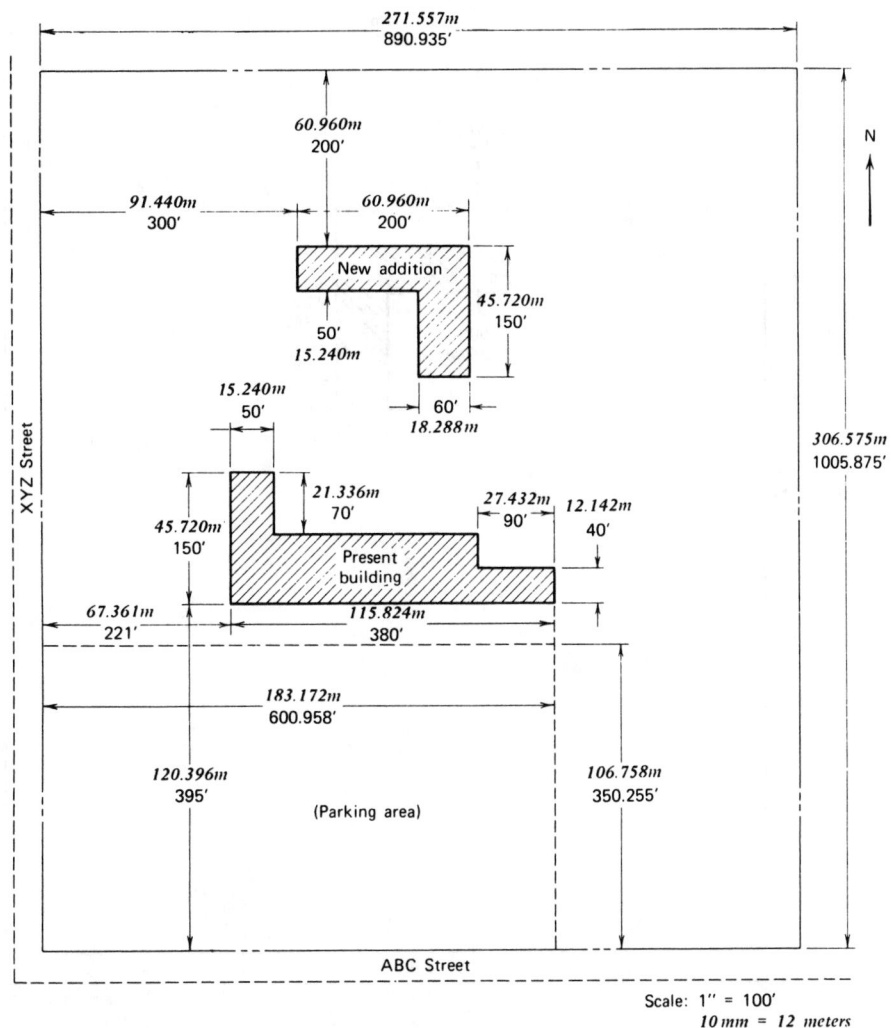

FIGURE 4.45 Plot view of proposed new building, no building currently on the property.

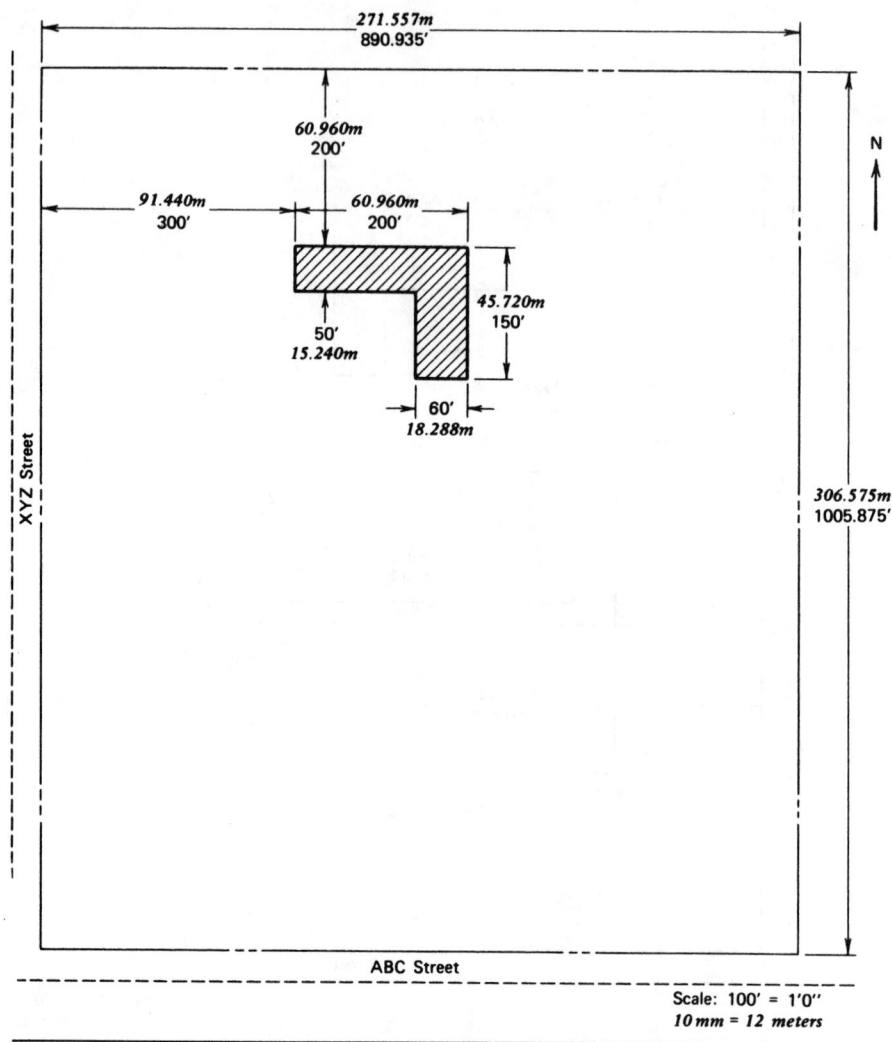

FIGURE 4.46 Plot view for an addition to present property.

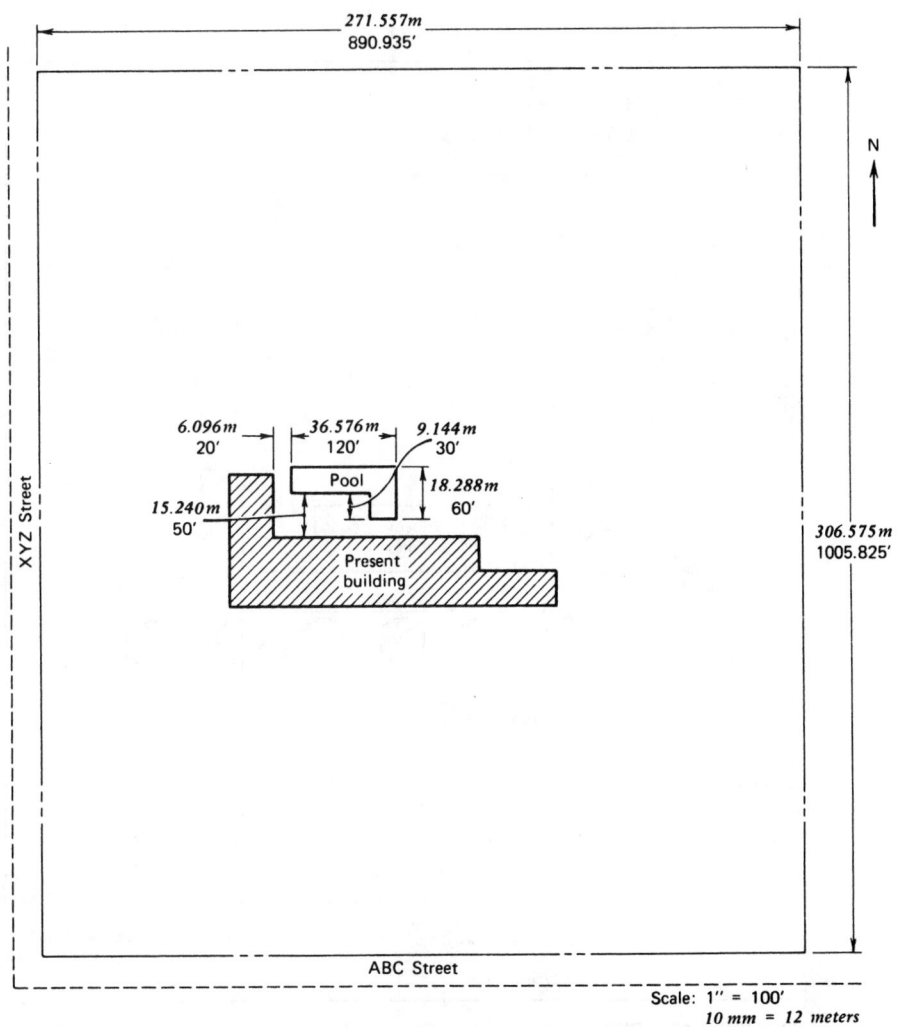

FIGURE 4.47 Plot view for the location of a new swimming pool on a parcel of land.

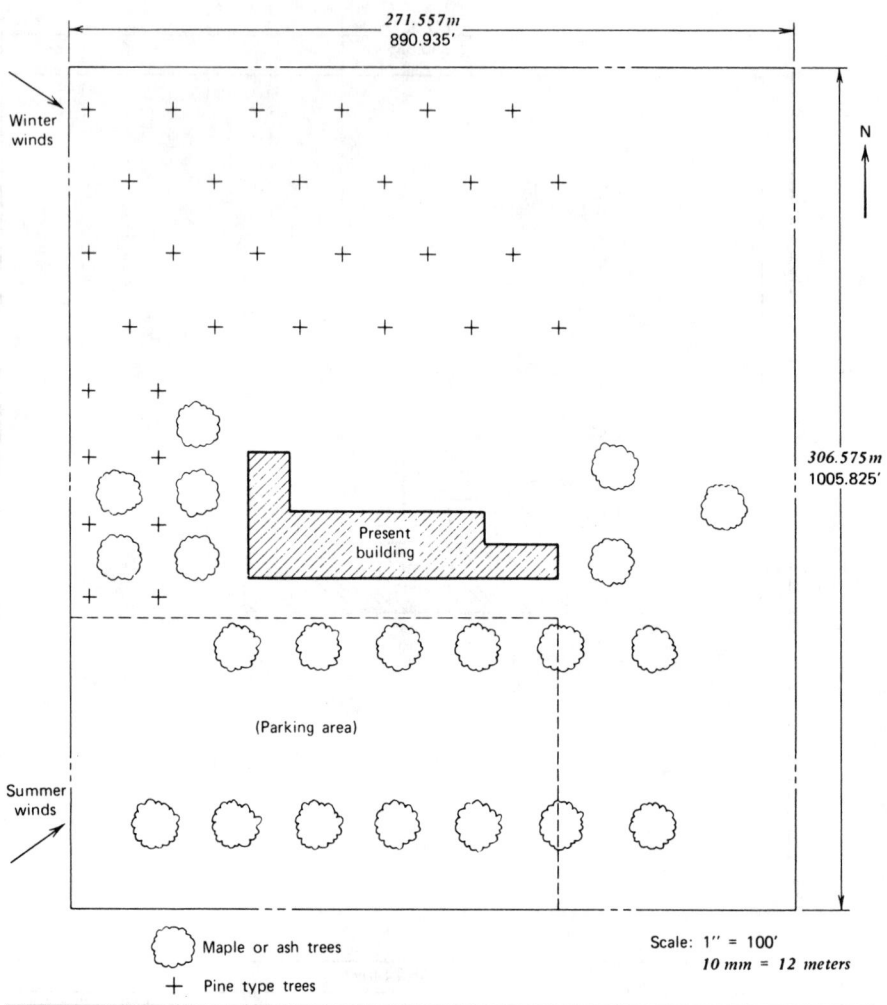

FIGURE 4.48 Plot view of new tree locations.

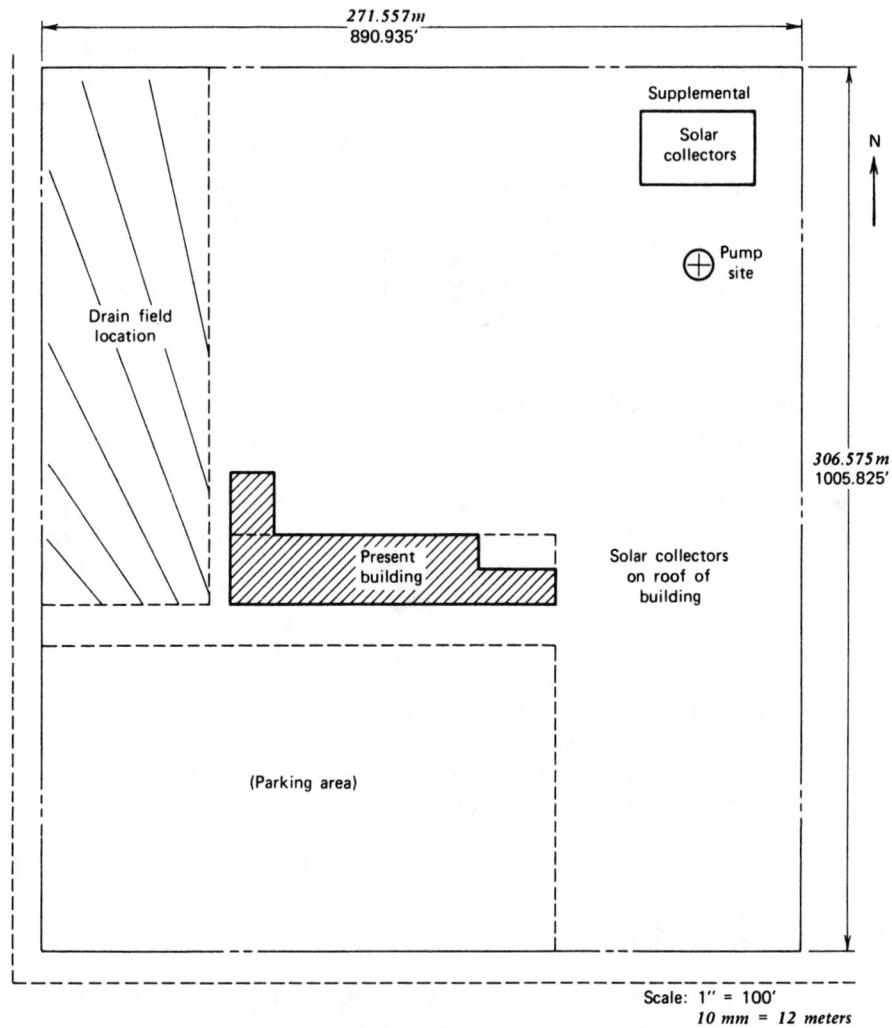

FIGURE 4.49 Plot view showing locations of proposed pump site, drainage field location, and solar collectors.

The written specifications provide valuable information regarding building equipment and its required preventive-maintenance schedules. Some hospitality managers and especially property managers/chief engineers develop preventive-maintenance and maintenance schedules directly from the building's written specifications.

Detailed blueprint and written specification reviews prior to the granting of construction or renovation contracts could reveal potential future maintenance problems. One example might be flashing, its size, material type, location, and fastening technique—poor flashing results in water leakage into the building between wall and roof lines.

MANAGEMENT SUMMARY

Some managers have minimal blueprint-reading knowledge. Before a hole is drilled into a wall, a current blueprint should be reviewed for hidden utilities. A check of the blueprint may quickly reveal if the capacities of the present electrical, water, sewage, heating, ventilation, and air-conditioning systems are adequate for a new addition, or if new systems will have to be added to the building.

Blueprints should be maintained (updated and stored in the engineering department). Too often, they are lost or left to become obsolete. Blueprints can be used for material requirements, for new layouts, and to estimate manpower requirements for current building operations. Blueprints are a great help to management in its efforts both to manage energy and to conduct a successful business.

QUESTIONS/PROBLEMS

1. Redraw one of the scaled drawings in this chapter to a larger scale. Then redraw it to a smaller scale.

2. A scale is 5/64" = 1'0"; convert this to an equivalent SIU scale.

3. Refer to Figure 4.4c, and prepare several alternative guest room layouts that will result in maximum carpet life within the room.

4. Refer to Figure 4.14, and determine the clearance between the walls if the outside walls are 0.75 unit thick and the interior walls are 0.30 unit thick.

5. Refer to Figure 4.16, and repeat the procedure in the preceding problem for walls that are:

    a. 1.5 units thick
    b. 2 units thick

6. Refer to Figure 4.20, and determine the amount of carpeting for Room 111 in:
    a. Square yards
    b. Square meters

7. If you were looking for a layout of the duct work of the heating, ventilation, and air-conditioning system and your chief engineer told you to look at the plan for the building, what could you conclude from this statement?

CHAPTER 5

COMPUTER APPLICATIONS FOR MAINTENANCE AND ENGINEERING

ABSTRACT

Computer applications can be made in various engineering and maintenance areas, including management, design, energy monitoring and control, fire safety, and security.

Computer application decisions will have to be made regarding capability, flexibility, user-friendliness, portability, and end-user support and service. Maintenance management applications must consider the capabilities of a system to handle work processing, develop facilities histories, accurately record and report maintenance cost accounting, and manage an inventory control system. Many energy-management systems are also computer based. The primary advantage of a central computer EMS is that large sections of the property can be controlled from one location and each room or grouping of rooms can be programmed for different environments.

***Key words:** ASCII; CAD; CAFM; capability; CATV; computer aided design and drafting (CADD); configuration; CRT; dot matrix printer; EMS; FMIS; hardware; I/O; kilobytes (K); megabytes (MB); memory; modem; operating system; peripheral; postscript quality; program; random-access memory (RAM); read-only memory (ROM); software; system; system unit.*

INTRODUCTION

Computer-aided management tools such as computer-aided design and drafting (CADD), computer-aided facility management (CAFM), and facility management information systems (FMIS), see Figure 5.1, will continue to develop and assist all levels of management and staff in the engineering-and-maintenance unit in forecasting, storing, and accessing more information faster. Computer technology is becoming more sophisticated with greater networking and integration of differing systems. Hardware, communications systems, fiber-optics, laser technology, laptop computers, and other information advancements still in development will continue to change, grow, and proliferate at any workplace around the world.

There are two primary reasons for developing a facility management information system (FMIS): first to save time and second to deal efficiently with complex and diverse data. A computer-based system can turn around reports much more rapidly, provide uniformity of data reported, and easily compile and consolidate corporate reports through a shared data file if a corporation maintains buildings in more than one location.

Computer applications for the engineering operation in a hotel, motel, or resort operation might be considered for managerial functions, design, energy monitoring and control, fire safety, and security. Unfortunately, a systemwide application is not often considered; rather, properties back into the use of a computer, in some cases ending up with many disconnected parts. In decisions relating to automation, the computer is not a solution but a tool. Nor is it the solution to maintenance problems ranging from poor employee performance to high operating costs. If employees are not producing effectively now, the problem is one of supervision; something a computer cannot correct. Computers can only give people the information they need to manage better; they cannot work miracles on their own.

The purchase of a computer system, which includes hardware (the computer itself and peripheral equipment) and software, is in almost all cases a cost-effective decision. The evaluation of a system should include: capability, flexibility, user-friendliness, portability, and end-user support and service.

Maintenance
    Work orders
    Preventive and corrective maintenance
Design and construction
    Existing and new construction documents
    Contractors, vendors, and suppliers
    Construction cost estimates
CADD system
    Building floor plans
    Construction drawings
    Equipment, furnishings, fixtures, and finishes

FIGURE 5.1 Facility management information system.

CAPABILITY

Capability is determining what the system needs to do, how it will best fulfill its function, and where it will be most valuable. It is no longer necessary to direct all the work to a large, central computer; complete systems can fit on a desk top, so the computer can be placed where the work is. Figure 5.2 illustrates factors that should be considered when assessing capability.

Externally, the system will include a keyboard for data and instruction input, a video (CRT) screen on which the user can observe and check input/output, a printer to record output in a permanent form, and some form of mass storage to hold programs and data until the system requires them.

Unseen, or internal, components are of equal, if not greater, importance. The internal parts are the processor, which performs the computing; memory, which holds whatever data and programs the operator is using at the moment; and input/output (I/O) circuits for communication between the computer and its peripheral devices. Circuits organized on a "bus" system, which lets one plug in other circuit boards to accommodate changing needs, are desirable.

One of the easiest ways to compare computer systems is to consider memory. Every computer needs memory to store both the programs it works with and the data it processes. This includes random-access memory (RAM) and read-only memory (ROM). The contents of RAM can be changed at any moment to make way for new programs or updated information that will not be required when the computer is turned off. ROM, however, does not change when the computer is disconnected. Because it is used mainly for programs that the computer needs for its own operation, it must be on tap the moment the computer is turned on.

The capacity of memory in a small business computer is measured in kilobytes, or K. One byte will hold one character of data, or approximately one instruction. A kilobyte is 1024 bytes (computers work in powers of 2, and 1024 is 2 to the 10th power [$2^{10}=1024$]). The capacity of a business computer might range from 48K (the minimum for most business applications) to millions of bytes (one million bytes equals 1 megabyte).

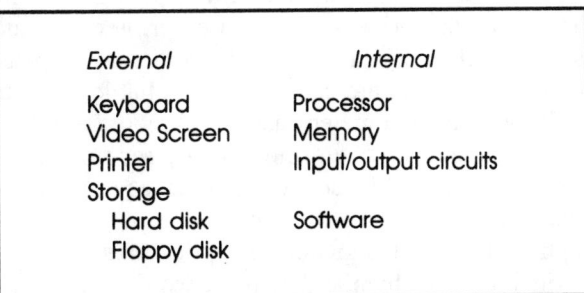

FIGURE 5.2 Factors influencing computer system capability.

The peripheral equipment that needs to be added to a system should also be considered as part of its capability. Peripherals, which often cost more than the computer, include terminals, disk drives, and printers. A terminal usually consists of a keyboard, video display screen, and circuits to communicate with other parts of the system. One-piece models, which are easier to move and often have fewer breakable cables, are not as easy to adjust for operator comfort as are those with separate screens and keyboards. Display screens typically should hold a minimum of 24 lines of 40 characters each. Terminals that display only uppercase letters cost less than those that also display lowercase letters; though adequate for some applications, they are limiting when reports must be printed or when quality printing is required. Computer keyboards usually include more keys than one finds on a typewriter. However, the basics should include a numeric keypad for fast, calculator-style number entry; cursor control keys to move the computer's activity to various spots on the screen; keys designated for special functions, such as deleting or inserting material on the screen; and user-programmable keys whose functions vary with the programs that call on them.

Terminals must also be able to communicate with their computers. Thus, the correct type of interface connection is important. Most computers and terminals communicate by the ASCII code, in which all visible characters are standardized. Invisible characters, though, such as the one that tells the terminal to clear its screen, vary with the terminal in use. It is particularly important to make sure any terminal and software purchased can work together.

Printer selection requires careful consideration of print quality, speed, type of paper, interface requirements, noise, and cost. Print quality varies considerably. Some printers produce characters similar to a typewriter, in that the characters are molded on a plastic or metal wheel (e.g., a daisy wheel), with short type bars radiating from the center, which is pressed against a ribbon to make an impression on the paper. Metal-wheel printers give better quality, but cost more. Wheels should be interchangeable for different typefaces.

The majority of printers are dot matrix impact or laser. Dot matrix printers compose letters from individual dots on a grid, or matrix. The more dots on the matrix, the higher the print quality. Laser printers produce much higher quality results. While early laser printers were slow, expensive, and difficult to operate, modern lasers are usually more reliable than other print technologies, in addition to being quieter, faster, and more flexible.

Usually, a major consideration when selecting a laser printer is whether to pay for postscript capability. This technology enables a PC to tell output devices exactly what to print. It allows for greater capability to vary type sizes and print graphics. For most engineering applications, the extra cost of this feature is marginal and worthwhile. For most word processing, spreadsheets, database reports, and forms, it is not necessary.

Font availability is another consideration. Some lasers offer only a few, while others provide several dozen as standard equipment. Without special fonts and sizes, the laser prints as well as a good typewriter, only faster. With varied fonts, the laser can produce output that looks professionally typeset, featuring headlines, footnotes, boldface, and italics. The standard fonts can often be supplemented at lower cost with soft fonts, which is software that must be loaded into the printer every time it is turned on. Hard fonts are stored in cartridges for instant use. Vendors sell cartridges containing dozens of fonts. The engineering unit should consider the need for varied fonts and select a printer that can handle its needs cost effectively.

Paper may come in sheets, rolls, or perforated fan-fold form. Printers with a friction feed (usually a roller platen system, like a typewriter's) have the capability for either sheet or roll. Fan-fold paper, with the removable strips of sprocket holes along each edge, is used in printers that also have a tractor-feed sprocket system. Friction feed allows for individual forms, letters, and so on, while tractor feed simplifies the rapid printing of long reports, which can be stripped apart and filed. The reliability and capacity of the paper-handling system should not be overlooked. Single-sheet capacities vary from 50 to as many as 500 sheets. Printers deliver their output either faceup or facedown and vary in their ability to handle paper and envelope sizes.

Disk systems are floppy or hard. Floppy disks are essentially of the same material as magnetic tape. Traditional magnetic hard disks were once limited to capacities of 5 or 10 megabytes and access times in excess of 65 milliseconds. While very large and fast in comparison to floppy diskettes, these hard disks now have been superseded by newer devices with storage capacities well over 2500 megabytes and access times well under 20 milliseconds.

Raw storage capacity is also important because much of today's best software requires several megabytes of disk space. Currently, 120-megabyte drives are the minimum for most new computers, and it has been estimated that nearly two million drives with 30-megabyte capacities were delivered in the late 1980s. It generally pays to buy twice the amount of storage space that might be required.

Optical disks are another form of technology that is entering the market. They offer massive storage capacities on the order of 500 to 2500 megabytes per disk. They are best used as archives for past records and reference materials. A whole year's worth of work orders or maintenance records might be placed on a single optical disk.

When considering floppy disks, rather than focusing on how many bytes a disk will hold, ask a salesperson how many typical files the disk will hold with the recommended software, and what each file can contain. The fewer disks an operator must juggle for each task, the less chance of human error.

A modem is another peripheral that may be essential for your capability needs. Through a modem, either external or internal, a computer system can communicate by telephone with distant data banks. The main considerations when selecting a modem are compatibility with industry standards and the baud rate, or operating speed, which must match the modem with which it is communicating. In the recent past, 300 baud was fast; now 1200- to 2400-, and 14,400-baud modems are becoming quite common. A 1200-baud modem will transmit a paragraph about twice as fast as a person can read it. Remember that a modem is not enough for computer communications. A PC also requires software to control the modem, to dial the number of the receiving modem, and to either send the data out over the telephone wire or receive and store incoming data.

Typically, the system purchased from the vendor is only part of the initial expense. Some systems are supplied without hardware. Other systems require additional software that must be purchased from other vendors. Site development requirements, such as wiring remote terminals and preparing a central computer facility, also must be included and vary from system to system.

A typical mistake when automating a maintenance-and-engineering function is to begin looking at software packages. Unfortunately, the decision to purchase a particular package is often based on the appeal of a particular portion of it. However, looking good and meeting organizational needs are not the same thing. An audit of the maintenance-and-engineering function should be completed. Included in this audit should be the applications of automation to maintenance, inventory control, budgeting, energy monitoring, facility design, word processing, and life safety. A clear definition of what the computer system must accomplish at each application is essential.

The results of the audit should be used to prepare a summary of software requirements for the maintenance-and-engineering system. Software requirements must be as detailed as possible, for they will be used to evaluate the suitability of vendor proposals or as the basis for developing custom software. However, they should also be written up at this point with an eye toward overall function rather than technical specification.

Once a facility's audit is complete, the engineer will have a good idea as to software capability requirements. Three basic software options are usually available to the engineer. They include in-house software development, purchasing a complete maintenance-and-engineering system, or contracting with a firm to lease computer services.

In-house software development offers the advantage(s) of customizing specific hardware applications and operating conditions, and easy revision. However, if it is essential that the system be up and running quickly, the other two options should be considered. Developing a software package in house is a lengthy process, often taking years to develop fully and debug. Other implementation options can provide a fully operational system in a much shorter time span.

Purchasing a complete maintenance management package is generally the quickest way to move an organization into the area of computerized maintenance-and-engineering management. Multiple packages are available. The selection of a commercially available software package trades off some flexibility. It is doubtful that any one program or combination of programs can match the maintenance and engineering needs exactly. However, with the current Microsoft® Windows® versions to most software programs, the user can easily select from among multiple applications available with a particular software product.

Contracting with a maintenance management organization for leased computer services might provide a quick way into computerized systems without a major investment in hardware, software, and personnel. Software and the primary hardware in leased systems are typically located at the vendor's facilities. Terminals and printers located in the maintenance-and-engineering unit are connected to the central computer equipment via phone lines. The vendor assumes responsibility for maintaining the computer systems and the software. The user pays a fee based on what maintenance programs are used, the number of terminals connected to the system, and the size of the maintenance-and-engineering unit's database.

The advantages of a leased system include lower start-up costs, faster start-up, minimal dedicated space for equipment, and fewer technically trained personnel in computer operations. The most serious drawback to a leased system is its high annual costs in comparison to other options. Fees for leasing computer services are greater than the annual operating costs associated with in-house-developed systems and purchased systems. However, for those organizations that do not have the resources to purchase and maintain their own equipment, leasing might prove to be the best option.

FLEXIBILITY

Some software is available for single-user applications only, and some for single- and multiuser applications. The latter must be given careful consideration, particularly if multiple terminals might be required in the maintenance-and-engineering unit. Multiple terminals might be required if simultaneous access and sharing of programs and data are anticipated. For example, perhaps one terminal is necessary to generate work orders, a second to back up the work-order generation process and to produce reports, and a third to be placed in the warehouse to handle the distribution, return, and receipts of materials and supplies. Multiuser software would be required in this system configuration.

Software with a Windows version also provides for increased flexibility in allowing multiple applications of the software to be in process simultaneously, depending on the hardware configuration.

USER-FRIENDLINESS AND PORTABILITY

If the computer system is to be a valuable management tool in the maintenance-and-engineering unit, it must be effective and easy to use. However, there might be a considerable difference between ease of use for a computer technician and ease of use for the manager and staff of the unit. User-friendly systems provide simple screen menus in a Windows format to describe system functions; step-by-step instructions for the use of a particular function; minimal keystrokes to enter complex data; easy-to-read output, whether it is a work order or a management report; and minimal "pencil" input from engineers when completing or closing out a work order.

Consider whether a particular software program presents new problems with hardware selection or modification. For example, a software package should be able to be used in an MS-DOS configuration.

END-USER SUPPORT AND SERVICE

What level of software support can be expected during installation and operation? Does the vendor provide training and telephone consultation? Can the software vendor assist in the development of report formats that will help address the technical requirements of the maintenance-and-engineering unit?

Despite vendor sales literature, start-up of a maintenance management package is no simple task. Personnel will have to be trained, data on facilities/equipment will have to be collected, and bugs in the software will have to be worked out. Depending on the nature of the system, installation time can last from a month to as long as a year.

Since software will become obsolete in a short time, also consider whether the software vendor is working to improve its product; and if product improvements are likely, what is the vendor's pricing policy on upgrades? Most vendors charge an annual fee to support their products. The fee typically includes assistance in the event of system trouble, updates to the software, and the annual licensing fee for the software. Annual fees range from 5 to 15 percent of the original purchase price for the system software.

MAINTENANCE MANAGEMENT

The computer can assist with work processing, facility histories, cost accounting, and inventory control.

WORK PROCESSING

The software selected should assist with work processing in recording, scheduling, monitoring, reporting, and ordering. While work orders must typically be entered into the computer manually, once entered, preventive-maintenance orders should be automatically generated at the specified interval. Some available software has preprogrammed preventive maintenance that can be customized or adopted as is. This feature can save considerable amounts of data entry time and may also call attention to preventive-maintenance practices that may not have been identified for a particular facility.[1]

Software should automatically recall individual maintenance procedures from memory. Simple programs search the backlog of preventive-maintenance orders and print those due for work, not taking into account the available staff to complete the work. However, scheduling provisions can prove invaluable in balancing the workload for the work force. Since the level of unplanned work has to be accommodated, the amount of planned work that should be scheduled each week will vary. The software that simply prints the listing of all work needed places the burden for balancing this workload on the manager. More sophisticated programs will perform this balancing function by analyzing the total workload and printing a schedule of planned and unplanned work that fully utilizes the available staff. Such programs will also assign priority in the work to be done according to the maintenance goals and priorities that have been created.

Most software programs have the capability to monitor work through to its completion. The program should be able to print a listing of all work in process that has been completed, not reported as complete, or deferred for a specific reason. However, some programs can also update individual equipment histories with the results of each preventive-maintenance order. The software should also have a provision to allow for the generation of new unplanned work orders.

Overall work orders:

    Each unit within the engineering operation
    Each building or facility area
    Scheduled completion by date/time
    Completed by specific employee
    Type of work (e.g., repair, replacement, modification)
    Dollar value
    Man-hour requirement
    Common equipment types
    Pending
    Overdue

Sort work by:

    Due date
    Shop
    Craftsman
    Priority

FIGURE 5.3   Maintenance management reports.

The reporting function of maintenance software must provide for considerable flexibility. Figure 5.3 illustrates various types of reports that might be made and sorted. Some software also contains an ad hoc query capability, which allows for the generation of custom reports. However, since the cost of the software may increase dramatically with this capability, a careful analysis of the type of reporting information required should be analyzed.

The software should be able to specify the supplies required for every planned work order and to track the supplies consumed for planned and unplanned work. However, the sophistication in this area may vary dramatically. The more sophisticated software can automatically update estimated inventory levels of key supplies, materials, and spare parts. This involves a file linkage between the planned work and inventory control data.

FACILITY HISTORIES

As work is processed, completion dates, man-hours, materials and supplies, parts, and so on, are recorded. This database forms a maintenance history for the facility and equipment. With certain software enhancements, interesting uses can be made of these data. For example, a record of facility data can improve the forecasting of future maintenance costs. Software enhancements might include automatically projecting costs per square foot (square meter), costs per maintenance visit, or costs by type of maintenance activity.

Software that can store the maintenance history of specific pieces of equipment is also a valuable management tool. Such information can assist in calculating repair or replacement cycles and in tracing potential maintenance-related causes for equipment failure. The more sophisticated software automatically links the planned preventive work that is performed on equipment with the unplanned work that might be performed, thus eliminating the need for dual data entry when calculating repair and replacement costs.

COST ACCOUNTING

The software should be able to report costs, which approximately total the actual expenditure of funds through the payment of payrolls and material invoices. Typically, accurate dollar costs of individual activities are necessary only when such work is to be reimbursed. Because of the tremendous expense associated with the consolidation of these two sets of records, most software tracks maintenance costs in parallel with a formal accounting system but does not directly link and reconcile the two systems.[2]

Labor is typically tracked by the number of man-hours expended on an individual maintenance activity. A total of all man-hours expended on activities during a week should equal the total number of man-hours available and the number of man-hours authorized by payroll. Most software will permit the name of an individual employee to be tracked through a special code that has been assigned to that person. If a considerable quantity of maintenance work is completed on a reimbursable basis (e.g., charged back to the department for which it was performed), then it is desirable to purchase a more sophisticated software with capability in this area. The degree of accuracy of total man-hour cost varies with the software.

Material costs include consumable supplies (lubricants and rags), raw construction materials (lumber and piping), and specific spare parts. Typically, software will not record a consumable against an individual work order unless used in major quantity or exclusively with a particular work order. Nor will it track the costs of using specific shop tools (saws, hammers, and drills) to individual maintenance activities. Such costs are usually tracked only when they are rented or purchased for a specific, one-time use. Raw construction materials should be tracked by the software to specific work orders.

However, the degree of accuracy or specificity of cost may vary. Usually, the exact inventory control cost is not worth the time necessary to determine the exact price and quantity. Spare parts required by a single piece of equipment can and should be charged to the equipment involved through an exact costing on the work order.

INVENTORY CONTROL

Most software has the capability of tracking materials through a formal inventory control system. Simple tracking involves an independent listing of item by name, part number, and quantity on hand. The more sophisticated system will coordinate purchases with increases to the computer inventory levels. As materials are consumed, the reported consumption is noted and reflected in the resulting inventory levels. However, computerized inventory control is accurate only if a periodic verification of recorded inventory as actual stock on hand is conducted.

COMPUTER-AIDED DESIGN AND DRAFTING

Ten years ago, most facility designers hardly knew what CADD (computer-aided design and drafting) was. A few had purchased the early systems, which were bulky and expensive. Computer-aided design was mainly the province of aerospace or automotive engineers. Today, just about everybody knows what it is: an electronic drawing system.

A typical computer-aided design and drafting (CADD) system includes a standalone mainframe or microprocessor computer, workstations with one or two terminals offering graphic and/or alphanumeric capabilities, ink or electrostatic drawing plotters, and printers.[3]

The strength of a CADD system is its ability to recall enormous amounts of unwieldy information. Thus, turnaround time of CADD drawings is much faster than that of drawings done by hand. Building systems can be quickly located when questions concerning maintenance, repair, and renovation must be explored. Even more important is the ability to experiment with and explore various alternate designs and uses of a facility. Walls, partitions, and furnishings can be moved in a matter of seconds to reveal alternate use of space. The accuracy of construction/renovation cost estimates also typically increases because of the accuracy of computerized specifications.[4] Once the design is in CADD, it can be output to a variety of media at any time. An entire drawing sheet, or a selected portion of it at fax size, can be requested and within minutes be supplied to the user.

CADD is more than just a drafting tool. Visualization and three-dimensional modeling packages are currently available for CADD systems. CADD systems can quickly provide an infinite number of views of a particular design. Techniques like animated walk-through help facility managers and users to understand what they are seeing.

CADD projects can be stored electronically, on disk or tape, and data for the original design can be recalled and updated, giving the user better design service value over the economic life of the project.

A CADD user needs to consider networking terminals. Terminals standing alone somewhat defeat the purpose of having multiple stations. Copying files from one terminal to the other can become a most time-consuming task. The network provides users with access to one common database and a central symbol library. In addition, data are easier to manage and everyone has access to the most current files. Multiple users can also have access at any time to any modems, scanners, plotters, and other tools that may be installed on terminals in the network.

For CADD to be successful, the user has to decide how the technology is going to help achieve business goals. Thus, before shopping for CADD software, analyze internal processes, problem areas, and the opportunities that CADD offers. Finding an easy-to-use and easy-to-learn CADD package is essential. If the software is not easy to learn, it will not be used and, in essence, not do what it needs to do. Consideration should be given to software with Windows as its graphical user interface. A Windows graphical user interface is easy to understand, and all such programs have the same basic look. Also, software with two- and integrated three-dimensional capabilities should be considered. This moves the software beyond a simple drafting tool, to a design tool. Typically, no single CADD package can do it all. However, the ability to translate files between different CADD packages is a must. AutoCAD® *I* is the current CADD industry standard. To coexist, software should be able to work with AutoCAD files. For example, VersaCAD™ 8.0 can translate files back and forth to AutoCAD.

Finally, buy the best hardware that can be afforded to support CADD. CADD builds up information quickly. This means an expanded hard drive, extra memory, high-resolution monitor, and high-speed graphics cards.

An investment in CADD systems in the past ran into the hundreds of thousands of dollars, with the equipment and software becoming obsolete rapidly. However, the availability of a CADD program for *Windows 95®* may introduce new users through lower prices. The inexpensive products include two-dimensional design software in the $300 to $600 range. In addition, the industry standard *AutoCAD®* can be purchased for under $5000. However, cost-effective alternatives include entering the CADD market gradually through overlay drafting; working with a CADD-equipped architectural firm on building renovation and construction; and/or setting up a workstation tied into a CADD computer through a service bureau with a CADD consultant.

ENERGY MANAGEMENT SYSTEMS

During the energy crisis of the mid-1970s, a number of products were introduced to assist hotels with the management of their energy costs. Owing to engineering and design flaws, the majority of these products did not live up to their promises. However, two basic types of guest room energy-management systems survived the 1970s and have matured into valuable management tools.

These two products are computerized centrally controlled systems (front-desk systems) and guest occupancy sensing systems.

With a computerized centrally controlled system, all guest room heating, ventilation, and air-conditioning (HVAC) units are connected to a computer at the front desk or in the engineering office via hard wiring, in-house CATV, power wiring, or something similar. Guests control room temperature with a thermostat located in the guest room from check-in to check-out. Thus, when a hotel has high occupancy and there is a relatively short time between check-out and the next check-in, there is little opportunity for savings. In essence, the computer cannot cycle the guest room into an energy-savings mode allowing room temperatures to increase slightly. Thus, most of the software in such systems programs HVAC unit on–off according to a time schedule (20 minutes on and 3 minutes off) when outside temperatures permit.

Occupancy sensing EMS systems seemingly may have the greatest potential for energy savings in the guest room since they know when the guest is present or absent. The early occupancy sensors used ultrasonic motion detectors, which sensed the movement of objects, without regard to the source of the movement, by detecting changes in reflected high-frequency sound transmitted into the guest room space. Without motion present, the software in such systems adjusts the room temperature to an energy-savings level. Once motion is sensed, the software in the system readjusts the room temperature to the setting established by the occupant of the room.

The technology on which most occupancy systems are now based utilizes passive infrared detectors, which sense the infrared body heat of the guest. Unlike motion detectors, these devices can distinguish between people and inanimate moving objects such as draperies or even the blades of a ceiling fan.

Most occupancy-based systems have an internal secondary thermostat to maintain room temperature at a comfortable, management-selected, energy-conserving level while guests are out. The guest has complete control of room temperature while in the room. When the HVAC unit is off, it is not consuming energy. Occupancy sensing systems will substantially reduce operating time since guests are out of the room more than they are in the room. Payback is generally under 2.5 years with a return on investment of 40 to 50 percent.

SUMMARY

In the maintenance-and-engineering unit, computer applications can be made in various areas, including management, design, energy monitoring and control, fire safety, and security.

In the consideration of computer applications, decisions will have to be made as to capability, flexibility, user-friendliness, portability, and end-user support and service.

Of particular importance is capability, which is a function of hardware and software, and which takes into account keyboard, video screen, printer, storage, processor, memory, input/output circuits, and maintenance-and-engineering function audit.

Maintenance management applications must consider the capabilities of a system to handle work processing, develop facilities histories, accurately record and report maintenance cost accounting, and manage an inventory control system.

While for most hospitality businesses a complete computer-aided design and drafting system may not be cost effective at this time, CADD presents considerable opportunities for cost savings in the design, renovation, and construction process. Thus, working with CADD-competent architects and engineers and other groups should be considered.

Many energy-management systems are also computer based. The primary advantage of a central computer EMS is that large sections of the property can be controlled from one location and each room or grouping of rooms can be programmed for different environments.

REFERENCES AND BIBLIOGRAPHY

1. Magee, G. H., *Facilities Maintenance Management*, R. S. Means Company, Inc., Kingston, MA, 1988.
2. Borsenik, F. D.."Computers: Software Review: MRI Property Management and Accounting Systems," *Journal of Property Management*, May 1989, pp. 62–64.
3. Monroe, L., "Focus on CADD Systems," *Buildings*, July 1984, pp. 103–108.
4. Borsenik, F. D., "CADD Systems: High-Tech Era Hits Hotel-Design Industry," *Hotel and Motel Management Magazine*, April 27, 1987, pp. 58–59.
5 Fizer, W. C., "The Cost of a Rented Room: When Your Guests Go Out Do Your Profits Go With Them?" *Lodging*, May 1994, pp. 79–81.
6. Weizer, N., G. O. Gardner III, S. Lipoff, M. F. Roetter, and F. G. Withington, *The Arthur D. Little Forecast on Information Technology and Productivity: Making the Integrated Enterprise Work*, Wiley, New York, 1991.
7. Floyd, S., *The IBM Multimedia Handbook*, Brady Publishing, New York, 1991.
8. Bunzel, M. J., and S. K. Morris, *Multimedia Applications Development, Using DVI Technology*, McGraw-Hill, New York, 1992.

QUESTIONS/PROBLEMS

1. Your supervisor hands you a memo that asks you to outline the essential issues of a specification for a computerized maintenance-management system for the engineering department. How should you respond?

2. What questions should be asked when considering the purchase of a maintenance-management software package?

3. What questions should be asked when considering hardware options for a maintenance-management system?

4. Write a memo to a software designer indicating the type of information that should be reported on a computerized work order and the type of management reports that the software must be capable of generating.

5. Develop a set of management specifications for an energy-management system.

CHAPTER 6

Courtesy of Computerized Security Systems, Inc.

LIFE SAFETY SYSTEMS

ABSTRACT

The manager should understand the importance of preparing for events that may threaten the life and property of guests and employees, as well as the assets of the business. The common problems center around fire protection and protection from criminal activity.

To determine whether a fire safety system is adequate, the manager must assess whether: codes have been followed; fire suppression systems are adequate; building design isolates toxic smoke and gas; the fire alert system is adequate; emergency exits can safely evacuate building occupants in a fire emergency; management of hazardous areas and equipment has been considered; and staff training programs and guest information programs include preparing for a fire emergency.

Protecting the lives of guests and employees, guest and employee property, and the assets of the business from the criminal actions of others includes a security survey that may reveal gaps in existing design and technology, particularly with respect to: building access; lighting of the building exterior and grounds; unsupervised parking areas; security of guest room doors, locks, and windows; key control; and protection provided for guest property.

Key words: Americans with Disabilities Act (ADA); analog-style smoke detection; automatic sprinkler; biometrics; candela; capture mechanism; carbon dioxide; carbon monoxide; Class A fire; Class B fire; Class C fire; closed-circuit television (CCTV); coded or computerized lock; deadbolt; deluge; detection; dry chemical; dry pipe; extended-coverage sprinkler; fast-response sprinkler; fire; fire pump; fixed temperature; flame detector; halogenated; halon replacement; hose line; Hotel and Motel Fire Safety

Act; ionization; life safety system; misting (fogging) system; multisensor detectors; Occupational Safety and Health Act (OSHA); photoelectric; pre-action; quick-response sprinkler head; rate-of-temperature rise; redundancy; solid-core door; standpipe; thermoelectric; wet pipe.

INTRODUCTION

There should be an understanding of the two systems that are critical for protecting the lives of guests, employees, and the general public who may visit and use the facilities of a hospitality establishment. A *life safety system* can be defined as a combination of technology and procedure for the early detection of, and reaction to, fire or other emergencies affecting human life. A *security system* may be defined as the combination of security hardware and people with a security awareness that serve to maximize the protection of persons in a hospitality facility from criminal activity.

In the hospitality industry, the life safety system is generally designed to protect the guest, minimize property loss, meet insurance requirements, and protect the establishment against the expense of litigation. During the 1980s, there were a number of tragic fires, which brought a major focus on the fire problem, especially within the lodging industry. In November 1980, 85 lives were lost in the MGM Grand Hotel fire in Las Vegas, Nevada. The considerable media attention, with actual "on-the-scene" coverage via television, elicited an unfortunate response among arsonists as they began to see the lodging industry as a target industry for their criminal activities. On December 31, 1986, an arson fire at the Hotel DuPont Plaza in San Juan, Puerto Rico resulted in the loss of 97 lives and focused the attention of the U. S. Congress on the need for legislation.

The Hotel and Motel Fire Safety Act of 1990 stated as its purpose, ". . . to save lives and protect property by promoting fire safety and life safety in hotels, motels and all places of public accommodation affecting commerce." The response of the lodging industry has been outstanding as all new construction has been fully covered by sprinklers and most high-rise properties have been retrofitted with sprinklers. The success of that response was measured in the spring of 1995 when the National Fire Protection Association determined that the fire statistic relating to hotels and motels was so minimal that it should no longer appear as a separate indicator in the residential category of its annual fire statistical report.[1]

The 1990s have seen a significant increase in crimes against persons on the premises of lodging establishments. Tragically, this represents a crime war against all residents of the United States. In 1994, the crime statistics were a national disgrace. Among U.S. residents 12 years and older, there were 10.9 million incidents of victimization through violence or personal theft. In addition, there were 32 million property crimes.[2] Sting operations by major television channels and considerable coverage in the daily newspapers and national journals pointed to hotels and motels as an industry with major crime problems. While there has been no national legislation to regulate this problem, the industry through its association, the American Hotel & Motel Association, in cooperation with the American Automobile Association, the American Association of Retired Persons, the American Society of Travel Agents, and the National Council for Crime Prevention, introduced an extremely effective "Traveler Safety Campaign."[3] The amusement and theme park, foodservice, and lodging segments within the hospitality industry have installed many security systems and have expanded training so as to provide maximum security to the patron, the employee, and the visiting public.

The purpose of this chapter is to introduce the hospitality professional to the technology that will provide maximum life safety and security protection for those being served by the hospitality industry. In the most litigious society in the world, it is critical that this matter be given full attention.

FIRE

In spite of considerable advances in fire protection technology and training, not a day passes in which there is not a fire in several hospitality establishments. Usually, such fires are in lodging or foodservice units. A report in 1981, which still holds true today, indicated that about 20 percent of those establishments will recover fully from the fire, and the remainder may suffer a loss of revenue that will never be recovered and may ultimately result in business failure.[4] In order to understand fire protection, the hospitality manager should ask the following questions:

1. Does the building comply with the appropriate codes and standards?
2. Are fire suppression systems adequate?
3. Does the building design isolate toxic gas and smoke?
4. Are fire alert systems adequate?
5. Does the exiting system facilitate safe evacuation?
6. Is hazardous equipment in the building properly managed?
7. Does the staff training program include responding to a fire emergency?
8. Does the establishment comply with the Egress and Fire Protection sections of the Occupational Safety and Health Act (OSHA) Standards?

CODES AND STANDARDS

In considering applicable fire standards for the hospitality industry, one must be aware of the impact of the Williams–Steiger Act of 1970, better known as the Occupational Safety and Health Act (OSHA). Since it focuses on the employee, there is a tendency to overlook it as also pertaining to the patron, guest, customer, or the general public. However, in the hospitality setting, the employee and public will be in common areas where the law applies to the employee and consequently will directly affect any nonemployee. The applicable OSHA Standards include Subpart E—Means of Egress and Subpart L—Fire Protection. The Means of Egress requirements are comprehensive and compatible with the stipulations under the National Fire Protection Association (NFPA) Life Safety Code 101. Under Subpart L, mandates refer to a portable fire extinguisher, fire detection systems, and employee alarm systems. Where specific installations are in place, OSHA will mandate certain maintenance and training procedures but generally does not require installation of the systems. These include standpipe/hose systems, automatic sprinkler systems, and fixed fire-extinguishing systems (general, dry chemical, gaseous agent, water spray, and foam).

The Hotel and Motel Fire Safety Act of 1990 applies only to those establishments that provide lodging and meeting space for federal employees. This law requires that as of October 26, 1996, 90 percent of federal government travel stays must be in facilities complying with the act. The law requires that all installations over three stories in height must be fully protected by sprinklers and must have single-station, hard-wired smoke detectors in each guest room. Properties of three stories or less may qualify by having only the single-station, hard-wired smoke detectors in each guest room.

Applicable codes are developed by state and local government units, and considerable differences can be found between one government agency and another with respect to fire code requirements. Most of the state and local fire codes in the United States are patterned after one of the codes listed in Figure 6.1. The fire codes listed in the figure elaborate on general fire safety regulations. A state or local government unit may adopt the entire model fire code, adopt it in part, or modify it to fit state and local concerns. For exam-

Code	Published by
Uniform Fire Code (UFC)	International Conference of Building Officials and the Western Fire Chiefs Association
National Building Code (NBC)	Building Officials and Code Administrators, International
Standard Building Code (SBC)	Southern Building Code Congress
Fire Prevention Code	International National Fire Protection Association
NFPA Life Safety Code 101	

FIGURE 6.1 Model fire codes in the United States.

ple, in 1981, after several hotel fires, Clark County, Nevada, adopted the Retroactive Life and Fire Safety Standards for Existing Buildings. This ordinance modified existing and prior codes to require hospitality buildings, as well as other buildings in the county, to follow tough new standards concerning emergency lighting, door closers, stairways, corridors, shaft and stairway enclosures, automatic sprinklers, elevator fire emergency control, HVAC (heating, ventilating, and air-conditioning) smoke control, evacuation route diagrams, and voice communication/ paging alarm systems.[5]

A periodic review of current research on the effectiveness of various protection methods is also very important. For example, the Factory Mutual Research Corporation, one of the independent firms involved in testing fire protection products and equipment, has corroborated over the years that in-room fire safety equipment is more effective than other approaches, such as corridor-only protection. In their tests, all in-room smoke detectors responded early enough to allow safe escape by room occupants. In-room sprinklers activated in time to suppress the fire and avoid appreciable damage. However, no corridor detector ever went off during the simulated fire test, which in some cases lasted up to 13 minutes (0.2167 hours).

The hospitality manager must ensure compliance with appropriate state and local codes. However, in the absence of such legal requirements, the manager should review model fire codes to determine what should be considered "reasonable care" for the protection of guests and employees. In addition, since code compliance means investing in products and equipment, care must be taken when considering such technology. The manager should also be concerned with how the products and equipment will perform in an emergency. A number of independent firms are involved in testing fire protection products and equipment. Testing is done to ensure that products such as smoke detectors and fire extinguishers perform as they are supposed to in an emergency. Some of the larger testing firms are Underwriters Laboratories (UL), Factory Mutual Research Corporation (FM), Southwest Research Institute (SwRi), and the Center for Fire Research of the National Institute of Standards and Technology (NIST).

The hospitality executive can look to these organizations for their listings of fire protection products and equipment that have been submitted for analysis and testing. Technology that performs favorably according to a standard, for example, a simulated fire condition, against which it was tested is listed as having performed satisfactorily in a simulated emergency. A "stamp," or insignia of the firm conducting the test, is affixed to the product. An example is the familiar "UL" label.[6]

FIRE SUPPRESSION

Figure 6.2 describes the effects created by the combustion process in a building fire.[7] One of the most deadly aspects of such fires is extreme heat.

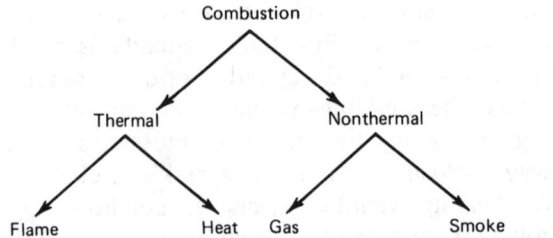

FIGURE 6.2 By-products of combustion.

In a hotel fire during the early 1980s, temperatures in excess of 1400°F (760°C) were reported. Temperatures above 140°F (60°C) can cause serious damage to the respiratory system, while 300°F (148.9°C) seems to be the maximum at which a person can breathe and survive. As heat is conducted to the lungs, a decrease in blood pressure results. The accompanying collapse of blood vessels leads to circulatory failure.

The extreme heat associated with a building fire can also cause severe body burns. As body skin temperature is increased, the ability of the body to reduce this temperature decreases. The body's ability to produce a cooling effect on the skin generally breaks down above 140°F (60°C). Thus, a second-degree burn might occur in one second if the skin temperature is raised to 158°F (70°C).

One of the purposes of a fire suppression system is to dissipate rapidly the excessive buildup of heat. Figure 6.3 shows combustion occurring with the right combination of heat, fuel, and oxygen. A fire suppression system is designed to eliminate one of these elements (heat or fuel or oxygen) and extinguish the fire.

Suppression technology utilized in the hospitality industry is classified as water based, carbon dioxide, halon replacement, or dry chemical.

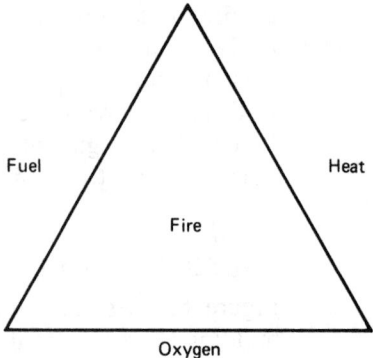

FIGURE 6.3 The fire triangle.

REDUNDANCY

A critical issue to be considered by senior management within the hospitality industry is the degree and level of redundancy to be installed in any and all of the systems reviewed in this chapter. In recent years, there have been spectacular examples of what happens when redundancy is not provided or when it becomes compromised. A "state-of-the-art" system was provided in a new hotel, including all the "bells and whistles"—auxiliary power, detection and alarm systems, full sprinkler suppression plus full water supply and pump capacity, emergency lighting, smoke exhaust and pressurization of stairwell capabilities, and so on. Within five months of opening, a transformer exploded and took the *adjoining* auxiliary power unit with it. Nothing worked! The system was compromised due to the poor location of the auxiliary equipment and the emergency lighting lacked a battery backup. This is a prime example of the redundancy to be considered by the hospitality management team. Consider an emergency lighting system tied in with the regular power, backed up by auxiliary power, backed up by a battery pack, and ultimately backed up by employees carrying flashlights to assist in evacuation. The level of redundancy becomes a senior management decision frequently affected by code and local regulations.

Water-Based Fire Suppression Systems

Water-based fire suppression systems typically used on Class A (wood, paper) fires include a combination of automatic sprinklers and standpipe/hose lines. Of particular concern to the hospitality manager should be whether the system is wet or dry pipe and whether the sprinkler heads have been properly selected and installed.

Wet-Pipe Sprinkler System.   A wet-pipe sprinkler system, as shown in Figure 6.4, is one that is filled with water at all times. In essence, behind each sprinkler head is water that is readily available to flow onto a fire. Many local codes require this system. However, it is also important to note that during months when the temperature drops below freezing for any extended period of time, portions of the system exposed to these temperatures may freeze. Frozen water can rupture pipes and create serious damage to the system and the property it is protecting. Thus, wet-pipe systems may require an antifreeze solution fill during freezing periods.

Dry-Pipe Sprinkler System.   In some locations where freezing conditions are a regular problem, dry-pipe systems are sometimes substituted if the code permits. Behind each sprinkler head (Figure 6.5) in a dry-pipe system is a charge of air. If any sprinkler head should activate, the air in the sprinkler pipe is discharged, releasing a water control valve, which causes water to flow into the sprinkler pipe and out through the activated sprinkler head(s).

Wet Pipe
System Operation

When sprinkler (A) opens, water discharging from the system lifts the Alarm Valve clapper (B) from its seat and flows through the alarm port (C), to the Retard Chamber (D), building up under the Pressure Switch (E) and sounding the optional Electrical Alarm (F). The optional Waterflow Indica-tor (G) also activates an alarm and shows fire location.

Water flows to the Water Motor Alarm (H), sounding a mechanical sig-nal. During surges or pressure fluxuations, the clapper opens momentar-ily, trapping excess pres-sure in the system and allowing only small amounts of water into the Auxiliary Valve and Re-tarding Chamber in order to prevent false alarms.

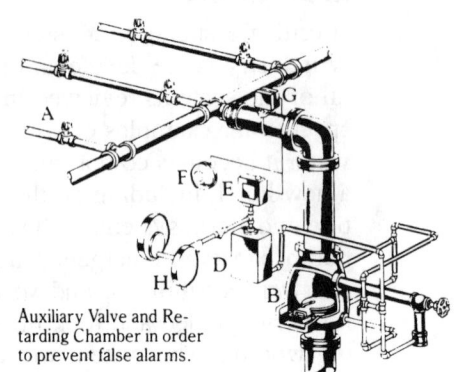

FIGURE 6.4   Wet-pipe sprinkler system (courtesy of the Viking Corporation).

Dry-Pipe
System Operation

When a sprinkler (A) activates, the system air pressure falls, opening the valve clapper (B) flooding the system. The build-up of water under the Pres-sure Switch (C) activates an optional Electrical Alarm (D). The flow of water from the Intermediate Chamber operates a Mechanical Alarm (E). In the open position, the Valve Clapper is latched out of the water-way in order to prevent water columning.

In larger systems, an accelerator (F) senses the rapid drop in air pressure caused by the actuation of a sprinkler and opens the Dry Valve faster.

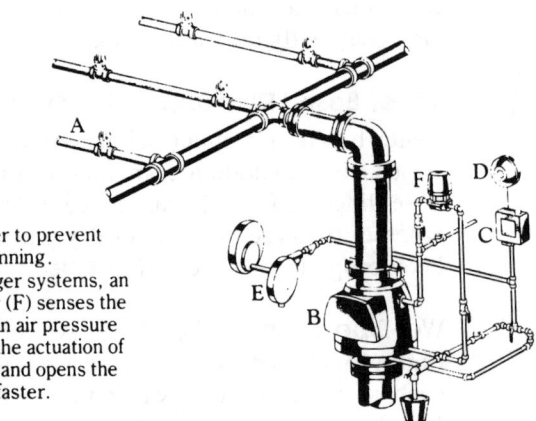

FIGURE 6.5   Dry-pipe sprinkler system (courtesy of the Viking Corporation).

Deluge Sprinkler System.   Dry-pipe sprinkler systems should not be con-fused with deluge systems. The deluge system could result in excessive water damage in a fire. Although the piping in a deluge system does not contain water, each sprinkler head in the system is open at all times. Thus, if water flows out of one of the sprinkler heads in an emergency, it will flow out of all the heads.

Since serious water damage can result from the activation of sprinkler heads, managerial personnel should be familiar with the location of all valves that control water flow to sprinklers throughout the building. It is typical for a standard sprinkler head at a pressure of 15 pounds per square inch (103.5 kilopascals) to distribute approximately 22 gallons per minute (1.4 liters per second), or at 30 pounds per square inch (207 kilopascals) to discharge 33 gallons per minute (2.1 liters per second)—for example, 0.17 gallons per square foot per minute (0.12 liters per square meter per second) on an area of 130 square feet (12.1 square meters).[8] A deluge system would have little, if any, use in a lodging establishment. Its only possible use might be in a heavy storage area where conventional sprinkler suppression would be overcome by the high concentration of flammable or combustible materials. This system is presented for the information of a future hospitality industry executive so there is an awareness of the availability of such an intensive and extensive water source. Usually, it is advantageous within the lodging situation, in particular, to focus the water in a limited area to rapidly extinguish a fire before it can critically involve a large fuel mass. Such an action would help in minimizing water damage.

Preaction System. Preaction systems are often used in portions of a building containing equipment that is particularly vulnerable to damage by water from a sprinkler. These systems are similar to a dry-pipe system but contain a supplemental fire detection device designed to detect a fire before water flows through the sprinkler head. This detection alarm activates and allows water to enter the dry pipe; at the same time, it sounds an alarm to alert personnel that an emergency exists. The extra time (between the alarm signal and the actual water flow through the sprinkler head), a matter of minutes, might be sufficient to put out a fire with suppression agents that will not damage equipment in the area.

Sprinkler Heads. The hospitality executive should be aware that there are different types and installations of sprinkler heads. Figure 6.6 shows typical sprinkler heads. The head in Figure 6.6a is a heat-sensing device. Sprinkler heads can be selected that activate at temperature levels ranging from 135 to 575°F (57.2 to 301.7°C). Careful consideration must be given to matching the head to the appropriate temperature condition. For instance, in an area where the ceiling temperature does not exceed 100°F (37.8°C), a head rated between 135 and 175°F (57.2 and 79.4°C) should be satisfactory. However, if the ceiling temperature in the area regularly exceeds 100°F (37.8°C) but does not exceed 150°F (65.6°C), a head rated between 175 and 225°F (79.4 and 107.2°C) would have to be utilized.[8]

In addition to the heat rating of the sprinkler heads, consideration must be given to their spacing and position. The National Fire Protection Association has developed sprinkler standards that show the maximum water coverage area for a sprinkler head. Generally, a standard sprinkler discharging 15 gallons per minute (0.95 liter per second) will cover a radius of 16 feet (4.9 meters) with a uniform flow of water measured approximately 4 feet (1.2 meters) below the deflector of the sprinkler.

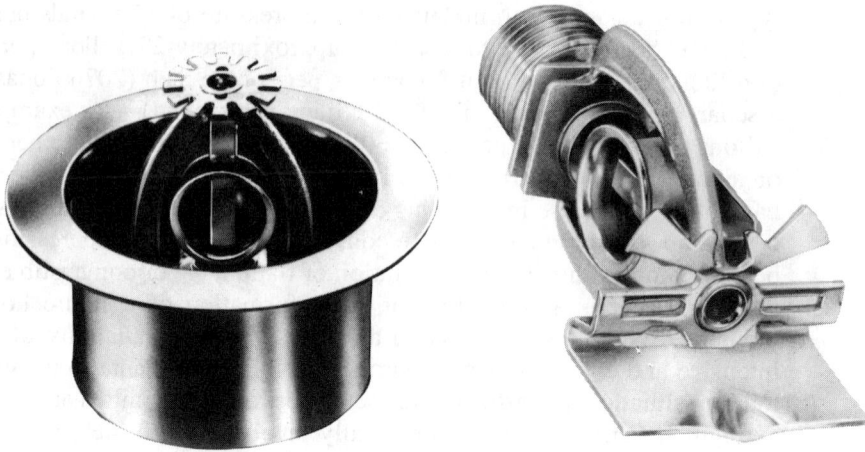

FIGURE 6.6 Automatic sprinkler heads (courtesy of Grinnell Fire Protection Systems Company).

Sprinklers are also designed to be installed in set positions on the pipe to which they are attached. The positions, as shown in Figure 6.6a and b, are either pendant or sidewall, respectively. In some instances, upright models are used if piping is exposed. The primary difference between the three positions is in the design of the deflector that determines the water discharge distribution pattern. Once the system is designed for a certain head position, it cannot be interchanged without modifications. For example, a pendant-designed head, which is to be installed below the sprinkler pipe, if installed in an upright position, would direct water upward toward the ceiling rather than downward onto a fire. (In Figure 6.6a, the pendant would be in a reversed position and the receptacle would be inset into the ceiling or soffit.)

For special applications, flush-mount, ornamental, cycling (on/off), and fast-response heads might be considered. If aesthetics are a concern, a flush-type or ornamental sprinkler can be used. The flush design minimizes the protrusion of the working parts of the sprinkler below the ceiling. Ornamental heads are decorated with special colored finishes that can blend with the decor of the area. Cycling heads, although relatively expensive ($20 to $40 for cycling heads and $3 per standard head), appear to offer great potential for lodging applications. This type of sprinkler is designed to cycle on and off automatically in response to changes in fire temperature. This type of head will minimize water damage while controlling and extinguishing a fire.

A fast-response sprinkler head should be considered for guest rooms where it is essential that water be distributed on a fire at the earliest possible moment, before any significant heat or smoke buildup is evident. This type of head has a high level of thermal sensitivity and is designed to reach the activation temperature rapidly in response to an early stage of fire development. This classification includes:

- *Residential sprinklers,* which have a fast response and are particularly effective against dwelling unit fires.
- *Extended-coverage (EC) sprinklers*, which provide a spray sprinkler with maximum coverage capability.
- *Quick-response (QR) sprinklers,* which provide a quick response and maximize the spray available for the suppression of a fire. This is one of the preferred sprinkler heads in conventional guest rooms in a lodging establishment.
- The combination of the above two heads is available as a *quick-response extended-coverage (QREC) unit.*
- For specific fire hazards, a *quick-response early-suppression (QRES) sprinkler* is also available.
- *Large drop sprinklers and early-suppression fast-response (ESFR) sprinkler head*s are among the other units available to address special needs within the hospitality industry.

The final point to consider in evaluating sprinkler heads is reliability. Once a sprinkler head activates, it must be replaced, thus making it difficult to test an installed sprinkler head. However, the independent testing laboratories mentioned earlier regularly run tests on various types of sprinkler designs, listing those that perform according to the standard against which they were tested. Only those sprinkler heads that have been listed should be installed.

Misting (Fogging) Systems. The suppression of fire through misting is being carefully considered as an alternative to halon, which is to be phased out by the year 2000. For years the fogging or misting system has been incorporated in some cooking equipment exhaust hoods. In the mid-1990s, attention focused on the misting technology and its potential application in elevator penthouses, computer sites, electrical equipment rooms, libraries, museums, and even in the guest room. A perforated tube is installed at the ceiling level around the entire contour of the room. Since it would be impossible to hold water in a perforated tube, the water mist suppression system may be activated by spot heat detection within the protected space. The system may operate at a high-pressure or low-pressure capacity. In one experiment with a guest room, a liter of water under high pressure was sufficient to suppress a room fire. The obvious reduction of water damage with the application of such a small quantity of water makes this a system worthy of investigation and review. As with any existing system that is being moved through research and development to a more extensive use, there are problems of water purity, possible clogging of the orifices in the tubing, and back-up capabilities, if required, to name but a few. Nevertheless, this is an alternative suppression system that should be considered for appropriate application within the hospitality industry.

Standpipe/Hose Systems. Most codes require standpipe/hose lines in addition to automatic sprinklers as a means of applying water. Such systems are classified according to the use for which they are intended. A Class 1 system is provided in a building for use by the fire department or persons trained in handling heavy streams of water—2.5-inch (63.5-millimeter) hose line. Class 2 systems—1.5-inch (38.1-millimeter) hose line—are provided for use by building occupants until the fire department arrives. All codes relating to fire protection establish the "authority having jurisdiction" as the final arbitrator of fire systems within a community. This is usually a fire commissioner or other individual of senior rank. It is judicious and just common sense to review plans for all systems with the authority that will ultimately provide or withhold approval of an installation. It should be noted that there are many jurisdictions where the authority having jurisdiction does not want employees to become involved in the use of standpipe/hose installations. Such authority may even require that there be no hose, but only the standpipe and connections for use by the fire service hose, only.

Where permitted, employee training is essential for using standpipe/hose fire protection systems. For example, 100 feet (30.5 meters) of 1.5-inch (38.1-millimeter) hose in a building corridor will generate a pressure of 65 pounds per square inch (448.5 kilopascals) at the outlet and 100 gallons per minute (6.3 liters per second) of water flow. For untrained personnel, this hose can be extremely difficult and dangerous to handle.

Local codes will usually dictate the location and number of standpipes. However, all portions of the building should be within 30 feet (9.2 meters) of a nozzle attached to 100 feet (30.5 meters) of hose. Outlets for larger-diameter hoses are reserved for use by the fire department and are located in stairwells, whereas smaller-diameter outlets and hose for use by building occupants are located in corridors. OSHA mandates that every 1.5-inch (38.1-millimeter) or smaller hose outlet used to meet the standard be equipped with hose connected and ready for use.

Care must be taken to ensure that hose stored in corridor locations is properly protected. Lightweight, woven-jacket, rubber-lined hose must be used for interior standpipe locations. The alternative, unlined linen hose, does not meet OSHA Standards and is unacceptable. The presence of such a hose during an OSHA compliance inspection could result in a citation and fine.

Other System Factors. If a water-based suppression system is in place in a building, regular inspections are essential. Figure 6.7 outlines the components of a system that should be included in the inspection. Recommended inspection frequencies are also shown in Figure 6.7.

Component	Frequency of inspection[a]
Fire pump	Monthly
Emergency water supply tank	Yearly test of float switch
Fire standpipe valves	Weekly
Fire standpipe, connections outside	Monthly
Sprinkler heads	Monthly visual
Sprinkler flow indicators	Semiannual
Fire alarm stations	Weekly visual
	Annual operation
Prealarm bells	Monthly
General alarm bells	Semiannual

[a]State and local codes will determine the specific frequency.

FIGURE 6.7 Typical components of a water-based fire suppression system requiring inspection.

A fire water pump is essential to provide required water pressure for an automatic sprinkler system. A manually activated fire water pump should be used only in locations where sufficient water is already available to sprinklers and standpipes. It is desirable to use an automatically activated fire water pump in a fire emergency. An auxiliary power source is mandatory.

Sprinkler and standpipe valves should be readily accessible, numbered, identified with labels indicating what they control, and there must be assurance that there is no leaking present within the system. (A flow alarm will provide that assurance—see the following discussion.)

Dry standpipe/hose connections that might be used by the fire department to pump external water to the upper floors of a building should be inspected to ensure that they are not blocked with stones or other debris. Hose lines stored within the building should be inspected to determine whether they have been damaged by moisture or vandals.

A sprinkler system is usually required to be equipped with an approved alarm (electronic bell, horn, or siren). This alarm should be tested to ensure that it operates if any of the following occurs: any water flow from a sprinkler, electric power supply failure to the fire water pump, or significant water pressure fluctuations in the lines.

Sprinkler heads should be inspected for any accumulation of mineral deposits, dust, paint, or other debris that could seriously hamper their activation. For example, if the sprinkler heads in a guest room that was recently repainted were not covered, they could be permanently damaged and require immediate replacement. The piping carrying the sprinkler heads should be inspected to determine if its pitch is correct, if there are loose pipe hangers, and if there is a proper antifreeze charge, where appropriate.

Finally, a critical component for the successful operation of a water-based suppression system is water. A careful assessment of the reliability of the system supply, capacity, and pressure during normal periods and unusual occurrences should be made. Connection to public water mains that feed on a grid pattern, or from two or more sources of water, is more desirable than from a single water main. In addition, the diameter of the main should be considered. Building mains less than 6 inches (152.4 millimeters) in diameter are usually unreliable unless serving a small lodging unit or a small free-standing restaurant.

Special reference should be made to NFPA 25, Standard for the Inspection, Testing, and Maintenance of Water-Based Fire Protection Systems. This places full responsibility upon the owner for all the functions noted in the standard's title. However, when the owner is not the occupant, the authority for compliance with this standard may be passed on to the occupant, management firm, or managing person through a lease agreement or other appropriate contract instrument. It should be further noted that the preceding tasks should be performed by staff that have developed competence through training and experience. Management must assure such competence.

Carbon Dioxide, Halon Replacement, and Dry-Chemical Systems

Hospitality industry properties may also include or be required to include carbon dioxide, halon replacement materials, or dry-chemical suppression agents as part of their fire protection system for Class B (flammable liquids) and Class C (electrical) fires. Carbon dioxide and halon replacement materials are gases that have been used for many years to extinguish fires involving flammable liquids, gas, and electric-powered equipment. Effective in 1995, the production of halon was reduced by 50 percent with complete phaseout of production throughout the world required by the year 2000. Halon is a contributor to the depletion of the earth's stratospheric ozone layer and a replacement material should be used. As previously noted, the misting technology holds great promise for the future and should be considered as an effective substitute for halon.

Dry chemical is a powder mixture recognized for its ability to extinguish fires in flammable liquids, such as kitchen grease. While dry chemical takes away the fuel supply from the combustion process, carbon dioxide and halon replacement materials make effective fire suppression agents, primarily because they reduce the oxygen content of the fire area to a point where combustion can no longer be supported.

These suppression agents have been used for many years in range hoods found in food preparation areas to extinguish fires occurring on cooking surfaces. Carbon dioxide and halon substitutes are also used in special hazard areas such as computer and electrical equipment rooms where an application of water could seriously damage equipment.

In selecting one of these suppression agents, the manager should not use dry chemical in installations that have electric relays and contacts because the chemical may coat electrical contacts of the equipment and make them useless. Also, since dry chemical is slightly corrosive, it should be removed from undamaged surfaces as soon as possible.

A principal concern with carbon dioxide and halon replacement materials has been their possible hazard to people exposed to the chemicals. Studies indicate that, in sufficient concentration, these chemicals can result in dizziness and can temporarily impair physical and mental capabilities.

Figure 6.8 outlines the normal maintenance concerns of dry-chemical, halon replacement, and carbon dioxide systems. Although workers performing this maintenance might be service-contract technicians, the equipment identified in Figure 6.8 should constitute the basic elements of a maintenance schedule.

Maintenance of dry-chemical, carbon dioxide, and halon replacement systems should include a regular weighing of the storage container holding the chemical. If loss of the chemical charge from the container is more than 10 percent, the container should be replaced.

The success of these systems in extinguishing fires depends on the height of the nozzle above the cooking surface. A periodic check is required to determine if the nozzles have been moved by employees, for example, a cook working at a range surface.

Most of these systems are also equipped with a spring-loaded activation mechanism that can be tripped manually or automatically if temperatures exceed a specified level. If the heat-sensitive link becomes covered with grease or other substances, it may not work. Maintenance should include, even if not required by the code, regular replacement of the link.

Component	Frequency of inspection*
Alarm	Annual
Shutdown devices	Annual
Storage container (pressure and weight)	Semiannual
Nozzles	Weekly visual
Direction	
Grease seals in position	
Fusible link	Monthly visual
* State and local codes will determine the specific frequency.	

FIGURE 6.8 Typical components of carbon dioxide, halon replacement, and dry-chemical fire suppression systems requiring inspection.

Portable Extinguishers

Water, carbon dioxide, halon replacement, and dry chemical can also be applied from portable extinguishers. However, when considering portable extinguishers, attention should be directed toward their installation and testing.

Portable fire extinguishers must contain suppression agents that are properly rated for the class of fire that might occur in the area. Figure 6.9 shows the relationship between the type of suppression agent and a potential fire.

The manager should also be aware that certain types of extinguisher designs are considered obsolete by most authorities and could cause potential injury to the users. Any type of extinguisher that must be turned upside down before the suppression agent can be applied to a fire should be removed from service. It has been determined that these extinguishers can explode if the discharge mechanism becomes blocked. In addition, these extinguishers, once activated, cannot be turned off.

Additional considerations should focus on who will use the extinguisher and where it will be used. For instance, a 2.5-gallon (9.5-liter) water-filled extinguisher weighs approximately 30 pounds (13.6 kilograms). This extinguisher would not be an appropriate selection for a housekeeper's cart. Figure 6.10 identifies normal discharge distances for various types of suppression agents and must also be considered when selecting extinguishers.

Type of fire	Typical suppression agents			
	Water	Carbon dioxide	Halon replacement	Dry chemical (A, B, C-triplex)
A A fire involving ordinary combustibles, such as wood, cloth, paper, rubbish, and plastic	✓		✓	✓
B A fire that occurs when flammable liquids, including paint, grease, oil, and gasoline, ignite		✓	✓	✓
C A fire involving live electrical systems, including malfunctioning motors, control panels, and wiring		✓	✓	✓

FIGURE 6.9 Fire suppression agents and their appropriate uses.

Suppression agent	Discharge distance[a]
Carbon dioxide and halon	6–12 feet (1.83–3.66 meters)
Water and foam	30–40 feet (9.15–12.20 meters)
Dry chemical	10–15 feet (3.05–4.58 meters)

[a]Presumes a minimum safe distance of 8 feet (2.44 meters) from a fire, and any wind to the back of the person operating an extinguisher.

FIGURE 6.10   Typical discharge distance for portable fire extinguishers.

When fire extinguishers are installed, locations should be chosen that facilitate easy access, are near exits, and are safe from damage generated by other activities in the area (e.g., carts being carelessly pushed down corridors and into extinguishers). It is also recommended that an extinguisher weighing over 40 pounds (18.2 kilograms) be no more than 3.5 feet (1.1 meters) from the floor and that those weighing less than 40 pounds (18.2 kilograms) be no more than 5 feet (1.5 meters) from the floor. Following these height guidelines makes it easy to use the extinguisher and reduces the chance of its being dropped as it is removed from its mounting.

Inspection and maintenance of portable fire extinguishers are essential. Each extinguisher should be weighed monthly to determine whether any chemical has been lost. Every 5 years, a hydrostatic test should be run on each unit to check for internal corrosion and damage that might not be visible. After passing a test and inspection, each extinguisher should be tagged to indicate the date it was inspected, who performed the inspection, and what was done. In addition, a tamper seal (e.g., lead and wire or plastic) should be affixed to the unit's discharge controls so that, by visual inspection, one can be reasonably certain it has not had unauthorized use. (The 5-year period applies to "wet" materials. In the case of the dry-chemical, dry-powder, or halon replacement materials, the canister requires a hydrostatic test on a 12-year schedule.)

Smoke/Gas Containment

The effects of heated air and fire gases are deadly. At a minimum, they result in obstruction of vision, disorientation, and loss of motor control. And, if inhaled, they contribute to immobility and respiratory failure.

One of the most serious problems in many buildings is the inability to isolate or contain toxic gas and smoke produced by a fire. During a fire, the temperature and pressure of the air near the fire are increased. This causes the air near the fire to flow away from the fire area, resulting in the movement of smoke and gas to other parts of the building.

Figure 6.11 indicates construction and remodeling practices that can lead to the spread of smoke and gas, a serious problem for lodging and institu-

Walls don't extend to underside of rated ceilings.
Holes or unrepaired damage in fire-rated walls.
Smokeproof enclosures not provided with adequate ventilation.
Non-fire-rated access panels on linen/trash chutes and electrical/plumbing chases.
No fire dampers in ducts penetrating fire walls.
No fusible links or self-closing devices on corridor or exit doors.
Plumbing and electrical chases extending from basement to roof without fire stops or seals.
Linen and trash chutes not properly rated.
Seismic joints.
No separation of elevator lobbies from corridors.
Absence of smoke detectors or similar detection in HVAC ductwork.
Using corridor makeup air for HVAC in guest rooms.

FIGURE 6.11 Problems contributing to smoke spread.

tional buildings. In a lodging or health-care facility fire, particular concerns are building exits and protection from smoke contamination of rooms not involved in the actual fire. Under the mandates of the Americans with Disabilities Act (ADA), a separate area of refuge is required. An exception was permitted in properties fully protected by sprinklers, but this comes under challenge from time to time. (The responsible hospitality executive will review this requirement to determine its current status.) These locations then become "safe areas" for guests or patients remaining in their rooms or for those attempting to use emergency exits and stairways to evacuate the building. Unfortunately, smoke-resistant passageways are compromised during renovations or modifications when piping, wiring, or openings for telecommunication equipment are made through enclosed walls and are not properly resealed.

Potential smoke contamination problems are increased when doors on utility access panels, guest rooms, stairways, and trash or linen chutes are not checked to determine whether they seal properly or whether they have been blocked open by employees working in the area, thereby increasing the chance of smoke seepage to "safe areas."

In addition, it is critical to the survival of the guests, customers, patients, clients, and employees in a fire emergency that the HVAC system stop automatically when smoke is detected. This prevents the system from circulating smoke into areas of the building not affected by the fire. There are sophisticated systems that will place the fire-involved area into an exhaust mode and start fans that will pressurize the stairwells. This will minimize smoke intrusion into the stairwell. Of course, as with any system involving people, the blocking of doors by exiting persons for fear of being trapped in the stairwell could create the very problem they are trying to avoid. The pressurizing would soon be overcome by the continuing introduction of smoke into the stairwell via the blocked doors.

DETECTION

A fire detection system in a building should consist of the elements identified in Figure 6.12. The most common detectable elements of a fire are heat, smoke, and radiant energy.

Heat Detectors

Heat detectors are the oldest form of automatic fire detection, dating back to the earliest use of automatic sprinklers in the 1860s. The automatic sprinkler, as previously discussed, includes heat detection and suppression capa-

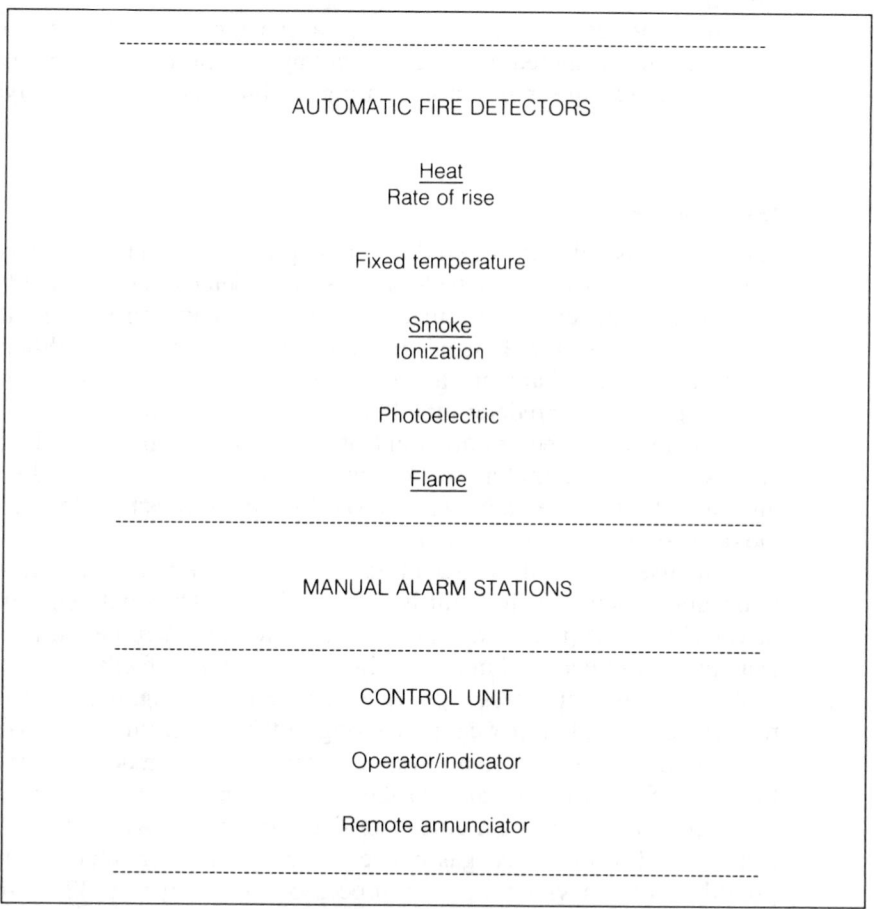

FIGURE 6.12 Components of a fire detection system.

bilities. Heat detectors that provide only an alarm and no suppression are also available.

A fixed-temperature detector activates when the heat-sensing element reaches a specified level. Management personnel must determine, as with automatic sprinklers, the normal temperature conditions in the area where the detectors are to be installed. Generally, the detector should be rated at least 25°F (13.9°C) above the maximum anticipated temperature.

The fixed-temperature detector located near the ceiling level will not initiate an alarm until the air temperature near the ceiling exceeds the design operation point. Therefore, in some instances, it is more desirable to utilize rate-of-temperature (heat)-rise detectors.

Rate-of-temperature-rise detectors will activate when the rate of temperature increase exceeds a particular value. For example, a rise in temperature exceeding 12 to 15°F per minute (0.1 to 0.2°C per second) could activate the alarm.

A thermoelectric detector contains a sensing element (thermocouple) that produces an increase in electric voltage as the temperature increases. The electric voltage is monitored and any abnormal increase activates the alarm.

Smoke Alarms

Figure 6.12 also identifies two different approaches to detecting smoke: ionization and photoelectric detectors. Ionization detectors use a small amount of radioactive material that ionizes the air in a smoke-sensing chamber contained in the detector. Ionized air conducts electric energy. When smoke enters the sensing chamber, the level of electric flow is reduced. When this flow drops below a predetermined level, the alarm is activated.

Photoelectric detectors are light-obstruction, or light-scattering, smoke alarms. This means that as smoke enters a sensing chamber, it disrupts the intensity of a light beam being received by a photosensitive device, causing the detector to activate an alarm.

A multisensory unit includes rate-of-temperature-rise, photoelectric, and ionization sensors. Such a unit is valuable in structures with concentrations of valuable items (museums, historic sites, etc.) and facilities in which there is a high risk of personal injury (as in most hospitality facilities).

A built-in microprocessor provides analog measuring, digital transformation of values, and numerical processing of the data from these two sources. The processor intelligence allows a decentralized alarm decision and avoids the flow of unnecessary data to the control panel. The presence of digital compensation within the multisensory unit adapts to environmental changes caused by dirt, humidity, gas concentration, and aging. One manufacturer provides a unit in which the microprocessor constantly runs 32 self-diagnostic checks providing important system maintenance and environmental information, which is stored in a resident nonvolatile memory. The resident memory provides a history, logging hours of operation, original and current sensitivity, ambient environment, job number, alarms, time and date, faults, and signal patterns just before the last alarm.

Many fire codes mandate automatic smoke detectors for guest and public areas in lodging units. Therefore, it is particularly important that the manager develop installation and maintenance procedures for these units. The normal maximum area of coverage for a single smoke unit is 900 square feet (83.7 square meters). However, these units cannot be mounted more than 35 feet (10.7 meters) apart, nor more than 18 feet (5.5 meters) from a wall, nor closer than 8 inches (203.2 millimeters) to a wall. National Fire Protection Association Standard 72, National Fire Alarm Code, provides excellent detailed installation assistance.[9] These automatic smoke detection units should not be located in areas where humidity is greater than 95 percent, or where air currents are excessive—greater than 15 feet per second (4.6 meters per second), or where there is excessive dust, or in kitchen and food preparation areas. Such conditions increase the chance of mistaken alarms and result in increased maintenance requirements.

In addition, special problems are encountered in guest rooms with low ceilings and where there is considerable smoking. In these areas, ionization smoke detectors will have to be installed that have a capacity to delay an alarm until the smoke source has been identified as hazardous. This capacity or "interrogation period" prevents the detector from transmitting an alarm condition to the control unit until the detector senses smoke for a preset period of time, normally in the 20- to 30-second range. The interrogation period enables the sensing chamber in the unit to be cleared of temporary conditions caused by lighting a pipe or cigar.

Analog-style smoke detectors have improved the efficiency of computerized detection systems. In addition to giving a basic alarm signal, these detectors also report the percentage of ionization (for ionization detectors) or the percentage of obscuration (for photoelectric detectors) at each polling by the central panel. If the central panel senses sufficient degradation in the head, it will declare a supervisory trouble alarm to indicate the need for maintenance. Analog heads also can be reset by a time-driven program to be more or less sensitive to smoke buildup as it might relate to building use or occupancy. However, restrictions are imposed on the central programming to prevent the system from falling below the minimum National Fire Protection Association recommendations for smoke sensitivity.

The manager should initiate a maintenance procedure for smoke detectors that includes as a regular test the introduction of a small amount of smoke into the unit with special test equipment recommended by the detector manufacturer. Regular maintenance should keep the unit dust free, inspect the electrical source, and ensure that the sensitivity adjustment on the unit has not been disturbed.

Flame Detectors

Flame detectors respond to radiant energy or flame. The flame detector responds very rapidly but only to energy that is visible. An object placed between a flame and the detector reduces its effectiveness.

When selecting automatic detectors, the manager must be aware of the types of fires that could be expected in the area to be protected. For example, heat detectors should be located in an enclosed space where a rapid buildup of heat could be expected from a fire. Photoelectric smoke detectors should be installed in areas where there is a strong possibility of a smoldering fire, for example, where there is a concentration of PVC-clad electric wiring. An ionization unit should be used if there could be a fire with little smoke, the type of fire that occurs with certain flammable liquids used in cleaning operations.

Other Alarms

A manual alarm station is provided in the detection system for a person to register an alarm if a fire is discovered in the vicinity. The manager should determine whether such units are located along escape routes and positioned so that they are visible at all times.

The activation of an automatic sprinkler should also initiate an alarm in the fire detection system. This type of alarm is facilitated by a water flow switch. The water flow switch should be located on the main supply piping to the sprinkler lines.

Guest room visual alarms are required under the Americans with Disabilities Act for the hearing impaired in a designated number of rooms (2% of total rooms with 20 rooms per 1000 rooms plus one room per each 100 rooms in excess of the 1000 rooms). Alarms are to be permanently mounted in place and must be activated by the building fire alarm system. The intensity and strobe frequency of lighting are a continuing issue. Alarms placed at 24 inches (0.61 meter) or more below the ceiling are required to be 110 candela minimum (the candela is a source light measurement term equivalent to 1383 lumens, or the light output of a 75-watt incandescent lamp; refer to Chapter 11 for additional lighting terms). Alarms placed at less than 24 inches (0.61 meter) are required to be 177 candela minimum (2225 lumens). The hospitality manager should be aware that the intensity and frequency of the strobe action of the alarm light may induce an epileptic seizure. Review this matter for current requirements.

Another dimension of the visual alarm is the expense of installation. The power requirements for the system exceed the low voltage level for the conventional alarm installation. One must either provide power boosters for the total alarm power grid or go to the expense of installing an additional alarm line dedicated to the visual alarms, only.

A *carbon monoxide detector* is required by law in Chicago, Illinois, and Albany, New York, with a number of other cities contemplating such a requirement. In the presence of equipment that is powered by fossil fuels, there is the danger of a malfunction that could result in the creation and spread of carbon monoxide in a facility. Since this gas is odorless, there is no way of knowing of its presence; frequently until it is too late to respond and exit from a contaminated area. With reference to the lodging industry, the law requires: "In every hotel and motel, one approved carbon monoxide detector shall be installed for every 10,000 square feet (930 square meters) of floor area, or fraction thereof, (a) on every floor on which a fossil fuel–burning boiler or furnace is located, and (b) on every floor in which sleeping rooms are heated by any type of warm air heating plant . . . that burns fossil fuel. Floor area shall be computed separately for each floor."

The model code for this mandate was enacted in Chicago in 1993 and amended in 1994. The National Fire Protection Association (NFPA) Code 720 Household Carbon Monoxide (CO) Warning Equipment Standard Committee has been organized and will be working toward codification of the manufacture, installation, and use of these devices. As this will be a continuing focus within the fire protection community, the hospitality manager should review the current requirements for his or her establishment in this regard.

Detection Control

The function of the control is to monitor and evaluate all components of the fire detection system, as well as the automatic sprinkler system and the public address and evacuation systems for the building. The control unit must be equipped with an emergency power supply since it has to operate in the event of a building power failure.

The operator/indicator terminal is that point in the fire detection system where an alarm anywhere in the system can be accurately located and identified by those responsible for monitoring the system. In a modern hotel, such terminals are located in more than one area of the building (engineering, security, front desk). The manager should ensure that the terminal is monitored 24 hours a day, 7 days a week.

Fire codes may require that terminals be located in the main lobby or in areas easily accessible to fire fighters. In these locations, the terminals or panels may have limited operating capabilities, possibly identifying only the general location of the alarm. In such cases, the terminal is called an *annunciator*. Annunciators are particularly useful in properties with multiple buildings, where annunciator panels are located at the entrance to each building, or in buildings with multiple floors and rooms per floor, where annunciator panels are placed at the entrance to each floor.

The primary operation/indicator terminal should be equipped with a printer that records: time, day, and type of alarm; time and date of alarm acknowledgment; time and date of system reset; time, day, and type of fault signals (mistaken alarms or problems with the system); and time and date of fault corrections.

With the continuing advances in microelectronics, fire alarm system manufacturers found that they can give each device connected to the system a unique identity by putting in a local transponder. These systems are called *addressable systems*. With the use of transponders, the need for a local panel is eliminated; each device reports directly to the central fire alarm panel. When a device alarms, it gives the panel its specific address and status. This style of system reduces the wiring requirement to a single pair of wires, connected to each device in either a daisy-chain or a T-tap style. The central panel polls each device in sequence and, if the device does not answer, it will annunciate a trouble condition.

Many modern fire detection systems are also equipped with a special alarm transmission device that can automatically link the building with the fire department. These communications are superior to the telephone message that can often be misunderstood or incorrectly transmitted because of the stress the caller may experience in a fire emergency. Added intelligence in the central panel also allows for English language messages for each alarm and a graphic floor plan showing the building structure and the alarm location. Advances in microelectronics technology have further introduced English language interfaces to allow for simple commands in a question-and-answer format. Graphic interfaces display information concerning point status (alarm, trouble), type of alarm (smoke detector, fire alarm [pull] station), number of alarms in the system, location of reporting unit (node), and a custom location label. Alarm, supervisory, and trouble conditions have dedicated knowledge push-button switches. Operation of the appropriate acknowledge switch silences the tone alert with the panel lights illuminated until all conditions in that category are restored to normal. Security access levels control the depth of the operator's interaction. On Level 1, the operator provides routine actions, whereas Level 4 covers sensitive operations and will provide a pass code. Display panels may also show floor plans with exact device locations, highlighting alarmed devices and the spread of smoke and fire.

EXITING

In a building there are three essential components that must be reviewed by the manager. The components are the way of exit access, the exit, and the way of exit discharge. A *means of egress* comprises the vertical and horizontal ways of travel throughout a structure from any location within that structure. *Exit access* is that portion of the means of egress that leads to an entrance to an exit. *Exit* is that portion of the means of egress that is constructed in such a manner as to provide a protected way of travel to the exit discharge. *Exit discharge* is that portion of the means of egress between the termination of the exit and a public way.

Adequate exit access further includes: number of exits, capacity of exit access, travel distance to an exit, protection of the exit access, and ease of determining the direction to an exit.

The discharge is the exit passageway, which must be protected by special construction and equipment to provide a safe means of traveling to the exterior of the building. Adequate exit discharge includes: capacity or number of persons that can utilize the exit, marking or identification of the most direct route to the outside, security, and lighting.

Although exiting is usually carefully regulated by code, Figure 6.13 suggests an overall guideline for evaluating the exit plan for a building.

ELEVATOR EQUIPMENT AND FOODSERVICE FACILITIES

The manager must also ensure that certain essential building systems are designed and maintained for fire safety. Of particular concern are the elevator system and the kitchen exhaust system.

Elevators

In a high-rise building, a critical building transportation system is the elevator. In a fire emergency, elevators can be deadly for people trying to use them. Elevator shafts may act as chimneys for toxic gas and smoke, and elevator controls can malfunction when exposed to extreme temperatures and dense smoke. In several hotel fires, elevators loaded with panicked guests have been sent directly to the fire floor by malfunctioning controls, exposing the occupants to deadly heat and toxic gas.

To ensure against such an occurrence, the elevator should be equipped with a capture mechanism. The capture mechanism, activated by the fire detection system, returns the elevator cars to a "safe area" and becomes inoperable unless activated by authorized personnel or fire fighters.

Foodservice Facilities

Food preparation facilities are considered to have a high risk of fire. One common source of kitchen fires is an improperly designed and maintained kitchen exhaust system, as reported by the National Fire Protection Association. The manager should evaluate the fire safety of a kitchen exhaust system by asking the following questions:

1. Have proper construction materials been selected? For example, the NFPA recommends: "The hood or that portion of a primary collection means designed for collecting cooking vapors and residues shall be constructed of and be supported by steel not less than 0.043 inches (1.09 millimeters), No. 18 MSG in thickness, stainless steel not less than 0.037 inches (0.94 millimeters), No. 20 MSG in thickness, or other approved material of equivalent strength and fire and corrosion resist-

Location:

(1) Exit access—Two separate exits are typically required from each floor or area of the building.

(2) Travel distance—Codes establish the maximum distance a guest or employee should have to travel before reaching an exit; for example, 150 feet (45.75 meters) is used in many codes.

(3) Discharge to the outside—Clearly marked from inside. Doors must swing open to the outside. The discharge area is clear and not blocked with vehicles, debris, or other material.

Protection:

Corridors leading to the exit, doors leading into the exit, and the exit passageway (for example, stairways) should be protected from penetration by flame, heat, or smoke during a fire emergency. Codes generally specify a minimum number of hours of fire resistance for the floors, walls ceiling, and doors for such areas. Care must be taken to ensure that such resistance is not compromised by remodeling, which may poke openings into walls, floors, or ceilings or add flammable interior finishes (for example, carpet, fabric, paint).

Capacity/Dimensions:

(1) Corridor width leading to an exit—Sufficient to ensure a smooth flow of guests and employees to the exit system. Generally, a minimum width of 44 inches (1.12 meters) at the narrowest point is required. However, it is most important that the clear width of corridors should not be reduced by built-in objects (ice and soda machines) or stored material (for example, carts, tables, chairs).

(2) Corridors/stairways leading to the discharge point—Such capacity is expressed in terms of persons per unit of exit width; for example, one unit of exit width is equal to 22 inches (0.59 meters) of clear opening. Generally, the capacity of all exits must equal or exceed the maximum number of persons on any floor or area in the building at any one time.

(3) Discharge point to the outside—Door widths are generally equal to or greater than the capacity of the exit system terminating at the discharge.

(4) Dimensions—Codes generally specify the headroom, slope of floor, door swing clearance, stair riser/tread height, landing size of all components considered part of the exit access, system, and discharge.

Identification:

(1) Lighting—For exit access, the exit discharge should be illuminated on a continual basis. Critical points include angles and intersections, corridors and passageways, stair ways, and landings of stairs and doors. Minimal lighting levels are generally published by code, for example, one footcandle (10.8 lux) measured at the floor. In the event of a single lighting unit failure, the basic lighting should not leave any area in darkness.

(2) Emergency power—Should be arranged so as to provide the required illumination automatically in the event of any interruption of normal lighting.

(3) Signs—Codes generally specify the size of letters; for example, 6 inches (152.4 millimeters) high, with principal strokes not less than ¾ inch (19.1 millimeters) wide; color, lighting level, and position of sign. All lighted exit signs should also be connected to the emergency power supply.

Note: Detailed discussion of exiting can be found in NFPA Standard Number 101 ''Life Safety Code.''

FIGURE 6.13 Checkpoints for the evaluation of an emergency exiting system.

stance."[10] Failure to use the proper construction materials could result in the collapse of the hood and duct when they are exposed to normal operating temperatures.[10]

2. Has the duct system been properly installed? Improper installations include: nonrated openings in fire walls; interconnections with other parts of the building ventilation system; dips or traps that collect residue; failure to exit grease-laden vapor as directly as possible to the outside of the building; failure to encase in fire-resistant material; improper clearance from combustible materials and adjacent buildings at the exit point; service to more than one floor in multistory buildings; and design that causes hot exhaust gas to blow across a roof surface rather than away from the roof. Any or all of the above design errors increase the chance of a serious problem if a fire occurs in the duct system.

3. Is grease removal and air movement adequate in the exhaust system? For example, grease extractors and filters should be tested and listed by a reputable fire research laboratory. Particular attention should be directed to the fire resistance of the construction materials of the filter. The filter frame should fit tightly but be easily removable for cleaning. The air velocity in the system must be sufficient to remove grease-laden vapors. The National Fire Protection Association recommends a minimum air velocity of 1500 feet per minute (7.5 meters per second).[10]

4. Is the fire suppression equipment adequate? As discussed previously, it is especially important that the suppression equipment be matched to the hazard. Dry-chemical, carbon dioxide, or halon replacement systems are widely used and recommended. Water mist or "fog" systems seem to be growing in popularity because of the ease of cleanup after activation.

5. Has the exhaust system received proper maintenance? A maintenance checklist should include these points: promptly remove grease accumulations on the hood, duct, and exhaust surfaces; never operate the system without filters in place; never use flammable solvents or cleaners on the exhaust components; never apply cleaning solvents to fusible links or other parts of the fire suppression system; ensure that all electrical components are properly secured before the system is cleaned; and ensure that, on completion of any maintenance, the fire suppression system and other system components are reactivated.

EMPLOYEE TRAINING

In the hospitality industry, fire prevention should be the responsibility of every employee. The first step in fire management is to provide the means to reduce fire damage through alarms and suppression. The second critical step is employee training. Figure 6.14 identifies the causes of most fires in the

Cause	Number	% of all building fires	Deaths	% of all fire deaths
Incendiary/suspicious	27,800	25.8	89	36.2
Electrical distribution	14,500	13.5	11	4.4
Cooking equipment	13,500	12.5	10	4.1
Smoking	11,200	10.4	68	27.6
Appliance, tools, or air conditioning	9,300	8.6	6	2.3
Heating equipment	8,500	7.9	17	2.3
All others	23,000	21.3	43	18.3
Total	107,800	100.0	244	100.0

Ranking based on analysis by the U.S. Fire Administration.

Source of Data: 1983–1987 National Fire Incident Reporting System and NFPA survey.

FIGURE 6.14 Major causes of fire in the United States (1983–1987).

service industry. These fire problem areas should be brought to the attention of all employees, particularly those who are responsible for the operation and servicing of various building equipment.

Fire training includes fire prevention, operation of fire suppression equipment, and alarm response. Each of these topics must be discussed with every employee. Additionally, there is currently considerable interest in the hospitality industry in the concept of an in-house fire response team. Generally, the fire response team includes at least two employees from every shift, with the duties of the fire response team chief being handled by the chief engineer and/or the director of security.

It is essential that members of the fire response team have hands-on familiarity with fire-fighting equipment, know all the exit locations in the building, and understand current evacuation procedures, as well as the operation of the building's evacuation alarm system. However, it should also be noted that the actions of the fire response team during an emergency are essentially limited to the time between the fire alert and the arrival of the local fire department.

OSHA has stipulated special training for employees who serve on a fire brigade, as this group of employees will essentially be called upon to fight structural fires. Location and distance from a municipal or volunteer fire department may necessitate the development of trained fire fighters, who will train at an approved fire fighter school, have access to approved protective equipment, and, in some instances, have fire trucks on the premises, as in a large resort complex. In most hospitality facilities, the fire response team will be preferred to the fire brigade.

Guest Safety

In addition to the fire training and/or education provided employees, the manager must never overlook the guests, customers, patients, members, and other building occupants. Fire codes will usually require the posting of exit and evacuation diagrams and instructions in guest rooms and in public areas of the building.

This information might be supplemented with information about the meaning of various alarm signals (alert versus evacuation), how guests will receive instructions in a fire emergency (by telephone or over a speaker in the guest room), and what to do if a guest is handicapped and needs special assistance (provide a special telephone number). Figure 6.15 shows the type of information that might be posted in the guest room.

SECURITY SYSTEMS

The cost of crime in the United States is estimated to be averaging $140 billion per year during the 1990s, with anticipated costs of $200 billion annu-

---

Diagram showing location of nearest exits and of manual fire alarm

Explanations:
Emergency equipment located in the room (sprinklers, smoke detectors, voice communication).
The meaning of audible and visual alarms that might be heard or seen.
Who to call in an emergency.

Safety precautions:

As soon as you are shown your room, locate the emergency exit.
Make a mental note of the direction in which you must leave your room and the path you must travel to reach the floor exit.
Familiarize yourself with the room you occupy. Get accustomed to the layout and furnishings.
Check the window and sliding glass door locations. Check to see if and how they open.
Put your room key where it's easy to locate in case you must leave in a hurry. You might need the key to return to your room if you can't exit the building safely.
In a fire emergency, never open a door without first determining whether it is warm to touch. If it is, do not open it.
Never use an elevator in a fire emergency.
On entering an exit stairwell in a fire emergency, make sure the door into the stairwell does not lock behind you.
If you encounter smoke during your escape in a fire emergency, do not attempt to run through it; retrace your steps to a safe passage or drop to your knees and stay close to the floor where there may be some air that is not contaminated with toxic smoke.

FIGURE 6.15   Guest room emergency information.

ally by the year 2000.[11] As indicated earlier in this chapter, because guests and customers in the hospitality industry might be vulnerable to robbery, assault, rape, and larceny, the manager should seriously consider the effectiveness of security personnel, procedures, and equipment. In view of the tremendous cost of crime to the nation, it is critical that the hospitality executive consider the amount and nature of investment to protect the guest, employee, general public, and assets of the individuals and the property. The following information will focus on desirable design practices and equipment that decrease the likelihood of crime.

RESTRICTED ACCESS

Countless lodging units and other related hospitality activities allow virtually unrestricted entry to the facility and unrestricted movement throughout the building. This is readily apparent with multiple lobby and stairway doors that are open 24 hours a day. Although fire safety dictates the number of exits a building must have, many of these doors can provide exits with restricted entry. Panic bars, fire locks with self-contained alarms, and other devices offer perimeter security without violating safety codes and interfering with emergency use of exits. Poor perimeter security, coupled with unsupervised hallways designed with recesses or places from which an unsuspecting guest or customer might be attacked, create potentially dangerous situations. The criminal will actually "shop" for vulnerable buildings, especially lodging units. Restricted access has a psychological impact on a potential offender. It signals a warning to outsiders that steps have been taken to block intrusions.

A significant development in an access-control system was achieved in 1996. This provides an answer to unauthorized entrance from nonlobby doors and the movement of unwanted persons via stairways, emergency doors, or employee-only doors. The system detects the movement of people in stairwells, entry through fire exit doors, and intrusion into employee-only areas. It protects against the propping of a door or opening from the inside to permit illegal entry and futher controls against unauthorized egress. Electromagnetic pressure holds the door against any pressure less than 1500 pounds; however, in a building emergency, the alarm will immediately release the electromagnet to permit emergency egress. The system further includes cameras (CCTV) and elevator-access systems. An added feature is a victim alarm and a distress signal for activation by a disabled person at each stairway door.

A door that has been violated announces a 20 second message, "Hotel Security is on the way. Legal prosecution will be made." Flashing strobe lights give futher evidence of the intrusion and an 85 decibel alarm sounds. The violation signals to a central control panel and continues to operate until reset—a procedure that requires only 30 seconds.

Extending the perimeter to the "outer bounds" of the property, there are other aspects of protection to be considered. Do circumstances indicate the need for fencing? Can such fencing be integrated with an infrared or microwave screening that would detect and alarm when intrusion was made by a person or persons scaling or otherwise penetrating the fence at other than a monitored entrance? Could the infrared or microwave technology be installed without the fencing to provide similar control against intrusion?

Are there situations in which one wishes to protect against an individual (a "peeping Tom," for example) from approaching a window or glass door area? A seismic detector might be considered to provide an alarm should the individual leave a path or walkway and approach through a garden or lawn area. Of course, this would be operative during night hours and there would be some unwanted alarms when animals moved through a monitored area. Sensitivity to weight could reduce such alarms.

In service areas of the structure, are doors and windows secured? Is adequate lighting provided in this section of the property? A door "hidden" in a darkened alcove could allow a criminal to work at leisure to break into the property. Review and restrict intrusion through skylights, roof hatches, ventilator shafts and vent openings, sewer and service tunnel entrances, outside stairways to basement entrances, and fire escape systems whether by stairway or exterior stationary ladder units.

LIGHTING

Adequate lighting is a psychological deterrent to criminal activity. On the other hand, a dimly lit area creates a situation that may actually encourage criminal acts against guests and customers or the property.

The only way to assess the adequacy of exterior building lighting is to inspect the facility during the evening hours. For instance, a parking area or walkway that seems to have a number of lighting fixtures during the day may look entirely different during the evening hours if, say, 50 percent of the lights are inoperable. Also, consider whether there are dark areas between the lighted areas and whether the lights automatically activate in response to changes in natural light levels or depend on employees' remembering to "flip the switch."

OSHA has established minimum illumination intensities in footcandles for all business enterprises. See Figure 6.16.

PARKING

Parking facilities need to be monitored in order to minimize such risks as hit-and-run accidents, vandalism, auto theft, and burglaries from automobiles. The security of a parking area is increased if the property utilizes uniformed security patrols, provides adequate lighting, and monitors the park-

Footcandles (Lux)	Area of operations
5 (53.8)	General site area (this would probably include parking lots).
3 (32.3)	Excavations and waste areas, accessways, active storage areas, loading platforms, and refueling areas.
10 (107.6)	General shop (e.g., mechanical and electrical equipment rooms, active storerooms, employee living quarters, lockers or dressing rooms, dining areas, and indoor toilets and workrooms).
30 (322.8)	First-aid areas and offices

FIGURE 6.16 Minimum OSHA lighting requirements.

ing areas with CCTV (closed-circuit television). In order to reduce the incidence of room theft and assault, high-rise buildings with connecting garages should be designed so as to require all persons entering the building from the garage area to pass a monitored security post or pass through a supervised lobby area or security device before they can enter guest areas. Problems occur when people can enter an elevator in the garage area and travel unnoticed to any floor in the building.

DOORS, LOCKS, AND WINDOWS

The manager should consider the following basic guidelines:

1. Solid-core doors are to be used from corridors or exterior openings. The average hollow-core wood door has a thin layer of wood stretched over a wooden frame that is stuffed with cardboard or a similar substance. Such doors may have secure locks, but an intruder can simply punch a hole through the door.

2. Hinges on all guest room doors should be concealed. If hinges are exposed to the corridor, the door can be removed by an intruder with a screwdriver and a hammer.

3. Solid metal door frames are to be used for guest rooms. Wood frames and hollow metal frames can be peeled or expanded to render the lock useless.

4. Deadbolt latches and locks, as shown in Figure 6.17, are to be provided on guest room doors. The bolt must extend from the door lock into a bolt receptacle in the door frame at least 1 inch (25.4 millimeters) and, preferably, 1.5 inches (38.1 millimeters).

5. The lock must automatically engage when the door is closed so that the room occupant or employee does not have to remember to engage the lock.

(a)

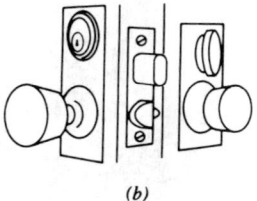

(b)

FIGURE 6.17 Deadbolt locks and latches. *(a)* Dead-latch lock with single-cylinder auxiliary deadbolt lock. *(b)* Cylinder bored spring-bolt and dead-bolt lockset.

6. Properties listed in the 23 area directories of the American Automobile Association (AAA) must have deadbolts on connecting room doors that have at least a 1-inch (25.4-millimeter) throw. If this security element is lacking, the property will not be listed by AAA.

7. A view port (peephole) should be considered for all guest room corridor doors at 5 feet (1.5 meters) from the floor and at 4 feet (1.2 meters) from the floor in rooms for the disabled. Many properties provide two viewports at varying levels to accommodate children and guests of lesser height. Install a lens that will provide at least a 180-degree view of the corridor at the room door. Be sure there is adequate lighting in the corridor to permit the guest to identify the caller.

8. Coded or computerized dead bolt locks, shown in Figure 6.18, are used instead of keyed locks on guest room doors. These locks provide the guests or employees with their own personal combination, which is added to the magnetic strip on an electronic room access card. If the card shows the correct combination, inserting it into the door releases the lock. If the card is lost or stolen, a new code is programmed by an in-house computer for that particular lock. A significant control has been added to most of the electronic room access cards in the form of an interrogator function. This permits an audit of room entries from the prior 40 entries to unlimited number of entries in some of the hard-wired, on-line electronic locking systems. The audit will reflect all entries and identify whether access was gained by the guest or a member of the hotel staff. This includes all entries by room attendants, bell staff, room service staff, engineering staff, and so forth.

FIGURE 6.18 Coded programmable lock (courtesy of Saflok Computerized Security Systems, Inc.).

9.   Window glass must be listed as burglary resistant by independent testing laboratories or protected with security screens.

10.   Windows less than 18 feet (5.5 meters) above the ground should be protected with special glass, grates, or security screens.

11.   Sliding glass doors are provided with special locks or are not used in the building. Special attention must be given to these doors; the glass is vulnerable, the aluminum frame is subject to prying, and the lock can be easily compromised with a screwdriver, pry bar, or hacksaw. A lock pin inserted through the door and frame provides additional protection and prevents the lifting of the sliding door unit from the tracks and out of the frame.

KEY CONTROL

Locks are useless without adequate key control. The manager evaluating the security of a building should ensure that keys to guest rooms are: unmarked and do not identify the property or room location in the property; stamped "Do not duplicate"; changed whenever a key loss is detected, or at least every eight months, regardless of key loss; and available to employees only on a carefully controlled basis (logs should be kept on who receives which keys and when they are returned, and a sign-out and sign-in procedure should be strictly adhered to).

However, even with the most stringent key controls, it may take a professional thief only a matter of seconds to record the impression of a room key in a bar of soap for later duplication or memorize the "cuts" on a key for future duplication. Questions must be raised as to who has access to the key codes and how frequently the codes are changed for particular rooms.

Coded or computerized locks seem to provide greater protection and key control. Such technology is usually divided into three categories: those systems that rely on what the person desiring access knows; those systems that respond to who the person is; and those systems that rely on what the person possesses.

Typical knowledge-based access control is the digital keypad. Relying on a personal identification number (PIN), the system requires that the person wishing to gain access provide a series of numbers. While such technology might be found on shipping/receiving doors and food/beverage freezers and pantries, it has not been widely used on guest room doors.

Personal identification technology is based on biometrics. Biometrics is a branch of biology that deals with its data statistically and by quantitative analysis. In a biometrics access control system, a mathematical characterization of an individual's unique feature is created. Called a template, this characterization can be of a fingerprint, retinal pattern, signature, hand geometry, or voice pattern. Obviously, a biometrics system provides the most security, since no two people have the same fingerprint, retinal pattern, or voice pattern. However, while they provide tremendous potential for the hospitality industry, current costs of some $3500 per door are beyond most budgets.

Examples of possession-based access control systems include the access card, or key card, and the key itself. The five most common types of access cards are punched, barium ferrite, magnetic strip, Weigand, and proximity.

Punched cards are covered with a series of holes representing the combination to a particular lock. Because of advances in electronic technology, possible problems associated with creating the key, and potential for counterfeiting such cards, other technology appears more suitable for hotel and hospitality operations.

Barium ferrite cards carry a magnetic code placed between layers of the card. Encoding is performed by vendors. Delaminating the card scrambles the chips, thereby rendering the card useless. The oldest of these technologies, it is vulnerable to magnetic fields and can be counterfeited by some relatively inexpensive machinery.

Magnetic strip cards, featuring a magnetic strip on the reverse side, are similar to automatic teller machine or credit cards. This is the least expensive technology for hotel facilities. While the card is vulnerable to erasure by magnetic fields, a key advantage is the ability of the hotel operator to buy an inventory of blank cards from a number of sources, obtain an encoding device, and produce the cards thereafter on site. This eliminates the lead time necessary when ordering from outside vendors. Encoding equipment can cost as little as $1500, whereas individual cards range from $1.50 to $3, depending on their features.

Weigand cards, thicker than the two previously mentioned cards, feature short wires laminated within the card. When inserted into a Weigand-type reader, the card's magnetic field registers a "Weigand Effect." More advanced types also incorporate a magnetic strip as an additional security enhancement, and one manufacturer even offers a plastic key instead of a card.

Proximity cards interface with an equally unique type of card reader permitting either contact or "hands-free" operation. Punched, barium ferrite, magnetic strip, and Weigand cards need to make contact with the system reader. Earlier versions of this technology had drawbacks that have now been largely overcome. The readers can be discreetly mounted within a wall and can sense a card from a distance of more than 2 feet (0.61 meter). They are more secure than magnetic strip or barium ferrite cards, but cost between $6 and $12 each.

Overall, card systems may range in price from $500 to $2000 per door.

In addition, with coded locks, particular attention should be focused on the number of lock entry levels and its memory capability. Lock entry levels are the number of different codes that can be simultaneously programmed into the memory lock, much like access codes to a computer program. For instance, a lock system with four entry levels would enable the property to assign codes to the guest, housekeeping, engineering, and security for a particular room. In addition, if a loss or theft should occur in a particular room, security should be able to read the memory of the lock by plugging a hand-held scanner into the lock; this provides a list, or printout, of the codes used to open the lock in the past hour or day.

New technologies in card design have been developed, but whether or not they will be adopted for widespread use remains to be seen. Pioneered in France, "smart cards" feature a very small microprocessor chip with computing power and information, enabling the card to perform certain calculations. The smart card could enable the user to gain access to a guest room, purchase items while in the hotel or area, turn on selected guest room technology (e.g., HVAC), and upon check out have a complete billing of charges. The smart card is very expensive—about $15 versus $1 for a magnetic strip card.

During the 1990s, there was a significant move on the part of many hotel and motel chains to require that all properties, both corporate and franchised, have electronic lock systems in place by specified dates. Some hotel chains disenfranchised individual franchisees who were unwilling to comply with this mandate. The result of this action was that by the mid-1990s over one million rooms of the three million rooms in the United States were equipped with electronic lock systems.

VALUABLES

Because problems can occur with key control or because of codes and ordinances, the manager may have to provide a safe or some other type of secure area at the front desk or in the guest room for the protection of expensive property such as cameras and jewelry. It is desirable for a safe to have:

1. A fire resistance rating established by an independent testing facility. The ratings in the case of fire specify the maximum temperature at which the safe will protect its contents and how long such protection can be provided at that temperature. Generally, the standard safe deposit box at or near the front desk does not provide this level of protection. If the needs of the guests dictate, consideration should be given to installing a vault or secured area that would have these fire-and burglar-proof ratings. The continuing movement of the lodging industry to properties fully protected by sprinklers supports the fire protection aspects of this requirement.

2. A burglary resistance rating established by an independent testing facility. This rating establishes the type of forcible entry the safe can withstand (hammer/bars, torch, explosives) and for how long. As noted in item 1, this matter requires special review by senior management.

3. The capability of in-room safes to be easily secured in a guest room so as to prevent the unit and its contents from being stolen. Remember, the innkeepers laws for the various states do not provide the limitations on liability that pertain to the safe deposit box system, which is under direct control of the establishment.

4. The ability to be easily and inexpensively rekeyed or recoded after each guest room occupancy.

SUMMARY

The manager should understand the importance of preparing for events that may threaten the life and property of guests and employees, as well as the assets of the business. The common problems center around fire protection and protection from criminal activity.[12]

To determine whether a fire safety system is adequate, the manager must assess whether: codes have been followed; fire suppression systems are adequate; building design isolates toxic smoke and gas; the fire alert system is adequate; emergency exits can safely evacuate building occupants in a fire emergency; management of hazardous areas and equipment has been considered; and staff training programs and guest information programs include preparing for a fire emergency.

Protecting the lives of guests and employees, guest and employee property, and the assets of the business from the criminal actions of others includes a security survey that may reveal gaps in existing design and technology, particularly with respect to: building access; lighting of the building exterior and grounds; unsupervised parking areas; security of guest room doors, locks, and windows; key control; and protection provided for guest property.

REFERENCES

1. *Fire Journal*, National Fire Protection Association, Quincy, MA, Vol. 89, No. 5, September–October, 1995.
2. *Bureau of Justice Statistics 1994*, Bureau of Criminal Justice Statistics, U.S. Department of Justice, Washington, DC, 1994.
3. *Traveler Safety Campaign*, Press Kit, American Hotel & Motel Association, Washington, DC, March 16, 1993.
4. "Traveler's Risk," *The Wall Street Journal*, Vol. CV, No. 10, July 15, 1981.
5. *Retroactive Life and Fire Safety Standard, for Existing Buildings* (pamphlet), Clark County Department of Building and Zoning, Las Vegas, 1981.
6. *Fire Protection Equipment Directory and Building Materials Directory, Fire Resistance Directory*, Underwriters Laboratories, Inc., Northbrook, IL (annual).
7. *Las Vegas Review Journal*, December 19, 1983. (These temperatures were reported by the Associated Press for the Cathedral Hill Hotel fire, which occurred in San Francisco, California, on December 18, 1983).
8. "Standard for the Installation of Sprinkler Systems," NFPA-13, National Fire Protection Association, Quincy, MA, 1994.
9. "National Fire Alarm Code," NFPA-72, National Fire Protection Association, Quincy, MA, 1993.
10. "Ventilation Control and Fire Protection of Commercial Cooking Equipment," NFPA-96, National Fire Protection Association, Quincy, MA, 1994.
11. Information Services Library, American Society for Industrial Security (ASIS), Arlington, VA, 1996.
12. The reader should also consider other management practices that enhance guest and employee safety, such as those specified for tap-water temperature in Chapter 12 of this book.

QUESTIONS/PROBLEMS

1. Determine the extent to which life safety is, or has been, a problem in the following types of facilities in your city:
   a. Lodging
   b. Foodservice
   c. Health care

d. Club

e. Institutional

2. As the new manager of one type of facility listed in the preceding problem(select one), you are preparing to conduct a fire inspection. Outline areas/equipment you would include in your inspection and your reason(s) for including them.

3. Assume you have been directed by the chief executive of your firm (select one from above) to prepare a preventive-maintenance checklist for the fire protection technology in the building and to explain why you included each technology.

4. As buildings are designed, constructed, and renovated, certain decisions can be made or procedures followed that decrease the likelihood of smoke spread in a fire emergency. Prepare a memo to the general manager describing these critical decisions and procedures.

5. You receive a telephone call from an insurance investigator representing the company that carries the liability insurance for your firm. Because of numerous liability claims (for property theft, assaults, rape) that the insurance company is paying for firms similar to yours, the insurance company is planning to conduct a security audit of each property it insures. The investigator will arrive tomorrow. Before the investigator arrives, the general manager wants you to conduct a preliminary security evaluation of the property and report back. Outline what you would include in your investigation.

6. If your chief engineer indicated that you could cut costs by replacing damaged doors in the building with hollow-core doors, what could you conclude from this statement?

CHAPTER 7

Courtesy of Howard Johnson's Hotels.

HEATING CONCEPTS AND HEAT MANAGEMENT

ABSTRACT

A manager must develop a basic understanding of heat and heating concepts before heat can be properly managed. Heat concepts are extremely important in the hospitality industry. Heat is used for building space comfort control; it is used to process food; it is used for sanitation; it is removed for building cooling and food preservation (food chillers and freezers). Heat management provides an environment that keeps customers happy and employees productive. Heat is expensive and the maintenance of heat generation systems can be very complex and costly. The key to heat management is an understanding of the limitations of the heat system. The key to low-cost heat is the correct combination of heat management and preventive maintenance.

Humidity

Key words: absorption coefficient; AFUE (annual fuel utilization efficiency); anticipator; boiler; Btu; Celsius; coal stoker; co-generation; condensation; conduction; convection; convection coefficient; convector; critical temperature; degree-day; dehydrofreezing; dry-bulb temperature; effective temperature; electric heat pump; electric resistance heat; emissivity; Fahrenheit; flue gas analysis; forced convection; fusion; heat; heat distribution system; heat exchanger; heat plant; heat transfer; heat transference system; heat transmission coefficient; HSPF (heating season performance factor); ignition system; insulator; kilocalorie; latent heat; low-E window; low-limit switch; plenum; radiant gas; radiant heat; radiation; radiation shape factor; radiator; relative humidity; safety switch; sensible heat; setback temperature; specific heat; sublimation; temperature; thermal conductivity; thermal resistance; thermostat; upper-limit switch; vaporization; watt.

INTRODUCTION

Heat is a form of energy. It is energy that the hospitality industry depends on in more ways than most people realize. People are aware of basic heating functions, such as heating buildings, heating water, and cooking food. Some even associate heat with refrigeration and air cooling. However, heat is also required to transport customers to and from hotels, clubs, health-care facilities, and restaurants. Internal-combustion engines, jet aircraft, and diesel trains depend on heat energy resources. Sanitation programs are still highly dependent on heat. Currently, the United States and other highly industrialized nations rely on adequate heat resources to maintain their living standards.

Few people have a fully developed awareness of heat, heating concepts, and temperature. A basic understanding of these terms is essential for controlling heat energy costs. Heat energy management includes heating, refrigeration, ventilation, and air conditioning, the subjects of this and the next three chapters.

HEAT AND TEMPERATURE

Many people use the terms *heat* and *temperature* interchangeably. Some may associate high temperature with heat and low temperature with the lack of heat. This impression is generally correct.

More precisely, heat must be associated with quantity, while temperature is related to intensity, or quality. Heat energy management is related to both terms. Heat is energy imparted to molecules, which causes an increase in their rate of movement. Observe the effects of adding the same amount (quantity) of heat to each of two beef roasts. One roast weighs 3 pounds (1.4 kilograms). Adding 100 heat units to this roast may increase its temperature from 50 to 100°F (10 to 37.8°C). Adding the same 100 heat units to a second, larger roast of 30 pounds (13.6 kilograms) will increase its temperature only from 50 to 55°F (10 to 12.8°C). See Figure 7.1.

Another way to view heat and temperature is to measure the temperature of 8 ounces (0.24 liters) of water. Now, consider a 42-gallon (159-liter) oil drum filled with water at the same temperature. Ask yourself: Which has the most heat energy? Heat refers to the quantity of energy.

TEMPERATURE

Temperature is used to control heat input. Temperature control is the fundamental heat-management technique available to us at the present time. Temperature control is the vital link among building heating, cooking, refrigeration, and air-conditioning energy-management systems. Through temperature, we control heat energy costs.

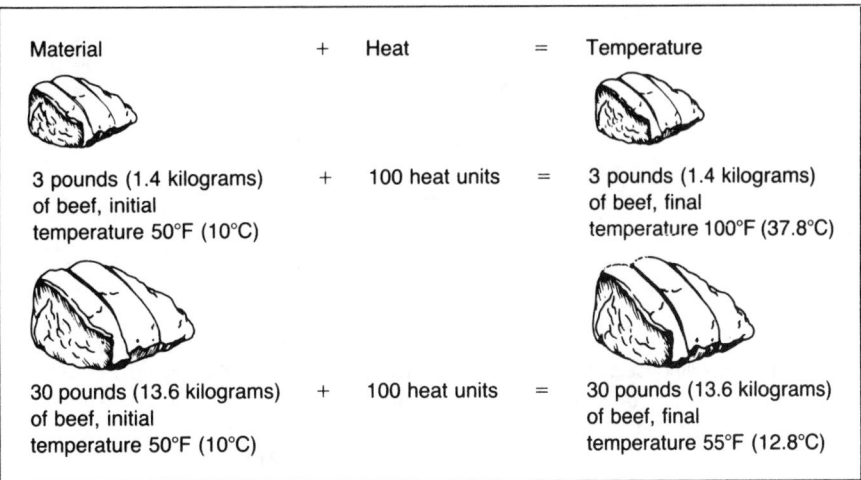

FIGURE 7.1 Heat and temperature effects.

There are two primary temperature scales, Fahrenheit and Celsius. The Fahrenheit scale is common in the United States and in some other English-speaking nations. Celsius is used throughout the rest of the world. The Celsius scale is the old centigrade scale.

Temperature scales are a function of the boiling and freezing points of water at sea level. Water freezes at 32°F (Fahrenheit) and 0°C (Celsius) and boils at 212°F and 100°C. These relationships are shown in Figure 7.2. The figure also shows how to convert from one scale to the other.

HEAT

Today, in the United States and a few other English-speaking countries, heat energy is measured in British thermal units (Btu). The watt is the Standard International Unit (SIU) heat measurement term. Heat energy can also be measured in kilocalories. The definition of heat is related to water. A kilocalorie is 1.16 watts, or the amount of heat required to increase the temperature of 1 kilogram of water 1°C (17 to 18°C). A Btu is the amount of heat required to increase the temperature of 1 pound of water 1°F (67 to 68°F).

TEMPERATURE AND MOISTURE

The general concept of moisture level and its effect on temperature will be briefly discussed in this section. The subject of moisture, or relative humidity, will be covered in Chapter 10.

One way to think about the interrelationship of moisture and heat is to observe its effects on the human body. Your body loses heat by one or both

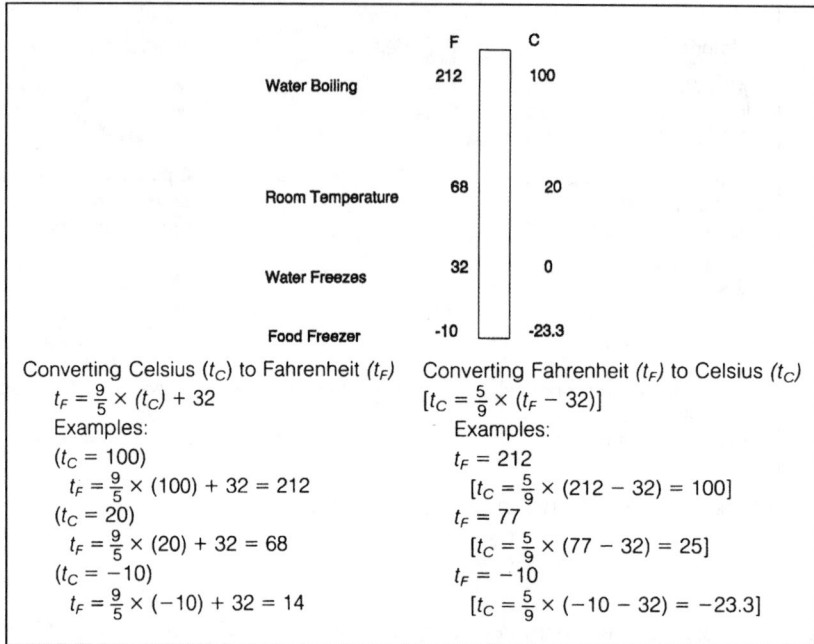

Converting Celsius (t_C) to Fahrenheit (t_F)

$$t_F = \frac{9}{5} \times (t_C) + 32$$

Examples:

($t_C = 100$)

$$t_F = \frac{9}{5} \times (100) + 32 = 212$$

($t_C = 20$)

$$t_F = \frac{9}{5} \times (20) + 32 = 68$$

($t_C = -10$)

$$t_F = \frac{9}{5} \times (-10) + 32 = 14$$

Converting Fahrenheit (t_F) to Celsius (t_C)

$$[t_C = \frac{5}{9} \times (t_F - 32)]$$

Examples:

$t_F = 212$

$$[t_C = \frac{5}{9} \times (212 - 32) = 100]$$

$t_F = 77$

$$[t_C = \frac{5}{9} \times (77 - 32) = 25]$$

$t_F = -10$

$$[t_C = \frac{5}{9} \times (-10 - 32) = -23.3]$$

FIGURE 7.2 Temperature relationships and conversions between Fahrenheit and Celsius.

of two methods—temperature and moisture effects. The body loses much of its heat because of its relatively high surface temperature, normally around 85°F (29.4°C). If the surrounding temperature is 75°F (23.9°C) or less, the temperature difference of 10°F (6.5°C) or more is usually adequate to dissipate body heat. If the environment is at the same temperature as your body or higher, your body must reject heat by an alternate method.

This alternate heat-loss method is loss of body moisture. Evaporating body moisture absorbs heat from the body surface, which directly cools the body. When the moisture level in the air is low (desert), the rate of evaporation is high, causing rapid body cooling. When the moisture level of the air is high, evaporation occurs at a much slower rate, which may cause some discomfort. Therefore, partial warming and cooling of the body can be controlled by regulating the moisture level of the air.

The percent relative humidity is the ratio of the amount of moisture contained in a given air volume to the maximum amount of moisture this air can hold (percent relative humidity is discussed in Chapter 10). On a hot day, air-conditioning temperatures can be relatively high—78°F (25.6°C)—if moisture levels are low, at say, 30 to 50 percent relative humidity, and people will feel comfortable. This results in lower air-conditioning requirements. By the same token, people can feel warm in the winter with lower temperatures—65 to 68°F (18.2 to 20°C)—when the moisture level of the air is high (50 to 70 percent relative humidity). The concept of producing an apparently higher or lower temperature by controlling air moisture is called the *effective temperature*.

These temperature/moisture relationships become very important in health-care facilities, especially in winter. Older patients frequently require higher environment temperatures—74°F (23.3°C) or higher. When moisture levels are controlled, higher effective temperatures can provide sufficient warmth at lower heating costs.

Heat energy management depends on a working knowledge of heat terminology. Heat terminology can be grouped under four basic headings: types of heat, heat transfer, sources of heat, and building heating systems.

TYPES OF HEAT

Products, or matter, can exist in one of three energy states: solid, liquid, or gas. The lowest energy state is the solid. In the solid state, product molecules are in a relatively stable position, vibrating in a confined space or within a lattice-structure position. As heat is added to the product, energy is absorbed by the molecules so that they vibrate faster and faster. Heat that increases the product temperature is called *sensible heat*.

Eventually, as more heat is absorbed, the rate of vibration reaches a critical temperature. The solid-state critical temperature is the freezing or the melting temperature. At this temperature, heat can be added to a solid, but its temperature will not increase until the entire mass of product turns into a liquid. The liquid state represents a higher energy level, as molecules are farther apart and have greater freedom of movement. The heat necessary to bring about a change of state in a product—for example, from a solid to a liquid—is called *latent heat*.

SENSIBLE HEAT

Sensible heat, when added to a product such as food or air, causes the temperature of the product to increase. When the temperature of a product decreases, sensible heat has been removed. Basically, sensible-heat changes can be indirectly measured by using a thermometer. The amount of increase or decrease in the temperature of a product depends on a product thermal property, the *specific heat*, and its weight. The specific heat is the amount of heat required to increase or decrease the temperature of a product one degree for each unit weight of the product. Representative specific heats are shown in Figure 7.3.

Foodstuffs	Specific heat	
	Btu per pound per °F	Watts per kilogram per °C
	Above freezing point	
Carrots	0.87	1.01
Chicken	0.80	0.93
Lean beef	0.77	0.90
	Below freezing point	
Carrots	0.45	0.52
Chicken	0.42	0.49
Lean beef	0.41	0.48
Nonfood items		
Air	0.24	0.28
Brick	0.22	0.26
Ice	0.50	0.58
Steam	0.48	0.56
Water	1.00	1.16

FIGURE 7.3 Specific heat of selected products.[1]

It should be noted that in Figure 7.3 the specific heat depends on the state of the product, that is, whether it is a solid, a liquid, or a gas. Thus, the same amount of heat could have different temperature effects for the same product weight; see Figure 7.3.

Food products are considered to be fresh (liquid) or frozen (solid); Figure 7.3 indicates the differences in the specific heats of three food products in fresh (liquid) and frozen (solid) states. Figure 7.4 shows basic heat relationships and examples that can be used to determine the amount of sensible heat involved in heating and cooling a product—in this case, beef.

LATENT HEAT

Most products have one critical temperature called the freezing point and another called the boiling point. Associated with each critical temperature is *latent heat*.

There are several types of latent heat: fusion, vaporization, condensation, and sublimation. The latent heat of fusion is the heat required either to melt or to freeze a product at a given pressure and temperature, its freezing point. The latent heat of vaporization is the heat required to vaporize a product at a given pressure and temperature, its boiling point. The latent heat of condensation is the heat that must be removed from a vapor to condense it to a liquid at a specific temperature and pressure. The latent heat of vaporization equals the latent heat of condensation at the same critical temperature and pressure. Some products proceed directly from the solid to the gaseous state, for example, dry ice at sea-level pressure; this is called the latent heat

Sensible heat = heat added to a product
Relationship when heating a product:

$H_S = c \times w \times (t_2 - t_1)$

H_S = sensible heat

c = specific heat

w = product weight

t_2 = final product temperature

t_1 = initial product temperature

Lean beef is to be heated from 40°F (4.4°C) to 160°F (71.1°); there are 10 pounds (4.54 kilograms) of beef; how much heat must be added to the product?
The specific heat of lean beef above freezing is 0.77 (0.90).

$H_S = 0.77 \times 10 \times (160 - 40) = 924$ Btu

$[= 0.90 \times 4.54 \times (71.1 - 4.4) = 272.4$ watts$]$

40 F (4.4 C)   160 F (71.1 C)

\+ 924 Btu =

(+ 272.4 Watts =)

10 Pounds   10 Pounds

(4.54 Kilograms)   (4.54 Kilograms)

No Cooking Losses

FIGURE 7.4 Sensible-heat requirements for heating beef.

of sublimation. Relationships between latent heat and critical temperature are shown in Figure 7.5.

The product latent-heat requirement depends on environment pressure. The pressure influence can be shown with two examples. It is known that water, which has a boiling point of 212°F (100°C) at sea-level pressure, boils at much lower temperatures in the mountains. The higher mountain elevation has a lower atmospheric pressure; thus, it is easier for the molecules to escape from the liquid to the gaseous state.

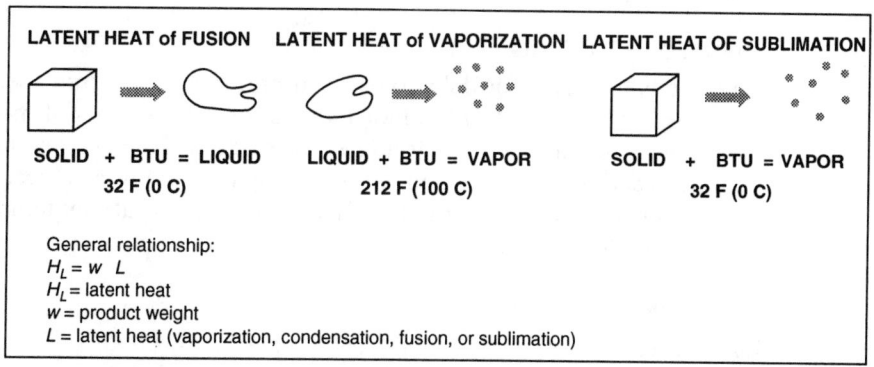

LATENT HEAT of FUSION   LATENT HEAT of VAPORIZATION   LATENT HEAT OF SUBLIMATION

SOLID + BTU = LIQUID   LIQUID + BTU = VAPOR   SOLID + BTU = VAPOR

32 F (0 C)   212 F (100 C)   32 F (0 C)

General relationship:

$H_L = w\ L$

H_L = latent heat

w = product weight

L = latent heat (vaporization, condensation, fusion, or sublimation)

FIGURE 7.5 Latent heat and critical temperature.

The boiling point of water is increased when pressure is increased. A pressure cooker provides this environment. Normal pressure cooking occurs at 5, 10, and 15 pounds per inch (34.5, 69, and 103.4 kilopascals), resulting in approximate boiling points of 220, 230, and 240°F (104.4, 110, and 115.6°C), respectively. At higher temperatures, food will cook and process much faster. The latent heat of vaporization will be different at each of these boiling points.

SENSIBLE AND LATENT HEAT: FOOD-PROCESSING APPLICATIONS

Heat Processing (Cooking) of Food

Sensible and latent heat are *both* involved when food is cooked. One can easily visualize the sensible-heat requirements of cooking. Increasing the temperature of fresh food from 40°F (4.4°C) to 140°F (60°C) requires sensible heat.

When food is cooked, it has volatile loss, which is a moisture loss. The volatile loss represents a latent-heat requirement. When foods are cooked, there are other changes that require latent heat. These are chemical changes that affect fatty and protein foods, especially meat products. Fats exist in fresh foods in the solid state. Fats melt at various temperatures. Melted fat may end up in the product drip, as dripping loss, or may remain in the food. When melted fat is cooled and changes back to a solid, it releases its latent heat, causing the temperature of the food to remain at a high level for a short time, even after the food is removed from the cooking environment. When a protein food is initially heated, proteins are partially broken down; this represents another energy (latent-heat) requirement. However, once proteins are broken down, there is no protein heat energy requirement when food is reheated. This is one reason why less energy and time are required to reheat previously cooked food. Generally, the heat requirements for these chemical changes—melting fat and breaking down proteins—are small compared to the sensible-heat and volatile-loss latent-heat requirements. See Appendix 7 for a complete discussion of cooking a food product.

Drying Food Products

Some foods are dried, or dehydrated, and preserved for future use. Drying removes over 95 percent of the moisture from food. The loss of moisture is a latent-heat requirement. If drying takes place at high temperatures, the chemical reactions mentioned in the preceding paragraphs also occur, which increases energy requirements. Food can also be dried at low temperatures through dehydrofreezing.

Dehydrofreezing of Foods

Dehydrofreezing is drying at very low temperatures. Food is first cooled to its freezing point, which requires the removal of sensible heat. Then it is frozen by removing its latent heat of fusion. The frozen product is then placed in a low-pressure environment, which changes the critical temperatures of food (both the melting and the boiling temperatures). Small amounts of heat are slowly added to the food to drive off the ice (a sublimation process) contained in it. The latent heat of sublimation is required for this process.

HEAT TRANSFER

The process of moving heat from a higher-temperature heat source to a lower-temperature product is called *heat transfer*. In some cases, one would like to increase the rate of heat transfer, such as in cooking food; in other cases, one would like to reduce the rate of heat transfer, such as slowing down the rate of heat loss from a building during the winter.

Heat can be transferred by three methods: conduction, convection, and radiation. In most cases, all three methods occur at the same time.

CONDUCTION HEAT TRANSFER

Conduction heat transfer usually occurs within solids, or from one solid to another when the two are in contact. Thermal energy imparted to a molecule causes it to vibrate. This molecule vibrates against a second molecule and, in turn, imparts energy to it; the second molecule then vibrates and reacts with a third, and a chain reaction develops. The amount of heat transferred depends on the temperature, the material and its thickness, and the surface area through which heat transfer takes place.

Heat energy flows from hot to cold, or from a high energy level to a low energy level. Hence, a temperature difference is necessary for heat transfer. Heat cannot flow from a low-temperature source to a high-temperature source. The larger the temperature difference, the greater the rate of heat transfer. Therefore, doubling the temperature difference doubles the rate of heat transfer by conduction. The surface area through which the heat is being transferred also determines the total amount of heat being transmitted. If one heat unit is transferred through one square foot (square meter) and if the entire surface is homogeneous, then 100 heat units will be transferred through 100 square feet (square meters) of the surface.

The material through which heat is transferred also affects conduction heat transfer. Different materials have different thermal conductivities, which define the ability of the material to conduct heat. Conductors have high thermal conductivities, and insulators have low thermal conductivities. Thermal conductivities are specified per unit thickness of the material, such as per inch (millimeter) of thickness. For example, if a material has a thermal conductivity of 1.0 for 1 inch (25.4 millimeters), the total thermal conductivity of 2 inches (50.8 millimeters) of the same material is not 2.0 but 0.5, because it requires twice as much energy to force the same amount of heat through the substance. This is why the thickness of insulation is increased: Doubling the thickness can reduce heat loss by 50 percent, and increasing the thickness by a factor of 4 reduces heat loss by 25 percent.

The conduction relationship and examples of conduction heat transfer are shown in Figure 7.6.

CONVECTION HEAT TRANSFER

The *convection heat transfer* process is complex compared with conduction heat transfer. Recall that conduction heat transfer involved the movement of

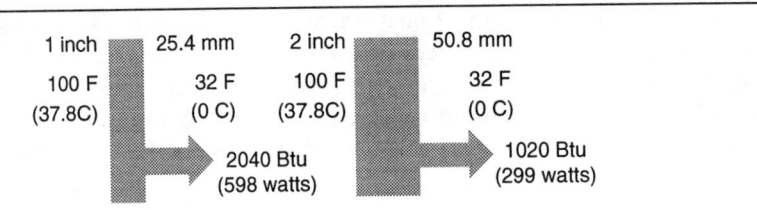

General relationship:

$$H_{conduction} = \frac{A \times K \times (t_2 - t_1)}{X}$$

$H_{conduction}$ = conduction heat transfer in heat units per hour

A = surface area of heat transfer
K = thermal conductivity of material through which heat is transferred
X = material thickness
t_2 = temperature of warmer side of material
t_1 = temperature of cooler side of material

Example:
A. Determine the conduction heat transfer through 1 inch (25.4 millimiters) of cork that has a surface area of 100 square feet (9.29 square meters), the temperature on one side of the cork being 100°F (37.8°C) and 32°F (0°C) on the other side, in one hour.

$$\text{Heat units/hour} = \frac{100 \times 0.30 \times (100 - 32)}{1} = 2040 \text{ Btu per hour}$$

$$\left[= \frac{9.29 \times 43.25 \times (37.8 - 0)}{25.4} = 593 \text{ watts per hour} \right]$$

B. Repeat the above for 2 inches *50.8 millimeters* of cork.

$$\text{Heat units/hour} = \frac{100 \times 0.30 \times (100 - 32)}{2} = 1020 \text{ Btu per hour}$$

$$\left[= \frac{9.29 \times 43.25 \times (37.8 - 0)}{50.8} = 299 \text{ watts per hour} \right]$$

Note: Increasing the insulation thickness by a factor of 2 reduces heat loss by 50 percent.

FIGURE 7.6 Conduction heat transfer relationship with examples of doubling the amount of insulation.

heat through a solid and the movement of heat between two bodies in contact with each other. The convection process also involves the movement of heat between two bodies, or surfaces; however, the body surfaces are not in contact. They are separated by a fluid. The fluid may be a liquid, such as water or cooking oil, or a vapor, such as air or steam. The complete convection process consists of three separate actions:

STEP 1. A hot surface conducts heat to an adjacent fluid layer, thereby increasing its temperature.

STEP 2. As the fluid is heated, its molecules, especially those adjacent to the hot surface, move faster and require a larger space in which to vibrate. This causes the fluid to move, as in convection currents or air drafts in a room. As the warm liquid moves from the hot surface, it is replaced by cooler portions of the remaining fluid, which are now heated by the hot surface. Thus, the fluid is continuously heated. The warmer fluid continues to move until it comes in contact with a cooler surface.

STEP 3. The warm fluid now in contact with the cooler surface again transfers heat by conduction from its fluid layer to the surface of the cooler body. Thus, the cool body is heated.

These combined steps are called convection heat transfer. The convection heat transfer process is dependent on the temperatures of the hot and cold surfaces, the area of these surfaces, and the heat transportability characteristics (convective properties) of the fluid. Large temperature differences between the surfaces increase the rate of heat transfer. Heat transfer can also be increased by increasing the area of the surfaces.

A common example of convection heat transfer occurs in an oven. Air is the fluid in the oven. The hot surface is the hot oven wall or an electric heat element. The air heat transportability is called the *convection coefficient,* which is about 1 Btu per square foot per degree Fahrenheit per hour (5.68 watts per square meter per degree Celsius per hour) for normal oven temperatures. The convection process can be increased if a mechanical pump or fan is used in the oven; this is called *forced convection.* With a fan, the convection coefficient is between 3 and 6 (17.04 and 34.08), averaging about 4 (22.72) for most energy-efficient forced-convection ovens.

Convection relationships and applications are shown in Figure 7.7.

RADIATION HEAT TRANSFER

The first two heat transfer processes covered solids in direct contact and solids separated by a fluid. Heat can be transferred from a hot surface (body) to a cold surface (body) not in contact with it by electromagnetic waves (equivalent to radio and television waves); this is called *radiation heat transfer.*

Oven 350 F (176.7 C)  Beef surface 215 F (101.7 C)

Beef surface area 3 sq. ft. (0.28 sq m)

General relationship:

$H_{convection} = A \times f_C \times (t_2 - t_1)$

$H_{convection}$ = convection heat transfer in heat units per hour

A = surface area of heat transfer

f_C = convection coefficient

t_2 = warmer temperature (fluid or product)

t_1 = cooler temperature (product or fluid)

Determine the amount of heat transferred to beef in a normal oven that is at 350°F (176.7°C); the beef surface temperature is 215 F (101.7°C), the convection coefficient is 1 Btu per square foot per hour per °F (5.68 watts per hour per square meter per °C), and the meat has a surface area of 3 square feet (0.279 square meters).

Heat units/hour = $3 \times 1 \times (350 - 215)$ = 405 Btu per hour

$[= 0.279 \times 5.68 \times (176.7 - 101.7) = 118.9$ watts per hour$]$

FIGURE 7.7 Convection heat transfer relationship.

The amount of energy transferred from the hot surface to the cold surface depends on all the following factors:

1. The radiative property of the hot surface. This is called *emissivity*, which varies with temperature and surface material. Generally, emissivity values vary from 1 (for dark-colored, rough-textured surfaces) to almost 0 (for mirror-like surfaces).

2. The radiative property of the cold surface. This is called the *absorption coefficient*. The absorption coefficient has characteristics very similar to emissivity.

3. The hot surface area, cold surface area, and distance and angle between the hot and cold surfaces, all included in the term *radiative shape factor.* When the hot surface is fully exposed to the cold surface, the shape factor will have a value greater than 0. If there is a shield between the cold surface and the hot surface, the shape factor is 0, meaning that the hot surface cannot radiate energy to the cold surface. For example, the roof of a building is a shield between the sun and someone in the building.

4. The temperatures of the hot and cold surfaces.

Radiation heat transfer computations can be complex; however, the relationships shown in Figure 7.8 can generally be used for building radiative-heat losses and gains.

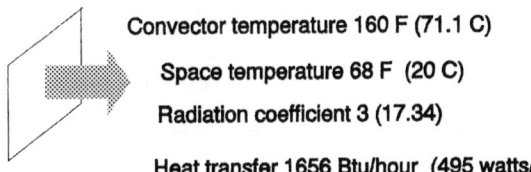

General relationship:

$H_{radiation} = A \times f_R \times (t_2 - t_1)$

$H_{radiation}$ = radiation heat transfer in heat units per hour for normal building temperatures

A = surface area of heat transfer

f_R = radiation coefficient

t_2 = warmer temperature

t_1 = cooler temperature

A convector is heated to 160 ° F (71° C) and is located in a 68° F (20° C) room. The convector has a surface area of 6 square feet (0.56 square meters) and the radiation coefficient is estimated at 3 Btu per square foot per hour per °F (17.34 watts per square meter per hour per °C). Determine the radiation heat transfer to the room.

Heat units/hour = $6 \times 3 \times (160 - 68) = 1656$ Btu per hour
$[= 0.56 \times 17.34 \times (71.1 - 20) = 495.1$ watts per hour$]$

FIGURE 7.8   Radiation heat transfer relationship for low temperatures.

COMBINED HEAT TRANSFER

Generally, all three heat transfer methods will occur at the same time. Conduction, convection, and radiation heat transfer effects are combined into a single *heat transmission coefficient (U)*. Some heat transmission coefficients are shown in Figure 7.9. If you know the design inside temperature of a building and the average outside temperature for its location, you can quickly determine building heat losses (see Figure 7.10).

INSULATION AND HEAT TRANSFER

The amount of heat necessary to provide a comfortable building temperature depends on the rate of building heat loss. This rate varies with building construction techniques, including the amount of thermal insulation. In the past, low-cost heat resources did not usually provide economic incentives to add insulation. Now, higher heating costs make moderate- and high-cost insulation feasible investments.

Several problems may arise when you try to determine adequate amounts of insulation. First, most economic insulation models or procedures assume a constant fuel cost. However, fuel costs are obviously not constant. They

Item	Heat-transmission coefficient	
	Btu per hour per square foot per °F	Watts per hour per square meter per °C
Single glass	1.13	6.42
Insulating glass with 0.25-inch (6.4-millimeter) airspace	0.65	3.76
Uninsulated frame wall with wood siding, 4-inch (100-millimeter) airspace	0.24	1.39
Fully insulated frame wall with wood siding, 4 inches (100 millimeter) insulation	0.053	0.31
Uninsulated wood-deck roof, 10-inch (254-millimeter) airspace	0.23	1.33
Insulated wood-deck roof, 8 inches (203-millimeters) insulation	0.029	0.17
Other insulators	0.22	1.25
Low emissitivity (E) glass	0.125	0.71
Smart glass		
Phenolic foam board-1 inch (25.4 millimeters)	0.121	0.68

FIGURE 7.9   Selected heat transmission coefficients. [2]

have risen in the recent past and will continue to increase in the future. Second, standard building construction techniques may limit the amount of insulation that can be placed within walls and roofs. Third, many modern buildings have been built with large amounts of window glass area, and solid glass is a poor insulator. Fourth, until recently, insulation has been used largely against winter cold. Today, however, when the interior climate of a building is controlled on a year-round schedule, utility costs for cooling should also be considered.

Insulation is now universally accepted as an excellent energy-management tool. It is easily placed in buildings under construction. The thickness of walls can be increased to accommodate any feasible insulation thickness. Roofs can be designed to contain amounts of insulation appropriate to the climate, as well as the space necessary to permit circulation of ventilation air to discourage condensation.

Insulators are rated by *thermal conductivity*, which should be as low as possible. Most insulators have thermal conductivities ranging from 0.12 to 0.33 Btu-inch per square foot per degree Fahrenheit per hour (0.68 to 1.87 watts-25.4 millimeters per square meter per degree Celsius per hour). The thermal conductivity value is for each unit depth of insulation measured in inches (millimeters). Insulation is normally purchased in incremental thick-

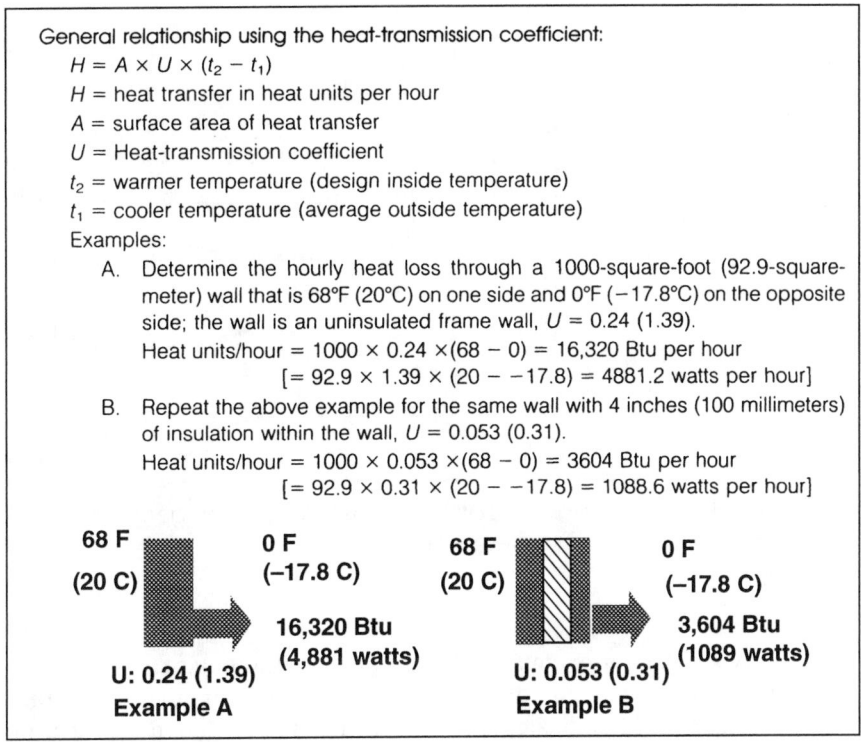

General relationship using the heat-transmission coefficient:

$H = A \times U \times (t_2 - t_1)$

H = heat transfer in heat units per hour

A = surface area of heat transfer

U = Heat-transmission coefficient

t_2 = warmer temperature (design inside temperature)

t_1 = cooler temperature (average outside temperature)

Examples:

  A. Determine the hourly heat loss through a 1000-square-foot (92.9-square-meter) wall that is 68°F (20°C) on one side and 0°F (−17.8°C) on the opposite side; the wall is an uninsulated frame wall, U = 0.24 (1.39).

  Heat units/hour = 1000 × 0.24 ×(68 − 0) = 16,320 Btu per hour
  [= 92.9 × 1.39 × (20 − −17.8) = 4881.2 watts per hour]

  B. Repeat the above example for the same wall with 4 inches (100 millimeters) of insulation within the wall, U = 0.053 (0.31).

  Heat units/hour = 1000 × 0.053 ×(68 − 0) = 3604 Btu per hour
  [= 92.9 × 0.31 × (20 − −17.8) = 1088.6 watts per hour]

68 F (20 C) 0 F (−17.8 C) 16,320 Btu (4,881 watts) U: 0.24 (1.39) **Example A**

68 F (20 C) 0 F (−17.8 C) 3,604 Btu (1089 watts) U: 0.053 (0.31) **Example B**

FIGURE 7.10   Heat transfer through a wall, showing the effects of insulation on heat loss.

nesses. The standard thickness for batt or roll insulation in the United States is 3.5 to 12 inches (88.9 to 305 millimeters). Insulation purchased in these standard depths is rated in *thermal resistance* units (R). For example, a specific type of insulation may be rated at 11 R for 3.5 units of thickness, or 30 R for 12 units of thickness. Another type of insulation may be rated at 13 R and 35 R, respectively, for the same thicknesses. The R for phenolic foam board is 8.3 per inch. Building codes normally specify the minimum thermal resistance for walls and roofs. The basic problem confronting the architect and the building owner is: What is the optimal amount of insulation?

Figure 7.11 shows the basic relationship between the cost of heating energy and the cost of insulation. The figure clearly shows that as the thickness of insulation increases, its cost increases; at the same time, the cost of heating energy decreases. The building owner should be interested in total costs: the sum of the annual cost of insulation and the annual heating cost. The figure shows that there is a minimum cost point, which corresponds to the optimal thickness of insulation.

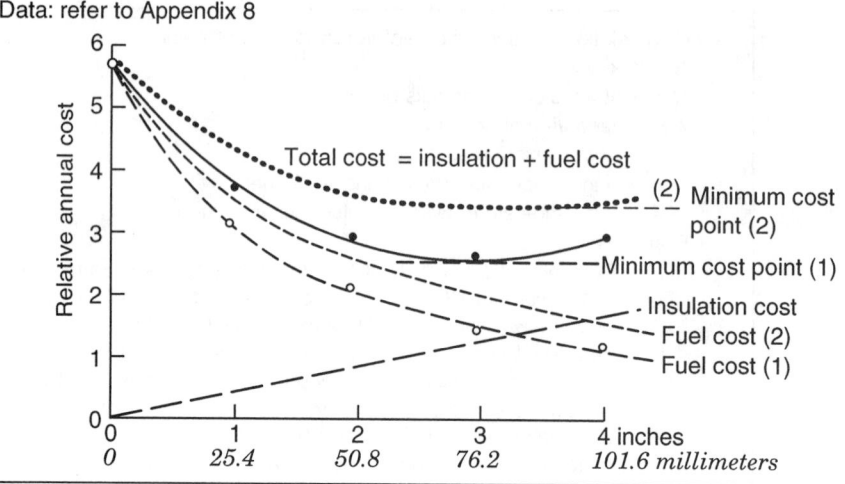

Data: refer to Appendix 8

FIGURE 7.11 Optimal insulation thickness for a given geographic location. (1) Normal fuel cost; (2) increased fuel cost.

A similar set of data applies to air conditioning. The optimal insulation thickness for air conditioning may be different from that for heating.

Figure 7.11 indicates the optimal insulation thickness for a given heat source cost, a specific heat system efficiency, a specified insulation cost, and a specific geographic location. Normally, the last three variables are defined at the time of construction. Once the building is built, the only major item that will vary in the future will be the cost of heat energy. Past trends indicate that energy cost will probably increase in the future. Figure 7.11 shows that optimal insulation thickness increases when heat energy cost increases. Hence, what is the optimal insulation thickness for the ownership life of the building?

Many authorities suggest that the estimate of building ownership life expectancy is extremely variable and difficult to estimate. (Building ownership life expectancy does not refer to the physical age or life estimate of the structure, but rather to the estimated number of years the building will be owned by the same person or group. For example, if you purchase a motel and sell it 5 years later, the ownership life is 5 years.) Building ownership life expectancy is a decision that must be made jointly by the architect and the owner of the building. However, it is recommended that the optimal insulation thickness for lodgings (hotels, motels), institutional buildings, apartments, clubs, and health-care facilities be based on energy cost projections 5 to 10 years from the time the building is built or purchased. The optimal insulation thickness for foodservice units should be based on a 3- to 5-year energy cost projection.

Appendix 8 shows how one would actually determine the optimal insulation thickness for the heating season, for the cooling season, and for combination heating and air-conditioning requirements. The same appendix shows the optimal insulation thickness for projected future energy costs.

MANAGING BUILDING HEATING SYSTEMS

SOURCES OF ENERGY FOR BUILDING HEATING

The average heating cost for a lodging establishment has little value because it has meaning only if a particular lodging establishment had an average geographic location, average construction and insulation, an average number of guest rooms and occupancy, the average customer with an average behavior—the list could go on.

Energy metering must be used to determine actual heating costs for a property. Only isolated data are available at the present time for buildings with actual energy metering. For example, total hotel energy consumption (including heating energy) has decreased from about 182,000 to a little less than 129,000 Btu per square foot per year (1,033,760 to 732,720 watts per square meter per year) for selected hotels during a 5-year period.[3] One hotel has reported that heating energy is 8.7 percent of its total energy consumption, but this excluded the operation of fans and auxiliary energy for controls.[4] Another hotel reported 13.1 percent of total energy consumption for heating, which included auxiliary energy for fans and controls.[5] Still another report stated that guest room and corridor energy consumption averaged 25 percent of the energy requirement for the total property.[6] Another report stated that metered actual energy consumption for a hotel indicated the following heating requirements: guest rooms and corridors, 47.3 percent of the total consumption of these areas; kitchen and laundry, 11.4 percent for heating; and lobby and service floors, 33.9 percent for heating.[7]

The only conclusion is that building heating energy for lodging establishments varies between 8 and perhaps 40 percent of the total energy consumption of the property. A best estimate is probably close to 25 percent for the typical U.S. lodging establishment. Foreign data are not available.

Foodservice building heating data are almost nonexistent. Foodservice properties are even more difficult to analyze than lodging establishments. The National Restaurant Association recognized eight different types of foodservice outlets in one study.[8] They measured (metered) total energy consumption of various types of establishments and made best estimates of energy consumption by functional areas in the unit: food preparation, sanitation, refrigeration, lighting, and HVAC (heating, ventilation, and air conditioning). Separate building heating energy is not reported. HVAC ranged from 20 to 38 percent of the total building energy consumption, averaging 25 percent.

Comparative measurements of energy consumption for building heating for other types of service industry establishments are not readily available. The best estimates would be that health-care and institutional buildings would be similar to lodging units; apartment complexes would be similar to residential or lodging units with very limited foodservice outlets; clubs would probably be similar to the average foodservice unit.

Building Heat Cost Model

The building heat cost model is a useful tool for effective heat management. The model is dependent on inside and outside temperatures, building construction and its heat loss characteristics, geographic location, heat system efficiency, and fuel cost. The model projects annual heating costs. Management can predetermine the effects on heat energy cost of each of the variables just listed. Management can also determine the potential savings of reducing building temperature, adding insulation, changing heating systems, switching heating fuels, or any combination of these factors.

Design Outside Temperature.
The average design winter dry-bulb temperature is a normal average-low temperature and is used to estimate the heat capacity of a building heating system. It does not represent the lowest temperature on record. The design winter temperature is a term fundamental to heating economy.

Building Temperature.
The building temperature is directly under the control of management. In the 1960s, design inside temperatures of 72 to 75°F (22.2 to 23.9°C) and higher were used. As energy costs increased, the design inside temperature was gradually reduced to a maximum of 68°F (20°C) and is expected to decrease to 65°F (18.3°C) or lower if energy costs continue to increase.[9,10] These design temperatures are as low as 60°F (15.6°C) in many European buildings.

Health-care facilities, lodging units, and 24-hour foodservice units are normally maintained at an average 24-hour temperature. Other types of buildings are operated at two temperature levels during workdays. If the building is not utilized on weekends, lower temperature settings are recommended when the building is closed. (See the discussion of temperature setbacks presented later in this chapter.) Some hotel corporations use three guest room temperature settings during the heating season.[9,10] Naturally, the highest guest room temperature (e.g., 70 to 72°F [21.1 to 22.2°C]) is for a sold guest room that is currently occupied. An occupancy sensor can be used to determine if the guest room is occupied. A second lower temperature setting (e.g., 65°F [18.3°C]) is used for a sold but unoccupied guest room, and the lowest temperature setting (e.g., 55 to 60°F [12.8 to 15.6°C]) is used for an unsold guest room. Normally, a computer linking the guest room thermostat, an occupancy sensor, and the front desk registration system is used for this guest room temperature control system.

Degree-Day. A degree-day is the difference between the average daily temperature for a 24-hour period and a base temperature. The degree-day is based on an assumed inside base temperature of either 65°F (18.3°C) in the United States or 60°F (15.6°C). The base temperature indicates that if the outside temperature is 65°F (18.3°C) or higher during the heating season, heating is not required; adequate heat will be given off by building appliances and occupants to maintain building temperatures of 65°F (18.3°C) or higher. Experience has proved that this is accurate even if inside the thermostats are set at 72 to 75°F (22.2 to 23.9°C).

The standard procedure for determining degree-days is simple and can be compiled for any location for any period of time. Most mass communication systems, such as radio, newspaper, and television, report daily high and low dry-bulb temperatures as recorded from ordinary thermometers. From these recordings, an average temperature is determined. This average temperature is subtracted from the base temperature—60 or 65°F (15.6 or 18.3°C)—and the result is the number of degree-days occurring for that 24-hour period. Only positive degree-days are considered.

This procedure is repeated each day throughout the heating season (September 1 to June 1 in the Northern Hemisphere) and accumulated for the entire season.

Building Construction Factors. The building's construction materials and techniques, and the resulting heat transmission coefficient, are among the most important factors affecting heating costs for a given location. Figure 7.9 indicates the heat transmission coefficients for various construction techniques for walls, roofs, windows, and doors.

The heat transmission coefficient, the surface area through which heat is being transferred, the design inside temperature, and the design outside temperature are all used to arrive at the heat loss through a particular section of the building. The accumulated results for each building section represent the total heat loss of the building in most cases. It is not recommended that the owner or manager make these computations for a building because the heating, air-conditioning, and ventilation engineer will consider both heat-gain and heat-loss factors for a building.

Appendix 8 shows the results of computations for various situations: a normal building with limited insulation and the same building with adequate insulation; a building with a high percentage of window glass surface area, the same building with double-glazed, or Low-E, windows, and the same building with minimal window area. Each building variation has different hourly heat losses. The heat-loss differences reflect the potential annual savings in heat energy and cost percentages among different construction techniques.

The final portion of the model relates to the cost of heating, which takes into account the overall efficiency of the heating system, the heat value of the fuel, and the unit cost of the fuel. This is also shown in Appendix 8 for the examples discussed here.

ENERGY SELECTION FACTORS FOR BUILDING HEATING

The primary heating-energy selection factor for a building should be the energy cost. The cost can be annual heating cost or, a much better criterion, life-cycle costing. This criterion considers not only the cost of the building's heating system but also all its related costs: repairs and maintenance, personnel requirements, fuel storage requirements and cost, insurance, and accident or hazard potential costs.

If special pollution control equipment is required for a specific fuel, then the cost of this equipment and its operation is considered in life-cycle costing. The availability of present heating fuels should not be a major fuel selection factor at least through the year 2005 on a national scale.

There are three primary building heat fuels currently being used in most properties. These are oil, natural gas, and electricity. The secondary building heat resources, used less frequently or in conjunction with primary fuels, are: city steam, solar energy, LPG, coal, and a fuel for co-generation. There are also auxiliary energy resources such as electricity, required for heat control systems, fans, and pumps; water, required for hot-water and steam distribution systems; and chemicals, required to treat water if water is an auxiliary energy resource. The reader should recall that each of these heat resources was described and discussed in Chapter 3.

HEATING SYSTEM SELECTION FACTORS

Several variables should be analyzed when considering a new heating system. These variables frequently include the following items: fuel availability, fuel storage requirements, heat recovery capabilities, temperature and moisture quality, fuel conversion efficiency, pollution standards, system cost, hazard potential and insurance, availability of new systems, employee skill requirements, and flexibility. It should be noted that during one 5-year system evaluation period, certain variables may be more critical than others, while other variables may have greater significance during the next evaluation cycle.

Fixed and variable system costs are usually related and must be analyzed by management when a heating system is selected.[9,10] A partial list of fixed costs includes installation cost, repairs, maintenance, fuel storage costs, pollution control equipment costs, taxes, and insurance. Variable costs include the remainder of the costs, the primary ones being the cost of fuel and auxiliary energy. A high fixed-cost system generally has a low variable cost; a low fixed-cost system generally has a high variable cost. Figure 7.12 shows these general effects. Also, note that there is a point at which the two total-cost lines cross, the *break-even point*. The figure is useful for determining break-even points between various fuels and systems.

Foodservice operations and smaller lodging and health-care units generally utilize lower fixed-cost heating systems; large institutional, lodging,

System *A* has a high annual fixed-cost and a low variable-cost.
System *B* has a low annual fixed-cost and a high variable-cost.

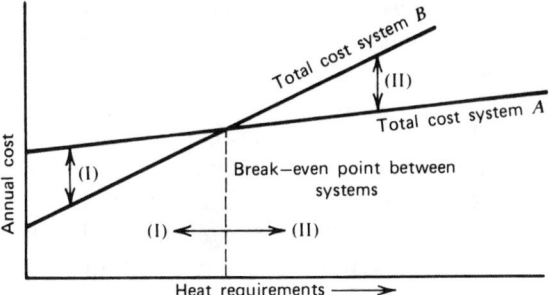

(I)   Best region for System *B*.
      Difference between Lines *A* and *B* represents annual savings of System *B*.
(II) Best region of System *A*.
      Difference between Lines *B* and *A* represents annual savings of System *A*.

FIGURE 7.12   The break-even point of high and low fixed-cost and variable-cost heating systems.

and health-care complexes generally use higher fixed-cost heating systems—because of their relative size, unit fuel cost becomes a major factor in economy.

HEATING SYSTEM COMPONENTS

The building's heating system includes conversion of an energy source to useful heat (a heat transference system) and a control network. If conventional fuels (coal, oil, or natural gas) are utilized, a *heat plant* is required. The type of heat plant depends on the fuel. Some heat energy sources, such as city steam and electric resistance heat, do not require a heat plant. The *heat transference system* could be warm air, hot water, or steam. All heat systems require a control network that depends on the heat plant and the heat transference system.

Heat Plants

Coal Stoker.   The most efficient and practical heat plant for coal is the *coal stoker*. The stoker automatically feeds coal and air into a combustion chamber at a controlled rate. Coal is usually fed by a screw-type device called an auger or by gravity flow from a coal storage hopper into the combustion chamber. A fan blows air into the combustion chamber. A conveyor belt is used in the combustion chamber to remove ash, allowing for a high percentage of heat to be extracted from the burning coal.

The efficiency of a coal stoker in proper adjustment is close to 70 percent. One problem with a coal stoker is the formation of clinkers—solid masses of coal ash. Another problem is that the coal stoker can produce a large quantity of pollutants. The amount of pollutants depends on the grade and quality of the coal.

Oil Heat Plants.   The oil heat plant is relatively simple compared to the coal stoker. There are several types of oil heat plants. In one, oil is pumped along with air into a combustion chamber. The combination of air (oxygen) and oil spray strikes a hot surface, the combustion chamber wall, whose temperature is above the ignition temperature of the fuel. Combustion results, liberating heat.

The grade of oil indicates the type of oil heat plant. There is generally very little difference between the various types of heat plants for the same grade of oil. However, the heavier grades of oil, the use of which is greatly restricted in the United States, are usually preheated before combustion.

Oil heat plants require an *ignition system*. The ignition systems are electric spark and electric hot-wire ignition.

Current U.S. federal regulations require a minimum efficiency of 78 percent (January 1992) for an oil furnace (oil heat plant with a warm-air heat transference system) and 80 percent (January 1992) for an oil boiler (oil heat plant with a hot-water or steam heat transference system). These heat plants are rated in terms of the *AFUE (annual fuel utilization efficiency)*. The AFUE is a percentage rating of expected performance considering losses up the chimney, cycling effects (heat plant heat-up), and losses from non-electric pilots during a typical year of operation. It is equal to the Btu heat output rating divided by the Btu fuel input rating during a representative heating season. Some oil furnaces in 1996 had AFUE ratings in excess of 90 percent. Likewise, some oil boilers in 1996 had AFUE ratings in excess of 87 percent.

Gas Heat Plants.   The gas heat plant is relatively simple. The same basic system is used for natural, SNG, LPG, and LNG gases. The only major difference is the gas orifice, which supplies gas to the burner. With large burners, air fans may be required to supply air to the combustion chamber. Burners are available in several shapes and configurations. Gas heat plant ignition is limited to electric spark and electric hot-wire systems.

Gas heat plants and all types of gas burners must be equipped with automatic shutoff valves in case ignition does not occur in the combustion chamber. Ash and pollution problems are minimal with gas heating plants.

Gas heating plants are also available with variable fuel feeding rates. Conversion kits are available to change heating plants from oil to gas, from gas to oil, or from one type of gas to another. Pollution control equipment on the exhaust system is normally not required.

Current U.S. federal regulations require a minimum efficiency of 78 percent (January 1992) for a gas furnace (gas heat plant with a warm-air heat transference system) and 80 percent (January 1992) for a gas boiler (gas heat plant with a hot-water or steam heat transference system). Some gas furnaces in 1996 had AFUE ratings in excess of 95 percent. Likewise, some gas boilers in 1996 had AFUE ratings in excess of 90 percent.

Other Heat Plants (Nonsolar).   City steam and geothermal energy sources do not require a heat plant because steam can be used directly to heat buildings, or it can be used to heat water for hot-water heat transference systems.

Electric resistance heat may or may not require a heating plant. If electric energy is converted directly to thermal energy in the room—in radiant panels, baseboard units, or space heaters—a central heat plant is not necessary. The central electric heating system requires a very simple heat plant, with only metallic or wire heat elements used to heat air or water. Both these systems are considered to be 100 percent efficient. These systems are classified as electric resistance heating systems.

The *electric heat pump* obtains building heat from two sources. The primary heat source is the outside environment, such as air, ground, or water. Electric energy is purchased to operate the heat pump, and a high percentage of this energy is released to the building. The electric heat pump is a type of refrigeration cycle.

Current U.S. federal regulations require minimum efficiencies for heat pumps. The heating cycle of the heat pump is rated in terms of the *HSPF (heating season performance factor)*. The HSPF represents the heating performance over an entire heating season and is equal to the total Btu of heat delivered divided by the total watt-hours (Btu equivalent) of electric energy used during a representative heating season. The HSPF for a combination heating–cooling heat pump must be at least 6.8 (January 1992) and at least 6.6 (January 1993) for a heat pump (single-package unit used for heating only).

Solar Heat Plants.   The final heat plant to be reviewed is the solar heat plant. Three primary techniques are currently used to collect solar energy: heating air, heating water, or producing electricity. In all three processes, a portion of the energy must be stored for use during the night.

Solar collection devices vary in efficiency and performance. If you plan to use solar heating, you should consider the following variables: solar inclination, the angle of the sun to the earth in your geographic area; the percentage of sun days; the type of solar collector; the desired temperature of the heat transference medium; and the cost. Collectors usually have a large collection surface area with respect to the area being heated. The absorption of energy is generally not very high with devices in current use, and solar heating systems normally have to be supplemented with alternate heat systems. The major solar-energy system problems are the cost of the system and the low level of performance.

Co-generation Heat Plants. Co-generation utilizes one heat resource, primarily natural gas—but also coal and oil—to produce both steam and electricity. Steam turbines yield steam for heating applications and also generate electric energy. Figure 7.13 charts the co-generation process.

Co-generation plants were used extensively in the 1950s and 1960s in large buildings and building complexes. They were introduced again in the late 1980s for smaller buildings, including some hotels of 200 to 300 guest rooms. These systems were economical when electric-energy costs were high relative to the cost of heat. Electric-energy costs, however, are a function of two factors: cost per unit and electric demand (these will be discussed in Chapter 11). It may now be practical to generate electric energy in an effort to reduce electric demand charges and—by fully utilizing the by-product of electric generation, steam—to heat and cool buildings. Co-generation systems are very expensive to install and maintain and are generally practical only when adequate supplies of natural gas can be obtained for extended time periods.

Heat Transference Systems

Several heat distribution systems are available. They are warm air, hot water, steam, and radiant. Any one of the heat plants just described could be used in conjunction with these systems.

Warm-Air Transference (Distribution) Systems. A primary heat distribution system is the *warm-air distribution system*, which is also used for air conditioning. The heating plant is used to warm air, which is then moved by means of a fan throughout the building. Air is supplied to rooms through supply ducts and returned to the heat plant for reheating through exhaust

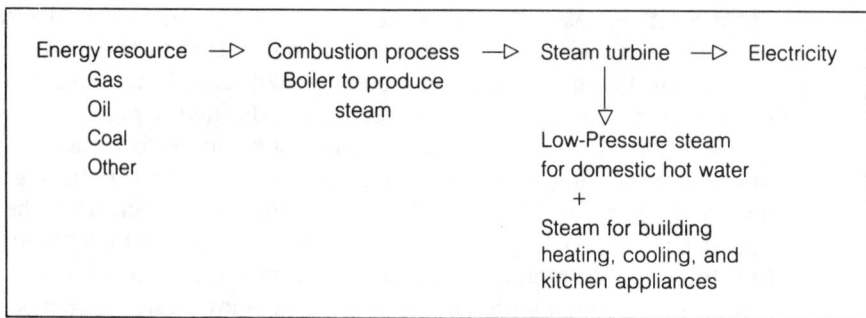

FIGURE 7.13 Co-generation system.

ducts from the rooms. The system can provide an excellent building environment. Moisture can be added to the air to conserve heat energy, air can be filtered, and controlled amounts of fresh air can be added to satisfy ventilation codes. It is also possible to utilize a *heat exchanger* between the air that is exhausted to the outside and the outside fresh-air supply to extract usable heat from warm exhaust air. Various schematic diagrams of these systems are shown in Chapters 9 and 10.

The major problems with warm-air heating are balancing the system (providing adequate air flow to each room) and building space requirements. This system is ideal for central air filtering and for removing tobacco smoke from rooms and public spaces. The amount of circulated air can easily be adjusted for summer cooling or winter heating requirements.

Hot-Water Transference (Distribution) Systems.

The primary advantage of this system is that large amounts of heat can be transported through pipes, which require little space. Water is moved through the pipes by pumps. Heat is released from the water to the room by baseboard heaters, convectors, radiant heating units, or plenum chambers.

Hot-water baseboard heaters are placed near outside walls of the room or under window areas. Thermostats control the flow of hot water to the units. If a water leak appears, it can be quickly repaired with a minimum of effort and time because the heating element is readily available in the room.

Hot water can also be piped to individual room heating units called *convectors*. The convector is a series of smaller pipes, similar to an automobile radiator. Air flows over these pipes and is heated. The pipes are hidden from the room occupants by a shield that has bottom and top openings: Cool air enters through the bottom openings, is heated within the device, and enters the room through the top openings.

Hot-water heat has been used as a *radiant heating system.* Hot-water pipes are placed in floors, walls, or ceilings. This system has a lower room temperature response rate than baseboard or convector systems because the entire floor, wall, or ceiling mass must be heated before the room is heated. Many of these radiant distribution systems were placed in the floor, which was not very effective for lodging and health-care areas because typical lodging rooms have a high percentage of floor area covered with furniture, which insulates the source of heat (the floor) from the room.

Hot water has also been used to heat air within a duct or *plenum* arrangement (an enlarged duct area). Heated air is then blown into the room. These systems are very similar to warm-air heating distribution systems and have the advantages of warm-air heating.

Hot-water distribution systems should be two-pipe systems; that is, hot water is supplied by one pipe, and cooled water is returned to the heating plant by a second pipe. Figure 7.14 shows two-pipe and single-pipe systems. Single-pipe systems should not be used because hot water and cool

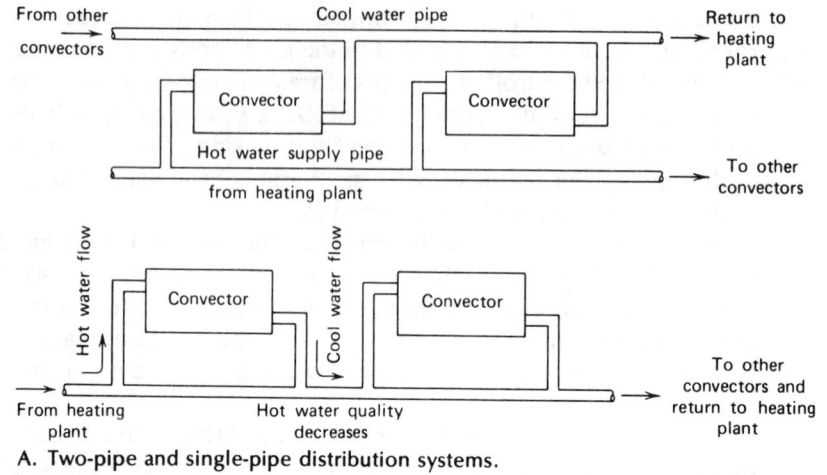

A. Two-pipe and single-pipe distribution systems.

FIGURE 7.14 Two-pipe and single-pipe hot-water distribution systems.

water are intermixed, which lowers the temperature of the supply water for each of the subsequent convectors on the supply pipe.

Hot-water distribution systems have some inherent disadvantages. Heated water must be treated so that it will not corrode pipes, valves, and fittings in the system. Water leaks may cause considerable damage in a building, especially if a pipe enclosed within a wall or ceiling area develops a leak. Additional ventilation and moisture control systems must be used for total building environment control. The heating plant is more complex because a boiler (water heater) is required. The total system is frequently more costly to maintain than warm-air heating systems.

Steam-Heating Transference (Distribution) Systems.

Steam-heating distribution systems are similar to hot-water heating systems. Water is converted to steam at the heating plant (boiler). Steam passes through a piping network to room *radiators* or convectors. The difference between a radiator and a convector is that the radiator pipes are exposed to the room, whereas the convector has a shield placed over the heating pipes.

Two-pipe distribution systems are recommended for steam heating. Steam changes back to water, and this water, called *condensate*, flows back, or is pumped, to the boiler through a second set of pipes.

Steam distribution systems can also be used with a plenum arrangement similar to the hot-water plenum system. Steam can also be used to heat water by means of a heat exchanger. Figure 7.15 shows such a system. This arrangement can provide multiple-temperature hot water for various sections of the building. For example, one heat exchanger can provide water at 120 to 140°F (48.9 to 60°C) for building heating, a second heat exchanger

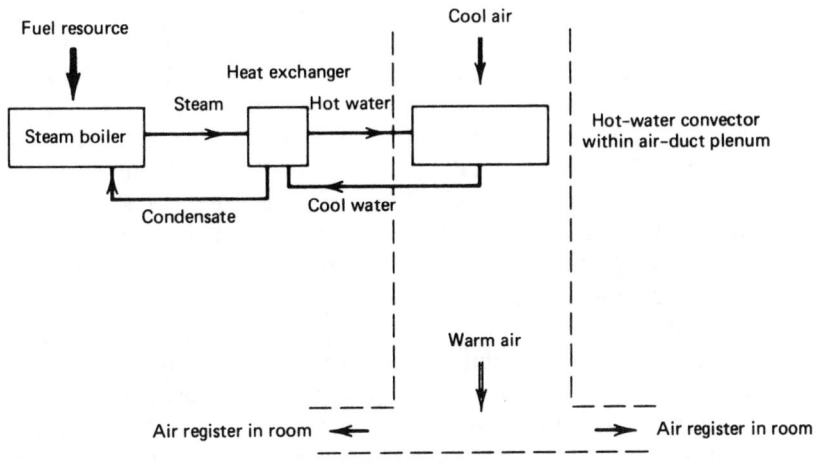

FIGURE 7.15   Steam hot-water-heated air plenum system.

can provide hot water at 100 to 120°F (37.8 to 48.9°C) for occupant use, and a third heat exchanger can provide water at 160 to 180°F (71.1 to 82.2°C) for washing dishes and pots and pans. A single heat exchanger can also provide all three water temperatures (see Figure 7.16).

Steam-heating systems require air eliminator valves and steam traps at each convector or radiator. The air eliminator valve releases air from piping, so that full steam flow occurs within the pipes. Steam traps are required to separate steam from condensate within piping. These devices require considerable maintenance.

Radiant Heat.   *Radiant-heat distribution systems* are complex and costly. Hot-water and steam radiant systems are used. They provide hot wall and ceiling surfaces; they are not used in floors.

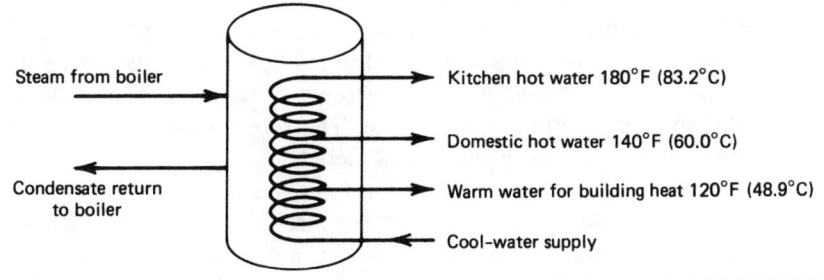

FIGURE 7.16   Steam hot-water heat exchanger providing three water temperatures.

Electric radiant systems are more frequently used in guest rooms, smaller meeting rooms, or other areas of variable occupancy and use. The electric radiant system consists of ceiling panels. This system provides for optimal temperature patterns in a room. Each panel may have a separate control.

Radiant gas or oil (kerosene) panels and heaters are also used in selected portions of a building. Halls, storage areas, or mechanical equipment rooms are frequently equipped with these radiant heaters. The exhaust gases from these heaters must always be vented to the outside. Individual units can be turned on as needed, can be operated independently of each other, and are equipped with separate thermostats.

There are other types of unit heaters, such as fireplaces, but they are usually considered as amenities rather than primarily as heating systems in the service industry. They provide intense temperatures and high building fire potential. When they are in use, room thermostats controlling the primary heat should be lowered and adequate makeup air must be provided to replace the air escaping through the fireplace flue. Whenever a fireplace is not in use, the flue damper must be closed to prevent warm building air from escaping to the outside.

Figure 7.17 shows various radiant-heat systems that are used in the hospitality industry.

Heat Control Networks

Thermostats. The room heat control switch, the *thermostat*, senses the temperature at its location and compares this temperature to a specified temperature, or thermostat setting. If the sensed temperature is lower than the thermostat setting, it will activate the room heating unit in larger buildings or the fuel supply to the heat plant in smaller buildings, such as freestanding foodservice units. Thermostats usually make use of bimetallic elements to sense temperature. They may be completely controlled by room occupants or preset and controlled by building personnel or a computer.

Thermostat calibration (adjustment control) is frequently poor. Thermostat accuracy can be off 0.5 to 5 percent, or more. Typical thermostats should be accurate to within ±1°F (±0.6°C). A 5-percent error at 70°F (21.1°C) can result in room temperatures that are 3.5°F (1.9°C) above or below the desired room temperature. Since each one-degree variation can influence heating cost by 1 to 3 percent or more, this can have a significant influence on building heating cost. Thermostats should be calibrated with a standard mercury-in-glass thermometer.

Zone thermostats can be used in large areas to provide an average temperature within those spaces. The major problem with zone thermostats is that the air temperature distribution patterns are difficult to adjust and control.

Room and zone thermostats can be connected to outside thermostats, or *anticipators*. These outside units measure the effects of outside temperature before they are felt within the building. Anticipators may overrule individual

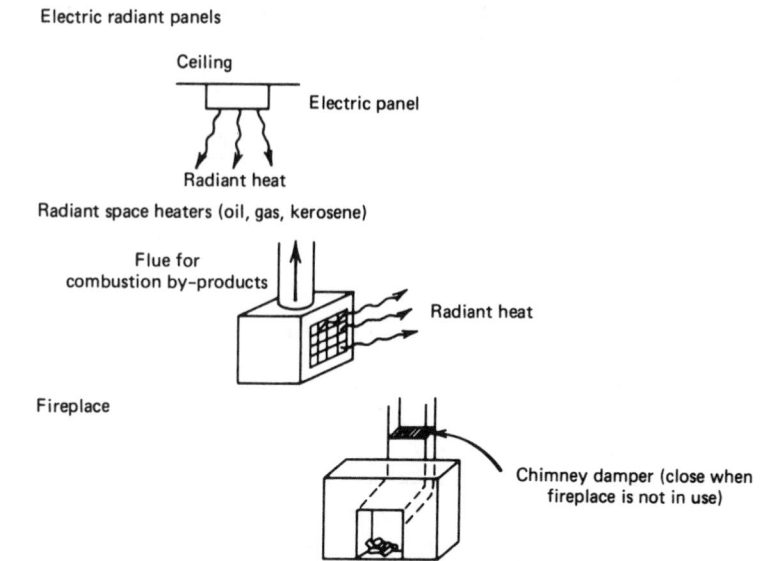

Electric radiant panels

Ceiling

Electric panel

Radiant heat

Radiant space heaters (oil, gas, kerosene)

Flue for
combustion by–products

Radiant heat

Fireplace

Chimney damper (close when
fireplace is not in use)

FIGURE 7.17   Several types of radiant-heating systems used in the hospitality industry.

or zone thermostats. For example, if a room thermostat calls for heat, but if it is rapidly warming up outside, the anticipator may not allow the heating plant to start its cycle.

Thermostats in the public areas of a building should be enclosed or key controlled so that only authorized personnel can change the settings. These thermostats are set to control both heating and cooling requirements.

Table 7.1 shows the potential heating energy savings if thermostat settings are reduced by 3°F (1.66°C),[11] 5°F (2.77°C),[11] or 7°F (3.88°C) for degree-days that vary from 1000 to 10,000. Example approximate degree-days for selected cities are: 1000 Corpus Christi, Texas, and Yuma, Arizona; 2500 Las Vegas, Nevada, Phoenix, Arizona, and Charleston, South Carolina; 7000 Detroit, Michigan, Des Moines, Iowa, and Buffalo, New York; 9000 St. Paul, Minnesota, and Bismarck, North Dakota.

Heat Plant Controls.   The thermostat, with its capacity to activate the heating system, serves as the communicating link between a room and a heat plant. The heat distribution system is controlled by the heat plant's *low-*

TABLE 7.1   Reducing heating temperature by various amounts

Heat degree-days	Potential percentage energy savings if thermostat is set back various degrees		
	3°F (1.66°C)	5°F (2.77°C)	7°F (3.88°C)
1,000	15	26	36
2,000	14	24	33
3,000	13	22	31
4,000	12	20	28
5,000	11	18	25
6,000	10	16	23
7,000	9	14	20
8,000	8	13	18
9,000	6	11	15
10,000	5	9	12

limit switch. The low-limit switch is activated when the heat plant reaches a predetermined temperature. At this temperature, fans or pumps in the heat distribution system are activated, sending heat to the room heat units.

The heat plant is also equipped with an *upper-limit switch.* This switch shuts off the flow of energy to the heat plant when the plant has reached a specified high temperature. Heat plants should be approved by Underwriters Laboratories, which specifies the maximum setting of the upper-limit switch-setting temperature. If Underwriters has not specified an upper setting, never exceed the manufacturer's recommended maximum. The system may not be safe above that limit.

There are usually other control devices that completely overrule the above-mentioned controls of the system. If the fuel ignition system is not working, a *safety switch* prevents fuel from flowing into the heat plant. If any portion of the complete system is dependent on electric energy, and if the electric service is interrupted, the entire system shuts down.

Figure 7.18 shows how the heating system control network is interconnected.

Computer Heat System Control. Various microprocessor chips are available for heat plants that link room thermostat, upper-limit and lower-limit switches, ignition system, and safety devices all in one unit. These may be preset by the manufacturer who sets your specifications, or they can be adjusted within established limits after installation. These units are excellent for foodservice units. However, larger buildings, such as lodging units, should consider computer-controlled heat systems. One aspect of a computer-controlled heat system was previously discussed in this chapter (thermostat settings for unsold, sold unoccupied, and sold occupied guest rooms).

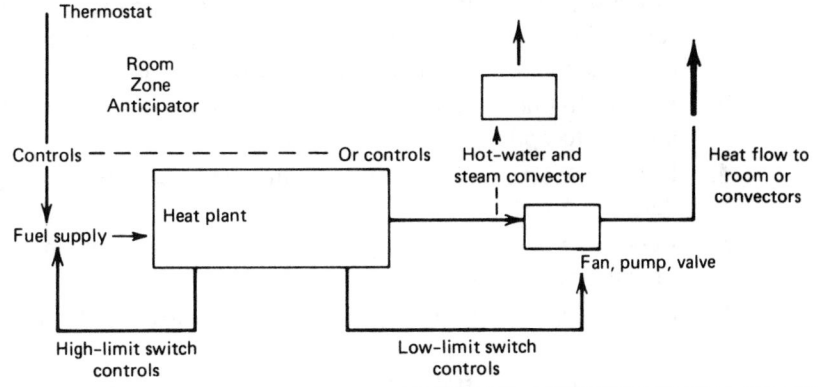

FIGURE 7.18 Heating system control network.

The potential energy savings for various setback temperatures are shown in Table 7.2.

A complete computer heat system control is capable of performing all or many of the following functions:[12]

1. Continuous monitoring of room and space temperatures throughout the building. Depending on computer capabilities, temperatures can be checked several times per hour.
2. Controlling room and space temperatures within specified limits throughout the week. Guest room thermostat settings were previously

TABLE 7.2 Potential heating energy saving percentages produced by setback temperatures (reducing temperatures in unoccupied spaces)

Heat degree-days	Setback temperature and percentage potential heat energy savings		
	60°F (15.5°C)	55°F (12.7°C)	50°F (10°C)
1,000	13	25	36
2,000	12	24	36
3,000	11	22	33
4,000	10	20	30
5,000	9	19	28
6,000	8	16	24
7,000	7	15	22
8,000	7	13	19
9,000	6	11	16
10,000	5	9	14

discussed. In addition to space temperatures for meeting rooms, those for public areas, dining rooms by sections, offices, and storage rooms can also be preset by a time schedule during the week.

3. Monitoring heat plant combustion by-products and adjusting fuel and air flow to optimize combustion efficiency.

4. Evaluating building heating requirements and optimizing the heat delivery system.

5. Recording energy consumption and correlating consumption to building heating requirements.

6. Controlling, if required, water chemistry for hot-water and steam heat systems.

7. Monitoring room status.

8. Monitoring life safety systems.

9. Scheduling heat system preventive-maintenance requirements and developing preventive-maintenance worker schedules.

10. Maintaining a heat system repair and maintenance log.

11. Providing information for heat system management reports.

This list is not all inclusive, as new software programs are continuously being developed for property management. The major problem with a computer heat system control is the cost of interfacing all monitored devices to the computer.

Heating System Maintenance

Two aspects of maintenance are reviewed in this text. One aspect, life-cycle system and maintenance costing, was discussed in Chapter 2. Life-cycle costing can be used to determine the feasibility of replacing a current heating system with a similar or alternate system when maintenance costs become excessive.

The second aspect of maintenance keeps the day-to-day heating system operation as cost effective as possible. This requires daily, weekly, monthly, and seasonal maintenance. Maintenance means more than just keeping the system in operation. Data must be obtained to determine the overall effectiveness of the system. These data can also be used in performance evaluations of the maintenance-and-engineering department.

The following data should be obtained:

A. System cost factors
1. Outside temperature. High and low temperatures should be recorded; from these, the number of degree-days can be developed, and heating costs can be determined and compared to the actual costs.
2. Fuel consumption records.

3. A complete listing of all repairs, indicating man-hours, parts that failed or were replaced, the cost of parts, and the total cost of the repair, including supervisory costs.

4. A complete maintenance schedule, indicating what was done, when it was done, and the related cost of the schedule.

5. A record of flue gas analysis and the corrective action taken.

6. An equipment adjustment record and the results of these adjustments.

7. Unit and total cost of heating energy, including auxiliary energy requirements of fans, pumps, motors, and other energy consumers in the system.

B. Building customer or client factors

1. Occupancy figures. If possible, energy requirements should be correlated with occupancy, sales, meals, customers, and employee counts. This information can be used for future projections.

2. Log of temperature complaints and the corrective action taken, including time and cost estimates.

Each item should be used to establish a better maintenance program for the heating system. The primary purpose of maintenance is to keep the heating system in operation and provide quality heat at a reasonable cost.

SUMMARY

Heat energy and temperature control are very important in the hospitality industry. Heat is involved with refrigeration, ventilation, and air-conditioning systems. A fundamental understanding of this chapter is essential so that the manager can effectively control all heat-related systems. Effective control implies saving money.

Heat, temperature, and moisture are all interrelated and affect customers and employees. Heat management provides an environment that keeps customers happy and employees productive. There are two basic types of heat, sensible and latent. These are related to the building environment. Equally important is an understanding of how heat can be moved, or transferred, within a building by conduction, convection, and radiation.

The basic heat resources in the hospitality industry are natural gas, oil, and electricity. These will probably continue to be the primary heat resources in the near future. Even if alternate energy resources are developed in the future, they will be used to provide oil and synthetic gases and to generate electricity.

The manager must understand the workings of the building heat system. This chapter pointed out that many systems require extensive maintenance. Generally, oil and natural gas resource energy systems require more closely supervised maintenance than electric heat systems. However, electric heating systems can have a high energy cost. The manager must be constantly on the alert for new system components that could be used to reduce heating energy costs.

REFERENCES

1. *Refrigeration,* Technical Publishing, Chicago, 1943.
2. American Society of Heating, Refrigeration and Air Conditioning Engineers, *Handbook of Fundamentals, ASHRAE Guide and Data Book,* New York, 1981.
3. *A Survey of the Energy and Water Use of Selected Hotels and Motels—1982,* Technical Services Center and Hospitality, Lodging and Travel Research Foundation, Inc., San Antonio, 1982.
4. *Summary Report of Energy Usage/Consumption—Analysis for Six Hotels and Motels,* Hospitality, Lodging and Travel Research Foundation, New York, 1981.
5. Aulback, R. E., *Energy Management,* Educational Institute of the American Hotel & Motel Association, East Lansing, MI, 1984.
6. Robach, Inc., Torrance, CA, 1984.
7. Turner, W. C., ed, *Energy Management Handbook,* Wiley, New York, 1982.
8. National Restaurant Association, *PREP Study,* Washington, DC, 1984.
9. Borsenik, F. D., *Holiday Inn, Inc.—Hotel Group Energy Management Program: Phase I,* University of Nevada, Las Vegas, November 20, 1989.
10. Borsenik, F. D., *Holiday Inn, Inc.—Hotel Group Energy Management Program: Phase II,* University of Nevada, Las Vegas, December 5, 1989.
11. Houston Lighting and Power Company, *Guide to Commercial Energy Efficiency,* Houston, October 1992.
12. Kirk, D, "Computer Systems for Energy Management," *International Journal of Hospitality Management,* Vol. 6, No. 4, 1987.

QUESTIONS/PROBLEMS

1. Select several recipes and convert the cooking temperatures and times to Standard International Units.

2. Refer to Figure 7.4, and repeat for ten 3-pound (1.36-kilogram) chickens.

3. Refer to Appendix 7, and repeat for chicken that has a 30 percent volatile loss.

4. Refer to Figure 7.6, and repeat for concrete and stone. Compare your results to those shown in the figure, and estimate the thickness of concrete required to provide the same insulating ability as the cork. The thermoconductivity of concrete and stone is 7.2 (1.038).

5. Refer to Figure 7.7, and compare the results to the deep-fat frying of beef at 300°F (149°C) with a convection coefficient of 6 (34.1).

6. Refer to Appendix 8, Parts A and B, and repeat for your geographic location. Also, determine the annual cost of heating the building at your location with coal.

7. Visit a local hospitality establishment and determine all of the following:

   a. The building environment temperatures for different function activity areas.
   b. The source or sources of building heat.
   c. The type of heating system utilized in the building.
   d. What type or types of heating system controls are used?
   e. The heating system maintenance requirements. Based on the information you have learned in this chapter, prepare a set of heating system recommendations that should reduce the annual heating cost of the building and report these to your class.

CHAPTER 8

Courtesy of the Board of Education, City of New York.

MANAGEMENT OF REFRIGERATION SYSTEMS

ABSTRACT

Refrigeration is the removal of heat by means of mechanical systems. Modern foodservice systems are very dependent on refrigeration (chillers and freezers) for the production and preservation of high-quality food and food products. Most hospitality buildings are dependent on refrigeration (air-conditioning systems) to produce a comfortable summer building environment. Refrigeration systems are costly to install, operate, and maintain. The selection of refrigeration systems components is critical for reducing initial system costs. Space temperature control is necessary to control and minimize operating energy costs. And a well-structured and managed preventive-maintenance program is required so the system can produce the desired space and building environment. These are the basic management objectives of this chapter.

Key words: *absorber; absorption refrigeration; American Society of Heating, Refrigeration, and Air Conditioning Engineers (ASHRAE); appliance heat load; chiller; chlorofluorocarbon refrigerant (CFC); compressed-air refrigeration; compressor, condenser; defrosting; drier; energy management system (EMS); Environmental Protection Agency (EPA); evaporative cooler; evaporator; expansion valve; forced-convection evaporator/condenser; freezer; generator; halocarbon refrigerants; hermetic unit; infiltration heat load; lithium bromide absorption refrigeration cycle; oil separator; product heat load; radiative cooling; refrigerant; refrigeration; solar absorption cycle; solar vapor compression cycle; strong brine; swamp cooler; transmission heat load; Underwriters Laboratories (UL); vapor compression refrigeration cycle; water-cooling tower.*

INTRODUCTION

This chapter deals with the removal of heat, or refrigeration. Air-cooling and food storage systems depend on adequate and economical refrigeration systems. Refrigeration is necessary for complete, year-round air-conditioned comfort for hotels, clubs, foodservice and health-care facilities, and institutional buildings in most regions of the United States. Refrigeration energy costs have been increasing, and many energy-management techniques have been developed and utilized to reduce these costs. The insulation model and most of the energy-saving techniques discussed in the previous chapter apply to refrigeration.

REFRIGERATION CYCLES

VAPOR COMPRESSION CYCLE

The most common refrigeration system is the vapor compression refrigeration cycle. It is a cooling cycle that has almost universal application and use. It can be used for food preservation and air cooling. It is efficient, with a moderate operating cost, and is easy to control. Installation costs are usually moderate and maintenance is generally high.

The complete vapor compression cycle is shown in Figure 8.1. The operation of the cycle depends on a product that has a low boiling point. The product is called a *refrigerant*. The refrigerant's boiling point must be low enough to absorb heat at low temperatures required for food chillers and freezers. As the refrigerant boils at a low temperature, it is absorbing heat (latent heat of vaporization). For example, if a food freezer is to be maintained at a temperature of 0°F (-17.8°C), the boiling point of the refrigerant must be lower than 0°F; if a food chiller is to be maintained at 40°F (4.4°C), the boiling point of the refrigerant must be lower than 40°F.

The boiling point of a refrigerant can be changed by varying its pressure. Increasing refrigerant pressure results in a higher boiling point; reducing refrigerant pressure causes it to boil at a lower temperature. The purpose of the vapor compression refrigeration cycle is to regulate pressure, allowing the refrigerant to absorb heat at one place and release it at another.

The vapor compression refrigeration cycle consists of four basic components: evaporator, compressor, condenser, and expansion device (see Figure 8.1).

Evaporator

The evaporator absorbs heat and must be located in the space that is to be cooled. It can maintain temperatures as low as the boiling point of the refrigerant. Hence, if you regulate the refrigerant pressure in the evaporator, you will regulate the temperature of the cooled space. Products that are

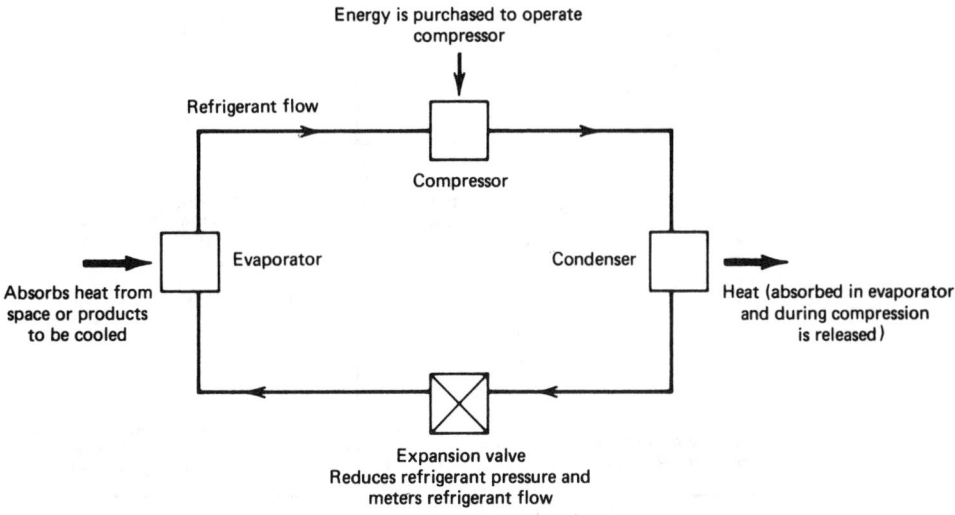

Energy is purchased to operate
compressor

Refrigerant flow

Compressor

Evaporator

Condenser

Absorbs heat from
space or products
to be cooled

Heat (absorbed in evaporator
and during compression
is released)

Expansion valve
Reduces refrigerant pressure and
meters refrigerant flow

FIGURE 8.1 The vapor compression refrigeration cycle. (See Figures 8.2 to 8.5 for a detailed description of each component of the cycle.)

warmer than the boiling point of the refrigerant are placed in a space, such as a freezer or chiller, that is to be cooled. Recall that heat flows from hot to cold; thus, the products are cooled. This product heat is absorbed by the refrigerant, which boils and absorbs the refrigerant's latent heat of vaporization. The heat gain of the refrigerant is equal to the heat loss of the cooled space and its contents. See Figure 8.2 for a visualization of this process.

The primary purpose of a refrigeration cycle is to absorb heat; this is done in the evaporator. The secondary purpose is to recycle the refrigerant. This is why the remaining portions of the cycle are required.

Compressor

The purpose of the compressor is twofold: to pump the refrigerant gas out of the evaporator and to increase refrigerant pressure. The compressor is activated by the evaporator temperature rise. As the refrigerant vapor passes through the compressor, or pump, its pressure and temperature are increased.

The pressure of the refrigerant is increased to raise its boiling point so that it can condense (change back to a liquid for recycling) at a higher temperature. Since the thermal properties of the refrigerant vary, the pressure requirements for this process vary.

Energy, in the form of electricity to operate a motor, is used to drive the compressor. This represents the major energy consumption component of the system. Sometimes it is the only energy requirement.

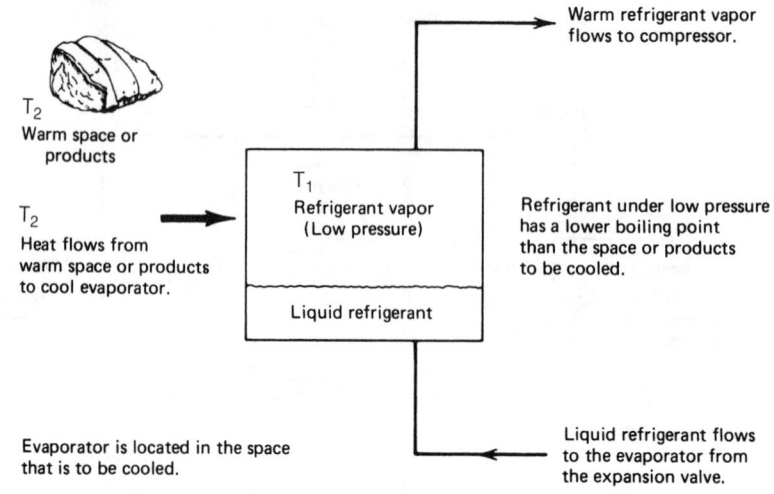

FIGURE 8.2 Evaporator: vapor compression refrigeration cycle. Heat flow from T_2 to T_1.

The compressor also adds some energy to the refrigerant. This results in a higher refrigerant temperature. See Figure 8.3 for an illustration of the compression process.

Condenser

The purpose of the condenser is to release the refrigerant heat that was absorbed in the evaporator and during compression. Condensers are usually placed in an air or water environment. The environment temperature must be lower than the refrigerant temperature and boiling point at the higher pressure as the refrigerant leaves the compressor. Hence, the refrigerant is cooled in the condenser, losing its latent heat of condensation, so that it returns to a liquid state. If environment temperatures are high, refrigerant pressures must also be high. Compressor energy requirements depend on the condenser environment temperature. Higher condenser environment temperatures require larger amounts of compressor energy, which reduce the efficiency of the system. The efficiency of the compression process can be increased when cool water is used to absorb heat at the condenser. It must be remembered, however, that water is energy and its cost must be considered. See Figure 8.4 for a visual description of this process.

A condensed refrigerant, with its high temperature and pressure, leaves the condenser and flows into the receiver for future use. Frequently, the lower portion of the condenser is used as a receiver, especially in small reach-in chillers and freezers and with some types of window air conditioners.

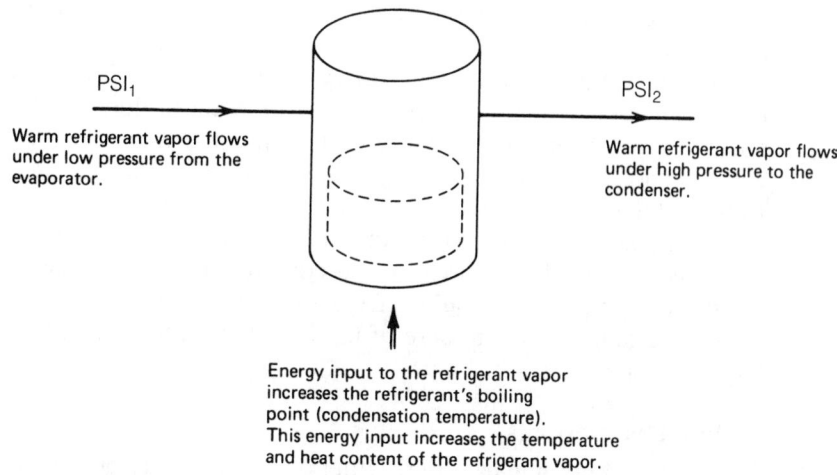

FIGURE 8.3 Compressor: vapor compression refrigeration cycle. Refrigerant enters at low pressure (PSI_1) and leaves at high pressure (PSI_2).

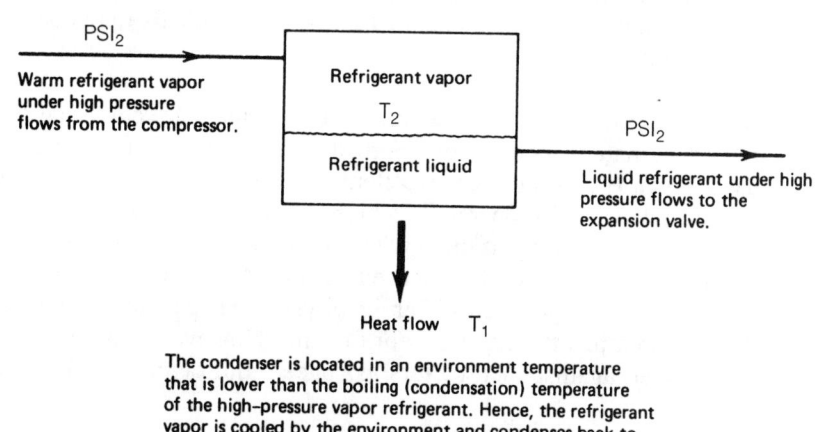

FIGURE 8.4 Condenser: vapor compression refrigeration cycle. Heat flow from refrigerant (T_2) to environment (T_1).

Expansion Device (Valve)

The refrigerant is now a liquid and is almost ready for reuse in the evaporator. However, its pressure must be reduced, which will reduce its boiling point. The unit that reduces pressure and controls the flow of refrigerant to the evaporator is the expansion device, or valve. Expansion valves can be adjusted to regulate the temperature of the evaporator. See Figure 8.5 for this process.

The expansion valve is the primary system control. It can also activate the compressor. When the valve allows refrigerant to flow into the evaporator, it permits the compressor to operate; when the valve closes, it stops the compressor. Temperature-sensing devices can also activate the expansion valve and the compressor.

In summary, a low-pressure liquid refrigerant absorbs heat in the evaporator; its pressure is increased at the compressor; it loses heat in the condenser; a high-pressure liquid refrigerant flows to the receiver; the expansion valve reduces the pressure of the liquid refrigerant as it flows back to the evaporator.

System Components

Chemical and mechanical driers (filters) are frequently placed in the refrigerant line to remove water that may accidentally get into the enclosed refrigerant piping network. Oil separators are used if there is a potential hazard from a mixture of oil and refrigerant. Oil could ooze from some type of compressors. In addition, various chemical separators can be added to the system if there is a chance that other chemicals may contaminate the refrigerant.

Forced-Convection Evaporators.

Evaporators are classified according to forced or natural convection. Forced-convection evaporators are generally used because they provide excellent temperature response. Forced-convection evaporators also operate at a higher temperature, which results in higher compressor operating efficiency. This efficiency gain is partially offset by the energy consumption of the fan used with the forced-convection evaporator.

Evaporators may also differ in physical shape and design. Shape and design can affect the efficiency of the unit. However, system efficiency must be weighed against such factors as space requirements, weight restrictions,

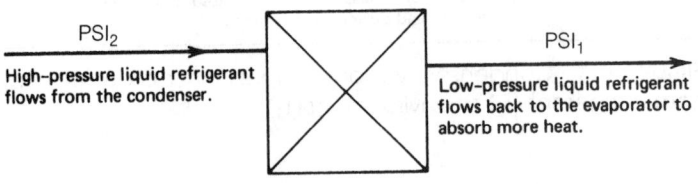

PSI$_2$

High-pressure liquid refrigerant flows from the condenser.

PSI$_1$

Low-pressure liquid refrigerant flows back to the evaporator to absorb more heat.

The expansion valve reduces the pressure of the liquid refrigerant. Hence, the refrigerant's boiling point is reduced. The expansion valve also meters refrigerant flow to the evaporator.

FIGURE 8.5 Expansion valve: vapor compression refrigeration cycle. Pressure reduction.

costs, and the proposed function of the unit. Generally, manufacturers provide the most effective physical shape and design for a given application.

Compressors. Three types of compressors are available. Small compressors are rotary-sealed "hermetic" units, which means that the compressor and its electric motor are combined in one component. These units are used in food chillers, freezers, smaller air-conditioning units, and small-area dehumidifiers. Maintenance of the hermetic compressor is simple, with minimal labor repair costs and high parts costs. These units usually have a long-life component warranty policy.

The most versatile compressor is the reciprocating unit, which is a piston moving in a cylinder, as in an internal-combustion engine. A reciprocating compressor is easy to repair but may require considerable maintenance. It is made in a variety of sizes and usually operates at a slower rate than the revolutions per minute (revolutions per second) of the electric motor that drives it. Therefore, a speed reduction mechanism is required.

Large compressors have a centrifugal design (like a jet aircraft turbine), are normally used only in large air-conditioning installations, and can be driven by electric motors or internal-combustion engines.

Condenser Types. Forced-convection condensers are used more often than natural-convection condensers because they provide fast heat dissipation and are smaller than equivalently heat-rated natural-convection units. Water and combination air–water condensers are also common. The water used in some water-cooled units can be recycled, as discussed later in this chapter. Condensers vary in design and physical shape.

Liquid refrigerant flows from the condenser to a receiving tank. The receiving tank holds the refrigerant until it is required by the evaporator, thus completing the refrigerant's flow through the vapor compression cycle. The receiving tank is a large vessel whose size, shape, and design have minimal effects on the efficiency of the system.

Expansion Valves. Expansion valves all produce the same effects and have about the same efficiency and performance ratings. Valve names indicate what they measure, and all are related to refrigerant pressure. There are pressure-sensitive valves; temperature-sensitive valves; float valves, which measure liquid-refrigerant levels in the system; and simple friction valves (friction reduces pressure, thereby lowering the refrigerant boiling point).

ABSORPTION REFRIGERATION CYCLE

The primary absorption refrigeration cycle used for air conditioning in the hospitality industry is the lithium bromide absorption cycle. Water is the refrigerant, which limits the minimum cold temperature of the cycle. The cycle is shown in Figure 8.6.

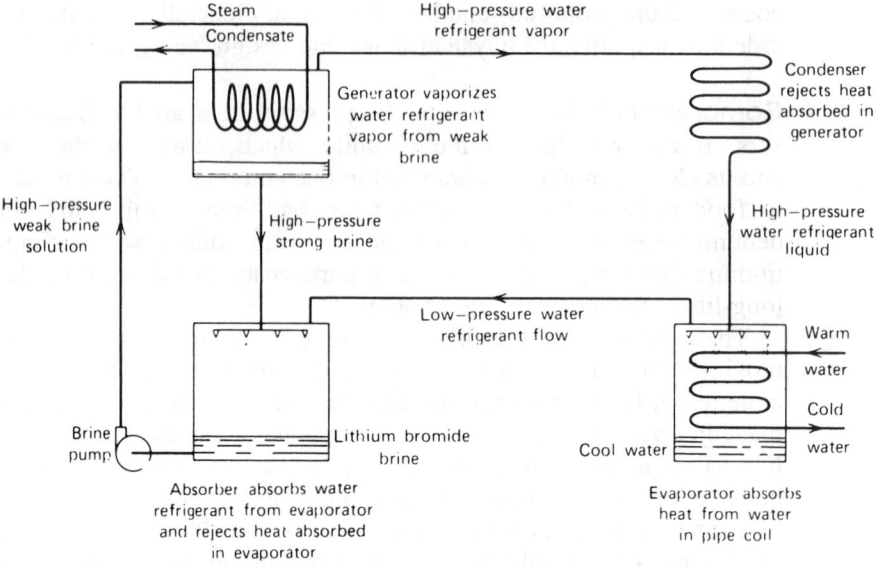

FIGURE 8.6 Lithium bromide absorption refrigeration cycle.

Cold water produced by the cycle is used to absorb heat from the building. Air, which cools the building, can be moved over a series of cold-water pipes with zone temperature controls (see Figure 8.7), or cold water can be piped to each room and individual room thermostats used to regulate air flow (see Figure 8.8). The latter system provides maximum room temperature response but has a higher installation cost.

The cycle consists of four basic components: evaporator, absorber, generator, and condenser.

Evaporator

The operation of the complete cycle can be analyzed by referring to Figure 8.6. Heat is absorbed at the evaporator by the water refrigerant. The water refrigerant is at an extremely low pressure and therefore has a low boiling point. Water changes to a low-pressure steam (water vapor) as it absorbs heat.

Absorber

Water vapor from the evaporator is attracted to and is absorbed by a salt solution contained in the absorber (salt attracts and absorbs water). A common salt solution is a lithium bromide brine. The latent heat of condensation is released by the water vapor refrigerant when it is absorbed by the lithium bromide brine and changes to a liquid (water). The absorber gets hot and must be cooled, just like the condenser in the vapor compression refrigera-

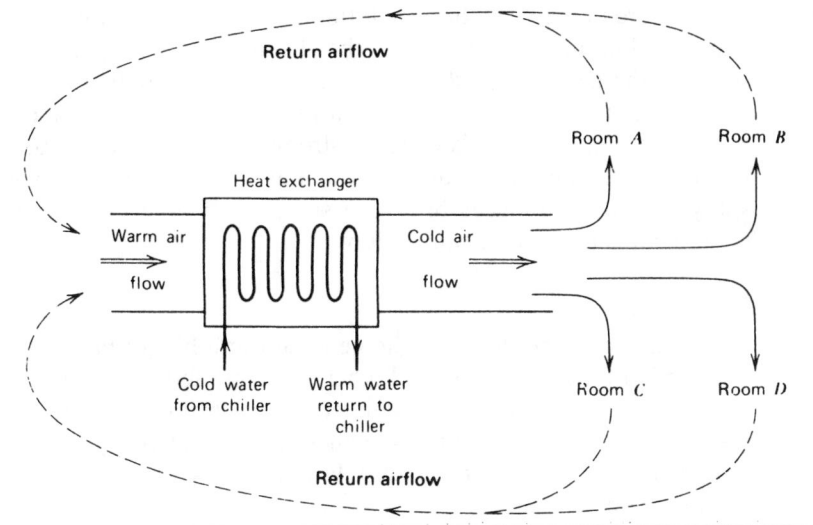

FIGURE 8.7 A cold-air distribution technique. One zone thermostat for all rooms.

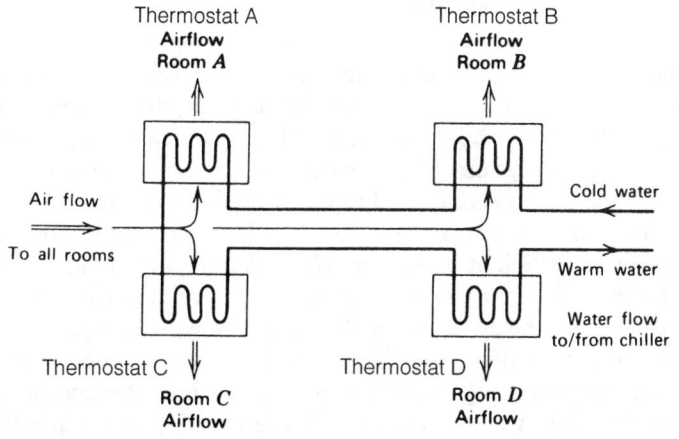

FIGURE 8.8 Individual control of cold air flow into each room.

tion cycle. When lithium bromide absorbs water, the brine solution is weakened and its attraction for additional water is reduced.

Generator

The weakened brine solution is pumped from the absorber and sprayed into the generator. Heat is added at the generator, driving off the excess water that was absorbed in the absorber as water vapor. Since the pump increases the pressure of the weak brine solution, water now has a higher boiling point than it had in the evaporator or in the absorber. Heat is normally supplied as steam in the generator, although any source of heat will allow the system to operate. The brine that is left has a high salt ratio—the excess water has been driven off—and it is called a strong brine. The strong brine flows by gravity back toward the absorber and is sprayed into the absorber. The spraying process reduces brine pressure, so absorber and evaporator pressure remains low and in equilibrium.

Condenser

The water vapor produced in the generator at a higher pressure proceeds to the condenser. Because of its higher pressure and resulting higher boiling point, water vapor can now be condensed, releasing the latent heat of vaporization that was absorbed in the generator at a relatively high environment temperature. The higher-pressure liquid leaves the condenser and flows back to the evaporator.

The water is sprayed into the evaporator, which reduces pressure on the water refrigerant. The cycle is now complete.

WATER-COOLING TOWERS

A water-cooling tower is used in conjunction with water-cooled condensers and/or absorbers. It cools the warm water flowing from the condenser or absorber so that it can be recycled back to the condenser and/or absorber. Figure 8.9 shows how a water-cooling tower can be used with an absorption refrigeration system. Condensers in the vapor compression refrigeration cycle can also be connected to water-cooling towers.

The cooling-tower operation is relatively simple and requires minimal energy for efficient operation. Water is pumped and sprayed into a confined air space. When water is sprayed into air, some of it will be evaporated, or absorbed by the air as vapor. As water changes to vapor, it must absorb heat, the latent heat of vaporization. The latent heat comes either from the air or from the remaining water being pumped into the cooling tower; thus, the nonvaporized water is cooled. This remaining cool water is fed back to the condenser for reuse. The water absorbed by the air must be replaced. Replaced water is called makeup water and is the only water that has to be purchased for the system to operate.

The efficiency of the cooling tower is greatly increased if any or all of the following conditions exist: a high outside air temperature, a low outside relative humidity, and increased air flow through the tower. Ideal water tower environment conditions exist in most desert regions of the world. However, cooling towers are generally used throughout the world.

Some building codes may require the use of water-cooling towers to conserve water with medium to large installations. The absorbed heat (warm

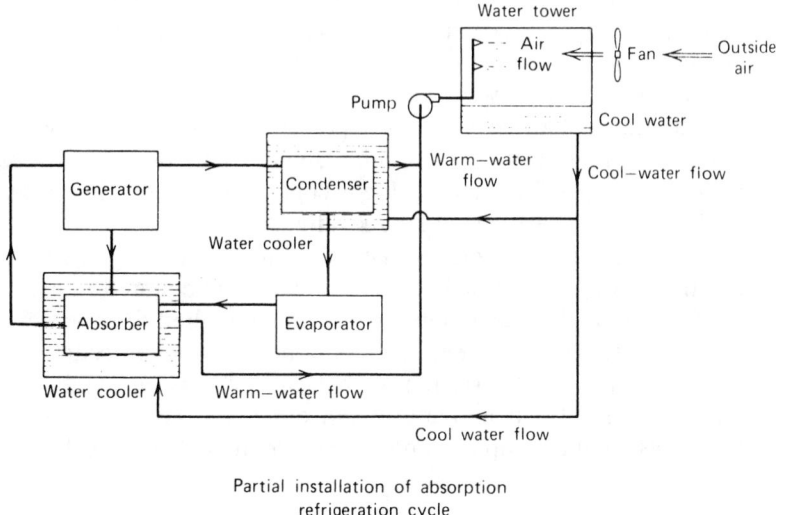

Partial installation of absorption
refrigeration cycle

FIGURE 8.9 Use of a water-cooling tower to cool a condenser and an absorber of an absorption refrigeration cycle.

water) can also be used to partially heat (preheat) domestic hot water in buildings.

SOLAR AIR COOLING

Solar cooling can be effectively used for building air cooling by using one of three systems: radiative cooling, solar vapor compression, and solar absorption. Each system must have an auxiliary backup energy system, which increases its maintenance, repair, and installation costs.

Radiative Cooling

A simple solar-cooling system is radiative cooling. Water is used to absorb building heat during the day and is circulated through pipes, plates, or other devices and allowed to radiate heat at night outside the building. Although the system works, it is dependent on several critical factors. A large water storage tank is required to absorb building heat during the day. A large radiative surface is required to lose heat during the evening. Cloudless nights are required so that the radiative surface is not shielded from the cold of outer space. The system is costly to install.

Solar Vapor Compression

A second, potentially feasible solar-cooling system operates like a vapor compression refrigeration cycle. The solar-energy system drives a compressor, so electrical energy is not required to operate an electric motor. Figure 8.10 shows such a system. A solar collector is used to heat a liquid or to change a liquid to a vapor. The heated liquid or vapor proceeds to a heat exchanger equipped with an auxiliary heater (a backup system) to heat a second fluid, changing it to a vapor. The heated second vapor drives an engine (similar to a steam engine), and a low-quality (low-temperature) vapor discharged from the engine is condensed in a condenser and continues back to the auxiliary heater for recycling.

You learned in Chapter 3 that solar energy can be converted directly to electric energy for immediate use. It can also be stored in electric batteries for future use. This technique may also be applied to solar vapor compression cycles. The heat engine mentioned in the preceding paragraph is replaced with an electric motor that can be powered with solar-produced electric energy (or from batteries) or directly from the present electric system. This technique appears more feasible than the relatively inefficient heat engine just described.

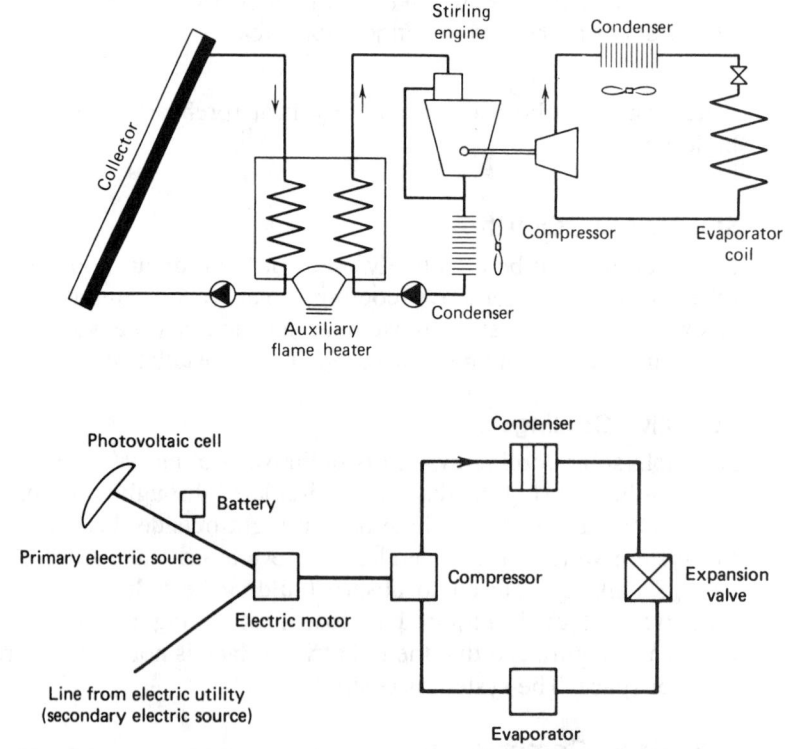

FIGURE 8.10 Solar vapor compression refrigeration cycles[1] (courtesy: S. V. Szokolay, *Solar Energy and Building*, Architectural Press, Ltd., London, 1975).

Solar Absorption Cooling

A third solar-cooling system is an absorption system. Figure 8.11 shows a solar absorption cycle. Like the lithium bromide absorption cycle, the cycle has four basic components. An evaporator absorbs heat from the area to be cooled. A liquid refrigerant absorbs its latent heat of vaporization, and its vapor is attracted to a chemical solution in the absorber. The refrigerant gas is absorbed by a chemical solution, and its latent heat of condensation is released. The liquid-refrigerant and chemical mixture flows to a generator, where solar heat is used to drive off the refrigerant as a vapor. The separated refrigerant gas proceeds to a condenser. The absorbing chemical flows back to the absorber for recycling from the generator, sometimes called a separator. The refrigerant gas is condensed in the condenser, and its pressure is reduced by an expansion device before it flows back to the evaporator. If sufficient solar energy is not available at the generator, an auxiliary form of heat has to be used as a backup heating system. The system is fairly efficient but requires a large solar-collection area.

Note: Figures 8.10 and 8.11 may appear to be from older or dated references, but it must be pointed out that the two solar system concepts have not changed. At the present time, the operation of solar vapor compression and solar absorption refrigeration cycles have not significantly changed since the mid-1970s.[1]

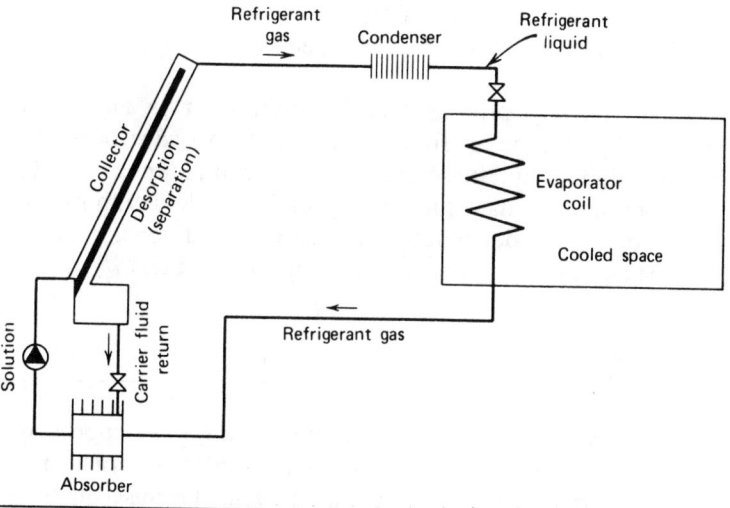

FIGURE 8.11 Solar absorption refrigeration[1] (courtesy: S. V. Szokolay, *Solar Energy and Building,* Architectural Press, Ltd., London, 1975).

ABSORPTION REFRIGERATORS

There are several additional techniques that can be used for cooling. The feasibility and potential use of these techniques generally depend on a low-cost energy source. One such system is an absorption system that can be used for food chillers and freezers. It is very similar to the previously discussed solar absorption cycle, except that a low-cost energy source, rather than solar energy, is used at the generator. The most common source of energy for these units has been either natural gas or LPG (propane or butane). These are frequently used as portable cooling units and are generally found in recreation vehicles.

COMPRESSED AIR

Air can be cooled by a compression-and-expansion process. Air is compressed to a relatively high pressure. The compressed air is quickly released to a space through an expansion valve. As compressed air is released, its pressure is suddenly released and it expands. The expansion process requires energy. This energy comes from sensible heat contained in the air in the space to be cooled, thus reducing the air temperature in the space. The primary compressed-air cooling application is with aircraft.

SWAMP, OR EVAPORATIVE, COOLERS

Used extensively in the southwestern United States and other desert regions, swamp, or evaporative, coolers operate like cooling towers and produce very cool, humid air. If the relative humidity of the air to be cooled is high, the process is not very efficient, which may restrict its use. Energy is required, in the form of water and electricity, to operate water pumps and an air fan.

In effect, any process that humidifies air is an evaporative cooling process. Spray-type air filters (see Chapter 9) have been used for years in larger buildings, and these units partially cool, humidify, and filter air. Many new cooling systems combine evaporative coolers with mechanical refrigeration cycles and, depending on fresh-air conditions, operate either system (see the energy-management section in this chapter).

REFRIGERANTS

Most refrigeration units are precharged with a UL-approved refrigerant by the manufacturer. The halocarbon family of refrigerants is generally used with vapor compression refrigeration cycles because of its excellent safety record. Local fire codes may also specify what refrigerants can be used in specific situations.

Halocarbon refrigerants are essentially nontoxic, noncorrosive, nonexplosive, and nonflammable. In addition, they have a relatively low specific volume—this means that the mechanical system can be physically small for a specific heat removal rate—and have moderate to low condensing pressures, that is, lower compression energy requirements. These factors make the halocarbon family fairly good refrigerants. One disadvantage is that special equipment and chemical analyzers are necessary to locate a refrigerant leak in the system. It is recommended that when an older nonhalocarbon refrigeration cycle is replaced, a new unit utilizing the halocarbon family of refrigerants be used as the replacement.

There are three primary refrigerant types, namely, R-11, R-12, and R-502, and two secondary refrigerant types, R-13 and R-503, used in the hospitality industry for vapor compression refrigeration cycles for air cooling, food chillers, and food freezers that are chlorofluorocarbons (CFCs). These are being phased out and are no longer being manufactured by international agreement. CFCs destroy the ozone layer around the earth when they are released to the environment. Special care and equipment must be used to capture these refrigerants when exhausted from current older equipment.[3] New vapor compression refrigeration cycles cannot use CFC refrigerants.

Substitute refrigerants are being developed and tested as replacements for CFC refrigerants. Generally, the substitute refrigerants are blends of halocarbon refrigerants, with UL classifications of R-22, R-152a, R-124, R-125, R-218, and R-290. However, not all new blends have been UL flammability tested and approved. The blend-type refrigerants are generally given a 400 number classification by ASHRAE (American Society of Heating, Refrigeration, and Air Conditioning Engineers). While these 400 classification refrigerants have met ASHRAE flammability test requirements and standards, not all have been classified by Underwriters Laboratories in early 1996.[4]

When purchasing new refrigerants or when replacing a CFC with an alternate refrigerant, you should specify that the refrigerant meet both UL and ASHRAE requirements. If there is any doubt about a specific refrigerant, check with the nearest Environmental Protection Administration (EPA) office.

Changing the refrigerant base, which had been R-11 and R-12 for over 30 years, leads to a large number of potential problems, all of which have not been solved at the time of this writing. The following are examples of potential problems: The field conversion standards and equipment for changing a CFC refrigerant to an alternate refrigerant have not been formally approved; only selected hermetic motor insulating materials have been approved for the new groups of refrigerants; compressor lubricants that can be used with motor insulating materials and the new blends of refrigerants are being developed and only a limited number of lubricants are currently approved; field testing standards for the new systems are being developed and tested; finally, remanufactured hermetic refrigerant compressor standards are being developed and a very limited number of compressor manufacturers are currently approved.

REACH-IN FOOD CHILLERS

Most reach-in refrigeration systems are predesigned and are reasonably efficient if properly maintained. Maintenance of the system is usually moderate and many units have a 7- to 15-year life. During its life span, the major repair is the replacement of the motor compressor unit. The condenser fan motor and interior air-circulating fan motors may have to be replaced once or twice during the unit's life span.

FOOD CHILLER SPECIFICATIONS

The basic rating factors for chillers are cubic feet (liters) or pounds (kilograms) capacity. The relationship between cubic feet (liters) and pounds (kilograms) is approximately 30 pounds per cubic foot (0.48 kilograms per liter). So, if one unit is rated in cubic feet (cubic meters), a factor of 30 (0.48) can be used to convert one rating to the other. The reach-in unit is driven by a sealed electric motor and rotary-type compressor unit (hermetic motor compressor) for the vapor compression refrigeration cycle.

The electric motor, and hence the driving system, will be rated in volts, amperes, and watts of electric energy (these electrical terms will be defined in Chapter 11). Ideally, you should purchase a unit that has the highest ratio of heat capacity to watts. A typical reach-in unit operates 16 to 18 hours per day.

If a manufacturer's model operates 16 hours a day, its heat-removal overload capacity is 8 hours of operating time. As the system could operate 24 hours per day, its overload potential is 50 percent.

Other factors will influence how long the compressor motor operates in one day. The manufacturer's specifications are based on certain well-founded assumptions. The interior design temperature is usually 40 to 45°F (4.4 to 7.2°C). Lowering the chiller temperature increases the operating time of the unit and its energy consumption. Another specification factor is the condenser environment temperature. Normally, an 80 to 90°F (26.7 to 32.2°C) temperature is assumed at the condenser. If the temperature of the room in which the condenser is located exceeds 90°F (32.2°C), two factors interact. First, the heat gain through the walls of the reach-in unit and the heat gain caused whenever the door is opened (infiltration) are increased, which increases compressor operating time. Second, the rate of heat transfer from the condenser to the room is reduced, which requires more time to condense the refrigerant. These factors lower the overall efficiency of the refrigeration unit and reduce its life.

The manufacturer must assume that the door on the reach-in unit will be opened at predetermined frequencies for set periods of time. If door openings and the length of time the door is kept open are not carefully controlled, operating costs could increase by 25 to 50 percent and the average chiller temperature could increase by 10 to 20°F (5.6 to 11.1°C) in a short time period, 2 to 5 minutes (120 to 300 seconds).

COMPONENT SELECTION FACTORS

Automatic Defrost

If the chiller temperature is to be maintained at 40°F (4.4°C), the evaporator will be maintained at 20 to 30°F (−6.7 to −1.1°C). Any moisture in the air will quickly freeze on the cold evaporator plates, which will lower the efficiency of the unit. Manufacturers usually provide an automatic defrost subsystem for the evaporator. Many chiller systems utilize a hot-gas defrost system. Hot gas is discharged directly from the compressor to the evaporator, bypassing both the condenser and the expansion device. The hot gas melts any ice that has formed on the evaporator.

A second automatic defrost system uses electric resistance wires placed on the evaporator. A built-in time clock allows electric energy to flow through the wires once every 12 hours to melt the accumulated evaporator ice. This system frequently has a higher energy requirement than the hot-gas defrost system.

Evaporator Selection

Reach-in units will have either natural- or forced-convection evaporators. Forced-convection units have fans in continuous operation, which circulate air within the chiller. This provides an ideal chiller temperature distribution. Dehydration of poorly packaged food items may be increased with this system. Forced-convection evaporators are set 10°F (5.6°C) below the chiller temperature. For example, if a 40°F (4.4°C) chiller temperature is desired, the evaporator temperature would be set at 30°F (−1.1°C) —40−10 = 30°F (+4.4−5.5 = -1.1°C). Even considering the total energy consumption of both the compressor motor and the forced-convection fan, the total energy requirement is frequently less than for a natural-convection evaporator.

The natural-convection evaporator depends on the movement of natural air currents caused by temperature differentials within the chiller. The evaporator is set 20°F (11.1°C) below the chiller temperature. For example, if a 40°F (4.4°C) reach-in temperature is desired, the evaporator temperature is set at 20°F (−6.7°C) —40−20 = 20°F (+4.4−11.1 = −6.7°C). This lower temperature increases the system operating costs because either a larger compressor motor is required or the system must operate for longer time periods for a specified heat-removal rate.

CHILLER MAINTENANCE

The temperature of the chiller should be checked with an accurate thermometer, such as a mercury-in-glass thermometer. Each degree of temperature error, that is, desired temperature compared to actual temperature, can significantly increase the operating cost of the unit.

You must keep the condenser clean and open to allow air to circulate around it. Dirt accumulations on the condenser serve as insulators and reduce the rate of heat transfer from the condenser to the environment. In most cases, periodic vacuuming of an air-cooled condenser removes most of the accumulated lint and dust. Kitchen grease may have to be removed by washing.

Do not place reach-in chillers near sources of heat. Heat produces a high environment temperature and increases the cost of operation. Also, do not place a reach-in unit near window areas where the sun's rays will strike any portion of the unit. The insulation used on reach-in units is excellent and has a high thermal resistance (R) rating; it is not very thick, usually 2 inches (50.8 millimeters).

REACH-IN FREEZERS

Reach-in freezers generally utilize the vapor compression refrigeration cycle to remove heat. Principles of operation for reach-in freezers are almost identical to the principles discussed for reach-in chillers, with the following exceptions.

Reach-in freezers can also be rated in cubic feet (liters) or pounds (kilograms). The conversion rate is 45 pounds per cubic foot (0.72 kilograms per liter). These ratings are usually reliable if the units are loaded with frozen items. Problems can arise, however, when freezing products. In order to freeze products, the latent heat of fusion must be removed from the product. This demand can be substantial and frequently overloads the refrigeration system.

Some manufacturers specify an additional factor: a freezing rate. A typical freezing rate is 2 to 3 pounds (0.9 to 1.3 kilograms) per hour. This amounts to only 48 to 72 pounds (21.7 to 32.6 kilograms) per day, which is only 1 to 1.5 cubic feet (28 to 42 liters) per day. If one has a 15-cubic-foot (420-liter) freezer, this represents a small percentage of the total capacity of the unit. Generally, when foodstuffs are being frozen, the compressor motor may operate up to 24 hours a day.

COMPONENT SELECTION FACTORS

Defrosting the Unit

Some units use the hot-gas defrost system described earlier. While this system has a low energy requirement, it can lead to large temperature differences within the interior of the freezer, which could partially thaw some food products placed near the evaporator.

The most common defrost system uses electric resistance wires. Every 12 hours, a time clock allows electric energy to flow through the resistance wires attached to the evaporator, and ice is melted.

Temperature Control

Because the quality and shelf life of frozen food are influenced by the unit's temperature, temperature control is critical in freezers. Freezer temperatures that are too low result in higher operating costs and greater food product dehydration. Freezer temperatures should be set with a mercury-in-glass thermometer, as indicated in a previous section. The unit should be set to operate in the temperature range -10 to $0°F$ (-23.3 to $-17.8°C$). A setting of $0°F$ ($-17.8°C$) is less costly to operate than a setting of $-10°F$ ($-23.3°C$) (see Figure 8.12).

Other Considerations

Most reach-in freezers have a natural-convection evaporator. This means that the actual temperature of the evaporator would be $-20°F$ ($-28.9°C$) for a freezer setting of $0°F$ ($-17.8°C$), or $-30°F$ ($-34.4°C$) for a setting of $-10°F$ ($-23.3°C$). These effects are also shown in Figure 8.12.

The various factors discussed for chillers also apply to freezers. However, these factors have more serious impact on the operating cost of reach-in freezers.

WALK-IN CHILLERS AND FREEZERS

Walk-in chillers and freezers are normally custom designed. Custom design includes prefabricated components that can be intermixed to satisfy several design variables. For example, one compressor may be used with a group of condensers and/or evaporators, or one condenser may be used with one of several compressors and/or expansion valves. These prefabricated component parts are considered to be custom designed.

Walk-in units are available in almost any size, from a small unit of 20 square feet (1.9 square meters) of floor area to very large rooms, such as refrigerated warehouses used in institutional complexes.

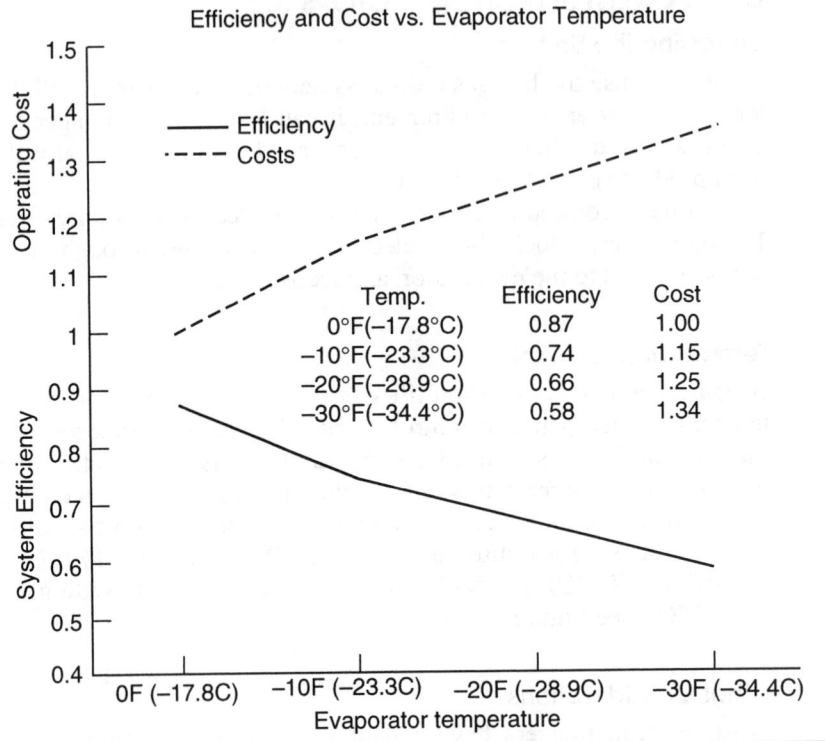

FIGURE 8.12 Operating cost and efficiency at different evaporator temperatures.

HEAT LOAD FACTORS

The size of the refrigeration unit depends on the heat load requirement. The heat load is a function of transmission heat, infiltration heat, appliance heat, and product heat. Refrigeration heat loads are determined for a 24-hour period in Btu per day (watts per day).

The transmission load includes the transfer of heat through walls, ceiling, floor, and doors. It depends on the temperature difference between the environment of the walk-in unit and its interior temperature, the unit's construction, and the amount of insulation. Appendix 9 shows how to determine the transmission heat load.

The infiltration heat load depends on the unit's volume and the temperature difference between the unit's environment and its interior. It also depends on the number of door openings per workday. Normal usage is assumed to be 6 to 8 door openings per work shift (8 hours). Heavy usage is 12 or more openings per work shift. The infiltration heat load increases by

50 percent between normal and heavy usage. These effects are shown in Appendix 9.

The appliance heat load consists of electric lamps and circulation fans for a forced-convection evaporator. The forced-convection evaporator fan, which is in continuous operation, provides a constant heat load. The electric lamp load depends on total lamp wattage and hours of operation. Normally, a lamp switch is located near the exterior door handle and is installed with an indicator lamp, which shows whether the inside lamps are on or off.

The product load is easy to estimate. A product sensible-heat load is considered. One way to minimize product heat loads is to schedule the delivery of products carefully. If all the products are received on the same day, they must all be cooled within the next 24 hours. If, however, the deliveries are spread over a three-day period, the product load is only about one-third. In addition, the lower chiller volume reduces the transmission and infiltration heat loads. These effects are also shown in Appendix 9.

The walk-in freezer has the same heat loads as the chiller. Its interior temperature is lower, which increases the transmission and infiltration heat loads. Although increased insulation is necessary to reduce the transmission load, it has no effect on infiltration and appliance heat loads.

Once again, the 16- to 18-hour unit operation rule is followed for walk-in units. The operating costs for various combinations of loads and the effects of these loads are shown in Appendix 9.

PLASTIC STRIP DOOR COVERINGS

In some foodservice operations, it may be necessary to keep the door to the chiller or freezer open for extended periods, for example, when there is excessive traffic into and out of the walk-in. In these situations, the chiller and the freezer are subject to a continuous convective-heat gain. Obviously, keeping a walk-in chiller or freezer door open any longer than necessary is not recommended.

If the walk-in door is kept open for any length of time, the additional heat gain is as shown in Figure 8.13. Every attempt must be made to minimize open-door heat gains. One technique is to use plastic door strips or curtains. The plastic strips hang from the top to the bottom of the door frame, reducing convective-heat gains to the walk-in. The potential energy savings are also shown in Figure 8.13.

OTHER DESIGN FACTORS

If a walk-in chiller and freezer are to be installed in an operation, you should seriously consider using the chiller as the entrance to the freezer, as shown in Figure 8.14. The figure also shows the net energy savings that result if the combination unit is used rather than separate freezer and chiller

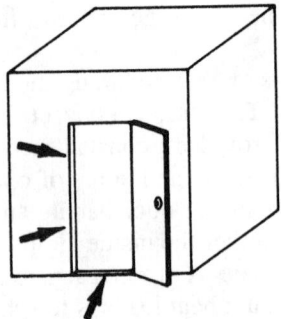 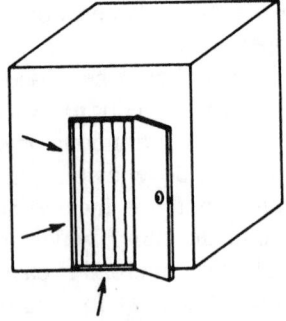

Heat flow

Walk-in with open door snowing large convective heat gain.

If the door is left open two hours per day for a 1000-cubic-foot (28-cubic-meter) freezer at 0°F (−17.8°C), the heat gain is 197,794 Btu per day (57,954 watts per day).

Heat flow

Same walk-in with open door and plastic strips hanging over door opening, showing reduced heat flow.

The same freezer will have a heat gain of 132,634 Btu per day (28,862 watts per day). Hence, the plastic strips reduce heat gain by almost 33 percent.

FIGURE 8.13 The use of plastic strip door coverings for walk-ins.[2]

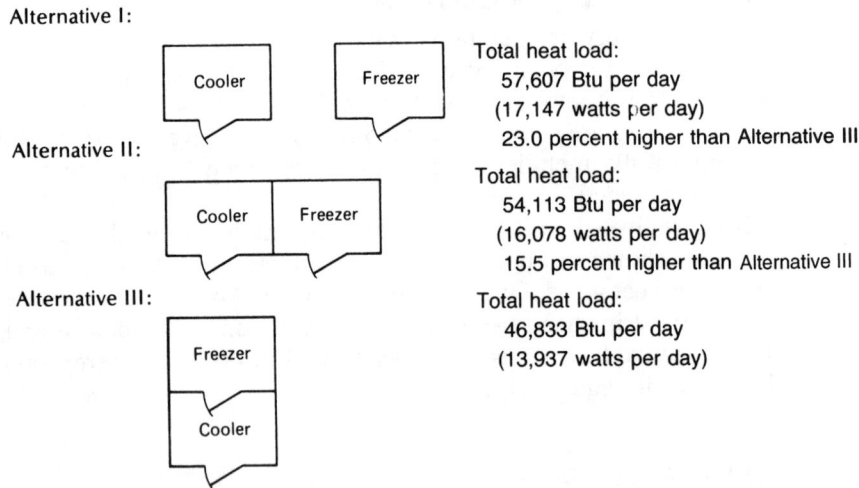

Alternative I:

Cooler   Freezer

Total heat load:
  57,607 Btu per day
  (17,147 watts per day)
  23.0 percent higher than Alternative III

Alternative II:

Cooler   Freezer

Total heat load:
  54,113 Btu per day
  (16,078 watts per day)
  15.5 percent higher than Alternative III

Alternative III:

Freezer

Cooler

Total heat load:
  46,833 Btu per day
  (13,937 watts per day)

FIGURE 8.14 Various freezer–cooler (chiller) combinations.

doors opening to a kitchen. It should also be pointed out that the chi...
slightly larger in a combination unit because of the second door opening in
the chiller; this reduces the storage capacity of the unit.

Energy costs can be reduced if a large number of reach-in units are
replaced with a single walk-in unit. Figure 8.15 shows this effect.

ENERGY MANAGEMENT AND MAINTENANCE

ENERGY-MANAGEMENT SYSTEMS FOR REFRIGERATION CYCLES

Considerable energy savings can be achieved if a property's refrigeration
systems are included in a computer-controlled energy-management system
(EMS). The system continually monitors cooled space temperatures, evaporator temperatures, condenser temperatures, and condenser environment
temperatures. As temperatures are continuously monitored in the cool areas,
an undesirable high temperature could activate an alarm if stored products
are in any potential danger. The system can also control expansion devices
and compressor operating times. If compressors are electrically driven, the
EMS can also control electric demand during a specified time period; for
example, it may not allow a compressor electric motor to start until another

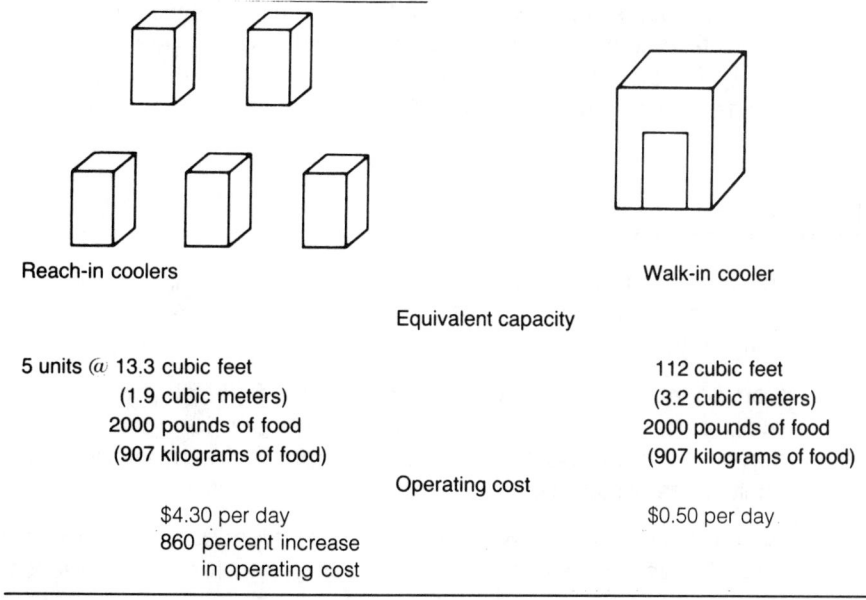

Reach-in coolers   Walk-in cooler

Equivalent capacity

5 units @ 13.3 cubic feet   112 cubic feet
(1.9 cubic meters)   (3.2 cubic meters)
2000 pounds of food   2000 pounds of food
(907 kilograms of food)   (907 kilograms of food)

Operating cost

$4.30 per day $0.50 per day
860 percent increase
in operating cost

FIGURE 8.15 Comparison of several smaller reach-in coolers and a single
walk-in cooler of the same equivalent capacity.

compressor motor is shut off. The same system could also control chiller or freezer entrances by personnel.

A trained refrigeration technician can quickly review EMS-monitored temperatures and identify if a refrigeration cycle is operating efficiently. If a particular unit is not performing to a specified standard, the technician can write a work order for the unit, indicating the components that should be checked.

The EMS will also control cooling-tower performance and regulate the flow of water through it or increase the amount of air flowing through it by controlling air fan speed. Also, if the environment wind speed is adequate, the electrically driven air fan can be shut off.

All of the preceding activities can be control programmed with several EMS units. A well-designed and maintained computer EMS can reduce refrigeration energy consumption by 20 percent or more; significantly reduce major refrigeration repairs and equipment downtime; significantly reduce product spoilage; and reduce refrigeration energy demand related costs by 25 percent or more, if electric demand cost rates are high. The major cost of the system is the interface between the computer control and measured temperature-related components. Throughout this chapter, various ideas were presented that resulted in reduced energy consumption for refrigeration systems. You should review the chapter, making a list of these energy-saving ideas and techniques. Compare your developed list with Figure 8.16.

This process should be repeated for the maintenance requirements of the total refrigeration system. Check your results with Figure 8.17.

Figures 8.16 and 8.17 should be used as energy-management guidelines and as a maintenance work schedule for refrigeration systems in a building.

SUMMARY

The focus of this chapter has been on the removal of heat, or refrigeration. The most common refrigeration system is the vapor compression refrigeration cycle.

Components of the vapor compression refrigeration cycle include the evaporator, compressor, condenser, and expansion valve. Most refrigeration units are precharged with a refrigerant by the manufacturer and typically utilize halocarbon refrigerants.

Another refrigeration cycle is the lithium bromide absorption cycle. This cycle includes an evaporator, absorber, generator, and condenser.

Both vapor compression and absorption may require a cooling tower to function correctly. The cooling tower operates in conjunction with water-cooled condensers.

Refrigeration cycles:

1. Low refrigerant condensation temperatures.
2. Use water for cooling condensers.
3. Forced-convection evaporator.
4. Size and shape of evaporator.

Water-cooling towers:

1. High outside temperatures.
2. Low outside relative humidity.
3. Increase air movement.

Use of solar coolers:

1. Absorption cooler.

Freon refrigerants.
High ratio of refrigeration capacity to watt consumption.
In many cases, 16-hour operation cycles.
Higher internal temperatures of coolers and freezers.
Reduce door openings of coolers and freezers.
Reduce ice thickness on evaporator.
Hot gas defrost.
Forced-convection evaporator.
Check thermostat on coolers and freezers.
Self-closing doors on reach-in coolers and freezers.
Keep condensers clean.
Keep refrigerators away from heat sources.
Maintain adequate clearance around reach-in coolers and freezers.
Increase insulation.
Purchase frozen food for freezers.
Reduce lighting requirements within coolers and freezers.
Reduce product loads.
Entrance to freezer through the cooler.
Reduce number of reach-in units.

FIGURE 8.16   Energy-saving techniques for refrigeration.

Solar air cooling might be effectively utilized as radiative cooling, solar vapor compression, and solar absorption.

Food chillers and freezers are also refrigeration systems and are either reach-in or walk-in. Most reach-in refrigeration systems are predesigned and are reasonably efficient. Important to the selection of reach-in freezers is the defrost unit and temperature control.

Walk-in chillers and freezers are normally custom designed. The size of these units depends on the heat load requirement. The heat load is a function of transmission heat, infiltration heat, appliance heat, and product heat.

Vapor-compression refrigeration cycle:

1. Electric motor for compressor
2. Driers in the refrigerant line
3. Oil separators
4. Chemical separators
5. Forced-convection evaporators—fan and water
6. Rotary compressor—simple maintenance
7. Reciprocating compressor—considerate maintenance
8. Gasoline or diesel engines for centrifugal compressor
9. Forced-convection condenser

Absorption refrigeration cycle:

1. Leakage of air into the system
2. Pump maintenance

Water-cooling towers:

1. Pumps
2. Fan

Solar air cooling:

1. Maintenance of the backup system

Evaporative cooler:

1. Water pump
2. Air fan

Refrigerant replacement for leaks
Reach-in refrigeration systems—minimal maintenance:

1. Maintenance increases as condensing temperature increases
2. Clean condensers

FIGURE 8.17 Maintenance considerations for refrigeration systems.

REFERENCES

1. Szokolay, S. V., *Solar Energy and Building*, Halsted Press, Wiley, New York, 1975.

2. Borsenik, F. D., *Minimum Savings When Using Plastic Strip Door Coverings Over Open Doors for Coolers and Freezers*, Special Report, Curton Industries, Inc., Catskill, NY, 1983.

3. Houston Lighting and Power Company, *Guide to Commercial Energy Efficiency*, Houston, October 1992.

4. Underwriters Laboratories, Inc., "Refrigeration News Notes—July, 1995," Northbrook Office, Engineering Services, Northbrook, IL, July 1995.

QUESTIONS/PROBLEMS

1. Discuss when one would use the vapor compression and the lithium bromide absorption refrigeration cycles for cooling.

2. When should the water-cooling tower be considered as part of a cooling system?

3. Discuss the potential use of solar refrigeration systems in buildings: lodgings, foodservice establishments, clubs, health-care facilities, and institutional buildings.

4. What items in Figure 8.16 could be immediately implemented in a foodservice operation with minimum cost?

5. Compare the preventive-maintenance factors in Figure 8.17 for refrigeration systems with those of systems used by a local lodging, foodservice, club, or health-care facility.

6. To what extent are plastic strip door coverings used in local foodservice establishments?

7. Visit a local foodservice operation and review its refrigeration systems. Obtain as much information as you can on these systems in order to do all of the following:

   a. List the number and sizes of all the refrigeration units (including air-cooling systems) used on the property.
   b. What are these systems used for?
   c. Determine if there are more efficient systems that could be used to replace the current systems.
   d. Develop an energy-management program for the establishment's cooling systems.
   e. Present your findings to the class or as a written report to your instructor.

CHAPTER 9

Courtesy of Hilton Hotels Corporation.

MANAGEMENT OF VENTILATION SYSTEMS

ABSTRACT

A smoke-free environment; airtight buildings; sick-building syndrome; energy-management systems for air flow, ventilation, and worker productivity; and ventilation to control the building's air environment are the main topics in this chapter. All are important issues for the hospitality manager. Each issue is addressed and solved by the appropriate application of fundamental ventilation concepts, system design, and management decision and action. While an adequate ventilation system can be specified, engineered, and installed, it must be maintained so it can deliver quality air and desired air flow.

Key words: air filter; air velocity; American Society of Heating, Refrigeration, and Air Conditioning Engineers (ASHRAE); canopy hood; central ventilation system; electronic filter (electrostatic precipitator); energy management system (EMS); equipment ventilation computation; floor area ventilation computation; fresh air; grease filter; grill; negative pressure; occupant method ventilation computation; pollution control filter; pressure losses; recirculated air; register; room ventilation system; room volume ventilation computation; sick building syndrome; smoke-free environment; ventilation; ventilation duct; ventilator hood; water spray filter; zone ventilation system.

INTRODUCTION

Management has a responsibility to provide clean, healthful air for customers and employees and in some cases a "smoke-free" environment. This chapter will familiarize you with various ventilation requirements (state and local codes and ordinances), provide you with basic technical information so that you can properly manage a building ventilation system, and show you how to reduce energy consumption while still providing healthful and comfortable air for customers and employees. In addition, a smoke-free environment will be stressed when appropriate. In some cases, a "sick-building syndrome" develops when insufficient fresh ventilation air is used.

Ventilation provides a controlled amount of air to a room or building. Several state and city codes[1] specify the amount of air that must be circulated through public spaces and in employee work areas, if it must be filtered, if it is smoke free, or if it is fresh air. The first state and local ventilation codes were approved to provide adequate air (oxygen) to sustain human life, to remove objectionable odors and dust, and to remove high-temperature and high-humidity air from a room or building. Some current ordinances specify that ventilation air must be sufficient to eliminate moisture condensation, which can cause slippery floors or unsanitary conditions, within employee work areas. Proper air movement and ventilation will reduce or eliminate these undesirable conditions and will provide a quality room environment.

Ventilation codes frequently have fresh-air requirements for selected building areas, such as kitchens. Fresh air is defined as "outside air," which may be hot, humid, or cold, lack moisture, or be polluted (outside plant pollen, auto emissions, or smoky air). Introducing untreated fresh air into a building, which can be done in some areas, can defeat several of the primary purposes for ventilating. Most building ventilation codes have been updated since the mid-1980s, after close to 50 years without significant changes.

Since the mid-1980s, many local government agencies, especially health departments, have enacted codes that either prohibit or restrict tobacco smoking in most types of hospitality buildings. Many foodservice units must provide for smoking and nonsmoking diner sections. Several casinos in Las Vegas, Nevada, are now nonsmoking and most have nonsmoking casino sections. Generally, one increases ventilation air if smoking is allowed; hence, ventilation air, in theory, could be reduced if smoking is prohibited. In practice, ventilation requirements have not been reduced in nonsmoking buildings or building sections. One air filter, the electrostatic unit, will completely remove all traces of smoke from the air; however, these units are generally not recognized in ventilation or health codes for smoke-free areas. In recent years, the American Society of Heating, Refrigeration, and Air Conditioning Engineers has worked with architects and several government organizations to develop practical and reasonable ventilation standards. Its efforts have been in the areas of simplified design procedures, operational standards, and systems that require minimal maintenance and repair. ASHRAE has also worked to reduce total building energy requirements. Several of these procedures will be discussed in this chapter and then applied to air conditioning in Chapter 10.

VENTILATION RATES

Ventilation rates (the movement of a specified amount of air) are generally covered in codes. Ventilation rates in the service industries frequently depend on the worker or customer activity level in a given section of the building. Therefore, ventilation could vary from one room to the next within the same building. A local code may specify one or more procedures for determining the quantity of ventilation air. Some of these procedures will be reviewed in this section. In all examples, the same size space will be ventilated, but the amount of specified air will vary according to typical code requirements.

ROOM-VOLUME VENTILATION COMPUTATION

A common ventilation rate is based on the gross volume of the space (length x width x height = volume). A code may specify a number of air changes per hour. Typical requirements range from 6 to 60 air changes per hour, fewer air changes being required for large public spaces (exhibition spaces), and more air changes being required for laboratories in health-care areas or food production areas. Codes may also specify summer and winter rates. Some codes specify minimum and maximum rates, the minimum usually applying to the winter heating season and the maximum to the summer.

Management must generally increase the minimum rate when smoking is allowed or when employees are performing heavy tasks. In most cases, the minimum rate is sufficient to provide adequate air to sustain human life and for any combination-type appliances (gas and oil appliances) that are in operation in the room.

Figure 9.1 shows an example of the room volume ventilation computation. This computation frequently provides the largest amount of ventilation air for a given space. You should note that the number and types of heat appliances are not considered in the example. So, although the calculation satisfies the ventilation code, the resulting temperature and moisture levels in the room could become very uncomfortable for customers and employees, resulting in a larger volume of ventilation air.

FLOOR AREA VENTILATION COMPUTATION

The second common ventilation computation depends on the room floor area. A typical code requirement is 0.5 to 12 cubic feet of air per minute per

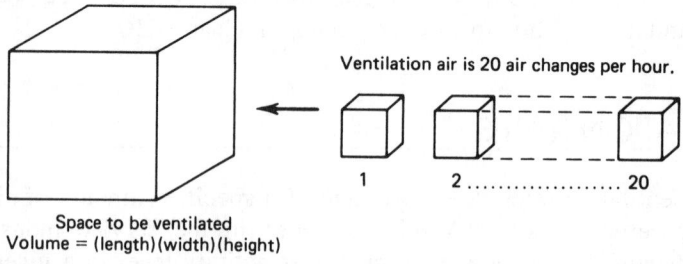

Ventilation air is 20 air changes per hour.

1   2 20

Space to be ventilated
Volume = (length)(width)(height)

A code requires 20 air changes per hour for a meeting room that is 30 feet (9.1 meters) wide, 60 feet (18.3 meters) long, and 10 feet (3.0 meters) high.

Ventilation rate = room volume × air changes
= 30 × 60 × 10 × 20 = 360,000 cubic feet per hour
(= 91.1 × 18.3 × 3.0 ×20 = 9991.8 cubic meters per hour)

FIGURE 9.1 Room volume ventilation computation.

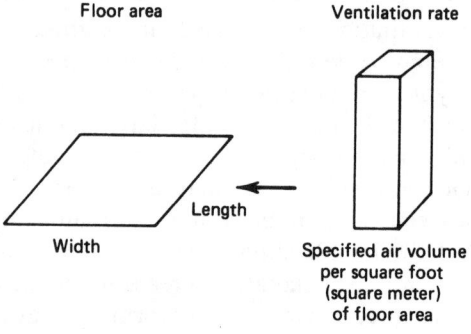

Floor area   Ventilation rate

Length

Width   Specified air volume
per square foot
(square meter)
of floor area

Refer to Fig. 9.1 for room-size data.

The ventilation rate is 6 cubic feet per square foot per minute (109 cubic meters per square meter per hour).

Ventilation rate = (floor area) × (ventilation rate)
=30 × 60 × 6 = 10,800 cubic feet per minute
(= 9.1 × 18.3 × 109 = 18,151.7 cubic meters per hour)

FIGURE 9.2 Floor area ventilation computation.

square foot (2.78 to 66.84 cubic meters per hour per square meter) of floor area. Figure 9.2 illustrates this method for the same space shown in Figure 9.1. These ventilation rates could be increased for the same reasons indicated for the previous example.

Many codes require that both room volume and floor area ventilation computations must be used to determine the ventilation rate. If you were the manager, how much air would you provide to the room? You should choose the larger of the two results because it satisfies both methods. You do not add both results.

OCCUPANT METHOD VENTILATION COMPUTATION

Some codes base the ventilation requirement on the number of occupants in a room. In some cases, the government agency inspector and the manager must reach a compromise with respect to the number of workers, patients, clients, or customers that may occupy a given space at any one time. (For example, in a foodservice kitchen, food servers are continuously moving back and forth from the dining room to the kitchen.) It would be very expensive to design a variable system that would automatically adjust to changing worker and customer levels. Local fire codes may specify the maximum number of people that can occupy a given space; in other cases, a health department inspector may set the maximum number of foodservice employees working in a specific area, and this is used as a ventilation occupancy base. The occupant method computation is shown in Figure 9.3.

Now, if a code specifies that all three of the previous methods must be satisfied, what does the manager do? As in the previous case, someone must determine all three ventilation requirements; then it is up to management to ensure that the largest amount of air is always provided. Once again, the largest amount of air will satisfy all three requirements.

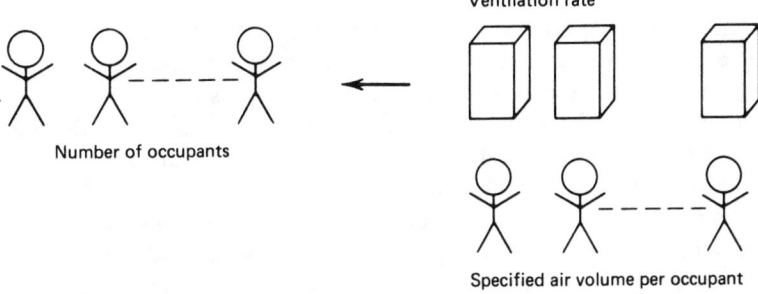

The room indicated in Fig. 9.1 will hold about 175 people. The ventilation rate is 10 cubic feet of air per minute per person (17 cubic meters per hour per person).

Ventilation rate = (number of occupants) × (ventilation rate)
= 175 × 10 = 1750 cubic feet per minute
(= 175 × 17 = 2975 cubic meters per hour)

FIGURE 9.3 Occupant method ventilation computation.

EQUIPMENT VENTILATION COMPUTATION

The final method for determining ventilation air depends on the types of equipment in a given area. This method usually applies to mechanical-equipment rooms, foodservice kitchens, and production areas. The volume of air depends on one or more of the following factors: physical size of the equipment, energy consumption rating, energy output rating, makeup air requirements (air required for gas or oil appliances), fire ordinances, safety requirements, construction of the building, and moisture being discharged from appliances. The list could lead to very complicated determinations of ventilation air. Yet management must ensure that all conditions are satisfied. Generally, the number and types of appliances are the primary factor in determining the ventilation rate for a foodservice kitchen. An example of this computation is shown in Appendix 10.

VENTILATION SYSTEMS

Once management has determined the proper amount of ventilation air, it must now select a system that will provide that amount of air. The architect or heating/cooling/ventilating engineer will design and specify the system components; there are several systems that could be used to provide the correct amount of air. The manager must be aware of the characteristics and limitations of these systems in order to make the proper selection. The manager is the one who has to maintain and operate the system after the architect and contractor finish their work and who is responsible for the output of the system, the right amount of clean, comfortable air to keep customers happy and employees productive.

The normal ventilation system consists of a network of air ducts that provide a path from the outside of the space to be ventilated to the space and back to the outside again. All modern systems use fans to move air. Older systems, especially in institutional buildings, some hospitals, and hotels, were dependent on natural-ventilation schemes that are now generally prohibited by ventilation codes. If not actually prohibited, they result in poor air distribution, questionable ventilation rates, and poor or nonexistent air filtration, at the same time requiring large amounts of costly building space (square feet [square meters] of floor space or cubic feet [cubic meters] of space volume).

CENTRAL VENTILATION SYSTEMS

A central ventilation system is shown in Figure 9.4. Figure 9.5 shows a complete system that can be used for heating, cooling, moisture control, air filtration, fresh air, exhaust air, recirculated air, combined fresh and recirculated air, and a heat exchanger between the exhaust-air and fresh-air supply.

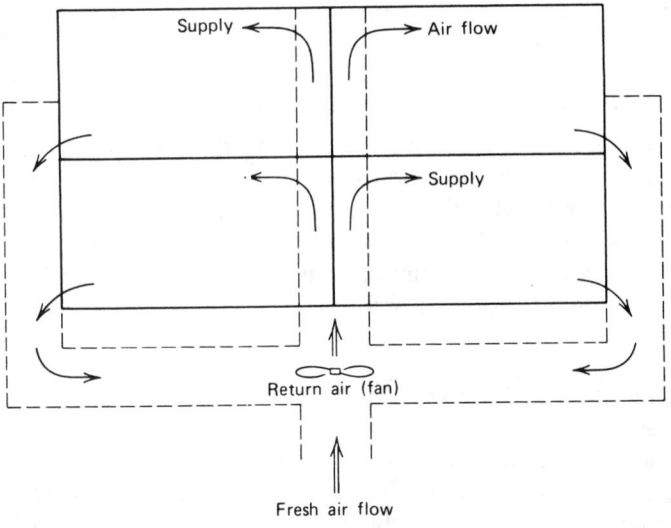

FIGURE 9.4 Central ventilation system for a building.

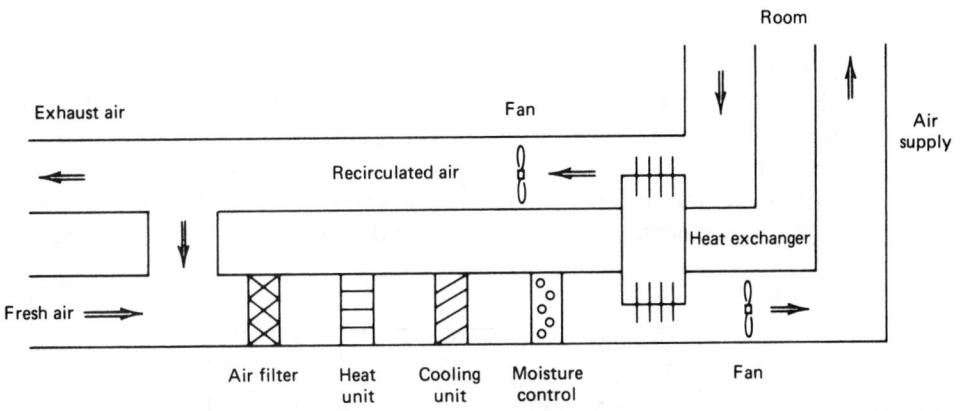

FIGURE 9.5 Ventilation system for complete environment control.

The various features in Figure 9.5 are optional, but they indicate how one system can be used for year-round environment control. This represents the ultimate system for modern building design.

The layout and configuration of the system appear very complex when several rooms are grouped together with a minimal number of heating and cooling units, air filtration units, and fans. Although a central layout is very practical, its application is limited when rooms, such as guest rooms, are to be opened or closed at random. If full or nearly full occupancy (more than

90 percent) is assured, the central ventilation/heating/cooling system is highly recommended.

Central ventilation is cost effective. Figure 9.6 shows a central ventilation system with separate room heating and cooling elements. With this installation, ventilation air moves through all the rooms at all times. Allowing air movement through all rooms eliminates a stale-air problem, which frequently develops with other ventilation systems. Although this system (Figure 9.6) is more costly to install than a central heating and cooling system, its energy cost can be minimized when rooms are not used. This is a very common system for smaller properties.

ROOM VENTILATION SYSTEMS

Many managers favor the unit or room ventilation system because, if a mechanical system fails, only one room is affected. When a central system fails, everything stops. With a room ventilation system, the engineer can repair the affected unit the next day; with a central system, an engineer must be on duty all the time to keep the entire system in operation. This can be very costly for a 150-room facility. Figure 9.7 shows a room ventilation system.

ZONE VENTILATION SYSTEMS

A third alternative offers some of the advantages of both the central and the room ventilation systems. The manager may select, install, or convert to a zone system for ventilation, heating, and cooling. It will cost more than the central system to install but less than the room system. Its maintenance and energy requirements are usually less than the room system but more than the

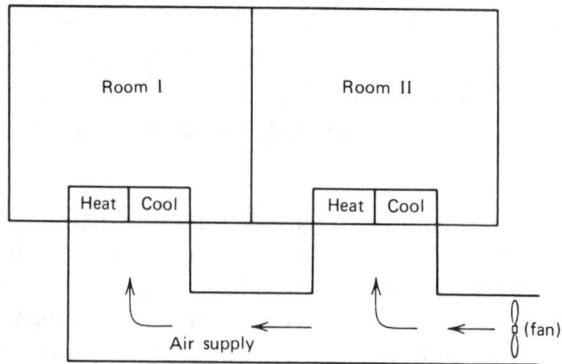

FIGURE 9.6 Ventilation system with separate heating and cooling elements in each room.

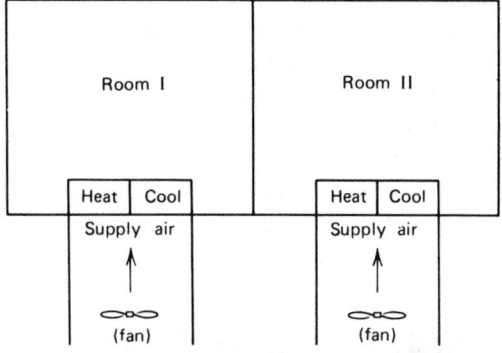

FIGURE 9.7   Separate ventilation system for each room.

central system, especially when occupancy or total building use is high. It is commonly used in modern buildings and frequently recommended for hospitality buildings. Figure 9.8 shows the zone system.

However, management must be very careful when using zoned sections of the building. Each level, or floor, of guest rooms is normally placed on a zoned ventilation, heating, and air-conditioning subsystem. For example, the following situation frequently develops in a lodging establishment. If

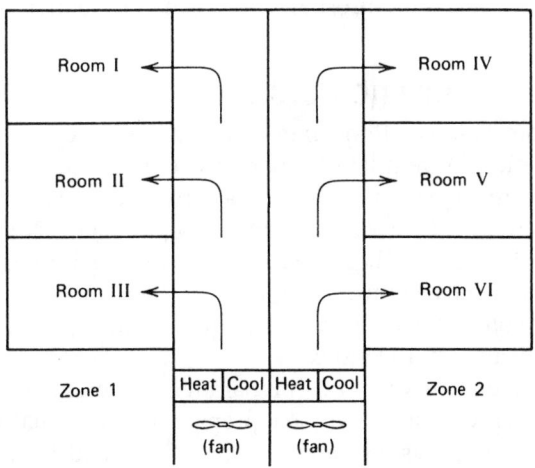

Installation of fan and heat/cool unit for a group of rooms with zoned ventilation

FIGURE 9.8   Zoned ventilation system.

one room is occupied on that floor, the ventilation, heating, and cooling systems are activated not only for the single occupied room but for each room on that level. If there are still unoccupied rooms at other levels in the hotel, why should a new level be opened for one or two occupied rooms? The $80 room revenue from one room is quickly lost when the total zoned system is placed in operation: This could cost from $7 to $8 per day per guest room.[2] Thus, 15 guest rooms would represent a total cost of $105 to $120. The example indicates that even at $80 revenue per room, two guest rooms must be sold just to recover the cost of heating or cooling that floor.

MINIMUM FRESH AIR REQUIREMENTS

During the 1970s and 1980s, ventilation rates were reduced to minimize energy requirements. Also, during this time period, new buildings were designed to be "airtight," that is, designed with minimum air infiltration (windows, doors, and walls). Recirculated air utilization was maximized to reduce air heating and cooling requirements. These design changes frequently contributed to indoor air quality problems (or "sick building syndrome").[3]

At the present time, the American Society of Heating, Refrigeration, and Air Conditioning Engineers (ASHRAE) recommends that 900 to 1200 cubic feet of air per hour (25 to 33.6 cubic meters per hour) be brought into the building for every occupant. This fresh air, if properly distributed within the building, should eliminate potential indoor air quality problems and maintain high levels of comfort and employee productivity.

KITCHEN VENTILATION SYSTEMS

The room volume, floor area, and number-of-occupant computations may be specified in ventilation codes for commercial foodservice kitchens. In addition, management should be aware that special and separate ventilation may be required for selected kitchen appliances. Normally, appliances and devices that give off heat and/or steam are required to have separate exhaust ventilation subsystems. Examples of these special appliances frequently include automatic dish-washing equipment, fryers, ranges, grills, broilers, steamers, and steam kettles.

Equipment for vegetable preparation, beverage dispensing, refrigeration, pot and pan washing, and meat preparation is normally excluded from separate ventilation system requirements. Oven and baking equipment requirements, as well as requirements for other types of equipment, vary with local ordinances. It is the manager's responsibility to know what the requirements are and how to satisfy them.

All kitchen ventilation codes assume that the manager or owner knows that air cannot be recirculated from the kitchen to other building sections.

Frequently, a percentage of the kitchen supply air can be taken from dining areas. This is done because the dining area is normally cooled and because exhausting this air through the kitchen will assist in keeping kitchen temperatures low. Most managers know that it can be costly to air-cool kitchens, which have very concentrated heat loads. This is why additional ventilation must be provided in kitchens.

Kitchens are normally maintained at a slightly negative atmospheric pressure. This keeps air constantly flowing into the kitchen from other building areas in order to confine odors and smoke to the kitchen. The slightly negative pressure is created by designing the ventilation system so that it exhausts more air than the amount being supplied. Depending on the volume of the room, exhaust air exceeds supply air by 1 to 5 percent; a larger percentage is used for small rooms and a lower percentage for large rooms. The next two sections show how this is done.

Ventilator Hoods

Figures 9.9 and 9.10 show two ventilation systems that can be used in food-service kitchens to produce negative kitchen pressure. (The scheme shown in Figure 9.7 could also be used if local ventilation subsystems are used for certain units of equipment.) Figure 9.9 illustrates kitchen equipment with its own ventilator hood, effective for that unit of equipment only, a system that is allowed in some areas. Each ventilator hood must be connected to a plenum exhaust duct (one large central duct receiving exhaust air from several ventilator hoods) and must be equipped with a grease filter. Manage-

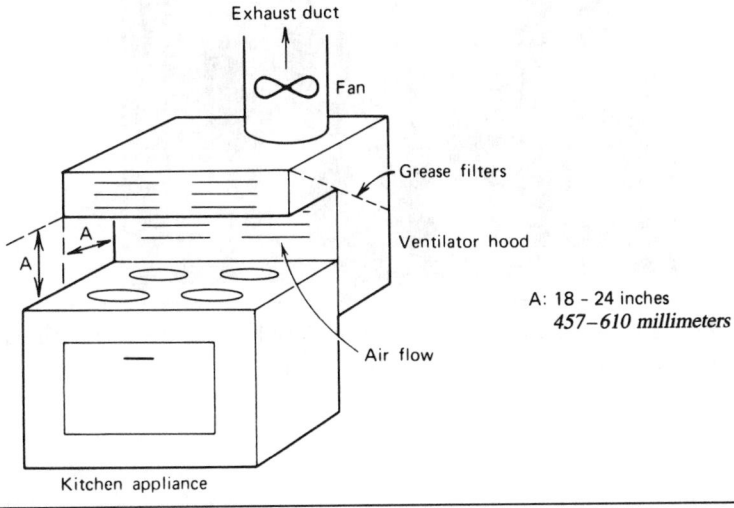

FIGURE 9.9   Ventilator hood for a kitchen appliance.

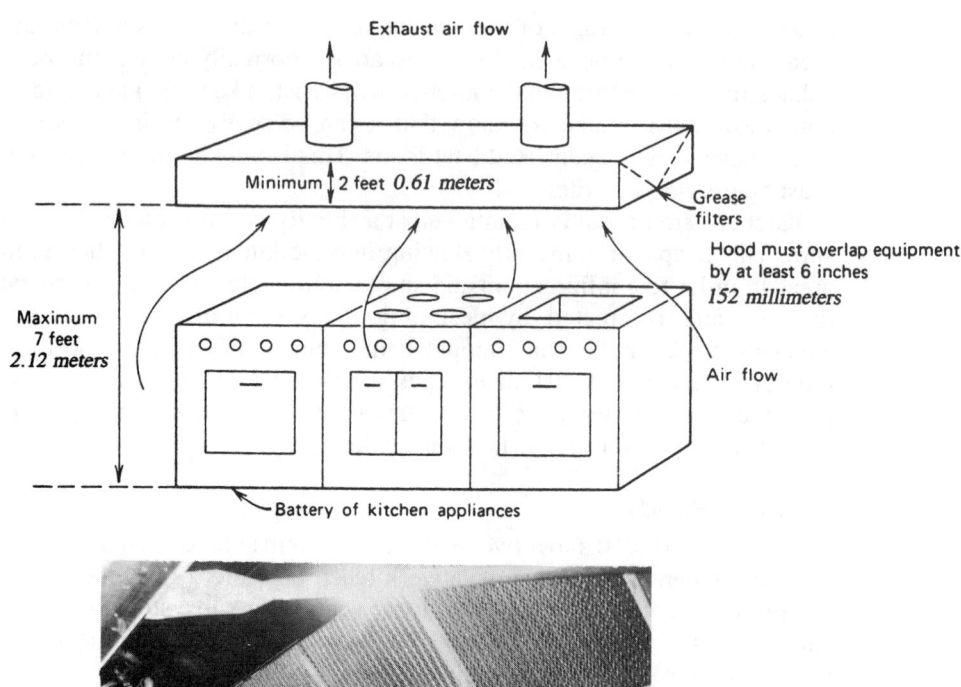

FIGURE 9.10 Canopy hood installation. Note the grease filters and the fire suppression nozzle at upper left.

ment can specify that grease filters should be physically small enough to fit in its automatic dish-washing machines. Filters should be cleaned each day, at the end of the daily dish-washing operations. An automatic fire extinguisher is usually required in each ventilator unit.

The manager can specify that all ventilator hoods must meet Underwriters Laboratories (UL) standards. Underwriters Laboratories has established the sizes of ventilator hoods and the maximum distances they can be placed from the surface of the equipment. It also specifies grease filter sizes, exhaust-opening dimensions, and minimum air flow. As each piece of equipment has its own custom-designed ventilator subsystem, it is not necessary to describe in detail the various sizes and shapes of the units. You must be certain that the local code allows ventilator hoods and that they have been approved by UL.

Canopy Hoods

Management's second alternative is to require canopy hood exhausts. Figure 9.10 diagrams a canopy hood exhaust system that is almost universally accepted by ventilation codes in the United States and in many foreign countries. Again, UL has prescribed certain minimal requirements for these units. Equipment that must have supplemental ventilation is frequently grouped together and placed under one hood. This technique greatly lowers the total cost of the canopy exhaust system. The canopy hood must also be equipped with a grease filter, and the hood must be connected to a plenum exhaust ventilation system. Separate fire suppression systems are frequently required for these units (see Chapter 6).

VENTILATION DUCTS

Ventilation systems require fans, which will be discussed in the next chapter, air transmission ducts, filters, and duct openings in the ventilated rooms.

Duct Insulation

Since many ventilation systems are included with heating and cooling systems, an excellent management decision is to insulate the air ducts with 1 to 2 inches (25.4 to 50.8 millimeters) of a high-quality insulator. Many round ducts are available with insulation affixed to them. Rectangular sheet-metal ducts are usually not insulated when purchased, and insulation must be added when the ducts are fabricated. The payback period for duct insulation is frequently less than one year. If ducts are long, the heat transmission losses and gains can be very high and can reduce the operating efficiency of the entire heating and cooling system. Some round ducts are constructed of fiberglass-type insulation by the manufacturer and have the additional advantage of noise absorption.

Pressure Losses

Most modern ventilation systems have fans for both supply and exhaust air. This provides for a positive air movement system throughout the building. The amount of air that can be handled by a duct depends on three factors: duct air velocity, duct size, and duct resistance, or friction. Duct resistance varies with duct size, air speed, and construction materials. Small ducts with high air velocities (speed) will normally have a high resistance to air flow. Resistance is also increased by adding more turns and loops in the duct system. You should be aware that high duct resistance means that larger-horsepower fans must be used to move the required amount of air for a room.

Air Velocity

Air volume, air velocity, and duct size (area) are interrelated (volume = velocity × duct area). The ventilation code heating and cooling requirements will specify the volume of air the system must handle. The velocity of air through ducts should vary between 300 and 4000 feet per minute (1.52 and 20.32 meters per second). Lower air velocities, with lower noise levels, are used for guest, patient, and client rooms. Higher velocities can be used in food production areas and mechanical-equipment rooms, where the employee activity levels are much higher and the users of the room will probably not be affected by high-velocity air and its noise level. In other areas, air velocity can vary between 500 and 2500 feet per minute (2.54 and 12.70 meters per second). Knowing the volume and velocity of air helps in determining the required duct size.

The preceding paragraph gives two recommended air speeds. If ventilation noise is a potential problem, then management should specify the lower air speed range because it generates less noise. If noise is not a problem, then system cost is reduced by specifying the higher air speed range, which results in smaller ducts. And if some noise can be tolerated, as in public spaces including dining rooms or where public address systems may be used, then management should select an air speed range somewhere in the middle, which has moderate installation costs. Noise will become a definite problem whenever air speed exceeds 3000 feet per minute (15.24 meters per second).

Management should also realize that duct heat gains or losses (especially when cooling the building) depend on the duct size. Larger ducts have higher heat gains and losses (regardless of insulation). This is another reason why you should always specify faster-moving air when possible. Associated with faster-moving air, however, is noise. Management must weigh noise against installation and operating energy cost.

REGISTERS AND GRILLS

The supply duct terminates in the room at a register. A register is a screen, or grate-type opening or air diffuser, that is visible within the room. The register has an adjustment feature, a damper, that allows the engineer to control the amount and direction of air flow to a room. Register efficiency depends on the ratio of free or open area (area allowing air flow) to the total or gross area of the register. If the percentage of open area is less than the size of the duct, air must speed up to move through the register. This increase usually generates noise. All you have to do is to specify that the register free area should be equal to the size of the duct. This will generally eliminate noise and reduce air flow resistance problems. In many cases, this free area can be 80 to 90 percent of the duct size if the duct air speed is less than 2000 feet per minute (10.16 meters per second).

Grills (screen or grate-type openings) are used on exhaust ducts. Dampers are not recommended for grills.

AIR FILTRATION

Although many ordinances do not require air filtration devices on fresh-air ducts, management has a responsibility to provide clean air for guests, clients, members, and employees. Therefore, fresh outside air should be filtered. All recirculated (nonfresh) air should also be filtered. Smoky air should not be recycled from one building section to another, especially to guest or patient rooms. A proper air filter can remove smoke. In addition, some sections of the building may produce excessive odors. Should you, as manager, allow this odor-polluted air to recycle throughout the building? If you are concerned about your customers, definitely not.

Most codes require some type of grease filter on exhaust ducts that lead from kitchen ventilator and canopy hoods. Air filtration has been perfected to such a point that small particles measured in microns (small fractions of an inch [millimeter]) can be effectively removed from air. Frequently, there are fewer air pollutants in building exhaust air than in fresh air, yet many ordinances require high percentages of fresh air. Fresh air can be more costly to purify than some recirculated air.

The type of air filter you select depends on the impurities you want to remove from the air.

DRY FILTERS

A very common filter that satisfies many public space ventilation codes is the dry filter. Its air flow resistance is relatively low; hence, the energy requirement to move air through it is low. It is not very effective, however, for small pollutant particles (odors, some airborne dust, or smoke). Air is forced through a series of openings, and particles are trapped within a mesh or screen, often made of fiberglass. When the filter is dirty, it is discarded.

Its effectiveness is increased slightly when it is treated with oil or certain other chemicals.

Many managers are now using reusable dry filters. These filters consist of a series of screens and are cleaned by washing. Their resistance to air flow is similar to that of the oil filter described in the next section, but they are not as effective as the disposable dry or oil filters. Reusable dry filters are also used as grease filters in canopy and ventilator hoods.

OIL-TREATED FILTERS

Oil filters or chemically treated filters are a little more effective than dry filters. They consist of a series of screens that are treated, or washed, with oil or chemicals. Air particles strike the screen and adhere to it. The filter is cleaned by washing and has a long life. Its resistance to air flow is fairly low, except when it is dirty.

WATER-SPRAY FILTERS

If smoke is a problem, water-spray filters are recommended. This filter also humidifies air and may lower air temperature (dry-bulb), thus cooling the air. Impurities are wetted by a water spray and rinsed from the air. The filter also removes dust and limited amounts of pollen and has moderate efficiency. Since water is sprayed against the direction of air flow, its resistance to air flow is moderate, but one must consider that it does more than filter air. You should also be aware that water (another energy source) is required and that electrically driven pumps (additional energy) are required for filtering. Thus, total energy requirements are high when compared with dry filters.

ELECTRONIC FILTERS

If you want almost pure, healthful air, the electronic (electrostatic precipitator) filter should be specified. It consists of a series of electrically charged grids, or screens. As air particles move through the screens, they receive an electrical charge and are attracted to the next grid, or screen, that has an opposite electrical charge. They have very low air resistance and a relatively low operating cost. They are cleaned by washing. Their chief disadvantage is a high installation cost. Although they are effective for most building-generated dirt, including plant pollens, they may not remove chemical pollutants from outside air.

Electronic filters will remove smoke from the air. Some ventilation, health, and building codes have recognized these filters; when properly installed within a room, such as a dining room, it is possible to mix smokers and nonsmokers within the same room. Recirculated air is filtered within the space. Fresh air is supplied per code requirements and exhaust air is filtered only if it is recirculated (another filter is required in this case).

OTHER FILTERS

If you have special pollutant problems such as odors, you may have to specify a special filter. These can be used with any of the filters previously discussed. Overall air-filtering efficiency increases when a combination air filter system is used. These combination systems are costly to install, and they increase air filtration system operating cost. These special filter combinations are not commonly used except for small rest rooms where odor problems may develop.

GREASE FILTERS

Most ordinances require grease filtration on kitchen exhaust systems. Metallic grease filters located in ventilator and canopy hoods remove a significant portion of kitchen grease. The filters are cooler than the grease condensation temperature, so grease vapors are cooled and condense on the filter. They have been very effective in controlling fire hazards in exhaust systems (see Chapter 6).

POLLUTION CONTROL FILTERS

Management may be required to install special filters on its heating plants. The purpose of these filters is to reduce discharges to the outside environment. Electrostatic devices can be used, which are very effective but very costly. Centrifugal filter devices will meet some pollution standards. Cartridge filters have met with some success and are becoming more efficient as improved high-capacity trapping screens are being developed. When gas (NG or LPG) is available, abundant, and can be legally used as a grease afterburner, it acts as an effective grease filter. Air grease washers have also been used in many areas and have met local air quality standards. However, you should be aware that each year new types of grease filters and other special filters are being developed and tested. The objectives of these new devices are to reduce filter installation cost and lower operating-energy requirements.

SMOKE-FREE ENVIRONMENT

Creating a smoke-free environment is a building renovation project. Smoke, especially tobacco smoke, is absorbed by materials, including painted surfaces, and is continuously emitted from these surfaces for extended time periods. A smoke-free environment is not established by banning smoking one day and calling the environment smoke free the next day.

In general, the creation of a smoke-free environment starts with a new building where smoking has never been allowed. If tobacco smoking has been allowed in a building or a building section, the following must be done before it can be called a smoke-free room or building. All fabrics and plastic-type coverings must be replaced—not washed or dry cleaned. This includes carpet, wall coverings, upholstered furniture fabrics, window drapes, curtains, and shades. If there is an absorption-type ceiling (sound absorbers of any type), they must be removed and replaced. Painted surfaces must be thoroughly washed and repainted. The ventilation ducts must be cleansed. All lighting fixtures must be cleansed of tobacco smoke and residue. In hotel guest rooms, mattresses must be replaced as well as all linens.

There cannot be any air flow from a smoke area to a smoke-free area. All exhaust ventilation ducts from smoke-allowed areas must discharge to the outside or can be recirculated back to the smoke-allowed areas. Exhaust air from the smoke-free areas can be recirculated back to either smoke-free or smoke-allowed areas. Creating and maintaining a smoke-free environment in areas where smoking was previously allowed or in buildings where smoking is allowed is very costly.

VENTILATION MAINTENANCE

Managers usually find that once the correct ventilation system is installed in a building, the maintenance of the ventilation system is relatively simple. A minimal amount of managerial maintenance can and will provide years of satisfactory ventilation service, low-cost operation, and an efficient system. The potential effects of a ventilation system on customers, patients, and clients are difficult to measure, and can only be effectively measured when the system is not operating properly. The effects of proper ventilation on employees can be significant: Productivity and morale are greatly influenced by comfortable temperature and moisture distribution within a room; even more important is proper air movement within confined spaces where employees must work for prolonged periods. These are primary management concerns.

Managerial ventilation maintenance includes keeping air filters changed or cleaned, electric-drive motors and fans in good condition, motor and fan bearings greased and oiled, ducts free from vibration, duct insulation in good repair, duct interiors clean, and the driving mechanism between the motor and the fan in excellent repair. If belt-driven connections are used between the fan and the motor, belt slippage must be kept to a minimum, as each percentage decrease of driving efficiency lowers the overall efficiency of the system by 1 percent or more.

An energy-management system may also include ventilation control. All of the following can be controlled with an appropriate EMS: Variable ventilation rates, obtained by using variable-speed electric motors driving ventilation fans. Variable mixtures of fresh and recirculated air, used to optimize air enthalpy (heat content), which results in reducing both heating and cooling requirements (this concept is fully discussed in Chapter 10). Stopping and starting the flow of ventilation air to selected building areas; occupancy sensors are used to detect if these spaces are occupied. Life safety; if combustion by-products are detected in the space or air ducts, the ventilation is shut off.

An EMS is most appropriate for kitchen and mechanical-room ventilation. Some ventilation codes specify air requirements for operating equipment, and air flow to these rooms must be increased when additional equipment units are in operation; EMS is thus connected to all equipment components and controls ventilation air by operating additional fans or by increasing fan air output through variable-speed electric fan driving motors.

SUMMARY

Management must be aware of local ventilation codes and carefully select the most practical ventilation system for each room or building section. It should be aware of, and minimize, factors that increase ventilation requirements.

The manager must also select an appropriate air filter for each building ventilation system. While air filter maintenance is minimal, it must be performed periodically to ensure clean air flow.

Management should also be aware that a smoke-free environment may become the accepted environment in the very near future (before the year 2000). Hence, if you are opening a new building in the next 5 years, it should be opened as a smoke-free building, or smoking should be restricted to well-defined areas. If you must convert to a smoke-free environment, a complete renovation is necessary to produce the desired effect. Building maintenance and housekeeping should be reduced in a smoke-free environment.

REFERENCES

1. Ventilation codes can be obtained upon request from the appropriate governmental agencies.

2. Laventhal & Horwath, CPA, *U.S. Lodging Industry,* Philadelphia (annual edition); Pannel, Kerr, Forster, CPA, *Trends in the Hotel/Motel Business,* New York (annual edition).

3. Houston Lighting and Power Company, Guide to *Commercial Energy Efficiency,* Houston, October 1992.

QUESTIONS/PROBLEMS

1. A room is 40 feet (12.2 meters) wide, 75 feet (22.9 meters) long, and 15 feet (4.6 meters) high. It has a summer heat gain equal to the winter heat loss of 160,000 Btu (46.880 watts) per hour. Determine and compare the various ventilation procedures for the room if the following requirements must be satisfied:

   a. 15 air changes per hour
   b. 8 cubic feet per square foot per minute (1146.4 cubic meters per square meter per hour)
   c. The room will hold 250 people; and each person must be supplied with 8 cubic feet of air per minute (113.4 cubic meters per hour)

2. Discuss and compare the following effects on ventilation and room/building environment:

   a. Central ventilation
   b. Room ventilation
   c Zone ventilation
   d. Use of fresh air in urban areas
   e. Influence of nonsmoking ordinances in public buildings
   f. Reduction of internal building temperatures during the heating season
   g. Increase of internal building temperatures during the cooling season
   h. Building heat gain

3. Determine the details of the local code or ordinance that establishes ventilation requirements for a lodging, foodservice, health-care, or club facility.

4. Determine the ventilation requirement for your classroom based on the appropriate section of a local code or ordinance.

5. Determine the type of ventilation system (central, room, or zone) that is most typical in your local lodging, foodservice, health-care, or club buildings.

6. Your instructor may assign this project along with Question 5 above. Determine the types of filters used by a local lodging, foodservice, health-care, or club building. Also determine why these types are used in the different building sections. Can you recommend more effective filters for this building? If so, explain your recommendations.

7. Discuss the effect of nonsmoking sections on the ventilation and air filtration requirements for the building you investigated in Question 6 above.

C H A P T E R 10

Courtesy of Howard Johnson's Hotels.

MANAGEMENT OF
AIR-CONDITIONING SYSTEMS

ABSTRACT

The heart of the HVAC (heating, ventilation, and air-conditioning) system is the air-conditioning component. It is the most costly component to install. It is greatly affected by building construction techniques and materials. Its air quality output can have very good or very poor effects on employees and customers. Its operating cost can be very high. Its maintenance requirements are generally the highest of all electromechanical systems within the building. Its design and use in the hospitality industry have added several months of operation to businesses in the warm and especially desert climates of the world. Property air-conditioning systems are assumed by customers and it is up to the manager to ensure that the systems will deliver quality air.

Key words: *absorption cooling system; air conditioning; air cooling; appliance heat gain; axial-flow fans; centrifugal fans; chilled-water compression system; comfort zone; dehumidifier; dew-point temperature; direct-expansion (DX) refrigerated air system; dry-bulb temperature; EER (energy efficiency ratio); enthalpy; enthalpy control; evaporative cooler; exfiltration; filter; gravity dampers; humidifier; HVAC; infiltration heat gain; latent heat of air; occupant heat load; positive pressure; precooler; preheater; psychometric chart; recirculated air; refrigerated air; reheater; relative humidity; residual heat load; SEER (seasonal energy efficiency ratio); sensible heat of air; solar heat load; thermostat control; total heat of air; transmission heat load; VAV; ventilation heat load; wet-bulb temperature; wind-chill effect.*

INTRODUCTION

The use of building cooling systems in the hospitality industry has greatly increased management's physical plant responsibility. If you are managing a modern building, it undoubtedly has some type of air-cooling system, even if it is only needed for a month or two during the entire year. Customers expect and demand a comfortable environment. Air cooling reduces the seasonal nature of many lodging and foodservice businesses.

AIR-CONDITIONING TERMS

There are three terms that describe the systems used to cool air: air conditioning, air cooling, and refrigerated air. Although some people think that these terms all have the same meaning, in fact each process produces a different building environment.

AIR CONDITIONING

Any treatment of the environment air within a building is *air conditioning*. Technically, a fan placed in a room to circulate air meets the air-conditioning definition. Filtering air is conditioning the air; heating is conditioning the air; cooling, humidifying, or dehumidifying are kinds of air conditioning. Thus, the process of changing any one of several properties of the air can be correctly classified as air conditioning.

AIR COOLING

Air cooling is any process that reduces air temperature. There are several air temperature reduction techniques. A fan blowing air over a bucket of ice water can be called air cooling. Evaporative coolers, or swamp coolers (actually water-cooling towers, which were explained in Chapter 8), are air-cooling techniques. The evaporative device lowers air temperature and increases the moisture content in the air. At one time, people living in dry desert climates hung water-saturated cloth over the open windows of structures. As hot, dry winds blew air through and around the water-saturated cloth hanging in a window, water was absorbed by the hot, dry air, thus cooling it. The method may have been primitive, but the effect was refreshing.

REFRIGERATED AIR

Refrigerated air is produced by a mechanical refrigeration cycle. The primary refrigeration systems are vapor compression and absorption cycles (see Chapter 8). The refrigerated-air system is capable of providing cool comfortable air at all times. It is also the most costly air-cooling system to install and operate.

HUMAN COMFORT TERMS

Four terms have been identified and are used to measure two fundamental heat properties of air: dry-bulb temperature, dew-point temperature, wet-bulb temperature, and relative humidity. These terms will be defined and discussed in the following sections. The basic heat properties of air are sensible heat and latent heat. Sensible heat refers to the hotness of air (temperature), or the rate of movement of air molecules. Latent heat refers to the moisture (water vapor) content of air. The comfort level of air depends on its sensible- and latent-heat contents.

DRY-BULB TEMPERATURE

The *dry-bulb temperature* is a measure of the rate of movement of air molecules. It measures the sensible heat of air. A conventional thermometer is used to measure dry-bulb temperature. As air molecules move faster, they have more energy and contain more sensible heat. See Figure 10.1. They strike the thermometer faster and more frequently, causing the thermometer to register higher temperatures. There is no common dry-bulb temperature that clearly divides uncomfortable from comfortable. This is why additional measurement terms are required.

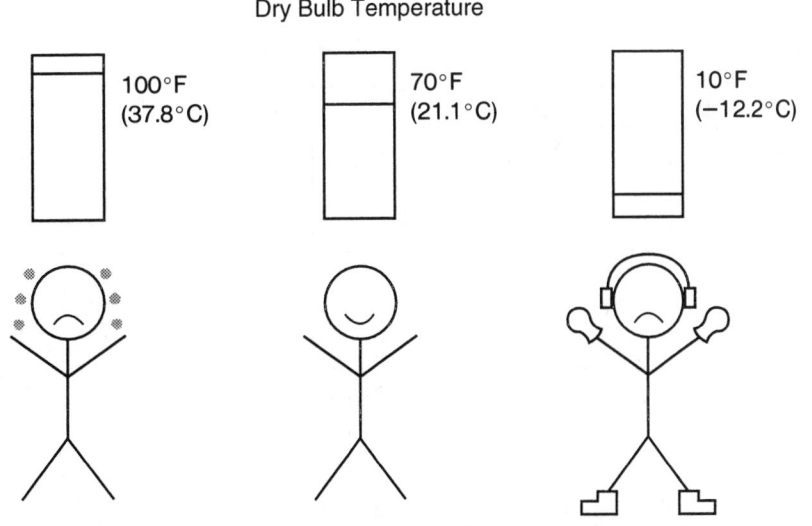

FIGURE 10.1   Dry-bulb temperature effects.

DEW-POINT TEMPERATURE

Whereas dry-bulb temperature measures the sensible heat of air, its latent-heat content is measured by the *dew-point temperature*. This is the temperature at which moisture will start to condense from the air. If the dew-point temperature is high, there is a large amount of moisture in the air.

High moisture levels can be very uncomfortable because the air's ability to absorb additional moisture is reduced. Your body loses heat through body moisture losses; and if the air cannot absorb this moisture you may feel uncomfortable. See Figure 10.2. This is one reason why dry air has a cooling effect. It is also the reason why we try to lower moisture levels during the summer to produce coolness and raise moisture levels during the winter to produce a warmer environment.

WET-BULB TEMPERATURE

One measure of the relationship between dry-bulb (sensible-heat) and dew-point (latent-heat) temperatures is the wet-bulb temperature. The *wet-bulb temperature* is a measure of the total heat content of the air (sensible plus latent heat). The wet-bulb temperature has various effects on people. Both high and low wet bulb temperatures are generally undesirable, as both can make individuals feel a moist warm or a dry cold; see Figure 10.3.

The wet-bulb temperature is measured in an unusual manner. The bulb end of a conventional mercury-in-glass thermometer is covered with a piece of cloth. The cloth is saturated with water, and the thermometer is exposed to the air. As the wet cloth loses moisture to the air, the temperature regis-

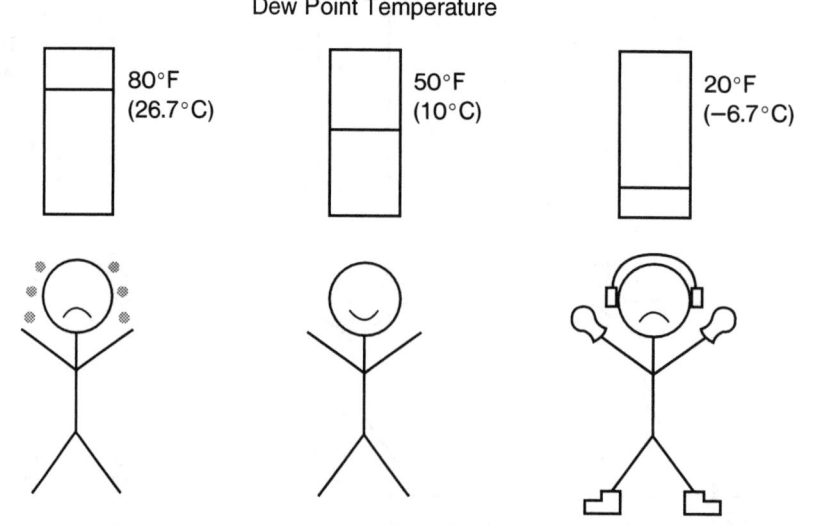

FIGURE 10.2 Dew-point temperature effects.

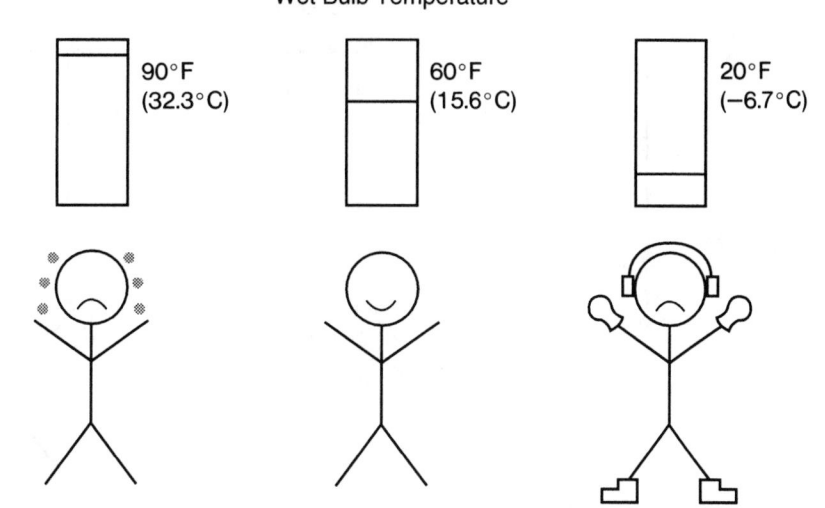

FIGURE 10.3 Wet-bulb temperature effects.

tered by the thermometer decreases. The wet-bulb temperature represents the lowest registered temperature that occurs when the moisture loss from the wet cloth is in equilibrium with the surrounding air. It is also the temperature that occurs when the moisture sensible-heat gain equals the water latent-heat loss to the air—hence, an equilibrium heat condition. It is a complex temperature relationship.

The wet-bulb temperature is relatively easy to measure. The next relationship, relative humidity, is easier to understand but is difficult to measure.

RELATIVE HUMIDITY

Many managers can quickly relate to two air comfort terms, temperature, which is actually the dry-bulb temperature, and relative humidity, often referred to simply as humidity.

The *relative humidity*, or, actually, percent relative humidity, relates two temperatures: dew point and dry bulb. The percent relative humidity is a ratio of the amount of moisture contained in a given volume of air (its dew point) to the maximum amount of moisture this air can hold at a given temperature (its dry bulb).

A low relative humidity means that the amount of moisture in the air is small, whereas a high relative humidity means that the air is holding a large amount of moisture. Either of these conditions can make you feel uncomfortable. See Figure 10.4. If the relative humidity is high (80 percent or higher), the ability of air to absorb moisture from your body is low. Therefore, you feel too warm during the summer when relative humidities are

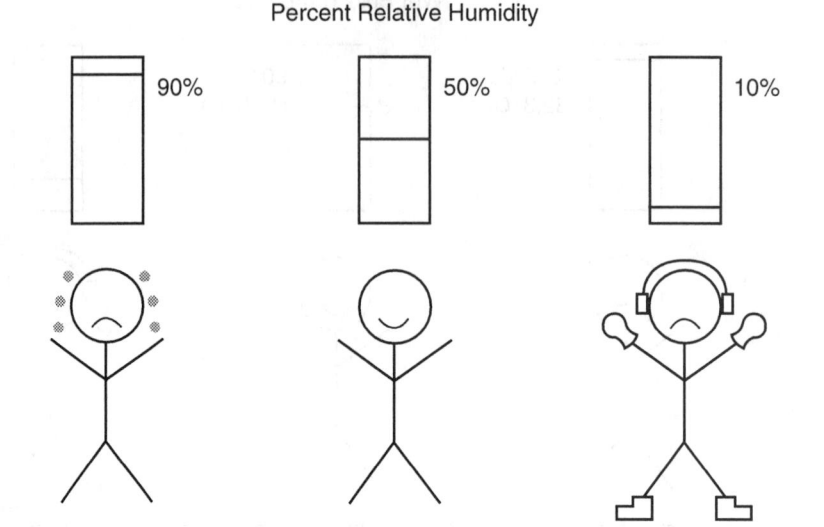

Percent Relative Humidity

FIGURE 10.4 Percent relative humidity effects.

high. Likewise, a high moisture level can make you feel warmer during the winter when relative humidities are low.

AIR MOVEMENT AND COMFORT

Most of you have probably heard of a wind-chill factor or index. The wind-chill factor is an equivalent comfort level that relates air speed and temperature. For example, if the outside temperature is about 0°F (−17.8°C) and if the wind is blowing at 40 miles per hour (64.4 kilometers per hour), this is equivalent to a temperature of about −40°F (−40°C). All this means is that you would feel as cold as if it were about −40°F (−40°C) and if there were no wind. Moving air makes you feel cooler. The wind-chill effect applies to both cold and warm environments. See Figure 10.5.

The ideal air movement rate is around 12 to 20 feet per minute (0.06 to 0.10 meters per second). A slower air movement is recommended in winter to reduce chill, and more rapid air movement in summer to increase chill. In the summer, a temperature of 78°F (25.6°C) can feel as comfortable as 75°F (23.9°C) if air is moving at about 16 feet per minute (0.08 meters per second). This slight air movement produces a 3°F (1.7°C) "chill."

TEMPERATURE AND MOISTURE EFFECTS ON CUSTOMERS AND EMPLOYEES

If a manager had customers who were all at the same age level and of the same sex, had the same social and economic backgrounds and experiences,

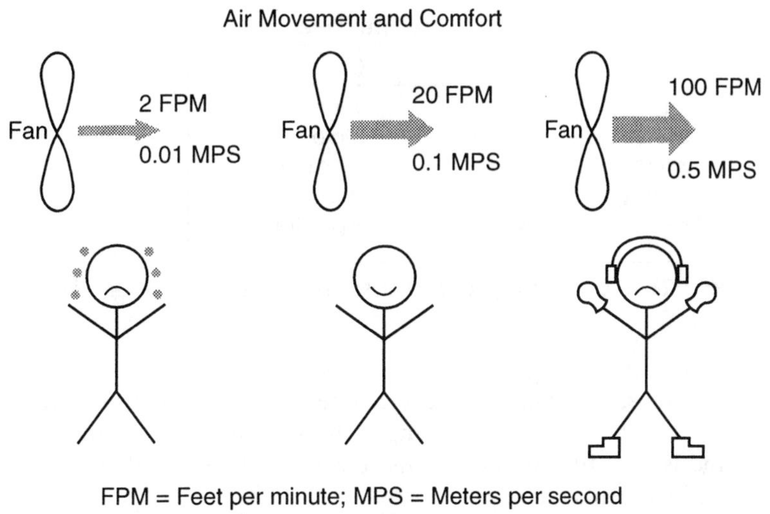

Air Movement and Comfort

FPM = Feet per minute; MPS = Meters per second

FIGURE 10.5 Air movement and comfort effects.

dressed the same, and consumed the same types of food, the manager could provide one building environment and all the customers would feel comfortable. Rarely, if ever, does this condition exist.

Generally, older people prefer higher building temperatures in the winter. Their comfort temperature in the summer depends on their dressing and eating habits, so it is difficult to establish a definite trend for summer building temperatures. Although many older people prefer higher summer building temperatures—75°F (23.9°C), rather than 72°F (22.2°C)—other older people are very sensitive to temperature.

The very young can quickly adjust to either cooler or warmer temperatures. People in the middle-age range are very sensitive to environment temperatures. Their comfortable temperature appears to depend on several factors, some of which are clothing, accustomed climate, genetic factors, activity level, personal health, diet, smoking habits, and beverage intake. Any of these factors or a combination of them may make a person inclined toward warmer or cooler temperatures.

Figure 10.6 provides some general guidelines that may be helpful in establishing environment temperatures for some hospitality industry building areas.

Lodging establishments are maintained at a variety of temperatures, depending on the activity level of the customers. The more active customers require lower temperatures. This rule is followed in all areas except the guest room. The bathroom of a guest room is generally warmer so that the facilities are warm to the touch. The bedroom portion is cooler so that the customers can sleep more comfortably.

Factor	Temperature	
	Warm	Cool
Age	Older	Young
Sex	Female	Male
Activity	Sitting	Working
Clothing	Light	Heavy
Diet	Low Calorie	High Calorie

FIGURE 10.6 Employee and customer temperature sensitivity.

Clubs, including foodservice operations and facilities, are probably maintained at much cooler temperatures than other segments of the service industries. Exceptions to this rule might be clubs that have older members and women's clubs.

Health-care facilities are usually maintained at higher cooling temperatures than any other segment of the service industries. The major reason is the amount and type of clothing worn by patients. Patients' rooms are maintained at higher temperatures because normally only sheets are used on beds. Other areas in hospitals can be maintained at lower cooling temperatures, especially in areas where patient and client use is minimal.

Nursing homes are also maintained at relatively warm temperatures because of the age of most of the clients. The temperature of the entire facility is almost constant. While this may be very comfortable for clients, the effect on employees is to lower their productivity, unless they are very young or are older.

Public space comfort control in institutional buildings is very difficult. The difficulty is compounded by two important factors. Management may be faced with a tug-of-war between the appropriate environmental conditions for workers and the customer or client environment, which may be totally different from that required by the employees. Thus, buildings may be relatively cool or warm. Classroom building temperatures are extremely variable. If the outside temperatures are very high, cool classroom buildings have a tendency to make students sleepy. Also, if the temperature is too high in a classroom, it could become very uncomfortable during class periods longer than, say, 50 minutes (0.83 hours).

Temperature can affect the productivity of employees. The general rules are very basic. Lower temperatures are required for high productivity in manual tasks. The reason is that the worker generates heat while performing heavy manual tasks and feels more comfortable as worker body heat is rejected at faster rates in cooler rooms. Lighter tasks are best performed at higher temperatures. Employee clothing also has a significant effect on optimal building temperature and worker productivity.

The guidelines in this section all assume relative humidity in the 30 to 70 percent range.

PSYCHOMETRIC CHART

The psychometric chart relates the three temperatures (dry bulb, dew point, and wet bulb) and relative humidity. To use the chart, you need to know only two of the four terms, for example, dry-bulb and wet-bulb temperatures and the other terms can be determined. The psychometric chart, how to use it, and applications to building air conditioning are shown in Appendix 11.

HEAT LOAD FACTORS

The cooling heat load depends on several heat sources: transmission and residual, solar, occupant, infiltration, appliance, and ventilation. An air-conditioning system is designed to remove the heat load, expressed in Btu per hour (watts per hour). The manager must realize that adding new heat sources to the building without making appropriate reductions in the building's heat load will strain the capacity of the system. Exceeding the system capacity generally results in an uncomfortable building environment.

The manager has some direct control over various building heat loads. Reducing the heat load reduces energy operating costs and equipment operating time, which reduces system maintenance and repair and increases equipment life (years before replacement). In order to control the heat load, the manager must have an understanding of how each heat source affects the heat load.

TRANSMISSION AND RESIDUAL HEAT LOADS

The transmission heat load is very similar to the winter heat transmission load. It depends on the interior and exterior temperatures, the heat transmission coefficient, and the surface areas exposed to the different temperatures. The transmission heat load is also related to two other heat loads—solar and residual.

The transmission heat load is based on an average-high outside temperature, the *design temperature*. If the walls and roof are heavily insulated, the heat transmission coefficient will be low and transmission heat gain minimal. The temperature difference (outside minus inside temperature) is not as great for cooling as it is for heating; so, for many sections of the country, optimal insulation thickness for heating may not be optimal for air cooling. In sections of the country where the cooling season is longer than the heating season and where summer temperature differences are greater than or equal to winter heating temperature differences, optimal insulation thickness is based on summer conditions. Management can use the optimal insulation model presented in Chapter 7 for determining the ideal insulation thickness for cooling. An example is shown in Appendix 11.

A building with a high heat transmission coefficient (U) has high heat gains; thus, if the maximum outside temperatures are reached at noon (1200 hours), the maximum heat gain occurs in the early afternoon. If the heat transmission coefficient is small, as for a heavily insulated building, the maximum heat gain may not occur until 6 P.M. (1800 hours), or later. This is why adobe structures are ideal in the desert. They are slow to warm up and slowly release their stored heat to the inside of the building, at a time when it is cooling off inside. (Recall that this was called passive solar heating in an earlier chapter.)

Closely related to the transmission heat gain is the building's residual load. The residual heat load is the heat contained within the building's furnishings and structural components. When the air-cooling system is first turned on, cooling energy must be provided to cool down the building's interior.

Wall and roof insulation, which is lightweight, has a low residual heat load, as do plastic-type lightweight furnishings. A building with a low residual heat load can be cooled in two hours or less, whereas a building with a high residual heat load, such as a concrete structure with upholstered furnishings and heavy drapes, may require four to six hours or longer to cool initially.

If an air-cooling system is continuously operated for 24 hours a day, the residual load has little effect on the cooling requirements. If the system is turned on and off on a frequent schedule, the residual load becomes important.

SOLAR HEAT LOAD

The solar heat is produced by direct and indirect solar heating of the building. While a solar heat gain is desirable during the heating season, its effects in summer can be very disruptive.

There are two solar heating effects. One effect produces instantaneous heat gains, as with glass surfaces (windows, doors, or walls). The other effect results when nonglass surfaces are heated by the sun.

Glass Surfaces

Much of the solar energy that strikes a glass surface will pass directly through it into the building. Some of the energy will be absorbed by the glass, which will radiate heat to the interior of the building, or the warm glass will heat building air by the convection heating process. Management can place exterior shields between the glass surface and the sun, which reduces or eliminates solar effects (recall radiation shields, which were discussed in Chapter 7). Mirror-tinted windows greatly reduce the instantaneous effects of the sun. Interior drapes allow solar energy to penetrate windows, but the instantaneous solar effects within the room are minimized, since the energy is absorbed by the drapes. The air volume between the glass area and the drapes acts like a greenhouse; it gets hot and most of the heat is dissipated to the room at a later time.

Glass window construction and placement decisions can significantly reduce instantaneous heat gains, thus reducing the size of the air-cooling system and its operating cost. Low emissivity (low-E) windows are better than single plate glass. East and west glass placement should be minimized to reduce instantaneous heat gains in summer.

Nonglass Surfaces

Solar energy also affects nonglass surfaces and can generate additional heat loads. Solar energy striking a nonglass surface may be reflected or absorbed. When absorbed by the surface, it increases the surface temperature; the heat is transmitted to the building's interior, as with heat transmission heat gain. Building insulation will reduce this solar heat gain.

The outside surface can be treated to reflect a higher percentage of solar energy, thus reducing solar absorption. Some reflective surface treatments are: smooth surfaces, light reflective colors or materials, heat shields (such as shade from trees), and keeping water on a flat roof. Management must realize, however, that most of these surface treatments will reduce desirable solar heating effects during the winter heating season.

OCCUPANT HEAT LOAD

Management must also consider the occupant heat load. It must estimate the number of customers, clients, patients, or club members, and the number of employees, and determine their activity level. The heat load depends both on the number of people and on what they are doing.

Management should also consider the clothing being worn by customers because it could result in increased or reduced room heat gains. Heavier clothing will absorb body moisture and prevent it from being absorbed within the room; when light or minimal clothing is worn, more heat will be absorbed by the room air. Management should consider, or encourage, a scheduled use of rooms that accommodate larger numbers of persons. In most areas, early mornings or late afternoons are desirable times for large gatherings, because solar heat transmission and ventilation and air-conditioning loads are usually smaller at these times. This practice could conserve air-cooling energy.

INFILTRATION HEAT LOAD

Infiltration is the movement of air through window and door frames and the movement of air from the outside to the inside through open doors and windows. You can select windows and doors that have very low infiltration heat gains. This not only reduces air-cooling requirements but also reduces heating requirements during the winter. The manager should have the architect supply infiltration factors for various door and window designs before deciding which units to install. The manager should also have the architect indicate the relative heating and cooling costs associated with each window and door unit. The manager can then weigh the increased unit cost (airtight windows and doors have higher initial costs) against the energy costs for heating and cooling.

You should also be aware that revolving doors and double-door entries greatly reduce infiltration heat gains when people are passing through open doors. If you have large customer movements, you should seriously consider these types of doors. The potential energy savings are shown in Figure 10.7.

Door and window frames and weather stripping wear with use and time or simply break down when exposed to the sun, wind, and rain for a number of years. The weather stripping on doors and especially windows must be periodically replaced.

There is one way almost to eliminate the infiltration factor for windows and doors. It is successfully used in many buildings. The ventilation system should produce a positive building pressure, except for kitchens, equipment rooms, and rest rooms, where negative ventilation pressure is recommended (see Chapter 9). The positive-pressure ventilation system results in *exfiltration*; that is, it blows cool air to the outside rather than allowing hot air to enter. This reduces poor air temperature distribution patterns (hot areas) around windows and doors, which is a very common problem in lodging guest rooms.

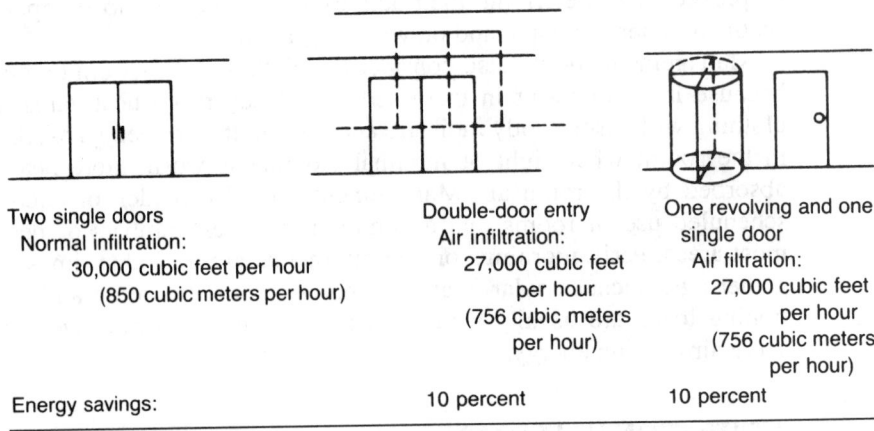

Two single doors
Normal infiltration:
    30,000 cubic feet per hour
    (850 cubic meters per hour)

Double-door entry
Air infiltration:
    27,000 cubic feet per hour
    (756 cubic meters per hour)

One revolving and one single door
Air filtration:
    27,000 cubic feet per hour
    (756 cubic meters per hour)

Energy savings: 10 percent   10 percent

FIGURE 10.7 Effects of using revolving and double-entry doors on infiltration heat gain for summer cooling.

Large windows in guest rooms should have an air-conditioning disconnect switch attached to them. When these windows are opened, the switch shuts off the room cooling system, as well as the heating system. This could significantly reduce air-cooling and heating requirements. It is essential that any guest room doors exiting directly outside be equipped with these switches.

A frequent cause of "sick building syndrome" is the lack of outside ventilation air. This may result because of zero air infiltration. Other factors that contribute to the syndrome are the installation of fixed windows (fixed windows cannot be opened) and the use of air curtains on outside doors. While these techniques minimize cooling and heating energy losses, provisions must be made for the introduction of fresh air to the building's environment. See Chapter 9, Appendix 11, and the following sections of this chapter for the appropriate mixtures of fresh and recirculated building air.

APPLIANCE HEAT LOAD

Operating appliances generate heat, known as the appliance heat load. The manager has some control over the appliance heat load in all rooms except guest rooms, where control is limited by the size of the appliance. In many rooms, the major appliances in operation are electric lamps that convert 75 to 95 percent of their electric energy consumption to heat. There are three basic controls that will reduce the appliance heat gain: reduce appliance operating hours, use more efficient lighting systems, and reduce light intensity. Figure 10.8 shows an example of changing from an incandescent to a fluorescent lighting system.

VENTILATION HEAT LOAD

The building cooling process uses cool air to absorb the building heat load (transmission and residual, solar, occupant, appliance, and infiltration). To

---

Room data: 30 feet (9.1 meters) wide, 60 feet (18.3 meters) long, and 15 feet (4.6 meters) high is maintained at 30 footcandles (30 lux).

  Incandescent lighting requirement: sixty-three 100-watt incandescent lamps.

    Total energy requirement = 63 × 100 = 6300 watts.

  Fluorescent light requirement: thirty-four 40-lamp-watt fluorescent lamps.

    Total energy requirement = 34 × 1.25 × 40 = 1700 watts.

Reduction in energy requirement by changing from incandescent to fluorescent lighting is 73 percent.

FIGURE 10.8 Effects on the cooling load of changing from incandescent to fluorescent lamps.

absorb this heat, cool air is produced and is allowed to circulate throughout the building by a ventilation system. Cool air, lower dry-bulb-temperature air, has the capability of absorbing large amounts of sensible heat, whereas cool air with a lower dew point has the capability of absorbing large amounts of latent heat. Hence, the makeup of the heat load, sensible and latent heat, is essential to determine the quality and quantity of ventilation air.

Ventilation air can be fresh air, recirculated air, or a mixture of the two when allowed by the ventilation code. This building cooling process is shown in Figure 10.9. Thus, the process cools air to some point (an estimated temperature and relative humidity) and, as the cool air absorbs building heat, its heat content, temperature, and relative humidity change. The ventilation air is then exhausted from the room or building. The exhausted air can be discharged to the outside, it can be recirculated, or mixed with fresh air and recirculated.

The heat removed from air as it is cooled in the air-cooling process is called the *ventilation heat load*. The size and operating cost of the air-cooling system depend on the ventilation heat load. The ventilation heat load depends on the amount of ventilation air, the air properties (temperature and relative humidity) before cooling, and the building cooling requirements.

Normal air-conditioning design suggests that the exhaust air leaving the room should be 80°F (26.7°C), dry-bulb temperature, at 50 percent relative

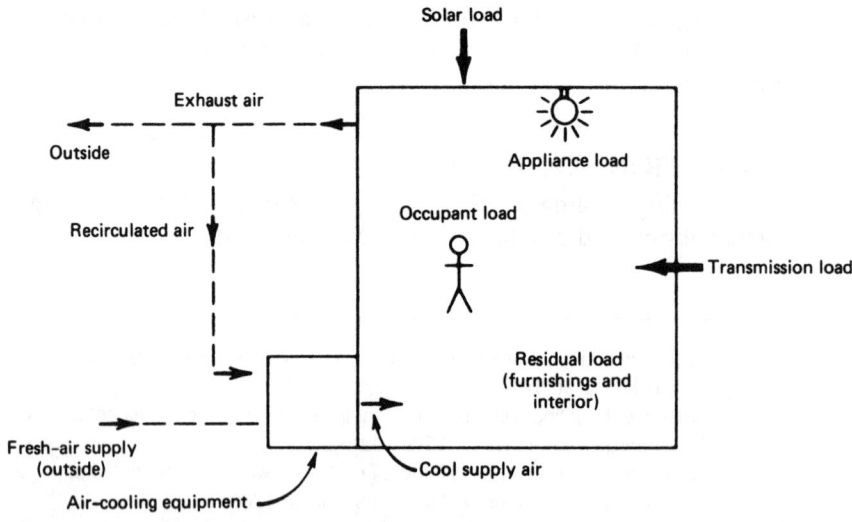

The cool supply air must have the capability to absorb all building heat loads. As the supply air absorbs the heat load, its enthalpy increases, and it leaves as warm exhaust air. The purpose of the air-cooling equipment is to cool outside/recirculated air down to such a point (enthalpy) that it can absorb the building heat load.

FIGURE 10.9   Building cooling process.

humidity. This suggested temperature and relative humidity provides a comfortable environment at a reasonable cost for most people. Most important, it satisfies over 90 percent of the air-cooling requirements in the hospitality industry.

A series of computations are required to determine the size of an air conditioner. A computational model is shown in Appendix 11. Low-cost computer software programs are available for most buildings and building uses. A new term is used in the model: *enthalpy*, or total air heat content, measured in Btu per pound (watts per kilogram). When air absorbs sensible and latent heat, its enthalpy increases, and when air is cooled, its enthalpy is reduced.

Enthalpy is related to the wet-bulb temperature. The effects of enthalpy on air-cooling requirements are as follows: a high outside enthalpy (fresh air) increases cooling requirements; a high recirculated-air enthalpy, that is, a high building heat load, also increases cooling requirements; and a low building temperature environment increases cooling requirements, as the cooling system must produce colder air (low enthalpy) to absorb the building heat load.

You can also compare the enthalpy of the fresh air to the recirculated air. If the recirculated air has a lower enthalpy, use this air rather than fresh air as ventilation air because it has a lower cooling requirement. If the fresh air has a lower enthalpy, which may occur after sunset, use fresh air for ventilation. Enthalpy-type semicomputer air flow controls can switch from one air source to another automatically. Computer control programs have preset temperatures for different functions and customer groups, for example, women's clubs (higher temperature), groups of older people (higher temperature), or young male sports teams (lower temperature). Appendix 11 shows the savings that can result from using such a control system.

AIR-CONDITIONING SYSTEMS

The complete air-conditioning system is shown in Figure 10.10. This system can do all the following: move air, mix fresh and recirculated air, filter air, heat, cool, add moisture, and remove moisture. Depending on the system components selected, the manager could end up with an air-conditioning system, an air-cooling system, or a refrigerated-air system.

This section will consider only air-cooling and refrigerated-air systems.

AIR-COOLING SYSTEMS

A very common air-cooling system used in the hospitality industry is the evaporative cooler. Evaporative coolers require two energy resources: electricity to operate a fan and water. You should recall that when water is

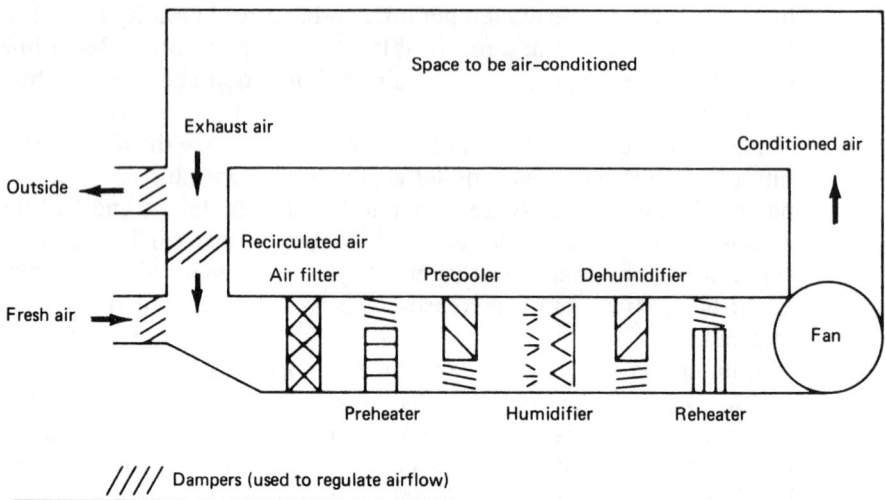

FIGURE 10.10 A complete, year-round air-conditioning installation.

absorbed by air, the air temperature (dry bulb) is reduced and the enthalpy is increased causing the percent relative humidity to increase. The total cooling energy requirement for this system is generally much less than the energy required to operate a refrigerated-air system.

As a bonus, the evaporative cooling process also filters air. However, evaporative cooling systems do not work when air is moist, high outside relative humidity. Air with medium to high relative humidity cannot absorb enough additional moisture to be cooled. Also, you would not want to circulate very humid air throughout a building.

Many managers install evaporative coolers in kitchens, laundries, or dry storage areas. In some cases, the evaporative cooler may be used only about one to two months each year, with refrigerated-air systems used during the remaining cooling period. The double cooling system is expensive to install, but energy savings can be very large during this time period, large enough to recover the cost of the system in less than 2 years.

Figure 10.11 shows a diagram of the evaporative air-cooling system for a room.

REFRIGERATED-AIR SYSTEMS

To ensure that cool, dehumidified air will be available throughout the cooling season, the manager should select a refrigerated-air cooling system. Currently, it is the most economical way to remove moisture from air. Air moisture condenses from air when it strikes a cold surface (an evaporator of a refrigeration cycle) and releases its latent heat of vaporization. Moist air

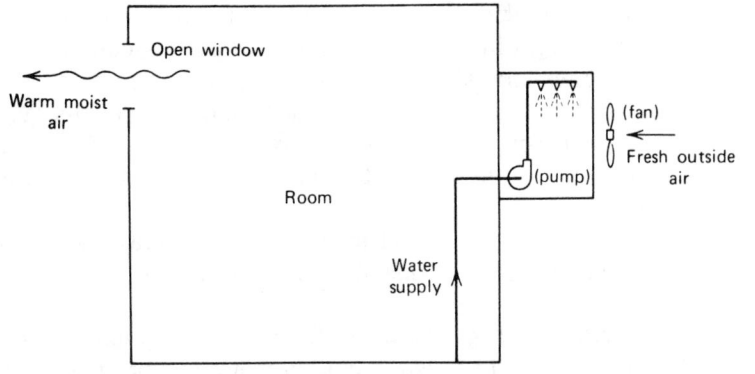

FIGURE 10.11   Evaporative air-cooling system for a room.

has a high dew point. The cold condensing surface (evaporator) must be below the dew-point temperature to reduce the air's dew point, thus dehumidifying the air.

Depending on cooling energy and initial cost requirements, the manager usually has a choice of two refrigerated-air systems: vapor compression or absorption cooling.

Vapor Compression Refrigeration Systems

The vapor compression refrigeration system was discussed in Chapter 8. The evaporator does the cooling in the cycle. Energy is purchased to operate the compressor and auxiliary components, such as fans, control systems, and water for water spray filters and humidifiers. Two types of vapor compression refrigeration systems are used: direct expansion (DX) and chilled water.

Direct-Expansion (DX) Refrigerated-Air System.   This system, which cools ventilation air directly at the evaporator, can be used for most cooling requirements. Each guest room or building section could have separate mechanical refrigeration systems. It is possible to cool an entire large building by this process. In a medium-sized facility, say, a hotel with 300 guest rooms, at least 10 and as many as 300 individual systems would have to be installed and maintained. Maintenance costs could be very high, and operating costs could also be very high if occupancy remained at a high level during the entire cooling season.

The system is basically simple. The evaporator is in the room or near the area that you want to cool. A fan is used to blow air over the evaporator. The air is cooled and is blown into the area to absorb the heat load. The system can cool fresh air, recirculated air, or a combination. The type of compressor used depends on the cooling requirements. Smaller units use a rotary compressor, and larger installations use a reciprocating compressor.

A word of caution about this system. As the evaporator is directly cooling air, any refrigerant leak at the evaporator allows the refrigerant gas to contaminate the air. You must check local building, ventilation, and fire codes to see if you can use the DX system and, if you can, what refrigerants can be used.

The DX system is very efficient for small areas and is the least costly refrigerated-air system to install. Its maintenance is moderate.

Chilled-Water Compression Systems.   A common system for medium- to larger-sized buildings is the chilled-water compression system. This system uses indirect evaporators. The basic vapor compression system is used to produce chilled water. The chilled water is circulated by pumps to areas that are to be cooled. Air is then blown over chilled-water indirect evaporators.

Smaller systems use a reciprocating compressor, while medium- to larger-sized systems use centrifugal compressors. The compressors are driven by electric motors.

These systems are relatively efficient when operated at 80 percent or higher heat loads, resulting in maximum cooling. Under these conditions, the compressor starts and operates for long time periods. System efficiency decreases when compressors are operated in short on–off cycles and when operating less than 50 percent of the time.

Absorption Cooling Systems

In the past, absorption cooling systems using lithium bromide absorption refrigeration (Chapter 8) were used primarily in large buildings and in some medium-sized establishments. Absorption cooling systems are now being installed in many smaller buildings, such as hotels with less than 100 guest rooms.

A manager who has city steam available should be encouraged to review this energy resource for use in operating the air-cooling system. While installation and maintenance costs for absorption cooling are moderate, energy operating costs are low if city steam is available, when compared to vapor compression system operating costs.

In all cases, the absorption cooling system produces chilled water. If city steam is not available, a heat plant is generally used to produce steam for the generator. The same steam boiler can be used during the heating months to heat the building, produce domestic hot water, and generate kitchen steam and hot water.

Figure 10.12 shows a common application of the absorption cooling system.

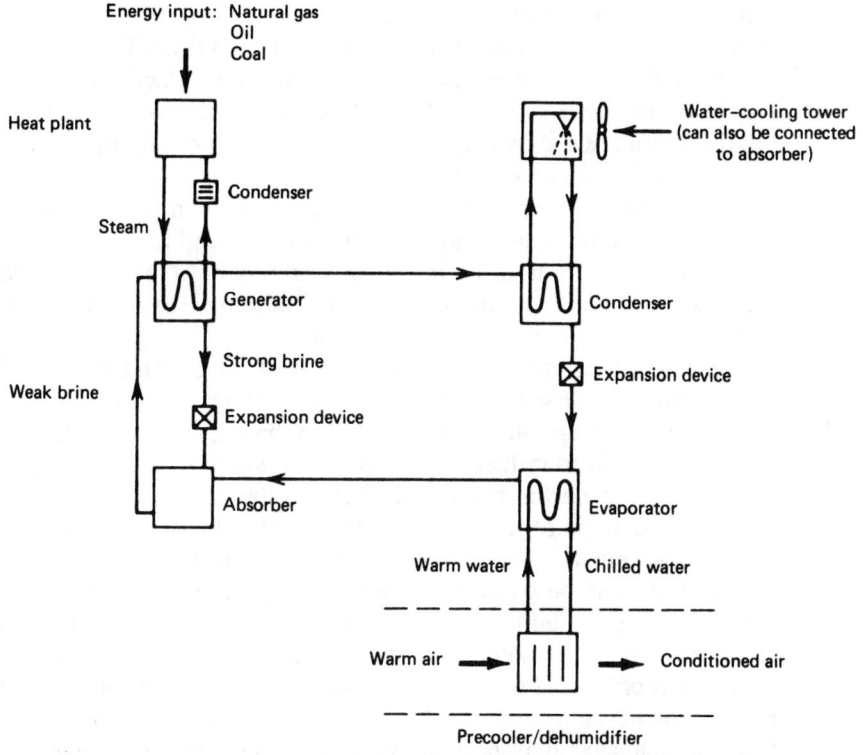

FIGURE 10.12 Air-cooling/dehumidifying system using lithium bromide absorption refrigeration.

AIR-CONDITIONING SYSTEM COMPONENTS

Air-conditioning system components include filters, preheaters, reheaters, precoolers, dehumidifiers, humidifiers, fans, and system air supply. Filters were discussed in Chapter 9. Various heaters, which can be used as preheaters or reheaters, were covered in Chapter 7. Precoolers and dehumidifiers are evaporators of refrigeration systems and were discussed in Chapter 8. Various types of humidifiers and fans are reviewed in this section, which concludes with a discussion of when each component is used in a complete air-conditioning system installation.

HUMIDIFIERS

Humidifiers add water to air. It is less costly to add water to the air than it is to remove water.

The evaporative cooler and water spray filter, which are essentially the same, are both humidifiers. These are the most effective air humidification techniques available to the manager at the present time. There are less effective humidification processes, but they seldom produce the needed results for the hospitality industry. (These other techniques, which seldom produce relative humidities above 30 to 40 percent, are used only in residential units and will not be discussed here.)

If your building has high moisture loads, you can take advantage of this situation if you recirculate air from the building and mix it with dry outside air. If the proper controls are installed, you may be able to take advantage of high moisture levels produced within the building (see the maintenance and energy-management section in this chapter).

The humidifier increases the dew point of the air and the resulting relative humidity to close to 100 percent. This is too humid to blow into a room. So, after the appropriate water is added to the air, its desired dew point, you must heat the air to reduce its relative humidity. Not much heat is required, but just enough partial heating to increase the dry-bulb temperature above the desired dew-point temperature. Heating should lower the relative humidity to an acceptable level of 70 percent or less. If the system is properly designed, air can be partially heated for very little cost. There are two heat sources within the building that normally provide enough heat for this purpose: Placing a fan motor in the air stream will partially heat air; if air is blown over or around fluorescent lighting fixture ballasts, the air will absorb heat from the lamp ballasts. If these techniques do not provide adequate heat, the manager may be required to heat air, obtaining heat from a heat plant or the condenser (absorber) of a refrigeration cycle.

FANS

The manager can select from two general groups of fans and also has a choice of three fans within each general group. Selection depends on several important factors: ventilation requirements, installation cost, energy consumption, noise, maintenance, air flow and duct system resistance, and, in some cases, weight (if fans are mounted in ceiling plenums or on a building roof).

The two general groups of fans are centrifugal and axial flow; see Figure 10.13.

Centrifugal Fans

Centrifugal fans are like wheels with spokes. The fan motor turns the wheel, and the air is sucked into the center—the supply duct supplies air to the fan center. The circulating motion of the wheel forces the air outward, greatly increasing its speed. The wheel is placed inside a housing, or enclosure, that has one exit opening. All the air going through the fan is forced out through

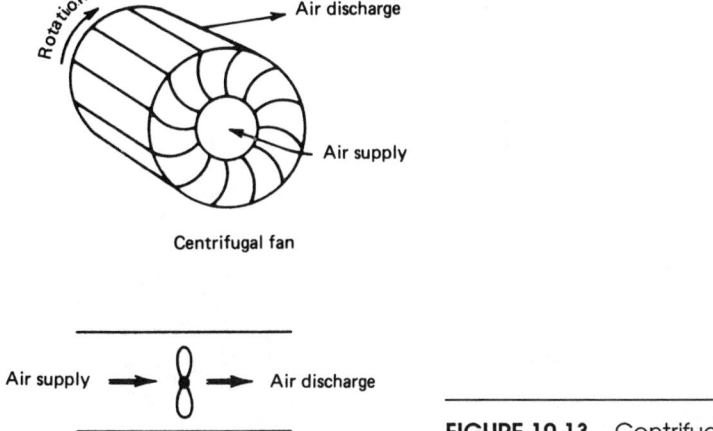

Centrifugal fan

Air supply → Air discharge

Axial flow fan

FIGURE 10.13 Centrifugal and axial-flow fans.

this exit opening. The air must make a 90-degree turn when going through this fan. The curvature of the fan spokes determines the type of centrifugal fan.

Managers, along with their architects and chief engineers, have generally selected centrifugal fans. This fan easily adapts to changing work requirements. For example, if a single fan is being used to supply air to several meeting rooms and if you close off one or more rooms because they are not being used, centrifugal fans will generally still provide adequate air flow to the open rooms. However, these fans are more costly to install, consume more energy, generate more noise, require more maintenance, and weigh more than axial-flow fans.

Figure 10.14 shows three types of centrifugal fans. Many managers select the forward curved-blade fan because of its ability to meet changing air flow and system pressure requirements, as in the meeting room example, and because of its low initial cost compared to other centrifugal fans. The backward curved-blade fan is the most energy-efficient centrifugal fan, generates minimum noise, and has the highest initial fan cost.

Axial-Flow Fans

Axial-flow fans are simple propellers placed in ducts or in a small duct section. The air simply rotates in the duct. Note the straight-line air movement in Figure 10.15. Duct configuration and propeller design determine the type of propeller fan.

Many managers select axial-flow fans for exhausting air from a room directly to the outside (see Figure 10.15) because of their low initial cost and high efficiency—high efficiency results from minimal duct resistance when the fan is discharging air directly outside as shown in Figure 10.15.

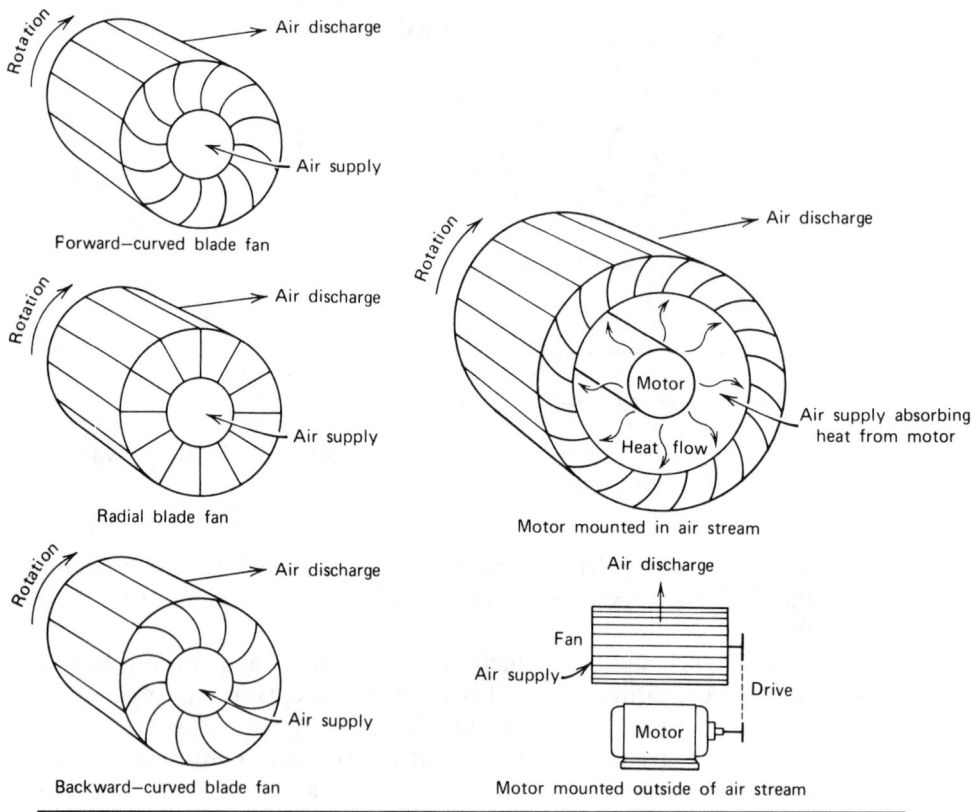

FIGURE 10.14 Centrifugal fans.

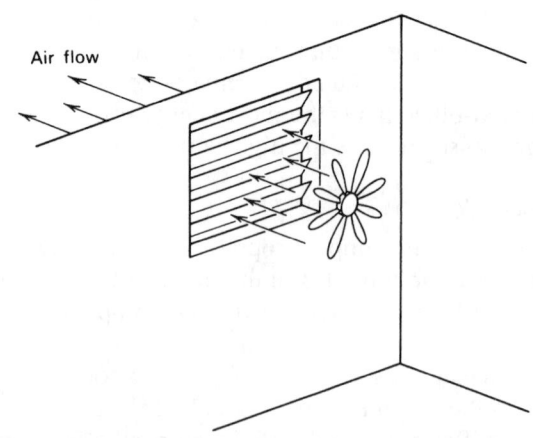

FIGURE 10.15 Use of propeller fan for the local exhaust of air.

The major disadvantage of axial-flow fans is that they do not perform well if a single fan is used for a group of rooms and a part of this area is closed off, as in the meeting room example.

Figure 10.16 shows various types of axial-flow fans.

U.S. GOVERNMENT STANDARDS

Window air conditioners are rated and measured by an EER (energy efficiency ratio). The EER is the cooling output in Btu per hour for each watt of energy input to the compressor. The minimum EER for a window-type air conditioner sold in January 1990 and later is 8.6. However, high-efficiency units with EERs of 10.0 to 12.0 are currently available. As an example, a window air conditioner with an EER of 12.0 requires 25 percent less energy to operate than a unit with an EER of 9.0; both units, however, would remove the same amount of heat from the space.

Central air conditioners and heat pumps are rated in SEER units. The SEER is the seasonal energy efficiency ratio, which reflects the entire cooling season and is equal to the total Btus of cooling delivered divided by the total watt-hours of energy used during a representative cooling season. The minimum SEER for a central air conditioner is 10.0, which became effective January 1992. Central air conditioners can be purchased with SEERs of 13.5 to 16.9 at the present time.

Heat pump units are rated in SEER units for the cooling cycle. A single-package heat pump must have a minimum SEER of 9.7, which became effective January 1993. The split-package heat pump must have a minimum

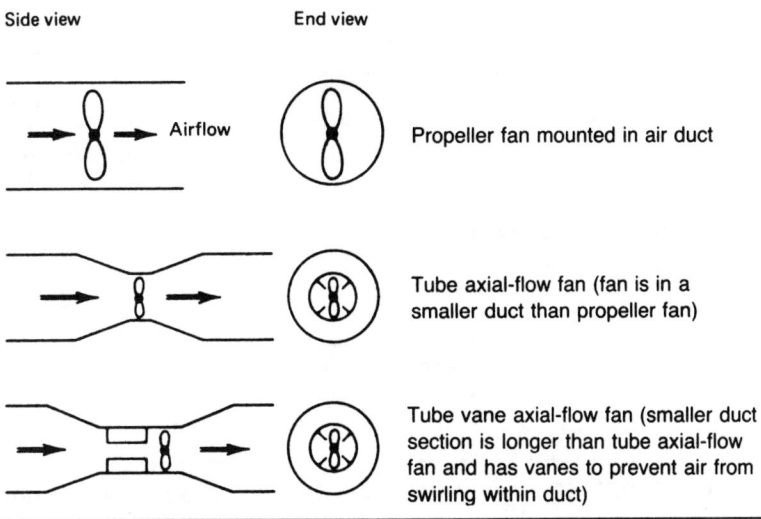

Side view   End view

Airflow   Propeller fan mounted in air duct

Tube axial-flow fan (fan is in a smaller duct than propeller fan)

Tube vane axial-flow fan (smaller duct section is longer than tube axial-flow fan and has vanes to prevent air from swirling within duct)

FIGURE 10.16 *Types of axial-flow fans.*

SEER of 10.0, which became effective January 1992. Typical high-efficiency heat pumps are available with SEERs of 11.3 to 16.4 at the present time.

COMPONENTS: WHEN TO USE WHAT

The complete air-conditioning system includes: fan, filter, preheater, precooler, humidifier, dehumidifier, fresh-air supply, recirculated-air supply, and reheater. Figure 10.17 shows what each component does. The figure also indicates the effect of each component on air temperature and relative

Component	Purpose	Temperature effects
Damper	Mixes air or bypasses a component (see Fig. 10.10)	Will act as a heat exchanger to heat or cool air.
Filter	Purify air.	Generally none, except for the water spray filter that increases dew point, but reduces dry bulb.
Preheater	Adds sensible heat to the air (generally used only during the heating season).	Increases dry bulb and wet bulb.
Precooler	Removes sensible heat from the air (generally used only during the cooling season).	Decreases dry bulb and wet bulb.
Humidifier	Adds water to the air.	Increases dew point and reduces dry bulb; this is generally a constant wet-bulb process. Air generally has to be reheated after humidification.
Dehumidifier	Removes moisture from the air (a difficult and costly process).	Reduces dew point, wet bulb, and dry bulb. Air generally has to be reheated after dehumidification.
Reheater	Adds sensible heat to air. This is generally required after either humidification or dehumidification because air has 100-percent relative humidity (is too wet to blow into a room). The fan motor or fluorescent lamp ballasts can be used for partial reheating.	Increases dry bulb and wet bulb.
Fan	Moves air.	Generally no effect, unless fan motor used as a reheater.

FIGURE 10.17   Complete air-conditioning system components and their purpose.

humidity. The figure does not indicate the amount of heating, cooling, humidification, or dehumidification actually required. You can get a general idea of what is to be used to produce desirable air by following the figure.

MAINTENANCE AND ENERGY MANAGEMENT

The air-conditioning system can be a costly system to maintain. Depending on the size of the building, or complex of buildings, several employees may work full time on the maintenance of the total air-conditioning system. Its repairs and maintenance cost can easily total 10 to 30 percent per year of its installation cost. If the maintenance cost approaches 25 percent of the initial cost per year for two consecutive years, the manager should have the chief engineer do a feasibility analysis for keeping the present system or replacing it (refer to Chapter 2 and its related appendixes for typical analysis techniques). The complete system is really three subsystems—heating, refrigeration, and ventilation—combined into one. System maintenance procedures are indicated in Appendix 11.

AIR-CONDITIONING ENERGY-MANAGEMENT SYSTEM (EMS)

Interfacing and controlling air-conditioning system components to produce air within the "comfort zone" has been a problem for chief engineers and building managers for years. Refer to Appendix 11 and Figure 10.17: How will each component affect either or both the sensible- and latent-heat content of the air? How will it do so in the space that is to be air-conditioned? The relationships can be very complex; for example, if the space heat load changes during the day, the space will get either warmer or cooler, which affects the exhaust-air temperature and moisture levels from the conditioned space. If this exhaust air is recirculated back through the air-conditioning system, this will affect each system component. In the past, chief engineers and their staffs had to learn how the air-conditioning system responded to changing heat loads; they drew on this experience to regulate system components to produce satisfactory air. It frequently took two air-cooling seasons to learn how system components respond to their controls.

The control system must quickly compensate for changing inside and outside air conditions. If controls respond properly, high-quality air is maintained and, more important, operating costs are minimal. Basic air quality controls are limited to temperature, moisture, and air flow measurements.

The basic control is the thermostat in the conditioned space. It starts or stops the air-conditioning system. Most thermostats measure only dry-bulb temperature. Enthalpy, dew-point, or relative-humidity controls must be used to control room moisture levels and to activate the humidifier, dehumidifier, or heater. If these latter controls are not used, the relative humidity can vary between 20 and almost 100 percent. Programmable thermostats are available that can be connected to room occupancy sensors and the front desk (see Chapter 7). As with room heating status controls, similar programmed room status temperatures can be set. For example, if the room is available but not sold, its temperature can be controlled at 85°F (29.4°C); if sold but not occupied, its temperature can be controlled at 80°F (26.7°C); and if the room is sold and occupied (as determined by an occupancy sensor), its temperature is set by the guest down to a management-programmed minimum, usually 72°F (22.2°C).

Ideally, the following controls should be used: wet-bulb temperature, or enthalpy; moisture control; and dry-bulb temperature. The wet-bulb-temperature sensing device (enthalpy control) measures both fresh, or outside, air, and recirculated air. It automatically sets dampers to regulate the amount of each kind of air and to minimize cooling or heating costs.

The moisture control device is in the conditioned air duct and measures dew point or relative humidity. This device regulates the humidifier or dehumidifier.

The dry-bulb temperature is regulated by an ordinary thermostat that controls heaters or coolers. Three separate units are required to provide quality air. Most buildings have one control (dry-bulb temperature). Some buildings have two controls (dry-bulb temperature and relative humidity), and a few have all three.

Measuring the temperature and moisture levels of air and adjusting precoolers, humidifiers, fan speed, and reheaters was a difficult process. Enthalpy controls (measurement of the total heat content of air) were introduced to regulate the mixture of recirculated and fresh air and to make system energy consumption more efficient. Initially, enthalpy controls resulted in limited success because system components had to be manually adjusted to compensate for changing air conditions. Later, data-processing systems were used to measure air quality at any point in the air treatment process (e.g., air temperature after precooling); if a system component was interfaced with the data-processing system, the system could be changed through manual adjustments to produce desirable air.

The control system can also be connected to a load-shedding program or electric demand program. The selection of an appropriate EMS can result in optimal air quality with significant reductions in energy consumption. In addition, if a component is failing, an alarm can be activated to notify the maintenance and repair staff of a potential problem. Many of these mechanical problems can be corrected before the occupants feel any significant changes in building air quality.

Gravity dampers can be installed in all ducts. When the fan is operating, the dampers are blown open, allowing full air flow; however, once the fan is off, the dampers all shut or close off the air ducts, which minimizes the gravity flow of air from warmer to cooler areas through the air duct network.

Finally, the manager should have the chief engineer investigate the use of a variable air volume (VAV) handling system with variable-speed fans. If additional cooling is required, the air speed can be increased to introduce more air flow to absorb the additional heat load. Likewise, when cooling requirements are reduced, the fan speed is reduced. In addition, this system provides a variable wind-chill factor.

SUMMARY

Air conditioning, air cooling, and refrigerated air involve mechanical systems that absorb or remove heat from a space to provide a comfortable environment for guests and employees. The comfort level is expressed as dry-bulb, dew-point, and wet-bulb temperatures and the percent relative humidity. The amount of building cooling depends on the heat load, transmission, residual, solar, occupant, ventilation, and appliance heat sources. The interrelations among mechanical systems, temperature–moisture measurements, and heat load are complex. A small change in any one of the factors can have significant effects on the other factors.

The manager must have an understanding of the air-conditioning mechanical components and how they relate to quality air to determine what could be wrong if the system is not delivering quality air. Most important, the manager must be aware that system maintenance must be carefully monitored to ensure that it will provide the desired building environment. These understandings are necessary so that the manager and chief engineer become a team, working together and not expecting the impossible, if the system starts to malfunction.

The complete system requires several energy sources: electric power, water, and, in many cases, a heat source, such as oil or gas. The customer may be allowed to control the space environment within preset temperature limits, which could have significant energy consumption effects. The complete relationships of temperature–moisture effects, energy consumption, component efficiencies, and heat load requirements all must be monitored and controlled with an appropriate energy-management system to minimize total energy consumption.

The previous chapters (heat, refrigeration, and ventilation) are combined to develop this chapter, perhaps one of the most important of the text addressing one of the most complex mechanical systems in modern buildings.

BIBLIOGRAPHY

1. American Society of Heating, Refrigeration and Air Conditioning Engineers, *1992 ASHRAE Handbook Systems and Equipment,* New York, 1992.
2. American Society of Heating, Refrigeration and Air Conditioning Engineers, *1993 ASHRAE Handbook Fundamentals,* New York, 1993.
3. Borsenik, F. D., *Holiday Inn, Inc.—Hotel Group Energy Management Program: Phase I,* University of Nevada, Las Vegas, November 20, 1989.
4. Borsenik, F. D., *Holiday Inn, Inc.—Hotel Group Energy Management Program: Phase II,* University of Nevada, Las Vegas, December 5, 1989.
5. Houston Lighting and Power Company, *Guide to Commercial Energy Efficiency,* Houston, October 1992.
6. Kirk, D., "Computer Systems for Energy Management," *International Journal of Hospitality Management,* Vol. 6, No. 4, 1987.
7. Piper, J. E., *Handbook of Facility Management, Tools and Techniques, Formulas and Tables,* Prentice-Hall, Englewood Cliffs, NJ, 1995.

QUESTIONS/PROBLEMS

1. Outside air is 90°F (32.2°C) and has a wet-bulb temperature of 75°F (23.9°C). Determine the relative humidity, dew-point temperature, and heat content of the air. (Refer to Appendix 11.)

2. Check the lighting currently used in a building and comment on the potential effects of changing light sources on:
   a. winter heating requirements (and cost factors)
   b. summer cooling requirements (and cost factors).

3. Discuss and compare the use of the various cooling techniques presented in this chapter in your local area. Extend the discussion to cover a different geographic area.

4. Air enters the air conditioner at 90°F (32.2°C) dry bulb and 10 percent relative humidity. Air leaves the air conditioner at 70°F (21.1°C) dry bulb and 60 percent relative humidity. The weight of the air is 5000 pounds (2267 kilograms). Determine the size of the air conditioner. Use

the psychometric chart to determine what air-conditioning system components are required and the air conditions, such as dry-bulb, dew-point, and wet-bulb temperatures, as air is discharged from each system component. (Refer to Appendix 11.)

5. Discuss the heat load factors for your classroom. How can these heat loads be reduced?

6. Review Figure 10.17 and discuss the components that would be required for your classroom to provide conditioned air.

CHAPTER 11

Courtesy of Hyatt Hotels.

ELECTRICAL NETWORKS
AND SYSTEMS

ABSTRACT

Electric energy is indispensable in the hospitality industry. Electric energy can be used for heat, light, and power. Normal building electric energy cost is close to two-thirds of the total energy budget for the building, so its control is essential for all energy-management programs.

The key to electric energy management is a knowledge of electric terminology and an understanding of fundamental electrical concepts. Gaining this knowledge and understanding is the principal objective of this chapter.

The primary use of electric energy is for the production of mechanical energy (power) through the electromechanical conversion in electric motors. Electric energy consumed by electric motors can account for up to 75 percent of the total electric consumption for larger properties (motors for HVAC, elevators, laundry equipment, food chillers and freezers, water pumps—just to mention some electric motor uses).

Electric energy for heat and lighting systems accounts for the remainder of the uses of electric power. While electric-to-heat conversion is generally very efficient (approaching 95+ percent), this can represent a costly heat resource. The use of electric energy for the generation of light is the most apparent use of electric energy. The electric–light conversion process is not very efficient at the present time. There are a large number of electric light sources, which produce all types of effects; especially interesting are the effects on surface color (building surfaces, food, and people).

Electric energy will continue to be a primary energy resource in the future, as nuclear-, solar-, geothermal-, and other-to-electric conversion processes will increase in the future, all resulting in abundant electric energy, which will eventually replace the dependence on natural gas and oil energy sources. Hence, the hospitality industry like other industries will

315

become more and more dependent on electric energy. The future hospitality manager has very little choice, he or she must learn how to manage electric systems for industry and management survival.

Key words: *alternating current (ac); ampere; anode; AWG (American Wire Gage); ballast; cable; capacitor; cathode; circuit; circuit breaker; circuit panel; cycles per second (cps); deferred energy charge; deferred energy credit; demand; demand equalization surcharge; direct current (dc); direct-current motor; distribution center; electrical service system; electronic heat converter; emergency energy system; fluorescent lamp; footcandle; fuse; ground; ground-fault circuit interrupter; high-intensity discharge lamp; horsepower; incandescent lamp; induction polyphase motor; kilowatt; kilowatt-hour; lamp; lighting system; lumen; luminaire; lux; master control switch; MCM; NEC (National Electric Code); off-peak; on-peak; "other" motor types; parallel circuit; power factor; resistance heater; rotor; series circuit; service wires; single phase (ac); single-phase motor; starter; stator; synchronous polyphase motor; three phase (ac); transformer; tungsten-halogen lamp; UL; volt; voltage drop; watt; wire.*

INTRODUCTION

The hospitality industry requires and uses large amounts of electric energy. The cost of electric energy remained at a relatively low unit-cost level until the 1970s. Since then electric-energy costs have increased by factors of 5 to 10. Now, the average hospitality industry manager spends two out of each three energy dollars for electricity.

This dependence on a single source of energy cannot be underestimated, and the value of electric energy in the hospitality industry is almost impossible to determine accurately. The industry is dependent on electricity for heat, light, and power. In addition, most building control systems operate electrically.

Worker and customer activity areas are dependent on electricity as a lighting source. To appreciate the industry's dependence on electricity for lighting, start to add up the number of electric lamps in guest rooms, guest bathrooms, halls, stairwells, meeting and conference rooms, dining areas, other public space, office space, and employee work areas, as well as for exterior safety lighting and decorative lighting. In the 1970s, most managers found that they could save electric energy by reducing the number and size of electric lamps. This was done with few or no customer complaints or losses in employee productivity. In the 1990s, light-efficient electric lamps were available for most building lighting requirements at reasonable costs.

Electric motors are the largest consumers of electric energy in our buildings. The total air-conditioning system discussed in Chapter 10 requires energy to drive fans, energy for cooling and heating air, energy for removing and adding moisture, and energy for the control system.

Management may also select electric energy as a heat source. While this can be an expensive form of heat, its convenience and ease of use make it desirable.

MEASUREMENT OF ELECTRICAL ENERGY

The basic electric-energy measurement terms are: watts (kilowatts, kilowatt-hours), amperes, and volts. Fortunately, most of the electrical-energy measurement terms used in the English-speaking countries are identical to metric and Standard International Units.

WATTS, KILOWATTS, AND KILOWATT-HOURS

The electric term *watt* is very important to management. It is a measure of the use of electrical energy. A high-wattage appliance has greater energy requirements and consumption than a low-wattage appliance.

The cost of electric energy depends on watt-hours (actually kilowatt-hours). The watt-hour is the rate of electric consumption. Watt-hour effects are shown in Figure 11.1. This figure shows different-wattage appliances, all consuming the same amount of energy during different time periods. Its message is very clear: When the appliance is not needed or required, turn it off.

Electrical energy is actually purchased by the kilowatt-hour. A kilowatt is 1000 watts. The kilowatt-hour is 1000 watt-hours, or 1 kilowatt being used for 1 hour. Figure 11.2 shows several appliances being operated for various periods of time, all consuming 1 kilowatt-hour of energy. All would have the same operating cost.

Watts depend on three factors: amperes, volts, and power factor.

AMPERES

Amperes measure the rate of electrical flow through a device or appliance. High ampere flow is directly related to high wattage consumption. The ampere is dangerous. If a very small number of amperes pass through your body, they could cause very painful reactions or even death. Many people can feel as little as 0.005 ampere, although this amount is usually not dangerous. However, 0.05 ampere could cause extreme pain or even death. (A 100-watt incandescent lamp requires over 0.800 ampere.)

Electric motors are rated in amperes. Many electronic devices are rated in amperes. Electric wires, fuses, and most electric switching devices are rated in amperes. Generally, if a device has a high-ampere requirement, its initial cost will be higher than a similar device with a lower-ampere requirement.

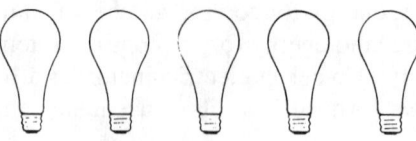

Lamps rated 200 watts each.
Lamps are in operation for 1 hour.
  $200 \times 5 \times 1 = 1000$ watt-hours

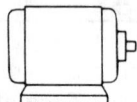

Electric motor rated at 500 watts.
Motor is in operation for 2 hours:
  $500 \times 2 = 1000$ watt-hours

Toaster rated at 1500 watts.
Toaster is in operation for 40 minutes (two-thirds hour):
  $1500 \times \frac{2}{3} = 1000$ watt-hours

FIGURE 11.1 Watt-hour consumption of various electric appliances.

$200 \times 5 \times 1 = 1000$ watt-hours = 1 kilowatt-hour

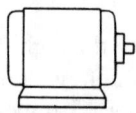

$500 \times 2 = 1000$ watt-hours = 1 kilowatt-hour

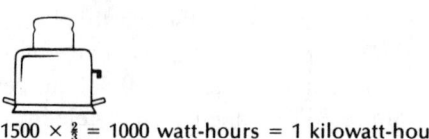

$1500 \times \frac{2}{3} = 1000$ watt-hours = 1 kilowatt-hour

FIGURE 11.2 Kilowatt-hour consumption of various electric appliances.

VOLTS

The *volt* is the unit of electrical potential. It is the pressure that causes electric current to flow. If volts are not available, there are no amperes or watts.

Many appliances and devices are rated in watts and volts, meaning that if the specified number of volts are supplied, the device consumes the indicated number of watts. Other appliances may be rated in volts and amperes, meaning that if the indicated number of volts are available, the rated number of amperes will flow through the device.

Some appliances, especially electric motors, may have dual ratings. An electric motor may be rated as follows: volts 120/140 = amperes 20/10. The correct interpretation of this rating is: (1) if the motor is supplied with 120 volts, it requires 20 amperes; (2) if supplied with 240 volts, it requires 10 amperes.

Generally, the initial cost of a device or appliance depends on its volt and ampere requirements. So if it is operated at a higher voltage, its ampere requirements are lower, and its initial cost is less.

TYPES OF ELECTRIC ENERGY

Appliances and devices may require different electric-energy sources. Small buildings may have very limited electric-energy capabilities, while larger buildings (hotels, institutional buildings, and health-care facilities) may provide several electric-energy sources. In this section, these sources will be briefly discussed, and management recommendations will be made for utilizing these optional resources.

DIRECT CURRENT

Direct current, or *dc*, has limited applications in the hospitality industry. Direct current provides a constant flow of amperes when a constant voltage is impressed on the amperes. Amperes change only if the electrical load changes or if the impressed voltage changes. Direct current is used in some security systems and for limited emergency energy use for selective devices, such as exit lighting.

For these uses, dc is probably provided by a battery, or a series of batteries. Many data-processing systems have backup dc sources. It is important to keep these systems in operation even when electric energy from the local electric utility is not interrupted. These backup devices are frequently long-life batteries that are automatically charged when electric energy is being supplied to the unit.

Direct current may also be generated on the property. This is done only for certain types of elevator motors. Some emergency lighting systems for public areas may also operate on dc power sources. In almost all cases, a battery energy source will be utilized.

ALTERNATING CURRENT

Hospitality industry buildings are supplied with *alternating current,* or *ac,* from the local electric utility. The manager must know the characteristics of the ac being supplied to the building by the local electric utility. All electric devices used within the building must be matched to the available energy. If they are not, serious problems can result, including the loss of all electric devices.

Most hospitality industry buildings are supplied with single-phase and three-phase alternating current.

Single-Phase Alternating Current

You can visualize single-phase ac by examining Figure 11.3. The figure shows a normal electric lamp connected to single-phase ac. The source of energy in this simple scheme is an ordinary wall outlet. The lamp cord has two distinct and separated wires; each wire is insulated to restrict the flow

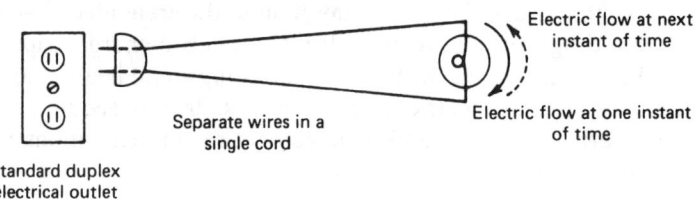

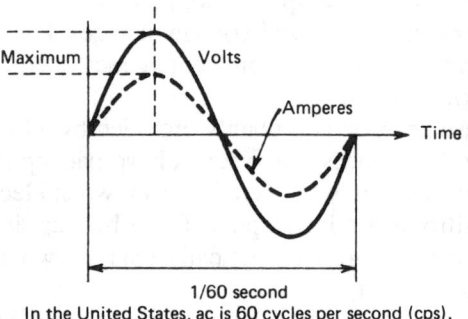

FIGURE 11.3 Single-phase alternating current.

of energy and to direct it to where you want to use it. The diagram shows each insulated wire as a separate line. One wire is connected to one side of the wall outlet and goes to the lamp, and the second wire is attached to the lamp and goes back to the other side of the wall outlet—notice that the plug at the end of the cord has two metal projections, one for each wire.

Electric energy flows along one wire from the outlet source to the lamp, through the light bulb, then back along the second wire to the wall outlet. This completes the *electric circuit.* You must have a complete electric circuit for energy flow: a source of energy (wall outlet), a path (wire cord), and a device (light bulb).

Electric-energy flow consists of amperes and volts. Amperes flow along the wire, and volts push the amperes. If you were to measure these units, you would do it as illustrated in Figure 11.4. Amperes are measured by an ammeter connected to a single wire. Volts are measured by a voltmeter connected between the two wires. A wattmeter, which is not shown, must be connected along and between the wires.

Figures 11.3 and 11.4 are diagrams for single-phase ac. This is the type of ac that is available for homes, apartments, lodging guest rooms, dormitory rooms, health-care patient rooms, and most public areas of buildings.

Alternating current means that the energy changes as it flows. The ampere reading is an average. The actual amperes vary as shown in Figure 11.5.

Alternating current can be generated at various cycles. The current common standard in the United States and in many foreign countries is 60 cycles per second (cps). So, Figure 11.5 represents one-sixtieth of a second. There are 60 complete cycles in each second. In some countries, ac is generated at 50 cps or less.

Single-phase ac is used for small electric appliances and devices. Three-phase ac is available in the hospitality industry for larger appliances and devices. A manager who has a choice between single- and three-phase energy should always choose three-phase because the initial equipment cost and the installation cost will be lower. Generally, operating energy cost is the same for both forms of energy.

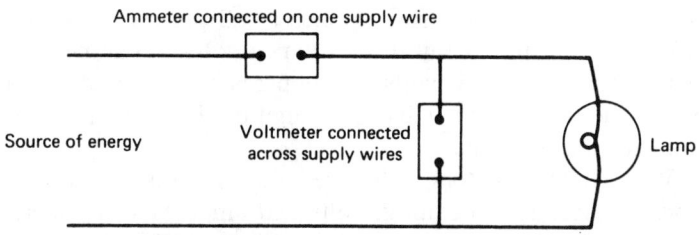

FIGURE 11.4 Measurement of volts and amperes.

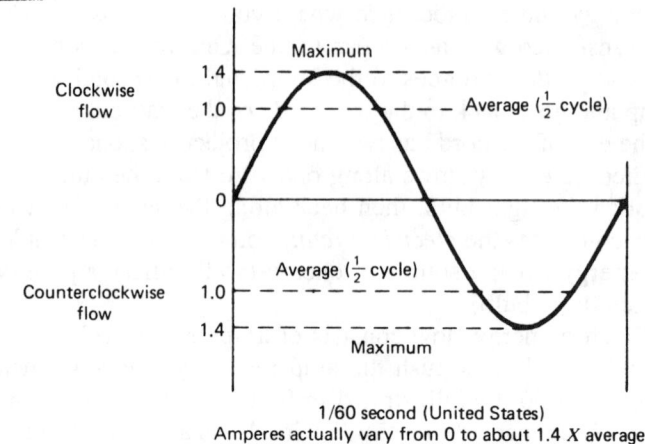

1/60 second (United States)
Amperes actually vary from 0 to about 1.4 X average.

FIGURE 11.5 Ampere flow for single-phase ac.

Three-Phase Alternating Current

It may be difficult to visualize what is happening with three-phase energy. It is basically the use of three separate single-phase energy sources combined into an energy supply network. Refer to Figure 11.6 and try to visualize the following: We need a special three-phase appliance. Let us look at a heating device such as a large oven. The heating device will have three separate heating elements. Figure 11.6 shows how the elements are supplied with energy. One energy source is used—a cable with four wires. Energy is flowing to the heating elements through a set of wires. Note the three separate energy paths (wires 1, 2, and 3). The fourth wire is a common wire that is used by all three paths. Amperes are flowing through each wire. Peak ampere flow and voltage occur at slightly different times along each wire.

Various wiring arrangements and resulting voltages are shown in Figure 11.7. Whenever three-phase energy is available, the manager should utilize it for all motors and electric heaters.

Power Factor

A *power factor* relationship applies to all phases of alternating current. It refers to the difference in time at which volts and amperes reach their peak or maximum values. If volts and amperes both peak at the same instant, the power factor is 1, or unity. See Figure 11.8, which shows the resulting wattage consumption.

When electric motors, inductive ballast fluorescent lamps, and other electronic devices are operating, volts and amperes will generally not peak at the same time; they are out of phase. Figure 11.9 indicates cases of amperes leading volts (capacitive power factor) and volts leading amperes (inductive

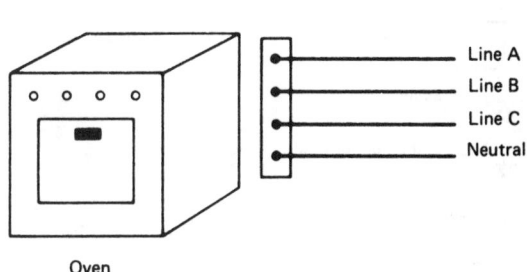

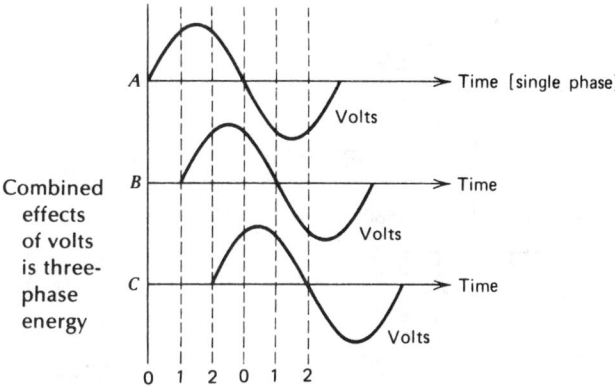

Note: Volts cross the time axis at three different times:
A axis, volts cross at time 0.
B axis, volts cross at time 1.
C axis, volts cross at time 2.

FIGURE 11.6 Differences between single-phase and three-phase alternating current.

power factor). The same figure also shows the resulting watts for these cases. Note that for the same amperes and volts that were shown in Figure 11.8, the wattage consumption is much lower. In these cases, only 80 percent of watts were produced by the same volts and amperes; thus, the power factor is 0.80.

The power factor can actually vary from 0 to, and including, 1, or unity. It normally varies from less than 0.60 to above 0.85. Electric utilities will usually impose a power factor surcharge on the electric bill whenever the power factor drops below a preset value, frequently 0.85.

The overall building power factor can be adjusted and improved. Generally, electric motors and inductive ballast fluorescent lamps will cause an inductive power factor. Electric condensers or capacitors are used in ac cir-

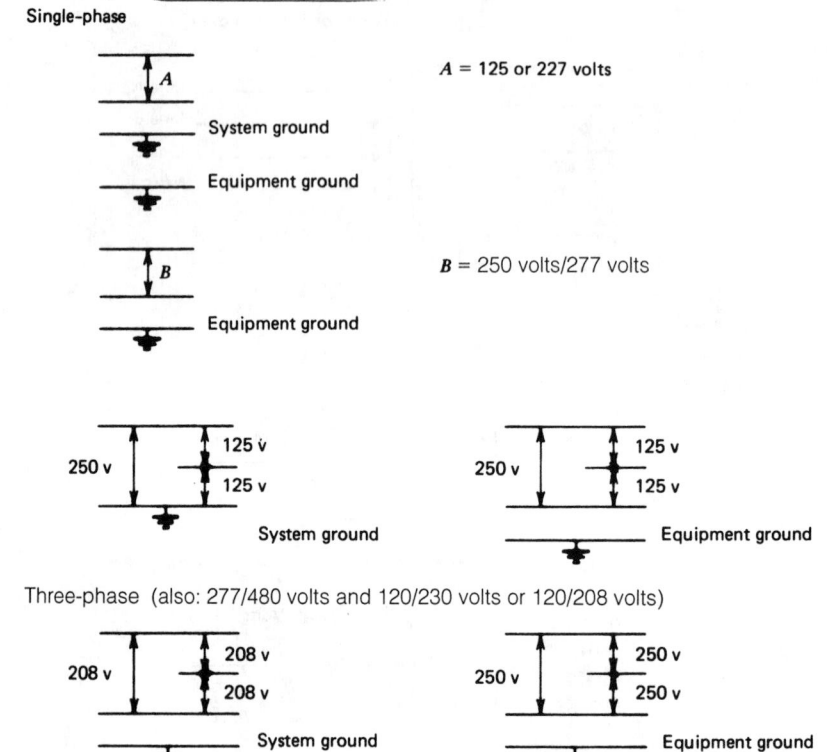

FIGURE 11.7 Typical electrical systems.

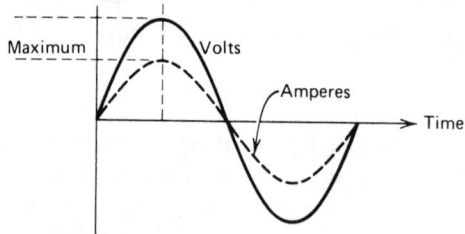

Volts and amperes cross the time axis at the same time.
Maximum volts and amperes occur at the same time.
$W = V \times I$
Appliance rated at 120 volts and 10 amperes:
$W = 120 \times 10 = 1200\ watts$

FIGURE 11.8 Unity power factor with alternating current.

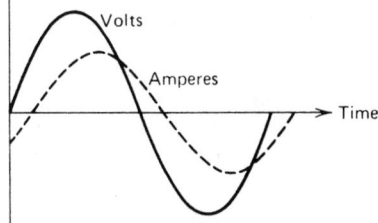

Volts leading amperes.

Volts and amperes cross time axis at different times; the time difference is related to the power factor.

The greater the time difference, the lower the power factor.

(a)

$W = V \times I \times pf$

where

     W = watts

     V = volts

     I = amperes

     pf = power factor

An appliance is rated at 120 volts, 20 amperes, and has a power factor of 0.8.

  Energy consumption = $120 \times 20 \times 0.8 = 1920$ watts

(b)

$w = (3)^{\frac{1}{2}} \times V \times I \times pf$

  Terms defined in Fig. 10.10)

A. A three-phase appliance is rated at 240 volts, 10 amperes, and has a power factor of 0.95.

Energy consumption = $(3)^{\frac{1}{2}} \times 240 \times 10 \times 0.95 = 3949$ watts

B. A single-phase appliance is rated at 240 volts, 10 amperes, and has a power factor of 0.95.

Energy consumption = $240 \times 10 \times 0.95 = 2280$ watts

(c)

FIGURE 11.9 *(a)* Alternating-current power factor less than unity; *(b)* relationship of power factor, volts, amperes, and watts for single-phase alternating current, *(c)* the energy consumption relationship for three-phase alternating current.

cuits to correct for these low induced power factors. And, depending on electric rate schedules, these corrective devices can have very short payback periods of less than 18 to 24 months.

Rarely does one find a capacitive-induced power factor, which is generally caused by large amounts of electronic equipment. Such power factors are corrected by adding inductive electric loads, such as continuous running electric motors on the building electric load.

The power factor corrective procedure is not shown in this text. The manager and chief engineer are strongly urged to seek the recommendations of the local electric utility if they are paying excessive surcharges because of low power factors.

WATTAGE CONSUMPTION FOR ALTERNATING CURRENT

Alternating-current wattage depends on all of the following: ac phase, amperes, volts, and power factor.

Single-Phase Alternating-Current Wattage

Some of you may have been exposed to the relationship and examples shown in Figure 11.9. It shows the relationship of amperes, volts, and power factor to watts. It allows the manager to compare energy requirements for various single-phase appliances.

Three-Phase Alternating-Current Wattage

The wattage consumption relationship for three-phase is also shown in Figure 11.9. It depends on amperes, volts, power factor, and an averaging factor. The averaging factor is required because volts and amperes of the three supply lines are not in phase. The averaging factor is nothing more than the square root of 3 (3 comes from the three-phase energy).

PURCHASING ELECTRIC ENERGY

This section will cover basic metering devices that will enable you, the manager, to read common meters. It will also cover typical electric rate schedules and will show you how to apply meter readings to determine an electric bill.

KILOWATT-HOUR METERS

Electric energy is purchased by the kilowatt-hour. Figure 11.10 shows the face of a common kilowatt-hour meter. The meter is basically an electric motor with a large circulating disk that rotates as energy is passed through the meter. A series of gears and dials records the number of revolutions

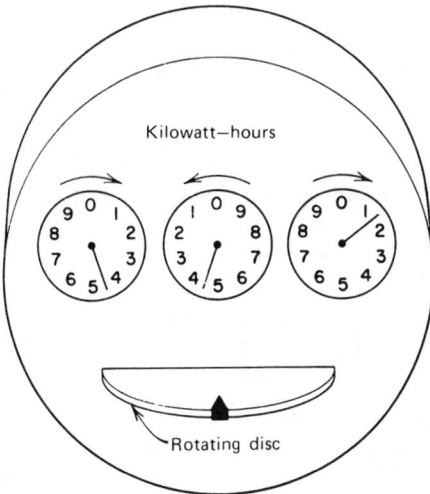

FIGURE 11.10 Typical kilowatt-hour meter.

made by the disk. A specified number of disk revolutions is equated to a kilowatt-hour. The face of the meter shows the counting and accumulation device used with most meters. If large numbers of kilowatt-hours are used during one purchasing period, one month, the meter may include a multiplier factor. Hence, one reads the meter and multiplies the result by the indicated factor and obtains the number of kilowatt-hours used during the time period.

The number of kilowatt-hours used during a period of time is the difference between the two readings (end of month and beginning of month), as indicated in Figure 11.11.

Many engineering departments purchase additional kilowatt-hour meters so that energy consumption readings can be made on individual units of equipment.

DEMAND METERS

Buildings in the hospitality industry frequently have a second meter, called the *demand meter*. The purpose of this meter is to record peak energy requirements. The demand meter registers either kilovolt-ampere or kilowatt requirements for any time period. The meter is designed with an instantaneous-demand hand that changes as building demand increases or decreases. The moving instantaneous-demand hand moves a semistationary hand that remains in the maximum-demand position. The meter typically records the maximum demand for a period of 15 minutes (0.25 hours). It is reset after it is read.

First-of-month reading, read the number the hand has just passed: 28535.

Last-day-of-month reading: 78702.
Energy consumption for the month: 78,702 − 28,535 = 50,167 kilowatt-hours.

FIGURE 11.11   Reading a kilowatt-hour meter on the first day and last day of the month and determining the consumption of energy for the month.

The utility must have the capacity and ability to provide kilovolt-amperes or kilowatt-hours at any required instant during the month. The utility estimates a certain electric demand for each building. It does not know when the maximum demand will be required. Now, if for some reason the actual demand exceeds the utility's estimate, additional energy input must be provided. The utility must have the capability to provide this additional demand. It can do this in one of two ways. It can increase its generating capacity, for short-term use (this represents a large capital expense), or it can purchase energy from another utility.

If the electric utility has excess generating capacity that is idle, this is a waste of investment. To recover this investment, it must increase its basic kilowatt-hour charges; so everyone is charged for idle equipment. If the electric utility does not have sufficient capacity to generate electric energy during periods of excess demand, it must purchase this energy from another utility. It has very little control over the rates charged by the second utility. Consumers must therefore pay demand charges.

POWER FACTOR METERS

Electric utilities must generate volts and amperes, yet they sell only watt-hours. This is because of the power factor previously discussed. Most electric utilities impose a low-power-factor surcharge. That is, whenever the power factor for a building drops below a predetermined value, usually 0.85, a surcharge is added to the bill. A power factor meter is shown in Figure 11.12.

FIGURE 11.12 Power factor, or phase, meter (courtesy of Nevada Power Company).

COMBINATION METERS

Figure 11.13 shows a combination meter. It will record and read out volts, amperes, demand, kilowatt-hours, power factor—all for 15-minute (0.25-hour) time intervals, for each hour in a 45-day period. All readings are kept on a continuous data-recording tape. The readout is transferred to a second tape, which is fed into a programmed computer. The computer digests the tape data and will print out all desired information. If the property requests these readouts, the electric utility may provide this information (a printout of the data).

A manager and chief engineer can analyze each day in 15-minute (0.25-hour) intervals during the past 30 to 45 days to determine peak energy consumption, demand, and when minimum power factors occurred. Then they must minimize electric consumption characteristics, that is, reduce demand and increase power factor.

ELECTRIC RATE SCHEDULES

Kilowatt-Hour Charges

Several electric rate schemes have been used for electric-energy charges. The simplest and most common rate is the flat charge per kilowatt-hour.

FIGURE 11.13 Combination electric meter (courtesy of Nevada Power Company).

The flat rate usually has two separate charges, on-peak and off-peak rates. On-peak refers to time periods when electric usage is very heavy; off-peak refers to the remaining time periods. Some electric utilities also have partial on-peak rates.

On-peak can apply to any time period of the day throughout the entire year or for selected months during the year. In the southwestern United States, on-peak generally refers to the late morning through early evening hours (e.g., 10 A.M. to 10 P.M. (1000 to 2200 hours) during the summer months, June through September). This is when air-conditioning requirements reach maximum demand. On-peak periods in the northern United States are normally during the daytime hours of the winter months, when heating and lighting requirements are very high. Electric utilities may have to purchase expensive electric energy from other utilities or may be forced to generate electric energy with backup oil or natural gas, which is generally expensive energy, to satisfy customer energy requirements.

Special electric meters must be used to record kilowatt-hours during on-peak and off-peak periods. Some electric utilities have several steps of on-peak rates. In effect, the cost per kilowatt-hour changes throughout the day, depending on when energy is consumed.

Figure 11.14 shows some examples of flat-rate kilowatt-hour charges and the potential effects of on-peak and off-peak pricing. Remember that these are rates that may not apply to your specific geographic area.

It should be noted that electric utilities do not have complete control over their rate schedules. A state or local government usually establishes a utility rate-setting board or commission, referred to in some areas as the Public

---

Customer service charge: $250 per month
Kilowatt-hour charges:
      Off-peak: $0.04 per kilowatt-hour
      On-peak $0.10 per kilowatt-hour

On-peak: 10 A.M.(1000 hours) to 10 P.M. (2200 hours), June–September; 20,167 kilowatt-hours used during period.

Refere to Figure 11.11 for monthly meter reading.

Electric bill computation:
      Service charge: $250.00
      Kilowatt-hours:
          On-peak: 20,167 x $0.10   2016.70
          Off-peak: 30,000 x $0.04   1200.00
      Total $3486.70

Meter reading from Figure 11.11 is 50,167.
Off-peak: 50,167-20,167 = 30,000

FIGURE 11.14 A flat-rate kilowatt-hour with off-peak and on-peak rate schedule.

Service Commission. The electric utility must apply for rate increases or decreases. During the public hearing, you can present a case for lower rates. You must present data and indicate the impact of the new or proposed rate on your business. While you may not be able to prevent rates from increasing, you may influence the rate-setting commission to keep rate increases to a reasonable level.

DEMAND RATES

In addition to charges for kilowatt-hours, most hospitality businesses must pay a demand surcharge for either kilovolt-ampere or kilowatt-hour maximum requirements during short time periods. The time period is usually defined as an average 15-minute (0.25-hour) period.

Demand surcharges may also be on-peak, partial on-peak, or off-peak. An example surcharge rate is shown in Figure 11.15. These surcharges increase your electric bill by the amount shown.

POWER FACTOR SURCHARGES

Many hospitality operations that have large buildings, such as hotels, health-care units, and institutional complexes, may also be subject to a power factor surcharge. This means that if your building power factor drops below a preset level (usually 0.85) during any average 15-minute (0.25-hour) time

Refer to Figure 11.14 for initial electric bill.

Electric demand data:

> Maximum on-peak demand 5:15 p.m. (1715 hours) on June 25 was 417 kilowatts.
>
> Maximum off-peak demand 2:18 a.m. (0218 hours) on June 8 was 659 kilowatts.

Demand costs:

> On-peak: $8 per kilowatt
> Off-peak: $1 per kilowatt

Electric costs:

Previous computations (Figure 11.14)	$3486.70
On-peak demand: $8 x 417	3336.00
Off-peak demand: $1 x 659	659.00
Total charges including demand surcharges	$7481.70

FIGURE 11.15 Demand surcharges affect the electric bill.

period during the month, your electric bill will increase. This is very similar to the demand surcharge discussed in the preceding paragraph.

These power factor surcharges could also apply to on-peak, partial on-peak, or off-peak periods and could have serious effects on your electric bill. One of the simpler surcharge techniques is shown in Figure 11.16. It is called a demand-equalization surcharge.

Other Electric-Energy Charges

The electric utility may also be authorized by the rate-setting commission to impose additional charges. Common additional charges are: customer service charges, deferred energy charges, environment pollution control charges, and taxes or franchise fees.

Customer Service Charge. A very common charge, the customer service charge, is usually a flat monthly fee paid by all customers. The amount is usually small compared to the total hospitality electric bill. This flat fee is assessed to cover such items as meter reading, bill processing, receipts processing, and losses from customers who do not pay their bills. This fee can vary from $5 to $450 per month.

Deferred Energy Charge. The public rate-setting commission must generally estimate future energy costs used to generate electric energy. The deferred energy charge is a correction technique used to compensate for either overcharging or undercharging customers in the past.

Refer to Figures 11.14 and 11.15 for initial electric bill and demand data.
Electric power factor data:

Minimum on-peak power factor 1:52 P.M. (1352 hours) on June 14 was 0.68.

Minimum off-peak power factor 4:58 A.M. (0458 hours) on June 21 was 0.75.

Power factor demand surcharge:

A power factor demand surcharge is made whenever the power factor drops below 0.85 during the month.
On-peak: $10 per unit
Off-peak: $1 per unit

Electric costs:

Previous computations (Figure 11.14)	$3486.70
On-peak surcharge: (0.85/0.68) x $10 x 417	5212.50
Off-peak surcharge: (0.85/0.75) x $1 x 659	746.86
Total charges including surcharges	$9446.06

FIGURE 11.16   Power factor "demand equalization" surcharge effects on the electric bill.

The deferred energy charge is usually assessed per kilowatt-hour. If the rate-setting commission has overestimated energy costs, the electric utility has consequently overcharged its customers. The future deferred energy charge is then adjusted as a credit on the electric bill for a set period of time (see Figure 11.17). This allows the electric utility to pay back its customers.

If the estimated energy cost was lower than the actual cost, the additional energy cost will be spread over future energy bills for a set time period (see Figure 11.17). Your energy bills will be higher in this more common case.

See Fig. 11.14 for basic data.
Example 1: The deferred energy charge is $0.0025 per kilowatt-hour
(total on- and off-peak)
$0.0025 × 50,167: $125.42
Example 2: The deferred energy credit is $0.0025 per kilowatt-hour
(total on- and off-peak)
$0.0025 × 50,167: $125.42 (credit)
Example 1 increases total electric charges by $125.42.
Example 2 decreases total electric charges by $125.42.

FIGURE 11.17   Deferred energy charges.

Environment Pollution Control Charge.   Most electric-generating plants are over 20 years old. When they were built, environment pollution control was minimal or nonexistent. In the United States, federal and state governments have passed pollution control laws and ordinances during the past 20 years. More recently, many foreign countries have followed suit. These laws require electric utilities to reduce environment pollutants, so that new generation facilities must be designed with proper pollution control equipment. For existing power plants, electric utilities have had to invest in new equipment to satisfy these new laws. The environment pollution control surcharge allows the electric utility to recover its investment and maintenance requirement for this equipment.

Taxes or Franchise Fees.   Some government agencies impose sales or use taxes that apply to total electric charges. Other agencies impose franchise fees. These taxes and fees increase total electric charges. The effect of this taxing will be shown in the next section.

Average Cost per Kilowatt-Hour

Although a rate schedule is used to determine the total electric charges for a building, it also serves another very important purpose. The total bill can be used to determine the average cost per kilowatt-hour. The energy operating cost of a unit of equipment can be determined, once the average cost per kilowatt-hour is known. Figure 11.18 shows how to compute the average cost per kilowatt-hour from an example electric bill.

The energy operating cost is very important to a manager who must purchase new equipment. Suppose that a manager who is considering a new air-conditioning unit for a meeting or banquet room has specified the heat removal rate and now has information on two units, both of which will remove the required amount of heat. Each unit has a different initial cost

---

Refer to Figures 11.14, 11.16, and 11.17 for initial electric bill, power factor demand surcharges, and deferred energy cost data. Local government taxes are 5 percent of total charges.

Electric costs:

Previous computations (Figure 11.16)	$9446.06
Deferred energy charge (Figure 11.17)	125.42
Taxes: 0.05 x $9571.48	478.57
Total charges including taxes	$10,050.05

Average cost per kilowatt-hour:
Total electric charges)/(Total kilowatt-hours)
($10,050.05)/(50,167) $0.2003

FIGURE 11.18   Total electric charges and the average cost per kilowatt-hour.

and each unit consumes a different amount of energy. See Figure 11.19 for an analysis of this situation.

THE ELECTRICAL SERVICE SYSTEM FOR BUILDINGS

Electric energy is supplied to a building by the electric utility by means of service wires. These wires are connected to various electric meters that measure kilowatt-hours, demand, and power factor; to a master control switch inside or outside the building; to a transformer; to distribution centers; to circuit panels; and to an emergency electric-generation system.

The master control switch is usually locked so that complete control is maintained. There must be a service access to the switch from the exterior of the building for the fire department and the electric utility. In case of fire, electric energy may have to be disconnected because of potential hazards

---

Data are obtained for two electric motors (A and B). Motor B has a higher operating efficiency. Both motors are rated at 5 horsepower. Both motors will operate 12 hours per day, 7 days per week, and 52 weeks per year (meeting room ventilation fan).

Energy cost (see Figure 11.18): $0.2003 per kilowatt-hour

Motor A:
      Initial cost: $250
      Estimated life: 12 years
      Energy consumption: 4.5 kilowatts
Motor B:
      Initial cost: $350
      Estimated life: 15 years
      Energy consumption: 4.25 kilowatts

Cost comparison:
  Motor A

Capital cost: ($250)/12	$20.83
Energy cost: 12 x 7 x 52 x 4.5 x $0.2003	3937.10
Total cost:	$3957.93

  Motor B

Capital cost: ($350)/15	$23.33
Energy cost: 12 x 7 x 52 x 4.25 x $0.2003	3718.37
Total cost:	$3741.70

Conclusion: Motor B should be purchased with a savings of $216.23 per year.

FIGURE 11.19   Cost comparison for two electric motors (Motor A, normal efficiency of about 82 percent; Motor B, high efficiency of about 87 percent).

caused by pumping water into an electrically energized building. The master control switch contains various types of system protectors, either fuses or circuit breakers, which are discussed in a later section.

The energy may flow to transformers, which reduce the voltage supplied by the electric utility. The transformer decreases high voltage supplied by the electric utility to the correct level to meet the needs and requirements of the building. The advantage of purchasing high-voltage energy is that many electric utilities discount the unit cost per kilowatt-hour if high voltage is purchased. Transformers are frequently placed in a fireproof vault.

After the energy is reduced to required voltage levels, it proceeds to distribution centers within the building. Separate fuses or circuit-breaker protection devices are found in the distribution center for each section of the building. In this manner, energy to any portion of the building can be disconnected without disrupting service in the remainder of the building.

Energy flows from each of the distribution centers to circuit panels. These panels serve as the final point of electric control for each outlet, motor, lamp, switch, and any other device located in that section of the building. Each of these devices or circuits has a separate fuse or circuit-breaker protection device.

Electric service entrances for a large building and a small building are shown in Figure 11.20. The ground network, as shown in the figure, is an essential portion of a complete system. The purposes of a ground are to pro-

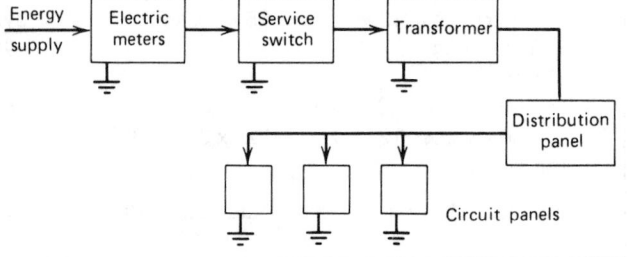

FIGURE 11.20 Electrical service for buildings.

Actual service entrance installation

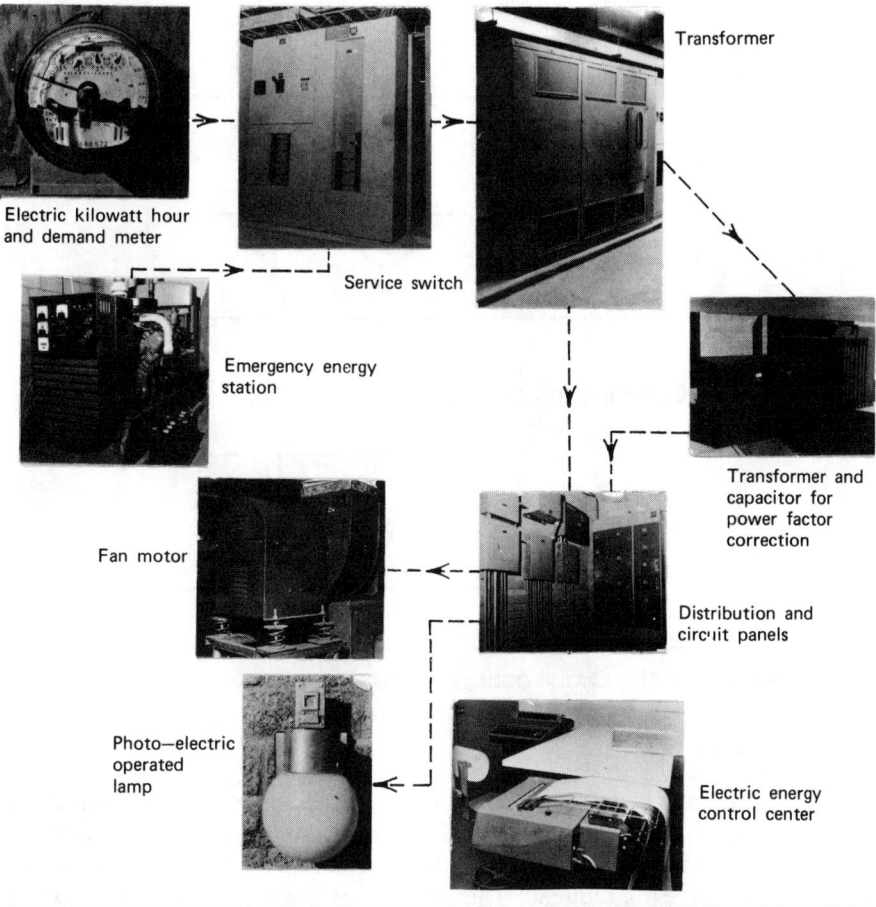

FIGURE 11.20 *(Continued)*

tect human life, appliances and devices, and the electric network. The ground serves as a potential path for unwanted, excessive, or dangerous energy flow. Each of the components in the electric service entrance is connected to the ground network.

ELECTRIC CIRCUITS

Electric appliances and devices may be connected to a source of energy by one of two wiring techniques—series or parallel circuits. Figure 11.21 diagrams several devices and appliances connected by each of these wiring techniques.

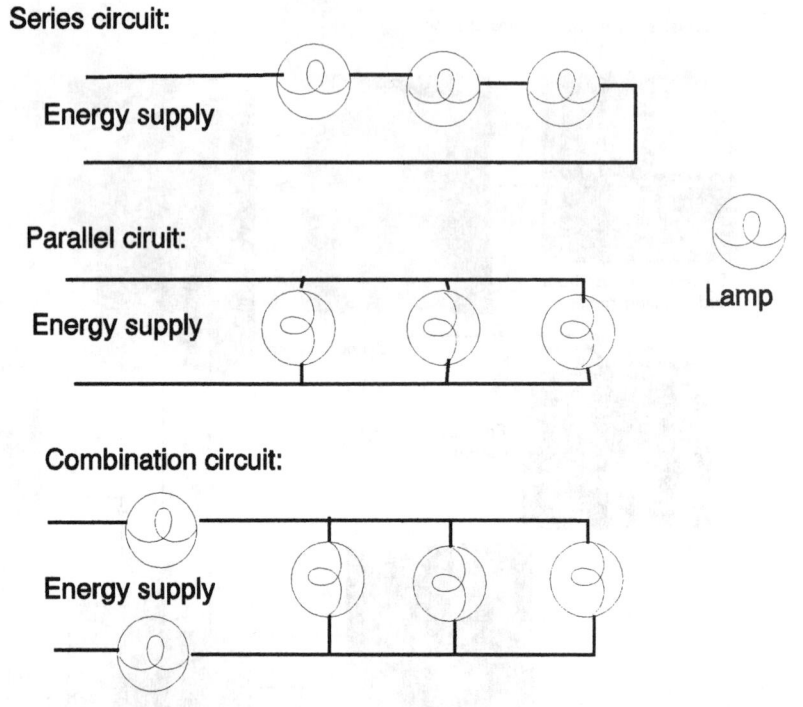

FIGURE 11.21   Circuit arrangements.

SERIES CIRCUITS

Each appliance has a resistance to electric-energy flow. With the series circuit, the effect of various resistances is cumulative; that is, as more devices are connected to the circuit, the overall resistance is increased and the flow of amperes is reduced. This circuit has limited use in the hospitality industry. Its primary use is for security systems and for lighting in large areas such as parking lots. Figure 11.22 shows a parking-lot lighting arrangement. If one lamp is broken, however, all lamps cease to operate because the circuit is broken.

PARALLEL CIRCUITS

The parallel circuit is the primary method of connecting appliances to electric energy. It allows each appliance to receive its required amount of energy (amperes and volts). It is shown in Figure 11.23. Switches and fuses are connected in series with the devices they control in the circuit. If a switch is off, or if a fuse is not operating, energy will not flow. As appliances are added to the circuit, the total energy requirement represents the sum of the individual wattages of each appliance as shown in Figure 11.23.

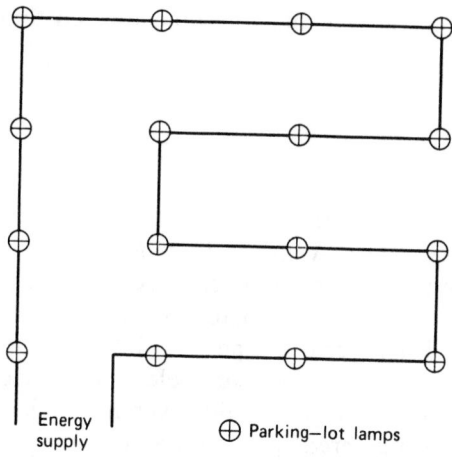

FIGURE 11.22 Use of series circuit for parking-lot lighting.

A. Circuit and appliances:

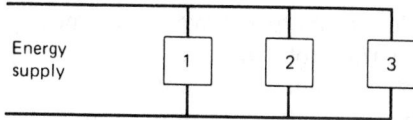

Appliance 1: 1000 watts
Appliance 2: 2000 watts
Appliance 3: 3000 watts
Energy source: 120 volts

B. Wattage requirement = sum of the wattages of individual appliances = 1000 + 2000 + 3000 = 6000

C. Ampere requirement $I = \dfrac{6000}{120} = 50$ amperes

FIGURE 11.23 Parallel-circuit energy requirements.

Voltage Drop

Electric wires resist the flow of energy, and this resistance must be considered in electric design. Wire is a series resistance. If the resistance of the wires is large, energy is required to force amperes through the wires; this loss of energy is called *voltage drop*. Voltage drop means that watts are consumed in overcoming the resistance of wires.

The manager must be aware that voltage drop is always present in electric circuits because perfect wires (zero-resistance wires) are not available. The manager can, however, specify one of several techniques to reduce voltage drop. The more common techniques are: use larger-sized wires (they have lower electrical resistance); restrict the number of appliances per circuit or use low-wattage appliances; operate dual-voltage appliances at the highest voltage; and design the system with a specified voltage drop. The effects of voltage drop are shown in Figure 11.24. Voltage drop can be costly but can be controlled by the manager.

PROTECTION DEVICES

Fuses

A fuse is a device that protects an electric network. It consists of a protection element that has a set resistance. Amperes flowing through the fuse generate heat. When a specified number of amperes is exceeded, the protective element gets hot and melts, stopping ampere flow. Fuses are rated in amperes. A fuse of a specified number of amperes will operate in a prescribed voltage range. Fuses may have replaceable elements. Once a fuse size is determined for a circuit, the manager should never allow a larger fuse to be installed in its place. Fuse sizes are dependent on the ampere capacity of the appliance or on the maximum ampere capacity of the wire, whichever is lower. Figure 11.25 shows some common fuses. Fuses are generally available in a variety of sizes.

Some appliances, especially electric motors, have large ampere demand when they are started. A small electric motor rated at 15 amperes probably will never get started if it is protected with a 15-ampere fuse. Its ampere starting requirement may be in excess of 30 or 40 amperes for a short time. Placing a 30-ampere fuse on the motor circuit allows the motor to start but sacrifices motor protection. A time-delay fuse rated at 15 amperes allows a short overload of amperes for start-up and also protects the motor under operating conditions.

If fuses are to be used, the manager should specify nontamperable fuses. These fuses come in two parts (see Figure 11.25). One part contains the fuse

---

1. Use large-size wires.
   Replace AWG 14 wire with AWG 12, because it has less electrical resistance.

2. Reduce the number of appliances per circuit.
   Each kitchen oven has a separate circuit.

3. Operate dual-voltage appliances at the higher voltage.
   Less amperes are required and there is less heat generation (resistance) at the higher voltage.

4. Design the wiring system with a lower voltage drop criteria.
   Use a 2 percent design voltage drop rather than a 5 percent design voltage drop. This will result in either (1) or (2) or a combination of (1) and (2) as shown above.

FIGURE 11.24   Voltage drop reduction techniques.

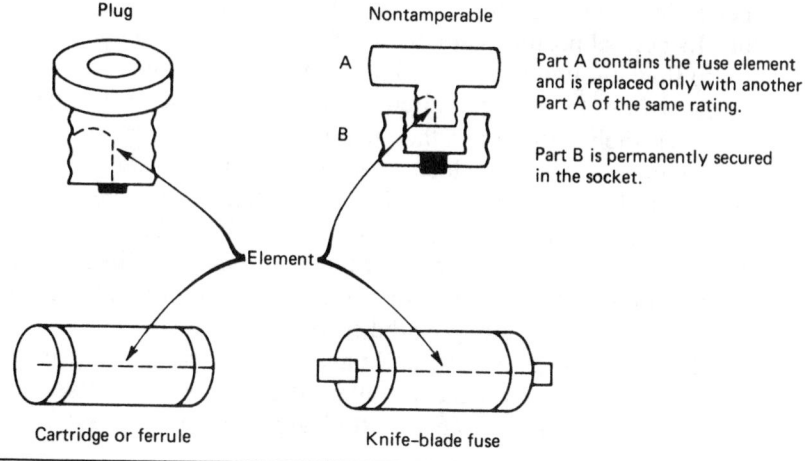

Plug

Nontamperable

A

Part A contains the fuse element and is replaced only with another Part A of the same rating.

B

Part B is permanently secured in the socket.

Element

Cartridge or ferrule

Knife-blade fuse

FIGURE 11.25 Example fuses.

element, which can be replaced. It is inserted into a second part, which, once placed in the fuse socket, cannot be removed. The nonremovable part will accept only the correct-size part containing the fuse element. Hence, a 15-ampere fuse comes in two parts, one containing the fuse element. These parts cannot be inserted into, or interchanged with, fuses of any other size.

Circuit Breakers

Circuit breakers are rated in amperes and are reusable. When their ampere specification is exceeded, they automatically trip off. Circuit breakers are designed to be turned on and off many times before they fail. They also cost much more than fuses. There are three types of circuit breakers: heat, electromagnetic, and ground-fault circuit interrupters.

Heat-Type Circuit Breakers

When excessive amperes flow through a device, they generate heat, with a resulting rise in temperature. The heat-type circuit breaker reacts to excessive heat by shutting off the flow of electricity whenever the circuit breaker reaches a specified temperature. To be reactivated, the unit must cool down to within the temperature operating range of the unit. These circuit breakers operate effectively on ac or dc.

Regular, or Electromagnetic, Circuit Breakers

Electromagnetic circuit breakers operate only on ac. They can be made in any size. They are much more expensive than fuses or heat-type circuit breakers of comparable sizes. The circuit breaker's external appearance is very similar to a wall switch. Unlike the on–off wall switch, the electromagnetic circuit breaker generally has three operating positions: on, reset, and off. Its normal positions are on or off, but if an excessive number of amperes try to flow through it, it trips to reset. When it is in the reset position, energy will not flow through the circuit. To reactivate the circuit breaker, it must first be switched to off and then to on.

The operation of the electromagnetic circuit breaker is much more complex than the heat-type circuit breaker. Alternating current flows through a coil of wire within the device. As ac flows, it produces an electromagnetic field within the coil. The force of the electromagnet directly corresponds to ampere flow. When the ampere rating of the circuit breaker is exceeded, the device trips to reset, stopping the current flow.

Most circuits in modern buildings are now protected with these circuit breakers. They are essentially nontamperable, and extra fuses do not have to be inventoried. They are an almost ideal protection device.

Ground-Fault Circuit Interrupters

In certain locations, such as bathrooms, outside energy service, swimming pools, and other areas indicated by local electric codes, special ground-fault circuit interrupters are required. These virtually eliminate all dangers of electrical shock. Ground-fault circuit interrupters measure ampere flow in both the basic supply wire and the ground. If there is any difference in energy flow between the two wires, the device trips to reset. The unit is reactivated by switching to off and then to on. Thus, two interconnected circuit breakers are included in one package. They are designed for maximum human protection. The unit also has a built-in testing device so that the circuit interrupter can be periodically checked to determine if the ground-fault component is working properly.

The ground-fault circuit interrupter is pictured in Figure 11.26. You may have seen these devices in bathrooms in place of regular wall outlets. In such locations, the interrupter protects only the outlet. If the unit is located back in the circuit panel, it protects all devices on the circuit.

WIRES

A common electric wire is shown in Figure 11.27. It consists of an electrical conductor, preferably copper, covered with an insulator. The purpose of the insulator is to confine electric flow to the conductor. Wire color coding is used so that the electrician can identify the different wires when connecting them at two or more locations within a building. The white insulated wire is usually attached to ground.

The diameter of the conductor determines the number of amperes it can safely carry. Insulation type and thickness specify the maximum voltage the wire can handle. Insulation type and thickness will also vary because of the

FIGURE 11.26 Ground-fault circuit interrupter (courtesy of Nevada Power Company).

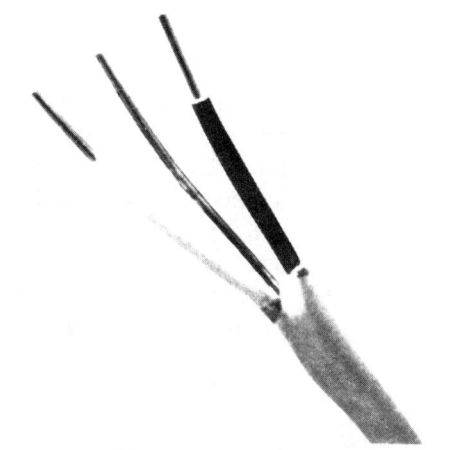

FIGURE 11.27 Electric wire (courtesy of Nevada Power Company).

environment to which the wire may be exposed. When specifying wires, you must specify the normal or expected environment.

Wires are generally rated in amperes. Figure 11.28 indicates normal maximum ampere flow for a copper conductor wire with thermoplastic insulation (type-T wire). Two wire diameter designation systems are used in the table. American Wire Gage (AWG) is used in the United States for small-

Wire designation	Wire size	Ampere capacity for type-T copper-wire insulation	Resistance of wire ohms per 1000 feet (305 meters)
AWG	14	15	2.575
AWG	10	30	1.018
AWG	8	40	0.641
AWG	0	125	0.102
MCM	300	240	0.036

FIGURE 11.28   Samples of size, amperes capacity, and resistance of wires.[2]

diameter wires. The MCM system, which measures thousands of circular mills, is used throughout the world for large-diameter wires. Figure 11.28 also shows wire resistance. Comparing the resistance of an AWG 14 wire to an AWG 8 wire (2.575 versus 0.641 ohms per 1000 feet [305 meters]), you can quickly determine the effects of small-diameter wires and the voltage drop concept previously discussed. Once wire is installed in a building, the manager must be careful not to exceed its ampere capacity.

Cable

Several conductors, each with its separate insulation, can be combined with additional insulation to form a cable. Various types of cables are available; their potential use is limited by local electric codes. Common building cables are nonmetallic sheathed, armored, and conduit (see Figure 11.29). The latter two have a metallic covering that is used as a continuous ground. When the local code allows, metallic cables are interchangeable within a building. Special cables are also available for waterproof installations, underground wiring, and communication systems.

CODES AND TESTING

NATIONAL ELECTRIC CODE

The National Electric Code (NEC) is published periodically by the National Fire Protection Association. It contains the most up-to-date safety standards in the field of practical electricity. The NEC is based on experience, on an outstanding safety record, and on recent developments in electric theory and application. Many local codes are based on the provisions of the NEC.

In addition to being used as a standard for local electric codes, manufacturers build electric equipment according to standards established in the

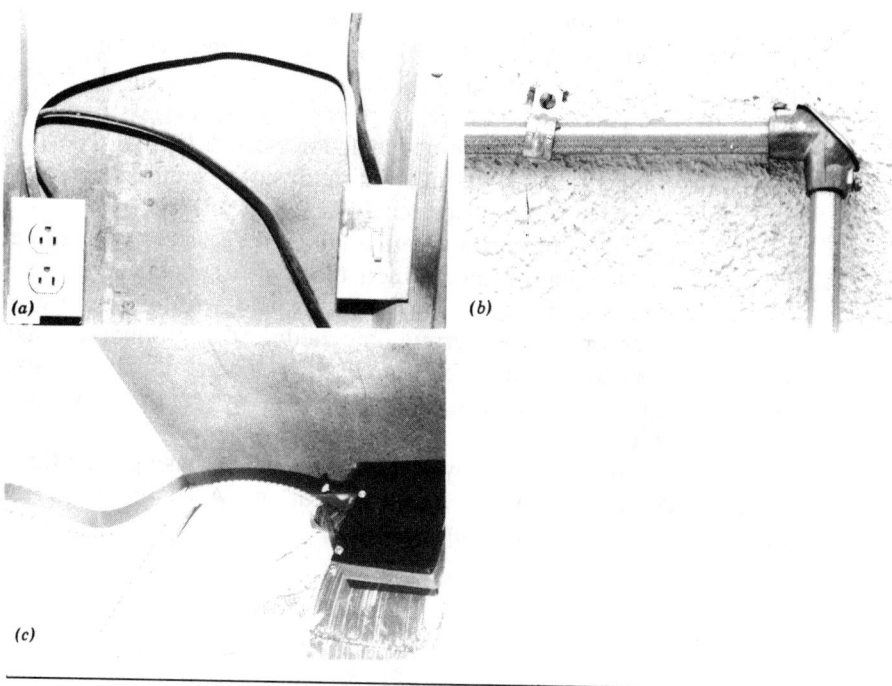

FIGURE 11.29 (*a*) Nonmetallic sheathed cable, (*b*) conduit, and (*c*) flexible steel cable.

NEC. When design approaches conflict, the NEC is generally cited as the ultimate authority. It is an excellent example of industry self-regulation.

The manager should always insist on following the NEC, except when local ordinances are more restrictive. Fire insurance companies use the NEC when determining insurance premiums for buildings. Any electric installation that is contrary to NEC recommendations usually results in higher insurance premiums.

UNDERWRITERS LABORATORIES

Underwriters Laboratories (UL) establishes test procedures; conducts tests on equipment, appliances, and devices; and approves tested items and unusual installations that are not covered in the National Electric Code or by its own standards.

A fundamental service provided by Underwriters Laboratories is its listing service. Electric device and appliance manufacturers may wish to have their devices approved by UL. They can submit their products to UL for testing. These products are subjected to a series of tests and must meet minimal performance standards to be listed. Representatives of UL may also purchase similar products at the retail and wholesale levels and spot-test them. If these products continue to pass the tests, they will continue to be listed; if not, they may be removed from the UL listing. The UL listing means that the products have met minimum safety standards and are generally satisfactory for "normal service."

Underwriters Laboratories offers additional services, such as certifying products and installations for which there are inadequate or nonexistent standards and specifications or an abnormal environment. Certification means that, according to current knowledge, the product or installation appears to meet minimum safety standards. The components and installation parts that make up the certified product must have had prior UL listings or UL certification.

UL listings may be used by the manager as purchasing specifications for products, devices, appliances, and installations. A UL listing, or certification, however, is not a warranty.

ELECTRIC HEAT

Electric heating provides the manager with an energy-efficient and very convenient source of heat. It is easy to control. It is extremely clean and nonpolluting. It generally has a low or minimal maintenance requirement, and repairs are easy to make. It offers several temperature options—high, medium, or low. Because of these advantages, it is a very popular form of heat in the hospitality industry. However, it may be expensive.

There are two general classifications of electric heaters; resistance heaters and electronic heat converters. Resistance heaters are the most common.

RESISTANCE HEATERS

Wires conducting electric energy have a resistance to the flow of energy. Electric-resistance heaters have wires with a relatively high resistance to electric-energy flow. Electric energy flowing through a resistance wire is converted to heat, causing the wire to get hot. Once its temperature exceeds the environment temperature, heat flows from the device to the environment. In pure resistance heating, the conversion of electric energy to heat energy is approximately 95 percent efficient.

Resistance heaters can be classified as high temperature, generally over 3000°F (1649°C); low temperature, 1600°F (871°C) or less; and medium temperature, 1600 to 3000°F (871 to 1649°C). The temperature ratings are not necessarily correlated to wattage ratings. Therefore, a manager can obtain the same number of heat units—Btu (watts)—from any of three heaters operating in a different temperature range.

High-Temperature Resistance Heaters

The most common high-temperature resistance heater is the ordinary incandescent lamp. The lamp generally converts about 95 percent of the electric energy input to heat output—the remaining 5 percent is light energy. Another common high-resistance heater is the quartz lamp. Its energy characteristics are equivalent to the incandescent lamp. Quartz is ideal because if water is accidentally splashed on it, quartz will not break.

These high-temperature resistance heaters are used in ovens, for food warmers in cafeterias, for space heating, and wherever a large amount of heat is to be concentrated in a small area. See Figure 11.30.

Medium-Temperature Resistance Heaters

Medium-temperature heaters are preferred by many managers because they feel that the lower operating temperatures, 1600 to 3000°F (871 to 1649°C), are safer than those previously discussed. The more common types are the quartz tube (the quartz lamp has sealed ends; the quartz tube does not) and various wire-type heaters found in some food-heating equipment and space heaters. When these units are in operation, the heating element glows with an orange or yellow color (high-temperature heaters usually show a white light). The conversion of electric energy to heat is again approximately 95 percent. See Figure 11.31.

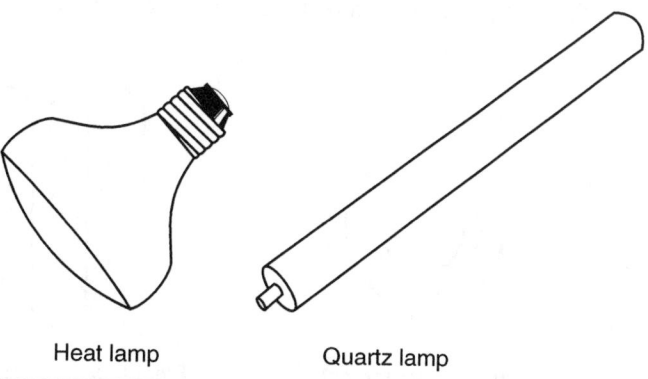

Heat lamp   Quartz lamp

FIGURE 11.30 High-temperature resistance heat sources.

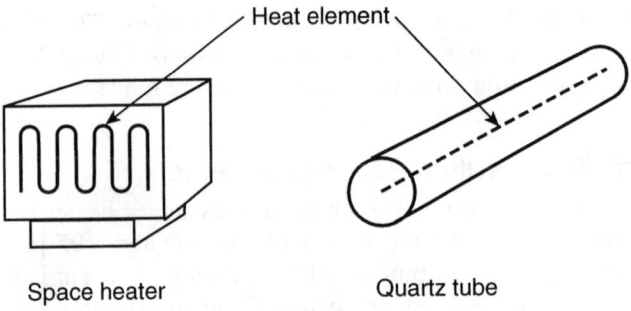

Space heater   Quartz tube

FIGURE 11.31   Medium-temperature resistance heat sources.

Low-Temperature Resistance Heaters

There are numerous types of low-temperature resistance heaters. The one you are probably most familiar with is the electric oven heater or the electric stove heating element. It consists of a resistance wire covered with insulation, with both wire and insulation sheathed in metal. When full voltage is impressed on it, it glows with a cherry-red color. This color signifies about 1600°F (871°C). These units are over 95 percent heat efficient. See Figure 11.32.

Other low-temperature heaters are wires that may or may not be insulated. They can provide very low temperatures, down to 40 to 55°F (4 to 13°C), and they are used to wrap around water pipes so that water contained within the pipe will not freeze when the environment temperature drops to 32°F (0°C) or less.

Maintenance of Resistance Heaters

The efficiency of electric heaters can be greatly reduced if the units are dirty. Dirt, dust, and lint can result in units that are only 50 percent efficient,

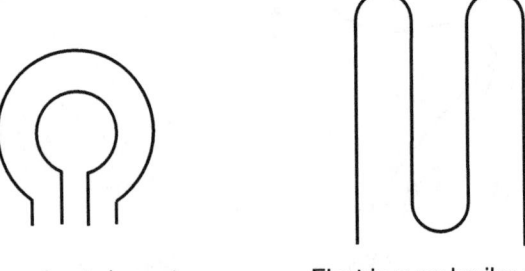

Stove heat element   Electric oven broiler unit

FIGURE 11.32   Low-temperature resistance heat sources.

which doubles the operating cost and increases the fire hazard of these units. If reflective surfaces are used in conjunction with the heat element, these surfaces must also be kept clean.

The normal resistance heater will last for thousands of hours. Generally, the elements are not repaired but are just replaced. Element replacement is very simple, almost as easy as replacing an electric lamp.

ELECTRONIC HEAT CONVERTERS

Electronic heat conversion systems have been extensively used for food preparation. The microwave oven is a good example. In comparison to normal ovens, it is very efficient (about 70 percent). Current microwave ovens have only a limited capacity and heat output per hour when fully utilized. This may be a restricting factor when a large number of items are needed in a short time.

Microwave oven surfaces must be clean because accumulations of dirt will absorb energy and decrease the overall cooking efficiency of the unit. Some units are available with built-in temperature-sensing devices that are inserted in food before the oven can be operated. When the sensor reaches a desired temperature, the energy source is automatically turned off. Repair costs on these units may be high.

Microwave units have also been used with varying degrees of success for thawing frozen foods. Foods are quickly thawed, thus greatly reducing preparation time while retaining a high quality that could be impaired with conventional thawing.

ELECTRIC LIGHTING

One of the primary uses of electric energy is for artificial lighting. In most buildings, lighting represents the second-highest electric-energy use, following electric-motor requirements. Older (pre-1980) lighting systems represent an inefficient use of electric energy. Various types of electric lamps range from about 5 percent to more than 35 percent efficient. The remainder of the energy is discharged as expensive and frequently unwanted heat. The overall lighting efficiency in the hospitality industry may be considerably less than the indicated percentage because of poor lighting characteristics in many buildings or rooms.

Light, its reflection, and object visibility are all interrelated. A light source radiates energy that you cannot see. Atmospheric air is transparent to light energy, which means that air does not absorb or reflect the energy passing through it. As light energy strikes a surface, it may be absorbed and converted to heat, which lowers lighting efficiency; the surface may transmit some of the energy (another energy loss); or light may be reflected. You see only reflected light.

Light-colored surfaces reflect a high percentage of the light striking them. A black surface reflects very little light; hence, it absorbs or destroys light energy. It is more difficult and costly to light darker-colored than lighter-colored rooms.

Light sources can also be different colors, which produce various qualities of light. Common light sources provide "white" light, which is the generation of all colors; so various objects lighted with white light appear natural or retain their real color. Red appears red when lighted with white light. Actually, the red object is radiated with all the colors from a white light source. The red object reflects only red light energy and absorbs nonred colors.

Insects are yellow-blind and cannot see objects that reflect yellow. Yellow to insects is like black to us. Hence, yellow light sources do not attract insects. Insects can see "black" light, which we cannot see. Therefore, black light sources are used for insect traps. Some street lights—for example, mercury-vapor lamps—attract large numbers of insects; others, such as sodium-vapor lamps, which generate yellow colors, do not appear to attract insects.

LIGHTING TERMINOLOGY

Lamps and Luminaries

A *lamp* is a source of light. A lighted candle is a lamp because it is a source of light. A flashlight is a lamp. The common electric lamps are incandescent and fluorescent. Lamps are available in different shapes and sizes.

A lamp is inserted into a lighting fixture. The combined lamp and lighting fixture is a *luminaire*. If an incandescent lighting fixture is capable of holding a 25-, 40-, 60-, or 75-watt incandescent lamp, the single lighting fixture becomes one of four luminaries. The general light output characteristics of the lighting fixture change with each size of lamp, resulting in different types of luminaries.

Lumens and Footcandles (Lux)

Lamp light output is given in *lumens*. A lumen is a quantity of light. One very good efficiency rating for lamps is the number of lumens produced per watt of energy input. This technique allows the manager to compare different lamps and the cost of lighting.

The lumen is the amount of light energy that strikes an area at a specific distance from a standard candle. If 1 lumen falls on a 1-square-foot area at a distance of 1 foot from a standard candle, it is called 1 *footcandle* of light intensity; or if 1 lumen strikes 1 square meter of surface at a distance of 1 meter from a standard candle, it is called 1 *lux*. Footcandles and lux refer to the intensity of light.

Room lighting design is based on footcandles (lux) and lumens. The relationship is shown in Figure 11.33. As you move farther away from the lamp, the lumens are spread over a larger surface area, so lighting intensity decreases. If correct lighting is not provided in an area, poorly lit objects can become hazards for guests, patients, or employees.

Lighting design depends on the footcandle (lux) intensity required at the work surface. Highly detailed work or work with high sight requirements demands high-intensity light for maximum worker productivity. Hence, lighting requirements vary with the task being done. Figure 11.34 shows some recommended light intensities for various tasks. These are based on extensive research and are hospitality industry standards.

RESISTANCE-TYPE LAMPS

Incandescent Lamps

One very common source of light is the incandescent lamp, which has a high-electric-resistance filament wire. As energy flows through the filament wire, it will incandesce, or glow. The emitted energy is visible light and heat.

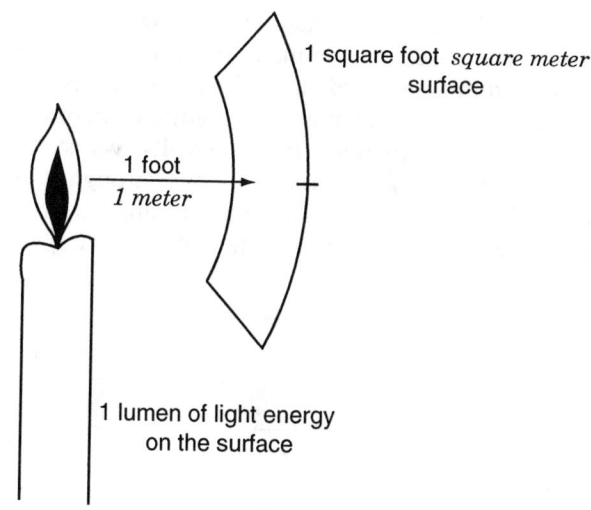

1 square foot *square meter* surface

1 foot
1 meter

1 lumen of light energy on the surface

Standard candle

Footcandle: *lux*

Relationship: 1 footcandle = *10.76 lux*

FIGURE 11.33 Comparison of footcandles and lux of lighting intensity.

Work area	Footcandles	Lux
Kitchen work area	30	322.8
Classroom	40	430.4
Bathroom	30	322.8
Hotel: general areas	10	107.6
Accounting and bookkeeping	100–150	1076–1614
Foodservice:		
Fast-food	40–50	430.4–538
Moderate-priced	10–20	107.6–215.2
High-priced	5–15	53.8–161.4

FIGURE 11.34 Recommended footcandle and lux intensities for selected tasks.

The lamp is available in a variety of shapes, bases, and operating characteristics. The more common shapes are A (standard or general service), PS (pear straight), C and F (flame), G (globe), PAR (parabolic), R (reflector), S (straight), and T (tubular). The bulbs may be clear or internally frosted and are generally available in a variety of colors. The two most common lamp bases are medium and 3 contact medium (a lamp with two filaments, which can be operated in combinations, for example, 30 watts, 70 watts, or 100 watts). Other bases include medium skirted, mogul, mogul 3 contact, mogul prefocus, miniature candelabra, candelabra bayonet, candelabra prefocus, intermediate, medium bipost, and medium side-prong.

Incandescent lamps are rated in volts, watts, hours (life expectancy in average operating hours), and lumens. Through lamp purchasing specifications and with knowledge of your building's voltage, you can take advantage of the operating characteristics of these lamps. Figure 11.35 shows the

	Supply volts		
	120	110	130
Lamp voltage rating	120	120	120
Effects:			
Watts	100	85	115
Lumens	1600	1300	2000
Life (hours)	1000	1500 or more	500 or less

FIGURE 11.35 Effects of voltage supply on operating characteristics of an incandescent lamp.

normal operating characteristics of a common incandescent lamp. Observe the 130-volt column. This column clearly shows how the basic lamp rating factors change when the lamp is operated at a higher than rated voltage. The second column shows the effects of operating the same 120-volt lamp at 110 volts.

You can purchase lamps rated at higher voltages, say, 130 volts, and operate them at your building voltage, say, 118 volts. In this case, column 2 of Figure 11.35 applies. You receive a little less light output, but lamp life expectancy is greatly increased and wattage consumption decreases.

The incandescent lamp radiates visible light that is rich in such warm colors as red, orange, and yellow. Hence, the lamps have a tendency to bring out the warm reddish color of food products, especially cooked meat and red and blush-color wines. Many foodservice operation interior color combinations are based on warm colors, which complement cooked meat items on the menu. Then, too, people look better in incandescent lighting, which highlights warm or pink flesh tones. The major disadvantage of incandescent lamps is their low light efficiency: They are only about 5 to 15 percent light efficient.

Figure 11.36 shows the relative shapes of a standard incandescent lamp (the A lamp), the R lamp, the PAR lamp, and the newest incandescent lamp, the ER lamp. The standard lamp shape, for example "A" shape, is not very effective as a down-light source, as light is emitted from the entire bulb. The R or PAR lamp concentrates the light emission by using an internal reflector surface. The new ER (ellipsoidal reflector) lamp concentrates light flow; hence, it directs 50 percent more lumens in a specified area. As a result 75-watt ER lamps can replace 150 watt R lamps. It is recommended that these lamps be tried before the mass replacement of all R and PAR lamps on the property.

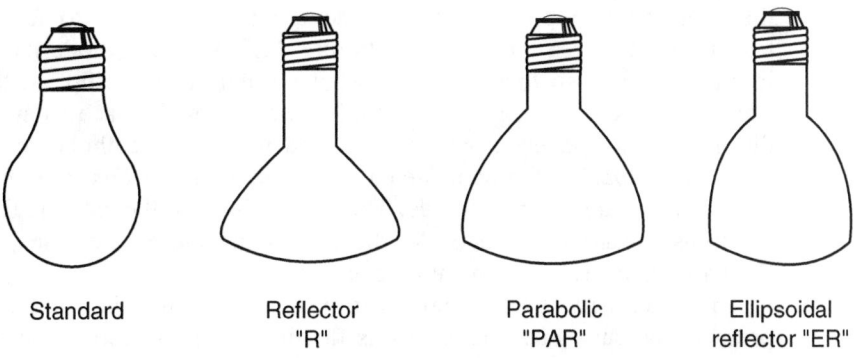

| Standard | Reflector "R" | Parabolic "PAR" | Ellipsoidal reflector "ER" |

FIGURE 11.36 Lamp shapes; ER is the most light efficient.

There are also lower-wattage PAR lamps available at the present time. It is recommended that 75-watt PARs be replaced with the new 65-watt PARs and 120-watt PARs replace the older 150-watt PARs.

Incandescent lamps range in size from 5 to 1500 watts. The life expectancy varies with the lamp type. The normal or standard incandescent has a rated life of 750 to 2500 hours. The reflector type incandescent lamps have rated lives of 2000 to 5000 hours.

Tungsten-Halogen Lamps

Another form of resistance lamp is the tungsten-halogen lamp, frequently called a halogen lamp. The life of a halogen lamp is generally greater than a normal-life incandescent lamp; its life varies from 2000 to 3000 hours. Its efficiency equals that of the most efficient incandescent lamp (12 to 15 percent light efficient), and its lumen output does not greatly decrease with its age; however, its initial cost is higher in comparison to an incandescent lamp. Whenever a single-lamp wattage requirement exceeds 200 watts, this lamp should be used in place of the incandescent lamp. Incandescent and halogen lamps have similar light quality characteristics and can generally be interchanged.

Halogen lamps are also available as reflector and nonreflector lamps. Generally, a 90-watt halogen can be used in place of a 150-watt conventional PAR incandescent lamp.

ELECTRIC-DISCHARGE LAMPS

Fluorescent Lamps

The fluorescent lamp is an electric-discharge lamp, which operates on alternating current, or simulated alternating current. The operation of the lamp is complex compared to an incandescent lamp. Like the incandescent lamp, the fluorescent lamp has a small filament, but its purpose is to heat an electric device called a *cathode* (see Figure 11.37). The cathode has voltage impressed on it, so that it becomes heated and "charged up" at the same time. The electric energy now actually flows through space as an electron discharge, and the electrons are attracted to another cathode-type device (called an *anode*) at the opposite end of the lamp. Electrons are constituents of atoms that are on the cathode. The high voltage at the cathode forces the electrons toward the anode. As the alternating current reverses, electron flow also changes between cathode and anode.

The space between the ends (within the glass tube) is filled with low-pressure mercury gas. The electrons flowing from one end to the other are absorbed by the mercury gas, and energy is emitted—for every action there is a reaction. Now, as this different energy passes through the glass tube

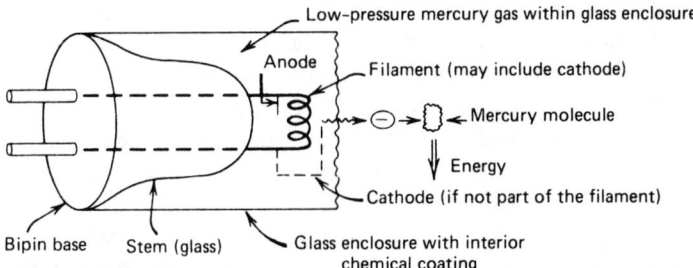

The heated cathode emits electrons that are attracted to the anode at the opposite end of the lamp (both ends are identical). The electron strikes a mercury molecule, which results in an emission of energy that is converted to visible light as it passes through the glass enclosure and chemical coating.

FIGURE 11.37 Fluorescent lamp operation.

with its chemically coated interior, visible light energy is produced along with low-temperature heat.

Light efficiency levels of 16 to 26 percent are obtained with a fluorescent lamp when generating "white" light. Its life, which is greater than that of a normal incandescent lamp, depends on the number of times the lamp is turned on. The optimal life is one start cycle and continuous operation, in which case it may provide efficient light for 16,000 to 24,000 hours, compared to 750 to 1500 hours for normal-life incandescent lamps. Its light efficiency decreases with age and hours of operation.

The color output characteristics of the lamp are variable and depend on the interior glass bulb coating. Almost every color of light can be produced. The use of warm-color-producing lamps is recommended in the hospitality industry, as their color emission is similar to incandescent lamps. However, warm-color-producing fluorescent lamps are less energy efficient than cool-color-emission fluorescent lamps. For example, a red-color-emission fluorescent lamp converts only 6 to 7 percent of its energy consumption to the production of light, whereas a blue-color-producing lamp is over 20 percent light efficient.

The light efficiency of the lamp decreases in cold and warm temperature environments. The lamp is designed for an 80°F (26.67°C) environment. Each 18°F (10°C) reduction in environment temperature reduces the light output by almost 50 percent. This is why they are very slow starting in cold temperatures, especially below freezing—32°F (0°C). When the temperature is very low, around 0°F (-17.78°C), the lamp may not start without external heating. Its shapes are limited to the familiar tube, U, circline, and the newer PL (compact twin tube) and SL (compact, double-folded, bent tube) types. The SL was designed as a replacement for the incandescent bulb and uses a medium incandescent (screw-in) base.

The lamp requires a special electric circuit for operation (see Figure 11.38). A ballast is required and some lamps need a separate starter. The common magnetic ballast, a wire wrapped around a piece of iron, causes an induction load, which causes volts and amperes to be out of phase; this is required for the electric-discharge effect. The ballast also provides normal voltage (about 120 volts) for starting the lamp and lowers the voltage (less than 100 volts) for normal lamp operation. This reduces the power factor.

Some older types of fluorescent lamps require a separate starter. The starter allows a filament to heat the cathode quickly so that the electric-discharge process can start. If any one of the three items that make up the lamp—lamp, ballast, and starter—malfunctions, the lamp will not work. Normally, the starter is the first item to fail in the circuit. It is always a good practice to replace the starter every time a lamp is replaced.

The instant-start fluorescent lamp eliminates the separate starter. These lamps usually have a smaller diameter, making it easier to start the electric-discharge process. As the lamps do not require a starter, it is easier to maintain the circuit.

Another type of fluorescent lamp is the rapid-start lamp. The cathode of this lamp is always kept hot even when the lamp is off. This is done through a special ballast-wiring technique. Although the lamp is quickly activated, it is consuming energy all the time; however, the consumption of energy is less when the lamp is off. These lamps have generally been replaced with instant-start lamps.

There are three other types of fluorescent lamps: slimline, high output, and self-ballasted. Flourescent lamps are available in various wattage ratings, ranging from 4 to 110 watts. A T12 lamp is 1.5 inches (38.1 millimeters) in diameter, each unit in the 12 rating being equal to about 1/8 inch (about 3 millimeters). Note, the same designation is also used for other

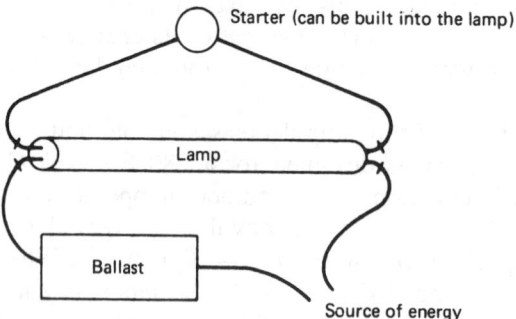

Starter is only used to supply high voltage to the lamp filament to start the lamp.
Ballast reduces lamp voltage after the lamp is in operation (emitting light).

FIGURE 11.38 Fluorescent lamp circuit.

types of electric lamps, a PAR40 incandescent lamp is approximately 5 inches (about 125 millimeters) in diameter.

Newer high light efficiency fluorescent lamps have been developed to replace the older F40 T12 (fluorescent 40 watt) type lamps. For example, the F32 T8 lamp provides the same number of lumens and consumes less watts and is smaller in diameter, 1 inch (25 millimeters). Whenever a ballast has to be replaced, this lamp should definitely be considered as a replacement. If a ballast does not have to be replaced and if a lamp fails, you should consider an F40 T10 lamp, which generates more lumens than the T12 lamp.

You should be aware that there is considerable variety among the standard "white" fluorescent lamps: daylight, cool white, warm white, and soft white are currently available.

If you are interested in highlighting food and red or other warm colors, the incandescent lamp provides an excellent light source. The warm-white fluorescent is the usual acceptable fluorescent alternative. However, if you want a lamp that blends with natural daylight from windows, the cool-white fluorescent lamp is ideal. Each fluorescent lamp type will produce a definite color tint, and it is recommended that you test lamp types in your surroundings before purchasing lamps and that you specify the exact type of lamp you find to be most desirable.

Fluorescent lamps require a ballast. The most common ballast is the magnetic ballast which is not very energy efficient. The U.S. government developed magnetic ballast standards and new units are much more energy efficient. These are designated with an *E*. Light dimmers cannot be used with magnetic ballasts.

Fluorescent lamps can be dimmed by installing an electronic ballast. The electronic ballast changes alternating-current cycles, which, in turn, changes the light output of the lamp.

Fluorescent lamp manufacturers have also improved the lamp's color-rendering capability so that they can be used in place of incandescent bulbs in settings where accurate color rendering is important. Such lamps—triphosphor film-coated fluorescent—offer an excellent source of light. A 4-foot triphosphor bulb costs about 25 percent more than a conventional F40 fluorescent.

Compact fluorescent lamps are available as one-piece screw-in units (to replace incandescent lamps) or as two-piece screw-in units. The one-piece unit has a built-in ballast and if either the lamp or the ballast fails, it is discarded and replaced with a new unit. The two-piece unit, on the other hand, has separate lamp and ballast units and either one or both units can be replaced. Generally, the compact two-piece fluorescent has a lamp life of 10,000 hours and a ballast life of 40,000 hours.

Compact fluorescent lamps can also be designated as ER lamps for down-lighting requirements. An ER diffuser component can be purchased for both one- and two-piece compact lamps. In addition, an ER compact fluorescent is also available (built-in ellipsoidal reflector). Similar to incandescent ER lamps, these are more light efficient than regular compact lamps.

High-Intensity Discharge Lamps

High-intensity discharge (HID) lamps are somewhat similar to fluorescent lamps. These lamps have a glass bulb with an internal glass, ceramic, or quartz tube filled with a gas that determines the type of high-intensity discharge lamp. There are electrodes (cathodes) at both ends of the tube. Electric energy arcs between the electrodes. Voltage is regulated by a ballast that serves the same function as in a fluorescent lamp.

Mercury Lamps. The most common high-intensity discharge lamp is the mercury lamp, frequently called the mercury-vapor lamp. High-pressure mercury gas is used in the arcing tube. The lamps are made in a variety of wattage. They have a very long life (12,000 to 24,000 hours). Their greatest life expectancy is for continuous operation. The light efficiency varies from 20 to 63 lumens per watt (compared to a normal incandescent lamp with 8 to 24 lumens per watt). The mercury lamp is generally the least efficient of the fluorescent and high-intensity discharge lamps. These lamps are available in the 50-to 1000-watt size range.

The ballast is usually very noisy and, as a result, is normally located some distance from the lamp. Some smaller mercury lamps have a self-contained ballast. These were developed as incandescent lamp replacements. These lamps are lower wattage, and ballast noise is minimal.

The mercury lamp requires a long start-up time (up to several minutes). In cold temperatures, the starting time may be even longer and starting more difficult. The mercury lamp is not as light efficient as a normal fluorescent lamp.

There are three types of mercury-vapor lamps; each produces different color effects. The clear mercury lamp makes people look greenish. Its use may make it difficult to find red and orange objects. These lamps are frequently used for very large-area lighting (in parking lots and warehouses), where color characteristics are not critical.

The white mercury lamp can make people look very pale, almost sickly, with its greenish-white cast. It illuminates red and orange objects very poorly.

The deluxe-white mercury lamp has color characteristics very similar to cool-white fluorescent lamps and can therefore be used for interior lighting. It has replaced the first two types of mercury lamps for sporting events and in large exhibition areas.

Metal-Halide Lamps. The metal-halide lamp is very similar in construction and operation to the mercury-vapor lamp. Metal particles are added to the mercury gas in the arcing tube. This generally improves the color response to objects, and light output is almost double the mercury-vapor efficiency, varying between 56 and 125 lumens per watt. Its life is generally similar to mercury vapor; under continuous operation, it may last up to 20,000 hours. Its color characteristics fall between the white and deluxe-white mercury lamps. Its color response is similar to the cool-white fluorescent lamp. New low-wattage metal-halide systems have just been introduced with more acceptable color and improved stability, thus widening the range of possible applications. These lamps are available in the 175-to 1500-watt range.

The start-up time for the metal-halide lamp is short (two to three minutes). The restrike time is very long, which should be of concern to managers. Restrike time refers to the time required to restart the lamp after it has been in operation and turned off. The entire lamp and its ballast must cool down, which could require 10 minutes.

High- and Low-Pressure Sodium Lamps.   Sodium lamps have a ceramic arc tube. Sodium is the arcing gas, and it provides a white-yellowish light. The high-pressure sodium (HPS) lamp, which is almost 35 percent light efficient, is currently one of the most efficient lamps available (61 to 140 lumens per watt). The life expectancy is very similar to the long-life mercury-vapor lamp (12,000 to 24,000 hours). Its start-up time is very similar to the metal-halide lamp, but its restrike time is only one-tenth that of the metal-halide lamp. If you do not mind the white-yellowish light produced by the lamp, it provides very low cost light. HPS lamps are available in the 35- to 1000-watt size range.

Low-pressure sodium (LPS) lamps, which produce 100 to 183 lumens per watt, are the most energy efficient light sources available at the present time. Their principal use is typically dusk-to-dawn security lighting. However, the lamps are monochromatic, which means that they emit only one color of the spectrum. While their golden glow reduces glare on roadways, it also washes out color, so making the correct choice hinges on whether driving accuracy or distinguishing colors is more important. LPS might be combined with other lamp sources to produce better color rendition. The rated life is 10,000 to 18,000 hours, and they are available in the 18- to 180-watt size range.

High-pressure sodium (HPS) is second in efficiency to LPS for outdoor applications. Its color-rendering properties, while not as good as white light sources, nevertheless allow for some color definition.

LIGHTING SYSTEMS AND DESIGN APPROACHES
Lighting Systems

Because of their higher light efficiency, fluorescent and HID, rather than incandescent, lighting should be used wherever possible. General uniform lighting can be provided by a variety of lighting techniques. Depending on what effects you wish to create, several lighting systems are available. They are direct, semidirect, diffuse, semi-indirect, and indirect. See Figure 11.39.

The most efficient lighting system is direct lighting (using ER lamps). All the emitted light is directed onto the activity area. This type of lighting is frequently found in institutional buildings because of its low installation and operating costs. Figure 11.40 shows a typical direct lighting system in a classroom or a meeting room.

Semidirect lighting diverts a portion of the light toward the ceiling (usually less than 40 percent), and a larger percentage is directed downward onto the activity area. This technique will highlight ceiling features and provide a soft-light effect within a room. Many meeting and conference rooms

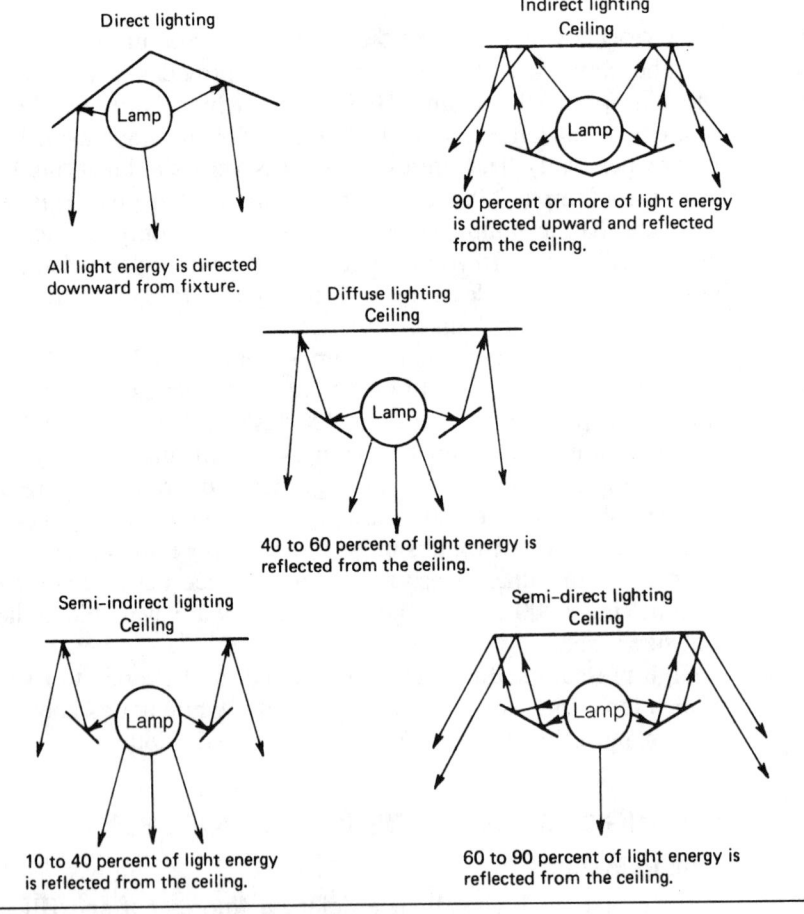

FIGURE 11.39 Example lighting systems.

FIGURE 11.40   Direct lighting in a classroom or meeting room.

use this type of lighting. This system is usually preferred over direct lighting by many hotel and foodservice managers. It is not as light efficient as direct lighting.

A diffuse lighting system directs approximately equal amounts of light downward onto the activity area and upward to the ceiling. This type of lighting is frequently used in public areas, including dining rooms and conference and meeting rooms, and in areas where it may be desirable to highlight ceiling features. The manager should be aware that the installation and operating cost of this system is frequently twice as great as for direct or semidirect lighting.

Generally, only direct, semidirect, and diffuse lighting are recommended for large areas and rooms. The remaining two lighting systems are recommended only for small rooms, where special effects are to be created or where the manager wants an especially relaxed mood, such as in guest rooms and cocktail lounges.

Indirect lighting reflects 90 percent or more of the emitted light from the luminaire to the ceiling and upper walls of the room. Therefore, light must be redirected from these surfaces down toward the activity area. Semi-indirect lighting directs between 10 and 40 percent of the light output directly to the activity area. These techniques are costly to install and operate for high footcandle (lux) intensities.

Lighting Design Variables

Room lighting design depends on several variables: type of luminaire (lighting fixture, lamp, and luminaire placement); room size (length, width, and especially height); color of surfaces (walls, ceiling, and floor); surface texture (smooth-glossy or rough); light intensity; room cleanliness; luminaire cleanliness; and room function. Each of these factors affects the amount of lighting energy required for a room and the initial cost of the lighting system.

Luminaries vary in physical shape. They are designed to produce a specific lighting system. Luminaries are rated by two primary factors: ease of housekeeping and light reflection characteristics. Light reflection, or utilization, characteristics are specified by the manufacturer. Luminaries with high light utilization coefficients should be used because fewer of these units will be required for a specific light level.

The luminaire light utilization coefficient also depends on the surface characteristics of the room. These characteristics include surface texture, color, and the relative size of the room. For example, larger rooms require fewer lumens per square foot (square meter) of floor area than smaller rooms. Lighter-color surfaces (walls, ceilings, and floors) require fewer lumens than darker surfaces. Smooth surfaces require less light than rough or textured surfaces.

The cleanliness of both the room and the luminaire can have significant effects on lighting costs. Dirt on the walls, ceiling, and luminaire absorbs and destroys light energy.

A variety of high light efficiency luminaire finishes and metal-plating techniques are available for maximizing the light produced by conventional lamps placed in luminaries. For example, in existing fluorescent ceiling-grid systems, high-reflectance aluminum-plated panels can be placed behind the lamps to increase the available light. The panels' reflective surface and special configuration direct 95 percent of emitted light into the room below. The increase in captured light is so substantial that one lamp can be removed from a three-lamp fixture with minimal reduction in lighting levels, or lower wattage lamps can be installed in the same lighting fixture.

Lighting Controls

Control technology has made important advances in recent years. By reducing the reliance on human activation and providing light when and where it is needed, these controls can help save energy at a low initial cost that is usually recovered within a few years.

Lighting controls can now be part of a software program that also controls the heating, ventilation, and domestic hot-water systems in a building. All electrical devices in these systems are connected through a common wiring system and speak a common computer language. An entire building's lighting system can be controlled by the central computer, which automatically adjusts lighting levels through preprogrammed schedules according to the current time and day.

A preset wall box system is another state-of-the-art control system. Used in conjunction with infrared motion detection (occupancy sensor), lights can be set to turn on only when an area is occupied or to shift automatically, by the use of timing devices, to activate a night security level.

Concealed intensity limit controls found behind the face plates of wall box dimmers are also useful for lengthening the life of incandescent bulbs. Typically, such bulbs have a life of 750 to 1500 hours. A wall box dimmer can be used to decrease the maximum level of voltage received by the bulb, thereby increasing its life.

Block switching is another type of control technology that can be used to create various lighting zones within one large space. Fixtures are switched in zones when they are installed, so that just a few of the lights in the room can be turned on at a time.

Large spaces can also be fitted with photocontrolled daylight compensation equipment, which measures available daylight and balances it with artificial light.

ELECTRIC MOTORS

The basic electric motor consists of three fundamental components: a stator, a rotor, and an auxiliary starting system. The starting system is probably the most complex mechanism in the motor.

The *stator* is the outer nonmovable shell of the motor. The stator consists of metal bars with insulated copper wires, which are wrapped or coiled around a single flat metal bar or group of bars. When electric energy passes through the wires, the metal bars become magnetized. If electric energy is flowing, say, from left to right, the metal bar becomes a "plus" magnet. If the flow of energy is reversed, moving from right to left, the metal bar becomes a "minus" magnet. Each bar or set of bars wrapped with a coil of wire is called a pole. (The terms north pole and south pole are frequently associated with magnets.)

A motor has sets of poles (a set is two poles). The internal motor wiring connects each set of poles so that as electric energy flows it produces a plus pole and a negative pole (see Figure 11.41). The poles in a set are 180 degrees apart.

Figure 11.42 shows a stator with two sets of poles (a total of four poles). Note that each set of poles is 180 degrees apart. The magnetization reverses each time electricity cycles, so the plus magnet changes to a negative magnet.

The rotating portion of the motor is called the *rotor*. It may consist of iron, steel, or copper bars and insulated copper wires. Briefly—and perhaps too simply—as electric energy builds up in the stator and produces a mag-

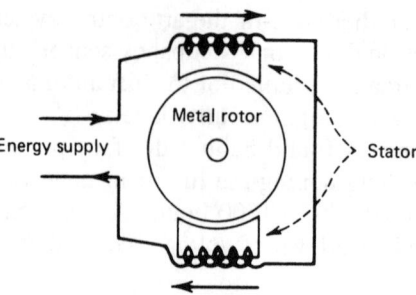

Energy flow produces a "plus" magnetic force
in the stator. This induces a "plus" magnetic
force in the upper half of the metal rotor, which
repels it from the stator.

Energy flow produces a "minus" magnetic force
in the lower stator. This induces a "minus" magnetic
force in the lower half of the metal rotor,
which repels it from the stator.

Connecting a mechanical load to the rotor, the rotor converts electrical energy to useful
mechanical energy. The stator continuously induces the same (plus or minus) magnetic force in
the rotor, which gives the rotor continuous motion.

FIGURE 11.41   Operation of a basic electric motor.

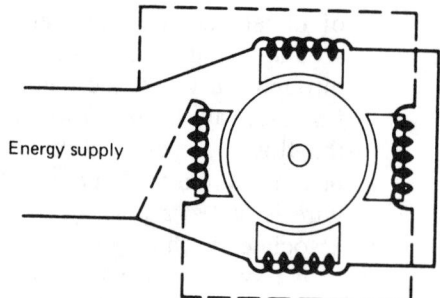

FIGURE 11.42   Motor stator with four
poles.

netic force, a similar magnetic force is established in the metal bars of the
rotor. This causes a repelling action between the rotor and stator.

If electric energy is supplied only to the stator, the stator's magnetic
forces will be induced in the rotor, hence the term *induction motor*. If electric energy is supplied to the rotor (this is done through devices called slip
rings or brushes), the rotor will have wires like those in the stator. As the
positive magnetic force develops in one stator pole, the same positive magnetic force develops in the rotor pole opposite the stator pole. Magnetism is

not induced in this case. Motors of this type are generally called *repulsion motors* in contrast to induction motors.

A metal shaft projects from one or both ends of the motor as part of the rotor. As the rotor turns, the metal shaft rotates. A gear or pulley can be mounted on the shaft. Either belts or chains can be driven by the shaft, which, when attached to equipment, cause it to operate, thus providing mechanical energy, or work. Thus, the process is completed: Electric energy through electromagnetic forces is converted to mechanical energy.

The electromagnetic pole effect causes amperes to lag behind volts with ac. The amperes are thrown out of phase, and this causes a power factor.

Depending on the type of motor and its load characteristics, special devices may be added to a motor to improve its starting ability, operating characteristics, and power factor. One of these special devices is a *capacitor*. This device can be used only with ac motors. The capacitor causes amperes to lead volts in an ac motor and brings the power factor back toward unity. The capacitor, in theory, does not allow electric current to flow through it. It consists of two sheets of metal separated by an insulator.

There are four classifications of motors: polyphase, single phase, direct current, and "other."

POLYPHASE MOTORS

The simplest and most economical electric motor is the polyphase, or three-phase, electric motor. Whenever three-phase energy is available, this motor should be used. The stator has three sets of poles. Each set of poles is fed with energy from each of the supply lines. The electromagnetic field builds up between each set of poles that are out of phase with each other. Polyphase motors generally do not require any special auxiliary devices for starting. As a result, they generally have a very low initial cost per horsepower. Operating costs depend on the efficiency of the motor.

There are two general categories of polyphase motors: synchronous and induction. Induction motors are the most common in the hospitality industry because they are low cost in comparison to other motors of equivalent horsepower and have universal application in the industry. Synchronous motors are essentially constant-speed motors—measured in rotor revolutions per minute, or rpm (revolutions per second, or rps). Synchronous motors operate with very little slippage between the electromagnetic fields of the rotor and stator. As a result, they operate with a high power factor and are generally efficient.

Synchronized Motors

The most common polyphase synchronous motor is the direct-current excited rotor motor. This motor has three-phase ac energy fed to the stator and dc energy supplied to the rotor. Regulating dc voltage on the rotor keeps it operating at rather constant rpm (rps) and improves its power factor. The motor can be made in any horsepower, so that its use is universal. It is generally used on equipment that is continuously operated, such as water-circulating pumps and ventilation fans. This motor can produce either a leading or a lagging power factor and, if the motor is large enough, it can be used to improve the building power factor.

A dc energy source is continuously required for the rotor. Direct-current batteries, vacuum tubes, transistors, rectifiers, or an MG set can be used for the dc energy supply. The term MG stands for ac motor (M) and dc generator (G). Alternating current is continuously fed to vacuum tubes, transistors, and rectifiers, which provides a sufficient source of dc for these rotors. If a large number of these rotors are to be operated, it may be more economical to install an MG set, which can also be used in conjunction with elevator equipment operated with dc motors.

Induction Motors

The largest group of polyphase motors are the induction motors. The motors may be special purpose or general purpose. Special-purpose types include motors required for frequent and rapid stopping (freight elevators). These motors are fairly efficient, operate with moderate power factors, have almost universal use and application, and are generally less costly than synchronous motors. The general-purpose induction motor is the most common motor used in the hospitality industry when three-phase energy is available.

SINGLE-PHASE MOTORS

Single-phase motors include: capacitor-start induction-run, capacitor-start capacitor-run, and special-purpose split-phase.

Capacitor-Start Induction-Run Motors

When a capacitor is connected to the starting poles of a basic induction motor, the motor is called a capacitor-start induction-run motor. The capacitor allows the motor to start heavy loads. These motors are usually between 50 and 70 percent efficient and have power factors that vary between 0.5 and about 0.70.

Capacitor-Start Capacitor-Run Motors

The capacitor-start capacitor-run motor has capacitors on the starting and running poles. This motor has characteristics and applications very similar to the capacitor-start induction-run motor; however, its efficiency frequently exceeds 75 percent. The running capacitor may also reduce rotor slippage, so the motor usually operates with less vibration and slightly higher rpm (rps). These motors are generally available in higher horsepower ratings than capacitor-start induction-run motors.

Special-Purpose Split-Phase Motors

Special-purpose split-phase motors are usually limited to 1/2 horsepower or less. The auxiliary poles have larger-diameter wires and hence can start moderate loads. They can be used on some small domestic laundry equipment and certain pumps. The outer motor shell and its mounting are frequently designed to fit a specific appliance, such as a small washing machine. Such a motor cannot generally be used for any other equipment.

DIRECT-CURRENT MOTORS

Direct-current motors form another complete group, or class, of motors. Energy must be directed to both the stator and the rotor with these motors. Slip rings or brushes are used to conduct energy to the rotor.

There are three types of direct-current motors: the shunt motor, which is a parallel-wiring arrangement between the rotor and the stator poles; the series motor, in which the rotor and stator poles are connected in series; and the compound motor, which represents a combination series-and-parallel connection between the rotor and stator. Generally, direct-current-motor rpm (rps) decreases with load. These motors are generally extremely efficient. Because dc is the energy source, their power factor is 1. These motors are variable speed. Regulating the voltage being supplied to the motor controls its speed.

Direct-current motors have the same universal applications as polyphase motors. They make ideal elevator motors because of the ease of regulating the supply voltage to the motor and the resulting speed of the elevator car.

OTHER TYPES OF MOTORS
Universal Motors

The universal motor is a special motor that operates with either alternating (single-phase) or direct current. It is similar to dc shunt and series motors. The motor is very efficient and also operates at a higher rpm (rps) when energized with dc. The universal motor has extensive applications and a very high starting-load capability. Motor speed control is provided by using a variable resistor or by variable electrical connections on the motor poles. Energy is supplied to the rotor by means of brushes.

Because of their ac and dc characteristics, many power tools utilize these motors. A worker can plug the unit into an ordinary outlet. When not in use, the device's dc battery is charging. When required for work in areas where extension cords are impractical or hazardous, the tool can be operated on its own stored battery power.

Repulsion-Start Induction-Run and Repulsion–Induction Motors

Another single-phase motor is the repulsion-start induction-run motor, which is very similar to the universal motor except that the brushes that supply energy to the rotor are used only for starting the motor. The starting load of this ac motor is very high. It operates like other induction-run motors, with similar power factors and efficiencies. Similar to this motor is the repulsion–induction motor, which has brushes in continuous operation, supplying energy to the rotor. Its operation is very similar to the universal motor, except that it is operated only on ac. Its uses and applications are like those of other single-phase motors. It can be used to start appliances and equipment under full starting load, as when starting compressors or fully primed water pumps.

Special-Purpose Motors

There is an entire group of special-purpose motors whose applications and general specifications are controlled by the National Electrical Manufacturers' Association and Underwriters Laboratories. These motors can be made for any unit of equipment and in most sizes; hence, they are almost custom made for the equipment. Efficiencies range between 30 and 90 percent, and power factors between 0.5 and 0.95. Actually, there are several thousand of these special-purpose motors.

ELECTRIC-MOTOR EFFICIENCY AND MAINTENANCE

The efficiency of an electric motor compares its energy requirement (watts input) to the mechanical work the motor is capable of performing, measured in horsepower (watts) output. For example, 746 watts is equal to 1 horsepower, and if 1000 watts of energy input is required to produce 1 horsepower of output, the motor efficiency is $746/1000 = 0.746$, or 74.6 percent.

The energy input that is not converted to useful output is converted to heat. Three primary factors result in low motor efficiency: the metal used for poles, internal wire sizes, and rotor bearings. Three metals are used for poles: iron, steel, and copper. Copper poles generally produce the most efficient and costly motors. Iron poles are used in low-cost and less efficient motors. The grade of steel determines the efficiency of steel-pole motors; generally, steel-pole motors are more efficient than iron-pole motors.

The diameter of copper wires influences motor efficiency. Small-diameter wires have more resistance than larger-diameter wires and result in less efficient motors. Motor bearings are usually ball-bearing, which are the most efficient, or sleeve types.

If you specify a motor efficiency of 80 percent and if the motor manufacturer delivers a motor of only 78 percent efficiency, the motor is usually discounted by an amount equivalent to future operating cost difference.

Motor maintenance is relatively simple. Keep motors lubricated (only the bearings are oiled or greased on a schedule set by the manufacturer). Lubrication frequently depends on operating hours. Properly maintained motors have been known to operate for 10 to 15 years or more.

EMERGENCY ELECTRICAL SYSTEMS

The hospitality manager who has public space available in the building must have the capability to provide temporary emergency electric power to selected areas of the building. While this may be a local requirement, most U.S. government agencies have insisted on this minimum safety requirement for many years. "Temporary" frequently refers to a power interruption. The building's emergency system must provide electric service for at least two hours.

The emergency energy system must be connected to the building energy system by means of an approved interconnect switch that keeps emergency energy from flowing back into the utility's power lines. The system must meet the National Electric Code requirements. The minimum requirements of an emergency system normally include: exit lighting from public areas; limited vertical transportation—at least one elevator in multiple-floor buildings; minimum lighting and ventilation provisions for interior areas or rooms in which large numbers of persons may congregate; and technical and operating rooms, as well as life-service systems, in health-care facilities; and emergency power for computers and security monitoring and alarm equipment.

Ideally, an emergency energy system should also provide adequate energy to operate the building's total security system, food coolers and freezers, and heating systems, except for total electric-heating systems. Some ordinances indicate that the emergency system must provide energy to selected areas and devices for a minimum of two hours, while others may have minimums of up to eight hours (health-care facility life-support and monitoring equipment and technical laboratories).

There are two basic forms of emergency electrical-energy systems: electric-battery and internal-combustion ac-generation systems. The type selected depends on the devices and appliances to be connected to the system.

ELECTRIC-BATTERY SYSTEMS

The battery system provides dc and with electronic simulators low-wattage ac. These ac converters are not very energy efficient and have the effect of oversizing the battery system for a given output. If dc is provided, only dc appliances can be operated; these would include, but not necessarily be limited to, dc and universal motors and incandescent lamps. This system would require each lighting system, or appropriate motor system, to be wired with separate circuits, so that energy would not become available to devices that could be damaged or destroyed with dc. An internal-combustion engine dc-generator system is another source of dc.

The battery system is probably the least expensive system to install in smaller buildings, such as freestanding foodservice units or clubs. Batteries do not require a large space and produce a minimum of operating noise. They are also pollution free. Batteries deteriorate with age, however, and must be constantly charged and replaced. The battery system could be very expensive for moderate-and large- load requirements, in, for instance, a hotel or health-care unit.

INTERNAL-COMBUSTION AC GENERATION SYSTEMS

For larger buildings, a feasible installation is the internal-combustion engine ac-generation system. The engine may be powered with diesel oil or gasoline.

This system has a long life, and emergency energy can be provided for long time periods. The system is ideal in that it produces ac at a voltage compatible with the components being supplied. Additional wiring is not required. The important aspect is to control the flow of energy to those units that are to be connected solely to emergency energy units.

This system can produce noise and excessive vibrations. Its pollution discharge level must also be controlled. Matching the anticipated electric load with the output of the system is critical: If overdesigned, the cost of the system can be excessive; undersizing the system results in overloading, which can quickly damage the system.

A single generator can supply all of the emergency power for a health-care facility for extended time periods (days, if necessary). Casinos frequently have emergency ac generators large enough to operate the entire casino, including its lighting, security system, HVAC system, and all electronic gaming equipment.

SUMMARY

Electric energy is indispensable in the hospitality industry. Most mechanical systems require electricity as a primary resource energy source and for complete or partial system control. In addition, electric energy can be used for heat, light, and power. Normal building electric-energy cost is close to two-thirds of the total energy budget for the building, so its control is essential for all energy-management programs.

The key to electric-energy management is a knowledge of electric terminology and an understanding of fundamental electrical concepts. Gaining this knowledge and understanding are the principal objectives of this chapter. You have learned a new vocabulary in this chapter, which should allow you to communicate—electrically speaking—with the chief engineer. You have been exposed to basic electric billing techniques, which will allow you to review and understand electric costs.

The use of electric energy is dependent on the building's electric network. It is complex, it is installed following industry standards and local building codes, and its electric output can be safely managed.

The primary use of electric energy is for the production of mechanical energy (power) through the electric-to-mechanical conversion in electric motors. Electric energy consumed by electric motors can account for up to 75 percent of the total electric consumption for larger properties (motors for HVAC, elevators, laundry equipment, food chillers and freezers, water pumps—just to mention some electric-motor uses).

Electric energy for heat and lighting systems accounts for the remainder of the uses of electric power. While electric-to-heat conversion is generally very efficient (approaching 95+ percent), this can represent a costly heat resource. However, frequently the benefits of electric heat outweigh the cost disadvantage.

The use of electric energy for the generation of light is the most apparent use of electric energy. The electric-to-light conversion process is not very efficient at the present time. There are a large number of electric light sources that produce all types of effects, especially interesting are the effects on surface color (building surfaces, food, and people).

Electric energy will continue to be a primary energy resource in the future, as nuclear-, solar-, geothermal-, and other-to-electric conversion processes will increase in the future, all resulting in abundant electric energy that will eventually replace the dependence on natural gas and oil energy sources. Hence, the hospitality industry like other industries will become more and more dependent on electric energy. The future hospitality manager has very little choice, he or she must learn how to manage electric systems for industry and management survival.

REFERENCES AND BIBLIOGRAPHY

1. Borsenik, F. D., *Holiday Inn, Inc.—Hotel Group Energy Management Program: Phase I*, University of Nevada Las Vegas, November 20, 1989.

2   Borsenik, F. D., *Holiday Inn, Inc.—Hotel Group Energy Management Program: Phase II*, University of Nevada, Las Vegas, December 5, 1989.

3. *Electric Power Monthly*, October 12, 1990, U.S. Department of Energy Information Administration, Office of Coal, Nuclear, Electric and Alternate Fuels, Washington, DC.

4. Houston Lighting and Power Company, *Guide to Commercial Energy Efficiency*, Houston, October 1992.

5. McPartland, J. F., J. F. McPartland III, J. M. McPartland, and G. I. McPartland, *McGraw-Hill National Electrical Code Handbook*, 18th ed., McGraw-Hill, New York, 1984.

6. Piper, J. E., *Handbook of Facility Management*, Prentice-Hall, Englewood Cliffs, NJ, 1995.

QUESTIONS/PROBLEMS

1. Check the electric appliances where you live, and list the type and wattage of each. Estimate the hours of operation each day for each appliance, and determine the watt-hour consumption of energy.

2. Refer to the preceding problem, and assume that you had a 120-volt battery. What ampere-hour rating would be required for a battery supplying the energy for your use?

3. How much more energy can be supplied with the same volts and amperes with three-phase, rather than single-phase, energy?

4. Refer to Figures 11.14 and 11.15, and determine the average cost per kilowatt-hour for a foodservice unit that consumes 25,000 kilowatt-hours (3000 on-peak) of energy per month. There are no surcharges or taxes.

5. Determine the device and circuit ampere requirements for the following devices if they are all on one circuit of 120 volts. Repeat for 240 volts.
    Appliance 1: 1500 watts, power factor 1.00
    Appliance 2: 1200 watts, power factor 0.75
    Appliance 3: 2700 watts, power factor 0.90

6. Refer to Figure 11.24 and determine the voltage drop if the ampere requirement is 20 rather than 25 amperes.

7. What wire sizes are required to handle the amperes in Problem 5? Base your answer on Figure 11.28.

8. Based on the information presented on lighting systems, what recommendations would you make regarding new construction or major renovations for each of the following types of hospitality industry buildings:
   a. Lodging
   b. Foodservice
   c. Health care
   d. Club
   e. Institutional

CHAPTER 12

Courtesy of Eastman Kodak Co.

WATER SYSTEMS MANAGEMENT

ABSTRACT

The water distribution and sewage drainage systems are the two most important modern building systems that are taken for granted and are least understood at the present time by building managers. Without question, a modern lodging and foodservice facility with its technological advances and equipment could not operate without a water supply and drainage system.

A potable water supply is essential in the hospitality industry. An adequate supply of clear sparkling water is assumed by the guest when checking into a lodging establishment and is essential for the proper preparation of food products. Such desirable water may not be supplied by a water utility and it is up to the hospitality manager to provide clear sparkling water. An understanding of quality water is required so that it can be provided.

Water distribution system knowledge is required by the hospitality manager so that the system can be designed, operated, and maintained to supply a continuous and adequate supply of water.

Water waste and sewage are created at the plumbing fixtures. A properly designed sewage drainage system must be designed and maintained to ensure that waste and sewage will be handled in the most sanitary manner. The major maintenance problem is clogged piping for drainage systems.

Swimming pools and spas are generally thought to be a guest requirement and occupy a significant percentage of the maintenance budget (chemicals, energy requirements for motors and water heating, and labor manhours). Pool use must be controlled to protect the facility owners.

The plumbing system is essential. It can become a major maintenance problem, especially with older buildings. As plumbing fixtures are added to the building, the drainage system is seldom renovated to accommodate the new requirements. These maintenance problems will not decrease in time, but they can be controlled.

375

Key words: *algae control; angle valve; auger; available water pressure; backwashing; building drain; building sewer; cartridge filter; centrifugal pump; check valve; combination system; diatomaceous-earth filter; disinfectant; distribution pipe; downfeed system; equivalent pipe length; expansion device; feet of head; filter; fixture branch; fixture drain; fixture operating pressure; fixture unit; friction pressure loss; gate valve; gear pump; globe valve; grains of hardness; grease trap; ground water; heater storage tank; heat exchanger; hot-water requirements; jet pump; key valve; National Standard Plumbing Code; needle valve; piping resistance; piping vibration; potable water; probable water flow; pump; reciprocating pump; riser; rod; rotary pump; sand or sand-and-gravel filter; semiconcrete pool; service pipe; sewage ejector; side-arm heater; snake; soil drainpipe; soil stack; steel reinforced concrete pool; storm drain; submersible pump; toilet (water closet); trap; turbine pump; upfeed system; vent; vinyl-liner pool; wading area; wading pool; waste drainpipe; waste stack; water distribution system; water hardness; water pH; water pressure; water softener; weir.*

INTRODUCTION

Energy distribution systems in hospitality buildings currently operate on three primary energy sources: fuel for heating, electric power, and water. Water is generally provided by a public utility. The hospitality industry is very dependent on a safe, potable water supply and a sanitary drainage network. There is increasing concern worldwide over supplies of potable water. Water has become a very important energy resource.

The primary sources of fresh water are rivers, lakes, and ground water. If rivers and lakes become polluted, our water resources become seriously restricted because more water must be extracted from the ground. This presents a potential problem, which could limit hospitality industry growth in some areas. The water table in many areas is falling, forcing water utilities to drill deeper wells to obtain increasing amounts of water. In effect, we are using ground water faster than nature can replenish it.

Water may have to be treated to make it potable, that is, safe for human consumption. The treatment process depends on the number and types of water impurities and the rate at which potable water is desired. This can be a costly process. The distribution network supplies water to where it is needed. The drainage network collects unwanted, or waste, water and delivers it to a processing center, where it can be treated, thus preparing it for recycling.

SOURCES OF WATER

The most common source of water for the hospitality industry is a water utility. A water main is usually buried underground just off your property line. You obtain a permit to run a building water main pipe across your property to the public utility water main. Water obtained from the utility has usually been treated to meet a local standard. It may be necessary, however, to provide additional water treatment to remove elements that could have undesirable effects on building equipment and services (such as dish washing, laundry, and swimming pools).

If a water utility does not service the property, water must be obtained from a river, an independent reservoir, or pumped from a well. A permit must be obtained to tap into these resources. There are usually strict regulations covering artificial open-water reservoirs.

What may be considered potable water in one geographic area may be classified as undrinkable in another. Definitions of potable water and minimum water treatment requirements usually depend on the source of water and its initial quality. This is why people who become accustomed to water in one geographic area may become ill when drinking potable water in a different area.

One water condition is extremely variable around the world—water hardness. It can cause a number of problems in the hospitality industry.

WATER HARDNESS

Water hardness is caused by calcium and magnesium salts, which are normally present in potable water. These are called hard salts because of two factors. First, when hard water is heated, salts will frequently precipitate out, causing a lime buildup within pipes and around plumbing fixtures or deposits on items being washed. Second, when water containing these salts is mixed with natural soap and some synthetic cleansers, the salts combine with cleanser chemicals and precipitate onto and within the products being washed. The resulting mixture is called "soap curd," a sticky substance that is difficult to remove from washed products.

In most cleaning processes, an overabundance of cleansing agents must be used to reduce or eliminate the effects of hard-water salts. This makes dish washing and laundering costly. The energy requirements of housekeeping tasks are increased when hard water is present since acidic and abrasive cleansers are required to remove lime buildup. The life of linens laundered in hard water is significantly reduced. Linens, dishes, and eating utensils washed in hard water will eventually become discolored, developing either a yellow or a brown cast.

Calcium salt deposits are harmful to hot-water heaters, boilers, and heat exchangers. The precipitate serves as a heat insulator and lowers the operating efficiency of the unit. Chief engineers must soften water used in heat exchangers and boilers. Water is treated with chemicals that combine with hard-water salts to form chemical buffers so that salts will not precipitate from water.

The more frequently used hard-water-salt eliminators are tanks filled with a synthetic chemical resin called *zeolite*. Zeolite has an affinity for hard-water salts and collects them on its surface. Hard-water salts removed from the water are replaced with a soft salt, such as sodium. Sodium salt is free-rinsing and does not create hard-water-salt problems. The zeolite resin eventually becomes saturated with hard-water salts and must be regenerated. Regeneration is a process that oversaturates the zeolite with a soft-water mixture, a brine. The soft salt replaces hard salts on the zeolite surface. Common table salt, sodium chloride, is used for regeneration. The zeolite process is practical and feasible because of the current low cost of sodium chloride and water. This process is shown in Figure 12.1.

There are two additional salt compounds that can be used to regenerate water softeners. A low-sodium salt has to be processed and should be used because of the harmful effects of sodium on the environment. Potassium chloride can also be used as a sodium chloride substitute for water softeners. Potassium replaces sodium in the soft water. As potassium is required in some human diets, this may be an ideal substitute in some cases. Potassium chloride has a higher cost than sodium chloride.

Many hospitality industry establishments soften only hot water. This is a questionable practice since mixing soft and hard water results in hard water with all its related problems. The softening of hot water may be practical in a foodservice establishment, when soft hot water is not usually mixed with hard cold water.

Water hardness is measured in grains (parts per million). Soft water has 0 grains (0 parts per million [ppm]) of hardness. The feasibility of a soft-water system generally depends on cleanser savings and the cost of treatment chemicals, water, and water-softening equipment. Generally, it is feasible to install automatic water-softening equipment if the water hardness is 20 or more grains (342 ppm).

WATER PUMPS

If water is not available from a water utility, then it must generally be pumped from a well, river, lake, or reservoir. The pumping process serves two purposes: (1) to supply water and (2) to overcome the friction, or piping resistance, of the water supply and distribution network. When water flows through a pump, mechanical energy is converted to water pressure, which allows water to overcome the resistance of the piping network.

Pumps may also be required to get water to a building's upper levels, because the water utility or water well pumps do not provide adequate water pressure.

WATER PRESSURE AND PUMPS

Normal atmospheric air pressure is approximately 14.7 pounds per square inch, or psi (101.4 kilopascals). If two columns of water are each exposed to

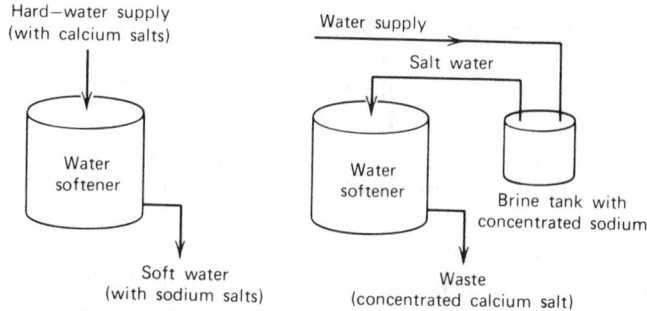

Hard—water supply
(with calcium salts)

Water supply

Salt water

Water
softener

Water
softener

Brine tank with
concentrated sodium

Soft water
(with sodium salts)

Waste
(concentrated calcium salt)

A. Normal tank use.

B. Regenerating the tank.

FIGURE 12.1 Water softening.

the same pressure, both columns will remain at the same level. If, however, the pressure on one column is changed, its water will seek a different level. Figure 12.2 shows what happens when one column of water is exposed to 14.7 psi (101.4 kilopascals), another to 13.7 psi (94.5 kilopascals), and a third to 15.7 psi (108.3 kilopascals). The difference between each of the three resulting levels is 2.3 feet (0.7 meter) for each psi (6.895 kilopascals). Hence, if the pressure is changed, the potential height of the water level is

2.3 feet per psi (0.7 meter per 6.895 kilopascals). This relationship exists because the weight of a column of water 1 square inch (645.2 square millimeters) in cross-sectional area and 2.3 feet (0.7 meter) in height is 1 pound (0.454 kilogram). It should be noted that the shape of the piping has no effect on the preceding relationships.

A pump eliminates air pressure from its supply pipe; this produces a vacuum that allows atmospheric air pressure to lift water (refer to Figure 12.2; the pressure *B* column has reduced pressure and water rises higher in the piping). As water is propelled through a pump, energy is imparted to the water, increasing its pressure. Thus, water rises in pipes.

The common types of pumps are jet, centrifugal, reciprocating, rotary, and gear.

JET PUMP

The jet pump is used to pump water from a well. It must be used in conjunction with a second pump (see Figure 12.3). The operating-energy requirement is generally high for the low initial cost of this pump. Typical pumping efficiencies vary from 15 to 45 percent. The water table must be within 100 feet (30.5 meters) of the ground surface.

CENTRIFUGAL PUMPS

The centrifugal pump has a rotating wheel mounted in an enclosure. Liquid flows into the wheel center and is forced to the outside of the enclosure by centrifugal force. These pumps are fairly efficient, reaching 80 percent in some cases.

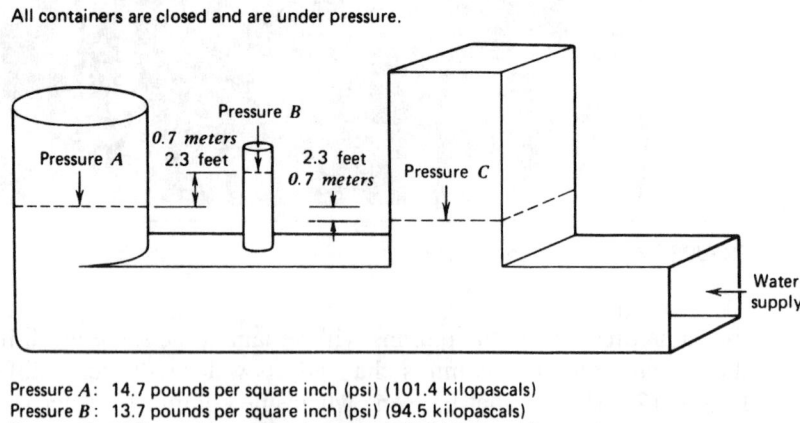

All containers are closed and are under pressure.

Pressure *A*: 14.7 pounds per square inch (psi) (101.4 kilopascals)
Pressure *B*: 13.7 pounds per square inch (psi) (94.5 kilopascals)
Pressure *C*: 15.7 pounds per square inch (psi) (108.3 kilopascals)

FIGURE 12.2 Height of water varies with pressure.

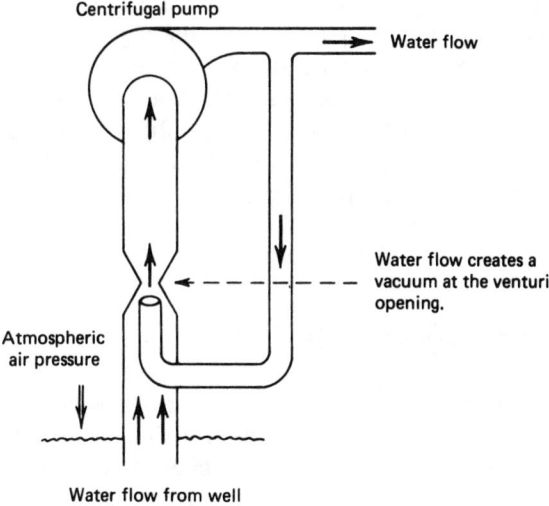

Centrifugal pump

Water flow

Water flow creates a
vacuum at the venturi
opening.

Atmospheric
air pressure

Water flow from well

FIGURE 12.3 Jet-pump operation.

Centrifugal pumps can be connected in a series network, in which one pump feeds a second, the second feeds a third, and so on. Each pump increases the pressure of the liquid being moved. Each pump may have its own electric motor, or one large motor can be used to drive a series of centrifugal impellers. If the centrifugal series pumps are located in a well and the motor is positioned at ground level, it is called a turbine pump. If a motor is also positioned in the well with the multistage impellers, it is called a submersible pump. Turbine and submersible pumps are very effective in pumping large quantities of water from a well and, because each impeller imparts a set amount of pressure, they are capable of exerting large amounts of pressure on water.

RECIPROCATING PUMP

The reciprocating pump provides a large lift potential, which means that it can be used in deep wells, it develops high water pressure, and it has moderate capacity. Its efficiency is relatively high, reaching 90 percent in some cases. It has a piston that moves back and forth in a cylinder, and it can be driven by an electric motor or internal-combustion engine. It is used only to move liquids (water) and gases (refrigerants).

ROTARY AND GEAR PUMPS

A rotary pump is normally used for the movement of semisolids or gases. Its efficiency level is very low at low rpm (rps) and eventually reaches 40 to 60 percent at high rpm. Its operation is similar to a single-tooth gear pump. It is not normally used to pump water. Its major use in the hospitality industry is with refrigeration systems or rotary compressors.

The gear pump, which consists of a series of rotating gears, provides accurate amounts of fluids and semisolids. It is a high-pressure-discharge, low-volume pump. It can obtain efficiencies of up to 65 percent. It is not normally used for pumping water. As a result, it has very limited use in the hospitality industry.

WATER AND SEWAGE CHARGES

The hospitality manager must be aware of water consumption and related sewage-processing billing techniques that affect his or her property. The most common water sewage rate schedule is a combination customer service charge and a flat-rate for each 1000 gallons (3785 liters). Such a rate schedule is shown in Figure 12.4.

The customer service charge could also vary with the size of the service pipe (the pipe supplying water to the property). Hence, the monthly service charge increases with the size of the service pipe. The flat-rate charge is currently being replaced with an increasing step-rate schedule. With this billing technique, there is a flat rate charge per 1000 gallons (3785 liters) up to a specified number of gallons (liters) called threshold 1; there is another higher flat-rate charge per 1000 gallons (3785 liters) from threshold 1 to a second threshold (threshold 2); finally, there is a third and higher flat rate per 1000 gallons (3785 liters) for all water consumption above threshold 2. Naturally, the number of thresholds could increase above 2. The effect of these thresholds is to encourage water conservation, because the water charges per 1000 gallons (3785 liters) increase with higher water consumption. See Figure 12.5.

Basic water rate schedule:

1. The minimum basic charge is a function of the size of the service pipe supplying water to the building; a 3-inch (762-millimeter) pipe may have a basic minimum rate of $250 per month.

2. There is a flat charge per 1000 gallons (3785 liters); assume that the charge is $1.25.

3. If the building requires 450,000 gallons (1,703,250 liters) per month, the charge for water is:

Minimum rate:	$250.00
$\dfrac{\$1.25}{1000} \times 450{,}000$:	562.50
Total charges per month:	$812.50

FIGURE 12.4 Water rate schedule.

Basic water rate schedule:

1. The minimum basic charge is a function of the size of the service pipe supplying water to the building: a 3-inch (762-millimeter) pipe may have a basic minimum rate of $250 per month.
2. The water charge for the *first threshold* is $1 per 1000 gallons (3785 liters) up to and including 100,000 gallons (378,500 liters) per month.
3. The water charge for the *second threshold* is $1.25 per 1000 gallons (3785 liters) for 100,001 gallons (378,504 liters) up to and including 300,000 gallons (1,135,500 liters) per month.
4 The water charge for the *third threshold* is $1.50 per 1000 gallons (3785 liters) for 300,001 gallons (1,135,504 liters) and more gallons per month.

Example water computation:

The building requires 450,000 gallons (1,703,250 liters) per month.

Minimum charge:	$250.00
First threshold charge:	
100,000 x ($1/1000)	100.00
Second threshold charge:	
200,000 x ($1.25/1000)	250.00
Third threshold charge:	
150,000 x ($1.50/1000)	225.00
Total water charges	$825.00

FIGURE 12.5 Water rate schedule with threshold limits.

Sewage charges depend on water consumption. One sewage billing technique is to double the water bill; thus, one-half of the bill is for water and the other half is a sewage-processing charge. A second system increases the basic water bill by 75 percent. This allows 25 percent of water consumption for grounds irrigation, swimming pools, and direct consumption that is assumed not returned to sewage lines for processing. A third system is similar to the second in that 80 percent of water consumption is estimated as sewage, and a flat distribution-and-processing fee is charged per 1000 gallons (3875 liters) of sewage. These three techniques are shown in Figure 12.6.

WATER DISTRIBUTION SYSTEMS

Figure 12.7 shows several water distribution systems used in the hospitality industry.

UPFEED SYSTEM

Figure 12.7A shows a common system used when the utility's water pressure is adequate to force water throughout a building of six floors or less in

Refer to Figure 12.4 for basic data:

A. Method 1. Double the water bill:

Water charges:	$ 562.50
Sewage charge:	562.50
Total per month:	$1125.00

B. Method 2. Sewage charge is 75 percent of the water charge:

Water charges:	$562.50
Sewage (0.75 × 562.50):	421.87
Total per month:	$984.37

C. Method 3. Sewage charge based on 80 percent of water consumption and a charge of $0.80 per 1000 gallons (3785 liters):

Water charges:	$562.50
Sewage $\left(\dfrac{\$0.80}{1000} \times 450{,}000 \times 0.8 \right)$:	$288.00
Total per month:	$850.50

FIGURE 12.6 Sewage charges based on water consumption.

height. The maximum number of floors that can be serviced with this system depends on the water pressure at the service pipe (the utility's water pressure), fixture pressure requirements, piping resistance, and the height to be serviced.

Fixtures require an adequate water pressure for water flow. Figure 12.8 shows the effects of ideal and inadequate water pressure. The effect of piping resistance will be discussed later in this chapter. The building height, or number of floors, is related to water pressure, and, if service pipe water pressure is not adequate, water may never reach a fixture located on the upper levels.

Upfeed System with Circulating Pumps

Figure 12.7B shows an installation similar to Figure 12.7A. It has a water-circulating pump, which increases water pressure. This is used when utility pressure or water well pump pressure is inadequate to overcome piping resistance or building height.

Figure 12.7C is similar to Figure 12.7B, except that it contains a return distribution pipe, which allows water to flow constantly throughout the system. This is frequently used on hot-water lines to provide an almost zero-wait time for hot-water supply.

DOWNFEED SYSTEM

A downfeed water distribution system is shown in Figure 12.7D. Water is forced or pumped to a storage tank located above the highest fixture level.

A. Upfeed system:

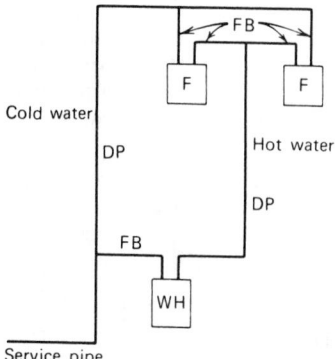

FB: Fixture branch
DP: Distribution pipe
F: Fixture
WH: Water heater

B. Upfeed system with a pump:

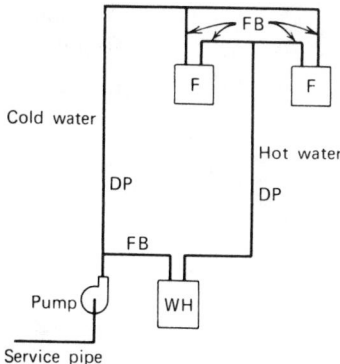

FB: Fixture branch
DP: Distribution pipe
F: Fixture
WH: Water heater

C. Upfeed circulating system with a pump (cold water only):

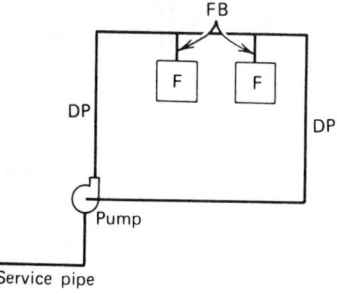

FB: Fixture branch
DP: Distribution pipe
F: Fixture

FIGURE 12.7   Water distribution systems.

D. Downfeed system (cold water only):

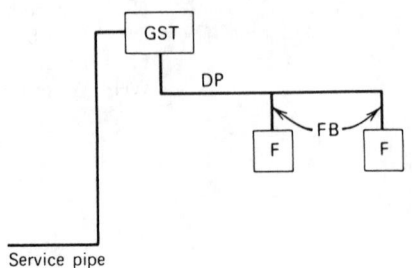

GST: Gravity storage tank
FB: Fixture branch
DP: Distribution pipe
F: Fixture

E. Downfeed circulating system (cold water only):

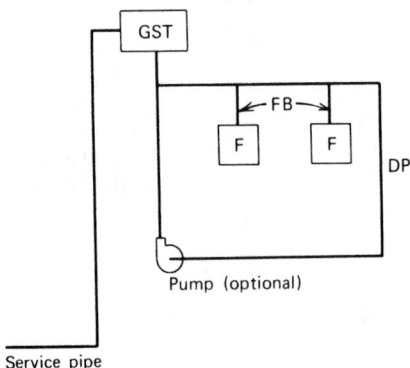

GST: Gravity storage tank
FB: Fixture branch
DP: Distribution pipe
F: Fixture

F. Combination system (cold water only):

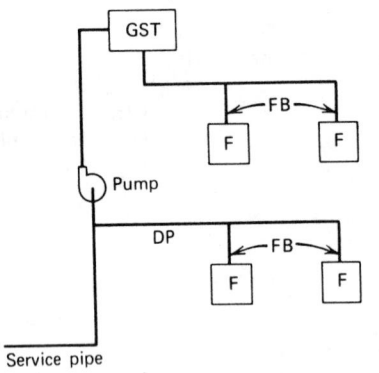

GST: Gravity storage tank
FB: Fixture branch
DP: Distribution pipe
F: Fixture

FIGURE 12.7 (Continued)

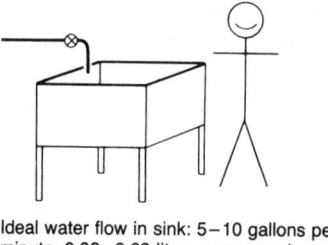 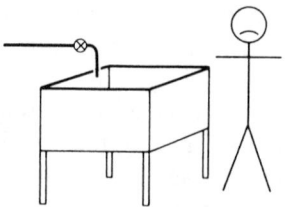

Ideal water flow in sink: 5–10 gallons per minute, 0.32–0.63 liters per second.

Inadequate water flow in sink: 1–2 gallons per minute, .06–0.13 liters per second.

FIGURE 12.8 Effect of ideal and inadequate water flow of a fixture.

When water is required, it flows by gravity from the storage tank to the fixture. Downfeed zones are used in very tall buildings. Zones will reduce high water pressure in the lower building levels caused by the height of the storage tank.

Downfeed Circulating System

Figure 12.7*E* shows a circulating downfeed system similar to the circulating upfeed system. This technique is frequently used with hot water to ensure adequate amounts of hot water at each fixture.

COMBINATION SYSTEMS

Figure 12.7*F* shows a combination upfeed–downfeed system. The upfeed system is used for the lower building levels and the downfeed system for the upper building levels. One of the circulating systems already discussed can also be used in conjunction with the system for hot water. This system is probably the most effective distribution system for multiple-floor buildings because water main supply pressure is utilized to the fullest extent and additional pressure for the upper levels is provided by pumps and an upper water storage tank.

PIPING

Piping includes pipes, pipe fittings, and valves.

Pipes

Pipes are identified as follows: main service pipe, which supplies water to the building; fixture branch pipes, which supply water to single fixtures; and distribution (branch) pipes, which supply water to fixture branches. Frequently, plumbers and blueprints refer to "riser pipes." A riser is a vertical distribution pipe that extends above the height of a shower head fixture branch (one or more building levels, or floors). See Figure 12.7.

The more common piping materials are copper and plastic. In older buildings, galvanized steel and brass were used, but these are generally being replaced with copper or one of several grades of plastic pipe. Copper is available in four grades: K (thickest piping), L, M, and DWV (thinnest piping—minimum diameter 1.5 inches [38 millimeters]). Grades K and L are recommended for water distribution pipes. The thin-wall DWV copper piping is used with plumbing drainage systems.

Several grades of plastics are available, such as acrylonitrile–butadiene–styrene (ABS) (plumbing drainage systems), polybutylene (PB) (cold and hot water and gas), polyethylene (PE) (cold water and gas), polyvinyl chloride (PVC) (cold water and gas), and chlorinated polyvinyl chloride (CPVC) (cold and hot water pipes that do not exceed 180°F [82.2°C]). The local plumbing code prescribes which piping materials are allowed.

Pipe Fittings

Various types of fittings are available that allow piping turns, piping connections, and the connection of pipes to fixtures, controls, and other devices. These fittings are either threaded or compression-type fittings, which include soldered connections for copper and solvent cement for plastic. Threaded fittings and connections are much stronger than compression fittings; hence, they are generally recommended for high-rise buildings. Water leak potential is about the same for both types of fittings under normal water pressures.

Valves

Valves control the flow of water. The correct valve must be used to minimize energy losses and for proper fixture operation and guest satisfaction.

Gate valves are used as on–off valves. They are operated in either completely closed or opened positions. Their resistance to water flow is minimal. These are used as shutoff valves on water mains.

Angle and globe valves are used for variable water flow. They have a high resistance to water flow when partially opened; thus, they restrict water flow. When completely opened, they have moderate resistance. These are used in lavatories, bathtubs, showers, and sinks.

Check valves allow water to flow only one way, have minimal resistance, and act as shutoff valves for reversed water flow. Fast-acting gate valves are key valves, which normally require only a 90- to 180-degree turn (quarter- to half-turn) on a handle to be fully opened or closed.

Needle valves are key valves used to control the flow of natural or LPG gases. They are generally found on gas kitchen equipment and provide very accurate controls. The main gas control valve is a key valve because it is fast acting.

FACTORS OF WATER DISTRIBUTION DESIGN

The primary purpose of this section is to make you aware of the principles of water distribution design. This will give you an understanding of how the system operates, variables affecting the system, how the variables affect the system, what can go wrong with the system, and, if a failure occurs, what the implications are and what steps may be necessary to correct the failure in order to have the system back in operation as quickly as possible.

NATIONAL STANDARD PLUMBING CODE

The National Standard Plumbing Code provides a format and a procedure for proper water distribution design. Like the National Electric Code, numerous sections of it are commonly adopted for local plumbing codes. The code reflects recent developments in technology, experience, and safety. The basic purpose of the code is to provide standardized plumbing procedures and recommendations, so that equipment, devices, and materials may be interchanged, and to act as an authority in case of differing opinions.

DESIGN VARIABLES

Plumbing design involves basic factors and assumptions regarding these factors. The design procedure is summarized in the following steps.

1. Determine the water pressure necessary to lift water to the highest plumbing fixture. See Figure 12.9.

2. Determine the fixture pressure requirement (pressure to overcome fixture valve resistance and for adequate fixture water flow). See Figures 12.8 and 12.9.

3. Determine the available water pressure. This can be obtained from the water utility for your property or measured at the service pipe.

4. Determine the pressure available to overcome piping resistance. This is step 3 minus the sum of steps 1 and 2; see Figure 12.10. If the result of this computation is positive, continue with the process. If the result is 0 or negative, a water-circulating pump must be added so the piping resistance can be overcome by water pressure; otherwise, water will not flow in adequate amounts from all the fixtures.

5. Determine the longest length of piping. You must follow the flow of water from the service pipe, where the available water pressure was measured, to the farthest fixture from the service pipe (the longest piping path). See Figure 12.10. Note: The longest length of piping does not have to be within the building, it may be found outside the building in a water irrigation system, for example.

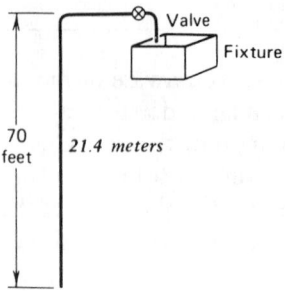

Water must be raised 70 feet (21.4 meters) and have adequate pressure to overcome the resistance of the valve and provide satisfactory water flow at the fixture.

The pressure requirement to overcome the valve resistance and insure adequate water flow is 15 psi (103.4 kilopascals).

The pressure requirement to lift water 70 feet (21.4 meters) is 30.4 psi (209.8 kilopascals).

The total pressure requirement is:

15 + 30.4 = 45.4 psi

(103.4 + 209.8 = 313.2 kilopascals.)

FIGURE 12.9   Water pressure requirement of a fixture.

Refer to Figure 12.9 for data on the pressure requirement of the highest fixture: 45.4 psi (313.2 kilopascals).

1. Water pressure at service pipe: 60 psi (413.7 kilopascals).
2. Available water pressure to overcome piping resistance:
      60 − 45.4 = 14.6 psi
      (413.7 − 313.2 = 100.7 kilopascals)
3. Longest pipe length: 150 feet (45.75 meters).
4. Equivalent piping length (pipe and piping fittings), the best estimate is 2 times the longest pipe length:
      2 x 150 = 300 feet
      (2 x 45.75 = 91.5 meters)
5. Friction loss per 100 feet (30.5 meters) of equivalent piping:
      14.6/(300/100) = 4.9 psi per 100 feet
      (100.7/(91.5/100) = 110.8 kilopascals per 100 meters)

If the available water pressure is 0 or less (negative), a water-circulating pump must be installed to increase water pressure. Step 2 above must be a positive result.

FIGURE 12.10   Pressure available to overcome the friction of the water distribution system.

6. Determine the equivalent length of piping. The equivalent length of piping makes an allowance for pipe fittings and valves. The resistance of a pipe fitting or a valve is given in linear feet of pipe. For example, a piping 90° elbow may be equivalent to 3 linear feet (0.915 meter) of pipe of the same size. In addition, larger-diameter piping has a lower resistance to water flow than smaller-diameter piping (larger-diameter pipe has a smaller circumference to cross-sectional area ratio). Not knowing the piping sizes at this point in the procedure, an estimate must be made regarding piping resistance. The normal procedure is to double the length of the longest pipe to arrive at the equivalent length of piping. The procedure will verify that this is correct or make an adjustment if this assumption is not correct. See Figure 12.10.

7. Determine the piping friction loss in psi per 100 feet of equivalent piping (kilopascals per 30.5 meters). See Figure 12.10.

8. Identify the water flow in gallons (liters) for each section of piping for the entire water distribution network. See Figure 12.11 for a partial view of a water distribution network.

9. Determine pipe sizes, by following one of two alternative techniques.

   Alternative A: Use the National Standard Plumbing Code tables for a specified type of pipe. First, the gallon (liter) flow along piping is con-

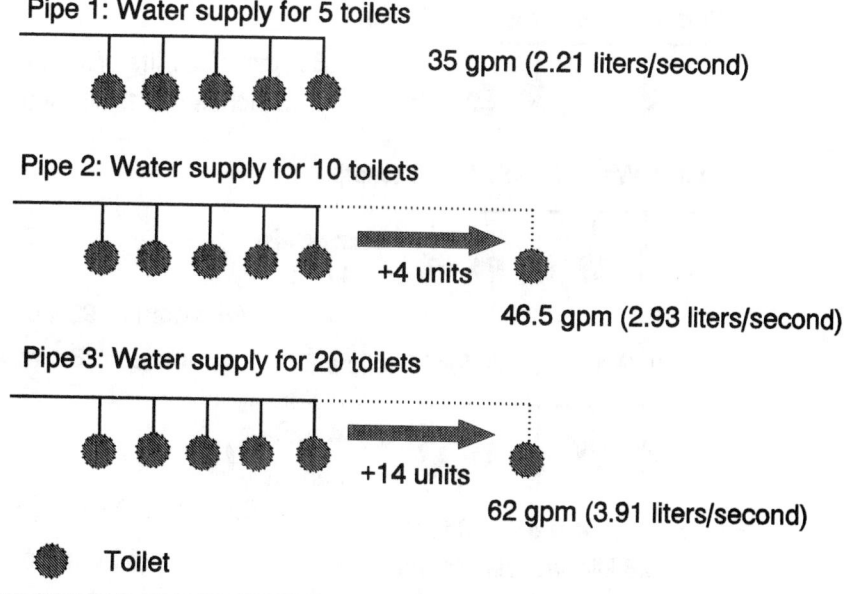

Pipe 1: Water supply for 5 toilets

35 gpm (2.21 liters/second)

Pipe 2: Water supply for 10 toilets

+4 units

46.5 gpm (2.93 liters/second)

Pipe 3: Water supply for 20 toilets

+14 units

62 gpm (3.91 liters/second)

● Toilet

FIGURE 12.11   Water demand and number of fixtures.

verted to probable water flow; as it is assumed that not all the plumbing fixtures would be utilized within a small time period, this is generally correct. Second, knowing the probable water flow and the piping friction loss (step 8), find the appropriate pipe table and select the pipe size for the specified water flow. See Figure 12.12 for an example.

Alternative B: Purchase a computer software program that will automatically convert gallon (liter) water flow to probable water flow and generate the correct pipe size for each piping section.

10. Verify that the assumptions were feasible. Once you have determined pipe sizes, the pipe fitting and valve resistance can be determined from the National Standard Plumbing Code and some computer software programs and compared to the estimate made in step 6. If the actual equivalent piping resistance does not exceed the estimate, the problem solution is accepted. If the equivalent resistance is higher than that estimated in step 6, the estimated resistance in step 6 is increased. Recompute steps 6 to 10 and continue until the estimated and actual equivalent resistances are the same or until the estimated is greater than the actual. See Figure 12.13 for an example.

Available Water Pressure Factors

The available water pressure is one of the most critical limitations on the design of the water distribution system. If water pressure is not adequate,

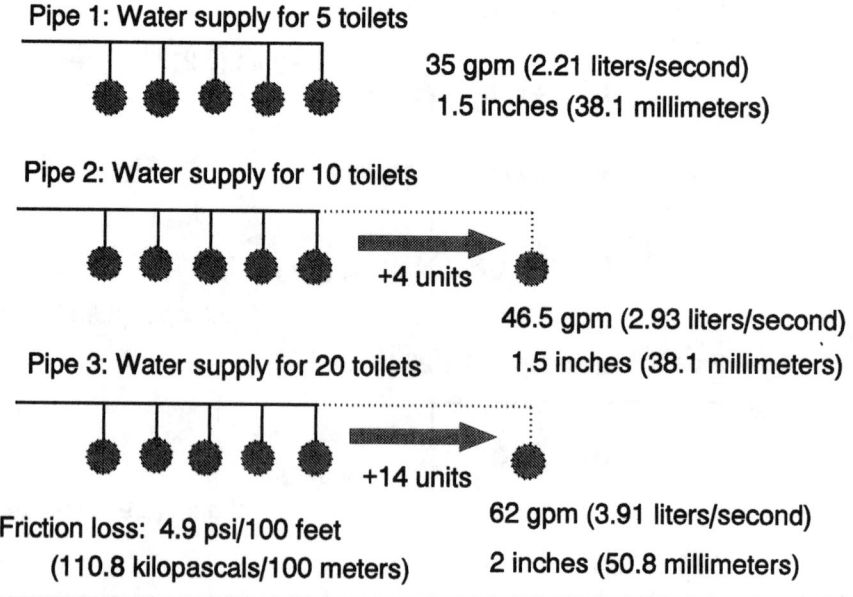

Pipe 1: Water supply for 5 toilets

35 gpm (2.21 liters/second)
1.5 inches (38.1 millimeters)

Pipe 2: Water supply for 10 toilets

+4 units

46.5 gpm (2.93 liters/second)
1.5 inches (38.1 millimeters)

Pipe 3: Water supply for 20 toilets

+14 units

Friction loss: 4.9 psi/100 feet
(110.8 kilopascals/100 meters)

62 gpm (3.91 liters/second)
2 inches (50.8 millimeters)

FIGURE 12.12 Water pipe sizes; refer to Figures 12.9 and 12.10 for data.

Refer to Figure 12.10 for data:
1. Longest pipe length: 150 feet (45.75 meters).
2. Equivalent piping length (pipe and piping fittings), the best estimate is 2 times the longest pipe length:

    2 x 150 = 300 feet

    (2 x 45.75 = 91.5 meters)
3. Friction loss per 100 feet (30.5 meters) of equivalent piping:

    14.6 /(300/100) = 4.9 psi per 100 feet

    (100.7/(91.5/100) = 110.8 kilopascals per 100 meters)
4. Water demand: 46.5 gpm (2.93 liters/second).
5. Pipe size: 1.5 inches (38.1 millimeters).
6. Piping resistance: resistance of all piping fittings and valves for 1.5-inch (38.1-millimeter) pipe is 145 feet (44.23 meters).
7. Total equivalent length of pipe and piping: 295 feet (89.98 meters).
8. Check on friction loss per 100 feet (30.5 meters) of equivalent piping:

    14.6/(295/100) = 4.95 psi per 100 feet

    (100.7/(89.98/100) = 111.9 kilopascals per 100 meters)

These are approximately equal to 4.9 and (110.8); hence, the original assumption was acceptable.

FIGURE 12.13 Checking on the equivalent length of piping; refer to Figure 12.10.

this will result in a more costly system. A high available water pressure may eliminate the use of water-circulating pumps or water storage tanks. It will also result in smaller-sized piping. Some buildings may have a water tower. If a water tower is higher than the plumbing fixtures, it serves as a downfeed system for the building. It will ensure an adequate and known water pressure for plumbing design. Water is initially pumped to the tower to fill it. The tower becomes the source of water for the water distribution system. The tower may also serve as a backup water supply system.

Friction Pressure Loss Factors

Generally, high available friction losses mean that smaller pipes can be used in the system, and low losses indicate that much larger pipes will be required. The friction loss can be any positive number (greater than 0).

If the friction loss is a small positive number and if circulating pumps are not used, there could be a problem when people are showering. Assume that a guest who is taking a shower has adjusted the hot and cold water flow to the desired temperature. Another guest in the same building section flushes a toilet, which has a very high cold-water requirement. The showering guest's cold-water supply is reduced, so that the shower water suddenly becomes very hot. This could be a serious problem.

HEATING WATER

The normal hot-water temperature requirements in the hospitality industry are: 110°F (43.3°C) maximum for domestic use, normal personal washing; 140°F (60°C) maximum for food production area sinks (it should be noted that this temperature could be dangerous for employees if they were to have their hands under the faucet when the water was turned on); 160°F (71.1°C) minimum for building heating or kitchen steam kettles or steamers; 180°F (82.2°C) for dish-washing equipment; and 80 to 100°F (26.7 to 37.8°C) for pools and spas. Kitchen appliances such as steam kettles and steamers will have an auxiliary water heater to increase water temperature. Some dish-washing equipment will have auxiliary water booster heaters if their supply water is not 180°F (82.2°C). In all cases, it is highly recommended to label fixtures supplied with water above 120°F (48.9°C) with a warning that the water is hot and dangerous.

Heating water can be costly. One primary effort in energy management is the reduction, whenever possible, of the temperature of hot-water heaters. In all cases, the hot-water storage tank and hot-water piping should be insulated.

STORAGE TANK INSULATION

Figure 12.14 shows the heat losses from a water storage tank at several temperatures. The same figure also shows the effect of increasing the insulation thickness on the storage tank by increments of 1 inch (25.4 millimeters). Increasing insulation thickness on the water storage tank and reducing water temperature will save energy.

Figure 12.15 shows three hot-water energy-management techniques. Technique A indicates the energy savings when reducing the water temperature. Technique B shows the energy savings when adding insulation and maintaining the same water temperature. Technique C generates the largest energy savings when reducing the water temperature and adding insulation to the storage tank.

PIPING INSULATION

There is another critical portion of the system that must be analyzed: the piping network and the potential energy savings that could result if these pipes were insulated. Figure 12.16 shows the effects of insulating various-size water pipes maintained at various water temperatures. The figure is based on 100 feet (30.5 meters) of pipe—a linear multiplier is used for various pipe lengths. See Figure 12.17, which shows the effects of reducing water temperature and adding piping insulation.

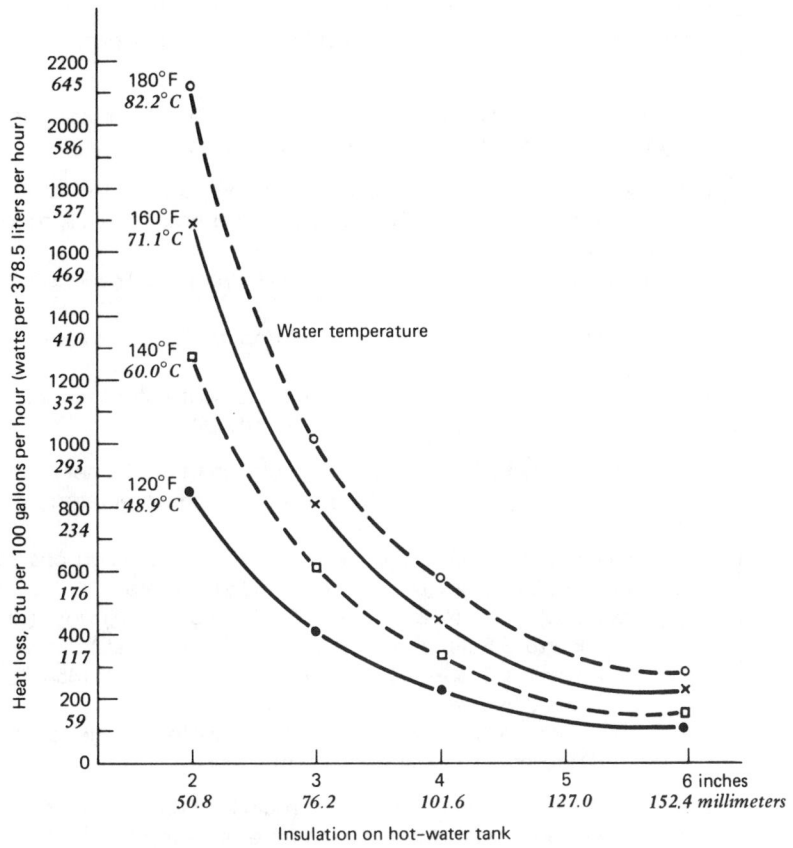

FIGURE 12.14 Heat loss per 100 gallons (378.5 liters) from a hot-water storage tank maintained at various temperatures (standard-size tanks).

HOT-WATER HEATERS

Common hot-water heaters include the unit heater storage tank, a side-arm heater, and a heat exchanger. The least efficient system is the heater storage tank, primarily because insulation around the unit is inadequate and the system has a low recovery rate. The heat recovery rate is the ability to heat water quickly. This unit is normally used as a dish-washing booster water heater, to raise the water temperature from 140 to 180°F (from 60 to 82.2°C), or in remote building areas where it is too costly to transport heated water over a long distance.

The side-arm heater can provide a very large quantity of water in a short time. It is connected to a water storage tank; Figure 12.18 shows such an installation. It has moderate efficiency and, when hot-water demand is mini-

Energy conservation techniques; refer to Figure 12.14 for data.

Initial data:
    Normal (2 inches insulation (50.8 millimeters)) hot-water storage tank of 500 gallons (1892.5 liters) maintained at 180°F (82.2°C).

1. Conservation technique A, reduce water temperature to 140°F (60°C).
        Heat loss at 180°F (82.2°C): about 2150 Btu/hour/100 gallons (about 630 watts/hour/378.5 liters).
        Heat loss at 140°F (60°C): about 1300 Btu/hour/100 gallons (about 381 watts/hour/378.5 liters).
        Energy savings: 2150−1300 = 850 Btu/hour/100 gallons (249 watts/hour/378.5 liters).
            Savings for 500-gallon (1892.5-liter) hot-water storage tank: 5 x 850 = 4250 Btu//hour (5 x 249 = 1245 watts/hour).

2. Conservation technique B, increase insulation from 2 inches (50.8 millimeters) to 4 inches (101.6 millimeters), no change in water temperature 180°F (82.2°C).
        Heat loss at 180°F (82.2°C): about 2150 Btu/hour/100 gallons (about 630 watts/hour/378.5 liters) with 2 inches (50.8 millimeters).
        Heat loss at 180°F (82.2°C): about 600 Btu/hour/100 gallons (about 176 watts/hour/378.5 liters) with 4 inches (101.6 millimeters).
        Energy savings: 2150−600 = 1550 Btu/hour/100 gallons (454 watts/hour/378.5 liters).
            Savings for 500-gallon (1892.5-liter) hot-water storage tank: 5 x 1550 = 7750 Btu/hour (5 x 454 = 2270 watts/hour).

3. Conservation technique C, increase insulation from 2 inches (50.8 millimeters) to 4 inches and reduce water temperature to 140°F (60°C).
        Heat loss at 180°F (82.2°C): about 2150 Btu/hour/100 gallons (about 630 watts/hour/378.5 liters) with 2 inches (50.8 millimeters).
        Heat loss at 140°F (60°C): about 375 Btu/hour/100 gallons (about 110 watts/hour/378.5 liters) with 4 inches (101.6 millimeters).
        Energy savings: 2150−375 = 1775 Btu/hour/100 gallons (520 watts/hour/378.5 liters).
            Savings for 500-gallon (1892.5-liter) hot-water storage tank: 5 x 1775 = 8875 Btu/hour (5 x 520 = 2600 watts/hour).

FIGURE 12.15 Effects of insulation and water temperature reduction on hot-water storage tanks.

mal or nonexistent, the heater supplies hot water to the storage tank for future use. The building's peak hot-water demand, the net usable capacity of the storage tank, and the water output of the heater must all be carefully balanced; otherwise, the system will perform like the unit heater storage tank discussed previously. The booster water heater concept is shown with a side-arm heater in Figure 12.19.

The heat exchanger is very efficient and is capable of providing various water temperatures for the building. Its installation is shown in Figure 12.20. The major disadvantage of a heat exchanger is that it is used with a building hot-water or steam-heating system. During the building heating months, it represents one of the most efficient water-heating systems available. The overall system efficiency is reduced during the nonheating season because a boiler must be operated to supply hot water or steam to the heat exchanger. Some buildings utilize a side-arm heater storage tank as a back-up system and for summer hot-water heating so that the main boiler does not have to be operated.

A solar water-heating system should be used whenever feasible to reduce energy cost. The system can be used to partially heat water, generally hot enough for guest use and especially for swimming pools and spas.

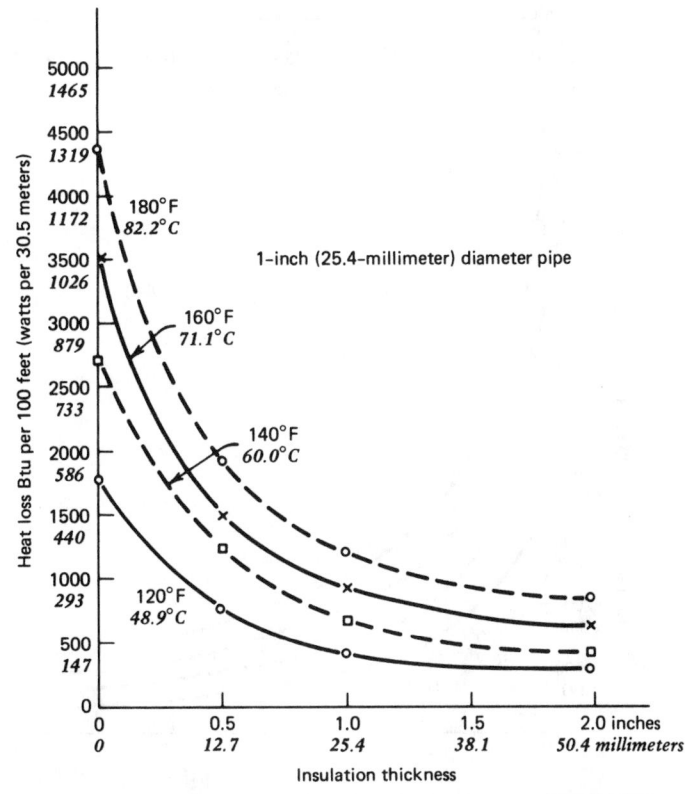

FIGURE 12.16 Heat loss per 100 feet (30.5 meters) of hot-water pipes of various water temperatures.

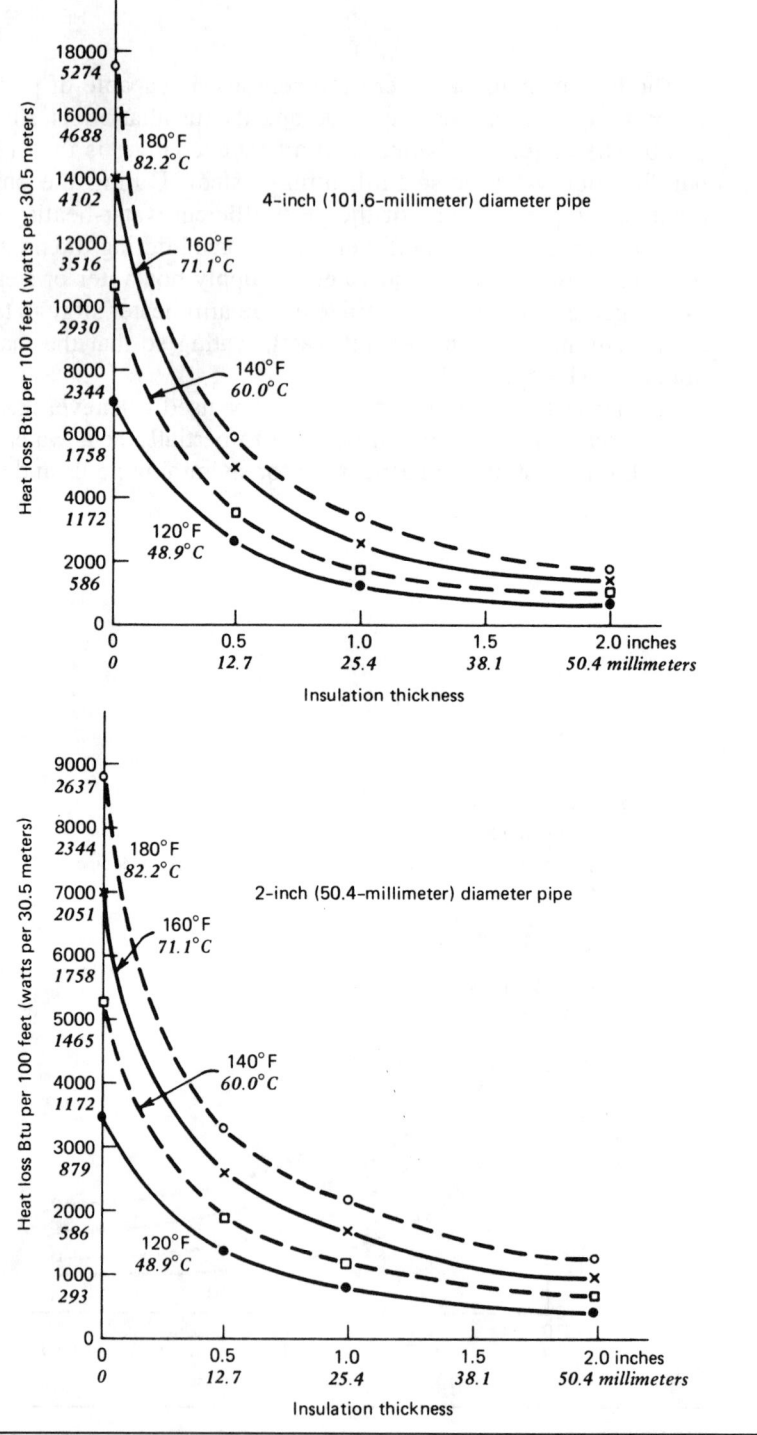

FIGURE 12.16 *(Continued)*

Energy conservation technique; refer to Figure 12.16 for data.

Initial data:

Normal noninsulated 2-inch (50.8-millimeter) water pipe 300 feet (91.5 meters) in length maintained at 180°F (82.2°C).

Conservation technique, increase insulation to 1 inch (25.4 millimeters) and reduce water temperature to 140°F (60°C).

Heat loss at 180°F (82.2°C): about17,500 Btu/hour/100 feet (about 5128 watts/hour/30.5 meters) with no insulation.

Heat loss at 140°F (60°C): about 2000 Btu/hour/100 feet (about 586 watts/hour/30.5 meters) with 1 inch (25.4 millimeters).

Energy savings: 17,500−2000 = 15,500 Btu/hour/100 feet (4542 watts/hour/30.5 meters).

Savings for 300 feet (91.5 meters) hot-water piping: 3 x 15,500 = 46,500 Btu/hour (3 x 4542 = 13,626 watts/hour).

FIGURE 12.17   Effects of insulation and water temperature reduction on pipe heat loss.

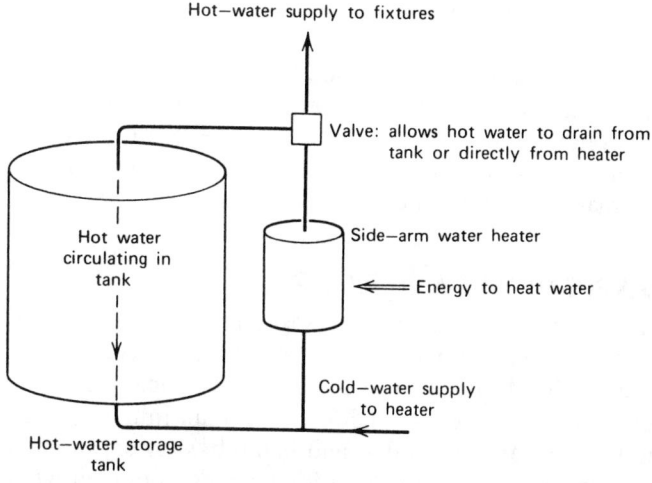

FIGURE 12.18   Side-arm heater.

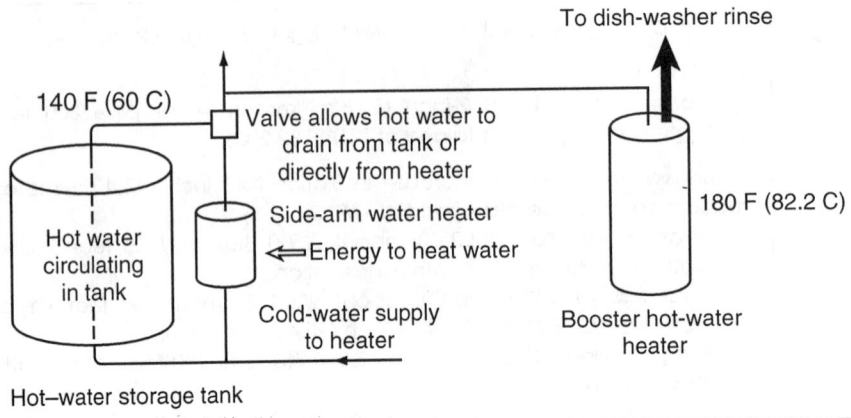

FIGURE 12.19 Side-arm heater with booster hot-water heat for dishwasher rinse.

WATER SUPPLY MAINTENANCE

The most common water supply maintenance problems are dripping faucets, piping vibration noise, and piping expansion noise. These are usually reported by guests or by an alert housekeeping crew or are found during management inspection of the property. In areas where labor costs are high, it costs more to repair these items than the resulting energy savings. There is no set cycle, other than the approximate age of the plumbing network, of such major piping failures as broken pipes.

LEAKING VALVES AND PIPING

Dripping faucets increase housekeeping costs and may be annoying to guests. If one additional minute (60 additional seconds) is required to clean fixtures with dripping faucets, and if additional cleaning chemical requirements are considered, the additional 3 man-minutes (180 man-seconds) per guest room (lavatory, toilet, and bathtub–shower combination) can become expensive, amounting to about $1 per guest room per week.

The corrective-maintenance procedure is simple. A valve seat washer usually has to be replaced. The need to replace a seat washer depends on its use, its age, the water temperature, its materials of construction, and the chemicals in the water supply. Normally, seat washers will last 1 to 5 years. The 1-year life can be assumed for heavy use, high water temperatures, and high water hardness. The task time for changing a washer is 3 to 10 minutes (0.05 to 0.17 hours), and washer costs vary from less than 5 cents to about 50 cents, depending on the valve and the fixture.

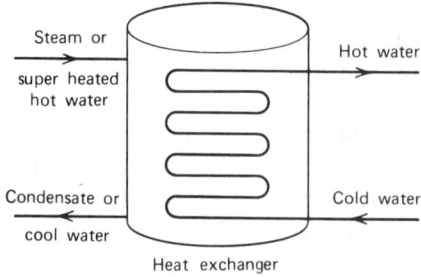

FIGURE 12.20   Hot-water heat exchanger.

The valve also has a stem washer, or packing. Its life is usually much longer than the seat washer. On average, a stem washer lasts 2 to 8 years; its life depends on the same factors that affect seat washers. The water loss is equivalent to a low runoff, and it can be observed only when the valve is open—when water flows through the faucet and leaks where the valve is attached to the sink or lavatory. A good maintenance department policy requires the plumber to replace the stem washer each time the valve seat washer is replaced. This requires only another 2 minutes (120 seconds) for most valves.

Water leaks that develop at piping connections are difficult to control. They must be visible and exposed, or large water losses may occur (since the effects of water damage must be observed before you know there is a leak). This is why all connections should be designed so that there are visible inspection points for periodic checks. The building preventive-maintenance program should inspect these points every 12 to 24 months.

PLUMBING VIBRATION NOISE

Plumbing vibrations can cause noise that is transmitted throughout the building. Since noise control is analyzed in another chapter, the only sources of noise that will be mentioned in this chapter are those that can be eliminated by plumbing-maintenance management. Hot-water piping can cause a noise problem. When pipes are heated by hot water, they expand, and rapid piping expansion can generate noise. Reduced hot-water temperatures and adequate piping insulation will solve this problem.

PIPING-EXPANSION PROBLEMS

Piping expansion can also cause pipes and connection points to separate. Provisions must be made to reduce this problem. While copper and plastic pipe are recommended in most new installations, these materials have the greatest expansion coefficients. One solution is to use piping materials that have low coefficients of expansion (pipes other than copper or plastic). Another solution is to install expansion devices, such as piping loops and expansion joints. These devices do not prevent materials from expanding, but they allow piping to expand at controlled points and eliminate undesirable expansion noises.

PLUMBING FIXTURES

The manager generally has little input regarding the number of plumbing fixtures to be installed and maintained. The National Standard Plumbing Code specifies the minimum number of plumbing fixtures for occupants and customers. These figures are guidelines and recommendations. Although many local ordinances adopt the guidelines stated in the code, others increase these minimums. The number of required plumbing fixtures for a space depends on the number of potential users and on the population density. The local fire marshal frequently determines the maximum number of people that may occupy a room at any given time. This occupant figure is normally used as a base for determining the minimum required number of plumbing fixtures.

Plumbing fixtures are grouped into various categories. One group includes toilets and urinals. These fixtures require large quantities of water when flushed, and water control valves must be carefully regulated to provide the minimum water flow for satisfactory operation, since any excess water represents an energy waste.

Nonconserving, older toilets use from 5 to 7 gallons (19 to 26 liters) per flush, accounting for almost 40 percent of indoor water use in lodging guest bathrooms. Low-flush toilets have a shallow trap design that allows water to siphon out of the bowl in lesser amounts than in older toilets. Low-flush toilets, defined here as toilets that use not more than 3.5 gallons per flush (13.2 liters per flush), must meet the performance standard A112.19.2M-1982 of the American National Standards Institute (ANSI). When low-flush toilets were first sold, there were some reports of the need for double flushing and that clogging in sewer laterals would increase. However, standard sewer pipe diameters and slopes, both inside and outside buildings, have been found to carry wastes adequately and with sufficient velocity to prevent clogging and double flushing has been minimized. This is because low-flush toilets maintain peak discharge rates comparable to nonconserving toilets, and it is peak flow that transports solids down the pipe.

Another group of fixtures allows the occupants to use water for washing or for equipment operation. These include, but are not limited to, lavatories (for washing face and hands); showers; sinks of all types, such as laundry trays and sinks, vegetable preparation sinks, and pot- and pan-washing sinks; dish-washing equipment; and swimming pools. Foodservice equipment and swimming pool equipment specifications are also covered in the National Sanitation Foundation Standards. Underwriters Laboratories is also involved with electrically related plumbing equipment.

Showers account for a significant portion of water consumed. Typical shower annual water consumption of 12,300 to 16,000 gallons (47,662 to 62,000 liters) can be cut to about 8100 gallons (31,388 liters) with a 2.5 gallon per minute (0.16 liter per second) shower head. Standard shower heads deliver approximately 8 gallons per minute (0.52 liters per second). While early shower head water reduction technology was usually found to be unsatisfactory, new water-saving heads are much improved. They can produce a powerful stream (mixed with air) and the sensation of abundant water. Similar to shower head technology, water-saving faucets are also available. Such faucets mix air with the water stream to produce the function and sensation of a larger volume of water.

DRAINAGE SYSTEMS

The drainage system is shown for one fixture in Figure 12.21. It is a gravity flow system, and atmospheric air pressure is required for its complete and safe operation. The figure also indicates basic piping terminology for the system.

SEWAGE FLOW AND PIPING

Traps and Vents

Waste, or sewage, drains from a fixture into a fixture drain through a trap. The trap contains a quantity of waste that prevents sewer gases from escaping from sewer lines back into the building. Wastes flow through the trap because the fixture liquid level is higher than the trap. Connected to the fixture drainpipe is a fixture vent. The vent allows air to circulate throughout the drainage system. This simple connection prevents wastes from siphoning from the trap by equalizing air pressure on both sides of the trap; hence, a quantity of water is always retained in the trap. See Figure 12.22.

Soil and Waste Pipes

The fixture drainpipe discharges into a soil or waste drainpipe. The difference between the two pipes is one of terminology only. A soil pipe can handle any building drainage, including human excreta (from toilets). The waste pipe can handle everything except human excreta. A single drainpipe can receive the discharge from several fixtures and is positioned at an angle

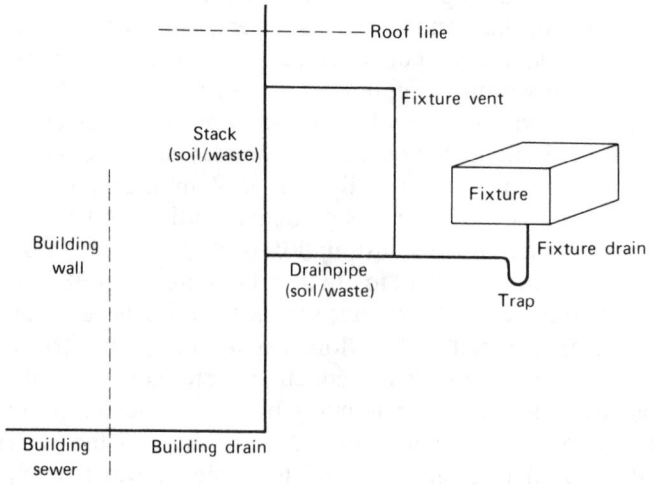

FIGURE 12.21 Drainage system for a single plumbing fixture.

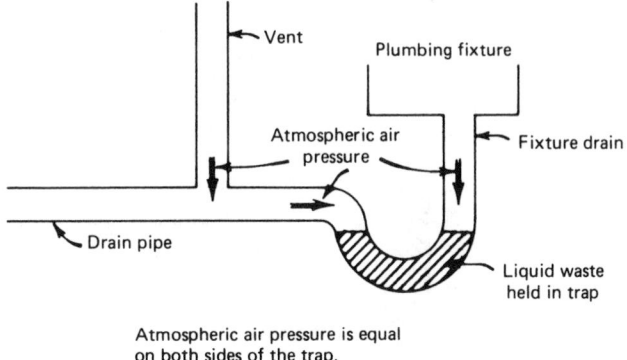

FIGURE 12.22 The trap.

(small slope measured at 1/4-inch vertical drop per foot of horizontal distance [19.4-millimeter vertical drop per 1 meter of horizontal distance]) that provides for continuous gravity flow in the system.

The drainpipe deposits wastes into a soil or waste stack or into a building drain. The stack's lower portion is a large, vertical drainage pipe, and its upper portion is a large vent that must extend through the building roof line. The stack discharges into the building's main drain, which eventually collects all building sewage. The building drain deposits sewage into a building sewer at the outside of the building wall. The building sewer deposits sewage into a private sewage disposal system or into a public sewer line that is located beyond the property boundary line.

Special Sewage Systems for Multiple Basement Levels

Some buildings have multiple basement levels, several of which may be located below the building sewer line (see Figure 12.23). Any plumbing fixture located below the building sewer line must discharge through a sewage ejector system. This system has an enclosed sewage collection tank. When sewage fills the tank, it may be pumped out to the building drain or forced by use of compressed air up to the building drain. Reverse sewage flow is prevented by using check valves.

Storm Drains

Drains from the building roof and parking areas usually discharge into storm drains. The technique of combining storm and sanitary sewage has been banned in many areas of the United States because it overloads the sanitary drainage system. Storm runoff cannot be drained into private sewage disposal systems. Storm runoff water can be stored, if enough land area is available, for irrigation purposes (this could be an important water resource for golf courses that purchase water).

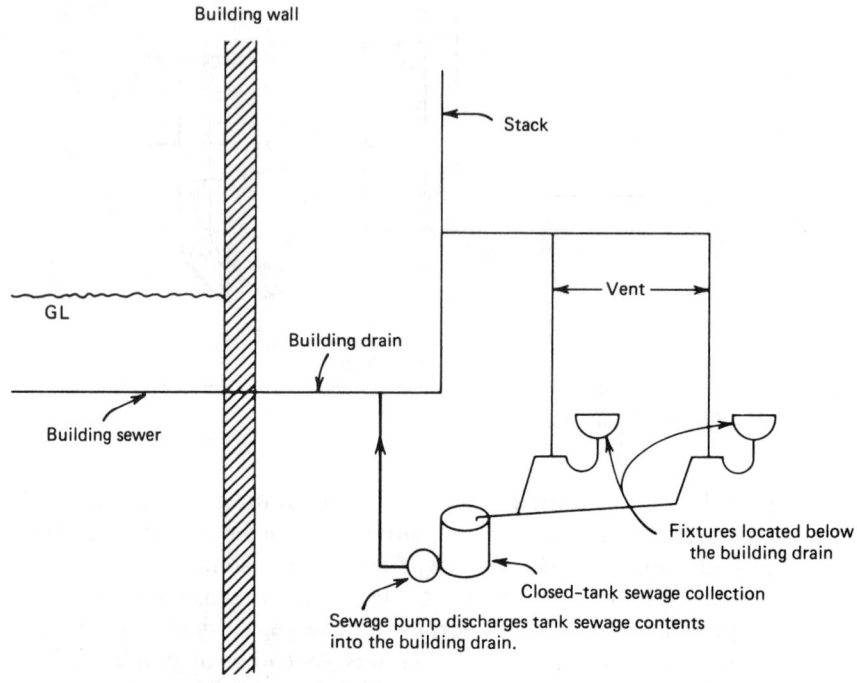

FIGURE 12.23   Sewage ejector.

Subsurface drainage is required in areas with high water tables or water-tight soil. This water is normally drained into sump holes and pumped into a storm drainage system, used for irrigation purposes, or, when allowed, pumped into the building sewer line. Again, this water cannot be discharged into a private sewage disposal system.

DRAINAGE DESIGN FACTORS

Drainage design is more complex than water distribution design. The major design problem is not overloading pipes (too many fixtures for a given pipe size). The design is based on the probability of a number or group of fixtures being discharged at the same time into the drainage piping.

Fixture discharges are given in fixture units. Fixture drainpipe sizes are indicated in the National Standard Plumbing Code, as are fixture-unit discharge ratings from various types of fixtures.

All drainpipes are rated in fixture-unit capacities. All you have to do is add up the number of fixture units discharging into any drainpipe and determine its size from an appropriate table in the code. Drainpipe sizes are also dependent on the number of toilets draining into a single pipe. In drainage design, there is one golden rule: A larger drainpipe can never, under any circumstance, drain into a smaller pipe. Hence, pipes are the same size, or larger, at each connection point in the direction of gravity flow.

Storm drainage system design is very similar to sewage design. The National Standard Plumbing Code provides tables that relate anticipated rainfall and surface area to piping size.

DRAINAGE MAINTENANCE

The maintenance of a properly designed drainage system should be minimal. In a gravity flow drainage system, the basic maintenance requirement is to keep the system open, that is, the piping clean and free from stoppages. Most maintenance tools are designed so that they can be inserted in piping and remove debris. Plumbers use augers, rods, and "snakes." These devices are flexible so that they will not coil within a pipe and will make turns as the piping turns. They may push the material to a larger pipe or break up the matter into smaller particles so that it can be flushed away; or they may be designed to collect matter so that it can be removed from the pipe. Various chemicals may work in traps and short sections of pipe to decompose clogging matter. Many chemical cleaners are only effective, however, if greasy materials have clogged the piping.

The major problem in foodservice operations is grease condensation within pipes. This problem is increased in traps and small-diameter pipes and is not as serious in large-diameter pipes. Frequently, grease traps are installed on equipment and serve as grease collection points. These traps must be cleaned on a periodic schedule.

Laundries have problems with lint, small articles of clothing, and soap, all of which clog pipes. The plumber's tools mentioned at the beginning of this section will effectively remove these obstructions in the pipes.

Building drains may become clogged with tree roots. These may have to be removed from the pipes periodically by using rooters, which cut off tree roots within the pipe. Chemicals may be added on a periodic schedule to discourage future root growth, or trees may have to be removed from the area.

SWIMMING POOLS

Pool design, construction, and maintenance in public settings (lodgings, resorts, clubs, schools, colleges, and health-care facilities) are strictly controlled by the local public health department. The equipment and their utility connections are frequently tested, and maintenance procedures are spelled out by the National Sanitation Foundation in its numerous standards. Underwriters Laboratories may be involved because of electric connections for lighting and motors. The public pool differs from the homeowner's pool in that continuous maintenance and inspection procedures and records are required by ordinances.

CONSTRUCTION TECHNIQUES

Several practical construction techniques are used for pools. Some construction techniques have resulted in lowering the initial pool cost to such an extent that any reasonable-sized property can now have a pool. The type of pool selected for a particular area or property depends on local conditions and potential pool use. Ground freezing can limit the types of pools for a particular area. High ground water tables can also have an effect. Local codes may specify acceptable pool types.

The most costly pool, for any given surface area and volume in gallons (cubic meters) of water, is the steel-reinforced concrete pool lined with a marine plaster finish or ceramic-type tile (sidewalls and bottom). They must be drained or heated during the winter months to prevent pool water from freezing. The concrete pool is probably the most durable pool. Concrete pools include those constructed with poured concrete, steel-reinforced concrete blocks, and Gunite-type construction. Gunite pools are most frequently found in the southwestern United States, where freezing is minimal.

Semiconcrete pools have concrete bottoms and fiberglass or stainless-steel sidewall construction. They cost less than concrete pools and provide satisfactory service. Some managers feel that the maintenance requirements are lower because the sidewalls are easier to clean.

Less costly still is the vinyl-liner pool. These may have steel sidewalls and a packed-dirt or concrete bottom. The walls and bottom are covered with a vinyl or plastic liner. The liner is available in various thicknesses, and its life depends on its thickness, its use, and the local weather conditions. The plastic liner can be repaired underwater and quickly replaced at a low cost. These pools can be built above or in the ground.

The least costly pool is an above-ground pool with a plastic liner and steel wall construction. These are generally used as temporary pools or as wading pools for children.

Pools other than concrete do not have to be drained if there is danger of water freezing, since metal walls and vinyl liners are capable of expanding with ice. Always check with the pool manufacturer for his or her recommendations for your specific area.

DESIGN FACTORS

Pools can be built in any shape and size. Some pools are sectioned so that very high water-circulation rates are maintained in one area, which can be used as a therapeutic pool or spa. The pool can be located outside or inside, or covered for year-round use. Decoration schemes are virtually unlimited. The pool wading area can occupy from 20 to 80 percent of the surface area of the pool. The depth of the wading area varies from 3 to 5 feet (about 1 to 1.5 meters). The pool's maximum depth depends on diving boards and platforms and on their height. Normal depths are 8 to 18 feet (2.5 to 5.5 meters).

Wading pools for children are also classified as pools and are subject to the same construction, maintenance procedures, and ordinances as regular pools. They can be located in the ground or at any ground level on the property.

SWIMMING REGULATIONS

It is very important for management to establish pool and swimming regulations. These must be posted and enforced. Seek the advice of the local public health department and your insurance adviser to help you establish correct, legal regulations. Legal counsel is generally advised, since lawyers are aware of recent court rulings and settlements regarding accidents and lawsuits.

Pool regulations must be posted at the entrance to the pool area, which must be fenced, within the pool area, and in the guest rooms of lodging and resort establishments. In the case of a private club, regulations should also be posted in locker rooms and included in all announcements concerning pool activities.

Pool regulations normally specify swimming hours, number of swimmers, permitted games, lifeguard posting, food and beverage consumption at the pool area, clothing requirements, towel availability, and child safety rules. The pool area should be well lighted at night to minimize accidents. Glass and breakable dishware should never be allowed in the immediate pool area. Drinking containers should be soft, colored, and disposable plastic or paper products rather than hard, clear plastic.

POOL AND SPA MAINTENANCE

Filters

The fundamental pool maintenance device is the filter. The filter removes impurities from water and keeps it clear and sparkling. The true test of adequate filtering is to toss a small coin into the pool at its average depth and to be able to distinguish one side of the coin from the other as its rests on the bottom of the pool. The filter must cycle pool water every six to eight hours. A water turnover cycle consists of forcing all the pool water through the filter in a specified time period. In a normal operation, one water cycle is required each day. If swimming activity increases, more than one water turnover cycle may be required. Or if blowing dirt or excessive rainfall or sunshine occur, the filtering rate must be increased. The local public health authority has the best recommendations regarding filtering cycles for a particular area—sometimes the cycle is specified in the local public health code.

Several types of filters are available, and all are about equally effective in removing impurities. Some filters require filter aids, such as diatomaceous earth. Others, such as sand or sand-and-gravel filters, do not require additional filter aids but have lower water flow rates. Cartridge filters are also effective; some types have high and others low water flow rates. The manufacturer's specifications must be followed for all filters. Pumps and the filter should be operated just long enough to keep the water clear and sparkling.

Filters must be cleaned. There is no set schedule. Follow the filter manufacturer's recommendations. Normally, pool water is used for cleaning the filter. Filters are cleaned by backwashing. The dirty water being drained from the filter is discharged to the waste drainage lines of the building through an indirect drainage system. When allowed, this water should be used for property irrigation purposes. Also when allowed, fresh water, rather than expensive, chemically treated pool water, should be used to clean the filter.

The diatomaceous-earth filter requires the filter to be recoated with the filter aid (diatomaceous earth) after backwashing. Sand, sand-and-gravel, and cartridge filters that do not require a filter aid become immediately available for use after the backwashing process. Just enough water should be used to clean the filter.

Pool Debris

Soil, leaves, insects, and debris will collect in the pool and must be removed. Some soil floats, so various types of nets can be used to remove it. Pools are usually equipped with, and required to have, a weir arrangement with a strainer, which is an opening at the water surface level in the pool, so that floating trash will flow into the weir opening, where it is collected and retained for manual removal. Weir openings are connected to the filter system of the pool. See Figure 12.24.

Large objects on the bottom of the pool can be removed with nets. Smaller objects and soil can be removed with various pool sweeps that operate with the filtering system. The sweeps force or blow the pool's bottom soil toward the main pool drain, or they keep the soil in constant agitation so it can be removed by normal water filtering. Manual vacuum cleaners are efficient, and an experienced worker can quickly clean the bottom and the sidewalls of the pool. Most vacuums are connected to the pool's filtering system. Leaf collectors that operate on normal building water pressure are also available and are effective for removing larger pieces of soil on the pool bottom. The sidewalls and the bottom of the pool should also be periodically brushed to loosen and remove soil clinging to these surfaces.

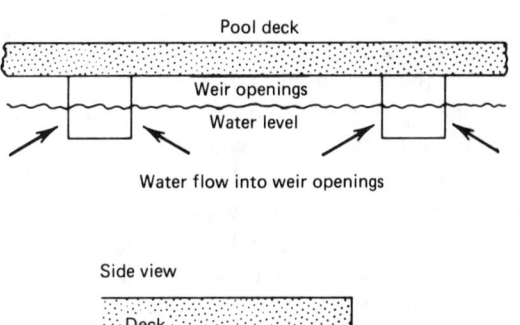

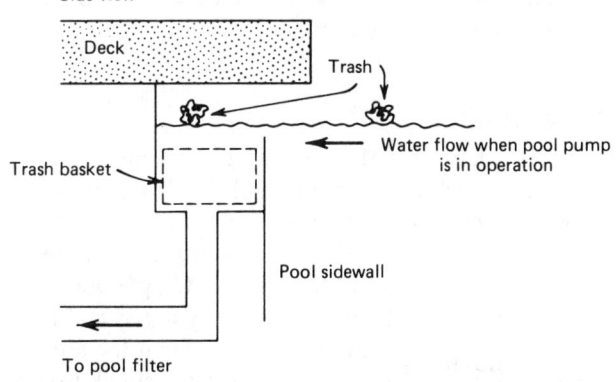

FIGURE 12.24 Pool surface weir openings to collect floating trash.

Chemical Treatments

All pools must be treated with appropriate chemicals. The primary chemical is a disinfectant that will destroy water bacteria. The disinfectant level varies with the type of chemical being used. Most ordinances require a residual chemical base of one to three parts per million. Test kits are available to measure this residual base. For public pools, records must be kept, logging the results of tests, the tester's name, and the amount and type of chemical added to the pool. The amount of disinfectant varies with the size of the pool, the weather, pool usage, the soil in the pool, the water condition and quality, and the quantity of water in the pool. Chemicals are available in liquid, powder, solid, and gas forms. The chemicals can be added manually, or suitable automatic feeders can be used.

The two common disinfectants are chlorine and bromine. Chlorine is the usual choice for pools, while bromine is used in heated spas. Bromine water treatment is generally more expensive than chlorine but does not leave as much residue on the pool sides or bottom, and it will not foam as much as chlorine with rapid water-circulating systems, such as those used in spas. Bromine levels are kept at one part per million, while chlorine levels are usually maintained at about two parts per million.

Chemicals are also used to control water acidity and alkalinity, referred to as water pH. The pH should be between 7.2 and 7.6, or slightly alkaline. If the pH exceeds 7.6, there probably will be water algae problems and swimmers may suffer minor skin and mucous-membrane irritations. Conversely, water will become uncomfortable when the pH drops much below 7.2. When the pH drops below 6.8, metal equipment will corrode. The amount of acid to correct for high pH, and the amount of alkaline to correct for low pH, depends on the type of corrective chemical used. These chemicals should be added only at specific rates and when the filter is in operation and the pool is closed to swimmers.

Algae Control

Algae are plant growths on the pool's sidewalls and bottom or within the water. Algae cannot be completely eliminated. They are introduced to the water from the swimmers' bodies or are blown into the pool. Rain also adds algae to the pool. All of the following encourage algae growth: sunshine, water temperatures above 80°F (26.7°C), pH above 7.8, and low disinfectant levels. Algicide can be used to destroy algae and may be added every 3 to 7 days during the swimming season. Disinfectants are excellent algicides. Shock treatments are used to kill algae; "shock treatment" means increasing the disinfectant level to 5 to 10 parts per million (the pool is closed until the level drops to 3 parts per million or less). Algae growth in some pools becomes so excessive that the pool water must be drained and the pool cleaned with acid chemicals, a process called acid washing.

Initial Water Treatment

Fresh water added to a pool is normally unstable; hence, it is difficult to control pH and disinfectant levels. Water stabilizers are required to counteract this effect. Water conditioners and other fresh-water chemicals and minerals may also be required to correct for initial water color. Various types of stabilizers and conditioners are available, and their use varies with local water conditions. The recommendations of other pool owners, a pool contractor, or the local public health authority should be followed for initial water treatment.

ENERGY CONSERVATION

A swimming pool kept in year-round operation consumes large amounts of energy. Every effort must be made to keep energy-related costs in line with the other services offered by the property.

Many pools are enclosed or partially enclosed for year-round use. An enclosure can reduce pool maintenance costs because the filter can be operated fewer hours a day; less chemical treatment is needed; algae problems are initially eliminated; pH is easier to control; less heat is required to heat the water and customer control is also easier when pools are enclosed since access doors can be locked when the manager decides to close the pool.

Pool enclosures are available in several styles and types; all are about equally effective with respect to maintenance factors. The enclosure requires adequate ventilation. Some enclosures are air conditioned.

Water surface enclosures and covers are also available. They are used to seal off the surface of the pool at night, when the pool is closed, or during adverse weather conditions. Some of these surface enclosures are classified as safety covers.

Pool heaters are usually costly to operate. Pool heaters are hot-water heaters connected in series with the water-filtering system. They are controlled by thermostats. They can be fueled with electricity, gas, or fuel oil. Solar heaters are ideal. Many areas have banned the use of both electric and natural-gas pool heaters. Solar heaters have virtually no operating cost when used in conjunction with the filter.

It is difficult to compare the operating cost of pool heaters because local weather variations can have a tremendous effect on heating cost. Pool water temperature, outside dry-bulb temperature, outside relative humidity, and wind conditions that cause water evaporation can all have tremendous cost effects. At night, radiation to outer space can be a significant factor and can result in a temperature drop of several degrees in pool water.

SUMMARY

The water distribution and sewage drainage systems are the two most important modern building systems that are taken for granted and least understood at the present time by building managers. Both are needed to obtain a building occupancy permit in the United States and in most countries throughout the world. Without question, modern lodging and foodservice facilities with their technology advances and equipment could not operate without a water supply and drainage system.

A potable water supply is essential in the hospitality industry. An adequate supply of clear sparkling water is assumed by the guest when checking into a lodging establishment and is essential for the proper preparation of food products. Such desirable water may not be supplied by a water utility and it is up to the hospitality manager to provide clear sparkling water. An understanding of quality water is required so that it can be provided.

Water distribution system knowledge is required by the hospitality manager so that the system can be designed, operated, and maintained to provide a continuous supply of water.

Hot water can be expensive, especially if water is overheated. In addition, hot water can be dangerous to guests and employees. Water for guest use should not exceed 110°F (43.3°C); 140°F (60°C) as kitchen hot water; 180°F (82.2°C) for dishwater rinsing, building heating systems, and as a water supply for kitchen steaming equipment; 103°F (39.4°C) for spas; and 80°F (26.7°C) for swimming pools. Solar water-heating systems should be used whenever feasible and all hot-water heating units and piping must be properly insulated to conserve energy.

Water waste and sewage are created at the plumbing fixtures. A properly designed sewage drainage system must be installed and maintained to ensure that waste and sewage will be handled in the most sanitary manner. The major maintenance problem is clogged piping for drainage systems. The two major sources of clogging are guest materials and food-related grease. Guest items dropped into sinks, bath–shower drains, and water closets are almost impossible for management to control; hence, as long as current fixtures are used, this will be a continuous maintenance problem. The control of food grease pipe clogging is possible to control partially through employee education programs, periodic chemical treatment (piping degreasers) of the affected fixtures and their related drainage piping, and frequent cleaning of traps.

Swimming pools and spas are generally thought to be a guest requirement and occupy a significant percentage of the maintenance budget (chemicals, energy requirements for motors and water heating, and labor man-hours). Pool use must be controlled to protect the facility owners.

The plumbing system is essential. It can become a major maintenance problem, especially with older buildings. As plumbing fixtures are added to the building, the drainage system is seldom renovated to accommodate the new requirements. These maintenance problems will not decrease in time, but they can be controlled.

BIBLIOGRAPHY

1. American Society of Heating, Refrigeration and Air Conditioning Engineers, *1993 ASHRAE Handbook Fundamentals*, New York, 1993.
2. Borsenik, F. D., *Holiday Inn, Inc.—Hotel Group Energy Management Program: Phase I*, University of Nevada, Las Vegas, November 20, 1989.
3. Borsenik, F. D., *Holiday Inn, Inc.—Hotel Group Energy Management Program: Phase II*, University of Nevada, Las Vegas, December 5, 1989.
4. Piper, J. E., *Handbook of Facility Management, Tools and Techniques, Formulas and Tables*, Prentice-Hall, Englewood Cliffs, NJ, 1995.

QUESTIONS/PROBLEMS

1. Determine the extent to which water softening is practiced by local lodging, foodservice, health-care, or club facilities. Also determine the types of water-softening systems and regeneration salts that are being used.

2. The normal water usage for a foodservice unit is 7.5 gallons (28.4 liters) of water per meal. What is the cost effect of reducing this water consumption to 5 gallons (18.9 liters) if the unit is charged $1.75 per 1000 gallons (3785 liters) of water for a one-year period? The foodservice unit serves 1000 meals a day. (Consider a month as 30 days.)

3. Compare the water distribution systems shown in Figure 12.7, and indicate when each system would be used in a multiple-floor building, such as a lodging unit, health-care facility, or institutional building.

4. Refer to Figure 12.9, and repeat for a building that is 325 feet (99.1 meters) in height.

5. Discuss and compare the advantages and disadvantages of using circulating pumps versus large-diameter pipes for a building.

6. Outline what you would include in a daily maintenance schedule for a swimming pool.

7. Determine the local health ordinances that apply to the operation of a swimming pool on a lodging or club property. Does the ordinance specify any maintenance procedures? What are they?

8. If you were reviewing a print of the proposed drainage route for a remodeling project in your building and it indicated that it was fixture–fixture drain–trap–stack, would this be correct?

CHAPTER 13

Courtesy of Hyatt Regency Hotel, San Francisco.

MANAGEMENT OF BUILDING TRANSPORTATION SYSTEMS

ABSTRACT

Vertical building transportation systems are required in all multiple-level buildings. At a minimum, stairs and fire-resistant stairwell structures and ramps are required. Usually, separate vertical-transportation systems are required for customer—client and employee—and product movement. These are costly systems to install, frequently up to 12 percent of the total building construction cost. System maintenance is included under building mechanical and electrical system costs (American Hotel & Motel Association Uniform System of Accounts for Hotels and Motels) and is difficult to separate from other electromechanical systems.

Energy management is difficult to control for vertical- and horizontal-transportation systems in buildings. Transportation systems are usually fairly efficient compared to other building systems, such as lighting, air conditioning, refrigeration, ventilation, and plumbing. Efficiency and operating costs may be improved, depending on which type of elevator machine is used. System efficiency is also frequently dependent on the manager's building maintenance policy. Good building layout can reduce the number of transportation system units and save energy.

The manager must be fully aware of the total building transportation system, and it must be fully operative when needed. Customers and employees are highly dependent on the system, especially in multilevel buildings.

Key words: balustrade; bumper; cable elevator; cables; car; clamping brake; collective control system; combplate; computerized control system; counterweights; dumbwaiter; electromagnetic brake; elevator machine; escalator; escalator controller; escalator machine; geared traction machine; gearless machine; guide rails; handling capacity; handrail; hydraulic elevator system; interval time; lower-limit switch; penthouse; people mover; pit; plunger; semicomputerized control system; shaft; sidewalk elevator; steps; tracks; traction drive; travel time; truss; upper-limit switch.

INTRODUCTION

Elevators, escalators, and stairs—ramps—are major vertical-transportation systems for passenger and product movement in buildings. Vertical-movement systems require energy; elevators and escalators are difficult systems to maintain and, in many cases, a costly building system to install. Almost as important are techniques for the horizontal movement of people and products. Actually, horizontal transportation involves the movement of more products and people but frequently receives little consideration. This chapter, while stressing vertical-transportation devices, will not overlook the important aspects of horizontal-movement techniques.

HIGH-RISE BUILDINGS

The problem of vertical transportation becomes very fundamental when one analyzes building economics and the feasibility of construction, maintenance, repair, operation, and control of long, horizontal buildings versus compact, multiple-floor, high-rise structures. It is frequently difficult to justify land cost and development requirements with horizontal construction. Trends in multiple-level automobile parking ramps indicate the economics of land development and use.

The high-rise structure also results in less employee walking time and greater movement efficiency (if an adequate vertical-transportation system is available). The lengths of plumbing and electric lines are also reduced in this type of structure. A quick look at heating and air-conditioning requirements shows that they are less costly in high-rise structures. Also, less customer and employee service centers are required.

VERTICAL TRANSPORTATION FOR TWO OR THREE FLOORS

Vertical-transportation costs and building construction costs are directly related in many types of structures. Recent laws stressing access and egress facilities for handicapped persons have increased these costs. These laws have changed construction requirements and require in-depth vertical-transportation analysis. For example, consider a two- or three-level motel. In the past, it was the practice to house handicapped people on the ground level to make it easier for them to move into and out of guest rooms. The typical two-level motel did not have elevator service, so handicapped people could not be housed on the upper level. Very few three-level motels had elevator service, as it was assumed that customers could and would walk to the third level.

Under current laws, if elevator service is not provided, walking ramps are mandatory between all building levels. Ramps can be very costly for a two-level building with no elevator service. Ramp cost for a three-level building is higher than some elevator systems. Thus, vertical-transportation devices that were once of concern only in high-rise structures must now be considered for many two-level hospitality buildings. As a result, a recent trend has developed toward multiple-level lodging construction.

HORIZONTAL MOVEMENT

Unfortunately, too much concern has been placed on vertical-transportation devices, and very little effort has been allocated to horizontal traffic flow and product movement. There are some exceptions; for example, hotel registration areas in Las Vegas and in some other gaming areas of the world are located adjacent to, or within, casino areas. Show lines in Las Vegas run right through the casino. In most gaming establishments, one must pass through the casino to enter foodservice units. The reason: Generally, casinos are more profitable.

In many other building areas, guests and customers walk long distances to move from one point to another. Very little attention has been devoted to the horizontal movement of people. Employee walking time is especially important. Take the simple case of 20 employees who spend 10 percent of their time walking from one area to another; this is equivalent to two employees who do nothing but walk all day. Reducing walking time to 5 percent saves the cost of one employee.

Not all walking time is considered unproductive; some managers state that an employee who is carrying a product is productive. Productive perhaps, but efficient? If 2000 pounds (907 kilograms) of food are moved in an 8-hour period at 50 pounds (27.7 kilograms) or less per trip, one should ask whether there is a more efficient way to move that food. Several older buildings have storage areas in one section, but the materials are used in another area. This results in an unproductive system.

VERTICAL-TRANSPORTATION TECHNIQUES

There are four principal techniques involved in vertical transportation: elevators; escalators; stairwells and passenger ramps; and gravity chutes, drops. The first three are utilized to some extent in most hospitality buildings. The last group should be used more extensively as an energy-management effort.

ELEVATORS

Well-managed passenger and freight elevators are two of the most dependable movement techniques utilized in hospitality buildings. Most ordinances in the United States and other industrialized nations have established very detailed safety programs involving government control and inspection of elevators. A single accident could have adverse effects on a hospitality building—especially a high-rise hotel or office building—for several years. Every management effort must be made to keep this vital transportation system in safe operating condition. Cost should not be a major factor. The safety record of elevators is outstanding, considering the millions of passenger miles (kilometers) traveled each day in these units and the complexity of elevator systems. A failure of any one of the several components could result in an accident.

Two basic elevator systems are used for the mass movement of passengers and freight. They are cable and hydraulic elevators. The more common elevator is the cable unit because it is fast, smooth, and quiet.

Cable Elevator Systems

The cable elevator system includes a shaft, guide rails, counterweights, shaft safety devices, elevator car, cables, and elevator machine.

Shaft. Elevators are positioned in vertical shafts that extend from the lowest level to at least the highest building level being serviced. A large vertical opening between floors, the shaft provides a natural chimney with the building and must be of fireproof construction. The fireproof aspects are designed to prevent fire from spreading within the shaft volume from one floor to the others and to prevent fire from escaping from one level into the shaft area. Fire detectors are required at each level; these will prevent shaft doors from opening at a fire level.

The lower portion of the shaft is the pit, and the upper portion is the control room. If the elevator control room is located on the roof of the building, it is called a penthouse, or roof house.

One factor leading to the high cost of elevator systems is the construction of the shaft. It is a separate building, with its own foundation. Hence, the rest of the building could collapse and the elevator shaft structure could remain upright.

Guide Rails. A vertical track system of guide rails is positioned in the shaft. The elevator car moves by wheels on the guide rails. The movement of the car wheels on the guide rails provides for quiet operation. Undesirable side movements, or vibrations, are normally caused by poor guide rail alignment, worn car wheels, or incorrect adjustments. Guide rails are permanently mounted in the shaft and normally get out of alignment only if the shaft foundation settles or construction cracks develop. Simple adjustments can correct minor problems. Wheel bearings are lubricated and sometimes replaced. A set of guide rails is also provided for counterweights.

Counterweights.   Moving in the opposite direction to the cable elevator car, counterweights are directly attached to the car by the cable; the elevator car is attached to one end of the cable and the counterweights are attached to the opposite end. The major purpose of counterweights is to offset the weight of the car and an estimated passenger load.

Moving the car and its passengers can create an energy requirement. This is reduced by counterweights. Actually, the energy requirement is to move the weight difference between the loaded, or empty, car and the counterweights. At times, energy is required to move a fully loaded car up or down; at other times, when the car is empty, energy is necessary to move the counterweights.

Shaft Safety Devices.   Several safety devices are located in the shaft area. There are two limit switches. A lower-limit switch is positioned at the lowest level being serviced and does not allow the elevator car to move below that level. Similarly, an upper-limit switch is placed at the highest serviced level. The limit switches disconnect the supply of electric energy to a system-driving motor and activate a braking system.

Another safety device is located in the pit. It is called the spring, or bumper. Usually, a combination spring/shock-absorber device is used that will absorb the energy impact of the car if by some remote chance the car ever advances below the lower-limit switch. This is a backup safety system that would greatly reduce damage and bodily injury if the cables and other safety devices were all to fail simultaneously.

A clamping safety system is also used between the car and the guide rails. This is a friction brake activated by a governor that measures the speed of the car. The safety clamps have a life of one use. They have to be replaced after they are activated.

Elevator Car.   Generally, passengers see only one component of the elevator system, the elevator car. The car should reflect the image and atmosphere of the building. Above all, it should be well maintained, because an ill-kept car could suggest a poorly maintained elevator system.

The car should be finished with materials that are easy to clean and maintain. Carpet is frequently used as the finish flooring. It should be replaceable carpet that can be easily removed for cleaning. The carpet will accumulate large amounts of dirt and will reduce the housekeeping costs in the upper portions of the building. A heavy carpet must be used so that its edges will not roll or curl and produce a tripping hazard. Carpet tears, cuts, frays, and loose strings are dangerous. Management should never allow damaged carpets to be used.

The car should be equipped with handrails for the passengers to grasp; handrail requirements vary with local ordinances. The car must be well lighted. Lights should be positioned and located so that passengers cannot remove the lamps. The glass bulbs should also be protected with an outer shell of unbreakable plastic or glass.

Car ventilation must be provided. Each car is normally equipped with an exhaust fan, so that air can be quickly removed. Some cars are equipped with music systems that provide relaxing music. If the building has a public address system for paging customers, clients, or guests, it should be connected to the car speaker, so that neither employees nor passengers miss an announcement because they are riding in the elevator.

Smoking is not permitted in elevators. A sign forbidding passengers to smoke should be posted at the car entrance, along with an ample supply of ashtrays or trash urns.

Cars are also equipped with a portion of the total elevator control network. Controls should be easy to read and use and must also be indicated in Braille. In addition to normal floor-stop controls and key-operated light switches, there must also be an overhead floor-level indicator, a stop switch, an alarm, a manual exhaust-fan switch (although some units have constant positive ventilation whenever the car is in operation), and an emergency telephone that is always connected to a 24-hour switchboard or any other 24-hour duty office within the building. If the car is large, a dual set of controls on each side of the door should be considered.

The car has a set of doors that open each time the car stops in conjunction with the shaft doors at that level. The doors are timed to open and close within a couple of seconds, except at the main or other specified levels, where the timing is longer. The control panel within the car has door "Open" and "Close" positions that override the timing device and can only be operated by someone in the car.

The car doors should also be equipped with, at a minimum, impulse or hydraulic door edges, which, when subject to the slightest pressure, prevent them from closing. Most newer systems have electric eyes, so that as long as the source and receiver path is blocked, the doors remain open. Electric-eye light paths are at a set level, however; they cannot see items caught higher or lower than that level. Hence, door-edge impulse or hydraulic edges should be used along with the electric-eye system.

Cables.   Attached to the structural frame of the car, cables are driven by the elevator machine and are attached to counterweights. Several cables are used, and each is capable of supporting the weight of the car and the counterweights. Several cables provide a margin of safety and also provide for more friction to move and to stop the movement of the car at the elevator machine sheave (defined in the next section) with a minimum of slippage.

Cable life depends on miles (kilometers) traveled, starts, and stops. Adequate lubrication also influences cable life. The single largest repair cost for many cable elevators is cable replacement cost. The first test of cable life is the visible wear of the cable, which is a steel rope consisting of many small wires. As the outer-cable-diameter wires wear and fray with use, this serves as the first sign of cable wear and replacement. A second measure of wear is miles (kilometers) traveled. The mileage (kilometer) performance ratio depends on building height and the number of floors being serviced. Hence, general rules cannot be established for the number of miles traveled versus cable replacement.

Elevator Machine.   Cables ride over the elevator machine sheave, which is a component of the elevator machine. The sheave is a large, multigrooved pulley; a single cable rides in each pulley groove. Two basic types of elevator machines are used with cable elevators: geared-traction and gearless-traction machines.

The geared-traction machine has an electric motor driving a series of gears to which the sheave is attached. Since gears are used with this machine, the resulting speed of the elevator car is dependent on the height of the building being serviced. For example, if the building is less than 15 floors (150 feet [45.75 meters]), the car speed varies between 50 and 200 feet per minute (0.25 to 1 meter per second). If the geared machine is used on taller buildings, its speed can go up to 400 feet per minute (2 meters per second) with a variable-voltage control system. It requires more maintenance than a gearless machine. Gears also wear because of friction, and are generally replaced on a 30- to 40-year life cycle. The driving motor for the geared machine is either an alternating-current polyphase motor or a direct-current motor. The elevator machine's motor control system is either a rheostatic or a variable-voltage control network.

The rheostatic control network provides variable car speed by controlling a series-resistance load with the motor. The ride may not be very smooth, because each time motor-winding resistance is reduced, there could be a slight jerk. A series resistance is also used to brake the speed of the motor and the car. Motors can also be wired in series and parallel circuits, and switching from one to the other provides additional motor and car speeds, in rpm (rps), with the same set of resistors. Rheostatic geared machines have operating efficiencies of less than 50 percent.

A better elevator machine control system is the variable-voltage unit. Older units usually require an MGM set if direct-current electric service is not available. The MGM set includes an alternating-current motor (M), driving a direct-current generator (G), which supplies energy for a direct-current motor (M), which drives the sheave. If the direct-current motor is connected to the sheave through a gear box or transmission, this unit is called a geared elevator machine. A controller regulates voltage on the direct-current motor, which controls car speed. The variable-voltage geared elevator machine frequently exceeds efficiencies of 50 percent.

The gearless machine has a direct-current motor directly connected to the sheave. The gearless machine motor is also used to brake or decelerate the car's movement. Gearless machines have the highest initial cost but lower maintenance and operating costs. The gearless machine has a long life; provides for a very smooth ride; can provide high car speeds, usually in excess of 400 feet per minute (2 meters per second); and can serve any number of floors, frequently above eight levels. At high speed, the gearless machine may attain operating efficiencies in excess of 60 percent. The efficiency can be increased with a solid-state control panel, which replaces the MG portion of the MGM set (it replaces the ac motor and dc generator).

Most cable elevators have an electromagnetic brake attached to the sheave. A direct-current-activated brake is most frequently used, which means that with alternating-current energy-driving systems an ac-to-dc conversion device—rectifier, vacuum tubes, solid-state control, or battery—has to be used to provide dc for brake operation. The electromagnetic brake is the most dependable braking device currently used on elevator machines.

Figure 13.1*a* shows the major components of the cable elevator system. Figure 13.1*b* shows the lower-cost hydraulic elevator. The figure clearly points out the common components of each system. The next section, which covers hydraulic elevators, will discuss only those system components that are different from cable elevators.

Hydraulic Elevator Systems

A review of Figure 13.1 shows that the shaft, car guide rails, shaft safety devices, and elevator car are similar or the same for both cable and hydraulic elevators. The hydraulic elevator does not have counterweights or cables. These are replaced with a plunger, which is part of the elevator machine. This is the basic difference between the two elevator systems.

Elevator Machine.   The hydraulic elevator machine operates an oil pump that is driven by an ac motor. The pump either forces oil into a hydraulic chamber, which lifts the car, or removes oil from the chamber, which lowers the car. Oil pressure causes a large piston, the plunger, to either rise or fall. The plunger is attached to the car floor. Maintenance of the elevator machine is minimal.

Other than this basic difference, passengers seldom know which type of elevator system they are riding in as everything looks the same. Other minor differences are car speed, energy requirements, and floor leveling. It is a low-car-speed (up to 200 feet per minute [1 meter per second]) system that is capable of servicing up to 75 feet (23 meters). Its energy requirements are relatively low and it is very safe.

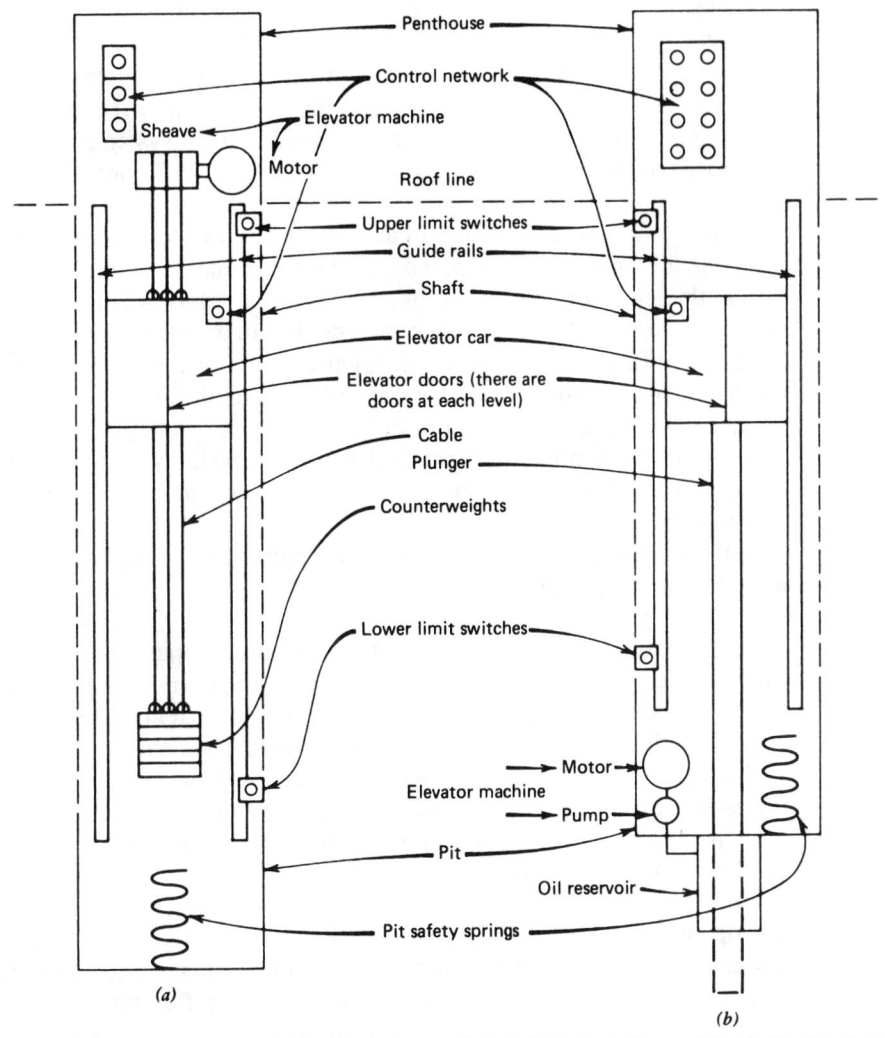

FIGURE 13.1   Cable and hydraulic elevator system components.

This system is used for low-cost passenger elevators in two- or three-floor buildings and for freight elevators.

Elevator Control Systems

The final major component of the elevator is the control system. This is not the elevator machine control but the overall control system, which includes all the push buttons on each of the levels to be serviced, the car's passenger-activated controls, the system that provides for elevator machine operation, and the interconnections among all the various safety and speed control devices.

The control system selected by the manager will be critical for passenger satisfaction and overall system efficiency and will affect system costs, including maintenance. The current common control systems are: collective controls, semicomputerized systems, and computerized controls.

Collective Controls.

Elevator car control became semicomputerized with the collective control system. This system eliminated operating personnel, except that elevator starters might still be on hand during building peak periods. The control unit has a memory device that collects and registers all calls, up and down, as well as passenger destinations, in separate (selective) memory units. Earlier collective control units could not distinguish up and down calls, only a request at a floor.

This system is no longer installed with new systems in the United States and has been replaced with more effective systems. However, it is still extensively used in foreign countries.

If the system has cars operating within defined building zones, it is called a multiple zoning system.

Semicomputerized Control Systems.

A semicomputerized (programmed traffic pattern control) system is used to operate a series of elevator cars. It can be partially programmed to handle heavy upward and downward traffic at peak periods throughout the day. It can also zone cars to various levels, with one or more cars serving selected levels, thus reducing customer waiting time. During off-peak periods, the program can shut down some cars, with the remaining cars reverting to the routine control system. The program can be manually overridden.

Computerized Control Systems.

Microprocessor-based elevator control systems were introduced in the 1970s. Before then, automated elevators were controlled by relays. These systems had little flexibility: In a two-terminal system, for example, the elevator car often had to go up before it could go down. In a 36-story building with three banks of elevators—one for floors 1–12, a second for 12–24, and a third for 24–36—if someone was waiting on the 25th floor to go down, and the car on 26 was assigned to the call, that car would have to go all the way to the top of the building before it could pick that person up. While the early microprocessor systems did not overcome this problem, current systems have. For one thing, they do not have to send a car up simply to get a passenger who is one or more floors down.

Fully computerized control systems attempt to minimize customer waiting time at any level. This system is the most costly to install and provides optimal customer service. Over an extended time period, maximum system efficiency and optimal customer service are obtained. Management can quickly program (with lobby control panels) the controlling computer to zone cars at any time and have cars return to high, medium, or low levels, or any combination, in the building. The manager can determine which cars operate when and how many are available at any time. Or the manager can revert to a semicomputerized operation at will. The major difference between this system and the semicomputerized one is that with this system the manager does the programming rather than using standard or limited programs. These systems are generally used in modern high-rise hotels and office buildings.

Switching from relays to microprocessors involves two choices—either overlay microprocessor circuits on top of the existing relay system or remove all the relays and start over. An overlay is less expensive and will cause less disruption in service, but may not deliver the high performance levels of a completely electronic system.

The decision should depend in part on the state of the overall elevator system. If the equipment is outdated or is no longer well suited to the demands placed on the building, the entire system should be considered for replacement. However, an overlay modernization can often be done in stages—dispatch first, followed by motion control. Keep in mind that some overlays are one shot, which means they cost less but offer less flexibility for the future.

With microprocessors, motion control performance also improves. The car will accelerate more quickly but also more smoothly; it will decelerate more smoothly; and it will do a better job of landing level with the floor.

The payoffs of microprocessor-based elevator control appear to be: (1) Speed, cutting corridor waiting times by 20 to 50 percent. (2) Flexibility, with easy upgrade once installed, since changes often involve only software, not hardware. (3) Easier maintenance, since electronic circuits have no moving parts to wear out; troubleshooting is simplified because the mechanic can find the source of the problem by plugging a diagnostic tool into the elevator's computer. (4) Better forecasting, since the system can be hooked up to the engineer's office, making it possible to get a good look at elevator traffic patterns.

In the future, microprocessor-based controls should be able to forecast when and in what system a problem is about to occur, and to call for help before anything goes wrong. Such systems are already beyond the conceptual stage.

Figure 13.2 is a summary of the major aspects of elevator control systems.

ESCALATORS

Vertical transportation is also provided by escalators, which are moving stairs. They are very effective for moving large numbers of people in short

Collective control	Car operators eliminated. Memory device collects and separates up and down passenger calls. Minimum recommendation for high-rise buildings. Starter use optional during peak travel periods.
Semicomputerized control	Control series of cars. Programmed for zoning cars. Eliminates operators and starters. Memory box similar to collective control
Computerized (programmed control)	Similar to semicomputerized control. Management can activate any control program it wishes.

FIGURE 13.2 Elevator control systems.

periods of time. Two units are usually required at each level, one moving upward and one downward. The escalator can be utilized even when not moving, since people can still walk up and down the large steps and grasp the handrails; thus, when inoperative they serve as open stairways. However, it must be noted that escalators cannot generally be used to replace stairs and stairwells required by building fire codes. The step "rise" (vertical distance between steps) for an escalator is much greater than on stairs. Also, building fire code stairwells must have fire-rated walls, floor, ceiling, and doors.

Escalators are usually designed to climb or descend at a 30-degree angle. In case of fire, the units can all operate one way to get people out of the building as quickly as possible, or they can be turned off if the fire is on a floor or floors serviced by the escalators. Many convention areas are serviced by escalators and are operated one way when meeting rooms are being filled or emptied, which doubles the capacity of the system. Once again, good building design will have escalators discharge passengers close to outside doors, beverage and dining rooms, meeting and exhibit rooms, and shops, or in a casino (entertainment) area.

Escalators do not eliminate the need for elevator service; they only reduce the required number of elevator cars and generally improve the quality of elevator service. Carriages, wheelchairs, and freight movement are all prohibited on escalators. An unfortunate aspect of an escalator is that it provides a natural chimney within a building and could be a fire hazard. This is why in many buildings escalators are staggered every three or four levels (see Figure 13.3); this design reduces the chimney effect.

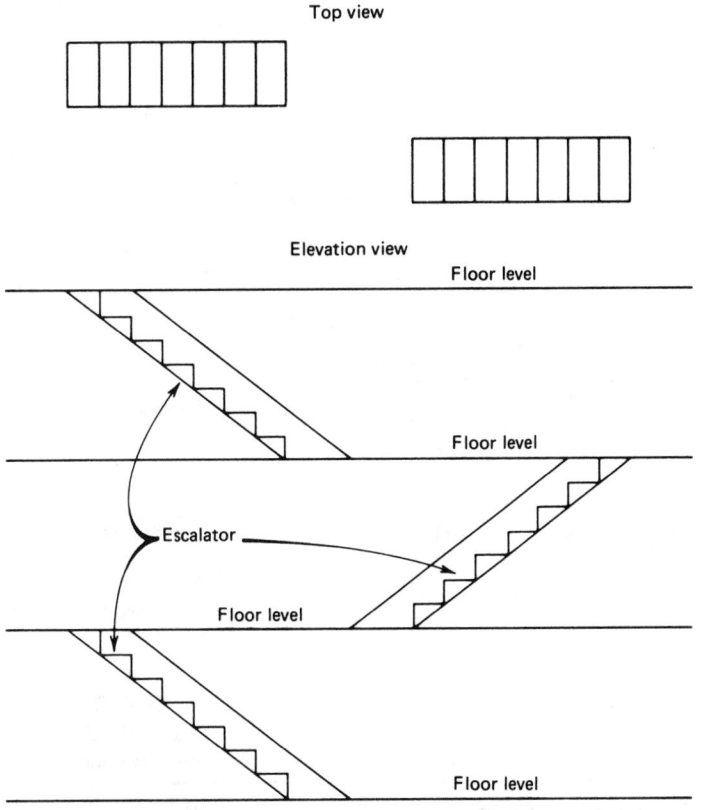

FIGURE 13.3 Staggering escalators to eliminate building chimney effects for fire protection.

The components of an escalator are in some ways similar to the elevator and in many cases much simpler, especially the driving machine and the control system (see Figure 13.4). The visible, movable portions are the steps and the handrail, which move at the same rate of speed. The steps rise and descend into and from comb plates, which look like large hair combs. The assembly around the steps and handrail is called the balustrade, which is concave so that clothing will not catch on its interior sidewalls. The balustrade is attached to the truss, which is the support system of the escalator. The steps ride on tracks, or guide rails. The steps and handrail are driven by the escalator machine, which is a geared-type apparatus. Alternating-current motors are used. The controller is a simple on–off–reverse switch. A governor shuts the system down in case of excessive speed. An emergency-

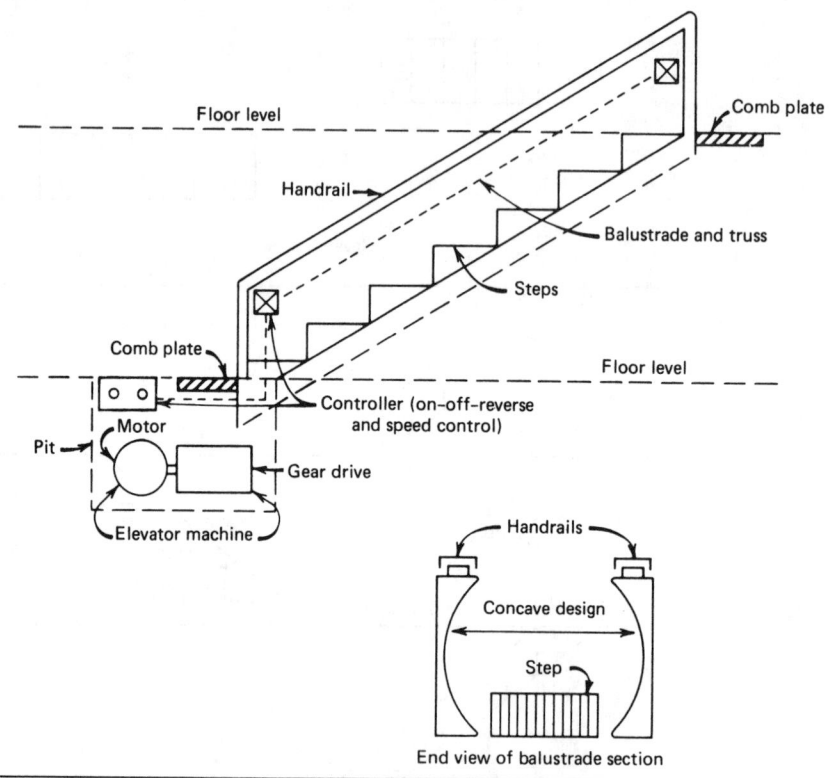

FIGURE 13.4 Basic components of an escalator system.

stop switch is located at both ends of the unit. The unit can normally be operated at one of two speeds, normal (90 feet per minute [0.45 meter per second]) and high (120 feet per minute [0.6 meter per second]). Passengers must be warned when the escalator is operated at high speed.

Escalators are generally available in one of two widths. The 32-inch (0.8-meter)-wide escalator can handle 4000 passengers per hour at 90 feet per minute (0.45 meter per second) and 5000 passengers per hour at 120 feet per minute (0.6 meter per second). The 48-inch (1.25-meter)-wide escalator can handle 6000 passengers per hour at the slower speed and 8000 passengers per hour at the higher speed.

There are various fire protection devices and techniques used with escalators. The purpose of these systems is to prevent fire from spreading from one level to the next and to protect escalator passengers. These systems (rolling shutter, smoke guard, spray-nozzle curtain, and sprinkler vent) were discussed in Chapter 6.

STAIRWELLS

The stairwell is another form of vertical transportation. All buildings must have stairwells enclosed in fireproof sections, so that people can safely exit upper building levels. The width and depth of the steps are specified by local building and fire codes. Stairwells must be well lighted—interior stairwells must have emergency lighting if adequate natural lighting is not available—and have handrails and nonslip steps. Normal construction is concrete and steel. Products, especially combustible items, cannot be stored or located in stairwells. Stairwells must generally exit close to a building exit door; if not, a fire-safe egress route must be constructed from the stairwell exit to the outside. (Once again, refer to Chapter 6 for additional fire safety aspects of stairwells.)

GRAVITY FLOW DEVICES

Gravity Chutes and Drops

Gravity can be used as a form of vertical transportation to move—actually to drop—materials. The fundamental purpose of chutes is simple: They save worker motions and increase employee productivity. Some multilevel health-care and lodging facilities frequently use gravity chutes for soiled linens and waste product movement.

Gravity chutes should be used for the free flow of incoming materials to work areas whenever possible and feasible. Serious consideration should be given to locating storage areas above the work area, so that products can be dropped on the exact point of use. The savings in time and energy can be significant.

Gravity should be used, wherever possible, for outgoing materials, such as garbage. Many establishments have installed garbage and waste collection rooms at lower levels and utilize drop systems from work areas. All collection points and horizontal movements are eliminated, or at least minimized, with this design.

Dumbwaiters

Although the dumbwaiter is a mechanical lifting and lowering device, it is not designed nor is it safe for passenger movement. Electric motors supply energy for lifting. Lowering is a slow, controlled form of gravity drop.

The dumbwaiter is a very simple cable-type elevator system. The car moves in a small shaft. It is usually used between two and four levels. Electric motors are geared or designed to rotate slowly, so that the car moves very slowly. Dumbwaiters can move finished products upward and then carry wastes on the downward return trip. Communication from one level to the next can be handled by means of a signal or voice transmitters.

Self-Leveling Storage Devices

Self-leveling equipment should also be used as much as possible, so that workers do not have to bend over and lift products. This equipment requires minimal maintenance and no energy. It is most frequently used for dish storage devices in foodservice operations.

FREIGHT ELEVATORS

Most freight elevators are cable-type, rheostatic, geared elevator machines with the lowest-cost control system, usually using a push-button operator or a collective control system. Hydraulic elevators may also be used. These units operate at low speeds, which is unfortunate, as they create considerable employee waiting and riding times.

The capacity of freight elevators is given in weight-pounds (kilograms). The relationship between total weight capacity and car platform surface area indicates the freight-class rating of the elevator. Door openings and controls are very basic compared to modern passenger elevators. In the United States, the employee safety aspects of the system are normally inspected by Occupational Safety and Health Administration (OSHA) investigators.

The basic types of freight elevators are the sidewalk elevator, which will service the main outside level and one or more basement levels, also used for platform lifts for stage shows; a light-duty elevator, which is a low-cost and low-capacity unit; a general-purpose freight elevator, which has a higher capacity than the light-duty freight elevator; and dumbwaiters, which are designed to move only products and normally have much lower weight capacities than light-duty freight elevators (previously discussed).

Sidewalk elevators and some light-duty freight elevators utilize a traction elevator machine located in the pit area of the shaft, which drives a cable directly connected to the sheave; hence, it winds or unwinds the cable on the sheave. Counterweights are not used with the traction elevator machine, and, since it services only two or three levels, its speed and cost are low.

VERTICAL-TRANSPORTATION DESIGN FACTORS

A complete vertical-transportation system for a building is usually designed by an elevator-manufacturing company representative, or elevator contractor. The design frequently yields several alternatives from which the manager can make a final decision. The manager must provide four basic factors to the designer relating to the desired quality of elevator service. These basic factors are handling capacity, travel time, interval time, and car location.

Handling Capacity

The handling capacity depends on the design interval time and car capacity. Elevator designs are based on a wealth of data accumulated over past years on building population densities at each level, passenger movement frequency, and peak travel periods. Alternate design plans are developed so that interval time specifications, car capacities, and number of cars can be interchanged. The design will even suggest the use of express and zoned elevators for high-rise buildings.

Travel Time

The most complex variable to analyze is travel time. This depends on several factors, each of which must be estimated or assumed and then related to other system variables. These factors are based on experience and previously developed data for similar buildings. A partial list of these factors includes: passenger loading time at the main level, car acceleration time, car decelerating time, passenger transfer (entering or exiting a car) at various levels, car running time, door opening and closing time, and express time from the last stop. Each factor interrelationship must be accurately evaluated because a miscalculation could result in one too few or one too many cars.

Interval Time

The interval time is one variable that greatly affects the quality of elevator service. The interval time is the average time difference between a passenger call for a car and the time the car arrives to pick up the passenger. Low interval times result in higher-quality service. Normal interval times usually vary from 25 to 120 seconds. Office buildings may have interval times as low as 25 seconds; first-class hotels have 40- to 60-second interval times for quality service, and other hotels have 50- to 70-second interval times; dormitories and apartments may have 70- to 120-second interval times.

Car Location

Once the number and capacity of the cars have been determined, building space requirements are known and a layout can be conceived. Several layout schemes may be suggested by the designer.

Elevators are frequently located as close to the front building doors as possible, as is normally the case in institutional buildings, office buildings, schools, and dormitories with limited occupant control. However, health-care facilities and lodging establishments must consider occupant control; hence, elevator service areas are not always located near entrance or exit areas. Lodging elevators are generally located near registration or reception areas. Many properties also locate specialty shops, including foodservice and beverage outlets, close to the elevators. The final decision for elevator location is made by the manager and architect and should be based on basic business objectives and the building theme being created.

HORIZONTAL-TRANSPORTATION TECHNIQUES

Horizontal passenger movement systems are normally restricted to moving walkways and halls or corridors.

MOVING WALKWAYS (PEOPLE MOVERS)

Moving walkways are very similar to escalators except that a continuous belt replaces the step arrangement. Moving walkways are also used on long vertical inclines. The normal maximum vertical rate of climb is 15 degrees. Wheelchairs or carts can be transported on moving sidewalks, which are capable of moving large numbers of passengers along long, narrow areas. To date, the most extensive use of these people movers has been in large airports. (Several hotels in Las Vegas have people movers, which take people into a hotel's casino area—you must walk back to the street when you leave the hotel.) Figure 13.5 shows a typical moving walkway, or people mover.

Walkway widths are the same or slightly less than escalator widths. A triple-width unit is not made (over 48 inches [1.25 meters]) because the middle person cannot hold on to the handrail. Moving walkways can move

FIGURE 13.5 Moving walkway, or people mover.

at higher speeds, up to 180 feet per minute (almost 1 meter per second) with a horizontal entrance and exit. Passengers must be notified when they enter on and egress from these high-speed moving walkways. The walkway speed decreases as the incline angle increases to the maximum speed of an escalator.

HALLWAYS AND CORRIDORS

Hallways and corridors are universally used as horizontal-transportation techniques. The width of the hall depends on the equipment and the number of people that are to move through it. If furnishings are placed in the hall, its width must be increased. Local building and fire regulations influence design and provide minimum widths and clearances between furnishings.

Doors should not open into the hall area, for several reasons. First, the opening of a solid door into a hall could prove dangerous to someone walking in the hall near the door. Second, in case of fire, people in a room may not be able to leave if they try to push a door against a mass of people moving in the hall. Frequently, an architect will make a very long hall wider in an attempt to reduce its apparent length. If heavy carts are to be moved in the hall, bumper guards should be placed on the lower portions of the walls to minimize cart damage. If the hall has an incline, or a few steps, handrails must be provided. In an effort to reduce housekeeping and floor-cleaning tasks, many designers use "line" effects, as shown in Figure 13.6. People tend to stay within lined areas.

Product Movement

In the hospitality industry, serious problems can arise when employees move products manually. Material-handling equipment should be used

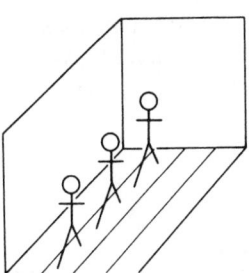

Lines encourage single-line flow.

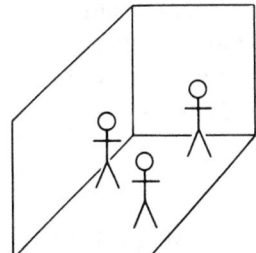

Wandering is encouraged with wall-to-wall floor coverings.

FIGURE 13.6 Line effects in a hall.

whenever possible, especially to move products to storage or from storage to a processing area; to handle the product during processing; to transport the finished product to the customer; to remove wastes to temporary storage; and, finally, to move wastes from temporary storage to a final collection-and-storage area within the property.

If the product must be moved, gravity or drop placement should be considered first. If this is not possible, the product should be moved in bulk; that is, one should move as much as possible at one time or all that is required for a given task for a work shift.

For short distances, two-wheel handcarts should be used with a platform size adequate to handle the largest or bulkiest container that has to be moved. For easy movement, the cart wheels should be large in diameter and width. If two-wheel handcarts are not large enough for the required single movement of goods and products, four-wheel carts or trucks must be used. One set of cart wheels should be capable of rotating 360 degrees so that the cart or truck can be completely controlled and be capable of very short turns. Four-wheel trucks should have a handle so that the truck can be pulled or pushed into position for heavy loads. The width and length of four-wheel carts should be controlled to fit on moving walkways and to fit on freight elevator cars (platforms).

Some four-wheel hand trucks can be used to retrieve items stored on pallets, in which case the truck is positioned under the pallet and the pallet is raised by a hydraulic platform onto the truck and then moved.

Mechanized trucks should be utilized for heavier loads or for long distances. These allow the driver to operate the device completely. If used within buildings where pollution and noise may be problems, electrically powered units should be used. Small internal-combustion engines (propane or natural-gas fueled) can be used outside or in well-ventilated areas where customer, patient, client, or guest travel is nonexistent, carefully controlled, or restricted.

Each of the systems described requires an employee to move with the products. A mechanized conveyor system can be used that does not require the employee to move with the product. The speed, capacity, vertical climb, and type of product being moved must all be carefully considered when selecting such a system.

ENERGY-MANAGEMENT CONSIDERATIONS

Emergency energy systems, as discussed in Chapter 11, must be provided for selected elevators. There must be at least one serviceable elevator that can reach all floors; in the case of a large number of levels with zone elevators, more than one elevator may have to be used so that all levels are serviced. Emergency power is usually nót provided for escalators or moving walkways because these systems can still be used when not in operation.

Elevators, escalators, and moving walkways usually do not consume a large number of kilowatt-hours and are not generally connected to a computer-controlled energy-management system. Both semicomputerized and computerized control systems, however, can be programmed to cycle elevators during high-energy-demand periods, so that selected units can be shut off manually to conserve energy (reduce electric demand). While kilowatt-hour consumption is not very high for these units, the instantaneous energy demand when several units are starting at the same time can be large and can have effects on demand surcharges. Energy demand must be considered with computerized demand control systems. It is also possible to limit the number of cars starting at any one time. If this is done, the quality of elevator service may be slightly reduced during these high-demand periods.

There is one final management factor that you must consider. It is transportation system fire protection. Refer to Chapter 6 for a complete discussion and review of these techniques.

SUMMARY

Vertical building transportation systems are required in all multiple-level buildings. At a minimum, stairs and fire-resistant stairwell structures and ramps are required. Usually, separate vertical-transportation systems are required for customer—client and employee—and product movement. These are costly systems to install, frequently up to 12 percent of the total building construction cost. System maintenance is included under building mechanical and electrical system costs (American Hotel & Motel Association Uniform System of Accounts for Hotels and Motels) and is difficult to separate from other electromechanical systems.

While the design of the vertical-transportation system is completed by the elevator manufacturer and is based on simulated and similar building actual data, the manager must decide on class of elevator service, decor, enhanced safety features, energy control system, and, with the architect, location within the building. The manager's decisions have a strong effect on the final elevator system and its projected performance.

Energy management is difficult to control for vertical- and horizontal-transportation systems in buildings. Transportation systems are usually fairly efficient compared to other building systems, such as lighting, air conditioning, refrigeration, ventilation, and plumbing. Efficiency and operating costs may be improved, depending on which type of elevator machine is used. System efficiency is also frequently dependent on the manager's building maintenance policy. Scheduled periodic lubrication reduces friction and energy requirements. Energy and demand charges can be saved by reducing the number of operating cars during specified time periods. Good building layout can reduce the number of transportation system units and save energy.

The manager must be fully aware of the total building transportation system, and it must be fully operative when needed. Customers and employees are highly dependent on the system, especially in multilevel buildings.

BIBLIOGRAPHY

1. McGuinness, W. J., B. Stein, and J S. Reynolds, *Mechanical and Electrical Equipment for Buildings,* Wiley, New York, 1980.
2. Bradshaw, V., *Building Control Systems,* Wiley, New York, 1985.

QUESTIONS/PROBLEMS

1. Why is analysis of horizontal and vertical transportation important in the hospitality industry? How can the business unit take advantage of the transportation systems on its premises?

2. What previously discussed energy concepts apply to vertical-transportation systems in buildings?

3. On the basis of the materials presented in this chapter, attempt to indicate elevator items and devices that should be checked, adjusted, and lubricated in a complete maintenance program.

4. Discuss the various elevator control systems, and determine when one system should be used in preference to another in various types of hospitality industry buildings.

5. Discuss and evaluate how a high-quality elevator service system differs from a lower-quality system for a building.

6. Analyze the need for escalator systems in various types of hospitality buildings?

7. If your elevator technician told you that he had been adjusting and aligning the guide rails on the system to keep the cars moving vibration free, is this a reasonable explanation for how he had been utilizing his time?

CHAPTER 14

Courtesy of Holiday Inns, Inc.

MANAGEMENT OF SOUND

ABSTRACT

Management has a sound responsibility in the hospitality industry. Its control and management can have positive and negative effects on employees, customers, clients, and guests. Building electromechanical systems are potential generators of sound and noise. There are numerous external sound sources that could terminate as building sound problems that must be resolved by management. Finally, employees and customers are potential sound sources that must be recognized and accounted for by management.

A building must be sound designed. If sound control is not designed into your building, you may be faced with a lifetime of sound problems. Sound can sometimes be controlled with minimum time, effort, and costs. At other times, sound can be controlled only with considerable effort and costs. And sometimes you cannot control noise effectively even if you spend large sums of money.

The management key to the sound problem solution is an understanding of sound characteristics. While undesirable sound is noise and could be potentially harmful to employees and customers, through prolonged exposure to intense sound, the proper control technique may minimize and eliminate this noise. Quality sound is also important to management. The correct message must be heard by all affected people, both employees and customers. This includes emergency announcements, speakers, entertainment sounds, and background music for increasing employee productivity and for guest enjoyment and relaxation.

Key words: annoyance; concave; convex; decibel (dB); hertz; masking; noise; noise criteria (NC); noise rating (NR); preferred noise criteria (PNC); reverberation time; sound; sound absorber; sound isolators; sound quality; threshold of hearing; worker sound effects.

441

INTRODUCTION

Hospitality buildings are generators of large amounts of sound and noise. Each operating electromechanical system produces sound. People working and talking increase the sound level of the building. Public address systems, radios, and television audio systems further increase the building's sound intensity. In addition, external sound sources, such as motor vehicles, airplanes, ocean surf, and wind, can penetrate the building and cause sound problems. We live in a world of sound.

Sound is a form of energy produced by a vibration. The energy must be transmitted through a gas, a liquid, or a solid to a receiver before it can be heard. Hence, there must be a vibration, a path, and a receiver to produce sound. If you eliminate the vibration, the path, or the receiver, you eliminate sound. Sound is managed by controlling the vibration source or regulating the energy path so that the energy level is acceptable to the receiver.

For you, as a manager in the hospitality industry, hardly a day will pass in which you will not have to deal with the effects of sound—or noise. (If you like what you hear, it is sound; if you do not like what you hear, it is noise.) You will have to manage sound—exterior sound transmission to the inside of the building and the sounds produced within your building. The more you know about sound, its terminology and its characteristics, the easier this difficult task will be. You live in a noisy world, but it is your job as manager to provide the best aural environment you can for your customers and employees.

When a guest is trying to sleep on an otherwise quiet night, he or she will not want to hear the dripping of water from a faucet, which was lost among the noise of the day, or the television audio and the talk of the evening hours.

Intense sound for extended time periods can be dangerous for employees. Intense sound even for short time periods may cause numerous employee errors and accidents. The manager must also be aware that one person's perception of quality sound could be different from another person's definition of quality sound. Each employee may react differently to various sounds. The manager should anticipate many of these employee reactions and learn to manage his or her employees. The materials presented in this chapter should provide the necessary knowledge to cope effectively with sound and related sound problems.

TYPICAL SOUND PROBLEMS

Generally a sound problem is a noise problem. Noise is unwanted or undesirable sound. There are two potential sound problems: the control of sound sources within a room and the transmission of external sound to a room.

ROOM SOUND PROBLEMS

Sound energy can be transmitted, reflected, or absorbed. Sound is produced by a vibration and transmitted by materials—gas, water, or solids. The transmission speed of sound depends on the transmitting media. Figure 14.1 shows the speed of sound through some materials and the time required to transmit sound 1000 feet (305 meters). Most of the sound generated within a room is transmitted through air to people.

Many room sound problems are caused by reflected sound and the lack of adequate sound absorbers. Other room sound problems are caused by the physical shape of room surfaces. Figure 14.2 shows the contrasting sound effects for concave and convex surfaces.

A concave surface will generally reflect sound energy to a specific area, thus reinforcing sound in that area, while convex surfaces are generally used to diffuse sound energy. Figure 14.3 shows how to take advantage of concave and convex surface effects in a larger room.

Sound is frequently controlled within a room by adding sound absorbers. When sound energy is absorbed, it is destroyed. The absorption of sound can become a complex problem because there are many different types of sound vibrations (see the sound frequency section in this chapter), and sound absorbers are designed to destroy specific types of sound vibrations (see the room sound treatment section in this chapter).

TRANSMISSION PROBLEMS

Sound that is generated externally, such as vibrating machinery in an adjacent room or highway noise, may cause sound problems within a room. This sound is generally heard as background noise and can be very irritating to the occupants of a room. These external sounds enter the room by transmission through structural components or, in some cases, through open doors and windows. Each room occupant may have a different tolerance for these transmitted sounds. Some occupants may be able to hear low-frequency or vibration sounds, others high-frequency sounds. You may be able to hear sounds that others cannot hear and may be deaf to other sounds. Hence, the

```
Speed of sound through:
   Air: about 1100 feet per minute (5.59 meters per second)
   Water: about 4700 feet per minute (23.88 meters per second)
   Steel: about 16,000 feet per minute (81.28 meters per second)
Time required for sound to travel 1000 feet (305 meters):
   Air: 54.55 seconds
   Water: 12.77 seconds
   Steel: 3.75 seconds
```

FIGURE 14.1   Speed of sound through various substances.

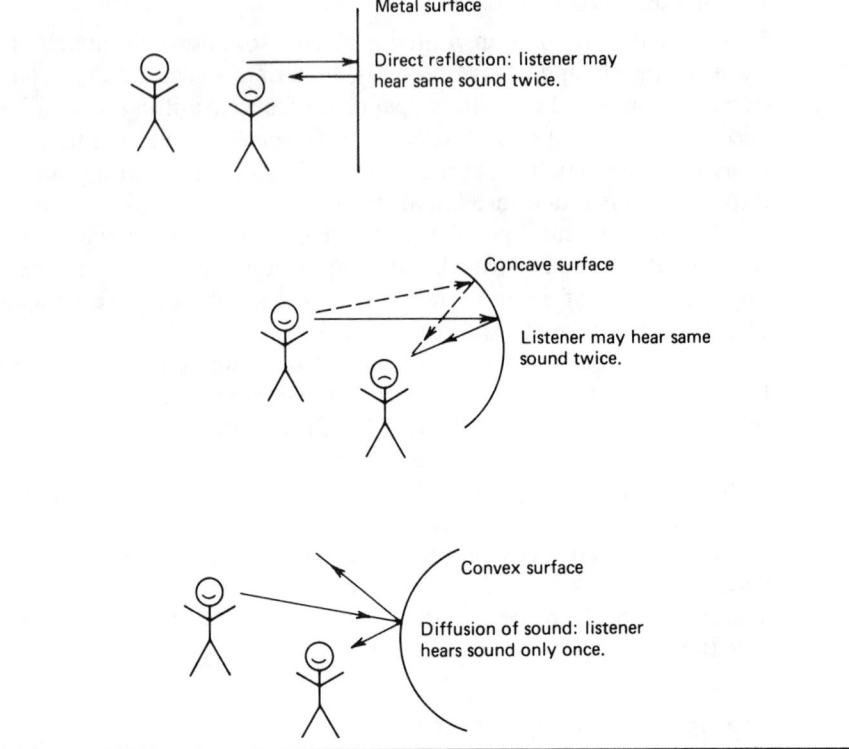

FIGURE 14.2 Reflected sound.

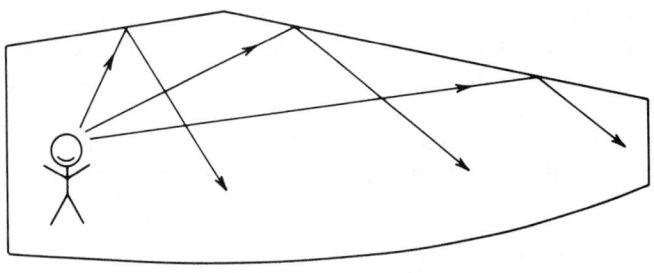

Using the ceiling to reflect sound
throughout the room.

FIGURE 14.3 Reflected sound in a larger room.

transmission of external sound to a room can be a complex and serious problem.

TERMINOLOGY

Sound and noise can be measured. There are two basic measuring techniques. One measures vibration intensity level, and the other measures vibrations per second, or frequency. The combination of both defines sound quality.

SOUND INTENSITY

Sound is energy. However, sound energy levels are extremely small in comparison to a watt or a Btu. For example, a person's threshold of hearing varies from 10^{-16} (0.0000000000000001) to 10^{-3} (0.001) watts per square centimeter. The latter is a painful sound for most people. If you shout at full voice intensity, the sound energy 5 feet (1.53 meters) from your face is 10^{-7} (0.0000001) watts per square centimeter.

A new measurement scale is introduced here, and you are exposed to centimeters for the first time. One inch equals 2.54 centimeters, and there are 10 millimeters in 1 centimeter. The centimeter is not an SIU measurement term.

One common sound intensity measurement scale is the decibel (dB) scale. The normal threshold of hearing is 0 dB. A jet aircraft engine produces 130 dB at a safe distance. The jet engine produces a sound energy intensity level 10 million-million times the threshold of hearing. The human ear is most remarkable since it can hear sounds between these energy levels (0 to 130 dB). The rustle of leaves is 10 dB, which is 10 times the threshold of the hearing energy level. Each 10-dB increase represents a 10-fold energy-level increase, so 20 dB is 100 energy units greater than 0 dB, and 30 dB is 1000 times the energy at 0 dB. Shouting at 5 feet (1.53 meters) is 90 dB, or 1,000 million times the energy level of 0 dB.

It is also possible to have negative decibel levels. Some people can hear in the negative range, especially young people. It should be noted that -10 dB has one-tenth the energy of 0 dB. Figure 14.4 shows examples of sound sources and relative sound energy output from these sources.

Sound intensity is reduced as it passes from its source across a room. This is because sound energy spreads out over a larger surface area as it moves from you into space, much as light does. Refer to Figure 14.5. If you are speaking at point A, the sound intensity at point B (listener 1) is 50 dB, and the intensity at point C (listener 2) is 44 dB. Listener 2 is twice as far away from you as listener 1. In other words, when the sound path distance is doubled the energy level is reduced by 6 dB.

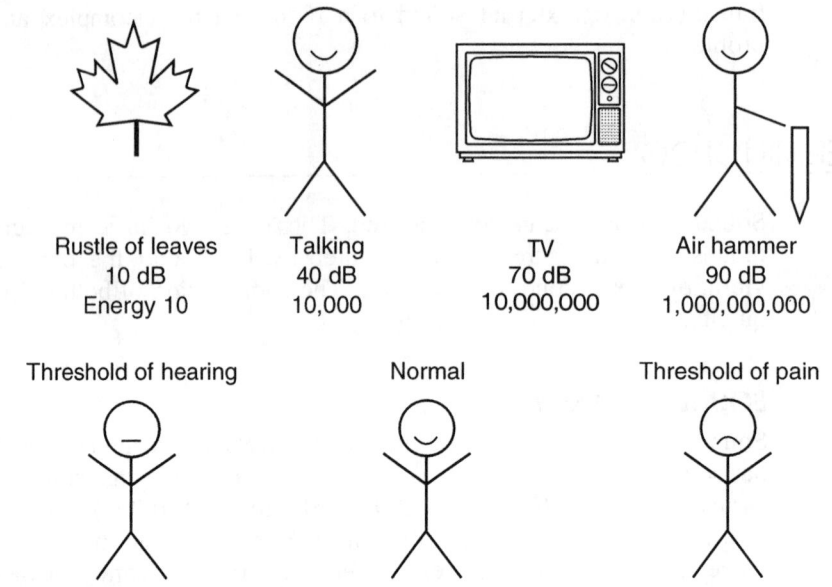

Rustle of leaves	Talking	TV	Air hammer
10 dB	40 dB	70 dB	90 dB
Energy 10	10,000	10,000,000	1,000,000,000

Threshold of hearing   Normal   Threshold of pain

FIGURE 14.4 Sound intensity from the threshold of hearing to the threshold of pain.

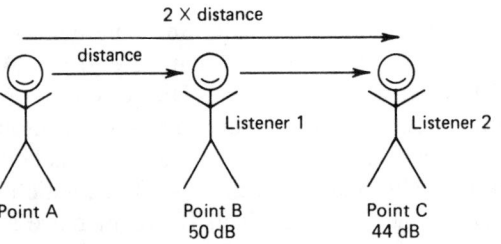

2 X distance

distance

Listener 1   Listener 2

Point A   Point B   Point C
50 dB   44 dB

FIGURE 14.5 Sound intensity decreases as sound energy passes across a room.

One additional sound intensity factor is important. This has to do with the additive effects of decibels. If a television set is tuned to 70 dB and a radio is adjusted to 70 dB and both are in operation in the same room at the same time, what is the cumulative effect? Do the decibels add up to 140? No. The net effect of both sound generators is 73 dB within the room. And if the television set is tuned to 70 dB and the radio to 60 dB, the resulting decibel level in the room is 70.5; the radio appears as background noise for the television set. The point is that decibel levels accumulate according to energy emission. Remember that a change from 60 to 70 dB increases sound energy by a factor of 10. The change, in the previous example, of 3 dB represents a doubling of sound energy. See Figure 14.6. Hence, turning on a radio next to the blast of a jet aircraft engine has an almost insignificant effect on the net energy emission of both units, as evidenced by the fact that the radio can be heard only by pressing it very close to the ear and thus eliminating the sound of the jet aircraft engine (background noise) from that ear. Buildings located next to airports are subject to the same phenomenon: As the aircraft fly low over the building, the noise generation exceeds more sounds and noise within the building, and one hears only the aircraft engines.

SOUND FREQUENCY

The number of sound vibrations per second is measured in hertz units. Low-frequency vibrations are harsh, deep sounds. Squeaky voices produce high hertz units. Humans can normally hear in the 20- to 20,000-hertz range. The hertz range of hearing, especially at the higher end of the scale, usually decreases with age. Some materials will absorb sound within specified hertz ranges. A combination of absorbers are used in some rooms to absorb and

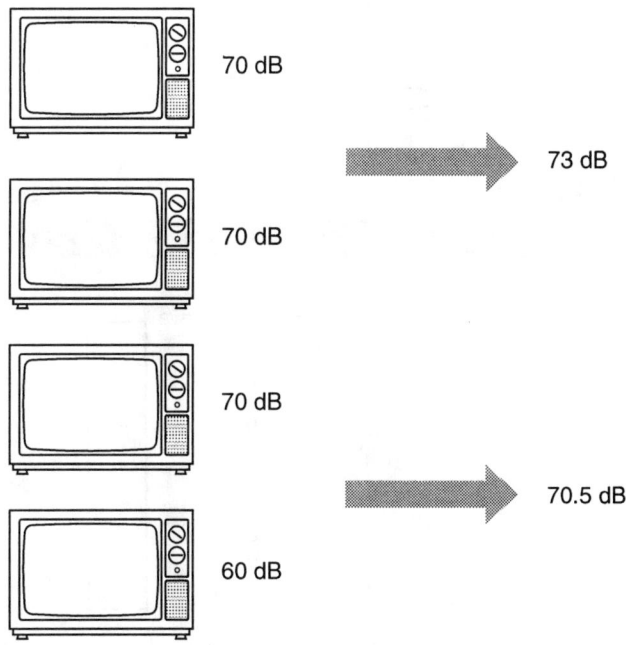

FIGURE 14.6 Additive effects of sound, a 3-dB increase doubles sound energy.

reduce sound frequency ranges. If a certain material absorbs sound in the 100- to 4000-hertz range, all sounds below 100 and over 4000 hertz units will be reflected back within the space or transmitted to other areas of the building. Knowledge of sound sources is required in order to control sound fully.

Materials have different coefficients of sound absorption. The coefficient varies with the frequency of the sound. For example, if the thickness of gypsum board is half an inch (12.7 millimeters), its sound absorption coefficient varies from 0.29 at 125 hertz down to 0.04 at 1000 hertz and then appears to improve as frequency increases. Heavy carpet on a foam pad has a low coefficient at 125 hertz (0.08) and increases as frequency increases, reaching 0.73 at 4000 hertz. Sound control can be partially effected by using the specified amount and types of absorbers in rooms. See Figure 14.7 for these effects.

The previous section stated that the threshold of hearing was 0 dB. Actually, it is 0 dB at 1000 hertz. For most people, the threshold of hearing varies with hertz units. At 50 hertz units, the threshold of hearing may be 50 dB. A pounding surf produces about 70 dB in the 20- to 90-hertz range.

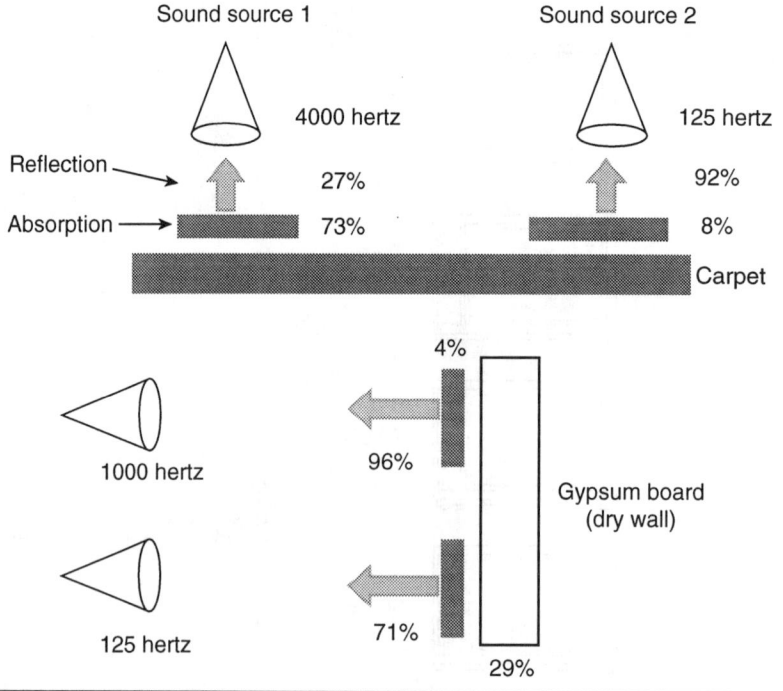

FIGURE 14.7 Sound absorption depends on material types and sound frequency (hertz).

Most people can hear −5 dB at 4000 hertz. Electric toothbrushes, vacuum cleaners, and singing birds produce 4000-hertz sounds. People have a hard time hearing in the 10,000- to 20,000-hertz range; higher intensities (dB) are required for one to hear in this range, as with lower hertz ranges. See Figure 14.8 for these effects.

SOUND QUALITY

The magnitude and frequency of sound determines its quality. High frequency combined with a large magnitude can be very uncomfortable to the human ear. High-decibel sounds at hertz units in excess of 20,000 cannot be heard by humans but can be heard by animals, as the silent whistle is heard by dogs. In some cases, a person can be deaf to certain hertz units at low decibels, but the same frequency is audible at higher decibel levels.

The ages of customers and employees are critical in determining if vibrations are sound or noise. Some sounds are potentially harmful to people. For example, you can withstand a sound at 100 dB for 20 minutes (0.33 hour) or less with no harmful effects. If people are exposed to this level for extended time periods, regardless of hertz units, permanent hearing damage can develop. Even a low 60-dB level can be harmful if the exposure is longer than eight hours. Earlier, we stated that a pounding surf produces about 70

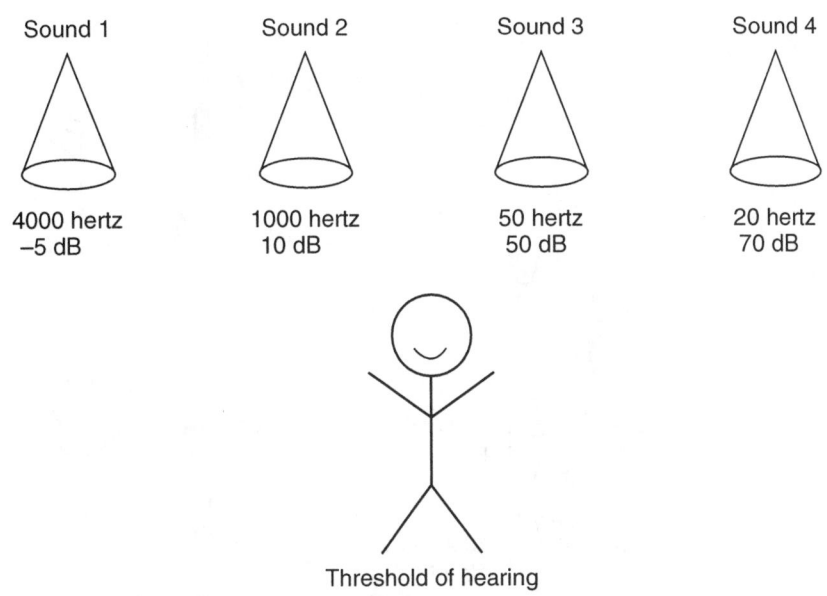

FIGURE 14.8 Threshold of hearing depends on both intensity (dB) and frequency (hertz).

dB. Hence, people exposed to this constant noise level can develop hearing impairment; their hearing can get so bad that they no longer hear the pounding surf after long exposures to it. Sound quality has no meaning to them in this range; everything is a hum.

Masking, another sound quality term, involves two sounds of the same intensity but different hertz units. Which sound will be heard? One hertz level will have to be increased in order to be heard or distinguished from the other. It becomes more difficult to distinguish hertz units if they are close together. Generally, high-hertz sounds will be heard over low-hertz sounds of similar intensities. Therefore, masking can be used to block out noise (unwanted sound of a similar decibel level). See Figure 14.9 for these effects.

Sound quality depends on how close together in time different sounds are heard. It takes time for you to distinguish between sounds. If two sounds are less than 10 milliseconds (0.001 second) apart, they cannot be distinguished. Most people have a hard time distinguishing sounds that are up to 50 milliseconds (0.050 second) apart and, at best, such sounds are poorly distinguished. This means that in order to distinguish one sound from another, the sounds must be received more than 50 milliseconds apart. If not,

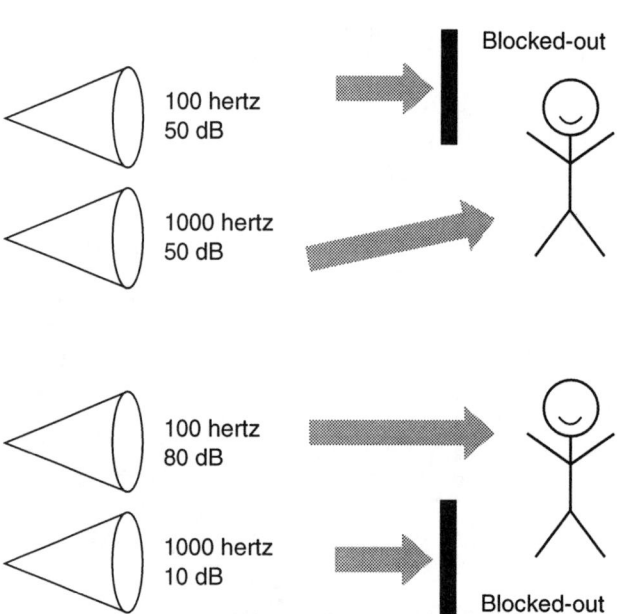

FIGURE 14.9 Sound masking depends on sound intensity (dB) and frequency (hertz).

sounds run together, resulting in poor-quality sound. See Figure 14.10 for these effects.

Sound quality also depends on reverberation effects. Reverberation depends on the size of the room you are in. Reverberation refers to the ability to distinguish between the original sound source and its reflection, or echo. If the reflected sound is received too quickly (less than 10 milliseconds), there is no lingering sound in the room and it is called a "dead" room. If the sound reflects back and forth several times before it is absorbed, the room will reverberate with sound and be "lively." There is a balance for the room called the reverberation time, which will be discussed in a later section.

NOISE

There are two aspects of noise that are of concern in the hospitality industry. One affects customers and the other affects employees. (The noise that affects employees is controlled in the United States by OSHA.)

Annoyance

Noise that affects customers is called annoyance. It can, in some unusual cases, be painful, but most of the time it produces psychological discomfort and is very distracting. General criteria regarding annoyance noise have been developed over the years.

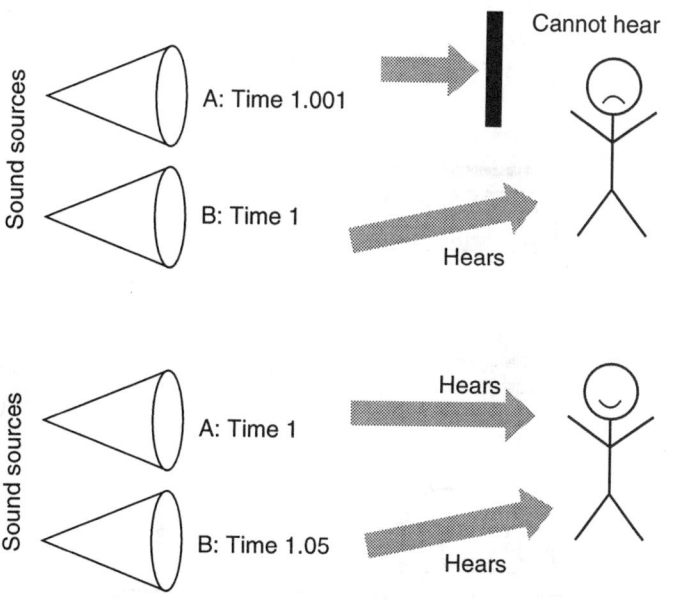

FIGURE 14.10   Distinguishing between two sound sources.

Loud noise is uncomfortable and distracting to customers. Therefore, keep noise intensity levels low. Noise also depends on hertz units. High-hertz noise is more distracting than low-hertz noise. A continuous noise is less distracting than intermittent noises at the same hertz and decibel levels. Hence, a barking dog or crying baby is more distracting than a radio continuously emitting sound at the same decibel level. See Figure 14.11.

Noise is less noticeable if it comes from a fixed location (an open window) rather than from several different and variable locations. See Figure 14.12. A customer can adjust to fixed-location noise. Finally, noise is more distracting if it transmits information (by radio, television, or public address system) than if there is no message noise, such as a hammer striking a metal pipe.

These noise factors become very important when a manager attempts to control noise within his or her building.

OSHA REQUIREMENTS

One of the concerns of OSHA (Occupational Safety and Health Administration) is to protect workers from a noisy environment. While most managers are aware that intense sound levels can cause temporary or permanent deafness, many are not aware that intense sound levels can also cause headaches, high blood pressure, and nervousness. Management has two

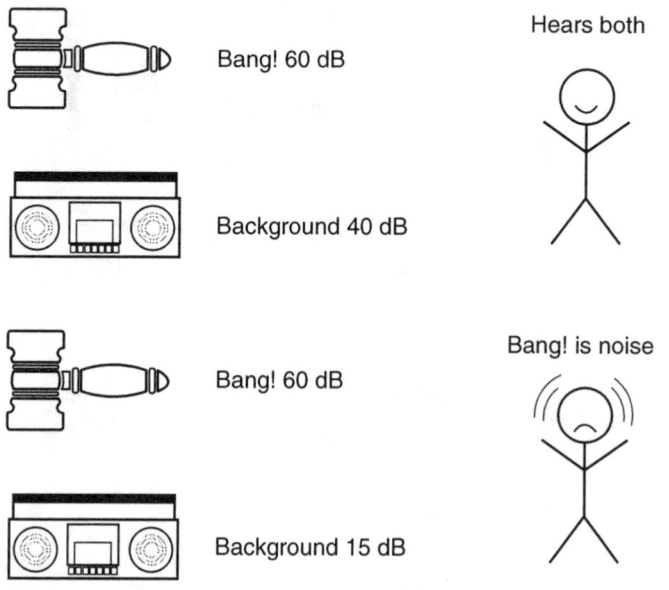

FIGURE 14.11 When is noise an annoyance?

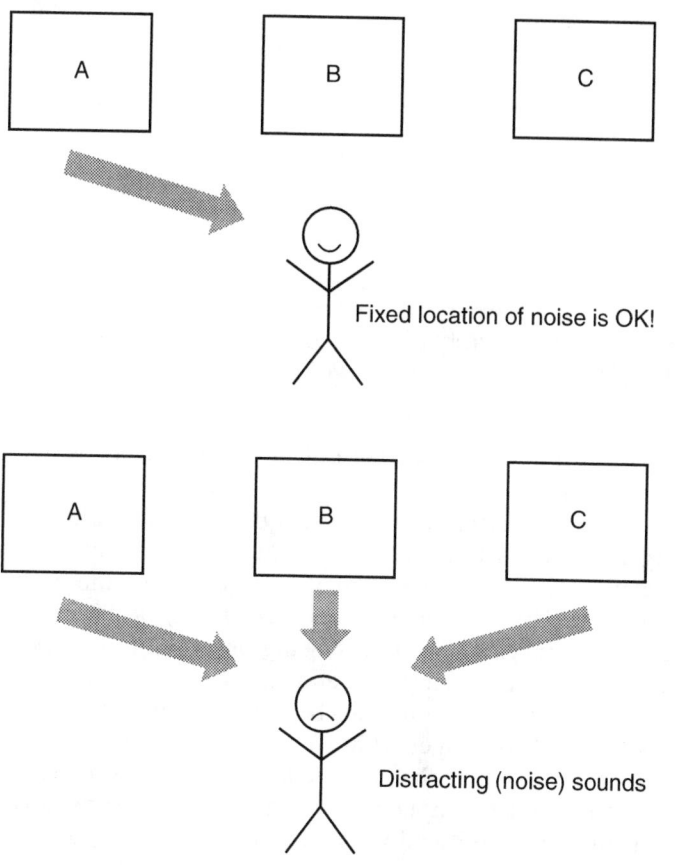

FIGURE 14.12 Sources of potential noise.

choices: to reduce the noise level or to provide hearing protectors for its employees.

As sound is transmitted throughout hospitality buildings, the best management alternative is to reduce noise at its source. Figure 14.13 shows noise exposures considered permissible by OSHA for various time periods. In addition, peak or impact noise cannot exceed 140 dB for any instant of time.

REVERBERATION TIME

Another basic sound term is reverberation time. The reverberation time is the time required for sound to be reduced by 60 dB, or to one-millionth (10^{-6}) of its original intensity. Its importance is in designing meeting, conference, and concert rooms and other spaces where large numbers of people

Duration per day, hours	Sound level, decibels
8	90
4	95
2	100
1	105
$\frac{1}{2}$	110
$\frac{1}{4}$ or less	115
Maximum	140

FIGURE 14.13 Permissible noise exposure (OSHA).[2]

may be present. The decibel reduction of 60 is an average desirable reduction for such rooms.

The reverberation time depends on the room volume, the sound-absorbing materials within the room, and the quality of these sound-absorbing materials. It also varies with the frequency of the emitted sound. If one knows the volume (length x width x height) of the room, the reverberation time will indicate if sound is being absorbed too quickly; if it is, and if a message warrants it, a public address system will have to be used so that the full impact of the sound can be heard by everyone in the room. In some cases, sound will linger within a room and become confused and disconcerting, indicating that the reverberation time is too long. The time can be adjusted by changing the number and type of absorbers within a room or by changing the amplification of the public address system. See Figure 14.14.

The reverberation time can be determined for various hertz levels; hence, one room can rapidly absorb low-frequency sound and allow high-frequen-

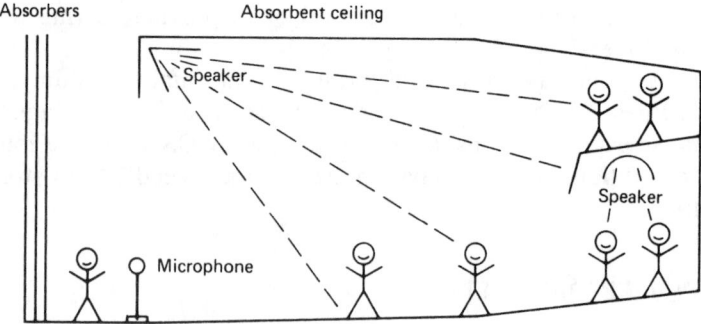

FIGURE 14.14 Using loudspeakers to direct sound and absorbers to control reverberation and echoes.

cy sound to linger. The opposite can also be true. The reverberation of different sounds can be controlled by changing materials, such as stage drapes. The lingering effect of stringed musical instruments is created through amplifiers, which produce long reverberation times.

SOUND TRANSMISSION MANAGEMENT

Generally, transmitted sound indicates an energy loss. If systems causing the vibrations were more efficient, less vibration would result and less sound and unwanted noise would be transmitted. The first step in sound transmission control is to adjust the unit or system to increase its efficiency, thus saving energy and reducing noise.

ROOM SOUND TREATMENT

Rooms should be treated to make them sound efficient. Efficient means that sound has adequate intensity to be heard properly within the room. Excess decibels, or at least a high percentage of them, should be absorbed within the room or by the building structure, so that they are not transmitted to other portions of the building as noise.

If operating equipment is a source of sound or noise in a room, special sound treatments are usually necessary at least to confine the noise to that room or area within the room. Rooms can be designed to meet specific background noise levels. A quiet room can be designed to provide a background noise of 20 dB or less, or 30 dB or less. A room designed at 70 dB or less would be fairly noisy. These are average design levels, and they vary with hertz levels.

These room sound designs are frequently based on *noise criteria curves* (NC designations). These criteria are used extensively in the United States. An NC-15 background noise curve is shown in Figure 14.15. Note that at low hertz levels, up to 47 dB are allowed, whereas at high hertz levels, only 11 dB are allowed for this design criterion (NC-15). The NC system was developed for the control of conversational sound in an office setting.

Another set of background noise curves has been developed in recent years. These curves are called *preferred noise criteria* (PNC) curves. The PNC-15 curve is shown in Figure 14.15. It should be noted that higher decibel levels are allowed at lower hertz levels, whereas lower decibel levels are allowed at higher hertz levels. This technique appears to overcome many NC-curve objections.

Not to confuse matters, the International Standards Organization has proposed a third set of curves called *noise ratings* (NR). It is not clear which set

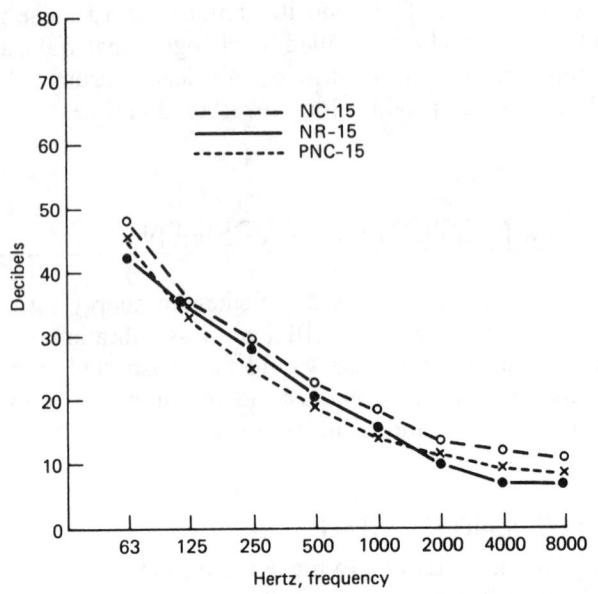

FIGURE 14.15 Noise criteria (NC), noise rating (NR), and preferred noise criteria (PNC) curves all with a 15 rating.

will finally be adopted for worldwide use. Figure 14.15 includes the NR-15 curve.

If you carefully review Figure 14.15, you should note that the NR-15 and PNC-15 lines cross the 15-dB intensity level at about 1000 hertz. The NC-15 curve crosses the 15-dB intensity level at about 2000 hertz. Also, the NC-15 line allows higher decibels at all hertz levels.

Mechanical equipment has a noise rating. The normal rating is in NC terms. A fan rated at NC-35 produces a maximum background noise that does not exceed the NC-35 curve at any hertz level. It may reach the NC-35 curve at only one hertz level and be well below the NC-35 curve at all other hertz levels. However, since it did reach the NC-35 curve once, it is rated at NC-35 (see Figure 14.16).

If several pieces of equipment are to be placed in the same room, the designer must have the complete noise generation ratings (decibel and hertz levels) for each unit of equipment and develop the NC room rating from these individual ratings.

The following recommendations should apply in the hospitality industry: Meeting and conference rooms, lodging guest rooms, private or semiprivate offices, and classrooms should be designed with a maximum NC-30, or PNC not to exceed 35; large offices, lobbies, retail shops, and most foodservice operations should not exceed NC-45, or PNC-40 to PNC-45.

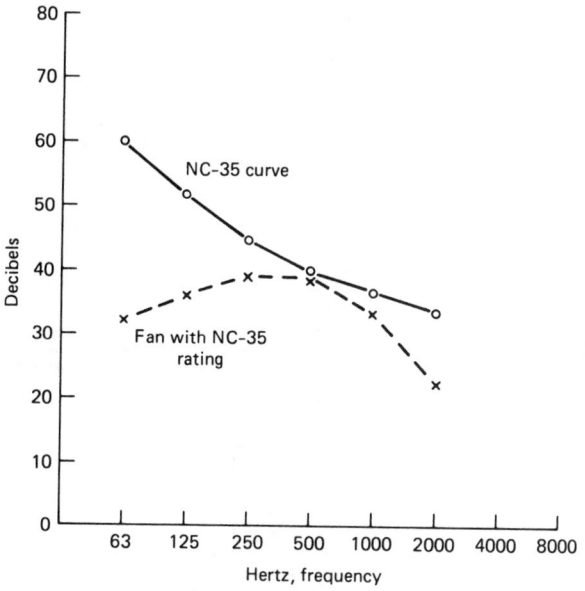

FIGURE 14.16   NC-35 rating for a fan.

ISOLATING SOUND SOURCES

Common equipment isolation techniques and devices are springs; resilient materials, such as rubber and cork; and separate equipment-mounting platforms. These devices absorb vibrations and convert them to heat. The absorber size, amount (volume or mass), type, and thickness depend on sound intensity and hertz levels. Often one must experiment with various devices to arrive at a correct combination. Figure 14.17 shows how this can be done for a unit of equipment.

ELIMINATING THE SOUND TRANSMISSION PATH

The final step, and frequently the most costly, is to eliminate the sound transmission path. If sound is being transmitted along water pipes, and the pipe cannot be eliminated, a compromise can be made. The pipe can be mounted at various points on resilient devices that may absorb a percentage of the vibration. As vibrations usually start at a water pump, the connection point of the piping to the pump can be made with resilient piping. This breaks the solid-metal path. If a large amount of sound is to be absorbed, a long length of rubber or plastic pipe is required; however, this may reduce the strength of the piping system. An alternative is to insert several short lengths of resilient piping along the path. If the second alternative is fol-

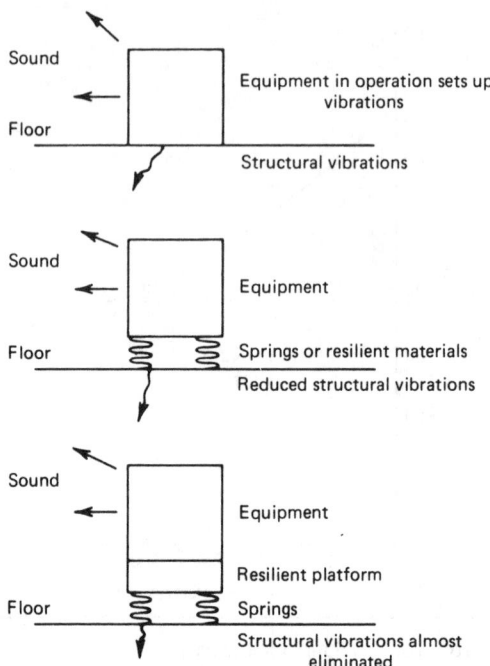

FIGURE 14.17 Isolation of a sound source.

lowed, make sure there are access areas to the pipe because the absorbed vibrations usually increase liquid leak potential at all connections. See Figure 14.18.

Air-conditioning and ventilation duct vibrations can be reduced with flexible connections. A portion of the interior of the ducts can also be lined with sound-absorbing materials. Special sound-absorbing diffusers, or registers, can also be used. Once again, the chief engineer may have to try a variety of techniques before the correct combination of devices is found.

Many noises can be transmitted through the building structure. Since these problems are expensive to correct, they are best dealt with in the design of the building. Mechanical-equipment rooms may be separated from the remainder of the building by placing sound absorbers between structural members (see Figure 14.19). It may also be necessary to construct a separate building for mechanical-equipment facilities; many health-care facilities, especially hospitals, have utilized this building design technique. Many Las Vegas hotels have also incorporated this measure into their designs. Several motels isolate mechanical-equipment rooms from the guest room structures by building isolation.

Sound transmission between adjacent, or a series of adjacent, rooms can be very distracting to guests in these rooms. This situation represents a very

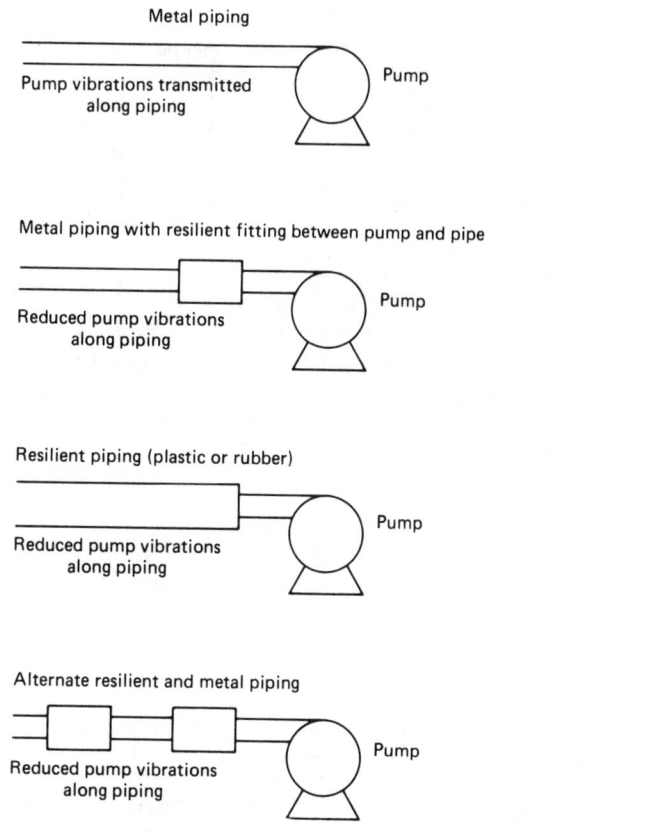

FIGURE 14.18 Reducing pump vibrations along piping.

common problem in lodgings, health-care facilities, dormitories, and office buildings. Sound produced in one room is transmitted to the adjacent room through common walls. As previously discussed, this may be heard in the adjacent room as background noise. If it exceeds the recommended NC or PNC rating, steps must be taken to reduce the transmitted sound between rooms. Figure 14.20 shows some normal sound reduction installations and their effects.

Impact noise can be especially annoying to customers and employees. It is best to cushion potential impact areas (kettles or metal utensils dropped on kitchen floors are good examples of impact noise). Carpet is an excellent absorber of impact noise, whereas stone or ceramic tile on concrete can transmit impact noise throughout an entire structure. If you cannot cushion the impact area, the solution to impact noise is very costly: You must use floating floors and properly suspended ceilings and provide a discontinuous type of structure. The costs are virtually prohibitive in existing buildings.

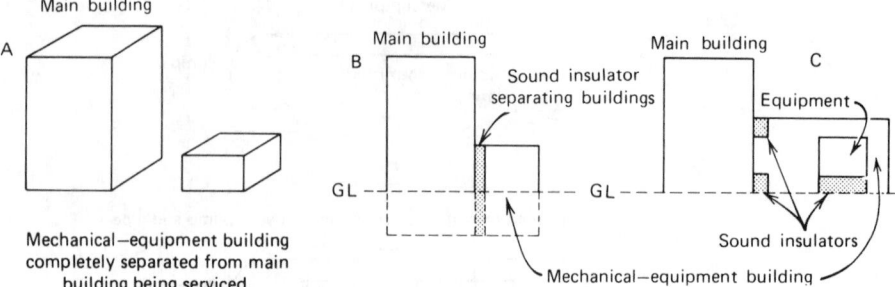

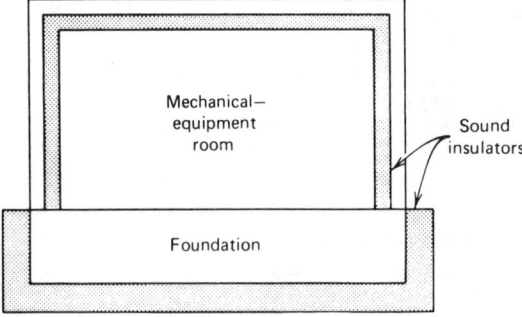

Mechanical–equipment building completely separated from main building being serviced.

A. Mechanical-equipment building completely separated.

B. Mechanical-equipment building sound-insulated from main building.

C. Sound insulators on main structural members between buildings, with additional insulation under each major component of equipment:

FIGURE 14.19 Techniques for separating mechanical-equipment rooms from the main building.

EXTERIOR NOISE

If exterior noises are a problem, they must be externally absorbed, or absorbed by the exterior building structure. The construction of the building is the key in many cases. Special sound-deadening sheathing can be placed on exterior walls to reduce or eliminate sound. This works fairly well for solid walls and doors, but windows and through-the-wall air-conditioning units may present a special problem. Single-pane glass will freely transmit external noise. Thermal windows with a vacuum between the panes of glass can effectively eliminate a sound path. However, special consideration must be given to window frames. Some exterior noise can be effectively reduced by using heavy drapes. Heavy fabric-lined walls are used in some lodging units; these control sound within the room and assist in reducing the transmission of outside noise.

3-inches (76.2-millimeters) solid concrete
with $\frac{1}{2}$-inch (12.7-millimeters) plaster on
both sides.
Sound transmission loss in decibels:

Hertz	Decibel Loss
500	44
1000	52
2000	58

Wall A

Wall rating 47

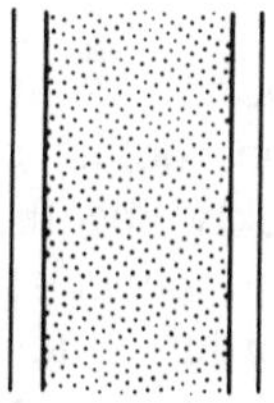

2 × 4-inch (50.8 × 101.6-millimeter) studs
with $\frac{1}{2}$-inch (12.7-millimeter) gypsum
wallboard with taped and finished joints.
Sound transmission loss in decibels:

Hertz	Decibel Loss
500	35
1000	42
2000	45

Wall B

Wall rating 41

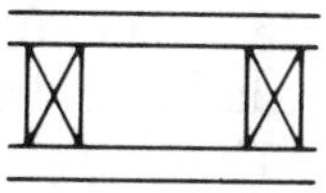

Metal studs $3\frac{1}{2}$ inches (88.9 millimeters)
and 24 inches (610 millimeters) on-center,
with $1\frac{1}{2}$-inch (38.1-millimeter) mineral
felt within wall, and 2 layers of $\frac{5}{8}$-inch
(15.9-millimeter) gypsum wallboard on both
sides
Sound transmission loss in decibels:

Hertz	Decibel Loss
500	51
1000	57
2000	57

Wall C

Wall rating 55

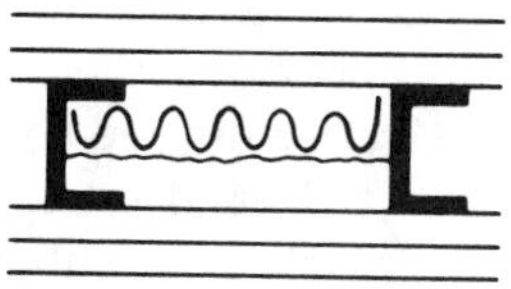

FIGURE 14.20 Reducing sound transmission between guest rooms.

Special consideration should be given to a building's location and its
landscaping. For example, locate the building away from a noisy road, and
use the area between the roadway and the building as a parking area rather
than locating the parking behind the property. Green belts—grassy areas
with trees—between noise sources and buildings are very effective. A parking ramp between the building and a noise source is also effective. If, however, these solutions are not possible, you must stop the noise at the structure's exterior walls.

SOUND CONTROL WITHIN ROOMS

Generally, sound control within a room depends on reverberation time. In some rooms, such as conference and meeting rooms, sound should be quickly absorbed. Longer reverberation times are acceptable for musical plays, concerts, and churches. Sound should be quickly absorbed in a recording studio and in hallways. It is best to have an architect—one who is well qualified to design acoustically efficient buildings for your industry—determine the reverberation time for a particular area. If it is too high, more sound absorbers will have to be placed in the area. Acoustical tile and padded carpets are excellent all-purpose absorbers. Frequently, the entire finish and furnishings of a room will have to be changed to produce desirable sound effects, especially if excessive plastic finishes and furnishings are used. Seldom in the hospitality industry is sound absorbed too quickly.

The shape of the room can also be designed to control sound. In some room areas, sound reflectors may be required, while other areas may require sound absorbers. The quantity and type of absorbers and reflectors depend on the purpose of the room and its activities. Each room activity may have different sound requirements. During a musical performance, for instance, furnishings, such as drapes, vary in weight and in the surface area to be exposed. Theoretical calculations can be made for different assumptions, but there is still an experimental factor, as well as overall experience, to be considered in design. At times, a room will have to be treated with special sound absorbers after it has been in use. See Figure 14.21 for an example of reflectors and absorbers being used at the same time.

Special sound effects can be generated with a public address, stereo, or any high-fidelity system. If a variety of activities are scheduled for a room, the public address system may be adjusted to produce either high- or low-hertz sounds to compensate for the overabsorption of certain frequencies. Thus, concert hall design is different from that of lecture and meeting halls, since the frequency of sound varies with its source. Because speakers and rooms vary, sound amplifiers must be adjusted for each event. Rooms are generally designed for set hertz levels.

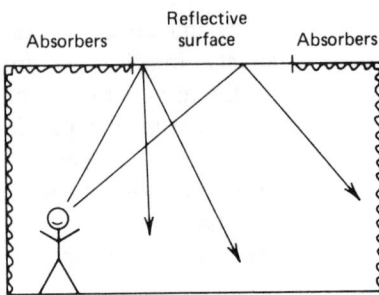

FIGURE 14.21 Using reflectors and absorbers in a meeting room.

If speech and music are to be simultaneously communicated to the audience, two public address systems may have to be used at the same time. Several may have to be used with some musical renditions because of the differing hertz ranges of various instruments, each of which may have to be amplified at different levels to produce the most desirable effect for listeners. The quality of the end product should be carefully considered. An average musical group could sound great with a good system and a great musical group could sound very poor with a low-quality sound system.

WORKER SOUND EFFECTS

Some musical selections will relax people; others will excite, anger, increase productivity, induce sleep, awaken, cause sound to linger—the list could continue. Musical selections as background sounds for workers are programmed at a set level. The worker can adjust to a given level of sound very quickly, and it is anticipated that such an adjustment will result in increased productivity.

A commercial foodservice kitchen can be too quiet, too noisy, or just right with respect to background sound and noise. If it is too quiet, workers may look around to see if others are working. When a kettle is dropped on a hard-surface floor, several workers will probably jump, or at least react, and productivity ceases. If workers can hear others talk, this will frequently result in lower productivity. Too much noise in a room can irritate workers. Accidents and errors usually increase. People must shout to be heard. Productivity decreases.

The ideal background sound is around 40 dB for people performing manual tasks. The hertz range depends on a worker's age, sex, education, social patterns, and background, to name only a few variables. At the 40-dB level, workers know that there is activity in the work area. On average, 40 dB is not too irritating to most workers. Their productivity increases at this decibel level and will be maintained at relatively high levels for extended time periods. Workers will still hear the dropped kettle, but they will not have to shout to be heard. They will not hear a person who is some distance away talking. They will generally adjust to the situation and the environment with a minimum of inconvenience.

SUMMARY

Sound is an important aspect of the hospitality industry. Its control and management can have positive and negative effects on employees, customers, clients, and guests. Building electromechanical systems are potential generators of sound and noise. There are numerous external sound sources that could terminate as building sound problems that must be resolved by management. Finally, employees and customers are potential sound sources that must be recognized and accounted for by management.

A building must be sound designed. If sound control is not designed into your building, you may be faced with a lifetime of sound problems. Sound can sometimes be controlled with minimum time, effort, and costs. At other times, sound can be controlled only with considerable effort and costs. And sometimes you cannot control noise effectively even if you spend large sums of money. You must recognize which category your building falls into. In some buildings, all three categories apply.

The management key to the sound problem solution is an understanding of sound characteristics. For example, in the simplest form, the sound source is a vibration, it must have a path, and there must be a receiver. Eliminating any one of the three requirements stops sound. Eliminate the vibration and there is no energy or sound. Eliminate the sound path so that sound cannot be transmitted; this can be done by installing sound absorbers, which destroys sound energy. Finally, if the receiver does not hear the energy, there is no sound. The sound could be redirected away from a person. The sound could be masked by utilizing background sounds.

While undesirable sound is noise and could be potentially harmful to employees and customers, through prolonged exposure to intense sound, one or a combination of the preceding techniques may minimize and eliminate this noise. Quality sound is also important to management. The correct message must be heard by all affected people, both employees and customers. This includes emergency announcements, speakers, entertainment sounds, and background music for increasing employee productivity and for guest enjoyment and relaxation.

Management has a sound responsibility in the hospitality industry.

REFERENCES

1. McGuinness, W. J., B. Stein, and J. S. Reynolds, *Mechanical and Electrical Equipment for Buildings*, Wiley, New York, 1980.
2. *Occupational Safety and Health Administration (OSHA)*, Table G-16, "Permissible Noise Exposures," Section 1910.95, amended June 3, 1974.

QUESTIONS/PROBLEMS

1. What are the major sound problems in each of the following types of buildings?
   a. Lodging
   b. Foodservice
   c. Health care
   d. Club
   e. Institutional

2. What can be done to correct a noise problem from a mechanical-equipment room located within a building?

3. How is the hospitality industry affected by various noise ordinances?

4. How can an establishment ensure that it will have a high-quality sound system within its building?

5. If a noise control committee were established in a hospitality-related business (select one segment of the industry), who should be included on the committee? Why?

6. If you were reviewing a blueprint for a remodeling project in a meeting room in your building and noticed a curved wall surface in the proposed plan, what questions, if any, would you ask about the impact of this design on the management of sound in the meeting room?

CHAPTER 15

Courtesy of Hobart Corporation.

FOODSERVICE EQUIPMENT MAINTENANCE

ABSTRACT

This chapter considers questions the hospitality manager should address when selecting and maintaining foodservice equipment for maximum utilization with minimum downtime. The following criteria for selecting equipment are critical: external dimensions, weight, compatibility, durability, utility requirements, maintenance requirements, and sanitation and safety. Preventive maintenance is essential for the mechanical equipment involved with food production, cooking, service, and beverage dispensing.

Key words*: Air Conditioning and Refrigeration Institute (ARI); American Gas Association (AGA); American Society of Mechanical Engineers (ASME); broiler; chlorofluorocarbon refrigerant (CFC); compatibility; convection oven; deck oven; disposal; durability; food cutter; fryer; gauge; griddle; grill; load-bearing capacity; microwave oven; mixer; National Board of Rules for Repairs; National Sanitation Foundation (NSF); peeler; plastic strip curtain; point of sale (POS); range; revolving oven; roll-in oven; slicer; stainless steel; steamer; steam kettle; thermostat calibration; Underwriters Laboratories (UL); utilities; ware-washing.*

INTRODUCTION

Foodservice equipment sales exceed $1.8 billion in the United States. However, the selection and maintenance of this equipment is often omitted from the training and education of foodservice managers. The consequence of this omission is that the equipment is ill suited for its intended purpose, is underutilized, and is not kept clean or operational.[1]

This chapter focuses on management guidelines for the selection and maintenance of foodservice equipment with the intended purpose of minimizing its operational costs and maximizing its productivity.

It is generally agreed that the foodservice menu establishes the variety and quantity of equipment required in a foodservice operation. Years ago, foodservice operations prepared and cooked all food from scratch. With increasing equipment and space costs and the availability of convenience and frozen foods, the need for certain types of equipment, such as peelers, grinders, meat saws, large mixers, and roll dividers, has decreased. There are currently several variations of four basic menus.

The basic menus include: steak house, or restaurants with food servers; health-care facility, or restaurants with cafeteria service; small health-care facility, or restaurants with limited menus; and school foodservice, or restaurants with fast-food service.[2] Figure 15.1 shows that while similarities exist, food production schedules for different types of menus require different types of foodservice equipment.

Foodservice equipment has been classified according to its functions: receiving, storage, preparation, cooking, baking, holding for service, and

Steak house or restaurants with foodservers		
Menu item	Schedule	Equipment
Soup	Prepared ahead	Steam-jacketed kettle
Steaks, chops	Cook to order	Grill and broiler
Salad and dressings	Prepared ahead	Refrigerator
Baked potato	Staggered baking	Convection or microwave oven
Rolls	Staggered baking	Convection oven
Butter	Ready to serve	Refrigerator
Ice cream	Ready to serve	Freezer
School foodservice or restaurants with fast food		
Entrée	Finish at serving time	Oven or steam-jacketed kettle
Vegetable	Staggered production	Compartment steamer
Salad	Prepared ahead	Refrigerator
Bread	Ready to serve	Room temperature storage
Butter	Ready to serve	Refrigerator
Dessert	Prepared ahead	Oven or steam-jacketed kettle or refrigerator or freezer

FIGURE 15.1 The influence of menu production schedule on equipment choice.

service.[3] Figure 15.2 presents a more detailed description of equipment within these classifications.[3]

The hospitality manager must initiate an inventory of existing equipment in order to select replacement equipment properly and provide for its maintenance. This chapter will consider guidelines for the selection and maintenance of the equipment identified in Figure 15.2.

FOODSERVICE EQUIPMENT SELECTION FACTORS

Figure 15.3 illustrates various factors that must be considered when selecting foodservice equipment. The asterisks in the table indicate those factors that can significantly increase equipment productivity or, if handled incorrectly, drastically increase maintenance cost.

EXTERNAL DIMENSIONS

Excellent reference material is available on layouts of foodservice facilities.[4] External equipment dimensions and clearances for such items as opening doors and handles determine equipment space requirements, and initial consideration of these factors will eliminate costly modifications in the facility to accommodate new equipment.

Food preparation	Serving
Cutters	Hot food
Mixers	Ice cream
Slicers	Ice equipment
Vegetable peelers	Beverage
Cooking	Coffee makers/urns
Ovens	Carbonated drink dispensers
Ranges	Cleaning
Griddles	Washers
Broilers	Dish
Fryers	Pot/pan
Steam-jacketed kettles	Glass
Steamers	Can
Toasters	Disposals
Waffle bakers	
Egg timers	

FIGURE 15.2 Categories of foodservice equipment.

Dimensions
   Internal
   External*
Weight*
Compatibility*
Durability*
Utilities*
Sanitation/safety*
Maintenance*
Capacity
Mobility
Ergonomics
Delivery period
Depreciation
Costs (initial, addition, installation)

FIGURE 15.3 Evaluation of food and beverage equipment factors.

*Significant for productivity and maintenance cost.

WEIGHT

The existing load-bearing capacity of floors, ceilings, and walls must be considered in relation to foodservice equipment requirements. A considerable investment may be necessary to brace a floor, ceiling, or wall to support the added weight of the equipment.

COMPATIBILITY

The technical expertise of the property management staff, the existing parts inventory, and the equipment and tools for maintenance and repair should be considered when selecting equipment. Bargain prices for equipment may not be such a good investment if additional staff training for maintenance is required or costly parts must be added to a stockroom inventory or expensive service contracts must be negotiated with an outside contractor.

DURABILITY

Another selection factor is durability. You should consider how construction materials will wear and whether they are appropriate for intended equipment use. Construction materials for foodservice equipment are usually metallic, plastic, or wood. Each of these materials has different durability characteristics.

Aluminum is a soft metal with little impact strength. Minor damage may result in a dent but may also penetrate the metal. In addition, although aluminum has a reputation for being "rust free," it is subject to corrosion when exposed to high-acid foods.

Stainless steel has high impact strength and higher corrosion resistance. There are more than 30 types of stainless steel used in foodservice equipment. Stainless steel that has high nickel and chromium with low carbon contents is more corrosion resistant and easier to weld than other grades.

Figure 15.4 illustrates examples of stainless-steel gauges (thicknesses) for the construction of foodservice equipment. Generally, gauges 8, 10, and 12 are used for bracing and supports, while gauges 12 and 14 are used in a table top. Gauges 14, 16, 18, and 20 are typically used in side panels or decorative facings. The other types of steel used in equipment construction include: plastic-coated, painted, laminated, and galvanized steel.

Figure 15.5 indicates a range of plastics and their application to foodservice equipment if durability is a selection factor.[5]

Wood has the advantages of being lightweight and relatively inexpensive compared to other materials, but it is permeable to bacteria, moisture, food odors, and stains. These negative factors restrict its use, except for tables and chairs. When wood is used for tables, the following selection factors should be considered: Hardwoods, such as maple and oak, are preferred to

Gauge	Inches	Millimeters
24	0.0239	0.6071
20	0.0359	0.9119
18	0.0478	1.2141
16	0.0598	1.5189
14	0.0747	1.8974
12	0.1046	2.6568
10	0.1345	3.4163
8	0.1644	4.1758

FIGURE 15.4   Stainless-steel gauges.

Type	Component of:
Acrylics	Food covers
Melamines	Dishes/countertops
Fiberglass	Trays/bus boxes
Polyethylene	Bowls/garbage cans
Polypropylene	Dishwasher racks

FIGURE 15.5 Plastics and their applications.

softwoods, such as pine, to bear the weight of food and containers, as well as people leaning on them; plastic-impregnated wood table tops are mar resistant. Wood chairs must be glued and reinforced with screws at stress points (where the back joins the seat and where the legs join the seat); legs should be reinforced by spreaders below the seat; chair arms must be securely fastened to the chair.

The mechanical components of equipment must also be durable. The waste disposal unit must be rugged enough to take most food scraps, and it should not have to be hand fed. A heavy-duty food cutter must have, at a minimum, a one-third-horsepower electric motor. If the equipment is not durable, it will not produce at the desired level, and its maintenance cost may be excessive.

UTILITIES

The operation of most foodservice equipment frequently depends on supplies of natural gas, propane, electricity, and hot and cold water. Adequate sanitary drainage and ventilation access are also essential. Perhaps you will have to specify an electric unit because it could be too costly to install natural-gas piping. Likewise, since natural gas is piped to the property but cannot be stored there, the natural-gas supply will possibly not meet demand during peak periods. If this factor were not considered, you would then have to install a supplemental propane standby unit.

Electrically operated equipment must be matched to the electrical limitations of the building. Wattage, volts, ac phases, and the connection plug are important factors.

Ware-washing equipment, steam-jacketed kettles, steamers, and vertical cutters/mixers have special plumbing requirements. For example, the dishwasher heater element is not designed to heat the incoming water. It is designed only to keep the unit's water tank hot and make up for the heat loss caused by dish absorption and aeration. This means that 140°F (60°C) water has to be supplied to the machine for washing; in addition, 180°F (82.3°C) water is required for rinsing and sanitation. This may necessitate booster water heaters near the machine, with water supply lines and floor drains.

A ventilation system capable of removing all waste products of combustion and cooking heat may also be necessary for some equipment. Some new units of equipment may require an additional ventilation system because the existing system cannot handle the additional load. Care should be given to selecting equipment that maximizes heat input and minimizes heat loss to food products. Such equipment will reduce building heat buildup and exhaust/ventilation requirements.

Foodservice equipment efficiency should also be an important selection factor. For example, open burner elements are generally more energy efficient than solid-top ranges and do not require preheating. However, if an open gas burner is used, a pot or kettle placed on the burner should be 1 inch (25.4 millimeters) larger than the burner diameter for maximum fuel efficiency. In addition, the gas flame should be adjusted to produce a blue flame and the flame must just make contact with the bottom of the kettle or pot. A flame "licking" up the side of the pot represents an energy waste. Also, since up to 30 percent of the gas used by an appliance is consumed by a pilot flame ignition, a pilotless ignition should be used. These factors point out that both equipment selection and operational practices are critical for conserving energy.

Because of the large amount of absorptive surfaces, metal, and insulation in ovens, only about half the energy that enters the oven finds its way to the cooked food. Thus, the most efficient ovens match the physical food size. High-efficiency ovens should have a minimum of 4 inches (101.6 millimeters) of insulation, maximum cooking capacity with minimum energy input, wrap-around heating elements rather than top and bottom elements, and wrap-around heating elements that are not part of a self-cleaning oven system.

Another energy-efficient device is a fluid griddle. Most griddles waste energy because it is difficult to keep the surface entirely covered with food; the uncovered surface radiates heat, resulting in a loss of energy. The fluid griddle uses fewer kilowatt-hours through a process that resembles the operation of a heat pump.

Plastic strip curtains can be used at receiving and walk-in refrigerator doors. When these are used as a supplement to the primary doors, heat gains can be reduced by 60 to 80 percent.

SANITATION AND SAFETY FACTORS

Organizations such as Underwriters Laboratories list products that conform to fire safety and electrical standards developed by the testing laboratory. The American Gas Association evaluates the safety of gas-consuming equipment. The National Sanitation Foundation's seal is widely recognized as a sign that equipment complies with public health requirements. Many manufacturers consider the standards of these organizations as minimum design and construction guidelines for foodservice equipment. Equipment purchasing specifications should include approval by these organizations.

MAINTENANCE FACTORS

When selecting foodservice equipment, you should consider its ease of cleaning, including means of access for cleaning. Equipment design dictates ease of cleaning. Reach-in refrigerators should have few, if any, interior seams. Spillage and food particles can collect at seams, creating a time-consuming daily maintenance chore which, if neglected, will lead to a sanitation problem. The same unit should have easily removable shelves for quick and efficient maintenance.

If moisture and condensation can accumulate on a floor surface under any unit of equipment, it should come equipped with a drip pan. The drip pan should be easily removable for cleaning.

The availability of spare parts and the level of expertise necessary to service equipment should also be selection factors. If existing property and equipment personnel are not qualified to maintain and repair the equipment, you should ask: What are the costs associated with a service contract?

The equipment's warranty should also be evaluated. The warranty usually specifies a certain protection period from defective workmanship. This time period can start when the equipment is installed or when it is purchased or shipped. Some manufacturers restrict the warranty period for both parts and labor. Labor repair costs are usually warranted for shorter time periods than replacement parts.

PREVENTIVE-MAINTENANCE CONSIDERATIONS

The increasing investment in foodservice equipment should dictate that equipment be properly maintained. The following is a sampling of preventive-maintenance practices designed to maximize equipment longevity and minimize periods when equipment is inoperative, or "down." Equipment identified in Figure 15.2 serves as the focus of this discussion.[6]

FOOD PREPARATION EQUIPMENT

The inventory of food preparation equipment may include mixers, cutters, slicers, and vegetable peelers.

Mixers

The size and number of mixers obviously depends on the output and types of items. The mixer, or vertical mixer, is essential for mixing food products. Most manufacturers ship the mixer ready to use. However, an initial inspection of the mixer's transmission oil may prevent a costly repair that will occur if the equipment is operated with an improper quantity of lubricants.

All mixer parts, including bowls, beaters, whips, and other accessories, must be cleaned daily. A weekly inspection of the oil level in the transmission case and an examination of the proper rotation of the planetary in gear-driven versions are also important. Some mixers are fitted with a power hub for attaching a vegetable slicer/shredder, power dicer, or meat chopper. Power hub functions may eliminate the need for other food-processing equipment.

Monthly maintenance routines include examinations of the bowl lift mechanism, greasing of all gear parts, and a check of all belts for proper tension. Every six months the mixer's oil pump should be inspected and the transmission oil reservoir drained and refilled with new oil. At this time, the beater shaft should be thoroughly cleaned, and the lubricant replaced. Some mixers use geared drive trains; some use V-belt drives; and some use a combination. Both have their advantages, and both, if properly maintained, will give years of uninterrupted service.

Food Cutters

This type of equipment is usually one of two varieties. One type has a series of entry points that cuts the food into various shapes according to such settings as slice, strip, chop, or bias. The other type, shown in Figure 15.6, has a removable bowl, which rotates in a clockwise direction as the food product is cut by knives turning downward in the bowl.

Cutters require daily cleaning of all entry points; hot water should be run through these points while the unit is operating. The cutting head guide, end bearing, spline shaft, adjusting ring, and slicer shaft are lubricated according to the manufacturer's recommendations.

In addition, blades may require sharpening. Remove blades carefully, and reposition them with the proper clearance, as recommended by the manufacturer.

In addition, it is important to check the lubricant level in the gear case each week, and more frequently if the cutter is heavily used. Monthly or more frequent checks for lubricant leaks and excessive gear noise in the

FIGURE 15.6　Food cutter (courtesy of Hobart Food Equipment).

bowl drive mechanism must be included in its preventive-maintenance schedule. The bowl drive gear should be lubricated annually.

Slicers

As with other equipment, one must take a careful look at the menu to determine what type of slicer is needed. Blade diameter, horsepower rating, and feed mechanism are key factors.

Blade diameters on most slicers range from 8 (203.2 millimeters) to 12 (304.8 millimeters) inches. A slicer with an 8-inch (203.2 millimeters) blade is quite adequate for slicing vegetables and most cold cuts. However, a 10 (254 millimeters) to 12-inch (304.8 millimeters) blade is required for slicing roasted meats, poultry, or large bricks of cheese or cold cuts.

Generally, the horsepower ratings of the motor range between 1/4 (250 watt) on small slicers to 5 (5000 watt) horsepower on fully automated slicers, the smaller horsepower ratings being more appropriate for light duty.

The simplest and least expensive models are equipped with a horizontal food carriage. In such models, the blade stands straight up. Food is placed into the carriage, a feeder grip is placed against the food, and the carriage is manually cued back and forth.

Slicers equipped with an inclined food carriage are the most common. The slicing blade is positioned at a 45-degree angle from vertical. Food is placed in the carriage and gravity carries the item being sliced toward the blade.

A slicer requires regular maintenance. The knife or slicing components should be cleaned daily. Electric slicers must be dismantled to be completely cleaned but should never be run through the dishwasher. This will most certainly result in costly repairs. If food tends to bounce around when cued back and forth, it is time to sharpen the blade. To clean and reassemble a slicer effectively takes from 5 to 10 minutes (0.083 to 0.167 hour), depending on how thoroughly the job is done.

Most manufacturers of slicers recommend that a few drops of lubricant be placed on the carriage slide rods weekly. The gauge-plate slide rods should be lubricated every month. All lubrication of this equipment, including its motor and drive gears, must follow the manufacturer's recommendations. For example, the manufacturer generally lubricates motor bearings prior to shipment, and these bearings are lubricated only once a year.

Peelers

The peeler, as illustrated in Figure 15.7, is used to peel potatoes, carrots, and other vegetables. Daily or more frequent cleaning, depending on use, is the principal maintenance. Insufficient cleaning results in an accumulation of dirt and vegetable starch that could reduce the cutting efficiency of the unit.

FIGURE 15.7   Portable peeler (courtesy of Hobart Food Equipment).

Examination of belt tension, electrical connection tightness, timer accuracy, and abrasive disk wear should take place monthly. Usually, motor bearings on this equipment are permanently lubricated by the manufacturer.

CLEANING EQUIPMENT

Cleaning equipment includes dishwashers and pot, glass, silver, and can washers.

Dishwashers

Because there are many different dishwasher designs, the literature received from the manufacturer is essential to a proper preventive-maintenance program.

Daily cleaning is important, particularly if the building has hard water. (Water-softening methods were discussed in Chapter 12.) Weekly maintenance should include removing any residue buildup of detergent from the unit's exterior. In addition, weekly cleaning and checking of thermostats and thermometers, and gauge calibration are essential. The unit's tank and drains must be inspected for leaks.

Monthly maintenance includes cleaning deposits from the heating elements and/or steam coils. Also, depending on the fuel source, the pilot light on gas-fired washers and the steam thermostat on steam-heated washers could require cleaning and adjustment. On a quarterly, or at least annual, basis, all motors and shafts should be lubricated, belts adjusted, and electrical connections tightened according to the manufacturer's specifications.

Pot, silver, and can washers require similar preventive maintenance.

WASTE DISPOSAL

A waste disposal grinds up materials so that they can be drained or deposited in the sanitary sewage system. Instructions for the use of this equipment should ensure that waste is fed into the unit in a continuous flow and that water is running into the unit at all times during disposal operation. In addition, procedures should be implemented that prevent any metal, glass, wood, cloth, plastic, mop strings, rubber bands, or cellophane from being accidentally dropped into the unit.

Weekly, the unit's cutter blocks should be examined for wear, motor bearings should be checked for unusual noise (turn the unit on and listen), and the unit's strainers should be cleaned. Annually, or more frequently if recommended by the manufacturer, the motor brushes and starting device should be examined for wear. Any required lubrication of motors can be done at the same time.

An increasingly important piece of technology is a pulping system. Such systems can dramatically reduce the costs associated with waste disposal. Additional discussion of such technology is found in Chapter 18 (see the section on solid waste systems).

DRY-HEAT COOKING EQUIPMENT

Dry-heat cooking equipment includes ovens, ranges, griddles, broilers, and fryers.

Ovens

Ovens are classified as convection, deck, microwave, revolving, and roll-in.

Convection Ovens. The convection oven differs from other types of ovens in that a fan introduces rapid circulation of heated air into the oven's cooking chamber. As illustrated in Figure 15.8, food can be cooked on a series of racks instead of an open hearth, enabling the entire oven volume to be efficiently used.

The convection oven can be electric or gas. Both models require daily cleaning of the interior cooking chamber. On a semiannual schedule, the electric model requires blower wheel-hub lubrication, inspection of the oven door for proper closing, and a check of all electrical connections for tightness. Lubricate the blower motor yearly, unless it is permanently lubricated by the manufacturer.

FIGURE 15.8   Gas convection oven (courtesy of Hobart Food Equipment).

Gas convection ovens require daily cleaning and monthly inspections of the pilot ignition system, burner air mixture, and flame height. The main burner flame should be a clear blue color with a definite inner cone at each port. If the flame is soft and yellow tipped, the burner air–gas mixture must be adjusted. Some models have a blower wheel, which requires semiannual lubrication. Check door alignment and electrical connections every six months.

A knowledge of programmable controls in the engineering unit will become important as the use of convection ovens with such control systems increases. Such controls increase the multitude of available preparation features, including cook and hold, which allow for slow, overnight cooking.

Combination ovens have also become more widely used in modern kitchens. Serving as a convection oven and steamer, they offer a type of versatility that is invaluable.

Deck Ovens   The deck oven, as shown in Figure 15.9, can be stacked, or "decked," to increase its capacity with minimal floor area requirements. Models may have one, two, or three decks. Electric and gas models are available.

Electric models require daily cleaning and semiannual inspection of electric connections and door alignment. The gas model requires a daily cleaning and a monthly examination of pilot and burner flame for proper adjustment.

Microwave Ovens   The microwave oven cooks food by converting microwave energy to heat within the food product. Electronic microwave tubes are located in the cooking chamber. Heat is generated within the food rather than from an outside source; hence, the oven remains cool.[4] A good application for microwave ovens is an alternative to vegetable steamers. Some models can effectively cook two 4-inch (101.6 millimeters)-tall full pans filled with vegetables at one time.

Most persons have, at one time or another, used a microwave oven. Most also know that the homestyle models are very underpowered for most commercial applications, with power ratings typically around 500 watts. Commercial facilities need to look to higher-powered models with a base rating of 750 watts. For cooking multiple portions, higher-powered machines are available in a full line of wattage ratings. Ovens are available in the mid-range level of 1200 to 1800 watts and a high-range level of 2100 to 2600 watts.

Basic models are equipped with a dial control used to set cooking times, whereas advanced models feature touch pads for setting times and cooking power levels. Many models are also equipped with programmable buttons that can be custom set to match items on a menu.

FIGURE 15.9   Six-pan bake oven (courtesy of Hobart Food Equipment).

The interior of the oven is another point to consider. Generally, the height of the oven cavity should not be a problem. However, the depth and width must be looked at closely to ensure that they are large enough to hold the cooking vessels necessary for the operations. Most oven doors today are hinged, either right or left, and all have interlocks.

Microwave ovens typically operate for years with only periodic cleaning of the oven cavity. The magnetron is the most fragile component of the system. However, less expensive, knock-off brands may be impossible or very costly to find replacement parts for or get serviced. Daily maintenance includes wiping up all spillage and surfaces in the cooking chamber with a mild detergent solution. Scouring pads and abrasive powders should never be used on any components or surfaces of the microwave oven.

Weekly, the unit's air filter should be washed in a mild detergent solution and dried. Oven exhaust ports should be inspected to ensure that they are open. Use a soft brush or toothpick to clear any blockage; then wipe the parts with a mild detergent solution. Inspect door seals for dents or damage. Each week, check door tightness and the interlock switch.

Semiannually, the blower motor requires lubrication, and a microwave (radio-frequency) leak test must be performed. This ensures that the waves are kept within the ovens.

Revolving Ovens.   The revolving oven uses a flat tray or multiple trays suspended between two reels that rotate the trays. Oven capacity may range up to 24 turkeys, 2000 potatoes, or 72 large pies per load.

These ovens can be fueled by gas or electricity. A daily and monthly maintenance program like those already discussed should be established to maintain electrical connections, burner adjustments, and motor lubrication. Weekly lubrication of the tray movement system is also required. A monthly inspection of the oil levels in gear boxes and related revolving drive mechanism is required.

Roll-In Ovens.   The roll-in oven is designed to receive portable racks containing food. The oven size determines the number of racks that can be accommodated. Both gas and electric models are available. A fan is also used to circulate air within the oven chamber. A water injection system is also available, which enables the oven to generate steam in excess of 300°F (149°C).

Maintenance involves daily cleaning of interior and exterior surfaces, weekly inspections of burners and electrical connections, monthly cleaning of the water injection nozzles, and quarterly lubrication of the blower shaft bearings. The electric motors are usually permanently lubricated by the manufacturer.

Ranges

Preprocessed foods have eliminated the need for the large battery of ranges found in foodservice facilities in the past. However, the range—electric and gas models—is still used when cook-to-order menu items are offered.

By definition, a range can be used to cook foods over burners or elements and bake/roast in its oven. When purchasing, think about whether the oven is actually needed. If a deck, convection, or other type of oven is used for roasting and baking, a cooktop (a set of burners/elements) can be purchased for much less money.

On the electric model, the most common arrangement is 12 x 24-inch (305 x 610-millimeter) hot plates. Pay close attention to the kilowatt rating of the elements and look for infinite range controls to ensure maximum cooking flexibility. There are also smart electric ranges that will automatically power down when a cooking vessel is removed or if a pot boils dry.

A daily cleaning of the top surface is required because grease can get between the plates. Check all electrical connections monthly.

On gas models, the available cooking surfaces may include open burners, uniform heat tops, graduated heat tops, and griddles. Uniform heat tops include two equal-sized plates, each with its own burner and controls. Heat is supplied over the entire surface of each section. The graduated heat top is provided with two open rings in the center of each top directly over the burners. Some burners are easier to remove for cleaning than others, and the easier it is to clean, the more often it will be cleaned. The newest innovation in gas burners is a system that delivers a mixture of gas and air. Conventional gas burners rely on the air available around the burner to support combustion; therefore, a grate design that allows heat to escape into the kitchen is also needed. The air/gas burner does not need ambient air to function properly, so it is surrounded by a set of rings that trap heat and deliver up to 50 percent more heat directly to the pots and pans. Such burners cook faster, use less gas, and keep the kitchen cooler.

Spark ignition is also standard on newer ranges. It helps lower energy costs by not continually burning fuel. Spark ignition also saves headaches, because pilot lights frequently blow out, which allows for a buildup of gas that could lead to an explosion.

Regular monthly maintenance of the gas burner must be provided. All surfaces are cleaned daily. Each week the burner box and top section of the heat top is removed and cleaned.

Griddles

The griddle, as shown in Figure 15.10, is a flat-top unit with surface heat being provided from beneath. Griddles are typically classified as counter top or roller top. The roller top is used primarily for cooking hot dogs. A series of fast-heating rollers turn the franks over at a slow, even speed. These rollers require a daily cleaning with a nonabrasive cleaner.

FIGURE 15.10 Gas griddle (courtesy of Hobart Food Equipment).

Counter griddles may be gas or electric models. The griddle surface of both models must be cleaned daily with a griddle stone or screen. Detergents and abrasive cleaners may damage the surface and must be avoided.

Electric griddles also require a monthly inspection of electric connections, and gas models require a monthly examination of gas ports, burner adjustments, burner valve lubrication, and pilot ignition. Roller-top griddles also require monthly lubrication of the rotor bearings of the motor (5 to 10 drops of #10 weight electric motor oil) and the gear box (1 tablespoon of #20 weight electric motor oil).

Electromagnetic induction cooking is available on griddles, ranges, and fryers. The key to induction cooking is the electromagnetic properties of the different alloys incorporated into the heat transfer surfaces. For example, a griddle section may be underlaid with an alloy that will heat up to a design temperature of 350°F (177°C), while another section, which uses a slightly different alloy, will heat up to 375°F (190°C). The entire cooking/heating surface heats to the design temperature. When strips of steak are placed on the griddle surface, the temperature of the surface drops and only the surface directly under the steak begins to draw electricity to recover to the design temperature. This means that the other portions of the griddle section will not overheat.

Broilers

Broilers are designed to cook by radiant (infrared) heat. The units are classified as either charbroilers or upright broilers and are available in gas or electric models.

Maintenance of the electric model chiefly involves periodic replacement of the heating elements and controls. The gas model requires inspection, adjustment, and cleaning of burner components.

Both the charbroiler and the upright broiler require daily maintenance. The charbroiler grates and the upright unit must be cleaned and the burner heat reflectors brushed free of all debris.

Fryers

Fryers include deep-fat fryers, tilting fryers and braising pans, and pressure fryers.

Deep-Fat Fryers. Figure 15.11 shows a deep-fat fryer, which includes heat elements, controls, and a fryer filter unit. Whether these fryers are heated by electricity or gas, the fat container and heating elements must be cleaned daily.

The electric deep-fat fryer also requires a monthly inspection of all electric connections and the high-limit thermostat. The high-limit thermostat is designed to shut off all energy to the fryer automatically if its temperature control thermostat malfunctions and if the temperature of the heating elements reaches 450°F (232.4°C).

Gas models require monthly inspections and servicing of the burner, pilot ignition systems, and high-limit thermostat. On the gas model, the high-limit thermostat shuts off gas flow to the unit if the temperature reaches 350°F (177°C).

The deep-fat fryer filter is used to remove carbon particles and sediment from cooking fat, so that the fat can be reused. If the fryer is equipped with

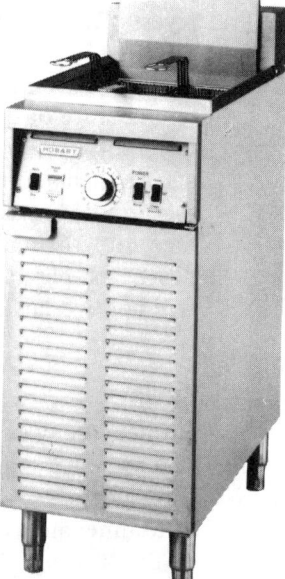

FIGURE 15.11 Convection fryer (courtesy of Hobart Food Equipment).

a drain valve, the filter unit is rolled under the drain, and fat is filtered through a filter cloth or paper and then pumped back to the fryer. If the drain is not available, the fat must be pumped out of the fryer through a filter into a container and then back to the fryer.

The filter pump requires daily maintenance. If fat is allowed to remain in the pump, it may congeal on pump gears and overload the pump motor. Quarterly, pump hoses must be checked for breaks, kinks, and weak spots. Electrical connections should also be checked for tightness.

New equipment has improved filtration systems, lengthening the life of cooking oils without carbonizing. Because the breakdown process is more gradual, less fat is absorbed by the product.

The new robot fryer offers significant labor savings and improved product quality. During off-peak periods, holding boxes are loaded with the product. The weight of the load will vary depending on the particular product, but it closely matches the load sizes used in most operations. An advantage of this product-loading requirement is that fry baskets will not overload with fries or other frozen items during peak periods of demand. Each load is consistent, which leads to improved cooking, minimal absorption of frying medium, and optimal quality product. The filled boxes are positioned in bays in the freezer compartment adjacent to the fryers. As requests for fries, chicken, or fish are entered into the POS (point of sale) computer system, the fryer's computer detects the need to cook a batch of product. A fry basket is automatically moved to the dispenser where the designated box of product is gravity fed into the basket. The basket then returns to the fryer and is lowered into the cooking position. After a predetermined time, the basket lifts and moves to the heated holding bin. After dumping, the basket is ready to accept the next load of product.

Tilting Fryers. Used for braising, frying, grilling, steaming, and thawing frozen foods, the tilting fryer can be freestanding, wall mounted, or counter mounted. Both gas and electric models are available.

Typical maintenance for a tilting fryer includes: daily cleaning (abrasive cleaners should never be used), monthly lubrication of the worm gear and bearing mechanism that allows the unit to be tilted, monthly inspections of electrical connections, monthly burner and ignition adjustments, and regular inspection of the high-limit thermostat to ensure that a 450 to 456°F (232 to 238°C) temperature is not exceeded.

Pressure Fryers. The pressure fryer is generally used for specialty items. Food is placed in the unit and fried under pressure by sealing a cover over the cooking pot. Maintenance of both gas and electric models involves a daily cleaning of the entire unit. Strong soaps or detergents, or caustics, must not be used.

Monthly maintenance includes adjusting burners, testing the unit's thermostat, and inspecting the high-limit thermostat. These fryers also have a filter system that needs regular cleaning.

STEAM-JACKETED KETTLES

A steam-jacketed kettle consists of two bowls, one sealed within the other. The bowls are separated by a space into which steam is introduced. When the steam condenses, it heats the inner kettle. These units may be stationary, tilting, or countertop.

Steam kettles range in size from small 32-ounce (0.908 kg) cookers, which are ideally suited for display cooking at raw bars, to mega kettles capable of processing 500+ gallons (1890+ liters) of food at a time. In most kitchens, a mix of kettle sizes and configurations makes the most sense. Small 20- to 40-quart (20- to 40-liter) countertop models are convenient for preparing multiple batches of soups or sauces throughout a meal period. Larger 60- to 80-gallon (225- to 300-liter) units support large batch production of foods, which are either held at a simmer in the kettle for service or held in steam table inserts in a warmer for use throughout a service period. Still larger kettles are used to support a cook/chill operation.

Daily maintenance includes cleaning the kettle and inspecting the supply steam line to ensure that supply pressure is never greater than the working pressure stamped on the kettle. If high-pressure steam is supplied to the unit, a pressure reduction valve is required. The high-pressure valve must be inspected each day.

The steam return line from the kettle to the boiler may include a steam trap, a swing check valve, and a gate valve. All these devices must be inspected each week.

Monthly, the gear and bearing mechanism on tilting kettles should be lubricated, the strainer in the steam return line should be cleaned, and the thermostat controlling heat buildup in the kettle should be inspected and cleaned. The steam trap must be cleaned each year.

STEAMERS

Such units are capable of steaming hundreds of portions of vegetables and other foods in a single batch, which is ideal for institutional operations or other volume feeders where large amounts must be cooked at one time. These units have found their way into many hotels, particularly in the banquet kitchens that service large ballrooms. A steamer consists of a sealed compartment where steam is allowed directly to contact the food being cooked. If the steamer is of the convection type, it can be opened at any time during the cooking cycle.

High-pressure steamers, which are capable of cooking in much less time than low-pressure steamers, were introduced with smaller cavities, making them well suited to à la carte operation.

The next development in steamers was the pressureless steamer, which offers operators the flexibility of opening and closing the compartment door during the cooking process.

A point to consider when purchasing a steamer is the volume of product that must be prepared. How many portions of steam table foods are served during a 15-minute (0.25-hour) period? For banquets, the number could reach into the hundreds; for à la carte operations, probably fewer than 30 portions of any accompaniment might be needed. Thus, high-pressure steamers are a good answer for à la carte operations. They are capable of cooking a half steam table pan full of vegetables in less than 4 minutes (240 seconds). The pressureless convection steamer will take roughly 50 percent longer to cook the same amount.

Steam is supplied by a boiler or a steam generator located below the cooking compartment. The steam generator can be energized by gas, electricity, or building steam. The steam coil boiler has a series of coils through which steam passes on its way to the cooking compartment. The steam must be "sanitary" since it comes in contact with food.

Maintenance of the steamer involves servicing or "blowing down" the boiler according to the manufacturer's instructions and removing any scale that may have accumulated from hard water. In addition, when the steamer is operating, it is essential that a proper water level is maintained in the boiler, that leaks are corrected before corrosion can start, that the low-water shutoff valve operates properly to ensure that the boiler stops operation if the water level drops below a safe level, and that the boiler's safety relief valve is functioning when the unit is under pressure.

Boiler servicing must conform to state and local codes because of the potential hazards of boilers. Servicing should also follow the ASME (American Society of Mechanical Engineers) Code and the National Board of Rules for Repairs.

SMALL EQUIPMENT

This category of foodservice equipment includes waffle bakers, egg timers, and toasters. This equipment may also be subclassified; for example, toasters may be pop-up or conveyor models.

Maintenance is typically minimal and focuses on daily cleaning. Other maintenance procedures must be scheduled. For example, pop-up toasters may have two to four bread slots. Bread is placed in the slot, a lever is pushed down, and bread drops into the heating chamber. When the preset heating cycle ends, the heat element shuts off and the toast pops up. In a conveyor model, bread is placed on a moving carrier or rack, which passes through a heat chamber, where moisture is removed from the bread, and then past a heat element, which toasts the bread. The pop-up unit is usually electrically operated. A conveyor model may operate on gas or electricity.

Daily maintenance with either type involves cleaning to remove bread particles. Care must be taken not to damage the heating element during cleaning or when removing any bread slices that jam in the unit while it is operating.

Inspections of all electrical connections and lubrication of the conveyor gear motor and conveyor chain are performed monthly. Gas models require monthly inspections of burner and pilot ignition components.

SERVING EQUIPMENT

Hot-Food Equipment

Hot-food or food-warming equipment is intended to maintain food temperature until it is served. The food is placed in a serving container and then placed in the unit while it is still hot.

Hot-food cabinets come in a variety of sizes and finishes. At a minimum, these cabinets should provide storage space for dishes on an undershelf. Cabinets can be specified with shelving on one or both sides of a hot-food table. Some cabinets are equipped with lowerators for holding plates, and in still others, the lowerators are heated.

Heated carving carts should be equipped with their own sneeze guards, a shelf for holding plates, gooseneck heat lamp, carving area, and hot well for holding sauces or other meal accompaniments. They should also be equipped so that the carver need not leave his or her station to get a backup roast.

There are a number of infrared heat lamp units that can be pressed into service for holding food hot for short periods. These top-heat units use infrared heat strips or lamps. Many of the units are freestanding and can be quickly set up wherever needed. One such product includes a sensing device that automatically shuts down heat lamps when no plates are in the pickup area. The sensor has a delay mechanism so that lights do not shut off immediately and a dimming mechanism helps to extend bulb life.

This type of equipment should receive daily cleaning of all food compartments. Monthly, all electrical connections are inspected for tightness. Thermostats are calibrated semiannually.

Ice Equipment

Ice equipment includes ice makers and ice dispensers. Both units have refrigeration systems. The ice maker can produce cubed ice of various sizes. The ice dispenser can form cubed, flaked, and block ice.

Cubed ice is made by applying water to an evaporator, which is divided like an ice cube tray. After the cubes have formed, the ice is harvested from the evaporator and the cycle begins again. For the flaked version, ice is scraped off the surface of the evaporator as it forms.

Self-contained machines integrate ice making and storage in a single unit. Modular machines allow a particular ice maker to be matched with a specified storage cabinet. Ice makers typically range in capacity from 50 to 4000 pounds (22.7 to 1816 kg) per day. However, the production capacity will vary depending on the temperature of the air flowing through the compressor and the inlet temperature of the water that flows into the evaporator. Also, while a machine might be capable of producing 400 pounds (181.6 kg) of ice in 24 hours, if the storage bin can only hold 50 pounds (22.7 kg) then that is the maximum amount of ice that one can have on hand at any given time.

Some manufacturers make storage bin interiors of stainless steel, while others use durable polyethylene. Ice bins that are fully insulated with an inch or more of foamed-in-place insulation will minimize melting.

The coating on the evaporator affects efficiency, ice quality, and sanitation. Evaporators made from plated galvanized steel may corrode over time, break down, and flake off into the ice. Some manufacturers utilize copper evaporators, which conduct cold readily and speed up the process. Others employ stainless steel, which is resistant to corrosion. Yet, another manufacturer coats its evaporator with a plastic that will not corrode or be harmed by cleaning solutions.

Some evaporators are designed so that cubes fall into the storage bin as individual pieces. In other machines, the cubes are held together by bridges, some of which break as the ice is dumped into the bin. The shape of the cube is perhaps the most important concern when purchasing a machine. Small, square or rectangular cubes pack together closely. In a glass, these cubes chill beverages quickly without watering down the drink excessively. On a salad bar, the small cubes pack closely around the food containers, helping to maintain optimal serving temperatures. Larger cubes chill beverages more slowly but will last for 15 to 20 minutes (0.25 to 0.33 hours). Thus, this type is suitable for glasses of water or other beverages that are refilled at the table.

Refrigeration systems were discussed in Chapter 8. The Air Conditioning and Refrigeration Institute (ARI) certifies certain claims about equipment that bears its seal. The ARI certifies the amount of ice that a particular model will produce under set conditions in a 24-hour period, the amount of water consumed per harvest, and the amount of water used by air-cooled units.

Environmentally friendly improvements to ice machines include refrigerants that are less destructive to the ozone layer and CFC-free foam insulation. In addition, some manufacturers have installed computerized controls in some machines designed to bring speed and accuracy to the ice-making process. Tied to the control is a set of four status lights on the front panel that indicate when the machine is making ice, harvesting, reaching maximum storage capacity, or malfunctioning. Inside the front panel is a digital readout that continuously displays evaporator and condenser temperatures.

Prechillers, designed for installation on cube machines, can increase production by up to 25 percent with no increase in operating costs. Prechillers take the dump water from the ice machine and use it to lower the temperature of the incoming water supply. Such chillers are easy to install, take up only a few square inches of floor space, and require very little maintenance. A prechiller is particularly useful in hot areas where the inlet temperature exceeds 70°F (21°C).

Daily maintenance should include cleaning the equipment's exterior; monthly, the condenser coils should be cleaned and the fan motor lubricated; the ice-making components should be cleaned quarterly.

Cleaning ice-making components is particularly important where water is hard. If the water has little or no dissolved solids, however, frequent silicone treatments of the freezing plate, where the ice is produced, may also be necessary to prevent ice from adhering to the plate.

Depending on the quality of the local water, single-line or multiple in-line cartridge filters will need to be installed and periodically replaced. Most ice machine leasing companies install filters on their equipment to extend the life of their investments. Another way to improve the purity of ice is to purchase an ice machine equipped with a purge valve that allows excess water to drain away at the end of each cycle. As the excess water drains away, it carries impurities with it.

Ice Cream Equipment

The soft ice cream machine makes a product used in cones, milk shakes, and other dairy desserts. Generally, a mix is added to a tank on the equipment, from which it is pumped under pressure to a freezing cylinder. The ice cream product is then drawn from a dispensing head.

Clean and lubricate this equipment daily according to the manufacturer's guidelines. Once a month, inspect electrical connections and clean the water supply strainer. On a quarterly schedule, clean the condenser and check for proper belt tension. Annual lubrication of compressor motors and bearings is generally required.

BEVERAGE EQUIPMENT

Beverage equipment includes coffee makers and urns, carbonated drink systems, and dispensers for products such as hot chocolate, juice, and tea.

Coffee Urns and Coffee Makers

The coffee urn includes a nonpressurized, vented water tank heated by electricity, gas, or steam. The heat source maintains an established water temperature regulated by a thermostat. Coffee is brewed in a liner next to the water tank. Water is automatically sprayed over the coffee grounds at measured intervals, with water flow controlled by a solenoid valve and a reset timer.

Back-of-the-house brewing still makes sense, but transporting coffee in small 12-cup serving pots wastes labor. An alternative is a system that brews up to 36 cups of coffee per batch into an insulated, transportable holding/dispensing tank. These double-jacketed stainless-steel units have foamed-in-place insulating layers. Single- or double-brew stations are available. At the touch of a button, a 12-, 24-, 36-, or 72-cup brewing cycle is initiated, and brew flows directly into the insulated tank.

Some machines are the pour-over type, but most require plumbing. However, consistent coffee depends on the amount of water per measure of ground coffee. Plumbed brewing systems should have a flow control unit, which regulates the amount of water no matter what the supply line pressure. If the level of coffee in the pot is different from cycle to cycle, a problem may exist. The flow control valve may be malfunctioning and the extra cup per packet of ground coffee means watered-down, substandard brew.

Typically, the brewing capacity of a single-tank, 36-cup batch coffee maker is 250 cups per hour, while a double-tank model can produce up to 400 cups per hour. Optional drip trays for each service area should be considered to keep the side stands dry with color-coded faucets to distinguish between regular and decaffeinated coffee or tea.

Automatic brewers that do not need paper filters have recently become available. Such brewers are equipped with two hoppers on the top of the system, one for regular and one for decaffeinated coffee. At the touch of a button, enough ground coffee for a half or full batch of coffee is augered into the brewing chamber. Hot water flows into the chamber and the brew flows through the metal filter plate and into the waiting pot. At the end of the cycle, the coffee grounds are washed away, either into a special trap or down the drain. The system can deliver a pot of coffee every 120 seconds for a total of 12 gallons (45 liters) per hour.

Among the hottest items of the 1990s are espresso machines. Some are fully automated and can produce up to 22 different types of espresso beverages, such as single shot, double shot, double latte, and single decaffeinate cappuccino, with the touch of a button.

Maintenance of coffee makers typically includes cleaning the solenoid valve, automatic-flow-control valve, strainer, spray arm, and spray nozzle. Once again, the frequency of such cleaning depends on water hardness and the buildup of mineral deposits. Gas units require burner and pilot servicing, while steam units require steam trap inspections.

Carbonated Drink Systems

This equipment includes a syrup tank, carbon dioxide gas tank, carbonator, and nozzles. Some systems have self-contained components, while others separate the syrup, carbon dioxide, and carbonator from the dispensing storage area.

In general, these systems require daily washing of all external surfaces of the dispensing station with a mild nonabrasive soap solution, weekly washing of drip pans and plates, and weekly removal of nozzles and valves for cleaning in a mild soap solution.

Examination of condenser coils and complete sanitizing of the system should take place monthly. Semiannually, filter water impurity strainers and various system valves should be inspected. If the system requires a water purifier to improve beverage taste, maintenance of this unit should follow the manufacturer's specifications.

Dispensers

This equipment includes hot-chocolate, juice, and tea dispensers. Hot-chocolate and tea dispensers mix a powder with water to brew these beverages. Primary maintenance includes daily cleaning of the dispenser and weekly examination of plumbing for leaks and of electrical connections for tightness.

The juice dispenser is designed to chill a product placed in a plastic bowl on the unit by a refrigeration system located at the base of the unit. Maintenance includes daily cleaning of the bowl, spray tube, impeller, and bowl cover. Lubricate the unit's pump motor and clean the refrigeration condenser quarterly.

SUMMARY

This chapter has considered questions the hospitality manager should address when selecting and maintaining foodservice equipment for maximum utilization with minimum downtime.

The following criteria for selecting equipment were stressed: external dimensions, weight, compatibility, durability, utility requirements, maintenance requirements, and sanitation and safety.

Preventive-maintenance schedules were recommended for the mechanical equipment involved in food production. cooking, service, and beverage dispensing.

REFERENCES

1. Kahrl, W. L., *Planning and Operating a Successful Food Service Operation,* Lebhar-Friedman Books, New York, 1979.

2. Jernigan, A. K., and L. N. Ross, *Food Service Equipment*, 3rd ed., Iowa State University Press, Ames, 1989.

3. Kotschevar, L. H., and M. E. Terrell, *Foodservice Planning: Layout and Design*, 3rd ed., Wiley, New York, 1985.

4. Kazarian, E. A., *Foodservice Facilities Planning*, 3rd ed., Van Nostrand Reinhold, New York, 1989.

5. Avery, A. C., *A Modern Guide to Foodservice Equipment*, rev. ed., CBI Book (a division of Van Nostrand Reinhold), New York, 1985.

6. Greaves, R. E., *Food Equipment Repair & Maintenance*, FERM Publishers, Rochester, NY, 1984 (a valuable reference of preventive-maintenance and repair procedures).

QUESTIONS\PROBLEMS

1. You are directed by your supervisor to prepare a maintenance plan for the foodservice equipment within a restaurant or health-care facility. Outline your approach for such a plan.

2. Determine the extent to which local foodservice managers include preventive maintenance in their management of equipment.

3. Many managers purchase foodservice equipment because it is the "best buy." Prepare a memo to your supervisor explaining why such equipment may not be the best bargain and may thus be an undesirable element of operations.

4. Discuss with a local supplier of commercial foodservice equipment the instructions/assistance it provides on the installation of one type of foodservice equipment described in this chapter.

5. Determine the extent to which a local health ordinance affects the installation and maintenance of foodservice equipment.

6. If you were discussing the purchase of food and beverage equipment with your chief engineer and he indicated that all such equipment must be purchased from the National Sanitation Foundation, what might you conclude from this comment?

CHAPTER 16

Courtesy of Holiday Inns, Inc.

MANAGEMENT OF
LAUNDRY SYSTEMS

ABSTRACT

Every 10 years, a property usually evaluates the feasibility of continuing as it has in the past versus adopting a new laundering alternative. This is particularly true for lodging, health-care, and institutional establishments. In each case, a thorough investigation is required to determine if the property should select one of the following alternatives: purchase linens and operate an on-premises laundry, purchase linens and use an off-premises commercial laundry, rent linens, use disposable products in place of linens, or use a combination of these alternatives.

It should be understood that the laundry industry is highly mechanized. The laundry consumes large amounts of energy, and it may place additional repair and maintenance requirements on the chief engineer and his or her staff. All these factors must be considered by the manager.

Key words: *combination linen service; commercial laundry service; disposable linen service; dryer; extractor; laundering cycle; laundering functions; linen rental service; multiple-suds principle; no-iron linens; on-premises laundry; soft-water requirements; 20°F (11.1°C) maximum- temperature-change rule; washer; water pH.*

INTRODUCTION

An on-premises laundry represents an investment of money, time, and human resources in many hotels, health-care facilities, clubs, and institutional establishments. A decision regarding an on- or off-premises laundry is frequently based on cost considerations. However, such a decision should also consider noneconomic issues.

A laundry department, depending on its size and staffing requirements, may be an independent department, much like marketing and sales, or a subdepartment. It is frequently found under the management control of an executive housekeeper. Because the department is heavily mechanized, it has extensive maintenance and energy expenditures.

The hospitality industry has gone through cycles in laundry management. There were years in which hotels, clubs, and institutions operated on-premises laundries. Then these operations were phased out. During this period, for a variety of reasons, more emphasis was placed on off-premises laundry service. A third cycle then developed, most recently in the mid-1960s, in which many units became totally dependent on off-premises facilities. In the 1970s and 1980s, a fourth cycle prevailed, as more hospitality industry units installed on-premises laundry facilities.

There are many reasons why the hospitality industry changed to on-premises laundry service. Economy is the basis of most decisions. The laundry has been viewed as an on-premises service for customers and clients. A minimal laundry was required to handle guest needs, and it was only logical to increase the size of the facility to satisfy the total laundry requirements of the hotel. Also, as some properties are located in remote areas, the on-premises laundry is a necessity for dependable linen management. Health-care facilities, some larger clubs, and even smaller foodservice units may have on-premises laundry services.

The development of no-iron linens and fabrics was a critical factor affecting the decision whether to operate an on-premises laundry. It is easier to launder no-iron fabrics. Equipment investment for facilities, employee skill levels, and hot-water and utility requirements were all reduced for no-iron products. Also, disposable table service is now common in many foodservice operations, and disposable linens are being extensively used in many hospitals and some health-care facilities. Therefore, a careful analysis must be made to determine the feasibility of installing an on-premises laundry.

LAUNDERING ALTERNATIVES

There are several laundering options, or alternatives, available to a manager: (1) renting clean linens from a commercial laundry, (2) purchasing linens and using an off-premises commercial laundry, (3) purchasing linens and installing an on-premises laundry, (4) using disposable products, and (5) using a combination of the preceding alternatives.

Many problems accompany each of these alternatives. Each alternative must be reviewed by management on a periodic schedule to determine the most feasible choice. Costs are continually changing, and what appears to be the best alternative one year could become a poor choice the next.

LINEN RENTAL

Managers can determine the types of linens they want to use and rent them from a commercial laundry, which may offer complete linen rental services. Payment is made for each item delivered to the property. Often, a commercial laundry will service a property up to a 100-mile (161-kilometer) radius on a daily schedule. There is a contract purchase charge for linens not returned. Many operations in the hospitality industry choose this alternative—especially smaller lodging units, clubs, foodservice units, and institutional buildings such as government agencies, churches, and office buildings. Some of the problems encountered with this alternative relate to emergency needs, delays in delivery, poor linen quality, and cost.

If a lodging property follows this alternative for laundering, the manager can follow one of several options for guest laundry requirements: provide no services, provide guest-operated laundry and dry-cleaning machines (usually coin operated on a revenue-sharing basis with a contractor), contract out guest laundry and dry-cleaning services, or operate a small on-premises laundry. While these specific options will not be analyzed in this chapter, the general analysis presented in this chapter would apply to them. Appendix 12 shows a partial analysis of these options.

COMMERCIAL LAUNDRY SERVICE

Many managers feel that this alternative is less costly than linen rental. You purchase linens and contract laundry services with an off-premises commercial laundry. You have complete control. However, a relatively large investment may be required to purchase, store, repair, and issue linens. The additional investment can be quickly recovered in many areas because commercial laundry charges are frequently based on the weight in pounds (kilograms) of laundered articles, and this may result in a lower unit linen cost than the rental alternative.

A major disadvantage is that linen inventory is frequently large, unless the commercial laundry is fairly close and has a dependable delivery schedule. The basic inventory rule followed by many properties is: one set of linens on the bed, one in the laundry, one on the shelf. Frequently, this rule is modified as follows: bed, laundry, shelf, and truck (which is used to transport linens).

This alternative also applies to guest laundry service.

ON-PREMISES LAUNDRY

This alternative requires a large capital investment. It also requires staffing and managing a laundry department. There are several costs associated with this alternative: depreciation of equipment and linens; building space charge; labor, administrative costs, and fringe benefits; repair and maintenance of equipment and space; energy costs (water, heat, sewage charges, and electricity); cleaning supplies; and taxes and insurance on equipment, linens, and the additional building space. However, because of the potential high cost of the alternatives previously discussed and with the acceptance of no-iron linens, many managers feel they can save money with an on-premises laundry.

DISPOSABLE LINENS

This alternative has several apparent advantages that should be considered. Disposable products are sanitary and convenient. They require less storage space. There is little danger of storage contamination and soiling while products are being moved within the property. The quality variance between products is minimal. Products have a fairly long shelf life. There are also disadvantages to disposable products, of which the most serious are unit cost, indirect costs associated with product disposal, customer acceptance, and employee training in the use of disposable products. The product disposal issue can be reduced by recycling disposable products.

Disposable products have been used in some health-care facilities for many years. Many properties use disposable products such as paper towels in rest rooms. Many managers are now using disposable employee uniforms and table service—napkins and table covers, especially custom-printed place mats. The industry trend is that while disposable products may have more future applications, managers will probably not replace traditional linens, such as bed sheets, pillowcases, towels, and blankets. These will probably be used in combination with one of the previously mentioned alternatives.

COMBINATION

The final option is to use a combination of systems for laundry management. There are certain areas where disposable products are most effectively used (public rest rooms), others where linens are better suited (bed linens), and some areas where a manager may wish to purchase or rent linens (employee uniforms) for special events. Many managers are currently utilizing this combination alternative for reasons of convenience rather than economy.

ECONOMIC FACTORS

Each operation must determine for its specific geographic location which alternative it should follow at a given time. Usually, the most important factor in selecting a laundry alternative is economy of operation, or feasibility. A survey of lodging managers revealed that essential laundering information was inadequate, incorrect, or not available.[1] Therefore, these managers concluded that a feasible decision about which alternative to follow is very difficult to make.

There are few general recommendations and guidelines that can be made regarding alternative selection. Each property must be analyzed as a separate case. It is very difficult to use a cost study from a property located in one region for another region, even if they are relatively close together, say, less than 100 miles (161 kilometers) apart. In the case of laundering, there are a limited number of reliable studies. The American Hotel & Motel Association, in conjunction with Cornell University, has published some excellent materials.[2, 3] (*Note:* Although these references were written years ago, there has been very little significant research done concerning laundering operations in recent years.) Basic information is provided—if certain assumptions are made—on which to make excellent decisions. A Michigan State University study covered lodging laundering practices and cost data in the United States.[1] (See the previous note.) In some areas, it may not be possible to consider all alternatives because complete rental services may not be available and there may not be a commercial laundry.

Item	Units (dozens)/guest room/year
Washcloths	$3^1/_2$
Face towels	$1^2/_3$
Towels	$1^1/_2$
Bath mats	$^1/_4$
Twin sheets	$1^1/_2$
Double sheets	$^1/_4$
Queen/king sheets	1
Pillowcases	$1^1/_3$

FIGURE 16.1 Selected linen requirements in dozens of units per guest room for an average U.S. lodging establishment.

PURCHASING LINENS

A lodging unit (health-care facility, dormitory) will initially purchase three or four complete sets of linens for each bed. However, the manager does not always know linen life expectancy. When does the manager start to purchase replacement linens? We know the wash life cycle for most linens. So, if the building occupancy were 100 percent and if there were no pilferage by guests or employees or early linen failures (rips and tears), you could calculate linen replacement cycles and determine an annual linen cost.

However, linen pilferage and linen failures do happen. Figure 16.1 shows data that will allow you to determine the number of selected linens you will purchase in an average year for a typical lodging unit (health-care and dormitory purchasing would be somewhat higher). The information was developed from lodging establishments in the United States and includes normal wash-cycle wear-out, industry pilferage, and early failure data. These data should be used to determine an annual linen requirement (see Figure 16.2 for an example 200-guest-room property).

Figure 16.3 indicates linen annual purchasing requirements for a lodging foodservice operation, and Figure 16.4 is an example using the information

Item	Units (dozens)/guest room/year
Washcloths	700
Face towels	334
Towels	300
Bath mats	50
Twin sheets	300
Double sheets	50
Queen/king sheets	200
Pillowcases	266

FIGURE 16.2 Selected linen requirements in dozens of units for an average 200-guest-room U.S. lodging establishment.

Item	Units (dozens)/foodservice seat/year
Table napkins	$1^{3}/_{4}$
Face towels	$2/_{3}$
Employee aprons	$1/_{2}$
Tablecloths	$1/_{4}$

FIGURE 16.3 Selected linen requirements in dozens of units per foodservice seat for an average U.S. lodging establishment.

Item	Units (dozens)/year
Table napkins	350
Kitchen towels	133
Employee aprons	100
Tablecloths	50

FIGURE 16.4 Selected linen requirements in dozens of units for a 200-seat foodservice operation for an average U.S. lodging establishment.

shown in Figure 16.3. To determine the annual cost of linens, one additional step is required. You must obtain purveyor bids for the number and types of linens you require.

LAUNDRY LAYOUT AND UTILITIES

This section and the one following apply only to an on-premises laundry. The suggested general space layout for a laundry is shown in Figure 16.5. It is most important to provide for one-way linen flow throughout the space and a final linen control point, the linen storage room.

The necessary laundry work areas are: receiving and sorting, general linen and uniform washing, extractor area, drying, ironing and folding, linen stor-

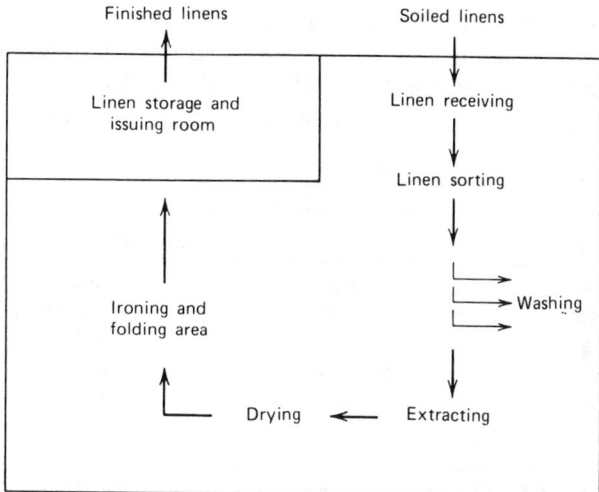

FIGURE 16.5 Suggested layout of general space for laundry installation.

age and issuing, linen repair (this is frequently included in the linen storage and issuing area), guest laundry, and dry cleaning for the property and guests.

Figure 16.6 indicates guidelines for space requirements and utilities. These are estimated requirements per guest room in lodging units. Variances from these estimates will exist because of equipment, linen soil to be removed, laundering procedures, and local practices.

SOFT-WATER REQUIREMENT

Most properties will soften water for the laundry. (Water softening was discussed in Chapter 12.) Hard water creates problems in the laundry.

Hard water contains salts that mix with soap and synthetic detergents to form a sticky substance called soap curd. This is a normal and natural chemical reaction involving hard-water salts and fats, oils, and alkali used in the manufacture of soap (or from linen soil). Soap curd sticks to linens, making them stiff and dirty. Soap curd builds up between linen fibers and causes fiber breakdown, thus greatly reducing linen life expectancy. In some hard-water areas, linen life expectancy is reduced by 50 percent or more compared to similar linens washed in soft water. Many establishments soften only hot water, which is satisfactory if only hot water is used in the laundry. Some washing formulas require medium-temperature water, a mixture of hot and cold water, and most rinse operations are cold water. The purpose of rinsing is to remove soap and other cleaning compounds from linens, but hard-water salts from unsoftened cold water may combine with soap entrapped in linens to form soap curd during rinsing.

The water-softening guidelines for a laundry are:

1. If the hardness is between 0 and 5 grains (0 and 85 ppm), synthetic detergents must be used for washing; water softening is not necessary. Synthetic detergents usually contain built-in water-softening agents to buffer, or soften, hard-water salts. Soap cannot be used when the hard-

Item	Requirements	
Space	4.5 square feet	0.42 square meter
Energy	3000 Btu	880 watts
Total water	8 gallons	30.2 liters
Hot water	4 gallons	15.1 liters
Cold water	4 gallons	15.1 liters
Linen (weight)	12 pounds	5.5 kilograms

FIGURE 16.6 On-premises laundry utility requirements per guest room (lodging) or patient bed (health care).

ness is much in excess of 0 grains (0 ppm) because excessive soap curd will be formed and rinsing will be difficult.

2. If the hardness is between 5 and 10 grains (85 and 171 ppm), a water-softening agent is required in addition to synthetic detergents. This procedure is generally less costly than installing a water-softening system for the laundry.

3. If the water hardness is 10 grains (171 ppm) or more, a complete water-softening system should be installed.

LAUNDRY EQUIPMENT CAPACITY AND COSTS

Figure 16.7 indicates the capacities of washing machines, extractors, dryers, and combination washer–dryers (used for uniforms, smaller linens, and guest laundry). Machine capacity is given in pounds (kilograms).

LAUNDRY LABOR AND SUPPLY REQUIREMENTS

Figure 16.8 shows estimated equipment and installation costs (assuming adequate utilities are available in the laundry area), laundry personnel requirements, and annual supply costs. The personnel requirements are total personnel (including supervisors for large properties—small units have working supervisors).

Item	Requirements	
Washer	1 pound	0.45 kilogram
Extractor	3/4 pound	0.33 kilogram
Dryer	1 pound	0.45 kilogram
Combination washer–dryer	1/2 pound	0.23 kilogram

FIGURE 16.7   On-premises laundry equipment requirements per guest room.

Item	Requirements/guest room
Equipment and installation costs	$100.00
Personnel	0.03
Annual supply costs	$52.00

FIGURE 16.8   On-premises laundry equipment and installation costs, personnel requirements, and annual supply costs per guest room for a lodging establishment laundry.

Figure 16.9 shows laundry equipment capacities and costs, personnel requirements, and annual supply costs for a 200-guest-room lodging establishment.

Appendix 12 compares the cost of various laundry alternatives based on the information presented in this chapter. It is only an example; you should not attempt to draw general conclusions from the appendix since cost factors vary significantly throughout the United States. Shown as a format for a feasibility analysis, it is accurate only for an area that has similar costs and for the indicated size of lodging unit with similar guest room and foodservice requirements.

LAUNDERING PRINCIPLES

CONVENTIONAL LINENS

Conventional linen laundering depends on wash and rinse cycles, water temperature and pH, fabric type, and soil characteristics.[2, 3] Water quality is especially important. There are many types of soil, with various reactions to water type and linen materials; hence, rules that cover all combinations cannot be given here. Only very general statements that have nearly universal application are made in this chapter.

Laundering Process

Because detailed scientific cleansing reactions are difficult to develop, the best local laundering practices are based on experience. It is known that the factors listed in the preceding paragraph are critical, but three other conditions are also known to affect laundering: cleanser concentration (ratio of cleanser to water and/or soil), time for cleanser to react with soil and linen

Item	Requirements/Costs	
Washer	200 pounds	90 kilograms
Extractor	150 pounds	68 kilograms
Dryer	200 pounds	90 kilograms
Combination washer–dryer	100 pounds	45 kilograms
Personnel	6 persons	
Purchase and installation costs	$40,000	
Annual supply costs	$10,400	

FIGURE 16.9 On-premises laundry equipment and personnel requirements; equipment purchase and installation costs; and supply cost for a 200–guest-room lodging establishment (see Figures 16.7 and 16.8).

material, and mechanical agitation. See Figure 16.10. Figure 16.11 shows the general laundering process.

pH

Assuming that soft water is available, the next critical factor is water pH. Various types of laundry water pH-measuring kits are available. However, water conditions are frequently stable for a given location, so one has only to measure the chemicals (weight or volume) for given volumes of water to adjust for pH. For example, if 2 pounds (0.9 kilogram) of a certain chemical will increase the pH of half a tub of water to a desired level, 4 pounds (1.8 kilograms) are required for a full tub of water.

There are normally six to eight different wash–rinse operations. Some of these operations are repeated several times in a given washing cycle. The pH is usually different for each operation. These are shown in Figure 16.12. The length of the wash cycle varies from 3 to 5 minutes (180 to 300 seconds). Seldom is a wash cycle more than 5 minutes (300 seconds). The effectiveness of the cleaning compound is greatly reduced after this short time period, and little additional soil is removed from linens in longer washing operations.

Examples of Laundering Cycles

Wash cycles vary with both the amount of soil and the type of linens. A few examples will be shown, which will indicate how both soil and linen types influence the cycle. Figure 16.13 shows a typical laundering cycle for heavi-

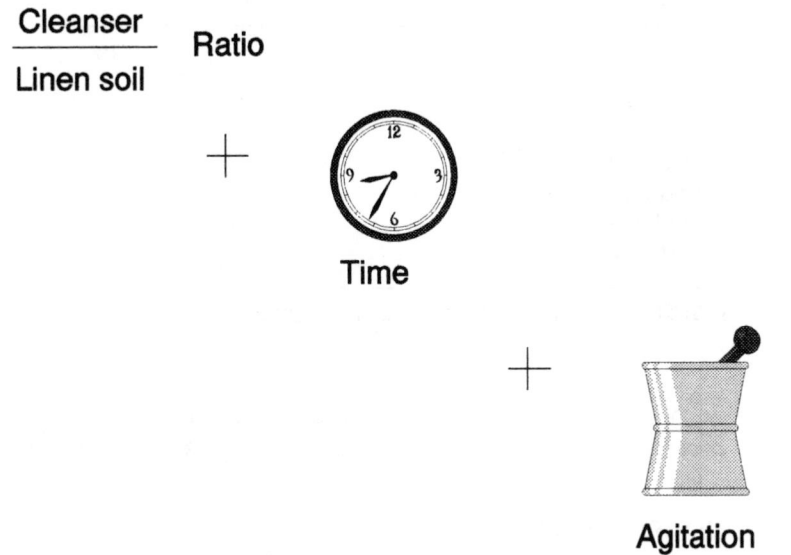

FIGURE 16.10 Laundering process factors.

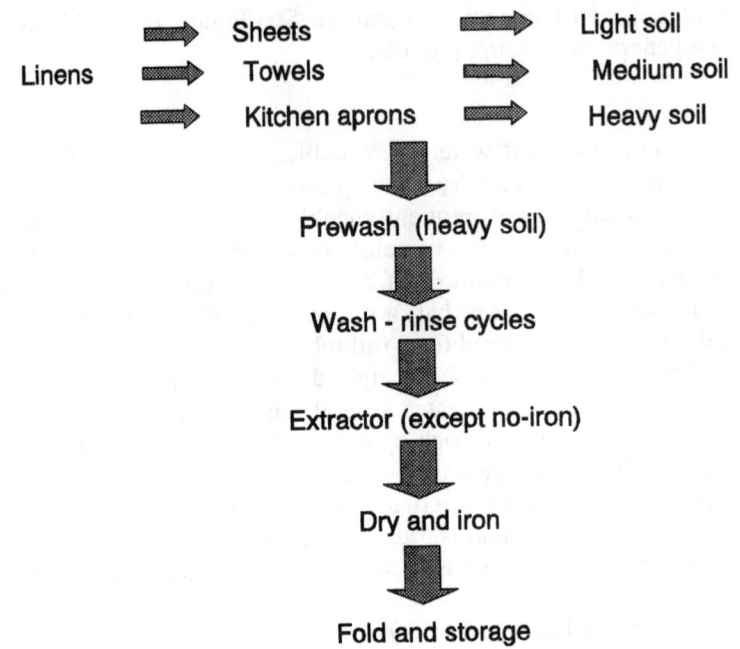

FIGURE 16.11 General laundering process.

Operation	pH
First wash (first suds)	11–11.6
Other washes	10.6
First rinse	10.0
Other rinses	<10.0
Neutralizing rinse	5.0
Final rinse (flatwork)	6.0
Bacterial-control rinse	4.0–4.5
Rust-stain-removal rinse	3.5–4.0

FIGURE 16.12 Wash–rinse operations and water pH.

ly soiled sheets, pillowcases, and towels. Figure 16.14 shows a laundering cycle for lightly and medium-soiled sheets, pillowcases, and towels.

NO-IRON LINENS

No-iron linens have changed the laundering alternative views of many lodging and health-care facility managers. Many managers have installed on-

Operation	Temperature
Initial wash	100°F (37.8°C)
Hot-water rinse	Maximum
Wash	150°F (65.6°C) + bleach
Hot-water rinse	Maximum
Medium-temperature rinse	1/2 hot + 1/2 cold
Cold rinse	Cold
Cold rinse	Cold
pH—see Figure 16.12	

FIGURE 16.13 Laundering cycle for heavily soiled sheets, pillowcases, and towels.

Operation	Temperature
Initial wash	100°F (37.8°C)
Hot-water wash	Maximum
Hot-water rinse	Maximum
Hot-water rinse	Maximum
Cold rinse	Cold
Cold rinse	Cold + bluing
pH—see Figure 16.12	

FIGURE 16.14 Laundering cycle for medium or lightly soiled sheets, pillowcases, and towels.

premises laundries because of the apparent ease of working with no-iron linens. It is felt that no-iron linens reduce laundering time and costs. However, experience has shown that savings are not always achieved.[1] Savings have resulted because of better laundry management; there are fewer management problems in the laundry when no-iron products are used.

Although managers of health-care units have wanted to use no-iron linens, they have been greatly concerned about whether these linens can be sanitized. Research has generally shown, however, that germ control has not been a problem with low-temperature washing and the lack of high heat in drying and ironing these linens.

USA L24 Standard

In the purchase of no-iron linens and fabrics, the USA L24 Standard should be met. Product quality, service, and life will be comparable to those of high-quality cotton linens and fabrics. These specifications generally require a mixture of 50 percent polyester and 50 percent cotton.[4]

The 20°F (11.1°C) Maximum-Temperature-Change Rule

No-iron laundering requires soft water for all washes and rinses. An especially critical factor for no-iron linens and fabrics is temperature control. The maximum temperature difference between two successive laundering operations is 20°F (11.1°C). This requirement also applies to drying the products. If the 20°F (11.1°C) temperature-difference rule is exceeded, wrinkled linens will result. These wrinkles can be removed only by repeating the complete laundering cycle.

Examples of Laundering Cycles

A recommended wash cycle for fabrics with light soil is shown in Figure 16.15. Figure 16.16 shows the recommended wash cycle for heavily soiled fabrics.

TRENDS AND MAINTENANCE CONSIDERATIONS

Automated laundering equipment is becoming very common in small, as well as large, on-premises laundries. Enhanced microprocessor technology provides for the programming of such variables as wash time, water levels and temperatures, and detergent injection, depending on the type of fabric.

Operation	Temperature
Wash	100–200°F (37.8–48.9°C)
Wash	100–200°F (37.8–48.9°C)
Rinse	100°F (37.8°C)
Rinse	100°F (37.8°C)
Extractor—maximum: 20 seconds	

FIGURE 16.15   Laundering cycle for medium or lightly soiled no-iron fabrics.

Operation	Temperature
Wash	120°F (48.9°C)
Wash	135°F (57.2°C)
Rinse	150°F (65.6°C)
Rinse	135°F (57.2°C)
Rinse	120°F (48.9°C)
Rinse	100°F (37.8°C)
Extractor—maximum: 20 seconds	

FIGURE 16.16   Laundering cycle for heavily soiled no-iron fabrics.

While it might be argued that the cost of repairing microprocessor machines is reason enough to select simpler units, the use of such technology continues to increase. And because of the difficulty of retaining laundry personnel, increasing emphasis is being placed on control technology that can be operated with minimal training requirements (inserting microprocessor printed circuit boards or selecting one of several cycles directly programmed on various machines).

Another trend in laundries is high-speed washer–extractors. This results in less moisture retention in fabrics and significant energy savings in drying time.

Laundering equipment requires considerable maintenance. Washer, extractor, and dryer drive trains (transmissions) require continuous service, because of the mass and weight of materials being agitated, accelerated to high-speed spins, and deceleration. Water pumps get clogged with linen fabrics (stockings) and must be disassembled, cleaned, and put back together. Filters must be cleaned daily. Electric driving motors of the appropriate size horsepower (wattage) ratings require minimal maintenance. Controlling units must be periodically replaced, because of misuse. A common control misuse is attempting to change the equipment setting after the cycle is started. This simple error is equivalent to the following automobile driving situation: driving down the road at a moderate speed and shifting the automobile automatic transmission into reverse; this results in a very high repair cost.

Laundry maintenance data are difficult to obtain. However, selected lodging studies have indicated that one full-time-equivalent maintenance person is usually required for the on-premises laundry for every 200 to 300 lodging guest rooms. This implies that two persons may be required to replace or repair a large washer drive train to get the laundry back into operation in a short time period. While, at other times, several days may pass before a laundry work order is processed.

SUMMARY

Decision making as to laundering alternatives is cyclic. Every 10 years, a property usually evaluates the feasibility of continuing as it has in the past versus adopting a new laundering alternative. This is particularly true for lodging, health-care, and institutional establishments. In each case, a thorough investigation is required to determine if the property should select one of the following alternatives: purchase linens and operate an on-premises laundry; purchase linens and use an off-premises commercial laundry; rent linens; use disposable products in place of linens; or use a combination of these alternatives.

Frequently, the selection of an alternative is based on costs, which depend on the size of the unit (number of guest rooms or beds). Several relationships, as well as industry cost data, are supplied in this chapter, which should serve as a guide to assist you in determining the best alternatives. Economic cost models must consider all basic costs but still provide you with the flexibility to analyze nonqualitative (noncost) information, such as personnel skills and selection, management problems, dependability of local services, and guest, customer, patient, and client input.

Linen-purchasing specifications, wear factors, theft control, and the amount of linens you could use in your operation are topics better addressed in a more specific study. Only guidelines of universal application are given here.

It should be understood that the laundry industry is highly mechanized. The laundry consumes large amounts of energy, and it may place additional repair and maintenance requirements on the chief engineer and his or her staff. All these factors must be considered by the manager.

REFERENCES

1. Borsenik, F. D., *Lodging Laundering Practices and the Feasibility of Using Disposable Linens in the United States*, Research Report, School of Hotel, Restaurant, and Institutional Management, Michigan State University, East Lansing, 1972. (Cost data were updated in this chapter to reflect 1995 costs and prices.)

2. Bradley, L. A., *The Selection, Care, and Laundering of Institutional Textiles*, Cornell University, School of Hotel Administration, Ithaca, NY, 1967.

3. *The No Iron Laundry Manual*, American Hotel & Motel Association, New York, 1970.

4. *USA L24 Standard*, American National Standards Institute, New York, 1963.

QUESTIONS/PROBLEMS

1. Determine space, equipment, and energy requirements for the laundry of a lodging establishment with 300 guest rooms.

2. Discuss the feasibility of each of the laundry alternatives discussed in this chapter for your location.

3. Determine the number of laundry personnel required to staff a laundry for a 300-guest-room lodging establishment, and analyze where

the laundry manager would best fit into the organizational structure of the establishment.

4. What noneconomic factors should be considered when selecting a laundry alternative for each of the following establishments?
   a. Lodging
   b. Foodservice
   c. Health care
   d. Club
   e. Institutional

5. Outline the components of the operational guidelines you would recommend for a laundry.

6. If your executive housekeeper told you that it would be more cost effective for the property to rent linen than to open an on-premises laundry, what information would you need to evaluate this statement?

CHAPTER 17

Courtesy of the Hyatt Regency, Dallas.

EXTERIOR SYSTEMS

ABSTRACT

This chapter addresses the basic principles of roofing, facades, windows and doors, signage, parking, and grounds management. Roof types might be flat or sloped and built-up, single ply, or metallic. The facade is the building's exterior walls. Windows and doors must be given the same amount of attention as the roof and facade. In the past few years, a number of technical innovations in glass and window design have enhanced their energy efficiency. There are four types of sign systems: identification, directional, informational, and regulatory. If the cost of land exceeds the cost of a parking structure, a parking deck will prove more economical: Lower land costs generally support on-grade parking. Landscape and grounds management is becoming a more significant part of hospitality building operations. A landscape that is both functional and attractive is the result of careful planning and analysis.

Key words: *Americans with Disabilities Act Accessibility Guidelines (ADAAG); alligatored; anodize; bitumen; built-up roofing (BUR); delamination; elastometer; ethylene interpolymer (EIP); heat mirror glass; infrared (IF); landscape architect; low E glass; polymer; sharkfins; superglass; supersmart glass; thermoplastic roof; threshold.*

INTRODUCTION

The exterior systems of hospitality buildings are becoming a larger part of the engineering responsibility. These systems, if left unattended or allowed to deteriorate, can cause significant damage to the interior of the building and can also result in customer dissatisfaction and inconvenience.

513

This chapter will examine the basic principles of engineering management as applied to roofing, facades, windows and doors, signage, parking, and grounds.

ROOFING

Overhead and out of sight, roofs are often left unattended in the overall management of a building. Their performance is frequently taken for granted. A roof is neglected until a problem is obvious and it stands a good chance of failing well before reaching design life. It is more than a roofer's self-respect that is on the line when he declares the roof is the most important integral component of a building. A roof protects everything else in the building from weather elements.

Every dollar of damage a roofing system sustains will typically result in at least another ten dollars of damage to the building below. A leaky roof does not drip down to an empty floor. It drips, instead, to ceiling fixtures, equipment, carpeting, and other expensive items within the building.

Unfortunately, a roof is subject to harsher conditions than any other part of a structure. It experiences the full direct impact of rain, snow, sunlight, and temperature extremes; it can be damaged by workmen and equipment, pooling water, and wind-driven dirt. Only regular inspections and maintenance will prevent these stresses from developing into serious problems.

The roof is composed of a deck and a covering. Decking is typically either wood, metal, cementitious wood fiber, structural concrete, lightweight insulating concrete, or gypsum. Coverings are either shingles, sheet metal, or membranes. Figure 17.1 identifies typical flat and sloping roofs.[1]

TYPES OF ROOFING

Built-up roofing systems (BURs) consist of overlapping layers of bituminous-saturated roofing felt. The various layers are cemented together with bituminous cement; and the top layer is generally coated with gravel, a mineral fiber, or a smooth surface coating. Coal tar pitch is reinforced with cellulose plies and covered with embedded gravel or slag.

Single-ply roofs are either elastomers, thermoplastics, or modified bitumens. Elastomers, if cured, are also known as a thermoset and might appear as vulcanized rubber. Uncured elastomers cure over time after the roof is installed and take on the properties of a cured elastomer.

Thermoplastic roofs are nonvulcanized—they soften when heated and harden when cooled. Common thermoplastics are polyvinyl chloride (PVC) and ethylene interpolymers (EIPs).

Fiberglass-reinforced roofs are composed of asphalt reinforced with a fiberglass mat and covered with embedded gravel or slag.

Flat Roofs
Built-up asphalt
Coal tar pitch
Single-ply sheeting
Fiberglass-reinforced
Sheet metal
Modified bitumen
Spray-on foam and coating
Single-ply membrane
Sloping Roofs
Composition shingles
Exotic shingle materials (wood, tile, slate, metal)
Mineral surface composition
Roll roofing
Sheet metal

FIGURE 17.1   Roofing types: flat and sloping.

Modified bitumen roofs include sheets of bitumen, modifiers, and a rein-forcement of either glass fiber felt or fabric. Self-adhering systems are cold applied by pressing the surfaces together; non-self-adhering systems consist of preformed sheets that usually are installed with hot asphalt or bitumen.

Steel and aluminum are the most common metallic roof materials.

Climates affect the roof type. In the South, for example, prolonged high temperatures and humidities attack the roofing membrane. A well-draining, light-reflecting membrane should be used. This may also reduce air-condi-tioning costs. In the North, high-strength roofing membranes with better elongation properties are best suited to resist the low-temperature stresses placed on a roofing system.

HISTORY AND INSPECTION

An effective roof management system depends on recording information about roof condition in a meaningful format on a regular basis. A good start-ing point for record keeping is a roof history. Figure 17.2 illustrates what information might be kept in the history. After these items are initially recorded, the roof history can be updated when inspections or repairs are made. This information helps ensure that any alteration will be consistent with the original specifications, and that materials used for repair or remod-eling will be compatible. It also helps pinpoint areas of ongoing problems so that long-term solutions can be found. A scaled aerial photograph is also a valuable tool for locating roof landmarks and dispatching contractors.

Regular inspections are essential to a preventive-maintenance program. The assumption that a roof is a "given" will be proven faulty when minor problems soon become major problems that consume valuable manpower.

As-built specifications and relevant changes
Roof plan showing location of all penetrations and roof-top equipment
As-built drawings of construction details directly related to the roofing system, such
  as flashing, deck, etc.
Minutes of pre-job conference, including list of persons present
Reports by job inspector during application, including weather conditions, materials
  used, code numbers on packaging, identifying areas completed each day
Materials manufacturer specifications and brochures for each component
All correspondence or notes between parties involved with the installation of the roof
Roof bonds or guarantees from manufacturer and/or roofing contractor
Report on previous maintenance inspections
Report on any corrective action taken
Record of any changes made to or on roof surface or substrate and copies of letter
  notifying roofing manufacturer of such changes
Record of new mechanical equipment installations and dates

FIGURE 17.2 Basic information for a roof history.

Roofs should be inspected in the spring to identify any problems that need to be corrected during the summer weather and in the early fall to correct any problems before winter.

The roof inspection should begin inside with a search for leaks, evident in discolored ceiling tiles, rust spots, peeling paint, or warped deck material. Unfortunately, by the time this happens, interior repair or redecoration may be required in addition to extensive repairs to the roof. Regular preventive maintenance can prevent leaks.

The inspection then moves to the top of the building. The first phase is a perimeter walk to assess general conditions and examine components at the roof's edge. Specifically, blocked drains, broken coping, loose or missing flashing, unsealed termination points, loose mortar, or deteriorated or open joints should be noted, for they create potential paths for water to enter the building.

Upon completion of a perimeter inspection, the roof should be examined section by section. Particular attention should be given to equipment penetrations, curbs around power fans, and skylights to make sure the flashing is complete and well adhered, providing no opening for water. Inspection around equipment wires will determine whether movement has opened holes in the roof surface.

A serious sign of a problem is ponded water on a particular section of a roof. Collected water can accelerate leaking and damage insulation. The weight of the water also adds stress to the supporting structure. A 1-inch (25.4-millimeter)-deep pond with an area of 100 square feet (9.3 square meters) weighs 520 pounds (236 kilograms), enough to cause the roof to sag eventually. Testing such sections with nondestructive infrared (IR) scan devices and nuclear moisture detectors, which are the X-rays of the roofing industry, will reveal if there is moisture in the roof.

Finally, the roof should be inspected for bare felt or delamination. Uniform ridges or "sharkfins" indicate waterlogged felt. Cracked or "alligatored" asphalt allows water entry. Tears or punctures in the coating or split laps in the membrane must be repaired to prevent deterioration of insulation underneath.

MAINTENANCE

The results of a roof inspection will facilitate maintenance decisions. Typically, minor maintenance will include: removing branches, leaves, and other debris from drain areas; resealing counterflashing, drains, metal work, equipment curbs, supports, and other rooftop accessories; and sealing small cuts or punctures and cracks.

Major repairs, including correcting the delamination of roofing felts, replacing cracked asphalt, or extensive foam replacement and recoating, are best left to qualified roofing applicators.

FACADES

The basic component of a building's facade is exterior walls. Moisture, water, pollutants, salt, and airborne contaminants that intrude into exterior walls cause a variety of costly problems.[2]

TYPES OF FACADE

Exterior wall coverings can be wood (shingles, weatherboard siding, plywood); concrete and masonry (brick, concrete, structural tile, stone, stucco); metal (corrugated iron or steel, aluminum, enamel-coated steel, protected metals); and mineral products (asphalt and fiberglass shingles, glass block).

There are many misconceptions about the durability of materials and the benefits of regular exterior maintenance. For example, stainless steel is not, in fact, stainless; though highly resistant to chemicals and corrosion, it does stain and once stains are embedded they are difficult to remove.

Stone, if maintained, will last indefinitely. However, if neglected, it will disintegrate in a short time. Unfortunately, because of atmospheric pollutants, some of the world's oldest buildings have deteriorated more in the last 40 years than they did over the centuries of their existence.

INSPECTION AND MAINTENANCE

Adequate maintenance depends in large part on geographic location. Highly urbanized areas, where emissions from cars compound acid rain (see the discussion in Chapter 18), demand more attention to maintenance than buildings in other areas. Foggy coastal conditions, which create heavy buildup of atmospheric salts and dirt, also create high maintenance conditions; in dry areas, the combination of limited rain, temperature fluctuations, and smog conditions are particularly damaging.

An annual inspection should include an examination for signs of leakage—for example, on masonry and metal buildings, mortar and expansion joints, metal seams, and any connections around windows, parapets, and stone caps.

Maintenance typically involves a cleaning or washing of the exterior surface. To ensure that no surface damage is sustained by the cleaning process, a test patch (20 square feet [1.86 square meters]) should be treated with the cleaning materials to ascertain potential chemical reaction and to determine the strength of cleaning necessary. A major and always damaging error in cleaning building exteriors is the use of an inappropriate product. For example, some chemicals applied to marble will clean it but will also turn it yellow. Fluorides will clean anodized aluminum but will ruin duranatic aluminum by stripping its electrolytic finish. A week's lapse is often necessary to judge the results of the cleaning test. Figure 17.3 illustrates a typical cleaning process.

Carefully selected and properly applied damp-proofing, waterproofing, and consolidation agents can help reduce maintenance. While a variety of protectors are available, including wipe-ons for anodized aluminum, most are designed for stone and masonry.

The effect of damp proofing on stone or masonry is to repel water by changing the contact angle between the water and the capillary pores. Silicone is the most often mentioned damp-proofing agent. Waterproofing can be accomplished in a number of ways, including joint waterproofing, paint, silicone, transparent waterproofer, and interior-wall-face waterproofing.

However, none of these alternatives can substitute for a well-constructed building, and none should be used to fill cracks in place of pointing or mortaring. Some coatings actually retain the dirt more than the uncoated masonry. There is some evidence that these coatings may actually cause greater deterioration than air pollution.

Select the mildest cleaning method for initial cleaning (for stone and masonry progress from handwashing to high pressure water to high pressure steam and chemicals)

Clean from the top of the building down

Minimize cleaner rundown and eliminate streaking by rinsing rundown immediately

Clean recesses but do not permit chemicals to puddle on horizontal surfaces or collect in joints and crevices

Avoid excessive rubbing

Use adequate water

Protect seals, gaskets, windows, and doors from strong solvents

---

FIGURE 17.3   Exterior facade cleaning principles.

Another aspect of facade maintenance is graffiti. This type of vandalism costs property owners millions of dollars annually for cleanup, not to mention irreparable damage. In the past, graffiti was almost impossible to remove effectively. The only alternatives were to repaint the defaced surface or, as a last resort, to sandblast the affected area. Sandblasting is costly and messy and destructive to the surface—it can be as debilitating as graffiti. In certain locations, sandblasting is against the law for environmental reasons.

Chemical graffiti removers can be effective in combating the problem. However, though often promoted by their manufacturers as "miracle" products that can remove anything and everything, this is an overstatement.

Graffiti removal depends on the type of surface on which it appears and the type of material that was used to apply it. Graffiti applied to masonry soaks into the surface and is very difficult to remove. Since a graffiti artist might use aerosol spray paint, felt-tip marker, nail polish, or shoe polish, several removers might be necessary. For example, the compounds typically involved in paints and inks can most effectively be removed using either a strong solvent-type compound or a strong caustic material or both. Both of these can damage the facade in the process of removing the graffiti. A small area should be tested before a complete application.

Typically, an alkaline/caustic stripper is applied to the total area to be cleaned and then is rinsed completely with high-pressure water. The alkaline stripper works especially well on porous surfaces because it is a slow-working product. It must remain on the surface for several hours or even overnight. The cleaner should be rinsed from the surface using high-pressure pumping equipment.

Solvent strippers will often remove various types of graffiti that alkaline strippers may not affect. Such strippers often work in as little as 15 minutes (0.25 hour) to one hour.

Graffiti problems can often be minimized by an anti-graffiti coating. Urethane-based graffiti control coatings are tough and allow several removals of graffiti with common cleaners before recoating becomes necessary. Removing graffiti from a protected surface is a much simpler process, often accomplished with one application of a removal product. The disadvantage of graffiti control products is that they may darken the surface. Thus, they should be applied up to a visible line on the building to make the darkening effect less noticeable. Penetrating sealers and water-repellent products can also protect a surface from graffiti, but because these products do not provide a continuous film over the pores of the masonry, graffiti is not nearly as easy to remove.

WINDOWS AND DOORS

Windows and doors must be given the same amount of attention as the roof and facade. Major problems associated with windows and doors include surface (frame) disintegration; swelling and warping; inferior hardware fasteners, weatherstripping, and workmanship.

WINDOWS

A building with windows is certainly something we take for granted. However, government estimates suggest that the equivalent of 1.7 billion barrels (270 billion liters) of oil are wasted every year on energy lost through windows. The most easily recognized shortcoming of glass is its poor insulation performance. A single pane of glass 1/4 inch (6.35 millimeters) thick, typical of many commercial and residential building windows, has 10 to 20 times the heat loss of an insulated wall.

Reducing the size and number of windows may reduce a building's energy load, but in the process may also drive customers and guests away. In the 1970s, many windowless structures erected to save energy were retrofitted with windows after negative responses from building users.

Window glass might be single pane, double pane, triple pane, low E, heat mirror, superglass, or supersmart.

Most window glass installed before the mid-1970s was single pane. A single layer of glass has an insulating value of about 1 R, making these windows very energy inefficient. Double-pane windows are two layers of glass with a sealed space between the layers. The first so-called thermal windows, rating about 2 R, began to appear in the early 1970s.

Triple-pane or triple-glazed windows, rated about 3 R, appeared for a time in the late 1970s but have largely disappeared in their original form of three layers of plain glass with sealed spaces between each glass. The significantly increased weight of the window can cause suspension or stress problems.

A relatively new type of glass is called low-emissivity (low-E) glass. These special windows, usually double glazed, have been available for several years and are rated 4 R if the space between the panes is filled with gas, usually argon. Without the gas, they rate about 3 R. The low-emissivity label results from a metallic coating on the glass that helps reflect heat. In cold climates, the coating is generally on the inner glass so heat is reflected back into the room; in warm climates, the coating goes on the outer pane to help minimize radiant heat, much like aluminum foil. The coating gives the windows a slightly dark tint, usually most noticeable from outside.

Heat mirror is one of several special window technologies developed by scientists at the Massachusetts Institute of Technology. A heat-mirror window has a colorless film of plastic suspended and sealed between two panes of glass. The plastic has a very thin metallic coating that reflects radiant heat and blocks out virtually all ultraviolet light. Argon gas is added between the panes for extra insulation, bringing the rating to 4.5.

Superglass windows have two heat-mirror films, suspended and sealed between two panes of glass. All spaces between the panes are filled with gas. The combination typically yields an R 8 insulating value.

Supersmart glass windows have a claimed R value of 9.09. They are manufactured with three layers of glass with sealed spaces in between. The outer glass layers have low-E coatings and the spaces between the outer and central glass are filled with argon gas.

Windows should be inspected regularly. For wood-frame windows, inspect loose-fitting frames, damaged frames and moldings, ill-fitting or broken sashes, deteriorated putty or trim, and hardware and other operating parts. For metal-frame windows, inspect rusting, warping, and sticking of the operating device.

The frequency of window washing depends on the environment but typically should occur at least twice a year. Washing speed varies but typically should occur at the rate of 300 to 400 square feet per hour (91.5 to 122 meters) per side, depending on location, window type, and ladder/equipment requirements.

DOORS

Exterior doors are subject to more abuse and weathering than interior doors. However, for both types, defects and corrective measures are similar.

Doors should be dusted periodically, the frequency depending on the environmental exposure conditions. At least twice a year, the door and frames should be washed using a mild detergent compatible with the material of the door. An expected average labor productivity for cleaning both sides of the door and frames is about seven doors per hour.

Doors should be inspected quarterly for: installation failures; deteriorated or damaged frames; paint or surface deterioration; material damage, such as cracked or broken glass; and broken or inoperative hardware.

An inventory should be maintained of door hardware, including door closing devices, lock sets, thresholds, bolts and screws, and so forth. The inventory should include: manufacturer, type and style, date purchased, date installed, contractor for installation, maintenance instructions, and chronological record of repair and replacement.

SIGNAGE

A sign system is a comprehensive collection of visual communication elements, consisting of four basic types: identification, directional, informational, and regulatory. Typically, the most important factor in signage is design. Unfortunately, it is a common practice to put up signs with little thought to the total impact of all the signs as an integrated system.

The major objectives to be accomplished by a sign system are:

1. Promoting the property's identity by subtly, but constantly, reminding the guests where they are.
2. Setting the mood, the lifestyle, of the property by using a well-thought-out and tasteful sign.
3. Supplementing the marketing effort by establishing a feeling of value in the visual perception of the property.
4. Providing information to guests about the location and use of the amenities to promote maximum use.
5. Regulating or influencing the user's behavior by advising what can or cannot be done.

A property contemplating the purchase of a new signage system should take steps to ensure that both the designer and the fabricator are knowledgeable about the type of material to be used (wood, native stone, metal); decisions in these areas can have a significant impact on cost, appearance, longevity, and versatility.

As a greater number of international visitors become part of a property's clientele, colors and symbols should be used. The four most prominent colors and their meanings are:

Green:	Safety and Escape
Red:	Stop, and Fire Equipment
Yellow:	Caution and Hazard
Blue:	Direction and Information

In *One World-One Language*, a brochure published by the American Hotel & Motel Association, a comprehensive list of international symbols for information, safety, warning, fire, prohibition, and telephone communication are illustrated.

Several key elements must be considered when designing an identification sign. It must:

1. Duplicate the property's logo, logo type, and colors as is practical.
2. Complement the architectural theme of the property through the choice of materials, colors, and details, even if the sign does not actually duplicate the architecture.
3. Be of proper scale for its environment. Obviously, it must be readable,

but it is important aesthetically that it not overpower or detract from its setting.

A sign system is best described as a family of graphic and visual communication devices, which are related by similar elements of materials, color, typography, shape, and overall design. In practical terms, this definition simply means that all the signs on a property should complement, not compete with, each other.

Signs are usually purchased in response to a specific need, with the tendency for each sign to be made without regard for other signs on the property. After awhile, this creates a jumbled look of colors, shapes, lettering styles, and quality levels. Such a problem is usually not even noticed by management and staff, for they do not depend on signs to inform them about the property; hence, they do not really pay attention to them. Because a signage system must be at once attractive and functional, its proper design is almost always a blend of creativity and practicality. Accordingly, implementing a new sign program consists of three phases, which includes planning, design, and execution.

In the planning phase, the property is studied to determine what signs are needed where. No concern is given at the time to what these signs will look like, as this occurs in the second, or design, phase. Signs might be categorized as identification, directional, informational, and regulatory.

Within each of these types, one would make additional distinctions regarding each particular sign. This would include a range of criteria: whether the sign would be seen by vehicular or pedestrian traffic, whether it identified something very significant or quite incidental, whether the viewer is being casually advised or strongly warned of something.

For example, of particular importance is a property's entryway sign. When locating this sign, consider right-of-way clearance, visual clearance, material, and landscaping. A sign placed beyond the property line onto the right-of-way can result in legal entanglements; if set apart from the building landscape, it also protrudes unnaturally.

After each required sign is identified, it will become part of a master sign schedule, itemized by sign types. From this schedule, a locator map is developed, which will show the location, message, and reading direction of each sign.

Visual clearance must also be considered. Modern signs tend to be large, so it is necessary to set them well back from road intersections. Traditional signs and their plantings call for flat gradients; contemporary designs frequently use rolling contours, often setting the sign on a carefully graded eminence. However, such a berm needs to be set back to allow ample corner visibility for all passing traffic. The sign must also be proportioned to its setting. It should be readable to travelers while they drive by at reasonable speeds.

The sign plan once developed should be reviewed by those departments that depend on signs in the course of their operations. By doing this review in the first phase of the sign program, participants can focus on message and location without the personal preferences, likes, and dislikes that may surface when subjective topics such as color and design are introduced. At the same time, this procedure provides the opportunity for more clearly distinguishing the functional needs of signage from the aesthetic and image considerations that are important to the marketing needs of the property.

Choosing sign material can be a problem. If a sign is reasonably close to a building, select materials that duplicate or are compatible with the building materials. If a sign is far from any building, select materials and a design style compatible with the surroundings. For example, native stone is always attractive for a pedestal; in wooded areas, native sawed or whole logs might be used. A white board sign, well lettered and properly maintained, can also be attractive and appropriate. Anodized or oxidized metals and dressed but not overly polished granite, marble, slate, or other types of stone are appropriate for signs if they reflect the surroundings.

Landscaping around an entryway sign determines the sign's ultimate attractiveness. A well-groomed sweep of ground from the nearest pavement up to and beyond the sign is the first consideration. The surface might be mowed lawn or desert sand, but it should look as if it receives constant grooming, including appropriate trimming around the sign base or at the margins of plantings abutting the sign. No matter how elegant and appropriate the entry sign and landscape design, inadequate maintenance can ruin the entire effect. Plantings should be selected to complement, not obscure, the sign; they should be properly proportioned to the sign and its base. For example, a narrow hedge of greenery around the base of a sign usually looks out of place.

Plant in broad sweeps, using unobtrusive but stylish, low-spreading species. If the plantings are to be higher than the sign, they should be planted well behind it. Do not bury a handsome sign in dense shrubbery; keep bushes yards away from the sign so the viewer has a feeling of depth.

Sometimes it is appropriate to have a trace of plant material on a sign. A base of ashlar limestone can make a sign look large and stark, but a trace of English ivy or Englemann's creeper will break up that harsh look.

It is essential that the person who decided to obtain, and has the authority to approve, a new sign system be responsible for reviewing the design concepts. After approval of the design concepts, including any modifications that can result from the review, the designer proceeds with the development of finished drawings. During this process, exact colors are selected, finished art is provided, layouts and dimensions are clarified, and specifications are developed. This complete package includes working drawings, specs, sign schedule, and locator map.

Sign manufacturers or vendors should be selected who can produce the type and quality of work that has been designed, and a negotiation or bidding process will determine who is selected. Depending on the size and scope of the project, it may make sense to produce samples or prototypes of some of the signs that will be used in volume. This enables all parties in the process to assess the appearance and function of an actual sign under real site conditions.

While installation is not a factor in a small sign program, it can have a significant impact on the function of the system in large programs. If signs are placed incorrectly, damaged in handling, or improperly installed, this will negate the significant effort and time devoted to planning and design.

PARKING, WALKS, AND DRIVES

The most common type of parking is on-grade. Where the size, configuration, and contours of a site are adequate to provide the required parking, on-grade is the least costly facility.

If the cost of land exceeds the cost of a parking structure, a parking deck will prove more economical; conversely, lower land costs generally support on-grade parking. In higher-density locations with accelerating land values, structured parking is generally the only choice. Structures include above-grade, below-grade, and composite parking.

Above-grade structured parking is a freestanding parking deck of two or more levels. The least expensive type of parking after on-grade, it provides optimum efficiency in terms of area, structure, and circulation. Below-grade is more expensive because of the structure and mechanical systems required.

Composite parking integrates above- and below-grade parking with the building above the structure. Typically, composite parking requires special ventilation and sprinkler systems, as well as a more elaborate facade.

Zoning laws usually establish minimum parking requirements. Three cars per 1000 square feet (93 square meters) is typical in suburban areas, fewer in urban areas, and more in low-density areas.

The *Americans with Disabilities Act Accessibility Guidelines* (ADAAG) calls for a sliding scale of accessible parking stalls from 4 percent in parking lots with 1 to 10 spaces down to 2 percent when the lot has more than 1000 spaces.

The parking space must be wide enough to allow a wheelchair user to open the door, transfer to the wheelchair, and easily exit to the walkway. This generally requires a 5-foot (1.5-meter)-wide access lane next to an 8-foot (2.5-meter)-wide stall. The access lane needs to be 8 feet (2.5 meter) wide in the case of van parking.

The efficiency of a parking structure has direct impact on the area per car required. Car module size and circulation are the two major factors in garage efficiency. Changes in parking/zoning codes, brought about in part by the decrease in standard car size and the increase in the number of compact cars, have resulted in a reduction in the parking stall size, thus decreasing the area required per car.

In most cases, concrete is the most efficient material for garages. Concrete obviates the problem of exposed steel and fire proofing in open, exposed garages while allowing for lower floor-to-floor height.

On-grade parking lot maintenance is an important aspect of property management. All parking lots, no matter how well designed and constructed, will deteriorate with the passage of time. The early detection and repair of minor defects is important. Cracks and other surface breaks, which in their first stages are almost unnoticeable, may develop into serious defects if not promptly repaired.

Keeping walks and drives clean and in good repair must also become part of the property's preventive-maintenance program. In order to keep repairs to a minimum, it is important to follow certain precautions. It is most important to ensure that harmful chemicals do not have contact with various surfaces (do not use salt to melt snow or ice on concrete; do not spill gasoline, kerosene, or other such liquids on asphalt surfaces).

Inspection should be made semiannually, preferably in the spring and the fall. Records should also be kept that detail the maintenance history of the surface. An inspection program designed to detect and repair cracks (alligator, reflective, shrinkage, slippage), pavement distortion, potholes, and skid hazard should be developed. Periodically, directional lines and other types of striping will have to be included in the preventive-maintenance program.

Repairs must be made as soon as possible after locating the defects. This is especially true with asphalt surfaces; because of the superimposed loadings and the nature of the material, once deterioration begins, further deterioration progresses at a rate faster than that for most materials. An important precaution that can be taken with asphalt surfaces is applying a sealer coat about six months after the surface has been constructed and one each year thereafter.

The ADAAG requires that the access lane from the parking area should lead to an accessible route that connects the parking area to the entrance. The accessible route should have no abrupt changes in level (bumps or steps) greater than 1/2 inch (3.25 millimeters), and ramps should be no steeper than a slope of 1 to 12.

No obstructions should hang over the accessible route that would present hazards to a person who has a visual impairment. The route should be a minimum of 36 inches (0.9 meters) wide to allow for people who use crutches or wheelchairs, and individuals carrying bags.

All walks on or around the site should have curb ramps where they cross curbs. They should be of a firm surface that is easily rolled upon and does not create a tripping hazard for somebody who has an even gait or uses crutches. Accessible walks should lead to the major entrances of the facility, which should also be accessible. At the front entrance, there should be an accessible drop-off, which has no changes in level, or a curb ramp. This makes it easy to roll carts, luggage, or wheelchairs from the vehicular area up to the entrance.

The entry doors must provide 32 inches (0.8 meters) of clearance when they are open at 90 degrees. This 32-inch (0.8-meter) clear width is required of all doors in new buildings, but is only a goal for existing buildings. For the most part, this will require a 3-foot (0.9-meter) door so there is adequate opening width when the door is open to 90 degrees. If there are vestibule doors, they must be designed and maintained so that they are easily negotiable by somebody who is carrying bags or is using a wheelchair or crutches.

LANDSCAPE AND GROUNDS MANAGEMENT

DESIGN

A landscape that is both functional and attractive, like a building with the same characteristics, is the result of careful planning and analysis. Because many grounds-management nightmares result from poorly conceived landscape plans, careful consideration must be given to evaluating the strengths and weaknesses of the site and containing grounds-management costs.

Most property managers will benefit from securing the services of a landscape architect to evaluate the site. A landscape architect understands soil, water, ornamental horticulture, and climatic factors and can also evaluate a site based on its proximity to markets, clients, and amenities. The landscape architect considers traffic patterns, access to highways, and other infrastructure conditions and availability to develop a landscape plan that capitalizes on all the site's strengths and minimizes damage to the natural environment. More than 40 states now require landscape architects to be licensed.[3]

There are countless landscaping strategies that can be adopted to minimize maintenance costs. However, as a rule of thumb, low-maintenance landscapes typically require the most costly capital expenditures at the outset.

Savings on maintenance costs can be realized by:

1. Using plants that, at maturity, are not much larger than when planted.
2. Using disease- and insect-resistant and drought-tolerant plants and

other materials that can be maintained without a great deal of human intervention.

3. Incorporating major planting beds, instead of grasses, into the landscape and avoiding annuals, which usually require a higher level of maintenance.

4. Spacing larger shrubs and trees closer together to minimize weeding.

5. Installing an automatic irrigation system.

6. Using only those grasses suitable for the climate and resistant to insect infestation and disease.

As illustrated in Figure 17.4, a substantial percentage of grounds-maintenance time and dollars will be expended on turf, tree, and shrub maintenance.

TURF

A turf-maintenance program includes mowing, fertilizing, liming, weeding, and irrigating. Mowing is usually the most costly phase of grounds maintenance; thus, it should be done as part of a routine maintenance program by trained personnel. Figure 17.5 illustrates some basic principles of a turf-maintenance program.

Fertilizers are plant foods that are applied to the soil to establish and maintain healthy, vigorous growth. Commercial fertilizers generally contain nitrogen, phosphate, and potash. The amount of each element required depends on the soil type, vegetation desired, and the climate. On commercial fertilizer labels, the first number indicates the percentage of available nitrogen, the second number indicates the percentage of available phosphate, and the third shows the percentage of available potash. For example, a 10-6-4 fertilizer contains 10 percent nitrogen, 6 percent phosphate, and 4 percent potash. The remaining 80 percent consists of inert materials.

It is important that the principal plant food elements be properly balanced when growing grasses and that this balance be maintained after the vegetation is established. The rate of application therefore varies and should be governed by the results of soil tests and the amount of rainfall.

Acid soils generally require liming to reduce their acidity and to increase the activity of important soil organisms. Lime is applied in the form of ground limestone, hydrated or burned lime, marl, oyster shells, and similar materials. Soil tests will indicate how much lime, if any, is required.

Weeds frequently invade turf as a direct result of inadequate maintenance. Although it is usually a relatively simple matter to kill most weeds, it is often difficult to prevent their return because of seed or unkilled portions of plants. There are many highly specialized matters involved in weed con-

Area/Operation	Frequency per Year		Time Required
TURF			
Mow 19" (0.48 meters) power	30	5	minutes* per 1,000 square feet
21" (0.53 meters) power self-propelled	30	4	(93 square meters)
48" (1.22 meters) power rider	30	29	minutes* per acre
72" (1.83 meters) power rider	30	24	
Edge trim and cleanup (with gas-powered equipment)			
Walks	30	25	minutes* per 1,000 linear feet
Shrub edge	10	60	(305) meters)
Fertilize			
Cyclone type	2	3	minutes* per 1,000 square feet
Weed Control		15	(93 square meters)
3-gallon (11.4 liters) hand pump	2	4	
Power rig 30" (0.76 meters) boom			
	2		
TREES			
Prune			
From ground	2	20	
Fertilize	1	30	
			minutes* per tree
Pest control			
Spray	3	20	
SHRUBS			
Prune	5	60	
Rertilize	1	5	minutes* per 1,000 square feet
Pest control	2	30	(93 square meters)

*Note:

5 minutes	= 300 seconds	25 minutes	= 0.42 hours	
4 minutes	= 240 seconds	60 minutes	= 1.00 hours	
29 minutes	= 0.48 hours	20 minutes	= 0.33 hours	
24 minutes	= 0.40 hours	30 minutes	= 0.50 hours	

FIGURE 17.4 Maintenance time for turf, trees, and shrubs.

trol; a complete program should be developed in cooperation with specialists before weed control projects are undertaken.[4]

In certain geographic locations where rainfall is not sufficient, irrigation will be necessary. Because of the costs associated with the purchase of water, careful consideration should be given to the use of moisture-sensing equipment.

TURF

Mowing
Keep mower blades sharp to minimize turf damage
Mow according to height rather than a fixed timetable: 1 to 1½ inches (25.4 mm to 38.1 mm) warm-season grass, 2 to 2½ inches (50.8 mm to 63.5 mm) cool-season grass

Fertilizing
Top dress cool-season grass in the spring or early fall
Top dress warm-season grass in the summer
Divide the annual amount into two or three applications per year

Liming
Quantities should be applied to correct excessive acidity from soil test samples
Fall application is most effective

Weed Control
Timely mowing of turf at proper height
Proper turf fertilization
Adequate irrigation

TREES AND SHRUBS

Protection from Equipment
Remove turf or soil and install a division strip to protect base from damage

Watering
Water deeply
Build dry wells around trees for watering tubes or pipes if the grade is to be changed.

Fertilizing
Spring application is most effective
Quantity dependent on trunk diameter or base

Pruning
Use clean, sharp tools
Avoid injury to adjacent growth, leaving cuts without lacerated edges
Seal cuts larger than a nickel with tree-wound dressing

FIGURE 17.5 Lawn, tree, and shrub maintenance principles.

TREES AND SHRUBS

Trees, once they have reached maturity, are one of the most expensive components of the landscape to replace. Basic maintenance for established trees and shrubs should include fertilizing, watering, and, in some cases, spraying. Periodic pruning will also become part of the maintenance schedule.

Watering trees and shrubs should be done only if rainfall is insufficient. Water enough to keep them healthy and to promote vigorous growth. Overwatering can be very damaging.

Trees should be encouraged to root deeply because the water supply will be more consistent and the roots will be less apt to feed on turf and gardens or to spread surface roots, which damage curbs and walks. However, because shrubs root at or near the surface, they must be watered at the surface.

Often, changes in a landscape can adversely affect existing plantings, in particular, trees. Typically, special protection must be provided for trees to survive exterior renovations. For example, most trees are sensitive to any important change in the depth of soil over their roots, particularly in high-rainfall areas and in clay soils. Thus, a breathing space (elevated concrete well and feeder tubes) will have to be provided for such plantings to survive.

The amount of fertilizing necessary is governed by the nature and condition of the soil in which plants are grown. After planting, the use of commercial fertilizers should be replaced with cow or steer manure to achieve maximum effectiveness and minimize damage to the plant.

Existing trees should be pruned to thin an overly dense crown, to shorten long or weak limbs, and to remove dead, dying, diseased, or injured wood. Pruning should be done during the season that produces the desired results. For example, spring-flowering plants are best pruned as flowers fade; summer- and fall-flowering plants are best pruned in the spring. Summer pruning tends to limit future growth; winter pruning often results in a vigorous burst of vegetative growth the following spring.

SUMMARY

This chapter addressed basic principles of roofing, facades, windows and doors, signage, parking, and grounds management.

Roofs are often left unattended in the overall management of a building. However, every dollar of damage a roofing system sustains will typically result in at least another ten dollars of damage to the building. The roof is composed of a deck and a covering. Roof types might be flat or sloped and built-up, single ply, or metallic. An effective roof-management system depends on recording information about roof condition on a regular basis.

The facade is the building's exterior walls. Moisture, water, and pollutants can cause a variety of costly problems. Adequate maintenance is determined in large part by geographic location and should consist of annual inspection and regular washing. Chemical removers can be effective in combating graffiti.

Windows and doors must be given the same amount of attention as the roof and facade. In the past few years, a number of technical innovations in glass and window design have enhanced their energy efficiency. Exterior doors are subject to more abuse and weathering than interior doors and should be inspected quarterly.

There are four types of sign systems: identification, directional, informational, and regulatory. Careful consideration should be given to signage design.

The most common type of parking is on-grade. If the cost of land exceeds the cost of a parking structure, a parking deck will prove more economical. Lower land costs generally support on-grade parking.

Landscape and grounds management is becoming a more significant part of hospitality building operations. A landscape that is both functional and attractive is the result of careful planning and analysis.

REFERENCES

1. Foley, J. M., "Roofing Design, Installation and Maintenance," *Buildings*, September 1985, pp. 132–136.

2. Bachner, J. P., *The Guide to Practical Property Management*, McGraw-Hill, New York, 1991.

3. Sternloff, R. E., and R. Warren, *Park and Recreation Maintenance Management*, 2nd ed., Wiley, New York, 1984.

4. Stutts, A. T., and F. D. Borsenik, "Turf, Trees, and Shrubs," *Maintenance Handbook for Hotels, Motels, and Resorts*, Van Nostrand Reinhold, New York, 1990.

QUESTIONS/PROBLEMS

1. Consult your local college or university operations-and-maintenance department or a hotel engineering department to evaluate its:
   a. Existing roof management plan
   b. Facade maintenance program
   c. Landscape and grounds management plan
   d. Parking facilities maintenance plan

2. Discuss the key elements of a roof management plan.

3. Evaluate the effectiveness of the signage used by your college or university, a local hotel, club, or hospital.

4. If your building has 500 windows, each measuring 5 x 10 feet (1.5 x 3 meters), how much time should be allocated in the maintenance

schedule for washing the exterior side? (Assume no special equipment or conditions are involved.)

5. If your grounds maintenance employees are compensated at the rate of $20.00 per hour, including benefits, estimate the annual cost of mowing a turf area of 2000 square feet (186 square meters) with a 19-inch (0.48 meter) mower compared to a 21 inch (0.53 meter) self-propelled power mower.

CHAPTER 18

Courtesy of Holiday Inns, Inc.

WASTE AND POLLUTION MANAGEMENT

ABSTRACT

This chapter considers the problems that solid waste, air pollution, and water pollution may present to the hospitality manager. The components of a management program to deal with the collection, treatment, and disposal of solid waste are considered, along with questions about the efficiency of solid-waste technology and equipment, such as motorized carts, compactors, incinerators, and disposal alternatives.

The chapter also considers the management problems of air pollution and acid rain, the importance of potable and recreational water, a management strategy for evaluating the present and future problems that water quality might present, and a description and evaluation of sewage disposal methods.

Key words: *acid rain; afterburner; agricultural gypsum; catchment area survey; cesspool; disposal fee; dumpster; effluent; fly ash; "green certification;" hydrilla; potable water; pulping; septic tank; soil absorption rate; toxic wastes; trash compactor; trash chute; Water Pollution Control Act.*

INTRODUCTION

The hospitality manager must develop a waste-management program and be aware of waste-management practices of other enterprises that may have an impact on the property. For instance, the management of solid wastes, that is, refuse and garbage, was not of great concern when disposal fees ranged from $7 to $15 per ton (907 kilograms). However, those fees now range from $11 to $20 or more per ton (907 kilograms), and they will continue to increase rapidly as the scarcity of landfills creates greater demand.

As public concern for the environment intensifies, the vision of corporate responsibility has broadened beyond its "good citizen" image of the 1980s to include ecology, conservation, recycling, and other environmental issues of the 1990s. Policymakers and industry have the challenge, responsibility, and mandate in the 1990s to bring market forces into harmony for environmental and social equity. With the advent of green labeling throughout parts of Europe and the Far East, the absence of a nationally recognized seal of environmental approval in the United States is increasingly conspicuous. In a Good Housekeeping and Roper Organization survey, 82 percent of the respondents confirmed that they would likely purchase a product with a "green certification." While green labeling has so far been linked to tangible products, it is only a question of time before it will encompass services.

Most state and local governments have or are developing stringent standards and regulations concerning water quality. Therefore, the hospitality manager must be concerned about the activities of the property that may pollute potable water as well as water supplies for recreational activities such as swimming, boating, and fishing.

The hospitality manager may also have to cope with the effects of such pollutants as sulfuric acids, nitric oxides, and sulfur dioxides. When these chemicals are mixed with air and combine with moisture, they result in a form of acid rain. Acid rain will corrode even durable surface building materials and can require that buildings be washed, a costly maintenance procedure.

This chapter will focus on property-management practices that directly and indirectly impact on problems generated by solid-waste management, air and water pollutants, and sewage disposal.

SOLID WASTES

The components of a management program to deal with solid wastes include collection and transportation within the facility and treatment and disposal outside the facility. A solid-waste-management program can also reduce the volume and toxicity of the garbage being sent to the landfill.

A facility survey is the key to an effective solid-waste-management program. The survey must identify: where solid waste is generated (housekeeping, food/beverage, engineering); the quantity of waste generated daily, weekly, and monthly; and the type of waste being produced, such as food waste, paper/rubbish, equipment parts, and scrap lumber. Once managers understand the source, composition, and volume of solid wastes, they can begin to address the most efficient methods of collection and transportation.

Collection and transportation are typically very labor intensive for a hotel, restaurant, club, or institution and can become very expensive. The efficiency of this operation may be improved with building trash chutes or by using motorized carts on the property.

TRASH CHUTES

In the design and renovation of buildings, especially high-rise structures, considerable thought should be given to the location of trash chutes within buildings. They should be centrally located and easily accessible to carts. Carts can be used to collect trash and transport it to the chute location. The chutes should deposit waste materials in a central storage area located at one of the lowest facility levels. Wastes should be directly deposited from the chute into carts to be carried to a dumpster or compactor servicing the building.

Many materials deposited in a trash chute are highly combustible, and local codes may require, or national standards recommend, that materials used to construct the chute, its doors, and termination point be carefully considered for fire and heat penetration.

Where trash chutes are utilized, they require maintenance to keep doors operating properly and regular cleaning to pass local sanitation and health-code requirements.

TRANSPORTING WASTES

Motorized carts can speed up the collection and transportation of solid wastes. However, this equipment also requires maintenance, such as charging the batteries of electric carts and complete motor or engine overhauls. In addition, staff training in safe operation of these vehicles is required.

Once materials have been transported to a central point, they can be disposed of directly into a dumpster, undergo compaction, or be incinerated. An open dumpster might best be suited for a facility generating a small volume of waste.[1] However, as the volume of waste increases, the cost efficiency of this system must be evaluated. Unless the property is hauling its own waste, there will be two components in a disposal fee. These include a tonnage (kilogram) fee based on the weight of the waste and a fee for each load hauled, regardless of weight. However, if waste is pulped, compacted, or incinerated before disposal, thus reducing the number of loads, hauling fees can be controlled.

Pulping is a relatively new technology for the hospitality industry. Such a system is designed to reduce paper/paperboard, yard materials, food, and plastics to a uniform, semidry pulp. Pulping is capable of handling 75 percent of the trash disposed. The system works by depositing waste into an input tray; it is then drawn into a whirling vortex of water and reduced to pulp by carbide steel cutters. It then enters a water press, where it is squeezed by a gear-driven helical screw to eliminate water through the screen sidewalls. A clean, moist pulp is discharged down a chute.

The system can be designed to fit under a counter or operate as a free-standing unit. Systems can be designed to situate the pulper in a kitchen area or in multiple building locations, with the water press on the disposal dock.

The savings of this system vary. A hospital in Illinois that typically serves meals to 500 people reduced meal waste to one garbage bag; and an employee cafeteria that serves 2600 to 3000 people at lunch reduced waste from 27 bags to 5 bags.

COMPACTORS

A trash compactor, such as the one illustrated in Figure 18.1, is typically located outside the building. Smaller versions, as shown in Figure 18.2, may be found in kitchen preparation or cleaning stations.

The compactor accepts raw waste and, by the use of hydraulic rams and plungers, reduces the volume of waste material by as much as 80 percent.

FIGURE 18.1 Stationary compactor (courtesy of International Dynetics Corporation).

FIGURE 18.2 Compactor for a foodservice operation (courtesy of International Dynetics Corporation).

The actual volume reduction depends on the type of waste materials placed in the compactor. Compactors are classified as stationary or self-contained. Stationary units include separate compaction and storage sections. As the storage section is filled with compacted waste, it can be disconnected from the compaction section, sealed, and hauled away for disposal. Extra wear is placed on the unit with each disconnect and reconnect. In addition, the risk of accidental waste spillage increases as the two components are disconnected.

The self-contained unit, which has a smaller capacity, combines the hydraulic compaction section and storage units together in the same unit. When waste is hauled away, both sections are transported, so that accidental spillage and disconnect/reconnect mechanical problems are reduced.

The manager should also consider: maximum unit capacity, required compaction force, size of waste deposit opening, and installation cost (available space without removing walls and doors and availability of a concrete pad on which the unit can be placed).

It is increasingly common to find units that provide compartments for sorting recyclable products and crushing them into 400- to 600-pound (180- to 275-kilogram) bales, greatly improving efficiency in refuse handling and cutting the number of trash pickups. Compacting recyclable products can improve the cost efficiency of hauls to the recycling depot.

INCINERATORS

Solid waste can also be incinerated. Small- to medium-sized incinerators are available that incorporate air pollution technology so that they meet legal requirements. Depending on the composition of the solid waste, incinerators can reduce the volume of waste by 85 to 90 percent. This results in reduced dumping and hauling fees. Incinerators may not be cost efficient unless a considerable volume of solid waste is generated on the property.

Incinerators, with the exception of the largest units, require a fuel source that will start and sustain waste product combustion. If waste material volume is large enough, incinerators can be equipped with heat recovery boilers for hot-water heating.

An incinerator typically requires licensed personnel for its operation and servicing to ensure that it operates within pollution control standards and local code requirements.

WASTE DISPOSAL

Waste disposal is also a component of a waste-management program. The landfill is the most common disposal method used in the United States. As the number of landfill sites decrease, large-scale incinerators may become the disposal points. The primary concern in disposal is transporting bulk, compacted, or incinerated waste to a disposal site. Two basic transportation options are available: hauling waste, utilizing personnel and equipment managed by the property; or contracting with a commercial waste hauler.

A cost-effective in-house system must have sufficient volume to keep in-house personnel busy five days a week. If waste volume is insufficient, a commercial hauler must be subcontracted for scheduled pickups. This agreement must be monitored to verify: the contracted number of pickups on the agreed day and time, dump container sanitation, and cleanup of the container area after a pickup is made.

In addition to the economic costs of dumping, in a time when landfills are rapidly filling up and shutting down, there is the problem that some solid waste (e.g., cleaning fluids, construction debris, discarded paint and solvents) will become toxic as it degrades and pose a threat to water supplies.

The costs can be minimized by reducing, reusing, and recycling. The solid-waste disposal plan should also include an assessment of: disposable versus reusable, reductions in chemical use, and extended product life.

For example, do not use paper or plasticware in restaurant outlets and employee dining rooms. Insist on reusable plastic, glassware, and silverware. In guest bathrooms, install amenity dispensers that can be refilled, eliminating small plastic bottles from the trash; and insist on items packaged in the least material possible.

In addition, take inventory of the detergents and cleansers currently being used to determine which ones are toxic. Substitute nontoxic products from the rapidly growing selection of environmentally safe cleaning products that work just as well. Some have included kitchen oil fats, motor oil, and car batteries in their recycling efforts.

Recycling programs also have an impact on the reduction of solid waste. Separated paper, plastic, glass, and metal that is picked up by haulers becomes the raw material for new paper, plastic, glass, and metal. Some creative recycling has included disposing of empty wine bottles to a wine-making supply outlet in the community catering to those involved in the home production of wine; the distribution of the live, potted evergreen plants found in many facilities during the holiday season to be replanted in the local community; and the disposal of discarded toilets from a retrofit to a local gravel company that pulverized them (e.g., the metal components were removed and recycled), using the crushed pieces as bedding for a new road. Recycling programs are most effective when a single individual in an organization is responsible for organizing, initiating, and monitoring the program. In successful programs, there are enough bins to separate waste properly, and the recycling bins are conveniently located and clearly marked.

AIR POLLUTION

Air pollution is an increasingly complicated problem. New pollutants are regularly found that could become harmful to people if prescribed levels in the atmosphere are exceeded. The major thrust of controls and regulations is directed at the manufacturing and chemical-processing industries, with the hospitality industry being essentially exempt from these controls at the present time in many areas of the United States.

Hospitality buildings discharge the by-products of combustion of heating fuels and certain impurities from their ventilation systems. Control of the initial input of fuel can affect the by-products of combustion. Ideally, natural gas should be used because its pollution discharge is insignificant. However, because the hospitality industry's supply of natural gas could be restricted or eliminated, some geographic areas must use fuel oil and liquid petroleum gas (LPG). The quantity and types of pollutants discharged by these heating fuels can be regulated by: purchasing low-pollution grades of fuel, which are in short supply and very expensive; increasing combustion efficiency, which reduces undesirable pollutants and conserves energy; and using available energy resources with existing systems. The last approach is being used by most establishments.

If rigid pollution codes are developed, control of air contaminants can become very costly. There is also concern that the efficiency of the overall heating and ventilation system will decrease as more controls are placed on it.

Initially, centrifugal devices were installed to remove fly ash and other solid particles from combustion exhausts. Now, chemicals must be removed from these same exhausts, which is costly. An example of this process is the controls on gasoline internal-combustion engines in automobiles. The discharge of various pollutants was established and controlled. The initial effect was that fuel consumption increased and other by-products of combustion became pollutants. The partial solution was to increase the efficiency of the total system. Hence, in the United States, mileage-per-gallon (kilometer-per-liter) requirements were established for new automobiles. These are forced efficiency standards that result in fewer pollutants. Heating fuels will come under more control in the future, which will contribute to the increased cost of heat sources in the hospitality industry.

Kitchen exhaust systems can discharge large quantities of vaporized oil into the environment. The immediate hazard is fire, because as oil is cooled, it condenses on buildings and outside surfaces. An afterburner system and many condensation techniques were developed for grease and oil to eliminate this problem. Afterburners in the exhaust system utilize natural gas to burn vaporized oil, and they worked very well. However, natural gas was restricted or eliminated, and these natural-gas devices became obsolete unless used with a more expensive fuel, such as LPG. These vaporized-oil discharges from hospitality buildings will come under more control in the future.

Air pollution is also having a significant impact on the maintenance of building exteriors. Because of the effects of acid rain, a growing concern of the hospitality manager should be the protection of the building from chemical attack. Acid rain refers to a family of sulfuric acids, nitric oxides, and sulfur dioxides that form when sulfur, a by-product of industrialization, large urban centers, and auto exhausts, unites with water. Unfortunately, the damaging chemicals in the air can often be transformed into corrosive elements simply by surface moisture.

Aluminum suffers pitting, which undermines the electrolytic coating protecting the base metal; this could require costly refinishing, spray coating, or replacement. Bronze is sensitive to acid rain, stainless steel can be "stained," and stone and masonry can be eaten away. Figure 18.3 suggests some maintenance guidelines for dealing with the problems of acid rain.

Adequate maintenance from these airborne pollutants may also depend on geographic location. Heavily urbanized areas where emissions from vehicles are concentrated, foggy coastal conditions with buildups of atmospheric salts and dust, and low-rain areas with temperature fluctuations and smog conditions may have more serious problems, requiring more frequent attention.

WATER POLLUTION

WATER STANDARDS

In 1962, the U.S. Public Health Service published standards for drinking water.[2] Most states and their local governments have enacted standards and/or codes pertaining to water quality that is considered potable—that can be utilized in food products or directly consumed. The quality of such water, if purchased from a public utility, is not usually monitored by a hospitality manager.

If the potable water supply comes directly from the property, from wells, reservoirs, or other private sources, water quality must become the hospitality manager's concern. Water quality refers to the relative bacteriological,

---

Inspect all exterior metal and masonry for signs of leakage.
Begin cleaning with the least harsh chemical and technology (ranges from hand-cleaning to high-pressure water, steam, or chemicals).
Test the chemical to be used in cleaning on a small section of the building for adverse reactions and effectiveness.
Start cleaning from the top down.
Do not permit chemicals to puddle on horizontal surfaces, joints and crevices.
Wash with the grain of the surface material, and avoid excessive rubbing.
Protect all seals, gaskets, windows, and doors that might be damaged by the solvents used in the cleaning operations.

FIGURE 18.3 Maintenance procedures for exterior building surfaces.

physical, radiological, and chemical characteristics of water in relation to its safe and desirable use by humans.[3] Potable water quality was discussed in Chapter 12. While bacteriological, or biologic, quality is probably the most serious management concern, the physical characteristics (such as taste, clarity, and odor) of potable water are important to guests and therefore to management.

Bacteriological characteristics are determined by counting the number of coliform bacteria present in a water supply. Although the coliform bacteria are nonpathogenic—that is, they do not cause disease—they are used to measure the pollution of water because they dwell in human intestines, have life cycles similar to disease-causing bacteria, and are more numerous and easier to detect. Typical quality standards in the United States permit only one coliform organism for each 100 millimeters of water, or about two bacteria in each cup of water.

Water treatment processes depend on the initial condition of the water. The most important treatment is that of disinfection. Chlorine-bearing compounds are widely used for disinfection. Calcium hypochlorite, available in tablet and powdered forms, is commonly used. However, chlorination of water should be handled by a system designed for commercial applications, a system that rapidly and continuously mixes water and chlorine. Guidelines used by many public health officers suggest that at least 2 ppm of free residual chlorine should contact the water for at least 20 minutes (0.33 hour) before treated water reaches the first customer.[4]

In 1977, Congress passed the Water Pollution Control Act, which decreed that all waters must be made safe for fishing and swimming. Following this legislation, state and local governments also established biological and physical quality standards for water that might be utilized for recreational activities.

POLLUTION SOURCES

The hospitality manager must carefully evaluate the present and future pollutants that may impact on a water supply being considered for potable and recreational uses. Water samples and tests, catchment area evaluations, and assessments of potential conflicts in use are techniques that may facilitate this evaluation.

Consult state health authorities in the initial evaluation of the biological and physical qualities of potential potable and recreational water supplies. If the water supply and system are going to be disapproved, it is better to know about it before millions of dollars are invested. Once approved, water should be sampled regularly. An ideal sampling program should involve continuous samples and analysis by means of automated equipment. Such a program is usually contracted to an independent test laboratory. If such a service is not available, however, health officials may approve manual sampling, but usually only if the sample accurately represents the water source and is of sufficient size for subsequent laboratory examination.[5]

The catchment area evaluations should consider present and future use of land areas comprising the watershed or feeder supply to the recreational or potable water supply. Septic-tank failures, construction site sediment, and runoff pollution from roadways, turf, and agricultural areas compound the water-quality problem, increasing water-management costs.

For example, approximately 25 to 30 acres (101,175 to 121,410 square meters) of drainage of catchment area is necessary to supply approximately 5 surface acres (20,235 square meters) of a lake. As the catchment area is developed, natural vegetation is stripped away for agricultural, residential, and even recreational purposes, such as play areas and parking areas. Thus, the potential for pollutants entering the lake's water supply increases. Cloudy water and aquatic vegetation may be visible signs of increasing pollutants.

Cloudy water results from clay sediment being introduced from the catchment area into the water supply. Although such a problem can be temporarily corrected by spreading agricultural gypsum (hydrated calcium sulfate) over the lake surface at approximately 12 pounds per 1000 cubic feet (192.25 kilograms per 1000 cubic meters) at specified intervals, these treatments drive up the maintenance costs of recreational water dramatically.

Aquatic vegetation such as algae and other water plants are also indicative of nutrient-rich water. The normal chemical nutrient is fertilizer that has been introduced into the body of water from the catchment area. Such chemicals are runoff pollutants from agricultural areas, residential property turf, and recreational facilities such as golf courses. Although the primary impact of the nutrient is on the physical quality of the water, biological impacts are also possible, depending on the pathogens present in the nutrient.

In the southeastern United States, the recreational value of fresh-water areas is being threatened by an aquatic plant known as hydrilla (*hydrilla verticillata*). This aquarium plant now infests more than half a million acres (about 200 million square meters) of lakes and rivers in Florida alone. The plant forms a nearly impenetrable mat of stems and leaves on the surface that makes swimming, boating, fishing, and waterskiing difficult and dangerous, if not impossible; clogs water intake systems; and provides a breeding habitat for mosquitoes and other pests.

Once established, treatments for hydrilla may endanger fish and wildlife; make the water unsuitable for human consumption and contact because of the toxicity and quantity of chemicals that must be introduced; and become costly, at $400 per water surface acre (about $100 per 1000 square meters) for a single treatment, with more than one treatment per year required.

CONFLICTING USES

A body of water has many uses (see Figure 18.4). The hospitality manager must determine which of these uses may impact on present and future water

> Aesthetic value
>
> Water surface sports (swimming, diving, waterskiing)
>
> Fishing
>
> Wildlife habitat
>
> Water storage (direct use as potable water supply, irrigation, livestock watering)
>
> Sewage treatment (oxidation pond, aeration lagoon, storage of treated effluent)
>
> Runoff control
>
> Sediment control
>
> Power generation
>
> Transportation

FIGURE 18.4   Potential use of water.

quality. For example, when considering the desirability of developing or redeveloping ocean front property, the manager must assess how water quality might be influenced by an off-shore oil or chemical spill in a commercial shipping lane. This could destroy the property's recreational potential.

On the other hand, a recreational activity may have negative consequences for other water uses. For instance, dredging to accommodate a hotel or a yacht club boat basin may adversely affect the area as a habitat for fish and waterfowl. Where recreational uses conflict with ecological concerns or with the interests of groups whose livelihood or quality of life depends on the existing ecology, federal, state, and environmental agencies, as well as local groups, make issuing of permits for development and compliance with regulations costly and time consuming.

SEWAGE DISPOSAL

Faced with skyrocketing water and sewer rates, many have learned that by reducing water flow, cash flow can increase. With a potential to save approximately 32 billion gallons (120 billion liters) of water per year, U.S. hotels gradually are phasing in effective indoor and outdoor water-saving measures. Water-saving devices include shower heads, faucet aerators, and water-saving toilets, which cut water flow in half at a minimum. If a public sewage line is not available or not capable of handling sewage discharges from the building you plan to construct, the planned facilities (hotel guest rooms, foodservice seats) may have to be reduced in number and size. Local codes regulate private sewage system tank capacity and drainage field requirements. In some cases, a temporary permit is issued that allows you to install a sewage disposal system on your property and operate it until a public sewer line becomes available. This can be a costly facility.

There are four general types of private sewage disposal systems: cesspools and chemical toilets, septic-tank/cesspool combinations, septic-tank drain fields, and complete filter systems.

CESSPOOLS AND CHEMICAL TOILETS

A cesspool is a large pit in the ground lined with concrete. The lining has openings in it underground. Sewage solids collect in the pit and are eventually decomposed by bacteria contained in the sewage and in the ground. The by-products are called *effluent*. The effluent drains through the openings into the adjacent soil. The immediate area around the underground pit, or cesspool, is usually lined with a layer of rock, a layer of gravel, another of sand, and, finally, local soil. As effluent passes through these layers of rock and soil, it is further decomposed and eventually processed, reverts to water, and reenters the water table.

The major problem with the system is that it can quickly become overloaded, in which case the immediate ground area around the cesspool becomes supersaturated with effluent, which rises to the surface, making it a very undesirable area. A second problem is that as additional solids are deposited in the pit, they may not be decomposed at a fast-enough rate, so that the pit quickly fills and must be frequently cleaned. These problems explain why cesspools are not generally allowed for anything larger than a household. They are not recommended for hospitality industry use.

Chemical toilets, which are above-ground cesspools, may be allowed on a temporary basis. They may be permitted on golf courses or for outside sporting areas. They are frequently unsanitary and unpleasant to use.

SEPTIC-TANK/CESSPOOL COMBINATIONS

A better system is the septic-tank/cesspool combination. The septic tank is a large, enclosed sewage-holding tank buried in the soil. Sewage flows in while effluent drains from the opposite side into a series-connected cesspool. Solids are retained in the septic tank. Some areas may permit a cesspool only when it is connected to a septic tank. This system is generally superior to, and more efficient in land use than, a cesspool system.

SEPTIC-TANK DRAIN FIELDS

A more efficient system, and one that generally eliminates a soil saturation condition, is the septic-tank/drain field disposal system. Adequate land area must be available for the system. The septic tank holds the solid sewage.

Effluent drains from the tank into a drain field, which is an underground semiporous piping network; that is, the pipes have openings so that the effluent can drain from the pipes into the adjacent soil. A layer of rock, such as crushed rock or small stones, is placed next to the semiporous piping network. A layer of gravel surrounds the rock layer. Sand or local soil is used as the next layer.

Septic-tank size and drain field area are based on the soil absorption rate and the drain field location on the property. Buildings cannot be placed directly on the drain field. The surface area above the drain field is usually planted with grass and, if the system is working properly, the effluent should never rise to the ground surface; therefore, it can be used as a grassy playground or recreational area. However, regular soil samples and tests of standing water should be taken. The septic-tank drain field is generally acceptable throughout the United States and foreign countries for small- and medium-sized facilities.

COMPLETE FILTER SYSTEM

The complete filter system, which is similar to many public sewage disposal systems, is used for large and medium-sized buildings and building complexes. With this system, large amounts of sewage can be treated on small land areas. It is expensive to install and maintain.

The filter system utilizes septic tanks or larger sewage-holding tanks, which receive sewage from the building sewer line. Solid sewage is separated from liquid sewage and is decomposed and changed to effluent. The effluent drains to a second holding tank, where it is further decomposed. The partially treated effluent drains to a distribution system that sprays the effluent into the air. The effluent falls on a layer of sand and gravel and percolates, or seeps, through it. As the effluent penetrates the sand-and-gravel filter, its color starts to clear, indicating that it is being purified. The effluent is treated further with a disinfectant, such as chlorine, which will destroy all remaining bacteria. It is then discharged into a river or reservoir.

Effluent may also be diverted to a pond for final purification, either with or without additional chemicals. The liquid that eventually leaves the pond can be pumped to a river or a lake; or it can be used, with health authority approval, as recycled water for a second recreational pond and eventually as a source of potable water. In all cases, testing procedures must be conducted to ensure safe water.

Energy can be obtained from a filter system as sewage gases are generated by decomposing sewage. These gases can be processed and are a potential source of LPG. The gases can be compressed and used to drive internal-combustion engines or turbines, which, in turn, drive electric generators to produce energy for pumping and for operating the sewage plant.

SUMMARY

This chapter has considered the problems that solid waste, air pollution, and water pollution may present to the hospitality manager. The components of a management program to deal with the collection, treatment, and disposal of solid waste were considered, along with questions about the efficiency of solid-waste technology and equipment, such as motorized carts, compactors, incinerators, and disposal alternatives.

The chapter considered the management problems of air pollution and acid rain. The chapter also focused on the importance to a hospitality manager of potable and recreational water, a management strategy for evaluating the present and future problems that water quality might present, and a description and evaluation of sewage disposal methods.

REFERENCES

1. Piper, J., "Waste Management Decision-Making," *Building Operating Management,* April 1985.
2. U.S. Public Health Service, *Drinking Water Standards,* Publication No. 956, Washington, DC, 1962.
3. U.S. Public Health Service, *Manual of Individual Water Supply Systems,* Publication No. 24, Washington, DC, 1962.
4. U.S. Public Health Service, *Environmental Health Practice in Recreation Areas,* Publication No. 1195, Washington, DC, 1965.
5. Young, R. A., *Plant Engineers Handbook,* American Institute of Plant Engineers, Cincinnati, OH, 1973.

QUESTIONS/PROBLEMS

1. Conduct a survey of solid-waste management for a local lodging or health-care facility.

2. Determine what type of trash compaction equipment is used by local lodging, foodservice, health-care, or club facilities. Describe preventive-maintenance schedules that have been developed for the compaction equipment.

3. What types of statutes/ordinances regulate the local hospitality industry's ability to incinerate solid waste?

4. Determine from state or local government agencies responsible for monitoring air quality the extent to which acid rain is a problem in

your geographic area. To what extent has the local hospitality industry included preventive building-maintenance practices, such as washing exterior surfaces, to reduce the problems that accompany acid rain?

5. Discuss with state or local health department officials the standards for potable water in your locale. What inspection procedure do state or local health department officials use when a building has a private source of potable water?

6. In reviewing the blueprints for a new guest room tower to be added to your existing high-rise hotel, identify the waste management issues that you would try and clarify from the blueprints.

Selected Conversion Units Used in This Book

English	Standard International Unit
Barrel (oil): 42 gallons	158.76 liters
Btu	0.293 watt
Btu-inch per hour per square foot per °F	144.2 watt-millimeters per hour per square meter per °C
Btu per cubic foot	77.44 watts per cubic meter
Btu per gallon	0.079 watt per liter
Btu per hour	0.293 watt per hour
Btu per 24 hours per cubic foot	10.3 watts per 24 hours per cubic meter
	0.010 watt per 24 hours per liter
Btu per pound	0.647 watt per kilogram
Btu per square foot per hour per °F	5.68 watts per square meter per hour per °C
Btu per square foot	3.151 watts per square meter
Btu per pound per °F	1.161 watts per kilogram per °C
Cubic feet per hour	0.028 cubic meter per hour
	27.96 liters per hour
Cubic feet per minute per foot	8.3 cubic meters per hour per meter
	304.56 liters per second per meter
Fahrenheit	$(°F - 32) \times (5/9)$ °Celsius
Feet	0.305 meter
Feet per minute	18.3 meters per hour
	0.005 meter per second
Feet per minute per square foot	0.005 meter per second per square meter
Footcandle	10.76 lux

English	Standard International Unit
Gallon	0.0038 cubic meter
	3.785 liters
Grain	17.1 parts per million
Horsepower	746 watts
Inch	25.4 millimeters
Mile	1.61 kilometers
Miles per gallon	0.43 kilometer per liter
Minute	0.0167 hour
	60 seconds
Pound	0.454 kilogram
Pounds per cubic foot	16.02 kilograms per cubic meter
Pounds per square inch	6.9 kilopascals
Revolutions per minute	60 revolutions per hour
	0.0167 revolution per second
Square inch	645 square millimeters
Square foot	0.093 square meter
Square yard	0.836 square meter
Time:	
8 A.M.	0800 hours
12 noon	1200 hours
2 P.M.	1400 hours
Yard	0.91 meter
$ per inch per square foot per year	$0.425 per millimeter per square meter per year
$ per pound	$2.21 per kilogram
$ per gallon	$264.17 per cubic meter
	$0.264 per liter

Replacement Cycles for Items That Fail

(Refer to Figure 2.22 for incandescent lamp mortality curve.)
    Additional data:

Average lamp life: 1500 hours
Estimated lamp use in meeting rooms: 180 hours per month, or 2160
(180 × 12) hours per year
Cost per lamp: $1.25
Labor cost for lamp replacement:
    Group lamp replacement: $2 per lamp
    Spot lamp replacement (including time to and from the job): $16 per lamp

There are three alternatives available to management for lamp replacement.

A. Alternative I is to replace lamps as they fail. This is called spot replacement. The costs associated with this alternative are

$$TC_I = \frac{H_E}{H_X} \times (L_1 + L_2)$$

where

TC_I = annual cost per lamp socket for spot replacement
H_E = estimated annual hours of lamp use
H_X = average hours lamp life
L_1 = lamp cost
L_2 = labor cost for spot lamp replacement

$$TC_I = \frac{2160}{1000} \times (\$1.25 + \$16.00) = \$24.84$$

B. Alternative II is to group-replace every 1500 hours and to spot-replace as lamps fail. The average life of the lamp is 1500 hours. This means that half the lamps will have to be spot-replaced between group replacements.

$$TC_{II} = \frac{H_E}{H_R} \times (L_1 + L_3 + P_R \times [L_1 + L_2])$$

where

TC_{II} = annual cost per lamp socket for group and spot replacement
H_E, L_1, and L_2 were defined above
H_R = lamp replacement cycle in hours
L_3 = labor cost per lamp for group replacement
P_R = probability of lamp failure between replacement cycles

$$TC_{II} = \frac{2160}{1500} \times (\$1.25 + \$2.00 + 0.5 \times [\$1.25 + \$16.00]) = \$17.10$$

Alternative II represents a savings of \$7.74 per lamp socket per year over Alternative I.

C. Alternative III is to group-replace every 1500 hours with no spot replacement. The problem with this alternative is that half the lamps will have failed by the time of group lamp replacement. The costs associated with this alternative are

$$TC_{III} = \frac{H_E}{H_R} \times (L_1 + L_3)$$

where

TC_{III} = annual cost per lamp socket for group replacement
All other terms were defined above.

$$TC_{III} = \frac{2160}{1500} \times (\$1.25 + \$2.00) = \$4.68$$

An improved management approach is to group-replace at a more frequent schedule if spot replacement of lamp failures is not practiced. Management may wish to group-replace every 1000 hours; at this replacement cycle, only 10 percent of the lamps would have failed. The cost associated with this policy is

$$TC_{III} = \frac{2160}{1000} \times (\$1.25 + \$2.00) = \$7.02$$

Management should identify critical lamp failure areas and spot-replace the lamps in these areas, and practice group replacement everywhere else.

Finally, if labor cost is of little concern, or if there is minimal labor cost difference between spot and group replacement, the advantage of group replacement is lost.

Replacement of Items That Wear Out

Figure 2.23 is an example of a maintenance-and-energy log for a unit of equipment. Figure 2.24 is a plot of the data shown in Figure 2.23. It should be noted that the cost of maintenance and energy is increasing. Cost data that follow this particular pattern can be analyzed to determine when the equipment should be replaced.

The first step is to determine the rate of increase for operating cost C. This is shown below.

Quarter of operation	Computation	Difference between two successive periods
1	100–0	$100
2	200–100	100
3	300–200	100
4	375–300	75
5	450–375	75
6	650–450	200
7	800–650	150
8	1175–800	375
9	425–1175	−750
10	600–425	175
11	800–600	200
12	1350–800	550
Total		$1350

Average rate of increase $(C) = \dfrac{\$1350}{12} = \$112.50$ per quarter.

Two other data are required to complete the procedure. The initial and equipment installation cost is defined as A. The estimated salvage value is defined as S. Shown here is a three-line nomograph. Find the value of C ($112.50) on the left scale (C scale). Next, find the $A - S$ value on the middle scale. Draw a line between these two points, extend it to the N (life) line to the right, and read the scale.

If $A = \$10,000$ and $S = \$5000$, N will equal 9 units, as shown. As the value of C was $112.50 per quarter, the unit value of N is in quarters. Therefore, keep the equipment for 9 quarters (2 years and 3 months); then replace it.

The equipment has its lowest quarterly cost at 9 quarters. If kept for shorter or longer time periods (8 quarters or less, or 10 quarters or more), its quarterly cost will be greater. The proof is shown below.

$$TC = \frac{(N - 1) \times C}{2} + \frac{(A - S)}{N}$$

where

TC = total equipment cost per N unit (quarter, year, or specified hours)
N = replacement period
C = rate of increasing operating cost
A = initial and installation cost
S = salvage value

For $N = 9$ quarters,

$$TC = \frac{(9 - 1) \times \$112.50}{2} + \frac{(\$10,000 - \$5000)}{9}$$

$$= \$1005.55 \text{ per quarter}$$

For $N = 8$ quarters,

$$TC = \frac{(8 - 1) \times \$112.50}{2} + \frac{(\$10,000 - \$5000)}{8}$$

$$= \$1018.75 \text{ per quarter}$$

For $N = 10$ quarters,

$$TC = \frac{(10 - 1) \times \$112.50}{2} + \frac{(\$10,000 - \$5000)}{10}$$

$$= \$1017.05 \text{ per quarter}$$

The minimum cost per quarter (minimum cost of ownership) occurred at 9 quarters.

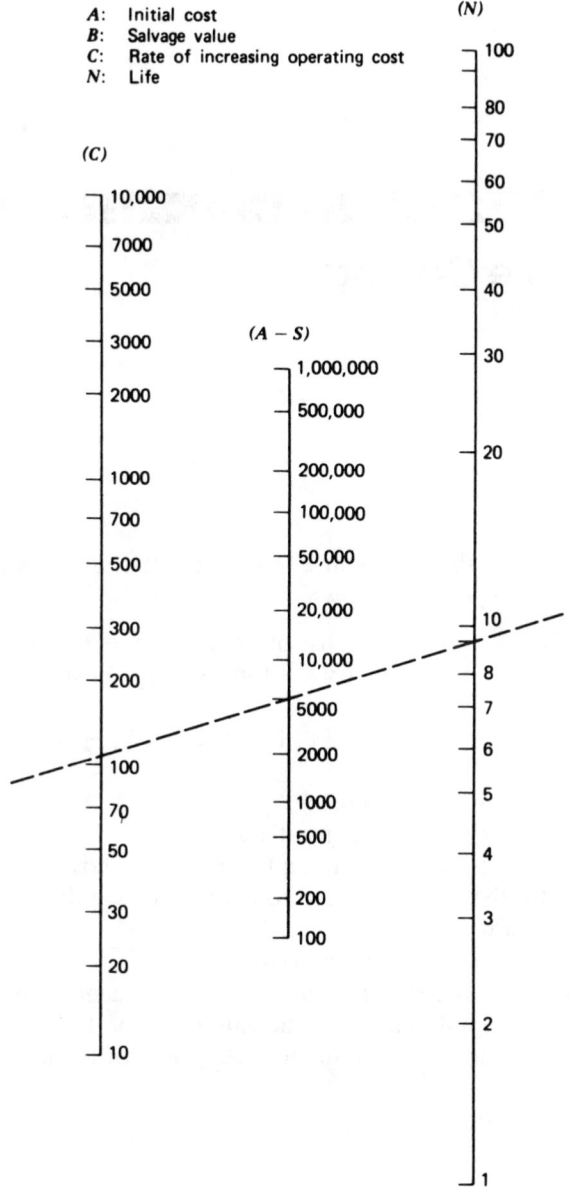

A: Initial cost
B: Salvage value
C: Rate of increasing operating cost
N: Life

APPENDIX 4

Life-Cycle Costing

The basic relationship that can be used to determine the present value of estimated building costs is shown below:

Total present costs = present cost of equipment + future maintenance and repair costs + future energy costs − salvage value

$$TC = A + B \times F_1 + C \times F_2 \times F_3 - S \times F_3$$

where

TC = total present value costs

A = initial cost including installation

B = estimated annual repair and maintenance costs

F_1 = factor that when applied to annual costs will equate these to present value

C = estimated annual energy costs

F_2 = factor that adjusts for the rising cost of energy; if energy costs are not expected to increase the value of F_2 is 1

F_3 = factor that when applied to (CF_2) or S will equate these to present value

S = salvage value

EXAMPLE

A hotel had an air-conditioning system that could continue to operate for another 10 years. Its present estimated value is $10,000. A check of its equipment log reveals that repairs and maintenance have been close to $1500 per year. Energy checks on the unit have shown that its energy costs are $3500 per year. Its anticipated salvage in 10 years is $500.

Factors: F_1 (N = years or periods, I = interest, discount percentage)

I

N	8	10	12	14	16	18	20
1	0.926	0.909	0.893	0.877	0.862	0.848	0.833
2	1.783	1.736	1.690	1.647	1.605	1.566	1.528
3	2.577	2.487	2.402	2.322	2.246	2.174	2.106
4	3.312	3.170	3.037	2.914	2.798	2.690	2.589
5	3.993	3.791	3.605	3.433	3.274	3.127	2.991
6	4.623	4.355	4.111	3.889	3.685	3.498	3.326
7	5.206	4.868	4.564	4.288	4.039	3.812	3.605
8	5.747	5.335	4.968	4.639	4.344	4.078	3.837
9	6.247	5.759	5.328	4.946	4.607	4.303	4.031
10	6.710	6.145	5.650	5.216	4.833	4.494	4.192

Factors: F_2

N	8	10	12	14	16	18	20
1	1.00	1.00	1.00	1.00	1.00	1.00	1.00
2	2.08	2.10	2.12	2.14	2.16	2.18	2.20
3	3.25	3.31	3.37	3.44	3.51	3.57	3.64
4	4.51	4.64	4.78	4.92	5.07	5.22	5.37
5	5.87	6.11	6.35	6.61	6.88	7.15	7.44
6	7.34	7.72	8.12	8.54	8.98	9.44	9.93
7	8.92	9.49	10.1	10.7	11.4	12.1	12.9
8	10.6	11.4	12.3	13.2	14.2	15.3	16.5
9	12.5	13.6	14.8	16.1	17.5	19.1	20.8
10	14.5	15.9	17.6	19.3	21.3	23.5	26.0

Factors: F_3

N	8	10	12	14	16	18	20
1	0.926	0.909	0.893	0.877	0.862	0.847	0.833
2	0.858	0.826	0.797	0.769	0.743	0.718	0.694
3	0.794	0.751	0.712	0.675	0.641	0.609	0.579
4	0.735	0.683	0.635	0.592	0.552	0.516	0.482
5	0.681	0.621	0.568	0.519	0.476	0.437	0.402
6	0.630	0.564	0.507	0.456	0.411	0.370	0.335
7	0.583	0.513	0.452	0.400	0.354	0.314	0.279
8	0.540	0.466	0.404	0.351	0.305	0.266	0.233
9	0.500	0.424	0.361	0.308	0.263	0.225	0.194
10	0.463	0.386	0.322	0.270	0.227	0.191	0.161

The chief engineer has an estimate for a new air conditioner that will consume only $2000 of energy in the next year. The installation cost of the equipment is $20,000. Its average repair and maintenance expenses will probably be $1000 per year over the next 10 years. It will have a salvage value of $5000 in 10 years.

Energy costs are expected to increase at 10 percent per year for the next 10 years. The current hotel interest rate (cost of borrowing money) is 14 percent. Should the chief engineer recommend the new air conditioner or keep the current unit?

ANALYSIS

Alternative I: Keep present unit.

A = $10,000
B = $1500
C = $3500
F_1 = 5.22 for 10 years (N) and 14 percent (I)
F_2 = 15.9 for 10 years (N) and 10 percent (I)
F_3 = 0.270 for 10 years (N) and 14 percent (I)
S = $500
TC_I = $10,000 + $1500 × 5.22 + $3500 × 15.9 × 0.270 − $500 × 0.270
      = $32,720.50

If this amount of money were placed in an account earning 14 percent interest, it would cover all present and future costs and have a balance of $0 after a 10-year period.

Alternative II: Purchase a new air conditioner.

A = $20,000
B = $1000
C = $2000
F_1 = 5.22
F_2 = 15.9
F_3 = 0.270
S = $5000
TC_{II} = $20,000 + $1000 × 5.22 + $2000 × 15.9 × 0.270 − $5000 × 0.270
        = $32,456.00

If this amount of money were placed in an account earning 14 percent interest, it would cover all present and future costs and have a balance of $0 after a 10-year period.

Comparison: The difference of $264.50 is very small—only 0.8 percent of the total costs of Alternative I. The chief engineer would probably recommend that the present unit be retained. Actually, both units are almost equally cost effective. However, if energy costs were to increase at a higher rate than 10 percent in the future, Alternative II would be more attractive.

General Comprehensive Energy-Management Program

A. Determination of current consumption of energy
   1. Establishment of an energy committee.
   2. Committee reviews current consumption of energy as well as past records.
   3. Committee develops a basic plan of energy conservation.
      a. General guidelines for Phase 1
      b. General guidelines for Phase 2
      c. General guidelines for Phase 3
B. Development and adoption of Phase 1 of the program
   1. Presenting Phase 1 to employees and obtaining employee feedback.
   2. Refining Phase 1, based on employee suggestions.
   3. Adoption of Phase 1; similar program indicated below:

HEATING SYSTEM

Use proper grade of coal.
Use appropriate grade of oil.
Use a fuel that is easily ignited.
Use day–night temperature settings.
Use work-off day temperature settings.
Lower internal building temperatures.
Make mechanical adjustments on system.

Adjust thermostat.
Guest room temperature control: 55°F (12.8°C) in unsold rooms; 65°F (18.3°C) in unoccupied sold rooms.
Public corridors and function rooms: night or unoccupied, as low as feasible 55°F (12.8°C); day temperature setting 65°F (18.3°C).

Control by-products of combustion emissions.

Remove ash from the heating plant.

Operate heating plant with long on-cycles.

Reduce coverings and furnishings over convectors and radiators.

Maximize natural-gas and fuel-oil-burner efficiency: adjust heating boilers, annually; adjust hot water boilers, semiannually.

Adjust, calibrate, and clean thermostats, annually.

Keep guest room drapes closed in unoccupied rooms.

REFRIGERATION

Lower refrigerant condensation temperatures and pressure.

Increase air movement in cooling tower.

Consider 16-hour operational cycles.

Raise internal temperatures for coolers and freezers.

Reduce the number of door openings for coolers and freezers.

Reduce ice thickness on evaporator.

Check thermostat on coolers and freezers.

Move refrigerators away from heat sources.

Maintain adequate clearance around reach-in coolers and freezers.

Purchase frozen food for freezers.

Reduce lighting requirements within coolers and freezers.

Reduce product loads.

Maximum evaporator ice thickness, 1/4 inch (6.35 millimeters).

Adjust, calibrate, and clean thermostats, annually.

Provide 2–3-inch (50–75-millimeter) clearance between reach-ins and walls or other equipment.

Operate chillers (walk-in and reach-in) at 40°F (4°C).

Increase freezer (walk-in and reach-in) temperature by 5°F (3°C).

VENTILATION

Use rooms selectively.

Correct free area of registers and ducts.

Balance air flow within the building.

Clean or replace filters when air flow is reduced by 10 percent.

Tighten and align fan belt drives.

AIR CONDITIONING (ITEMS NOT PREVIOUSLY CONSIDERED)

Day–night temperature settings.

Work-off day temperature settings.

Increased building temperatures.

Reduced activity level of occupants during hottest part of day.

Time of use of building and rooms.

Accurate and adequate controls.

Guest room temperature control: 85°F (30°C) for unsold rooms; 80°F (27°C) for unoccupied sold rooms.

Public corridors and function rooms: increase temperature by 5°F (3°C).

ELECTRIC APPLIANCES

Operate for shorter periods of time.
Check energy consumption.
Minimize electrical demand.
Minimize operation of several
electric motors at one time.

Maintain adequate repair-and-
maintenance policy.
Reduce number of appliances on a
circuit.

ELECTRIC HEATERS

Keep heaters clean.
Keep reflectors polished.
Keep heaters open to the area
being heated.

Rather than replacing with another
electric heater, consider a natural-
gas replacement.
Clean electric ovens every day,
when in use.

LIGHTING

Cover windows with light-colored
drapes at night.
Reduced light intensity.
Minimize use of incandescent
lamps.
Use incandescent lamps for warm-
color effect.
Do not use fluorescent lamps in
cold environment.
Minimize use of rapid-start fluorescent lamps.
Do not use incandescent lamps
above 200 watts.
Minimize use of mercury-vapor
lamps in favor of fluorescent
lamps.
Use metal-halide rather than
mercury-vapor lamps.
Use high-pressure sodium lamps
whenever possible.
Use direct lighting whenever
possible.

Use semidirect lighting rather than
diffuse lighting.
Use diffuse lighting rather than
semi-indirect lighting.
Use semi-indirect lighting rather
than indirect lighting.
Clean light fixtures.
Clean walls and ceiling.
Utilize larger rather than smaller
rooms whenever possible.
Place outside lighting on a time
clock control.
Reduce light intensity to the lowest
safe level.
Utilize motion or infrared light
controller sensors for function
rooms.
Use screw-in fluorscent lamps in
place of incandescent guest room
light fixtures when possible.
Use energy-efficient incandescent
lamps.

MOTORS

Operate motors at higher voltages
whenever possible.

Operate motors at rated loads.

WATER

Balance water pressure to needs of
building.

Utilize subsurface water for
irrigation.

Reduce temperature of hot water.
Eliminate water leaks.
Reduce pipe noise.
Utilize storm runoff water for irrigation whenever possible.

Reduce public rest room and guest room hot-water temperature to a maximum of 115°F (45°C), or lower when possible.

SWIMMING POOL OPERATION

Keep filtering time to a minimum.
Utilize waste water from filter backwashing, when acceptable, for irrigation.
Use fresh water for backwashing the pool filter.
Do not heat pool water over 80°F (26.7°C).

Set the maximum spa temperature at 103°F (39°C), ideally at 102°F (38°C).
Limit filter operating time to 8–10 hours per day, if feasible.

4. Implementation of Phase 1, one step of the energy conservation program at a time.
5. Measure the results.
6. Feedback of the results to employees.
7. Energy monitors may be appointed to reinforce the program.
8. If necessary, the adoption of an employee reward-and-penalty system.

C. Development of Phase 2
   1. Presenting Phase 2 to employees and obtaining employee feedback.
   2. Refining Phase 2, based on employee suggestions.
   3. Adoption of Phase 2; similar program indicated below:

HEATING SYSTEM

Regulate proper moisture.
Insulate feasibly.
Consider conversion to alternate sources of energy.
Direct use of fuel rather than electric heat.
Use city steam (by-product of electric energy generation).
Use gas whenever allowed and available.
Reduce glass areas.
Use double-glazed and thermal windows.
Use economizers in heating plant.

Use heat wheels to extract heat from exhaust air.
Use outside thermostat anticipator.
Install occupancy sensors in public areas and all function rooms to regulate temperature settings.
Install boiler soft-water systems.
Consider water-to-air heat pumps, rather than air-to-air heat pumps.
Consider heat wheels or heat exchanger to extract heat from all of the following: kitchen exhaust air; kitchen/laundry hot-water drains; laundry dryer exhaust.

Install and adjust pollution control equipment.
Preheat oil prior to combustion.
Size heating plant and system to building requirements.
Increase use of solar energy.
Control fresh-air input.

REFRIGERATION SYSTEMS

Use water for cooling condensers.
Use proper sizing and shape of evaporator.
Use solar coolers.
Use halocarbon refrigerants.
Use units that have a high ratio of refrigeration capacity to watt consumption.
Use hot-gas defrost systems.
Use forced-convection evaporators.
Install self-closing doors on reach-in coolers and freezers.
Increase insulation around coolers and freezers.

Install computer temperature controls.
Install enthalpy controls.
Replace weather stripping around doors.
Replace weather stripping around windows when necessary.

Enter freezer through cooler.
Reduce number of reach-in units.
Investigate the use of refrigerant and compressor oil chemical additives for vapor compression refrigeration systems; some of these additives lower operating energy requirements.
Install hot-gas defrost systems.
Install self-closing doors for all chillers and freezers.

VENTILATION

Use separate ventilation systems for each room or group of rooms.
Use separate modular heating and cooling for rooms.
Utilize cool air from remainder of building for kitchen ventilation.
Add thermal insulation on ducts.
Utilize larger ducts.

Reduce turns and loops in the duct system.
Correct air velocity in ducts.
Correct free area of registers and ducts.
Install efficient air filters.
Use combination air filter systems.

AIR CONDITIONING (ITEMS NOT PREVIOUSLY CONSIDERED)

Consider demographic characteristics of customers and employees.
Install feasible amounts of insulation.
Reduce residual heat load of the building.
Reduce window areas.
Use shields for windows.
Use light-colored surfaces.

Change type of lighting.
Use recirculated air whenever feasible.
Consider potential use of evaporative coolers.
Install fresh-air heat exchangers.
Install correct type of fan.
Use heat from the fan motor to heat air when needed.

Control use of fresh air for ventilation.

Use revolving and double doors.

Install weather stripping around windows and doors.

Establish controls and regulations concerning windows and door openings.

Install variable-speed fans.

Use evaporative coolers for employee areas, including kitchens, rather than mechanical refrigeration systems.

Use ventilation motors as supply air reheaters.

APPLIANCES

Install lower-wattage devices for the same tasks.

Utilize computer demand control devices when feasible.

Use parallel circuits for lighting.

Use large wires to reduce voltage drop.

Use higher voltages on appliances.

Install devices to increase the power factor in the building.

Investigate power factor improvement technology, if paying a power factor penalty on electric bills.

Consider low-temperature dishwashing systems.

Consider low-temperature laundry systems.

Replace gas pilot ignition with electric ignition.

Use microwave ovens for single entrée meal preparation.

ELECTRIC HEATING DEVICES

Switch to other forms of heat.

Utilize electronic heating for small-unit heating.

Utilize nonelectronic heating for large-quantity heating.

LIGHTING

Reduce reflective lighting.

Reduce amount of glass.

Use light-colored surfaces.

Use higher-voltage incandescent lamps.

Use tungsten-halogen rather than incandescent lamps whenever possible.

Use luminaries that are light-reflective efficient.

Replace incandescent lamps with fluorescent lamps.

Use fluorescent lamps for cool-color effects.

Use light-colored walls and ceilings.

Use smooth surfaces rather than textured surfaces for lighting.

Replace incandescent lamps with energy-efficient fluorescent lamps when possible.

Use low-voltage quartz halogen lamps when possible.

Use occupancy sensors for lighting control.

MOTORS

Consider use of capacitor-start induction motors to improve power factor of building.

Specify high grades of steel in motors.

Utilize polyphase motors whenever possible.

Utilize synchronous motors whenever possible.

Use direct-current motors whenever possible.

WATER

Utilize soft water whenever possible.

Soften hot and cold water.

Balance water demand and pump capacity.

Balance pump lift capacity with correct type of pump.

Use reciprocating pumps for large water requirements.

Provide adequate pressure at fixtures for full water flow.

Balance water pressure to the needs of the building.

Reduce pressure by using resistors, or smaller-size pipes.

Install water-circulating pumps to ensure adequate water flow.

Combine upfeed–downfeed systems in multiple-floor buildings.

Use threaded fittings for high water pressure.

Match water flow control to the appropriate type of valve.

Reduce the length of piping.

Reduce the number of fittings and valves.

Consider the potential use of a water tower.

Select and install fixtures with low water demand.

Use larger-diameter pipes when possible.

Increase amount of insulation around hot-water tanks.

Insulate hot-water pipes.

Reduce length of hot-water pipes.

Use larger-diameter hot-water pipes.

Use side-arm heaters or heat exchangers for heating hot water.

Consider use of some type of pool enclosure.

Install solar heaters for partial hot-water heating for pool and hot-water requirements.

4. Implementation of Phase 2, one step of the energy conservation program at a time.
5. Measurement of the results.
6. Feedback of the results to employees.
7. Energy monitors may be appointed to reinforce the program.
8. If necessary, the adoption of an employee reward-and-penalty system.

D. Development of Phase 3
   1. Presenting Phase 3 to management and obtaining management feedback.
   2. Presenting Phase 3 to employees and obtaining employee feedback.
   3. Refining Phase 3, based on management resources and employee suggestions.

4. Development of a time schedule for the completion of Phase 3.
5. Continued reinforcement of Phases 1 and 2.
6. Adoption of Phase 3; similar program indicated below:

HEATING

Install moisutre control system.
Install adequate amounts of insulation throughout the entire building.
Consider conversion to alternate sources of heat.
Install feasible solar-heat collectors for building heating.
Consider new building location to reduce heat losses.
Reduce window areas in walls and skylights.
Install thermal windows.
Install more efficient heating plants.

Install pollution control equipment that increases heating efficiency.
Install smaller-sized heating plants.
Install heat exchangers between supply and exhaust air.
Reposition heating convectors and radiators in rooms.
Install two-pipe systems for hot-water and steam-heating systems whenever they are being used in the building.
Install an EMS.

REFRIGERATION SYSTEMS

Change to more efficient systems.
Increase use of water-cooling towers.
Installation of solar coolers whenever feasible.
Purchase refrigeration units that have a high ratio of refrigeration capacity to energy consumption.
Install hot-gas defrost systems.
Relocate coolers and freezers to areas of low heat.

Increase amount of insulation on all coolers and freezers.
Change purchasing patterns for fresh and frozen foods.
Redesign freezers and coolers so that entrance to the walk-in freezer is through the cooler.
Eliminate all possible reach-in units.
Install an EMS.

VENTILATION

Convert from central ventilation to local or zoned systems.
Provide separate-room or zoned heating-and-cooling systems for rooms.
Design ventilation system so that exhaust cool air moves through the kitchen before being discharged.

Install insulation on all heating and cooling ducts.
Replace small, high-velocity ducts with larger ducts.
Install more efficient air filters.
Install an EMS.

AIR CONDITIONING (ITEMS NOT PREVIOUSLY CONSIDERED)

Change building design and furnishings to reduce residual heat load of building.

Install window shields for summer cooling; make sure they are removable to assist in winter heating.

Change orientation of windows to reduce summer-cooling requirements and assist in winter heating.

Install reflective surfaces on outside walls, or paint them a light color.

Install adequate controls so that system adjusts automatically for recirculated and fresh air, depending on temperature and humidity of fresh air.

Install revolving and double doors.

Change to more efficient lighting systems.

Install more efficient fans.

Reposition fan motor so that its heat can be used to advantage.

Install variable-speed fans.

Install an EMS.

APPLIANCES

Purchase more efficient appliances.

Install computer control device for energy demand control.

Rewire building with larger-size wires, or add new circuits and reduce load on present circuits.

Install variable capacitors or inductors that automatically compensate for low power factor.

Consider installing high-voltage transformers within building to obtain lower energy rate from electric utility.

HEATING APPLIANCES

Use electric heaters only when forced to.

Consider using electronic heating devices for small-unit cooking.

LIGHTING

Change to more efficient lighting systems.

Change to direct or semidirect lighting.

Redesign rooms and interior of building to include highly reflective surfaces whenever possible.

Reduce the number of small rooms in the building.

Install an EMS.

MOTORS

Change motors to include those units that will improve the building power factor.

Purchase high-voltage motors.

Balance load and energy output of motors.

Purchase motors with high efficiencies; use as a purchasing specification.

WATER

Install water-softening equipment, when required.

Install more efficient pumps.

Balance pressure requirements of building.

Consider the use of different water distribution systems that reduce energy requirements.

Change piping materials, fittings, and valves so that a more efficient system is installed (less friction).

Consider the use of a water tower in place of water-circulating pumps for multifloor buildings.

Install plumbing fixtures that have reduced water demand.

Install larger-diameter pipes.

Insulate all hot-water pipes.

Install side-arm heaters or heat exchangers for water heating.

Install solar heaters for swimming pools.

Install complete pool enclosures.

7. Implementation of Phase 3, one step at a time.
8. Measurement of the results.
9. Feedback of results to management and employees.
10. Appointment of energy monitors to reinforce the program.
11. Reevaluate the schedule as energy costs change.
12. Consider the use of a bonus system for outstanding department or employee-group-area energy conservation.
13. Maintain an energy conservation employee-reward suggestion system.

APPENDIX 6

Part A:
Fixed and Variable Energy Consumption (An Application of Linear Regression)

The objective of linear regression (least-squares procedure) is to estimate accurately energy requirements for sold guest rooms. The procedure develops a straight-line equation ($Y = A + BX$)

where

Y = estimated energy requirements, Btu (watts)

X = rooms sold

A and B are constants

B is the variable coefficient. Its value indicates the energy requirement per sold room.

A is the fixed coefficient. Its value represents the energy requirement when zero rooms are sold (energy is still required for public areas).

The number of observations = N.

The data in the first table following were obtained over a 10-day period from a 300-guest-room hotel with limited foodservice and conference facilities. The equation is used to estimate the energy consumption (Btu) for each of the days in the original data; the results are shown in the second table following.

X = Rooms sold

Y = Energy consumption, M Btu

N = Sample size, days

N = 10

ΣX = 1850

X = 185
ΣX^2 = 400,000
ΣY = 571
Y = 57.1
ΣY^2 = 34,681
ΣXY = 116,550
B = 0.1890M
A = 22.14M
Y = 22.14M + 0.1890M $\times$ X, Btu
(= 6.487M + 0.0554M $\times$ X, watt)

	Energy consumption (Y)	
Rooms sold (X)	Btu (millons)	Watts (millions)
300	78	22.85
50	32	9.38
250	69	20.22
100	39	11.43
200	62	18.17
150	51	14.94
275	73	21.39
125	45	13.19
225	66	19.34
175	56	16.41

	Energy consumption (millions)		Variance	
Rooms sold (X)	Actual	Estimated	Units (millions)	Percent
300	78	78.84	+0.84	+1.08
50	32	31.59	−0.41	−1.28
250	69	69.39	+0.39	+0.57
100	39	41.04	+2.04	+5.23
200	62	59.94	−2.06	−3.32
150	51	50.49	+0.49	+0.96
275	73	74.12	+1.12	+1.53
125	45	45.77	+0.77	+1.71
225	66	64.67	−1.33	−2.02
175	56	55.22	−0.78	−1.39
Average			+0.11	+0.31

The actual data and energy estimate equation are plotted and shown in the first graph in this appendix.

The correlation coefficient (goodness of fit of the predicting equation to the actual data) is 0.9966. A perfect correlation coefficient is 1.000; thus, the equation can be used as a management control technique. The allowable energy variance is ±2.63M; hence, any variance greater than +2.63M or less than −2.63M would require an explanation from the chief engineer. Note that all the actual variances shown in the graph fall within the allowable variance range.

The first graph also shows the fixed and variable energy consumption for the property. When the occupancy (rooms sold) is 0, the property's energy consumption is 22.14M Btu. This amount of energy is required to heat/cool public space, to provide minimum heating/cooling to guest areas, to provide minimum water requirements, to keep security systems and outside and interior lighting of public spaces functioning, to keep the pool in operation, and for all other energy consumption systems that do not relate directly to customer requirements.

Any energy reduction improvements (changing to more efficient lighting or heating/cooling systems) should result in the reduction of this fixed consumption. A fixed energy reduction goal of 10 percent could now be measured and its results compared to a new data plot. A 10 percent fixed energy reduction program should reduce energy consumption by (0.10 × 22.14M) 2.21M energy units. The new fixed energy consumption should be (22.14M − 2.21M) 19.93M energy units. (See the second graph in this appendix for

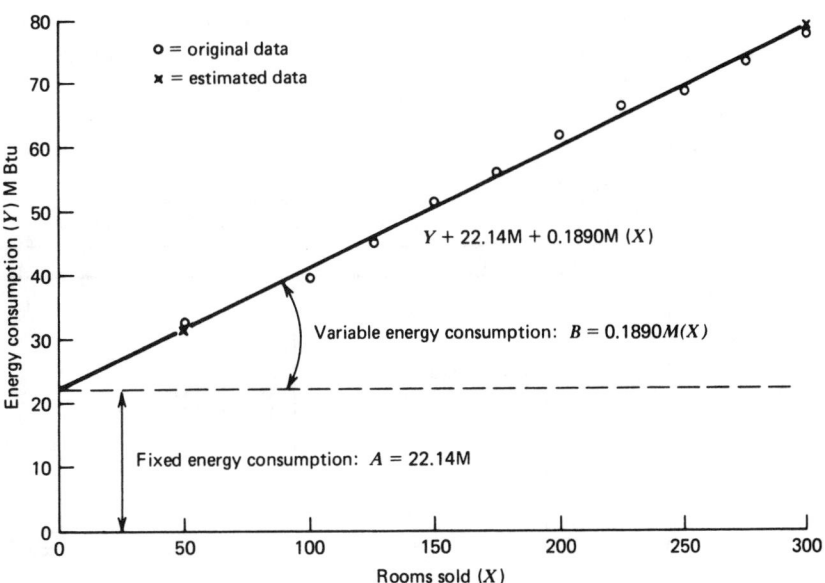

such a comparison; it shows the original energy consumption and the proposed new fixed goal.)

The variable energy consumption per sold guest room is B 0.1890M energy units. The sale of each guest room will increase energy consumption by 189,000 Btu. This includes energy consumed in the guest room (lighting, appliances, water consumption, heating/cooling requirements), plus guest transportation requirements (elevator), foodservice energy, and the energy requirements of other facilities.

A variable energy reduction goal of 10 percent would result in reducing B from 0.1890M, or 189,000 Btu, per sold guest room to 0.160M, or 160,100 Btu. This result is also shown in the second graph. More efficient guest room lighting, thermostat heating/cooling controls, improved efficiency guest use appliances, and efforts at energy conservation on the part of guests should all be reflected in a lower B coefficient.

If the A coefficient (22.14M) is compared to the property energy consumption (Y) at the average property occupancy (assume 70 percent, which is equal to 210 sold guest rooms), the estimated energy consumption would be 61.83M Btu. Comparing the fixed energy consumption (22.14M) to the total (61.83M) results in a ratio of 35.81 percent (22.14M/61.83M = 0.3581). Many chief engineers report that fixed energy consumption varies between 25 and 60 percent; it is almost 36 percent in our example. The lower ratio (25 percent) generally applies to properties with minimum guest services, whereas the 60 percent ratio applies to full service properties, such as resort hotels. It is important to know this ratio for a property, so that the manager and chief engineer can initially concentrate energy efforts in the fixed or variable energy consumption areas of the property. Hence, if the fixed energy consumption ratio is over 50 percent, initial energy conservation efforts should be directed at the fixed systems (public areas).

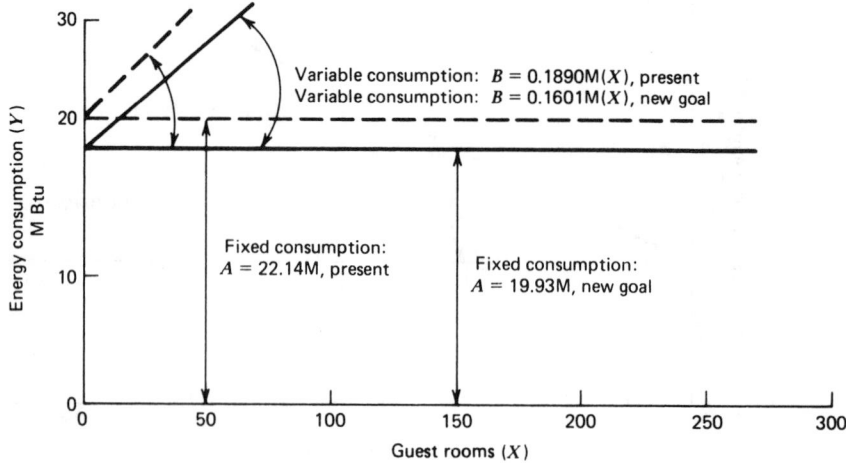

Part B:
Energy Management with
Multiple Regression

You are encouraged to refer to one of the several computer software spreadsheet programs (some of the common programs are Lotus® 1-2-3, Quattro® Pro, or Excel®) when solving multiple regression problems. Detailed problem procedures are not shown in this appendix; only the initial data and final results are shown.

Data shown below are taken from a Holiday Inn property located in the Southwest. The hotel has 367 guest rooms and provides full guest services (foodservice, function rooms, laundry, gift shop, elevator service, swimming pool and spas). There are approximately 150,000 square feet (about 14,000 square meters) of building space. Guest rooms have individual heat pump units and public space has central hot-water heat. Natural gas is used for cooking and an evaporative cooler is used in the kitchen.

The multiple regression technique is shown for electric KWHR data only for a 12-month period. The hotel variables are: (B) occupied guest rooms per month; (C) breakfast covers per month; (D) lunch covers per month; (E) dinner covers per month; (F) banquet covers per month; (G) heating degree-days per month; and (H) cooling degree-days per month. Degree-day data were determined by the local National Weather Service bureau for the period.

Kilowatt-hour Consumption versus Variables								
Month	KWHR Actual	Occp— Rooms	Breakfast	Lunch	Dinner	Banquet	Heat DD	Cool DD
Jan	290000	5400	3600	3200	3700	3700	980	0
Feb	250000	5000	3600	4100	3700	4100	740	0
Mar	230000	8400	5900	5600	5700	6600	675	0
Apr	225000	6400	4700	3900	5300	4900	380	0
May	230000	7500	5500	4700	4300	5200	140	0
Jun	275000	9500	6900	4300	6100	5800	0	125
Jul	390000	8400	6100	3800	6100	2700	0	265
Aug	365000	8400	6300	4000	6900	4300	0	175
Sep	285000	8400	6600	4400	5800	5400	100	40
Oct	270000	8200	4800	4400	2900	4000	320	0
Nov	230000	6700	4000	4400	4200	4600	700	0
Dec	300000	5900	3800	4300	3400	4500	925	0

Multiple Regression Results				
Regression Output				
Constant	(A)	217014.5		
Std Err of Y Est		28960.75		
R Squared		0.893043		
No. of Observations		12		
Degrees of Freedom		4		
Coefficients				
X Coefficient(s)	Std Err of Coef		t-test	
−7.83222	(B)	6.101396	−1.284	
55.21756	(C)	7.162274	7.710	Sig
−4.00898	(D)	15.24426	−0.263	
−5.65421	(E)	6.746165	−0.838	
−38.2478	(F)	8.492194	−4.504	Sig
103.0878	(G)	23.37128	4.411	Sig
281.7556	(H)	97.86443	2.879	Sig

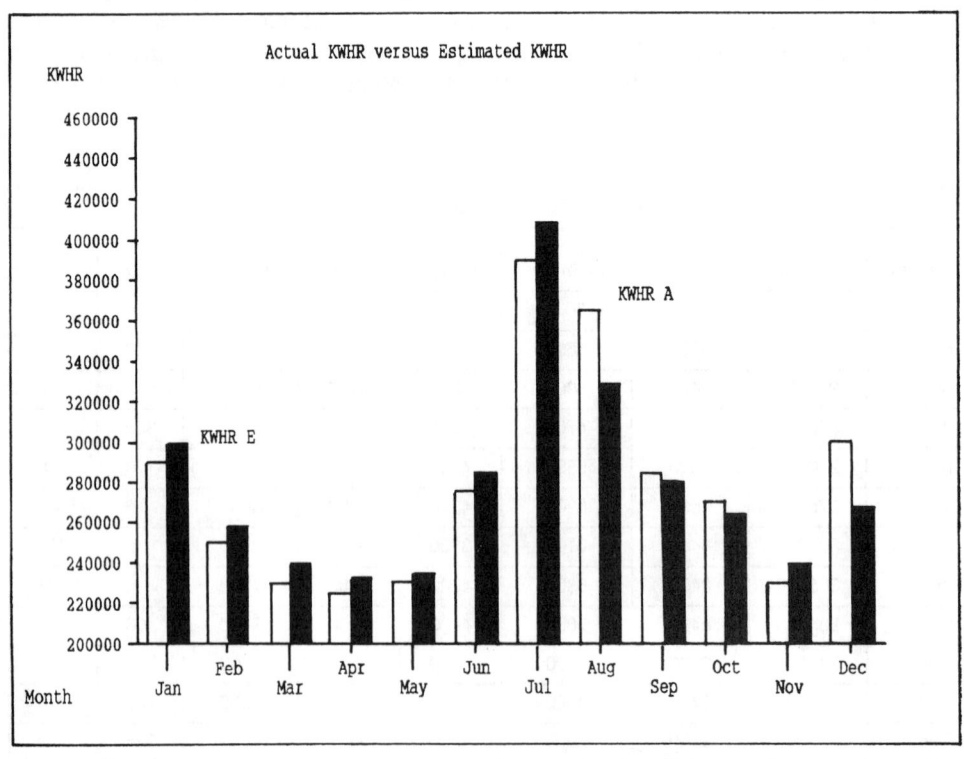

Actual KWHR versus Estimated KWHR

Multiple regression generates the following estimating equation:

$$Y = A + B \cdot (\text{Occupied rooms}) + C \cdot (\text{Breakfast covers})$$
$$+ D \cdot (\text{Lunch covers}) + E \cdot (\text{Dinner covers}) + F \cdot (\text{Banquet covers})$$
$$+ G \cdot (\text{Heating degree-days}) + H \cdot (\text{Cooling degree-days})$$

The coefficients A through H are obtained from the computer software program and are shown to the left. Y is the estimated KWHR. Multiple regression also produces statistical standard errors, which can be used to determine if hotel variables are significant and the overall error for Y. The monthly KWHR estimates are also compared to actual KWHR with a bar graph. A short discussion concludes the appendix.

KWHR Comparisons		
Month	KWHR Actual	KWHR Estimate
Jan	290000	299264
Feb	250000	258748
Mar	230000	239477
Apr	225000	232568
May	230000	234358
Jun	275000	285263
Jul	390000	409722
Aug	365000	328886
Sep	285000	280267
Oct	270000	263795
Nov	230000	240243
Dec	300000	267409

The preceding tables show KWHR consumption for 12 months, hotel operating information, degree-days for heating and cooling, multiple regression results, a bar graph showing actual KWHR versus estimated KWHR consumption, and a table of KWHR actual and estimated. The regression correlation coefficient for the multiple regression technique is 0.945 ($R^2 = 0.89304$), which is a fairly good estimate for the preceding data. The multiple regression table also shows *t-test* and significance results. The significant results are: breakfast covers, banquet covers, heating degree-days, and cooling degree-days. This indicates that only these data should be used for estimating KWHR consumption and that one should eliminate occupied room, lunch cover, and dinner cover data and repeat the multiple regression analysis. One should also check for colinearity of the data before completing the final multiple regression computations.

APPENDIX 7

Energy Requirements for Cooking Food

FOOD DATA

Weight: 10 pounds (4.54 kilograms) of fresh beef

Specific heat: 0.75 (0.87)

Initial temperature: 40°F (4.4°C)

Average final temperature: 160°F (71.1°C); this means that the outside product surface temperature will be about 220°F (104.4°C) and the interior product temperature will be 140°F (60.0°C).

Product losses: There will be close to a 30 percent product loss made up of dripping and volatile losses. The amount of each depends on the processing technique (high-temperature processing usually results in a higher volatile-loss ratio). It will be assumed that half the losses will be volatile and half drippings. Dripping losses include product moisture and fat losses.

The heat requirements of these losses are essentially latent-heat requirements. The volatile losses are a direct latent-heat process as product moisture (liquid) is changed to a vapor, or gas. The normal latent heat of vaporization is very close to 1100 Btu per pound (712 watts per kilogram) of volatile loss.

The drip latent-heat requirements are essentially the energy requirements to change the beef fats from the solid to the liquid state (liquid fat can then drip from the product). The typical latent-heat requirements are close to 60 Btu per pound (38.8 watts per kilogram) of product fat.

Other product heat requirements: When meat is cooked, its proteins are broken down. This also represents a latent-heat requirement. The energy requirement for protein breakdown is about 100 Btu per pound (64.7 watts per kilogram) of protein.

Note: Once meat protein is broken down (this is an irreversible process), the energy requirement is 0 when the product is reheated, whereas the fat latent-heat requirements are retained when meat is reheated. As the product cools, liquid fat still present in the meat changes back to the solid state from the liquid state, thus releasing heat back to the product (keeping it warm) even when it is removed from the source of heat (oven).

HEAT REQUIREMENTS

Volatile: About half the product weight loss is assumed to be volatile. The total product loss is 30 percent:

$$0.30 \times 10 \: pounds = 3 \: pounds$$
$$(0.30 \times 4.54 \: kilograms = 1.36 \: kilograms)$$

The volatile loss is 1.5 pounds (0.68 kilogram). The latent heat of vaporization is about 1100 Btu per pound (712 watts per kilogram); hence, the volatile heat requirement is

$$1.5 \times 1100 \: Btu = 1650 \: Btu$$
$$(0.68 \times 712 \: watts = 483.5 \: watts)$$

Drip: This consists of liquid losses, primarily water, salts, and liquid fats. The liquid fats are latent-heat losses. All the product solid fats change to liquid fats at about 135 to 150°F (57.2 to 65.6°C). If the product has 20 percent fats, the latent-heat requirement for this change is

$$Weight: 0.20 \times 10 = 2 \: pounds$$
$$(0.20 \times 4.54 = 0.91 \: kilogram)$$
$$Heat: 2 \times 60 = 120 \: Btu$$
$$(0.91 \times 38.8 = 35.2 \: watts)$$

Protein: If the product has 20 percent protein, the total protein heat requirements are

$$Weight: 0.20 \times 10 = 2 \: pounds$$
$$(0.20 \times 4.54 = 0.91 \: kilogram)$$
$$Heat: 2 \times 100 = 200 \: Btu$$
$$(0.91 \times 64.7 = 58.6 \: watts)$$

Total latent-heat requirements:

$$H_L = volatile + fat + protein$$
$$H = 1650 + 120 + 200 = 1970 \: Btu$$
$$H = 483.5 + 35.2 + 58.6 = 577.3 \: watts)$$

Sensible-heat requirements:

$$H_S = W \times C \times (t_2 - t_1)$$
$$H = 10 \times 0.75 \times (160 - 40) = 900 \: Btu$$
$$[H = 4.54 \times 0.87 \times (71.1 - 4.4) = 263.7 \: watts]$$

Total sensible- and latent-heat requirements:

$$H_T = H_S + H_L$$
$$H = 900 + 1970 = 2870 \; Btu$$
$$(H = 263.7 + 577.3 = 841 \; watts)$$

The preceding is only the product heat requirement. It does not indicate how fast the product will be heated (cooking time). Product cooking time depends on the product heat requirement (as indicated earlier), the product surface temperature (220°F [104.4°C]), oven or heat source temperature, product surface area, and on the heat transfer characteristics between the oven and the product. These factors are investigated in various parts of Chapter 7.

Annual Heating Requirements and Thermal Insulation Economy

A: Normal building construction
    1. Data
        Wall area = 4000 square feet (371.6 square meters); U = 0.24 (1.36)
        Roof area = 10,000 square feet (930 square meters); U = 0.23 (1.31)
        Glass area = 4000 square feet (371.6 square meters); U = 1.13
            (6.42)
        Note: U = heat transmission coefficient.
        Oil heat: 140,000 Btu per gallon (10,837.5 watts per liter) $1.50 per
            gallon ($0.396 per liter)
        Degree-days: 7000 per heating season base temperature 65°F (3888.9
            base temperature 18.3°C)
        Heat system efficiency: 75 percent
        Inside design temperature: 68°F (20°C)
        Outside design temperature: 0°F (−17.8°C)

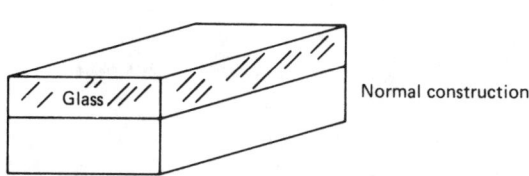

Normal construction

2. Heating requirements

H_{wall} = 4000 × 0.24 × (68−0) = 65,280 *Btu/hour*
[H = 371.6 × 1.36 × (20− −17.8) = 19,124 *watts/hour*]
H_{glass} = 4000 × 1.13 × (68-0) = 307,360 *Btu/hour*
[H = 371.6 × 6.42 × (20− −17.8) = 90,275 *watts/hour*]
H_{roof} = 10,000 × 0.23 × (68−0) = 156,400 *Btu/hour*
[H = 930 × 1.31 × (20− −17.8) = 46,052 *watts/hour*]
H_T = H_{wall} + H_{glass} + H_{roof}
H = 65,280 + 307,360 + 156,400 = 529,040 *Btu/hour*
(H = 19,124 + 90,275 + 46,082 = 155,451 *watts/hour*)

3. Heat units per heating season

$$H_S = \frac{H_T \times DD \times 24}{t_2 - t_1}$$

where
H_S = heat loss per heating season
H_T = building heat loss per hour
DD = heating season degree-days
24 = constant (24 hours per day)
t_2 = inside design temperature
t_1 = outside design temperature

$$H_S = \frac{529,040 \times 7000 \times 24}{68 - 0}$$

H = 1307 × 10^6 *Btu/season*

$$(H = \frac{155.451 \times 3888.9 \times 24}{20 - -17.8} = 384 \times 10^6 \text{ } watts/season)$$

4. Annual heating cost

$$C_H = \frac{H_S \times C_F}{E \times H_F}$$

where
C_H = heat cost per season
H_S = building heat loss per heating season
C_F = fuel cost per unit
E = heat system efficiency
H_F = fuel heat value per unit

$$C_H = \frac{1307 \times 10^6 \times \$1.50}{0.75 \times 140,000} = \$18,668 \text{ } per \text{ } heating \text{ } season$$

$$(C = \frac{384 \times 10^6 \times \$0.396}{0.75 \times 10,837.5} = \$18,668 \text{ } per \text{ } heating \text{ } season)$$

B: Energy-efficient construction
1. Data construction and heat data similar to part A with the following exceptions:
   Wall area = 7000 square feet (651 square meters)
   Roof area = 10,000 square feet (930 square meters)
   Glass area = 1000 square feet (93 square meters)

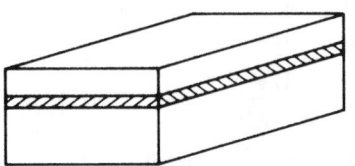

Energy efficient construction
has less glass area in
walls

2. Heating requirements
$$H_{wall} = 7000 \times 0.24 \times (68-0) = 114,240 \; Btu/hour$$
$$[H = 651 \times 1.36 \times (20- -17.8) = 33,467 \; watts/hour]$$
$$H_{glass} = 1000 \times 1.13 \times (68-0) = 76,840 \; Btu/hour$$
$$[H = 93 \times 6.42 \times (20- -17.8) = 22,569 \; watts/hour]$$
$$H_{roof} = 10,000 \times 0.23 \times (68-0) = 156,400 \; Btu/hour$$
$$[H = 930 \times 1.31 \times (20- -17.8) = 46,052 \; watts/hour]$$
$$H_T = H_{wall} + H_{glass} + H_{roof}$$
$$H = 114,240 + 76,840 + 156,400 = 347,480 \; Btu/hour$$
$$(H = 33,467 + 22,569 + 46,082 = 102,088 \; watts/hour)$$

3. Energy savings over normal construction
$$H_{saving} = 529,040 - 347,480 = 181,560 \; Btu/hour$$
$$(H = 155,451 - 102,088 = 53,363 \; watts/hour)$$

$$Percent = \frac{181,560 \times 100}{529,040} = 34.3$$

Hence, reducing building wall glass area will result in a 34.3 percent energy savings (also annual heat savings of 34.3 percent).

C. Optimal heating insulation for walls and roof
1. Basic relationship

$$X_{net} = \sqrt{\frac{DD \times 24 \times C_E \times K_I}{C_I \times 10^6}} - \left(\frac{K_I}{U_P}\right)$$

where
X_{net} = economical insulation thickness to be added to present building
DD = degree-days
24 = constant (24 hours per day)
C_E = energy cost per million heat units

K_I = thermal conductivity of insulation to be added to present building
C_I = installed cost of insulation per year per unit thickness
U_P = heat transmission coefficient of present building

2. Additional data

$$C_E = \frac{\$1.50 \times 10^6}{0.75 \times 140,000} = \$14.29/10^6 \ Btu$$

$$(= \frac{\$0.396 \times 10^6}{0.75 \times 10,837.5} = \$48.71/10^6 \ watts)$$

K_I = 0.32 Btu-inch per square foot per hour per °F
(= 46.1 watt-millimeter per square meter per hour per °C)
C_I = \$0.012 per square foot per inch per year (20-year life)
(= \$0.0051 per square meter per millimeter per year)

3. Optimal insulation
[0.235 is the average U of the roof (0.23) and the walls (0.24).]

$$X_{net} = \sqrt{\frac{7000 \times 24 \times \$14.29 \times 0.32}{\$0.012 \times 10^6}} - \left(\frac{0.32}{0.235}\right)$$

$$= 8.00 - 1.36 = 6.64 \ inches$$

$$X = \sqrt{\frac{3888.9 \times 24 \times \$48.71 \times 46.1}{\$0.0051 \times 10^6}} - \left(\frac{46.1}{1.335}\right)$$

$$= 203.20 - 34.5 = 168.70 \ millimeters$$

D. Optimal insulation for walls and roof and thermal windows
   1. Basic data
      Assume that 6.64 inches (168.7 millimeters) of insulation with a K_I = 0.32 (46.1) can be added to walls and roof.

      The resulting U's of the walls and roof are
         Walls: U_P = 0.24 (1.38)

$$R \ (added \ insulation) = \frac{6.64}{0.32} = 20.8$$

$$New \ R \ (wall) = 20.8 + \frac{1}{0.24} = 25$$

$$New \ U = \frac{1}{R} = \frac{1}{25} = 0.04 \ (0.23)$$

Roof: U_P = 0.23 (1.32)

$$New\ R\ (roof) = 20.8 + \frac{1}{0.23} = 25.1$$

$$New\ U = \frac{1}{R} = \frac{1}{25.1} = 0.04\ (0.23)$$

U of thermal windows (low E): 0.22 (1.26)

2. Heating requirements and cost for normal construction (see part A)

$$
\begin{aligned}
H_{\text{wall}} &= 4000 \times 0.04 \times (68-0) = 10,800\ Btu/hour \\
[H &= 372 \times 0.22 \times (20- -17.8) = 3234\ watts/hour] \\
H_{\text{glass}} &= 4000 \times 0.22 \times (68-0) = 59,840\ Btu/hour \\
[H &= 372 \times 1.26 \times (20- -17.8) = 17,718\ watts/hour] \\
H_{\text{roof}} &= 10,000 \times 0.04 \times (68-0) = 27,200\ Btu/hour \\
[H &= 930 \times 0.23 \times (20- -17.8) = 8085\ watts/hour] \\
H_T &= H_{\text{wall}} + H_{\text{glass}} + H_{\text{roof}} \\
H &= 10,800+59,840+27,200 = 97,840\ Btu/hour \\
(H &= 3234+17,718+8085 = 29,037\ watts/hour)
\end{aligned}
$$

Heating cost

$$H_S = \frac{97,840 \times 7000 \times 24}{68 - 0} = 242 \times 10^6\ Btu/season$$

$$(= \frac{29,037 \times 3888.9 \times 24}{20 - -17.8} = 71 \times 10^6\ watts/season)$$

$$C_H = \frac{242 \times 10^6 \times \$1.50}{0.75 \times 140,000} = \$3457\ \text{per season}$$

$$(= \frac{71 \times 10^6 \times \$0.396}{0.75 \times 10,837.5} = \$3459\ per\ season)$$

This represents a savings of $21,783 − $3457 = $18,326, or 84.1 percent, when compared to part A.

3. Heating requirement for construction indicated in part B

$$
\begin{aligned}
H_{\text{wall}} &= 7000 \times 0.04 \times (68-0) = 19,040\ Btu/hour \\
[H &= 651 \times 0.23 \times (20- -17.8) = 5660\ watts/hour] \\
H_{\text{glass}} &= 1000 \times 0.22 \times (68-0) = 14,960\ Btu/hour \\
[H &= 93 \times 1.26 \times (20- -17.8) = 4429\ watts/hour] \\
H_{\text{roof}} &= 10,000 \times 0.04 \times (68-0) = 27,200\ Btu/hour \\
[H &= 930 \times 0.23 \times (20- -17.8) = 8085\ watts/hour] \\
H_T &= H_{\text{wall}} + H_{\text{glass}} + H_{\text{roof}}
\end{aligned}
$$

$$H = 19{,}040 + 14{,}960 + 27{,}200 = 61{,}200 \; Btu/hour$$
$$(= 5660 + 4429 + 8085 - 18{,}174 \; watts/hour)$$

Savings over part A (normal construction)

$$H_T = 529{,}040 - 61{,}200 = 467{,}840 \; Btu/hour$$
$$(= 155{,}451 - 18{,}174 = 137{,}277 \; watts/hour), \text{ or 88 percent}$$

E. Optimal cooling insulation for walls/roof
   1. Data
   Cooling degree-days

2000 per cooling season, base temperature 80°F
(1111.1 per cooling season, base temperature 26.7°C)
Energy cost is $0.145 per kilowatt-hour; each watt of energy will remove the equivalent of 10 watts of heat from the building. Hence, 1 kilowatt of energy input will result in $10{,}000 \times 3.413 = 34{,}130$ Btu of heat removed

$$C_E = \frac{\$0.145 \times 10^6}{34{,}130} = \$4.25/10^6 \; Btu$$

$$(C = \frac{\$0.145 \times 10^6}{10{,}000} = \$14.49/10^6 \; watts)$$

K_I and C_I were given in part C.

   2. Optimal insulation thickness

$$X_{net} = \sqrt{\frac{2{,}000 \times 24 \times \$4.25 \times 0.32}{\$0.012 \times 10^6}} - \left(\frac{0.32}{0.235}\right)$$
$$= 2.33 - 1.36 = 0.97 \; inch$$

$$X = \sqrt{\frac{1111.1 \times 24 \times \$14.49 \times 46.1}{\$0.0051 \times 10^6}} - \left(\frac{46.1}{1.335}\right)$$
$$= 59.18 - 34.54 = 24.64 \; millimeters$$

Hence, the additional 6.64 inches (168.7 millimeters) of insulation required for heating is more than adequate for cooling.

Note: One should determine the optimal insulation requirement for both heating and cooling and use the larger of the two results for the building; in the preceding case, heating requirements were dominant.

Refrigeration Heat Loads and Their Effects on Equipment Requirements

The refrigeration heat load consists of four separate heat gains: transmission, infiltration, appliance, and product. The transmission heat gain depends on the physical size of the cooler/freezer and its construction. The infiltration heat depends on how long and on how many times the cooler/freezer door is opened. There are two potential appliance heat gains: lamps and their time of operation and air circulation fan motors. The product heat gain can be a critical factor as will be shown.

The rating and energy consumption of the refrigeration equipment depends on two major factors: the total daily heat gain and the evaporator temperature. The following example should give you a general idea of how the heat gain affects the equipment rating and its resulting energy consumption. It will point out how energy can be saved through management.

A. The transmission heat gain (H_T)

    1. Walk-in chiller basic data (see the diagram)

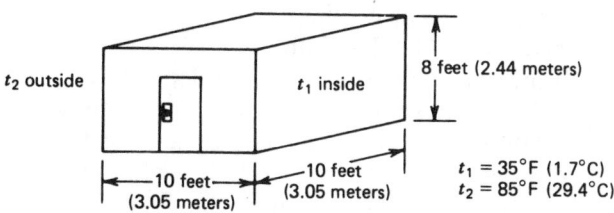

        $t_1 = 35°F$ (1.7°C)
        $t_2 = 85°F$ (29.4°C)

Door, walls, ceiling, and floor: $U = 0.053$ (0.300)

2. The gross surface area for walls and door, ceiling and floor is

$A = 4 \times (10 \times 8) + (10 \times 10) + (10 \times 10) = 520$ square feet
$[= 4 \times (3.05 \times 2.44) + (3.05 \times 3.05) + (3.05 \times 3.05)$
$= 48.37$ square meters$]$

3. Transmission heat gain

$H_T = 520 \times 0.053 \times (85-35) = 1378$ *Btu/hour*
$[H = 48.37 \times 0.3 \times (29.4-1.7 = 401.9$ *watts/hour*$]$

4. Food chiller heat gains are computed for a 24-hour period

$H_T = 1378 \times 24 = 33{,}072$ *Btu/day*
$(H = 401.9 \times 24 = 9645$ *watts/day*$)$

B. The infiltration heat gain (H_I)
  1. Each time the cooler door is opened, there will be an interchange of cool air leaving the cooler space with warm air replacing it. Naturally, the longer the door is left open, the greater the exchange of warm and cool air. Also, more frequent door openings will increase the air exchange. The refrigeration unit must have the ability to quickly cool the warm air that has entered the space; otherwise, the walk-in interior temperature will increase, which will affect the quality and storage life of the food products within the space.

    One of two operating conditions must be assumed regarding infiltration heat gains. The first is called "normal room usage." This assumes that a person enters and leaves the walk-in space no more than once per hour and that the total door-open time will not exceed 10 seconds. The second condition is called "heavy room usage," which could result in an open-door time of 60 seconds per hour. Both effects will be shown in part E.

    If the second condition limitation is exceeded, the manager should seriously consider installing plastic (or comparable) strips over the door opening (see Figure 8.15).

  2. Infiltration computation

$$H_I = V \times F_I$$

where
    H_I = infiltration heat gain
    V = volume of cooler/chiller space
    F_I = infiltration factor. This factor depends on V, t_2, and t_1
    F_I = 18.4 Btu per 24 hours per cubic foot (chiller space)
    $(F_I$ = 190.3 watts per 24 hours per cubic meter) for normal room
        usage
    F_I = 27.6 Btu per 24 hours per cubic foot
    $(F_I$ = 285.5 watts per 24 hours per cubic meter) for heavy room
        usage

$$V = 10 \times 10 \times 8 = 800 \ cubic \ feet$$
$$(= 3.05 \times 3.05 \times 2.44 = 22.7 \ cubic \ meters)$$

Normal room usage

$$H_I = 800 \times 18.4 = 14{,}720 \ Btu/day$$
$$(H = 22.7 \times 190.3 = 4319 \ watts/day)$$

Heavy room usage

$$H_I = 800 \times 27.6 = 22{,}080 \ Btu/day$$
$$(H = 22.7 \times 285.5 = 6480.9 \ watts/day)$$

It should be noted that the difference between the two F_I factors is $27.6 - 18.4 = 9.2 \ (285.5 - 190.3 = 95.2)$, or a 33 percent reduction in energy consumption, which could be obtained through management guidelines (controlling person movements into the chiller).

C. The appliance heat gain (H_A)

The appliance heat gain depends on the energy rating of the appliance and hours of operation.

Two appliances are located in the cooler: an electric lamp rated at 75 watts and a 200-watt electric motor driving the forced-convection evaporator fan. The electric lamp is on 6 hours per day and the fan motor is operated 24 hours per day.

$$H_A = W_A \times hours$$

where

W_A is the appliance heat (watts or Btu) rating

Lamp heat output

$$H_{A1} = 75 \times 3.413 \times 6 = 1536 \ Btu/day$$
$$(= 75 \times 6 = 450 \ watts/day)$$

Fan motor output

$$H_{A2} = 200 \times 3.413 \times 24 = 16{,}382 \ Btu/day$$
$$(= 200 \times 24 = 4800 \ watts/day)$$

Total appliance heat gain

$$H_A = H_{A1} + H_{A2}$$
$$= 1536 + 16{,}392 = 17{,}918 \ Btu/day$$
$$(H = 450 + 4800 = 5250 \ watts/day)$$

D. The product heat gain (H_P)

This analysis will consider two alternatives. Alternative I is to purchase 6000 pounds (2721 kilograms) of food at one time every 3 days. Alternative II is to purchase 2000 pounds (907 kilograms) of food each day. The initial food temperature is 50°F (10°C) for both alternatives.

The food temperature must be reduced to the cooler temperature in 24 hours or less for a maximum quality and shelf life.

1. Alternative I

$$H_{PI} = 6{,}000 \times 0.8^* \times (50-35) = 72{,}000 \; Btu/day$$
$$(H = 2721 \times 0.93^* \times (10-1.7) = 21{,}003 \; watts/day)$$

Note: * average specific heat

H_{PI} is the product heat gain for the first day (the day the products are placed in the cooler). The product heat gain for the second and third days will be 0.

2. Alternative II

$$H_{PII} = 2000 \times 0.8^* \times (50-35) = 24{,}000 \; Btu/day$$
$$(H = 907 \times 0.93^* \times (10-1.7) = 7001 \; watts/day)$$

Note: * average specific heat

Note: The total product heat gain for the first day is 72,000 Btu (21,003 watts) for Alternative I versus 24,000 Btu (7001 watts) for each day for Alternative II. The product heat gain remains 24,000 Btu (7001 watts) for each day for Alternative II, whereas it decreases to 0 for Alternative I. Hence, the total product heat gain for a 3-day period is equal for both alternatives. Do not be misled by this simple comparison.

The physical size of the cooler for Alternative II is much less than for Alternative I because more space is required to store 6000 pounds (2721 kilograms) of food products. Hence, Alternative I will have higher transmission, infiltration, and probable appliance heat gains for each of the 3 days. The net result is that the total energy consumption following Alternative I is about 42 percent higher than Alternative II. Likewise, because of the higher heat gains, larger equipment components (compressors, evaporators, condensers, and expansion valves) are required. These have a higher cost. The walk-in for Alternative I will also have a higher initial cost. The combined initial cost effect is that the cost requirements of Alternative I are about 160 percent higher than those of Alternative II.

E. Total heat gain (H_{total})
  1. Normal room usage and purchasing food each day

$$H_{total} = H_T + H_I + H_A + H_{PII}$$
$$H = 33{,}072+14{,}720+17{,}918+24{,}000 = 89{,}710 \; Btu/day$$
$$(H = 9645+4319+5250+7001 = 26{,}215 \; watts/day)$$

The refrigeration unit rating depends on the heat-removal rate and on the evaporator temperature. The heat-removal rate is based on a 16- or 18-hour rating factor.

Btu per hour (16-hour base) = 89,710/16 = 5607
[watts per hour (16-hour base) = 26,215/16 = 1638]
Btu per hour (18-hour base) = 89,710/18 = 4934
[watts per hour (18-hour base) = 26,215.6/18 = 1456]

These ratings assume that the 24-hour heat gain is removed in a 16- or 18-hour time frame. This means that the compressor will operate 16 or 18 hours per day (idle 8 or 6 hours per day). If required, the compressor could operate 24 hours per day, implying the refrigeration unit could remove an additional 50 or 33 percent heat gain.

Generally, the 16-hour design base results in a slightly larger and more efficient refrigeration system. The resulting energy cost difference between the two bases is usually less than 2 percent.

2. Heavy room usage and purchasing food every 3 days

$$H_{total} = H_T + H_I + H_A + H_{PII}$$
$$H = 33,072+22,080+17,918+72,000 = 145,070 \; Btu/day$$
$$(H = 9645+6480+5250+21,003 = 42,378 \; watts/day)$$

Btu per hour (16-hour base) = 145,070/16 = 9067
[watts per hour (16-hour base) = 42,378/16 = 2648]
Btu per hour (18-hour base) = 145,070/18 = 8059
[watts per hour (18-hour base) = 42,378/18 = 2354]

3. The second refrigeration rating factor is the evaporator temperature. The evaporator temperature is lower than the cooler space temperature, so that heat will flow from the cooled space to the evaporator. Two types of evaporators are available: natural convection and forced convection. The evaporator temperatures are shown below.

   a. Natural convection

$$t_{E\text{-}NC} = t_C - 20°F$$
$$(t = t_C - 11.1°C)$$

   where

$$t_{E\text{-}NC} = \text{evaporator temperature, natural convection}$$
$$t_C = \text{cooler or chiller temperature}$$
$$20 \, (11.1) = \text{constant that applies to natural convection}$$

   Hence,

$$t_{E\text{-}NC} = 35 - 20 = 15°F$$
$$(t = 1.7 - 11.1 = -9.4°C)$$

b. Forced convection

$$t_{E\text{-}FC} = t_C - 10°F$$
$$(t = t_C - 5.6°C)$$

where

$t_{E\text{-}FC}$ = evaporator temperature, forced convection

10 (5.6) = constant that applies to forced convection
Hence,

$$t_{E\text{-}FC} = 35 - 10 = 25°F$$
$$(t = 1.7 - 5.6 = -3.8°C)$$

4. Complete refrigeration unit specifications. Several alternatives are now available for the manager (for normal room usage and purchasing food each day).

a. Btu per hour (16-hour base) = 5607
   [watts per hour (16-hour base) = 1638.5]
   Evaporator (natural convection): +15°F (−9.4°C)
b. Btu per hour (18-hour base) = 4934
   [watts per hour (18-hour base) = 1456]
   Evaporator (forced convection): +25°F (−3.8°C)
c. Btu per hour (16-hour base) = 5607
   [watts per hour (16-hour base) = 1638.5]
   Evaporator (forced convection): +25°F (−3.8°C)
d. Btu per hour (18-hour base) = 4934
   [watts per hour (18-hour base) = 1456]
   Evaporator (natural convection): +15°F (−9.4°C)

REFERENCES

1. American Society of Heating, Refrigeration and Air Conditioning Engineers, *Handbook of Fundamentals, ASHRAE Guide and Data Book,* New York, 1985.

Equipment Ventilation Example Computations

There are two general ventilation computation procedures that may apply to equipment located in one room. These procedures may apply to food production rooms or mechanical rooms in the hospitality industry. In this appendix, these procedures will be applied to a food production kitchen. One common ventilation computation is called the hood system (Part A), the other the nonhood system (Part B).

If the local ventilation code requires that equipment be installed under hoods, the procedure shown in Part A must be followed. However, both procedures should be applied, and the one that results in the largest air requirement should be selected.

A. Hood system ventilation computation
    1. Basic data
        a. Equipment that must be installed under an exhaust hood is generally placed side by side in a line or back to back, as shown in the figures.

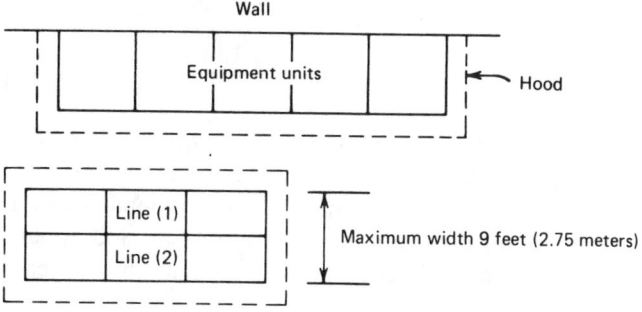

The exhaust hood must overlap the equipment line at both ends and at the front by at least 6 inches (152.4 millimeters). Hence, if the equipment line is 50 feet (15.25 meters) long and 5 feet (1.53 meters) wide, the minimum hood size is 51 feet (15.56 meters) by 5.5 feet (1.68 meters). The gross hood area is 280.5 square feet (26.14 square meters).

Each equipment line is 25 feet (7.63 meters) long. The maximum equipment width is 9 feet (2.75 meters). The hood size for this arrangement is 10 feet (3.05 meters) by 26 feet (7.93 meters) or 260 square feet (24.19 square meters).

b. The typical ventilation requirement for an equipment hood is to exhaust air at 100 feet per minute per square foot (0.50 meter per second per square meter) of gross hood size.

2. Ventilation computation

$$Exhaust\ air = A_H \times V_R$$

where

A_H = area of hood
V_R = ventilation requirement, 100 (0.50)

a. Single-line equipment arrangement:

$$Exhaust\ air = 280.5 \times 100 = 28,050\ cubic\ feet/minute$$
$$(= 26.14 \times 0.5 = 13.07\ cubic\ meters/second)$$

b. Back-to-back equipment arrangement:

$$Exhaust\ air = 260 \times 100 = 26,000\ cubic\ feet/minute$$
$$(= 24.19 \times 0.5 = 12.10\ cubic\ meters/second)$$

The hood exhaust-air requirement should now be checked with the basic kitchen ventilation computation (see Figure 9.1, room volume computation). For example, if the equipment with specifications just listed is in a kitchen that has a volume of 40,000 cubic feet (1120 cubic meters), the 28,050-cubic-feet-per-minute (13.07-cubic meter-per-second) exhaust corresponds to about 42 air changes per hour.

$$Air\ changes/hour = \frac{28,050 \times 60}{40,000} = 42.08$$

$$(= \frac{13.07 \times 3600}{1120} = 42.01)$$

Most kitchen ventilation codes require 30 to 60 air changes per hour. If a code specified only 30 air changes per hour, the additional 12.08 (42.08 − 30) air changes are supplemental equipment requirements. If 60 air changes are required, an additional exhaust system would be required because only 42.08 air changes could be exhausted through the hoods.

B. Nonhood system ventilation computation

1. Basic data

The basic equipment can be located throughout the kitchen. Kitchen equipment ventilation requirements follow.

	Ventilation requirement	
Item	Cubic feet per minute	Cubic meters per second
Conveyor (flight) dish-washing machine	2000	1.00
Range section	900	0.42
Coffee urn	600	0.28
Fryer	650	0.30
Three-deck oven	1200	0.56
Steam kettle	300	0.14

2. The following units of equipment are located in the kitchen with their ventilation requirements:

	Ventilation requirement	
Item	Cubic feet per minute	Cubic meters per second
1 Conveyor (flight) dish-washing machine	2,000	1.00
3 Range sections	2,700	1.26
2 Coffee urns	1,200	0.56
3 Fryers	1,950	0.91
2 Three-deck ovens	2,400	1.12
5 Steam kettles	1,500	0.70
Total	11,750	5.55

3. Equivalent air changes per hour for a 30,000-cubic-foot (840-cubic-meter) kitchen:

$$Air\ changes/hour = \frac{11,750 \times 60}{30,000} = 23.5$$

$$(= \frac{5.55 \times 3600}{840} = 23.8)$$

Note: Part B computations usually require less air than part A computations.

Optimal Insulation Thickness for Cooling; Psychometric Chart; Computational Model for Air Conditioning

A Optimal insulation thickness for cooling.
   (Refer to Appendix 8, part E, for basic relationships.)

   1. Data
      Cooling degree-days

   3000 per cooling season, base temperature 80°F
   (1666.7 per cooling season, base temperature 26.7°C)

   Energy cost during the cooling season averages $0.145 per kilowatt-hour. Each watt of energy will remove the equivalent of 8 watts of heat from the building. Hence, 1 kilowatt of energy input to the air-conditioning machine will result in 8000 × 3.413 = 27,304 Btu (8000 watts) of removed heat from the building.

$$C_E = \frac{\$0.145 \times 10^6}{27,304} = \$5.31/10^6 \, Btu$$

$$\left(= \frac{\$0.145 \times 10^6}{8,000} = \$18.125/10^6 \, watts \right)$$

   K_I = 0.32 Btu-inch per square foot per hour per °F
   (K_I = 46.1 watt-millimeter per square meter per hour per °C)
   C_I = $0.012 per square foot per inch per year, for 20-year life

(C_I = \$0.0051 per square meter per millimeter per year, for 20-year life)

U_P = 0.50 (2.84) (concrete block, drywall, and glass construction)

2. Optimal insulation thickness

$$X_{net} = \sqrt{\frac{3000 \times 24 \times \$5.61 \times 0.32}{\$0.012 \times 10^6}} - \frac{0.32}{0.50} = 2.64 \text{ inches}$$

$$\left(= \sqrt{\frac{1,666.7 \times 24 \times \$18.125 \times 46.1}{\$0.0051 \times 10^6}} - \frac{46.1}{2.84} = 64.72 \text{ millimeters} \right)$$

B. Psychometric chart and comfort

Figure A11.1 shows a special psychometric chart that relates three temperatures and relative humidity. To use the chart, you need to know only two of the four terms, for example, dry-bulb and wet-bulb temperatures. Draw a straight line connecting these two temperatures and extend it to the next two scales; then, read the dew point on its scale and the relative humidity on its scale. Various examples are shown in Figure A11.2. (Do not bother with the "Heat content" section in the table at this time; it will be referred to later.)

After you have repeated the operations indicated in Figure A11.2, you are now able to read the chart. The chart is used to determine outside air conditions that are critical in the air-conditioning process. The National Weather Service normally maintains two sets of temperatures for various locations in the country. These are average high summer dry-bulb and wet-bulb temperatures. Knowing these data, you can now use the chart to determine the dew-point temperature and the percent relative humidity. Later in this section, you will be referred back to this chart to make these calculations. This operation is required to determine the size of an air conditioner for a property.

Figure A11.3 shows an enlarged view of one section of the chart and indicates the general comfort area for a larger percentage of people. If you provide a building environment in this area, it will satisfy most people. Generally, the less humid region, with lower dew points, should be used for people who are performing manual tasks. The degree of comfort is approximately the same at each point in the region. You should be aware that air movement is assumed to be between 15 and 20 feet per minute (0.08 and 0.10 meter per second) on this chart.

C. Air-conditioner size computational model.

1. Building heat-removal requirements: refer to Figure 10.7 for a visual of the heat requirements. Someone — usually a professional engineer (PE) — determines each of the building heat loads. Assume that such

Heat content		Wet bulb	
watts/kilogram	Btu/lb	°F	°C
31.5	49	85	29.4
28.3	44	80	26.7
25.1	39	75	23.9
21.9	34	70	21.1
19.3	30	65	18.3
17.4	27	60	15.6
14.8	23	55	12.8
12.9	20	50	10.0
11.6	18	45	7.2
9.6	15	40	4.5
8.4	13	35	1.7
7.1	11	30	−1.1
5.8	9	25	−3.9

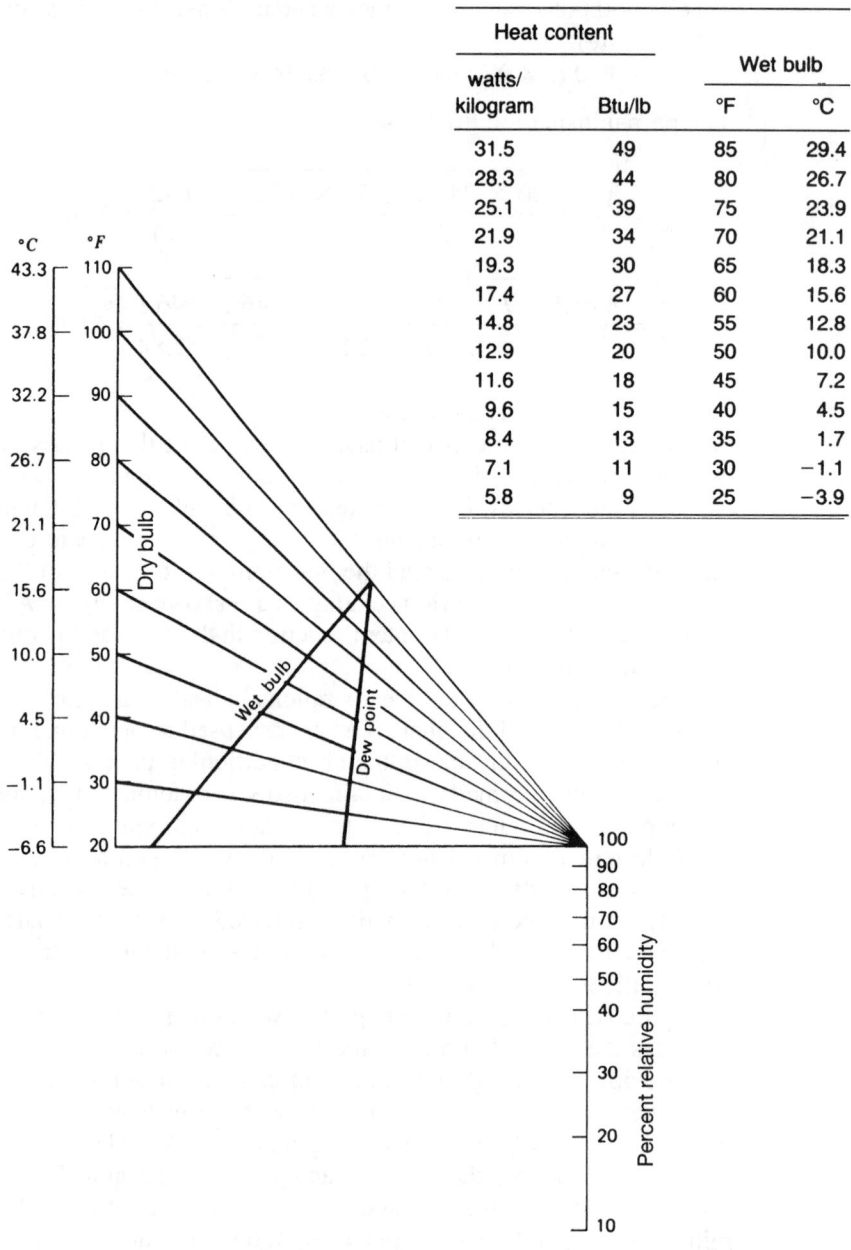

FIGURE A11.1 Psychometric relationships between dry-bulb, wet-bulb, and dew-point temperatures, and percent relative humidity.

Heat content		Wet bulb	
watts/ kilogram	Btu/lb	°F	°C
31.5	49	85	29.4
28.3	44	80	26.7
25.1	39	75	23.9
21.9	34	70	21.1
19.3	30	65	18.3
17.4	27	60	15.6
14.8	23	55	12.8
12.9	20	50	10.0
11.6	18	45	7.2
9.6	15	40	4.5
8.4	13	35	1.7
7.1	11	30	−1.1
5.8	9	25	−3.9

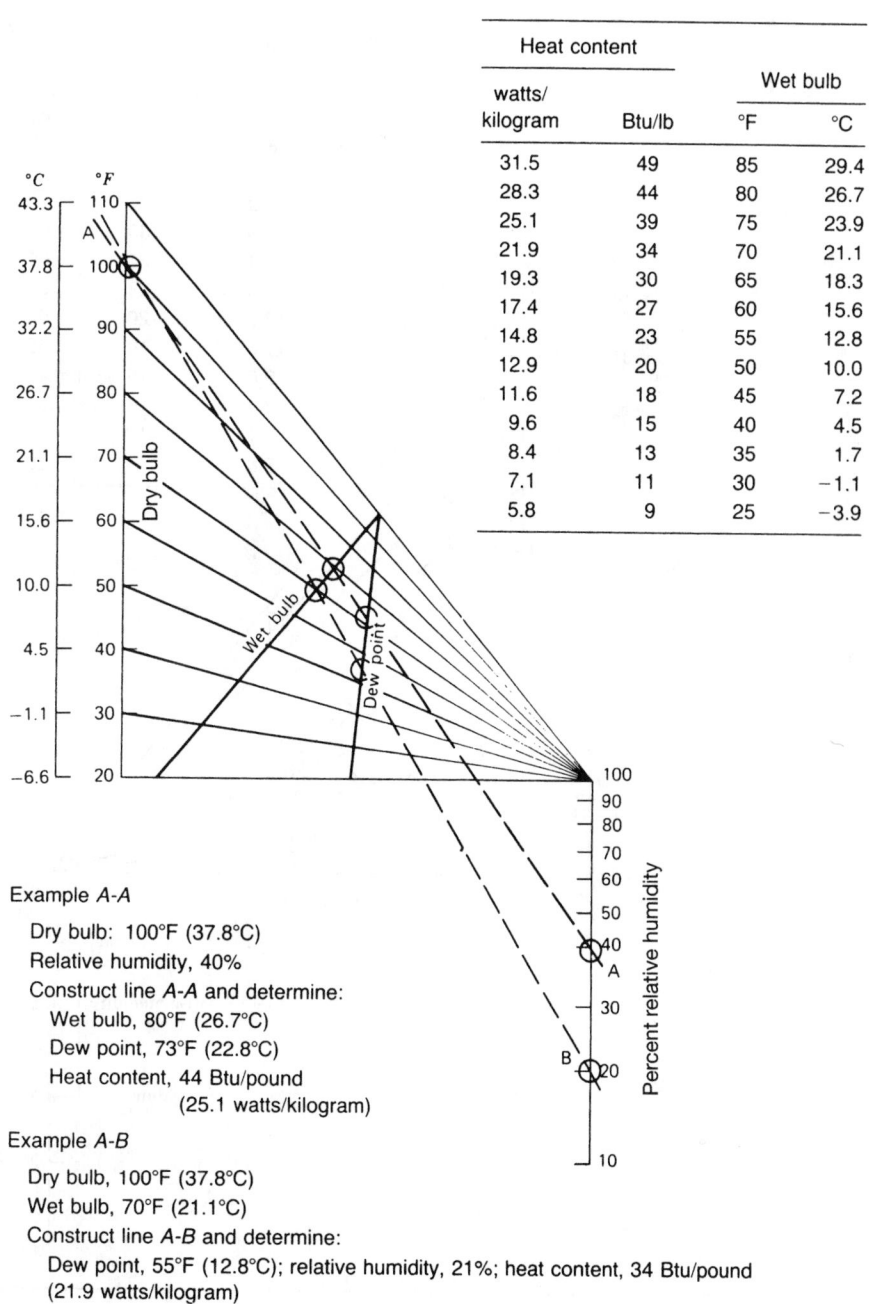

Example *A-A*

  Dry bulb: 100°F (37.8°C)
  Relative humidity, 40%
  Construct line *A-A* and determine:
    Wet bulb, 80°F (26.7°C)
    Dew point, 73°F (22.8°C)
    Heat content, 44 Btu/pound
          (25.1 watts/kilogram)

Example *A-B*

  Dry bulb, 100°F (37.8°C)
  Wet bulb, 70°F (21.1°C)
  Construct line *A-B* and determine:
    Dew point, 55°F (12.8°C); relative humidity, 21%; heat content, 34 Btu/pound
    (21.9 watts/kilogram)

FIGURE A11.2 Examples showing the use of Figure A11.1.

Heat content		Wet bulb	
watts/ kilogram	Btu/lb	°F	°C
31.5	49	85	29.4
28.3	44	80	26.7
25.1	39	75	23.9
21.9	34	70	21.1
19.3	30	65	18.3
17.4	27	60	15.6
14.8	23	55	12.8
12.9	20	50	10.0
11.6	18	45	7.2
9.6	15	40	4.5
8.4	13	35	1.7
7.1	11	30	−1.1
5.8	9	25	−3.9

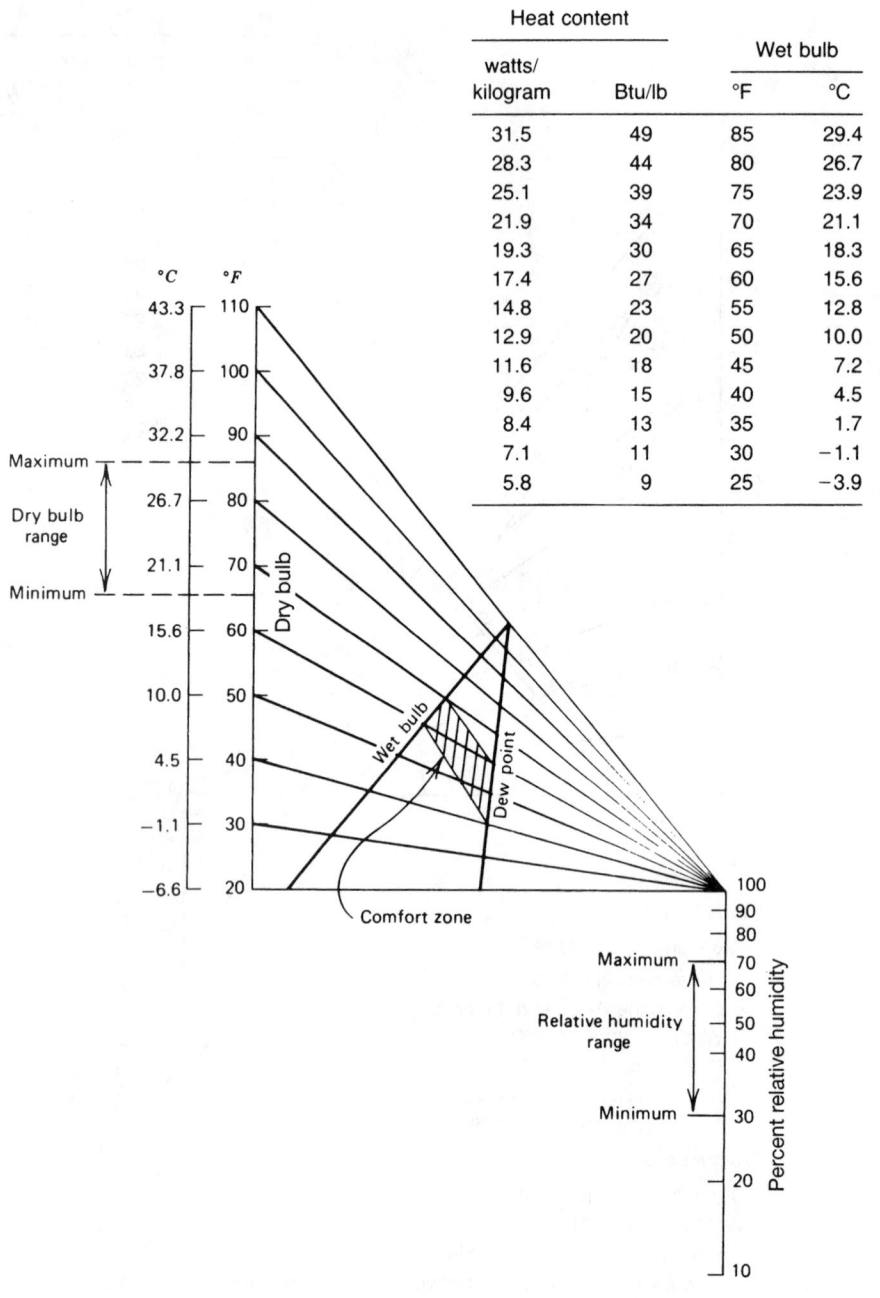

FIGURE A11.3 Human comfort zone.

a determination has been made and that the maximum heat load occurs at 4 P.M. (1600 hours) and is indicated below.

Heat gain	Btu per hour	Watts per hour
Transmission	50,000	14,650
Solar	30,000	8,790
Appliance	35,000	10,255
Infiltration	20,000	5,860
Occupant	40,000	11,720
Total	175,000	51,275

The cool supply air to the room or building (see Figure 10.7) must have the capability of absorbing this amount of heat.

2. Ventilation requirement: ventilation air is determined by one of the computational methods described in Chapter 9. For our purposes, assume that the maximum amount (per local code) of air is 200,000 cubic feet per hour or CFH (5600 cubic meters per hour, or CMH). This is the amount of air available to absorb the 175,000 Btu (51,275 watts) per hour of building heat gain.

The volume of ventilation air must be converted to pounds (kilograms) of air for computational purposes. The following equation is used:

$$W = 0.075 \times CFH, \text{ } pounds/hour$$
$$(= 1.216 \times CMH, \text{ } kilograms/hour$$
$$= 0.075 \times 200,000 = 15,000 \text{ } pounds/hour$$
$$(= 1.216 \times 5600 = 6810 \text{ } kilograms/hour)$$

3. Air design specifications
   a. Inside, or recirculated air: air-conditioning design specifies the maximum or optimal conditions of the room exhaust air (recirculated air, see Figure 10.7). This is generally 80°F (26.7°C) dry bulb, with 50 percent relative humidity.

   The corresponding wet-bulb temperature is 67°F (19.4°C). [Draw a straight line through the 80°F (26.7°C) dry-bulb point, left vertical scale on Figure A11.1, and the 50 percent relative humidity point, right vertical scale, and note the intersection on the wet-bulb scale.]

   Having obtained the wet-bulb temperature, use the enthalpy table on the upper right portion of Figure A11.1, and determine the appropriate air enthalpy. It is 31.5 Btu per pound (20.4 watts per kilogram). This represents the maximum heat content of the exhaust air from the building or space being cooled.

b. Outside, or fresh air: for this example computation, outside air conditions are assumed to be 95°F (35°C) dry bulb and 80°F (26.7°C) wet bulb. The enthalpy of the outside air is read directly from Figure A11.1. It is 44 Btu per pound (28.3 watts per kilogram).

c. Air entering the air conditioner: there are several options available to the chief engineer controlling the air flow to the air conditioner (see Figure 10.7): all fresh-air flow; all recirculated-air flow; or a combination of fresh and recirculated air, for example, 50 percent fresh air and 50 percent recirculated air. With the combination alternative, the percentages must add up to 100. The effects of these alternatives follow.

The computational equation for determining the enthalpy of the air entering the air conditioner is

$$h_3 = h_1 \times F_1 + h_2 \times F_2$$

where

h_3 = enthalpy in Btu per pound (watts per kilogram) of the air entering the air conditioner

h_1 = enthalpy in Btu per pound (watts per kilogram) of the fresh air

F_1 = decimal equivalent of the percentage of fresh air entering the air conditioner ($0 \leq F_1 \leq 1$)

h_2 = enthalpy in Btu per pound (watts per kilogram) of the recirculated air

F_2 = decimal equivalent of the percentage of recirculated air entering the air conditioner ($0 \leq F_2 \leq 1$)

$$F_1 + F_2 = 1.0$$

d. Example computation: building exhaust air: 80°F (27.6°C) dry bulb; 50 percent relative humidity; enthalpy is 31.5 Btu per pound (20.4 watts per kilogram). Fresh air: 95°F (35°C) dry bulb; 80°F (26.7°C) wet bulb; enthalpy is 44 Btu per pound (28.3 watts per kilogram).

1. 100% *fresh air supply*:

h_3 = 44 × 1.0 + 31.5 × 0.0 = 44 *Btu/pound*
  (= 28.3 × 1.0 + 20.4 × 0.0 = 28.3 *watts/kilogram*

2. 100% *recirculated air supply*:

h_3 = 44 × 0.0 + 31.5 × 1.0 = 31.5 *Btu/pound*
  (= 28.3 × 0.0 + 20.4 × 1.0 = 20.4 *watts/kilogram*

3. 50% *fresh air* + 50% *recirculated air*:

h_3 = 44 × 0.5 + 31.5 × 0.5 = 37.8 *Btu/pound*
  (= 28.3 × 0.5 + 20.4 × 0.5 = 24.4 *watts/kilogram*

4. Enthalpy of air entering the room or building being cooled (supply air to room or building): the air entering the space to be cooled must have the capability for absorbing the building heat gain (load). This air is also the same air that leaves the air conditioner (see the diagram).

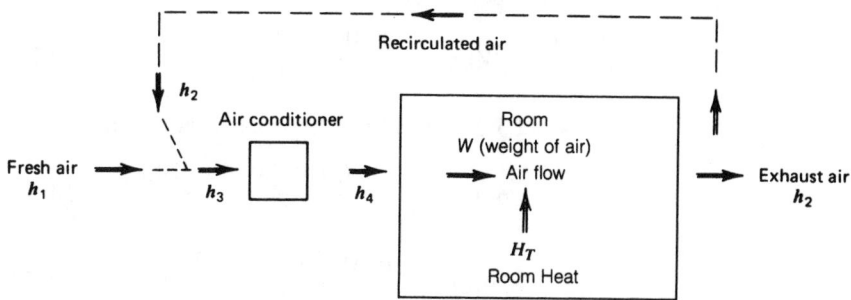

This computation will determine h_4. This air (W) with an enthalpy of h_4 will absorb H_T and end up with an enthalpy of h_2. The basic equation has the following form:

$$H_T = W \times (h_2 - h_4)$$

Solving for h_4:

$$h_4 = h_2 - \frac{H_T}{W}$$

Substituting the information obtained earlier results in

$$h_4 = 31.5 - \frac{175{,}000}{15{,}000} = 19.8 \; Btu/pound$$

$$\left(= 20.4 - \frac{51{,}275}{6{,}810} = 12.9 \; watts/kilogram \right)$$

5. Size of the air conditioner: the air-conditioner size is given in horsepower or tons. The sizing equation is

$$Horsepower, \; tons = \frac{W \times (h_3 - h_4)}{12{,}000}$$

$$\left[Watts = \frac{W \times (h_3 - h_4)}{4.713} \right]$$

where
W = weight of air
h_3 = enthalpy of air entering air conditioner (see the diagram)
h_4 = enthalpy of air leaving air conditioner (see the diagram)
12,000 (3516) = constant (Btu [watts] per hour)

Computation:

1. $h_3 = 44$ (28.3) for 100 percent fresh air

$$Horsepower = \frac{15,000 \times (44 - 19.8)}{12,000} = 30.3$$

$$[Watts = \frac{6810 \times (28.3 - 12.9)}{4.713} = 22,252]$$

2. $h_3 = 31.5$ (20.4) for 100 percent recirculated air

$$Horsepower = \frac{15,000 \times (31.5 - 19.8)}{12,000} = 14.6$$

$$[Watts = \frac{6810 \times (20.4 - 12.9)}{4.713} = 10,837]$$

3. $h_3 = 37.8$ (24.4) for 50 percent fresh and 50 percent recirculated air

$$Horsepower = \frac{15,000 \times (37.8 - 19.8)}{12,000} = 22.5$$

$$[Watts = \frac{6810 \times (24.4 - 12.9)}{4.713} = 16,616]$$

Note 1: It should be observed that when the outside enthalpy is greater than the building exhaust-air enthalpy, the minimum size of air conditioner occurs when the building exhaust air is supplied to the air conditioner. Hence, building exhaust air is recirculated through the air conditioner for maximum cooling. This is normally done when the building space is pre-cooled. However, when occupants are present, the local ventilation code, specifying a minimum quantity of fresh air, such as 50 percent, applies. Then, only minimum fresh air should be supplied to the air conditioner.

If a maximum-size air-cooling system is installed — 30.3 horsepower (22,252 watts) — and if all recirculated air is used for cooling, the refrigeration cycle will operate only 48 percent of the time:

$$\frac{14.6}{30.3} = 0.48 = 48\%$$

$$\left(\frac{10,837}{22,252} = 0.48 = 48\% \right)$$

Note 2: The preceding example shows why enthalpy controls are very feasible. One control is placed in the exhaust-air duct and a second in the fresh-air supply. These controls measure both enthalpy sets and allow the air with minimum enthalpy to flow to the air conditioner. The system is fixed to provide for minimum fresh-air requirements specified by the ventilation code. In the preceding example problem, the controls would vary from 50 to 100 percent fresh air if the code required a minimum of 50 percent fresh air. If the outside air cooled during the night, the enthalpy control would gradually regulate the dampers to allow more and more fresh air. At times, the cooling system may not be required because the outside air can absorb all the building heat.

Note 3: It is very possible that the horsepower (watt) computation may produce a negative number. This implies air heating. Most air heating would require an addition of water to the air (adding water to air is actually a heating process that increases the dew-point and wet-bulb temperatures, as well as the relative humidity). This may occur in dry desert climates and allows one to use evaporative (swamp) coolers for building cooling. (See Chapter 10 for a discussion of these units.)

Analysis of Various Laundering Alternatives for a 300-Guest-Room Lodging Establishment with Foodservice

A. On-premises laundry installation data and costs

    1. Annual linen requirements are shown in Table A12.1.

Table A12.1   Annual linen requirements for a 300-guest-room lodging establishment with foodservice

Item	Dozens per year
Washcloths	1050
Face towels	500
Towels	450
Bath mats	75
Twin sheets	450
Double sheets	75
Queen/king sheets	300
Pillowcases	400
Table napkins	525
Kitchen towels	200
Employee aprons	150
Tablecloths	75

    2. Annual linen costs are shown in Table A12.2.

Table A12.2 Annual linen costs for a 300-guest-room lodging establishment with foodservice

Item	$Cost per unit	$Annual cost
Washcloths	$1.50	$18,900.00
Face towels	4.00	24,000.00
Towels	6.00	32,400.00
Bath mats	12.00	10,800.00
Twin sheets	9.00	48,600.00
Double sheets	15.00	13,500.00
Queen/king sheets	25.00	90,000.00
Pillowcases	4.00	19,200.00
Table napkins	3.00	18,900.00
Kitchen towels	3.00	7,200.00
Employee aprons	10.00	18,000.00
Tablecloths	20.00	18,000.00

3. Equipment space and utility requirements
   a. Space requirement (see Figure 16.6): 1350 square feet (125.6 square meters)
   b. Energy requirement (see Figure 16.6): 900,000 Btu (263,700 watts) per hour
   c. Water requirements (see Figure 16.6): total water, 2400 gallons (9060 liters) per hour; cold water, 1200 gallons (4530 liters) per hour; hot water, 1200 gallons (4530 liters) per hour
   d. Equipment requirements (see Figure 16.7): washer capacity, 300 pounds (136.2 kilograms); dryer capacity, 300 pounds (136.2 kilograms); extractor capacity, 225 pounds (102.2 kilograms); combination washer–dryer capacity, 150 pounds (68.1 kilograms)
   e. Equipment costs (see Figure 16.8): about $30,000; assume a 10-year life; hence, $3000 per year
   f. Space charge: $15 per square foot ($161.25 per square meter) per year; total annual costs, $15 × 1350 ($161.25 × 125.6) = $20,250
   g. Energy costs: $0.145 per kilowatt-hour (including demand charges); 450,000 watts is the maximum electrical load; assume that the actual electrical utilization is 50 percent of full load, or 225,000 watts; the total electric charge is as follows:

$$225,000 \times \frac{\$0.145}{1000} = \$32.63 \text{ per hour}$$

h. Water charge: water requirement is 2400 gallons (9060 liters) per hour. If water cost $2.50 per 1000 gallons (3785 liters), the hourly charge is as follows:

$$2400 \times \frac{\$2.50}{1000} = \$6.00 \text{ per hour}$$

$$9060 \times \frac{\$2.50}{3785} = \$6.00 \text{ per hour}$$

i. Sewage charges: sewage charges are $1.00 per 1000 gallons (3785 liters); sewage charges are as follows:

$$2400 \times \frac{\$1.00}{1000} = \$2.40 \text{ per hour}$$

$$9060 \times \frac{\$1.00}{3785} = \$2.40 \text{ per hour}$$

j. Equipment repairs and maintenance: repairs and maintenance will average 15 percent of the original equipment installation cost, the cost is as follows:

$$0.15 \times \$30,000 = \$4500 \text{ per year}$$

4. Supply costs (see Figure 16.8): $15,600 per year
5. Personnel requirements and costs (see Figure 16.8): 9 persons are required; workers are paid an average (including supervisors) of $8 per hour plus an average of 25 percent in fringe benefits; hourly personnel costs are as follows:

$$9 \times \$8 \times 1.25 = \$90.00 \text{ per hour}$$

6. Other costs: insurance and property taxes are based on linens, equipment, and space values. These costs will average 3 percent of the value of these items.
7. Total annual costs and cost per guest room (the laundry is in operation 48 hours per week, 52 weeks per year) are shown in Table A12.3.

B. Costs of purchasing linens and using a commercial laundry
    1. Linen costs (refer to part A): $319,500
    2. Space charges (use one-third of part A charges): $6750
    3. Insurance and taxes (linen and space value): $9788
    4. Commercial laundry cost
        a. Pounds (kilograms) to launder each year: 12 pounds (5.44 kilograms) of linen per occupied guest room per day (Chapter 16, Reference 2):

Table A12.3 Annual on-premises laundry costs for a 300-guest-room lodging establishment with foodservice

Item	Cost per year
Linen	$319,500
Equipment	3,000
Equipment repairs and maintenance	4,500
Space charge	20,250
Energy:	
Electric	81,444
Water	14,976
Sewage	5,990
Supplies	15,600
Personnel	187,200
Other costs	11,093
Total	$660,853
Annual cost per guest room	$2,202.84

$$Weight = 12 \times 300 \times 365 = 1,314,000 \; pounds$$
$$(= 5.44 \times 300 \times 365 = 596,556 \; kilograms)$$

b. Average laundry cost is $0.25 per pound ($0.55067 per kilogram):

$$Cost = \$0.25 \times 1,314,000 = \$328,500 \; per \; year$$
$$(= \$0.55067 \times 596,556 = \$328,500 \; per \; year)$$

5. Total, excluding guest laundry provisions: $664,538 per year
6. Annual cost per guest room, excluding guest laundry provisions: $2215.13

C. Linen rental alternative
   1. Annual linen requirements and costs are shown in Table A12.4.
   2. Space charge, equal to commercial laundry space charge: $6750
   3. Total annual costs, excluding guest laundry provisions: $756,180
   4. Annual cost per guest room, excluding guest laundry provisions, $2520.60

D. Disposable linen cost
   1. Annual linen requirements and costs are shown in Table A12.5.
   2. Space charge, equal to linen rental space charge (see part C): $6750
   3. Total annual costs, excluding guest laundry provisions: $1,373,590
   4. Annual cost per guest room, excluding guest laundry provisions: $4578.63

E. Conclusions
The on-premises laundry has the potential to take care of guest laundry and dry-cleaning requirements, as well as other linens not included in this analysis, such as employee uniforms. These requirement costs would

Table A12.4 Annual linen rental requirements and costs for a 300-guest-room lodging establishment with foodservice

Item	Units	$/unit	$ Cost
Washcloths	260,000	$0.15	$39,000
Face towels	260,000	0.20	52,000
Towels	200,000	0.50	100,000
Bath mats	140,000	0.75	105,000
Twin sheets	141,800	0.40	56,720
Double sheets	26,000	0.60	15,600
Queen/king sheets	92,200	0.80	73,760
Pillowcases	260,000	0.30	78,000
Table napkins	630,000	0.12	75,600
Kitchen towels	60,000	0.50	30,000
Employee aprons	45,000	0.75	33,750
Tablecloths	90,000	1.00	90,000

Table A12.5 Annual disposable linen requirements and costs for a 300-guest-room lodging establishment with foodservice

Item	Units	$/unit	$ Cost
Washcloths	260,000	$0.25	$65,000
Face towels	260,000	0.30	78,000
Towels	200,000	1.00	200,000
Bath mats	140,000	1.25	175,000
Twin sheets	141,800	0.80	113,440
Double sheets	26,000	1.00	26,000
Queen/king sheets	92,200	2.00	184,400
Pillowcases	260,000	0.50	130,000
Table napkins	630,000	0.20	126,000
Kitchen towels	60,000	0.75	45,000
Employee aprons	45,000	1.00	45,000
Tablecloths	90,000	2.00	180,000

have to be added to the other alternatives, such as those given in parts B, C, and D. Guest laundry would also produce some income that could be used to offset a portion of the total cost of an on-premises laundry.

The preceding analysis is only an example of the total analysis. Prices, costs, and linen requirements can vary significantly from one geographic area to another. The costs used in this appendix were updated from Chapter 16, Reference 1.

GLOSSARY

Absorber: a component of a refrigeration cycle (absorption cycle) that contains a salt solution that absorbs a vapor refrigerant. Upon absorption, the refrigerant releases its latent heat of vaporization.

Absorption coefficient: the ability of a cold surface to absorb heat.

Absorption cooling system: cooling air with an absorption refrigeration cycle, usually the lithium bromide absorption cycle.

Absorption refrigeration: a refrigeration cycle that uses gas as an energy resource to operate the generator. It is used for food chillers and freezers.

Acid rain: a family of sulfuric acids, nitric oxides, and sulfur dioxides that form when sulfur, a byproduct of industrialization, large urban centers, and auto exhausts, unites with water.

Active solar heating: the absorption of solar energy using electromechanical systems.

Afterburner: a gas-fired kitchen exhaust filter used to ignite vaporized kitchen oil/grease byproducts.

AFUE (annual fuel utilization efficiency): the AFUE is a percentage rating of expected performance considering losses up the chimney, cycling effects (heat plant heat-up), and losses from nonelectric pilots during a typical year of operation. It is equal to the Btu (watt) heat output rating divided by the Btu (watt) fuel input rating during a representative heating season.

Agricultural gypsum: a chemical that has the potential for clearing water clouded by certain types of sediment.

Air conditioning: any treatment of the air, including movement, filtering, heating, cooling, humidifying, dehumidifying, or mixing fresh with recirculated air.

611

Air Conditioning and Refrigeration Institute (ARI): an organization that certifies the capacity of cooling equipment.

Air cooling: any process that reduces the temperature of air.

Air filter: any device that removes impurities from air, usually ventilation supply air. It may also be required on exhaust air systems, such as a grease filter.

Air velocity: the speed at which air moves through ducts, registers, grills, and space. Usually, duct air speeds are between 300 and 2000 feet per minute (1.5 and 10 meters per second).

Algae control: a procedure that keeps water plant life (algae) to a minimum. Chemicals are required to control algae. The most effective algae control is to keep the disinfectant level at 1 ppm or higher.

Alligatored: roofing that has a rough surface similar to the texture of alligator skin.

Alternating current (ac): generally, the type of electric energy supplied by an electric utility. Amperes and volts vary with time and reverse through electric devices.

Alternative I: refers to a complete on-premises maintenance-and-engineering department for a property. Typically, larger properties of 300 or more guest rooms with complete food and beverage services, complete meeting and conference facilities, and possibly resort-type recreational facilities have a complete on-premises department.

Alternative II: refers to a limited on-premises maintenance-and-engineering department with limited staff. Service contracts are typically used for selected equipment and control systems. This alternative is generally followed for properties of 150 or more guest rooms with a variety of food and beverage operations, some meeting and conference space, and some recreational facilities.

Alternative III: refers to a one- or two-person maintenance department. Personnel perform minimal maintenance functions and a large number of service contracts are required for adequate building maintenance.

American Gas Association (AGA): an organization that develops standards for gas operated equipment (safety and operating standards), and also does equipment research.

American Hospital Association (AHA): a professional organization that develops hospital and related health care industry standards.

American Hotel & Motel Association (AHMA): a professional organization that develops lodging industry standards.

American Society of Heating, Refrigeration, and Air Conditioning Engineers (ASHRAE): the organization that has (1) developed non-CFC refrigerant standards and a new 400 series of refrigerants that are blends of approved halocarbon refrigerants; (2) developed minimum fresh air ventilation standards that should eliminate or greatly reduce the "sick building syndrome" effects caused by insufficient fresh ventilation air.

American Society of Mechanical Engineers (ASME): develops maintenance standards for steam operated equipment.

Americans with Disabilities Act (ADA): U.S. federal law that sets modification and design facility standards to ensure disabled people rights and access; also states occupational qualifications (physical/mental requirements for employee titles).

Americans with Disabilities Act Accessibility Guidelines (ADAAG): U.S. federal requirements for companies conducting business with the U.S. government. In Chapter 17, the guidelines cover parking spaces and parking area sizes, access lane and route, and width of building entry doors.

Ampere: rate of electric energy flow.

Analog-style smoke detection: basic alarm signal plus reports percentage of smoke in each building area.

Angle valve: a water control valve used on fixtures for variable water flow. Water usually makes a 90-degree turn when passing through the valve.

Annoyance: noise that affects customers, for example, painful, high-hertz sounds or sound from a fixed location.

Anode: a device in an electric discharge lamp that attracts electrons emitted from the cathode.

Anodize: apply a protective film to light metals such as aluminum.

Anticipator: an outside thermostat that measures how fast the outside temperature is changing and overrides inside thermostats.

Appliance heat (gain) load: the heat gain from electric lamps or fan motors in a food chiller or freezer. Heat released from building appliances, including electric lamps.

Architect: a person who is responsible for developing blueprints.

ASCII: American Standard Code for Information Interchange, ASCII is a seven-bit-plus-parity code established by the American National Standards Institute to achieve compatibility among different computers and terminals.

Auger: a flexible spiral device that is inserted in drainage pipes to collect or push clogging debris to larger piping.

Automatic sprinkler: a device that is heat activated and connected to a system of plumbing piping through which a sufficient quantity of water can be distributed on a fire to extinguish it (removing heat) entirely or prevent its spread.

Available water pressure: the water pressure measured at a service or distribution pipe.

AWG (American Wire Gage): wire diameter sizing index. Used in the United States for smaller-diameter wires.

Axial-flow fans: a family of fans similar to propellers.

Backlog work order: a work-order request that cannot be completed at the present time because a replacement part is not in inventory or an employee trained to complete the work-order request is not on the property at the time of the request. The backlog work order is scheduled as a routine or regular work request when the replacement part is received or when the trained employee reports to work.

Backwashing: the filter cleaning procedure that allows pool water to flow in a reverse manner to force collected impurities from the filter screen or from layers of sand to an indirect waste connected to the drainage system.

Ballast: a component of an electric discharge lamp circuit that allows full circuit voltage to be impressed on the filament to get the lamp started and reduces the circuit voltage once the lamp is producing light. It is a series electric load that causes these lamps to operate with a power factor less than 1.

Balustrade: the concave assembly between the steps and handrail on an escalator system. The balustrade is designed to prevent clothing from snagging on the escalator structural assembly.

Benchmark: (1) A changing goal or work standard used in a Total Quality Management program. (2) A permanent marker that is used as a reference point when showing surface elevations or contour lines on survey and plot views.

Biomass energy: the production of synthetic oil or SNG from wastes, such as garbage and sewage.

Biometrics: access control technology based on a fingerprint scan.

Bitumen: asphalt.

Blueprint: a series of visual pictures, usually of a building, one of its structural components, or any item or equipment placed in a building. Blueprints may also be drawn of a parcel of land. Included with blueprints are written specifications.

Boiler: a heat plant that is used to heat water or generate steam.

Broiler: radiant food cooker; includes char-broiler and upright broilers.

Btu: a heat energy measurement term. It is the amount of heat required to increase the temperature of 1 pound of water 1° F.

Budget: a financial goal or objective.

Budget (comparison) report: a comparison of actual expenses and budgeted expenses with explanations for any expenses that are in excess of allowable variances.

Building drain: a horizontal drainpipe that collects wastes from fixture drains, drainpipes, and stacks and discharges the waste outside of the building to the building sewer.

Building sewer: a horizontal drainpipe that collects wastes from the building drain and discharges the wastes to the public sewer or to a private sewage disposal system.

Built-up roofing (BUR): overlapping layers of bituminous-saturated roofing felt.

Bumper: a safety device located in the pit. Sometimes called a spring.

Cable (electric): two or more wires with additional insulation. Common building cables are nonmetallic sheathed, armored, and conduit.

Cable elevator: a mechanical vertical-transportation system for a building that includes a shaft, penthouse, pit, guide rails, counterweights, cable, elevator machine, controls, and a car for passenger and/or product movement.

Cables (elevator): the car-suspending device for the cable-type elevator system. One end is attached to the car and the other to the counterweights. The cable rides over the elevator machine driving sheave.

CAD: computer-aided design; the process of digitally creating engineering drawings and capturing part geometry using a variety of interactive devices and programming techniques; examples are AutoCAD® and VersaCAD® 8.0

CAFM: computer-aided facility management.

Candela: a measurement of light intensity at the light source.

Canopy hood: a supplemental ventilation exhaust system for a single unit or an entire group of adjacent pieces of equipment. Frequently required on selected food production equipment.

Capability: determining what the system needs to do, how it will best fulfill its function, and where it will be most valuable.

Capacitor: a device that quickly stores up electric energy and releases the energy. Frequently used on ac electric motors to improve the starting ability of the rotor under mechanical loads. May also be used in electronic equipment to block the flow of unwanted or undesirable types of electric energy (a filter).

Capture mechanism: a device or technique that returns an elevator car to a fire-safe level after the fire alarm is activated.

Car: the device in which passengers ride in an elevator system. Or the platform on which products are placed for vertical movement with an elevator system. Normal passenger cars have handrails, lighting, a ventilation system, a passenger control network, emergency communication system, and doors.

Carbon dioxide: a nonaqueous extinguishing agent that smothers a fire by removing oxygen in the vicinity of discharge to the point where it will no longer support combustion.

Carbon monoxide: a gas produced by the incomplete combustion of carbon atoms. The complete combustion results in carbon dioxide. Carbon monoxide is an odorless and toxic gas.

Cartridge filter: a swimming pool filter that has a fine meshed screen that collects water impurities.

Catchment area survey: an evaluation of present and future land uses in a particular area as to how they might impact on recreational and potable water quality.

Cathode: a device in an electric discharge lamp that emits electrons.

CATV: cable access television.

Celsius: the SIU temperature scale. Water freezes at 0°C and boils at 100°C at sea-level pressure.

Central ventilation system: a single set of supply and exhaust fans and ducts that continuously provides ventilation air to an entire building.

Centrifugal fans: a family of fans similar to spoke wheels. When rotating or turning, they suck air into their centers and discharge air at one point on their circumference.

Centrifugal pump: a type of pump that consists of a spoke wheel moving within an enclosure. When the wheel turns or rotates, a vacuum is created in its center; as water passes through the pump, its pressure is increased by centrifugal force.

Cesspool: an in-ground pit, lined with concrete, that has periodic openings. Sewage solids collect in the pit and are eventually decomposed by bacteria contained in the sewage and in the ground.

Check valve: a one-way water valve. It only allows liquids to flow one way through it.

Chief engineer evaluation: determining the effectiveness of the chief engineer, usually by using various reports.

Chilled-water compression system: cooling air with chilled water. The chilled water is produced with a vapor compression refrigeration cycle.

Chiller: a food storage area (walk-in or reach-in) that maintains a 40 to 45°F (4.4 to 7.2°C) temperature.

Chlorofluorocarbon refrigerant (CFC): the group of refrigerants that, when released to the atmosphere, destroy the protective ozone layer around earth. These are currently banned around the world and must be replaced with safe substitute refrigerants.

Circuit: a source of energy, an energy path (usually wires), and a device (usually an energy consumer such as an electric lamp).

Circuit breaker: similar to a fuse except that the element activates a switch that interrupts energy flow. Hence, elements are not replaced but the switch is reset to reactivate the circuit. Heat-type (ac and dc) and electromagnetic (ac) circuit breakers are available.

Circuit panel: final control point for individual building and area circuits.

Clamping brake: a safety device placed between the guide rails and car that is activated by a governor that measures car speed.

Class A fire: involves ordinary combustibles found in every property (wood, paper, rubbish, cloth).

Class B fire: occurs when flammable liquids including paint, grease, oil, and gasoline ignite.

Class C fire: involves live electrical motors, controls, panels, and wiring.

Clearance: the actual dimension between walls or openings, or between a floor and a ceiling. Wall dimensions (thickness) are not included with a clearance dimension.

Closed-circuit television (CCTV): assists in deterrence, surveillance, apprehension, and prosecution. A basic system includes a camera, monitor, and connecting cable.

Club Managers Association of America (CMAA): a professional organization that has a manager certification program, which includes education, professional, and service requirements.

Coal stoker: a coal-burning heat plant that feeds air and coal into a combustion chamber at specified rates.

Coded or computerized lock: a keyless locking system that is hard wired to the building electric system or standalone with batteries. It is activated by an individual card, much like a credit card, with a combination of holes punched in the card or several layers of information encoded on the card's magnetic strip.

Co-generation: the use of one energy resource to generate electric power and heat. The heat is usually a by-product of electric power generation that is utilized to heat water or heat or cool a building.

Co-generation system: an on-premises energy system that consumes one or more fuels to generate heat and electric power.

Collective control system: an elevator system that records all up and down passenger calls and passenger destination calls. Operators are not required to control car movements. Starter use is optional during peak movement periods.

Combination linen service: a commonly used hospitality laundering alternative in which the hospitality unit may rent specific types of linens (employee uniforms), may purchase other types of linens and utilize the services of a commercial laundry for washing these products, may operate a smaller on-premises laundry for specific linens or for guest laundering, and may also use disposable products (public rest room towels).

Combination system: a water distribution system that is partially upfeed and partially downfeed.

Combplate: a component of an escalator system located at each level serviced by the escalator. Steps descend and rise from the combplates. They have the appearance of a hair comb.

Comfort zone: that part of the psychometric chart in which a person will feel the same degree of comfort with different dry-bulb, dew-point, and wet-bulb temperatures and different relative humidities.

Commercial laundry service: a laundering alternative in which a hospitality unit has a commercial laundry wash and clean and possibly repair linens at a fixed cost per repair and per pound (kilogram) of washing, or at a rate per unit of linen. With this alternative, the hospitality unit purchases linens.

Communication: a function of management that keeps everyone informed of what has happened or of future plans and activities.

Compatibility: matching the technical expertise of the property management staff, the existing parts inventory, and equipment and tools for maintenance and repair should be considered when selecting equipment.

Compressed-air refrigeration: a cooling technique that increases the pressure on air, and then quickly releases the pressure of the air allowing it to expand, thus absorbing heat.

Compressor: a component of a refrigeration cycle that increases the refrigerant pressure. Normal compressors are rotary, centrifugal, and reciprocating and are usually driven by electric motors.

Computer-aided design and drafting (CADD): able to recall large amounts of information and present data in existing or revised formats such as building diagrams.

Computer energy control: usually a computer-controlled energy-management system, which is a combination time clock, load cycling, and electric demand system. Such a system can be frequently expanded to control or monitor other building or personnel functions.

Computerized control system: an elevator control system that utilizes a computer for a group of cars. Each car has a collective control system. In addition, the system will minimize customer waiting time, provide optimal customer service, maximize system efficiency, zone cars, and place cars in or out of service.

Concave: a curved surface that concentrates sound energy.

Condensation: the latent heat that must be removed from 1 pound (kilogram) of vapor (gas) to condense it at the critical temperature. The latent heat of condensation and the latent heat of vaporization are equal at the same critical temperature.

Condenser: a component of a refrigeration cycle that releases the heat absorbed by the refrigerant to the environment. Condensers are usually air or water cooled.

Conduction: the transfer of heat within or from one solid surface to an adjacent surface.

Configuration: a list of the devices installed in the system unit and a description of how those devices operate.

Contour line: an equal-elevation line on a plot or survey view. Any point of the line is a set number of feet above or below an arbitrary point called a benchmark.

Control: a function of management that establishes and maintains operational standards.

Convection: the transfer of heat from a hot surface to a cold surface, which is separated by a fluid (liquid or gas). This fluid is actually heated by the hot surface; the fluid then heats the cold surface.

Convection coefficient: air heat transportability, which is about 1 Btu per square foot per degree Fahrenheit per hour (5.68 watts per square meter per degree Celsius per hour) for normal oven temperatures.

Convection oven: a gas or electric device that forces air, by a fan located at the rear of the oven, over and around food racks. Allows roasting and baking to take place faster and at lower temperatures.

Convector: a device located in a space through which hot water flows and releases heat to the space.

Convex: a curved surface that disperses sound energy.

Counterweights: a series of weights attached to one end of the cable, which offset the car and passenger weight to reduce energy requirements to move the car.

Critical temperature: the temperature at which a product changes from one energy level to another. For example, the freezing and boiling points are critical temperatures.

Cross-training: training a worker for multiple tasks, such as training an electrician to do plumbing maintenance tasks.

CRT: cathode ray tube; vacuum tube used in a video terminal screen.

Cycles per second (cps): generally, ac is supplied at 60 cps in the United States. The frequency at which alternating current changes.

Deadbolt: a lock design in which part of the lock extends from the door to a receptacle within the door frame, so that it cannot be pushed back externally but only by operation of the lock itself.

Decibel (dB): a measurement of sound intensity. A 10-dB change is a 10-fold change in sound energy; therefore, 30 dB is 10 times the energy of 20 dB, or 70 dB is 10 times the energy of 60 dB.

Decision making: a function of management that is involved in problem-solving alternative selection.

Deck oven: a roasting or baking oven that can be stacked, or decked to increase capacity without increasing floor area. On electric models, each deck is independently controlled.

Deferred energy charge: an additional electric billing charge that compensates the electric utility for fuel charges above a normal cost. Usually based on kilowatt-hour consumption.

Deferred energy credit: an electric billing credit for fuel charges below a preset cost. A compensation to the electric energy consumer, usually based on kilowatt-hour consumption.

Defrosting: the removal of ice from an evaporator used in food chillers and freezers. May be hot-gas or electric resistance defrost. The hot-gas system circulates high-pressure refrigerant gas from the compressor to the evaporator.

Degree-day: refers to the relative coldness of a geographic location and the heat requirements for building heating. Actually, it is the average outside temperature compared to 65°F (18.3°C) during the winter heating season. Each degree below 65°F (18.3°C) for 24 hours contributes one degree-day.

Dehumidifier: a device that removes moisture from air, or removes latent heat from air. Usually an evaporator of a refrigeration cycle.

Dehydrofreezing: freezing food by removing its latent heat of fusion, then slowly heating it under a low pressure to add its latent heat of sublimation, which dries the product (moisture is removed from the food during this process).

Delamination: when a roof begins to separate into layers as a result of climatic changes or age.

Deluge: a type of fire sprinkler system in which each sprinkler head is open. Upon activation of the system, water flows through each head regardless of whether a fire emergency exists at each sprinkler head.

Demand: the instantaneous electric-energy requirement. It is usually the average energy requirement for a 15-minute (0.25-hour) time period. Demand may be measured in kilowatts or kilovolt-amperes.

Demand equalization surcharge: demand and power factor energy surcharges are determined with one computation.

Detail view: a large-scale plan or elevation view of equipment, furnishings, or interior walls. It may also show the assembly of structural components.

Detection: acknowledgment of a fire from manual (guest or employee) or automatic (heat, smoke) technology.

Dew-point temperature: the temperature at which moisture will start to condense from the air. It is a measure of the latent-heat content of the air.

Diatomaceous-earth filter: a swimming pool filter that has a fine meshed screen coated with a filter aid called diatomaceous earth.

Dimension: length, width, or depth (height) of a room or structural component.

Direct current (dc): generally, the type of electric energy supplied by chemical batteries. Volts and amperes are constant for the same electric load at all times (in contrast to volts and amperes that change with time for the same electric load with alternating current).

Direct-current motor: a motor that only operates with dc that is fed to the stator and rotor. The common types are series, shunt, and combination.

Direct-expansion (DX) refrigerated air system: directly cooling air with the evaporator of a vapor compression refrigeration cycle.

Disinfectant: a bacteria-killing chemical added to pool water. It is usually chlorine or bromine.

Disposable linen service: a laundering alternative in which a hospitality unit purchases disposable linens (frequently paper-type products) for its use and disposes of the used products.

Disposal: a motor-driven device that uses water to carry food waste products into a shredder or grinder that reduces the waste into 1/8-inch (3 millimeters) pieces, which are flushed into the drainage system.

Disposal fee: the cost associated with having solid waste hauled off site. Usually includes a charge for tonnage based on the weight of the waste and a charge for the number of required trips.

Distribution center: an electric device that breaks down the flow of energy to different building sections. The center will contain protection devices for each building section.

Distribution pipe: any pipe that supplies water within a building.

Dot matrix printer: composes letters from individual dots on a grid, or matrix. The more dots on the matrix, the higher is the printer quality.

Downfeed system: a water distribution system in which water flows from an overhead reservoir to the plumbing fixtures.

Drier: a device used on a refrigeration cycle that removes water from the refrigerant.

Dry-bulb temperature: the temperature measured by an ordinary mercury-in-glass thermometer. Refers to the sensible-heat content of air.

Dry chemical: known as ordinary or multipurpose extinguishing agents. Ordinary dry chemical is used to combat Class B and C fires. Multiple-purpose dry chemical is appropriate for Class A, B, or C fire.

Dryer: a piece of laundering equipment in which linens are dried (moisture is removed from the linens). Dryers can be set or programmed to operate for various times and/or temperatures during drying. They are usually gas, electric, or steam heated. Dryers are rated in pounds (kilograms) of dry linens.

Dry pipe: a type of fire sprinkler system that contains air under pressure. Upon heat activation of an individual sprinkler, the pressure is reduced to a level whereby water pressure on the other side of the dry pipe valve can cause it to open.

Dumbwaiter: a freight elevator system designed to move products between levels within a building.

Dumpster: a waste collection device.

Durability: material wear factor and if materials are appropriate for equipment use.

EER (energy efficiency ratio): the EER is the cooling output in Btus (watts) per hour for each watt of energy input to the compressor. It is the standard of performance for window-type air conditioners.

Effective temperature: the concept of producing an apparently higher or lower temperature by controlling air moisture.

Effluent: a by-product resulting from the decomposition of sewage products. Effluent can be purified by soil-borne bacteria.

Elastomer: rubber-like synthetic polymer such as silicone rubber.

Electrical service system: the building system that receives and distributes electrical energy within the building. It usually includes service wires, electric measurement meters, master control switch, transformer, distribution centers, and circuit panels. The ground may also be considered as a component.

Electric demand controller: an energy control system that only allows selected electrically operated devices to operate within a specified maximum electric load. Therefore, one unit may not be supplied with electric power until another electric unit stops operating.

Electric heat pump: a refrigeration cycle that extracts heat from air, ground, or water and discharges the heat to a building.

Electric resistance heat: the direct conversion of electric power to thermal heat by using electric resistance elements, including light bulbs.

Electromagnetic brake: an electrically operated sheave brake used with cable elevator systems.

Electronic filter (electrostatic precipitator): an electric air filtration device that electrically charges air impurities and attracts the charged particles and collects them, thus removing them from the air.

Electronic heat converter: a device that converts electric energy to microwaves that will heat products. The most common industry device is the microwave oven.

Elevation view: an exterior view of a wall or the outside of a building. It shows the blueprint reader how the outside will appear.

Elevator machine: the mechanical driving system used in elevator systems.

The system may drive a sheave for cable systems or an oil pump for hydraulic systems.

Elevator starter control system: an elevator control system used for a group of elevator cars in which each car has an operator control system. A starter (person) is used to direct passenger movement to the cars and a starter indicates when cars may leave the main building level.

Emergency energy system: an on-the-premises electrical energy source. Typical emergency energy systems include battery (dc) or internal-combustion (ac) generation systems. Selected public and critical building areas may have to have on-the-premises electrical systems.

Emergency work order: a request for work that has emergency status, or the work request must be handled as quickly as possible.

Emissivity: the ability of a hot surface to radiate heat.

EMS: energy management system, either manual, mechanical-electrical, or computer control.

Energy expenses: an expense category in the Uniform System of Accounts for Hotels. Typical expense items are the cost of fuel, electricity, water and sewage, and steam.

Energy goals: management energy reduction objectives that may be based on energy consumption percentage reduction.

Energy/maintenance correlation: the relationship between equipment maintenance and energy consumption. Generally, if maintenance is adequate, energy consumption will be minimized.

Energy management: the efficient use of fuel, electricity, and water resources.

Energy obsolete: refers to a building that is not energy cost effective. It is too costly to renovate or restore as an energy-efficient building.

Engineering: the effective use of workers, materials, systems, and capital to provide customer services.

Enthalpy: a measure of the heat content of air. It includes both sensible and latent heat. *See* **Wet-bulb temperature.**

Enthalpy control: a device that measures air enthalpy and controls air flow.

Environmental Protection Agency (EPA): an agency of the U.S. federal government that develops, tests, establishes, and regulates environment protection standards.

Equipment inventory card: a file that contains specified data and information for a unit of equipment. Normally, each piece of equipment valued above $100 will be inventoried and should have an inventory card.

Equipment ventilation computation: a quantity-of-air computation that provides a set amount of air per piece of equipment during a stated time period (minute or hour).

Equivalent pipe length: the resistance of pipes and pipe fittings in a water distribution system.

Escalator: a mechanical vertical-transportation system between building floors. It is a one-way passenger movement system. The components include steps, handrails, combplates, balustrade, truss, tracks, driving machine, and a controller.

Escalator controller: the on–off and emergency switch and governor speed control system for an escalator.

Escalator machine: a geared-type driving device that drives the steps and handrails for an escalator.

Evaporative cooler: a device that sprays water into the air, thus humidifying and cooling air. *See also* **Swamp cooler.**

Ethylene interpolymer (EIP): a form of a thermoplastic roof.

Evaporator: a component of a refrigeration cycle that is located in a space that is to be cooled. The evaporator absorbs heat from the space through a refrigerant.

Executive chief engineer: a chief engineer for a medium or larger property who is a department head and who practices the functions of management.

Exfiltration: the movement of building air through and around windows and doors, usually caused by producing a positive ventilation pressure (air supply exceeds exhaust air and air moves from the interior of the building to the outside).

Expansion device: a device that absorbs piping expansion when piping is heated by hot water. May be an offset, a loop, or any other device that does not allow piping to extend beyond a specified length.

Expansion valve: a component of a refrigeration cycle that reduces refrigerant pressure and regulates refrigerant flow to the evaporator.

Extended coverage sprinkler: a fire-water sprinkler that discharges water farther than a normal sprinkler head, that is, in excess of 8 feet (2.44 meters).

Extractor: a piece of laundering equipment that removes excess water from linens prior to drying, usually by using centrifugal force. Extractors are rated in pounds (kilograms) of dry linens.

Facility manager: an administrator who has the building maintenance and engineering responsibilities for a larger property.

Fahrenheit: a temperature scale used in the United States and some other English-speaking countries. Water freezes at 32°F (0°C) and boils at 212°F (100°C) at sea-level pressure.

Fast-response sprinkler: a fire-water sprinkler that has a high level of thermal sensitivity and is designed to reach the activation temperature rapidly.

Feet of head: another water pressure measurement term. Water under a 1-pound-per-square-inch pressure (6.9 kilopascals) will lift water 2.3 feet (0.7 meter) in height.

Filter: (1) A device that removes impurities from air. (2) A device that collects water impurities from swimming pools, usually diatomaceous-earth, sand or sand-and-gravel, or cartridge types. The purpose of the filter is to keep the pool water clear and sparkling.

Fire: the result of heat, oxygen, and fuel.

Fire pump: a centrifugal pump used to provide water under pressure for a fire protection system.

Fire wall: a fireproof wall located within a building. It is used to contain a possible fire to a section of the building.

Fission: the current nuclear process for the generation of electric power. Fission is the splitting of the uranium atomic nucleus, which results in the release of large amounts of energy. This energy is used to convert water to steam, which drives electric-generating turbines.

Fixed temperature: a type of heat detector that produces an alarm when the detecting element reaches a predetermined fixed temperature.

Fixture branch: a distribution pipe that supplies water to a single fixture.

Fixture drain: the drainage pipe that receives the discharge from a single plumbing fixture.

Fixture operating pressure: water pressure requirement of a plumbing fixture to provide adequate water flow.

Fixture unit: a quantity of water. Fixtures are rated in fixture units of water demand.

Flame detector: activates when radiant energy (visible or invisible to the human eye) is detected.

Floor area ventilation computation: a quantity-of-air computation that provides a set amount of air per square foot (square meter) of floor area during a stated time period (minute or hour).

Flue gas analysis: usually a chemical test conducted on a heat plant that measures specified combustion by-products. The purpose of the analysis is to increase combustion efficiency.

Fluorescent lamp: an electric discharge lamp that produces light energy with a cathode that emits electrons, which are attracted to an anode. The emitted electrons strike mercury molecules with the result that electromagnetic energy is converted into light. Common fluorescent lamps are instant start, rapid start, rapid start high output, and rapid start very high output.

Fly ash: a by-product of combustion consisting of solid particulates. These can normally be filtered from the combustion discharges through centrifugal filters.

FMIS: facility management information system.

Food cutter: a motor-driven device of floor or bench variety, either provided with multiple entry points that cut or slice food products into various shapes or of the type that contains a rotating bowl that passes products through a set of rotating horizontal knives, which turn downward into the bowl.

Footcandle: the intensity of light at a surface.

Forced convection: using a pump or fan to increase convection fluid movement and increase the rate of convection heat transfer.

Forced-convection evaporator/condenser: evaporator/condenser equipped with fans or pumps to circulate the environment coolant (air or water) over the condenser, or cooled space environment over the evaporator.

Fossil energy resources: oil, gas, and coal, including shale oil, synthetic oil, LPG, and SNG.

Freezer: a food storage area (reach-in or walk-in) that maintains a temperature below the freezing point of food. It is usually maintained between −10 and +10°F (−23.3 and −12.2°C).

Fresh air: outside air.

Friction pressure loss: the amount of water pressure that is available to overcome piping resistance.

Fryer: models include deep fat, tilting, and pressure. Heated by gas or electricity with a tank containing a cooking oil into which the food product is immersed. Tank depths and types vary depending on the type of food product (fish, doughnuts, chicken, potato).

Full scale: a zero-dimension reduction. Hence, a 10-foot (3.05-meter) distance is shown as 10 feet (3.05 meters) on a blueprint. Normally, full scales are only used for smaller items or components.

Fuse: a circuit protection device. A fuse element melts when excessive amperes flow through the element. Elements must be replaced. Normal fuses are plug, nontamperable, time delay, ferrule, and knife blade.

Fusion: (1) The union of atomic nuclei to form heavier nuclei, which releases large amounts of energy. This energy is used to produce electric power. Fusion has minimal pollutants, including radioactive wastes. (2) The latent heat that must be removed from 1 pound (1 kilogram) of liquid to freeze a product at the critical temperature. Also, the latent heat that must be added to 1 pound (1 kilogram) of solid to thaw a product at the critical temperature.

Gate valve: a water flow control device that is operated completely open or closed. It is used as a shutoff valve on water distribution systems.

Gauge: refers to the thickness of sheet metal, especially stainless steel.

Geared traction machine: a cable elevator machine in which the electric driving motor drives a series of gears that drive the sheave.

Gearless machine: a cable elevator machine in which the electric driving motor is directly attached to the sheave.

Gear pump: a special pump that is used to increase pressure on liquids. It is capable of dispensing accurate amounts of liquid.

Generator: a component of a refrigeration cycle (absorption cycle) that heats a salt solution, driving off the refrigerant contained in the salt solution as a vapor or gas.

Geothermal: the extraction of heat (energy) from hot subsurface sources, such as hot water, steam, or hot rock layers. The present problem with this energy source is the production of pollutants.

Globe valve: a water control valve used on fixtures for variable water flow; straight-through valve in contrast to the angle valve.

Goal: an objective; a standard of performance. Ensures that customers, guests, employees, and other constituencies are able to visit or work in a certain type of location and, along with that, a specific type of environment.

Grains of hardness: a measurement of the amount of water hardness. One grain is equal to 17.1 parts per million. One grain or more is considered to be hard water.

Gravity dampers: when the fan is operating, the dampers are blown open, allowing full air flow; however, once the fan is off, the dampers all shut or close off the air ducts.

Grease filter: usually a metallic air filter that removes and collects vapors from exhaust air by grease condensation.

Grease trap: a trap designed to collect kitchen grease so that it can be removed when the collection device is filled. Its purpose is to prevent grease from condensing within drain pipes.

"Green certification:" environmental safe products and resulting by-products.

Griddle: a metallic, ground, polished plate with raised edges or gutters to catch and drain grease or liquid to a trough or pan or a series of rollers. Typically heated by gas or electricity.

Grill: (1) The beginning of the exhaust duct located in a room or space. It is usually a screen or grid arrangement. (2) Available as counter or floor models, which include: electric char (the food product is directly in contact with the elements that are heated), charcoal (removable bottom pan contains heated charcoal, which radiates heat to the food products on the above grill), gas (burners above a heat reflector, but below a heat-radiating element; food products are placed on a grate above the radiant element), gas char (contains permanent coals with gas burners located below coals and food product on grill above the coals), and upright (vertical model with an opening at the front, and gas-heated radiant ceramic or electric heating elements at the top of the container; food product is placed on a sliding adjustable grill set under the radiant heaters).

Ground: a secondary wire attached to a device for human, device, and circuit protection. The wire is physically attached to the ground water table and will conduct accidental energy flow from a defective circuit to the ground. Also a path for unwanted, excessive, or dangerous energy flow. Each device must be connected with a ground wire.

Ground-fault circuit interrupter: an electromagnetic type of circuit breaker that measures the difference in ampere flow between wires and activates a switch stopping energy flow if there is a difference. Usually required in bathrooms, outside energy service, and for all swimming pool electric devices.

Ground water: water contained in the ground. The depth of water in the ground depends on the local water table.

Guide rails: the vertical track system enclosed by the shaft. The track system called guide rails allows the elevator car to move from floor to floor.

Halocarbon refrigerants: a family of safe and essentially non-toxic refrigerants.

Halogenated: extinguishing agent stored as a liquid but discharged as a gas, leaving no corrosive residue. Used to protect electric and electronic equipment.

Halon replacement: halon is to be phased out by the year 2000. At the present time there is not a universally accepted product to completely replace halon. Substitute chemicals such as dry-chemical and carbon dioxide may be used. In addition, a misting or fogging technique appears to be a highly acceptable halon replacement.

Handling capacity: an elevator design factor that is dependent on passenger movement frequency, peak travel periods, and the population density at each serviced level within the building.

Handrail: a component of an escalator system on which passengers can grasp while riding on the steps. The handrails move at the same speed as the steps.

Hardware: (1) Physical equipment as opposed to programs, procedures, rules, and associated documentation. (2) Contrast with software.

Heat: a form of energy that is usually dependent on temperature differences. Heat is an energy quantity term, whereas temperature is an energy quality term.

Heat distribution system: an electromechanical system that is used to move heat from the heat plant to the space to be heated. Typical systems include warm air, hot water, and steam.

Heater storage tank: a container that is used to heat and store hot water for future building consumption.

Heat exchanger: (1) A heat transfer device that is used to extract heat from warm air (water) and heat cool air (water). (2) A type of water heating storage system that is capable of producing hot water at several different temperatures. It requires a continuous heat supply such as steam or super-heated water from a heat plant to heat water.

Heat mirror glass: a window construction with two panes of glass enclosing a suspended plastic with a metallic coating that blocks out radiant heat and almost all ultraviolet radiation.

Heat plant: a required heating system component when oil, gas, or coal energy resources are used. The fuel burns in the heat plant and heat is extracted to warm air or water or to produce steam.

Heat transfer: the movement of heat from a high-temperature source or product to a low-temperature source or product. This may be done by conduction, convection, or radiation.

Heat transference system: a heat distribution system.

Heat transmission coefficient: a term that measures the combined effects of conduction, convection, and radiation heat transfer. Usually, a wall or roof should have a low heat transmission coefficient.

Hermetic unit: a rotary compressor. Both the compressor and its driving motor are housed as one basic component; hence, if either fails, the entire unit (compressor and motor) is replaced.

Hertz: a measurement of the frequency of sound energy, or the number of vibrations. Some absorbers are only effective within specific hertz ranges.

Hidden lines: dashed lines used to show important structural components that are hidden from view.

High-intensity discharge lamp: an electric discharge lamp similar to a fluorescent lamp. Common types are mercury vapor, metal halide, and low- and high-pressure sodium.

Horsepower: an electric-motor rating factor. One horsepower is equal to 746 watts.

Hose line: connects to a standpipe to provide a means for manual application of water on a fire. Class 1 systems (2.5-inch [63.5-millimeter] hose connections) are provided for fire department use, and Class 2 (1.5-inch [38.1-millimeter] hose lines) are provided for building occupants until the fire department arrives.

Hotel and Motel Fire Safety Act: beginning of a national code that will limit the properties in which federal employees can stay to those that are fully sprinkled.

Hot-water requirements: the building hot-water demand for water. Hot water is usually supplied at 110°F (43.3°C) to 120°F (48.9°C) for domestic use (personal bathing and washing), 140°F (60°C) for kitchen fixtures, 180°F (82.2°C) for dish-washing rinsing, 80°F (26.7°C) for swimming pools, and 100°F (37.8°C) for spas.

HSPF (heating season performance factor): the HSPF represents the heating performance over an entire heating season and is equal to the total Btu (watts) of heat delivered divided by the total watt-hours (Btu equivalent) of electric energy used during a representative heating season.

Humidifier: a device that adds water to air, or increases the latent-heat content of air. Usually an evaporative cooler or water spray device.

HVAC: heating, ventilation, and air-conditioning system.

Hydraulic elevator system: a mechanical vertical-transportation system for a building that includes a shaft, penthouse, pit, plunger, elevator machine, controls, and a car for passenger and/or product movement.

Hydrilla: an aquatic plant that can render a body of water unsuitable for recreational purposes.

I/O: input-output circuits; communication between computer and peripheral devices.

Ignition system: any technique that will start the combustion process. Usually includes oil or gas pilot lights, electric sparks, or hot wires.

Improvement: enhancement of an operation; reduction of the operating cost of a facility.

Incandescent lamp: an electric light source that produces light from a filament that glows, or incandesces, when electric energy flows through the filament.

Induction polyphase motor: usually, a three-phase electric motor in which the stator induces magnetism to the rotor. The usual types are general purpose and special purpose.

Infiltration heat (gain) load: the heat gain by air movement through an open door or around a closed door in a food freezer or chiller. Infiltration may be reduced when using plastic door strips. Heat gain caused by the movement of outside air through and around windows and doors.

Infrared (IF): a roof-scanning device that indicates potential trapped moisture in roofing membranes.

Insulator: a material that has a high electrical or thermal resistance.

Internal customer: another department or an employee from another department, in contrast to a guest, client, or patient.

Interval time: an elevator design factor that is dependent on the average time between a passenger call for a car and car arrival.

Inventory control: refers to keeping an adequate number of supply parts on hand and to issuing parts and supplies according to an approved procedure.

Ionization: a type of smoke detector that includes a radiation source that ionizes the air flowing into a sensing chamber, causing electrical energy to flow between two electrodes. Smoke particles entering the chamber decrease the conductance between the electrodes and cause an alarm to be activated.

Jet pump: a device that is capable of pumping water. This pump has a venturi opening; when water under pressure is forced through the opening, a vacuum is established. This pump type requires the use of another pump that will increase water pressure so water can be forced through the venturi opening.

Journeyman status: a Total Quality Management department program rating term; the program rates above novice and below master.

Key valve: a fast-acting gate valve.

Kilobytes (K): capacity of memory of a computer. One kilobyte is 1024 bytes.

Kilocalorie: a kilocalorie is 1.16 watts, or the amount of heat required to increase the temperature of 1 kilogram of water 1°C (17 to 18°C).

Kilopascal: SIU pressure measurement term. Sea-level pressure is 100 kilopascals.

Kilowatt: 1000 watts.

Kilowatt-hour: consumption of 1000 watts during a 1-hour time period. Electric energy is purchased by the kilowatt-hour.

Kitchen steward: a foodservice person who is frequently given kitchen equipment maintenance responsibilities.

Lamp: a source of light. Usually, an electric light source such as an incandescent or fluorescent lamp.

Landscape architect: a professional who understands soil, water requirements, ornamental horticulture, and climate and develops a theme that complements the property's physical facilities. May be licensed.

Latent heat: the heat required at the critical temperature to cause a change in the state of a product, for example, to freeze or thaw a product.

Latent heat of air: heat contained in air moisture, measured by the dew point or relative humidity of the air.

Laundering cycle: a recommended washing procedure for various linen groups with different soiled conditions. The cycle indicates the number of washes, including water chemistry and temperature, and the number of rinses with specified water chemistry and temperature.

Laundering functions: those activities involved with laundering, including receiving and sorting linens, prewashing and washing, extracting, drying, ironing and folding, repairing, inventorying, and issuing linen-type products.

Leadership: a function of management that refers to the manager's ability to get the work done.

Life-cycle costing: the present value estimation of all future asset costs that includes the time value of these costs. This procedure is used to determine the most feasible (least costly) alternative.

Life safety system: a combination of technology and procedure for the early detection of, and reaction to, fire or other emergencies affecting human life.

Lighting system: refers to the relative amounts of light that are directed downward or upward (toward the ceiling and upper walls) from luminaries. There are five lighting systems; they are direct, semidirect, diffuse, semi-indirect, and indirect. However, only the direct, semidirect, and diffuse are recommended in the hospitality industry.

Linen rental service: a laundering alternative in which a business purchases the use of various clean linens. While the business does not own the linens, it is responsible for their replacement if lost or damaged. The rental rate per unit depends on the type of linen.

Lithium bromide absorption refrigeration cycle: a mechanical system that will remove heat from a space or products contained in that space. Such a system has four basic components: evaporator, absorber, generator, and condenser. The normal energy source to operate the cycle is steam, which is supplied to the generator.

LNG: liquified natural gas. Exposing natural gas to a very high pressure causes it to condense. The pressure must be reduced prior to burning the gas.

Load-bearing capacity: ability of a floor, wall, or ceiling to support weight of equipment without damage or collapse.

Load cycling system: an energy control system that only allows selected pieces of equipment to operate for specified time periods.

Lower-limit switch: a safety switch located below the lowest serviced building level located in the elevator shaft. Once the car exceeds the lower-limit switch, the elevator machine is shut off.

Low-E window: low-emissivity window. The R (thermal resistance) of such a window is between 3.5 and 4.5 (20 to 25.6 watts). It has two panes of glass, one of which is coated on one side with a reflector to infrared energy.

Low-limit switch: a heat plant switch that controls the heat distribution or transference system. It controls fans, pumps, or valves.

LPG: liquid petroleum gases, such as propane, butane, and isobutane.

Lumen: a quantity of light. The amount of light energy emitted from a standard candle 1 foot (0.305 meters) from the candle on 1 square foot (0.093 square meters) of surface. Lamps are rated in lumens.

Luminaire: a lighting fixture and a lamp.

Lux: the intensity of light at a surface. The SIU equivalent of footcandle.

Maintenance: keeping a building in repair so management can continue to provide customer services, which the building was intended to deliver.

Management inspection: checking on the physical condition of the property.

Management report: a record of the department's performance for a specified time period. It frequently includes a budget comparison report and a work activity report.

Manpower forecast: an estimate of future manpower requirements.

Masking: refers to two sounds at different hertz levels. Generally, a person can hear one source but not the other; therefore, one sound source is masked or undistinguishable.

Master control switch: the main building electric control center, including main protection devices.

Master status: a Total Quality Management department program rating term; the program rates above journeyman and may be considered as world class.

MCM: thousands of circular mills wire diameter sizing index. Used in the United States for larger-diameter wires.

Mechanical view: usually a plan view showing one electromechanical system such as electric, plumbing, ventilation, heating, air conditioning, or fire protection.

Megabytes (MB): 1,048,576 bytes.

Memory: the part of a system where data and instructions are stored. Memory size is measured in kilobytes (K) or megabytes (MB).

Microwave oven: stand or counter mounted with foods being heated or cooked by electromagnetic waves, which are absorbed by the food and converted to heat. Different from conventional ovens in that the heat is being generated within the food product from an outside source. The oven remains cool while the food product is heated from within.

Misting (fogging) system: high- or low-pressure water discharged through small perforations in a tube or piping around a potential fire load. The water discharges as a mist or fog of very small water particles. Small quantities of water are required to extinguish a fire. The system is activated by a fire sensor and the system acts like a deluge water sprinkler system.

Mixer: a motor-driven device with a vertical shaft or spindle having multiple speeds on which various accessories can be attached for slicing, shredding, grating, and grinding meat. They range in capacity from 5- to 20-quart (5- to 20-liter) bench models to 140-quart (130-liter) floor models. Matching mixer capacity and bowl capacity is essential to avoid costly repairs. For example, a 20-quart (20-liter) bowl should not be used on a 5-quart (5-liter) mixer.

Model: a reduced-scale rendering of a building, equipment, or component parts.

Modem: external or internal device through which a computer can communicate with a distant data bank.

Modification: to alter the facility or facility component to accommodate a new function or objective.

Multiple-suds principle: a series of washes at various chemical conditions (different pH and cleansers for each wash) and a series of rinses at various chemical conditions (different pH and various whiteners for each rinse). Generally, each wash varies from 3 to 5 minutes (180 to 300 seconds). Research has indicated that more soil is removed from linens under these conditions and times than for longer wash and rinse cycles.

Multisensor detectors: a fire sensor that includes rate-of-rise temperature, photoelectric, and ionization units. The unit is designed for maximum worker and guest protection.

National Board of Rules for Repairs: contains maintenance procedures for steam equipment.

National Restaurant Association: a professional organization that develops foodservice industry standards.

National Sanitation Foundation (NSF): develops standards for foodservice equipment, which are frequently adopted by public health agencies as requirements for the installation and operation of commercial foodservice equipment.

National Standard Plumbing Code: a nongovernment list of plumbing installation recommendations. It contains acceptable water system and drainage system design procedures.

NEC (National Electric Code): contains permissible electrical installation techniques. It is based on experience, safety, and recent electric developments. All or part of the code may be adopted by local governments for their electric code.

Needle valve: a special variable-flow valve used to control the flow of gases.

Negative pressure: frequently applies to food production areas that are adjacent to dining rooms. Produced when the space exhaust air is greater than the space supply air.

No-iron linens: generally linens of 50 percent cotton and 50 percent polyester treated with a chemical resin that leaves the linens in a wrinkle-free condition after prescribed washing, rinsing, and drying. These linens require no ironing or minimal ironing.

Noise: unwanted or undesirable sound. Noise to one person is not necessarily noise to another person.

Noise criteria (NC): a noise measurement procedure that depends on intensity and hertz levels. NC-15 means that noise is 15 dB at normal-speech hertz levels but relative decibels will be higher at lower hertz levels and lower at higher hertz levels. Equipment is usually rated in NC units.

Noise rating (NR): a noise measurement procedure similar to NC and PNC.

Novice status: a Total Quality Management department program rating term; the program rates below journeyman and may be considered as the lowest program rating.

Occupant heat load: heat released from the building's occupants.

Occupant method ventilation computation: a quantity-of-air computation that provides a set amount of air per room or space occupant during a stated time period (minute or hour).

Occupational Safety and Health Act (OSHA): U.S. federal law that establishes safety/health standards and record keeping requirements for employees.

Off-peak: a specified time period in which electric energy is purchased at minimum rates. On-peak and off-peak rates may apply to kilowatt-hour, demand, and power factor.

Oil separator: a device used on a refrigeration cycle that removes oil from the refrigerant.

On-peak: a specified time period in which any consumption of electric energy will result in a premium energy charge.

On-premises laundry: a laundering alternative in which a hospitality unit installs and operates its own laundering facility. It also purchases and maintains its linens.

Operating system: software that controls the execution of programs; examples are Microsoft ® Windows ® and DOS.

Operator control system: an elevator control system in which an operator (a person, either a passenger or an employee) is required to control door openings and closings, car movement, and car speed.

Organization: a function of management that assists management in getting required work done.

OTG (ocean thermal gradient): extracting energy from deep layers of water when the water layers have different temperatures. Present technology suggests that this energy could be used to generate electric power or to produce hydrogen.

"Other" motor types: these include universal, repulsion-start induction-run, repulsion–induction, and special-purpose motors.

Parallel circuit: a wiring technique in which devices are connected between the wires supplying energy to the circuit. This technique allows each device to receive its full voltage requirement. Hence, if one device malfunctions, it has no effect on the other devices.

Passive solar heating: using building structural components for the absorption of solar energy. The absorbed heat is then released within the building. Passive solar systems are nonmechanical heating systems.

Peeler: floor- or bench-mounted motor-driven device to peel root vegetables. Requires electricity, water, and a drain.

Penthouse: the upper portion of the elevator shaft. Generally, the penthouse is on the roof of the building and encloses the elevator machine and control system.

People mover: a horizontal-transportation system similar to an escalator system, except that a belt is used rather than steps for passenger movement.

Peripheral: equipment that needs to be added to a computer system. Included are disk drives, terminals, and printers.

Perspective view: usually a three-dimensional view of equipment, furnishings, or structural components. It usually includes two elevation views and one plan view on a single drawing.

Phase 1: an easy-to-implement energy program. Such programs require little or no investment and have payback periods of less than 1 year for any investment.

Phase 2: an energy-management program that may require moderate investments in energy control devices or energy-consuming devices. The investment payback period is usually between 1 and 3 years.

Phase 3: an energy-management program that requires investments in energy control devices or electromechanical systems that have investment payback periods of 3 to 5 years.

Photoelectric: a type of smoke detector that activates when smoke enters the sensing chamber and obscures or scatters a light beam passing through the chamber.

Piping resistance: the friction or resistance to piping water flow.

Piping vibration: usually caused when piping is heated with hot water.

Pit: the lower portion of the elevator shaft; it contains springs or bumpers. The pit of the hydraulic elevator system also houses the elevator machine.

Planning: a function of management that develops problem-solving alternatives used in the decision-making process.

Plant maintenance: health-care building maintenance expenses.

Plan view: a top-side view, usually of a room or a group of rooms, showing the floor, walls, windows, and permanent equipment.

Plastic strip curtain: installed at the entrance to a walk-in chiller or freezer to reduce the heat gain when the door remains open as food products are removed or added.

Plenum: an enlarged section of a ventilation duct, usually enlarged to hold convectors or radiators.

Plot view: a plan view of a parcel of land showing the proposed location of a building, or building addition, changes in landscaping, or other essential items.

Plunger: a component of a hydraulic elevator system that is attached to the car floor and lifts or lowers the car from level to level within the shaft. It replaces the cable and counterweights of the cable elevator system.

Pollution control filter: a special filter that can remove specific by-products of combustion, such as chemicals, solids (smoke particles), or odors.

Polymer: synthetic substance consisting of giant molecules formed from smaller molecules of the same substance.

Positive pressure: caused by supplying more air than is exhausted from a space.

Postscript quality: technology that enables a computer to communicate with a printer and direct its output in terms of type size and print graphics.

Potable water: safe drinkable water. Water fit for human consumption. There is no uniform standard definition for potable water. The definition of potable depends on what is available in a particular area; therefore, specific water standards can vary. What is considered potable in one area could be nonpotable in another area. Water that has been certified as safe for human consumption.

Power factor: a measure of the relationship between volts and amperes in alternating current. Power factors vary between (and including) 0 and 1. If volts and amperes reach their maximum values at the same time, the power factor is 1. The dc power factor is always 1.

Preaction: a dry sprinkler system. If a supplementary fire detection device (heat sensor) is activated, water flows into the piping before a sprinkler is activated. No delay is experienced when a sprinkler is activated by the heat of the fire.

Precooler: a device that reduces the temperature of air, or removes sensible heat from air.

Preferred noise criteria (PNC): a noise measurement procedure similar to NC, except that higher decibels are allowed at lower hertz levels and lower decibels at higher hertz levels.

Preheater: a device that partially heats air, or adds sensible heat to air.

Pressure losses: refers to air resistance flow through ducts and filters. Fan energy is required to move air through these resistance elements.

Preventive maintenance: scheduled periodic maintenance of building electromechanical systems, such as oiling bearings every three months, or checking elevator safety components each month, or conducting efficiency tests of equipment on a set time schedule.

Probable water flow: the conversion of fixture units to gallons of water per minute based on the probable use of water for a series of fixtures.

Product heat load: the heat gain from products placed in food chillers (sensible heat) and freezers (sensible and latent heat if the products are frozen in the unit).

Program: a sequence of instructions that a system can interpret and execute.

Property manager: an administrator who has the building maintenance and engineering responsibilities for a larger property.

Property operation and maintenance expenses: a maintenance/engineering expense category in the Uniform System of Accounts for Hotels. Typical expense items include: payroll, building maintenance, electric and mechanical equipment maintenance, furniture repairs, painting and decorating, waste removal, and other department-related expenses.

Property renovation: restoring a building or any of its parts to an acceptable standard so it can provide intended services.

Psychometric chart: a chart that shows the interrelationships of dry-bulb, dew-point, and wet-bulb temperatures and relative humidity.

Pulping: a waste compaction technique that grinds wastes with water and reduces the excess water. This technique reduces waste volume by 75–80 percent.

Pump: a device that creates a vacuum and increases water pressure through mechanical forces.

Quad: one quadrillion Btu (10^{15} Btu) (0.293×10^{15} watts). An energy measurement term that is equivalent to about 172,000,000 barrels (27.3×10^9 liters) of oil. World energy consumption was 360 quads (105.5×10^{15} watts) in 1994.

Quick-response sprinkler head: a sprinkler head that provides a very fast response and maximizes the spray available for fire suppression. This is one of the preferred sprinkler heads in conventional lodging guest rooms.

Radiant gas: oil or kerosene heater.

Radiant heat: usually a high-temperature heat unit placed in a room, such as an electric lamp, gas, or oil (kerosene) heater. Radiant heat also includes hot-water, steam, or electric resistance units placed in ceilings, walls, or floors.

Radiation: the transfer of heat from a hot to a cold surface by electromagnetic waves (surfaces are not in contact and there is no fluid used to transfer heat).

Radiation shape factor: refers to the percentage of radiant heat transferred from a hot surface to a section of a cold surface.

Radiative cooling: a solar cooling system in which water absorbs building heat, which is then circulated to devices that are exposed to the cool outside night air. The heated water is allowed to cool.

Radiator: a device located in a space in which steam condenses, thus releasing heat to a space.

Random-access memory (RAM): memory needed by a computer for new software and programs that the user may wish to operate.

Range: electric or gas device with a heated top surface or burner on which containers of food products are cooked. Types include small compact, restaurant weight/size, heavy duty series, taco range (accommodates heavy-duty pans up to 18 x 26 inches [457 x 660 millimeters]), Chinese range (width determined by dimensions of woks and bowls, allowing 6-inch [152.4-millimeter] space between them), compact cooking center, and stock pot.

Rate-of-temperature rise: a type of heat detector that produces an alarm when the rate of temperature increases beyond a predetermined value (usually 12 to 15° F per minute [0.1 to 0.2°C per second]).

Read-only memory (ROM): memory in which stored data cannot be modified by the user except under special conditions.

Reciprocating pump: a type of pump that has a piston moving within a cylinder.

Recirculated air: room or building exhaust air that is returned to a room or building as ventilation supply air. Such air is usually at least filtered.

Redundancy: a backup system.

Refrigerant: a substance that has a low boiling point; hence, it is capable of absorbing its latent heat of vaporization at a low temperature.

Refrigerated air: air cooling using mechanical refrigeration systems, usually a vapor compression or absorption refrigeration cycle.

Refrigeration: the removal of heat from a space or products using electromechanical systems, such as a vapor compression refrigeration system.

Register: the duct termination device on an air supply for a room or space. It may have an air flow regulator or deflection device called a damper.

Reheater: a device that partially heats air, or adds sensible heat to air, usually to reduce its relative humidity. Air can also be preheated by mixing cool air with recirculated air.

Relative humidity: the ratio of the actual moisture contained in air at a specific dry-bulb temperature to the moisture potential of air at the same dry-bulb temperature.

Renovation: the restoration of a building or any part of the building so it can efficiently render customer services.

Repair: to return a device or facility to its former state or to meet a business goal or objective.

Repair and maintenance log: a record of all repairs and maintenance performed on a piece of equipment. This may be kept on the reverse or back side of the equipment inventory card.

Replacement: is performed when equipment or a facility component has reached the end of its useful life.

Replacement cycle for items that fail: determining the specific schedule for replacing various items in an effort to minimize costs.

Replacement cycle for items that wear out: determining the specific time when an asset should be replaced to minimize costs.

Residual heat load: heat flow from the building's furnishings and structural components to the building's interior. The heat load caused by cooling the interior of a building.

Resistance heater: an electric device that has an element that gets hot and releases heat when energy flows through it. Common resistance heaters are high, medium, and low temperature.

Return on assets (ROA): a Total Quality Management department rating term. It is a ratio of business profit to business assets.

Reverberation time: the time for sound to be reduced by 60 dB, or one-millionth of its original intensity. The reverberation time can be different at various hertz levels.

Revolving oven: gas or electric device with a "ferris wheel"–type rotation of trays held in the oven. Provides an ideal combination of convected and conducted heat energy for cooking food products.

Riser: a vertical distribution pipe that extends above the height of a shower head or through one or more floors in a building.

Rod: a flexible device that is inserted in drainage pipes to break up and/or push clogging debris to larger piping.

Roll-in oven: a gas or electric convection oven designed to receive removable racks. Food products for roasting or baking are placed on pans, which are placed on the removable oven racks. The capacity of the oven determines the number of racks that can be added to the oven in a particular cycle.

Room ventilation system: a single set of supply and exhaust fans and ducts that continuously provides ventilation air to one room. Hence, each room has a separate independent ventilation system.

Room volume ventilation computation: a quantity-of-air computation that provides a set number of room volume air changes per hour.

Rotary pump: a special pump used to increase pressure on gases or semi-solids (some food items).

Rotor: the movable part of an electric motor that is used to drive connected machinery or devices. Electrically produced magnetism is frequently induced from the stator to the rotor, which causes the rotor to be repelled from the stator.

Routine maintenance and repairs: regularly scheduled building repairs and maintenance, such as responding to a guest room repair request or a walk-through light bulb replacement in public areas.

Routine work order: a request to have work done that is completed as quickly as feasible and is not considered to be an emergency work request.

Safety switch: a heat plant or distribution system switch that shuts down the heating system in case of a system malfunction.

Sand or sand-and-gravel filter: a swimming pool filter that collects water impurities as water is passed through layers of sand and gravel.

Scale: a dimension reduction factor applied to actual distances to reduce their length, so long distances can be shown on blueprints. A common U.S. scale is 1/4-inch=1 foot (6.35 millimeters = 0.305 meter). Hence, a 10-foot (3.05-meter) distance is reduced to 2.5 inches (63.5 millimeters) on a blueprint.

Section view: a cutaway view of a wall or other structural components, usually indicating how components are assembled.

SEER (seasonal energy efficiency ratio): the SEER is equal to the total Btus (watts) of cooling delivered divided by the total watt-hours of energy used during a representative cooling season. It is the performance standard for central air conditioners and the cooling cycle for a heat pump.

Semicomputerized control system: a semicomputerized elevator control system used for a group of cars. Each car has a collective control system. The computer can control car movement during peak passenger periods.

Semiconcrete pool: an in-ground pool that has a bottom constructed of steel-reinforced concrete. Its sidewalls are constructed of fiberglass or stainless steel.

Sensible heat: the heat required to change the temperature of a product, usually within a given state such as solid, liquid, or gas.

Sensible heat of air: heat that causes the temperature of air to increase or decrease, usually measured with an ordinary thermometer. *See also* **Dry-bulb temperature.**

Septic tank: an in-ground sewage container that must be periodically pumped out and the effluent hauled off site or be connected to a cesspool or drain field.

Series circuit: a wiring technique in which devices are connected along a wire in a string or line. The same number of amperes flows through each device in this circuit. Resistance to energy flow is additive; hence, adding devices to the circuit reduces ampere flow. If one device fails, energy will not flow in the circuit, so nothing works.

Service contract: a maintenance function assigned to nonbuilding staff for a specified period of time for a fee.

Service pipe: the main water supply pipe for a building.

Service wires: electric conducting wires that supply energy from the electric utility to the circuit panels.

Setback temperature: reducing the temperature in nonoccupied rooms by specified amounts.

Sewage ejector: an enclosed waste collection device that collects waste from fixtures located below the building drain. Wastes are generally pumped to the building drain when the device is filled.

Shaft: a component of an elevator system. The vertical opening between elevator car serviced building levels. It contains the vertical track system in which the car rides. The upper portion is the penthouse and the lower portion is called the pit.

Shale oil: oil reserves contained in rocks (a vast U.S. oil reserve). The major problem is how to extract oil economically from the shale.

Sharkfins: roofing ridges that are uniform in size that indicate waterlogged felt.

"Sick building syndrome": a condition that arose in the 1980s with the design and construction of energy efficient air-tight buildings, which resulted in employee sickness. The major cause is insufficient fresh ventilation air.

Side-arm heater: a type of water heater storage tank used in moderately sized lodging and foodservice units. It has a separate detached water heater and a storage tank.

Sidewalk elevator: a freight elevator system designed to move products from a basement level to the exterior building street level.

Single phase (ac): normal electric energy supplied to guest rooms, homes, and apartments. A form of alternating current in which each device is supplied with energy along two wires from the source of energy.

Single-phase motor: a type of motor in which the stator induces magnetism to the rotor. The normal types include split-phase induction, capacitor-start induction-run, capacitor-start capacitor-run, shaded-pole induction, and special-purpose split-phase motors.

SIU: Standard International Unit. In the case of blueprints, millimeters are used in place of inches and meters in place of feet.

Slicer: used to slice a variety of food products such as onions, cheese, meat, and tomatoes. Either bench- or stand-mounted with a motor-driven stationary round knife and plate for gauging slice thickness. Furnished with a knife sharpener.

Smoke-free environment: a space where smoking is not allowed and where all traces of tobacco smoke and residue created by smoking have been removed.

Snake: a mechanically powered rod. *See* **Rod.**

SNG: synthetic natural gas. A gas extracted from oil or coal, which has properties very similar to natural gas.

Software: programs, procedures, rules, and any associated documentation pertaining to the operation of a system.

Soft-water requirements: hot and cold water are usually softened for all laundering procedures; this is especially important for no-iron linens. However, synthetic detergents have enough water softeners to handle up to 5 grains (85.5 ppm) of water hardness, water-softening chemicals may have to be added to water if its hardness is between 5 and 10 grains (85.5 and 171 ppm), and water-softening equipment must be used for 10 or more grains (171 ppm or more) of hardness.

Soil absorption rate: also called percolation. The ability of soil to handle effluent generated by a private sewage disposal system. Essential when determining septic-tank and drain field size.

Soil drainpipe: a drainpipe that collects wastes from two or more fixtures.

Soil stack: a vertical drainpipe that collects wastes from drainpipes and fixture drains and extends from the building drain through the building roof.

Solar absorption cycle: similar to the lithium bromide absorption refrigeration cycle. Solar energy is used to generate steam, which is fed to the generator.

Solar heat load: either the instantaneous solar heat gain through exterior glass surfaces or the heat gain caused by solar heating of the building's structural components that eventually transfer the stored heat to the building's interior.

Solar vapor compression cycle: similar to the vapor compression refrigeration cycle. Solar energy is used to drive the compressor by either a steam engine or the direct conversion of solar energy to electric power.

Solid-core door: made of solid wood, usually a minimum of 1 inch (25.4 millimeters), without the use of fillers (cardboard, newspapers).

Sound: a form of energy that depends on a vibration, a transmission path (such as a gas, liquid, or solid), and a receiver.

Sound absorber: a surface that destroys sound energy. Various absorbers may only be effective for specific sound vibrations.

Sound isolators: devices or techniques that attempt to eliminate the sound path. Examples are mounting equipment on springs, resilient materials, or separate platforms.

Sound quality: depends on both hertz and intensity. For example, high-hertz and high-decibel sounds are uncomfortable; hence, they produce poor-quality sound.

Specific heat: the amount of heat required to increase the temperature of the unit weight of a product one degree.

Stainless steel: a type of metal with high strength and corrosion resistance that is utilized in the construction of foodservice equipment.

Standard deviation: a statistical computation of the dispersion of data about a mean (average). If the data have a normal distribution (bell-shaped curve), the standard deviation generates a range about the mean that includes various percentages of the data.

Standpipe: provides a means for manual application of water to fires in buildings. Generally designed to facilitate the fire department's provision of water on the upper floors of high-rise buildings.

Starter: a component of an electric discharge lamp circuit that allows full voltage to be impressed on the filament to get the lamp started. Once the lamp is in operation, it serves no functional purpose.

Stator: the nonmovable part of an electric motor. It consists of operating and frequently starting poles.

Steamer: sealed compartment where steam is in direct contact with the food product. Model must be approved for direct contact and not contaminated.

Steam kettle: two bowls sealed, one within the other, with a space between for the introduction of steam. The amount of steam surface is called jacketing. Styles available are either direct steam connected, generated steam from a boiler, or self-contained. The self-contained style has a permanent supply of chemically pure water with no direct water connection required. Capacity ranges from a table top oyster cooker of 1 quart (0.946 liters) to kettles of 200 gallons (757 liters).

Steel-reinforced concrete pool: an in-ground pool constructed of concrete and steel reinforcing rods. The concrete is covered with a marine plaster.

Steps: a component of an escalator system on which passengers ride while moving between floors. Steps move on tracks.

Storm drain: an outside horizontal drainage pipe that collects storm runoff water from building roofs, parking lots, and other surface water.

Strong brine: an absorbent used in an absorption refrigeration cycle, usually lithium bromide.

Structural wall: a wall that supports upper building levels or other building structural components. It generally cannot be removed.

Sublimation: the latent heat that must be added to 1 pound (1 kilogram) of solid to vaporize a product at the critical temperature.

Submersible pump: a form of centrifugal pump in which the pump and its driving motor are suspended in water when it is in operation.

Supersmart glass: a window glass construction that has three panes of glass. The outer glass consists of low E glass units. The spaces between the glass layers are sealed and filled with argon gas.

Survey view: a plan view of a parcel of land showing everything currently located on the land parcel including underground and overhead utilities or other important items. The survey view is usually drawn and certified by a licensed surveyor.

Swamp cooler: similar to a water cooling tower. A device that sprays water into the air, thus cooling the air that is blown into a space to be cooled. These devices work very well in a hot-dry climate. It is also called an evaporative cooler.

Synchronous polyphase motor: usually, a three-phase-type electric motor that operates at a specified number of revolutions. The normal types are direct-current excited-rotor, reluctance rotor, and hysteresis motors.

Synthetic oil: oil produced from coal or biomass wastes.

System: a functional unit consisting of a system unit, all attached devices (keyboard, display, printer, and others), and software.

System unit: the part of a system that contains the processing unit and devices such as diskette and fixed disk drives.

Temperature: a measurement of the speed at which molecules move. It is a heat quality term.

Thermal conductivity: the ability of a material to conduct heat. A heat insulator has a low thermal conductivity.

Thermal resistance: an insulator rating term. The ability of a product or material to retard heat transfer. The opposite or inverse of the heat transmission coefficient.

Thermoelectric: a type of heat detector that includes a sensing element that produces an increase in electric potential in response to an increase in temperature.

Thermoplastic roof: softens when heated and hardens when cooled.

Thermostat: a heat control switch that measures temperature and activates radiant heaters, convectors, radiators, or heat plants.

Thermostat calibration: adjusting a thermostat to minimize the difference between temperature setting for desired activation or termination of heat- or cold-producing equipment and when the unit actually begins or ceases to operate.

Thermostat control: a device that measures temperature and either controls air flow or components of an air-conditioning system.

Three phase (ac): normal electric energy supplied to larger buildings. A form of alternating current in which each device is supplied with energy along at least three wires from the source of energy.

Threshold: same as doorsill. A length of wood, masonry, and so on along the bottom of a doorway.

Threshold of hearing: the minimum sound that can be heard by an individual. The threshold depends on both hertz and decibels. For example, if one can hear 20 hertz at 70 dB and 4000 hertz at −5 dB, his or her threshold is −5 dB.

Tidal energy: extracting energy from the tidal-movement action of water masses. Present technology suggests that this moving water could be used to generate electric power.

Time clock system: an energy control system that uses time clocks to turn equipment on and off.

Toilet (water closet): a plumbing fixture designed to receive human excreta.

Total heat of air: a measure of the sensible- and latent-heat content of air, usually measured by the wet-bulb temperature. *See also* **Enthalpy**.

Total Quality Management: a systematic method of developing products and services that meet the needs and expectations of customers. The maintenance department serves a very important role in keeping the product at the guest expectation level.

Toxic wastes: wastes that cannot be decomposed naturally in the environment, such as some acids, solvents, and many petroleum products.

Tracks: a component of an escalator system on which the steps ride.

Traction drive: the drive system frequently used for sidewalk elevators. A cable is directly attached to the sheave, which is driven by a geared electric motor.

Transference losses: energy requirements for fuel ignition and combustion to operate a heat distribution system.

Transformer: a device that increases or reduces electric voltage. Building transformers usually reduce voltage.

Transmission heat load: (1) The heat gained through walls, ceiling, floor, and doors of a walk-in or reach-in chiller or freezer. (2) Summer heat flow from the exterior of a building through its structural components to the building's interior.

Trap: a downward looped section of piping that retains liquid wastes, so that sewer gases cannot escape back into the building.

Trash chute: a vertical duct discharge outlet in a building. Openings are located at one or more building levels. The duct discharges into a collection device (dumpster). These must be fire rated (duct and door designs).

Travel time: an elevator design factor that is dependent on passenger loading time, car acceleration and deceleration times, passenger transfer time, car door operating time, and car express time.

Truss: the vertical structural support system for an escalator system.

Tungsten-halogen lamp: an incandescent type of lamp.

Turbine pump: a form of centrifugal pump that is used to pump water from deep wells. The pump mechanism is located in the well and underwater, but the driving motor is located on the ground surface.

20°F (11.1°C) maximum-temperature-change rule: the maximum temperature difference between two successive segments of the laundering cycle for no-iron linens. If a 20°F (11.1°C) temperature difference is exceeded during laundering, the no-iron resins may "set up," that is, harden or result in stiff linens, and the linens may wrinkle after drying (wrinkles are then difficult, if not impossible, to remove from the linens).

UL: Underwriters Laboratories establishes electric device standards, performs device testing, and provides a listing service for devices that meet its standards. It also performs a certification service in which it approves of safe installations for which there are no safety standards.

Uniform System of Accounts for Hotels and Motels: a series of accounting definitions and accounting formats, procedures, and ratios developed by the American Hotel & Motel Association.

Upfeed system: a water distribution system in which the water pressure is adequate to force or lift water to each fixture.

Upper-limit switch: (1) A heat plant switch that will shut off the fuel supply when the heat plant exceeds a specified temperature. (2) A safety switch located above the highest serviced building level located in the elevator shaft. Once the car exceeds the upper-limit switch, the elevator machine is shut off.

Utilities: energy resources and connections, such as, electric, water, steam, gas, propane, and sewage connections.

Utility wall: a wall that contains one or more of the following building utilities: electric components, water–sewage–fire sprinkler–natural-gas piping, heating–cooling–ventilation components, or communication components.

Value added per employee (VAE): a measure of the increase in product value after an employee services or repairs a product.

Vapor compression refrigeration cycle: a mechanical system that will remove heat from a space or products contained in that space. Such a system has four basic components: evaporator, compressor, condenser, and expansion valve.

Vaporization: the latent heat that must be added to 1 pound (1 kilogram) of liquid to vaporize a product at the critical temperature.

Variance: an acceptable difference from a standard or goal. It may be expressed as a percentage of the standard or goal.

VAV: variable air volume handling system with variable-speed fans.

Vent: a piping network that allows atmospheric air pressure to circulate on the sewer side of traps, thus preventing the siphoning of liquid wastes from traps.

Ventilation: providing a controlled quantity of air to a space or entire building. Generally, a mechanical system consisting of fans, ducts, registers, grills, and filters is required.

Ventilation duct: an air transmission device, usually used in ventilation systems to supply and exhaust air to and from rooms.

Ventilation heat load: cooling fresh or recirculated air so it has the capacity to absorb the building heat load.

Ventilator hood: a separate ventilation exhaust system for each piece of equipment. Frequently required on selected food production equipment.

Vinyl-liner pool: an in-ground or above-ground pool that has steel sidewalls and a vinyl liner covering the sidewalls and bottom.

Volt: unit of electric potential. Volts push amperes through a device.

Voltage drop: the reduction of circuit voltage caused by electric wire resistance. This undesirable effect can be reduced by using larger wires, by restricting the number of devices on the circuit, or by operating the appliances at a higher voltage.

Wading area: the pool area that varies from 3 to 5 feet (0.92 to 1.525 meters) in water depth. It usually covers 50 to 80 percent of the surface area.

Wading pool: a pool of any construction technique that has a maximum depth of 18 to 36 inches (0.46 to 0.92 meter).

Ware washing: includes a variety of equipment designed to clean dishes, glassware, pots, and garbage cans. Dishwashers can be under-the-counter models, door type, or flight type (dishes move through the machine on a conveyor).

Washer: a piece of laundering equipment in which linens are washed and rinsed. The machine may be programmed for different wash and rinse cycles, including wash and rinse times, and will dispense various chemicals for each of the wash and rinse cycles. Washers are rated in pounds (kilograms) of dry linens.

Waste drainpipe: a drainpipe that collects wastes from two or more fixtures, except human excreta–type fixtures.

Waste stack: similar to a soil pipe, except that it cannot collect human excreta-type discharges.

Water-cooling tower: a device that releases condenser or absorber heat to the environment. Generally, water absorbs heat at the condenser or absorber and is sprayed into an environment. This spraying cools the water.

Water distribution system: a piping system that supplies and distributes water within a building to plumbing fixtures.

Water hardness: refers to the amount of calcium and/or magnesium salts contained in the water. These salts when combined with natural soap produce soap curd, a product that sticks to linens and eating utensils, making them look dirty (brownish or yellowish). Water hardness is measured in grains.

Water pH: (1) A measure of the acidity or alkalinity of pool water. The pH should be maintained between 7.2 and 7.6, or slightly alkaline. (2) A measure of water alkalinity or acidity for washing and rinsing laundering cycles. Washes usually require a pH of 10.0 to 11.6, while rinses usually vary from 3.5 to 6.0.

Water Pollution Control Act: U.S. federal act that decrees that all waters must be made safe for fishing and swimming. U.S. local governments establish water quality standards in accordance with the act.

Water pressure: the force created by a column of water. A column of water 2.3 feet (0.7 meter) in height creates a pressure of 1 pound per square inch (6.9 kilopascals).

Water softener: a device that will remove hard-water salts from water. One water-softening process is the zeolite technique that replaces normal hard-water salts with a soft salt (sodium) that is free-rinsing from linens and utensils.

Water spray filter: an air filtration device that sprays water into an air stream. Various impurities will absorb water and fall from the air stream. This device removes smoke from the air and will humidify air.

Watt: an SIU heat measurement term. Consumption of electric energy. Depends on amperes, volts, power factor, and phase if ac.

Weir: a swimming pool water surface opening that allows pool water to circulate through a screen-type basket through piping and a pump to the filter. It is designed to collect floating debris from the water surface.

Wet-bulb temperature: the temperature at which sensible and latent heat are in equilibrium in air. It is a measure of the total heat content of air.

Wet pipe: a type of fire sprinkler system that contains water under pressure at all times. In a fire emergency, individual sprinklers are activated by heat, and water flows through the sprinklers immediately.

Wind-chill effect: the cooling effect produced by air movement.

Wire: an electric conductor covered with insulation. The normal conductor is copper. The type of insulation usually indicates the wire type; for example, type-T wire means a copper conductor is covered with thermoplastic insulation.

Work activity report: a management summary of the various work completed by the maintenance-and-engineering department for a specified time period.

Worker sound effects: providing background sound that is not distracting to workers. This is done to maintain worker productivity.

Working chief engineer: a chief engineer for a smaller property who serves as a supervisor department head and who has technical expertise in one or more areas of maintenance (e.g., a plumber).

Work order: a request to have work done.

Work plan: a schedule of the department's planned activities for a specified time period. The chief engineer may have his or her work plan approved by management.

Work priority: the assignment of a work request as emergency, routine, or backlogged work.

Work productivity: the actual work output of the department. Work output is usually compared to man-hour output or payroll input.

World class: refers to about 2 percent of the world's hospitality maintenance-and-engineering departments that are considered to be outstanding with respect to a set of industry benchmarks.

Written specifications: a series of instructions that accompany blueprints. They usually include information that is difficult to show on blueprints.

Zone ventilation system: a single set of supply and exhaust fans and ducts that continuously provides ventilation air to a group of rooms. Each zone operates separately and independently of other zones.

INDEX